Cromwell's Navy

Cromwell's Navy

The Fleet and the English Revolution
1648–1660

BERNARD CAPP

CLARENDON PRESS · OXFORD
1989

Oxford University Press, Walton Street, Oxford OX2 6DP
Oxford New York Toronto
Delhi Bombay Calcutta Madras Karachi
Petaling Jaya Singapore Hong Kong Tokyo
Nairobi Dar es Salaam Cape Town
Melbourne Auckland
and associated companies in
Berlin Ibadan

Oxford is a trade mark of Oxford University Press

Published in the United States
by Oxford University Press, New York

British Library Cataloguing in Publication Data
Capp, Bernard
Cromwell's navy: the fleet and the English
Revolution, 1648–1660.
1. Great Britain. Royal Navy, 1509–1660
I. Title
359'.00941
ISBN 0-19-820115-X

Library of Congress Cataloging in Publication Data
Capp, B. S.
Cromwell's navy: the fleet and the English Revolution, 1648–1660
/Bernard Capp.
Bibliography: p.   Includes index.
1. Great Britain—History—Commonwealth and Protectorate,
1649–1660. 2. Great Britain—History—Puritan Revolution,
1642–1660. 3. Great Britain—History, Naval—Stuarts, 1603–1714.
4. Great Britain. Royal Navy—History. 5. Cromwell, Oliver,
1599–1658. I. Title.
DA425.C24   1989   941.06'3—dc19   88-38180
ISBN 0-19-820115-X

Typeset by Litho Link Limited, Welshpool, Powys
Printed in Great Britain by
Biddles Ltd., Guildford and King's Lynn

For Helen and Michael

PREFACE

I FIRST thought of writing this book almost twenty years ago, and it has been a long time in the making. Since the days of Gardiner and Firth the history of the navy has been written almost exclusively by naval specialists, a common development as history has grown ever more fragmented. They have by no means overlooked this period, as seven large volumes of documents in the Navy Records Society attest, but they have rarely sought to relate its history to the dramatic events taking place ashore. The immense bulk of surviving evidence has discouraged other historians from venturing into unknown waters. A curious historiographical warp has resulted. While the politicization of the New Model Army has always been readily accepted (though differences remain over its timing and extent), it is generally assumed that the navy was almost untouched by the revolution, and continued to see its role as merely keeping the foreigner at bay. This always struck me as something that ought to be demonstrated rather than assumed, and whenever I chanced across such officers as Capt. Owen Cox, Fifth Monarchy supporter and devotee of astrology, the suspicion grew that there might be more to the Commonwealth navy than simple patriotism. So my venture into maritime affairs — perhaps a rash undertaking for a Warwickshire landlubber — was not primarily to tackle a period of naval history *per se* but to explore a relatively uncharted aspect of the English Revolution. The Commonwealth navy was the product of that revolution, and its growth, leadership, character, and deployment all reflected that central fact.

My book focuses on two aspects: first, how the mariners influenced and were influenced by the political and religious developments of the period, and second, the social world they inhabited (though I have concentrated here on what was distinctive in a revolutionary age rather than attempting to provide a comprehensive survey of shipboard life in the seventeenth century). I felt it necessary to provide some narrative account of naval operations, partly because the naval wars of the 1650s were closely related to the security and maintenance of the regime at home, and partly as a reminder that the mariners' responses to events ashore have to be to set in the context of almost continuous war at sea. I have given less space to naval administration, which has been well described by others, from the excellent pioneering work of Oppenheim to the recent important theses of Dr Hammond and Dr Cogar.

The title of the book echoes Firth's *Cromwell's Army*, though the two works are very different in approach. The title, I admit, is somewhat unfair to the Rump, which played the major part in expanding and remoulding the fleet. Cromwell, however, was the lucky beneficiary, grasping its full potential and repeating the benefits of the international prestige it brought in its wake, and in the later 1650s the navy was as closely identified with his name as the army itself.

I am grateful to the British Academy for a grant towards the costs of research, and to the University of Warwick for sabbatical leave and for acquiring a considerable body of research material on microfilm. I would also like to acknowledge a debt to Dr David Davies, whose thesis on the Restoration navy is to be published, and to the authors of the other theses I have consulted. Dr N. A. M. Rodger's *Wooden World* appeared when this book was almost complete but made me look again at many of my previous assumptions. I am also grateful to the many libraries which have provided assistance, and especially to the Stepney United Reformed Church for permission to consult the early church-book in its possession. It would be nice to remember Samuel Pepys too, who planned a book on the same subject over three hundred years ago. Given the many other calls on Pepys's time and energy it is not surprising that his book remained unwritten, but he eased my task by saving and collecting many of the key manuscript sources.

I have added (in square brackets) the date a publication was acquired by the London bookseller George Thomason whenever it seemed significant or was needed to distinguish between two works with the same title. The spelling of quotations has been modernized throughout. Dates are given in the Old Style, though the year is taken as beginning on 1 January.

Marcus Rediker's important work, *Between the Devil and the Deep Blue Sea* (Cambridge, 1987), appeared too late for me to use in preparing this book.

B.C.

January 1988

CONTENTS

Abbreviations   xi

1. Introduction   1

PART I

2. The Revolt of 1648   15

3. The Navy New-Modelled   42

4. Gunboat Diplomacy and War, 1652–1660   73
     i. The Dutch war   73
    ii. France and the war with Spain   86
   iii. The Baltic crisis   106

5. Politics and the Navy, 1649–1658   115

PART II

6. Naval Officers: A Social Profile   155
     i. Commissioned officers: selection   155
    ii. The anatomy of the officer corps   162
   iii. Promotion and patronage   179
    iv. Authority   190
     v. Turnover   195
    vi. The warrant-officers   201

7. The Floating Commonwealth   212
     i. The ship's community   213
    ii. Public and private interest   230
   iii. The quality of life   243

8. Manning the Fleet   258
     i. Volunteers and the press   258
    ii. The seamen's grievances   275
   iii. Desertion and mutiny   282

9. Saints Afloat? Religion in the Fleet — 293

   i. The officer corps — 293
   ii. The ministry at sea — 307
   iii. Religion and the seaman — 321

PART III

10. The Navy and the Restoration — 331

11. The Legacy of the Commonwealth — 371

Conclusion — 395

Sources — 402

Index — 407

ABBREVIATIONS

A and O	C. H. Firth and R. S. Rait (eds.), *Acts and Ordinances of the Interregnum* (1911).
BDBR	R. L. Greaves and R. Zaller (eds.), *Biographical Dictionary of British Radicals in the Seventeenth Century* (1982–4).
Blake, *Letters*	*The Letters of Robert Blake*, ed. J. R. Powell (NRS, 1937).
BL	British Library.
Bodl.	Bodleian Library.
Burton, *Diary*	*The Diary of Thomas Burton Esq.*, ed. J. T. Rutt (1828).
CCSP	O. Ogle *et al.* (eds.), *Calendar of Clarendon State Papers Preserved in the Bodleian Library* (Oxford, 1869–1970).
Chaplain, 'Bourne'	W. R. Chaplain, 'Nehemiah Bourne', *Transactions of the Colonial Society of Massachusetts*, xlii (Boston, Mass., 1952–6).
CJ	*Journals of the House of Commons.*
Clarendon, *History*	Edward Hyde, Earl of Clarendon, *The History of the Rebellion*, ed. W. D. Macray (Oxford, 1888).
Clarke MS	Clarke MSS, Worcester College, Oxford.
Clarke Papers	*The Clarke Papers*, ed. C. H. Firth (Camden Soc., 1891–1901).
Coventry MS	Coventry MSS (Bath Papers, Longleat).
Cromwell, *Writings*	*The Writings and Speeches of Oliver Cromwell*, ed. W. C. Abbott (Cambridge, Mass., 1937–47).
CSP	*State Papers collected by Edward, Earl of Clarendon* (Oxford, 1786).
CSP Col.	*Calendar of State Papers, Colonial.*
CSPD	*Calendar of State Papers, Domestic.*
CSPV	*Calendar of State Papers, Venetian.*
Davies	G. Davies, *The Restoration of Charles II, 1658–1660* (San Marino, Calif., 1955).
DCW	J. R. Powell and E. K. Timings (eds.), *Documents Relating to the Civil War, 1642–1648* (NRS, 1963).

EHR	*English Historical Review.*
FDW	S. R. Gardiner and C. T. Atkinson (eds.), *Letters and Papers Relating to the First Dutch War, 1652–4* (NRS, 1899–1930).
Firth	C. H. Firth, *The Last Years of the Protectorate, 1656–1658* (1909).
Gardiner, *CP*	S. R. Gardiner, *History of the Commonwealth and Protectorate, 1649–1656* (1903).
HMC	Historical Manuscripts Commission.
HS	Harleian Society.
LJ	*Journals of the House of Lords.*
MM	*Mariner's Mirror.*
NMM	National Maritime Museum, Greenwich.
NRS	Navy Records Society.
Oppenheim	M. Oppenheim, *A History of the Administration of the Royal Navy . . . from MDIX to MDCLX* (1896).
Penn, *Memorials*	G. Penn, *Memorials of Sir William Penn* (1833).
Pepys, *Cat.*	J. R. Tanner (ed.), *A Descriptive Catalogue of the Naval MSS in the Pepysian Library* (NRS, 1903–23).
Pepys, *Diary*	*The Diary of Samuel Pepys,* ed. R. Latham and W. Matthews (1970–83).
Powell, *Blake*	J. R. Powell, *Robert Blake: General-at-Sea* (1972).
PRO	Public Record Office.
Sandwich, *Journal*	*The Journal of Edward Mountagu, First Earl of Sandwich,* ed. R. C. Anderson (NRS, 1929).
Thurloe	T. Birch (ed.), *A Collection of the State Papers of John Thurloe* (1742).

Place of publication is London unless otherwise stated.

I

Introduction

THE royalist statesman and historian Lord Clarendon once remarked that Cromwell's enormous power in England was as 'nothing compared with his greatness abroad'.[1] Clarendon had found by bitter experience that the Protector's magnificent navy, even more than the celebrated army, had made him feared and courted throughout Europe. The Venetian secretary too had noted in 1655 how it was bringing him 'friendship and repute in every part of the world'.[2] This powerful naval force had been built up by the Rump Parliament in the years after 1649 as essential for the new republic's survival. Quickly recognizing the potential of its new weapon the Rump had then turned the fleet against its commercial rivals, the Dutch, waging England's most successful war of the century. Cromwell as Protector employed the navy even more boldly in far-flung and ambitious schemes.

Yet for Cromwell, as for the Rump, the navy always existed primarily to defend the regime at home and keep the Stuarts at bay. To make sense of naval history in this period we therefore need to place it squarely in the context of domestic politics. Equally the domestic political history of these years has a naval dimension often overlooked. While historians have always recognized the army's political importance they have been less conscious of the navy's role, and most modern studies of the interregnum indeed give far less coverage of naval affairs than did Gardiner and Firth.[3] One

[1] Clarendon, *History*, vi. 94.
[2] *CSPV 1655–6*, 48.
[3] Even Gardiner once thought the navy was largely neutral in the civil war (C. D. Penn, *The Navy under the Early Stuarts* (1970; 1st pub. 1913), 268; cf. C. H. Firth in *MM* xii (1926), 239), though he more than compensated for this later. The theses of Baumber, Kennedy, and Cogar help to set the record straight; little of their work has appeared in print, but see D. E. Kennedy, 'Naval Captains at the Outbreak of the English Civil War', *MM* xlvi (1960) and idem, 'The English Naval Revolt of 1648', *EHR* lxxvii (1962). Hammond's thesis plays down the political aspects except during the crisis of 1659–60.

purpose of this book is to reintegrate the navy's story with the main currents of English history: to examine how each influenced the other, and how far radical ideology—whether political or religious—affected the fleet. One of its central arguments is that the navy was a highly politicized, partisan force—a fact deliberately signalled at the time by the practice of naming new warships after civil war victories. The officer corps was drastically remodelled in 1649 and later, with ideological criteria playing a key part in the process. Every interregnum regime recognized how much it depended on the fleet's political reliability, and each saw the need to mould a navy that was Puritan and parliamentarian as well as patriotic. This assessment contrasts sharply with some recent 'revisionist' studies of the New Model Army, which have challenged the traditional picture of it as a hotbed of radical ideas. In the context of current debates the thesis advanced here is thus 'counter-revisionist': while the army may have been less swayed by ideology than we used to think, our assessment of the navy needs to be revised in the opposite direction.[4] The second major aim of the book is to explore social structures and relationships within the fleet, and within each ship's company. The navy formed a community as populous as the largest provincial towns of the period, and the web of relationships binding officers and seamen together was both subtle and complex, far removed from the blunt tyranny of popular tradition. This is a field still relatively unexplored. Military and naval history ought to be, and can be, part of the social historian's terrain.[5]

During the civil war the naval contribution to the parliamentary cause was secondary. Victory was decided on land. The fact that Parliament had control of the navy was none the less vital in making victory possible. If the king had retained control of the fleet the royalists could have blockaded London, and the resulting economic dislocation might easily have generated enough popular pressure to force Parliament into peace on almost any terms. During the war the navy's undramatic work in protecting commerce kept up the

---

[4] See esp. M. Kishlansky, *The Rise of the New Model Army* (Cambridge, 1983). I believe Kishlansky greatly overstated his case. See the important material assembled by Robert Temple in 'The Original Officer List of the New Model Army', *Bulletin of the Institute of Historical Research*, lix (1986), 50-77.

[5] The best and most recent study is N. A. M. Rodger, *The Wooden World: An Anatomy of the Georgian Navy* (1986); earlier surveys include C. Lloyd, *The British Seaman, 1200–1860: A Social Survey* (1970 edn.). The subject has attracted few historians who are not naval specialists.

level of customs revenues and helped finance the war-effort. The navy was an effective deterrent to any foreign monarch tempted to send help to Charles. It assisted land campaigns by transporting supplies and reinforcements and by providing a mobile artillery. It played an important role in maintaining the outposts at Hull and Plymouth, and contributed to the capture of Bristol and Newcastle. The earl of Warwick, as Lord High Admiral, and his vice-admiral and successor William Batten provided vigorous and effective leadership.[6]

During the interregnum the navy's role was far more spectacular. The rulers of continental Europe were horrified by the execution of the king in January 1649 and all repudiated the new Commonwealth. The navy was thus needed to protect England from possible invasion and to force foreign powers to recognize the new regime. Over the next eleven years it was almost continuously in action, both defensive and offensive. It fought against royalist privateers and against the French (1649–55), Portuguese (1650), Dutch (1652–4), Spaniards and Flemings (1655–60), and North African corsairs. Even the barest summary conveys the unprecedented breadth of these operations. The fleet pursued Prince Rupert's squadron to Ireland, Portugal, and the Mediterranean (1649–50); it reduced the Channel Islands, Barbados, and Virginia (1651–2), and waged England's first major war at sea, against the Dutch (1652–4). Blake led an expedition to the Straits (1654–5) while Penn took another fleet to the Caribbean to assault the Spanish American empire. Blake and Mountagu blockaded the Spanish coast in 1656, and Blake destroyed a Spanish Plate fleet in the Canaries the following year. A smaller force under Stokes remained off Spain and in the Straits in 1657–9, while the main fleet was blockading the Flemish coast. In 1659 Mountagu led an expedition to the Baltic, an early example of gunboat diplomacy designed to protect English interests in the war between Denmark and Sweden. In addition the navy protected merchant shipping in home waters and as far afield as the Iceland and Newfoundland fisheries, St Helena, and the Mediterranean. And it maintained constant patrols in the Channel, successfully blocking royalist plans for incursions from the continent.

[6] J. R. Powell, *The Navy in the English Civil War* (1962); *DCW*; Baumber, thesis; Kennedy, thesis. Kenyon's remark that the navy was 'more ornamental than useful' to Parliament is very misleading: J. P. Kenyon, *Stuart England* (2nd edn., Harmondsworth, 1985), 159–60.

At first the navy was poorly equipped for the tasks ahead, both in human and material terms. Part of the Channel fleet had revolted in 1648 and joined the royalists in the Netherlands, and disaffection was rife in the ships which remained. Much of this book is concerned with the Commonwealth's endeavours to create a new, loyal officer corps and a body of orderly and contented seamen, supported by a committed and efficient administration ashore. The rest of this introduction is devoted to a brief survey of the other major aspects, in particular the navy's dramatic increase in size and the problems this raised. A fleet that had been sufficient to contain the cavalier threat in the 1640s was too weak to face the hostility of the whole of Europe. At the beginning of 1649 the Rump had only fifty warships, plus a few light shallops and ketches.[7] In the past the state had reinforced the navy in times of emergency by hiring armed merchant ships, as was done during the Armada campaign and, more recently, during the civil war; the summer guard for 1643, for example, had comprised thirty warships and forty-four hired merchantmen.[8] The Rump too hired merchant shipping on a considerable scale. But the interregnum also saw a massive increase in the number of ships owned by the state. Between 1649 and 1660 the navy added some 216 ships to its force, an unprecedented expansion.[9] About half of them—110—were former prizes, mostly Dutch with others of Portuguese, French, Spanish, Flemish, and even Swedish and Genoese origin. Towards the end of the Dutch War Thurloe could gleefully boast, 'We are able to fight them with their own ships.'[10] Far more significant was the huge building programme which the Rump undertook. It ordered five new warships as early as March 1649. Twenty ships of the third, fourth, and fifth rates were added in 1650–1 —quite large and well armed by the standards of the time, and more manoeuvrable, versatile, and cost-effective than the great ships favoured by Charles I in the 1630s.[11] The outbreak of war with the Dutch in

[7] R. C. Anderson, *Lists of Men-of War, 1650–1700: Part 1, English Ships, 1649–1702* (2nd edn., no date), 5–8.

[8] *DCW* 69–72.

[9] Anderson, *Lists*, 11–20.

[10] S. von Bischoffshausen (ed.), *Die Politik des Protectors Oliver Cromwell* (Innsbruck, 1899), 161. Thurloe estimated that 120 of the captured Dutch ships were men-of-war.

[11] *CSPD 1649–50*, 59, 82; Anderson, *Lists*, 11–12. The following examples give some idea of relative sizes: *Naseby*, 1st rate, 80–6 guns, 1230 tons; *Swiftsure*, 2nd rate, 60–4 guns, 898 tons; *Essex*, 3rd rate, 48–60 guns, 652 tons; *Preston*, 4th rate,

1652 brought a further acceleration: in September the Rump approved a plan to build thirty more warships.[12] The results of this twin-track policy were impressive. At the battle off the Gabbard in 1653 the English were able to assemble a formidable force of 118 vessels.[13] The total naval forces prepared for service that year amounted to no less that 180 ships.[14]

Cromwell's navy was largely inherited from the Rump. The Spaniards wisely avoided fleet actions, so it was possible to scale down the building programme. A number of small, fast vessels of shallow draught were built to match the Flemish privateers, and several prizes of this type were added during the later 1650s.[15] Larger ships were still being constructed too, if at a less hectic pace. The magnificence of the *Tredagh*, a third-rate built in 1654, overwhelmed a Venetian ambassador who crossed the Channel in her the following year. 'If your Serenity had a dozen like it in your fleet,' he wrote home, 'no naval power could stand against them.'[16] The year 1655 saw the launching of the great *Naseby*, attended by a throng of political leaders. The first ship of the first rate to be built since 1637, it symbolized both the domestic and imperial roles of the new navy. It was known at first, unofficially, as the *Great Oliver,* and John Evelyn noted with distaste that it carried on its prow an effigy of 'Oliver on horseback, trampling six nations under foot, a Scot, Irishman, Dutch, French, Spaniard and English . . . a Fame held a laurel over his insulting head; and the Word, *God with us*'.[17] Three years later another first-rate was launched and named the *Richard,* after Cromwell's eldest son, a further reminder of the navy's importance to the regime.[18] Not all the ships added during

40–50 guns, 516 tons; *Mermaid,* 5th rate, 24–32 guns, 286 tons; *Drake,* 6th rate, 12–16 guns, 146 tons. Manning levels fluctuated widely according to circumstances. As a very rough guide Pepys's figures for 1660 average about 500 men for a 1st-rate, 300 for a 2nd, 200 for a 3rd, 130 for a 4th, 90 for a 5th, 50 for a 6th: Pepys, *Cat.* i. 256–63.

[12] *CJ* vii. 186, 222; *CSPD 1651–2,* 429, 493; *CSPD 1652–3,* 55.

[13] *FDW* v. 20 gives 105 ships under Deane and Monck, increased by 13 when Blake's squadron arrived: Blake, *Letters,* 215.

[14] Bodl. Clarendon MS 47, fo. 183.

[15] Anderson, *Lists,* 18–20.   [16] *CSPV 1655–6,* 111.

[17] Ibid. 36, 48; *The Diary of John Evelyn,* ed. E. S. de Beer (Oxford, 1955), iii. 149–50. The effigy was derived from that of the Saxon King Edgar on the *Sovereign*: J. Charnock, *A History of Marine Architecture* (1801–2), ii. 281. Cromwell and his Council were present at the launching.

[18] Anderson, *Lists,* 20. Richard attended the launching: *CSPV 1657–9,* 209; *Mercurius Politicus,* 20–7 May 1658.

the interregnum were still in service in 1660, of course. Twenty had been wrecked, burnt, or blown up accidentally; twelve had been captured, mostly small escorts seized by heavily manned Flemish privateers; three had been destroyed in action; and many Dutch prizes were sold in the later 1650s as superfluous to current requirements.[19] Even so, when Pepys surveyed the navy at the Restoration he was able to list 161 ships owned by the state, 135 of them warships of the first to sixth rates: a naval force such as no English monarch had ever possessed.[20] None of England's neighbours could match it. In France, Mazarin had allowed the powerful navy he had inherited from Richelieu to run down, till by 1661 it numbered only about twenty vessels. Spanish sea-power had never recovered from the devastating defeat by Tromp off the Downs in 1639; though Flemish warships and privateers were highly successful in raiding commerce the Spanish navy never dared challenge the English fleet in this period. Only the Dutch could set out a fleet comparable in size and strength to England's. Their peacetime force of forty ships, established in 1648, could be rapidly reinforced in an emergency, but the battles of 1652 to 1653 showed that even the Dutch navy was no longer able to match the more strongly built and heavily gunned English vessels.[21]

The Commonwealth's urgent need to build up the navy in the years after 1649 is clear; but why did it turn away from the traditional practice of hiring merchantmen? In many respects this had worked well, for ships trading to the Straits, East Indies, and Americas were generally strong and well armed. The Rump did continue to employ merchant shipping extensively for coastal protection and escort duty. But the conflict with the Dutch inaugurated a new age of naval warfare, characterized by great fleet engagements in which merchant vessels proved very vulnerable. Their commanders were understandably reluctant to engage the enemy in such circumstances, as the flag-officers Ayscue and Penn complained bitterly in 1652. The 'baseness of spirit' of merchant commanders contributed to Blake's defeat at Dungeness in December that year,

[19] Anderson, *Lists*, 11–20.
[20] Pepys, *Cat*. i. 256–63.
[21] For a general survey see *The New Cambridge Modern History, iv, 1609–1648/59*, ed. J. P. Cooper (Cambridge, 1970), ch. 7; C. W. Cole, *Colbert and a Century of French Mercantilism* (1964), i. 451, (cf. i. 456–7 for Colbert's subsequent expansion); J. I. Israel, *The Dutch Republic and the Hispanic World, 1606–1661* (Oxford, 1982), 268–70. On the Dutch: *FDW* i. 57–8, v. 4.

and Blake and his captains begged the state to employ only its own ships in future, adding that if it had to hire some merchantmen too they must never be allowed to form more than one-fifth of the fleet. The Council accepted this advice, resolving to add prizes to the navy and use them in preference to hired merchantmen wherever possible.[22] The state was not able to dispense with merchant ships altogether during the Dutch war, but Cromwell discharged them as soon as peace was signed and pursued his ambitious designs against Spain using state-owned ships alone.[23]

The caution of merchant owners and commanders was natural, for in hiring their ships to the state they risked their estates as well as their lives. The Rump, following tradition, contracted to pay owners a fixed sum and made them responsible for supplying guns, ammunition, and powder. When a ship was being hired for coastal protection this arrangement promised the owners a reasonable chance of profit, but it was pitifully inadequate in the new conditions of naval warfare. The owners of the *Hannibal* refused to renew her contract on the old terms of 1653, complaining that the cost of powder alone expended in actions such as the recent battle off Portland would quickly swallow up the whole of the hire.[24] Traditional contracts also laid down that owners had to bear the loss if a ship was destroyed or captured, a fate increasingly probable.[25] Many commanders were themselves part-owners, and with their estates tied up in their ships they were likely to be doubly cautious. Most owners insisted on naming the ship's commander, seeing this as the best way to preserve it from the enemy and from embezzlement by the crew. Fear of embezzlement was a major concern, a point well made by Capt. Richard Badiley, a staunch parliamentarian, in a letter he sent to the Admiralty Commissioners about a hired ship belonging to a friend; Badiley begged them to appoint a commander who was not merely a 'fighting man but a person that will husband such things as belong to the ship, without which the owners were better [to] break her up than let her go into the service'.[26]

[22] J. Nickolls (ed.), *Original Letters and Papers of State* (1743), 86–7; *CSPV 1647–52*, 283; Clarke MS 1/12, fo. 14; *FDW* iii. 92, 147, 167–8, 178, 308.

[23] *CSPD 1654*, 144.

[24] Bodl. Rawlinson MS A 185, fo. 75.

[25] *FDW* iii. 394; for a typical contract see PRO SP 18/17/19. If a ship was sunk, the owners were paid for its hire only for the period actually served.

[26] SP 18/60/41; cf. *CSPD 1652–3*, 401.

The remedies for these problems would seem straightforward. In January 1653 Nehemiah Bourne, a senior official, urged the Admiralty to give owners 'some assurance of encouragement in case their ships shall be lost in fight,' and this was done in subsequent contracts.[27] The Rump also insisted on appointing its own commanders, heeding the advice of Blake and Penn.[28] This policy was widely enforced in 1653, though (as previous attempts had indicated) there were many problems to be overcome. Some commanders who were part-owners refused to take other ships, even far better ones. Owners too might refuse to sign a contract unless they kept the right to appoint the ship's commander, and if the state insisted they could deploy a variety of obstructive and time-wasting devices to render its hire worthless. And the owners were not the only problem, for sailors who had volunteered to serve under one captain sometimes deserted when they found a stranger set over them.[29] The state, with very limited administrative resources, often found it hard to impose its will.

In the unique circumstances of the interregnum there was also a political risk in using merchant shipping. 'Malignant' owners were likely to be uncooperative, and 'malignant' skippers might prove unreliable in action. Several of the merchant ships Richard Badiley pressed into service in the Straits in 1652–3 had commanders of this kind, and he found them truculent and openly hostile to the government.[30] Merchant commanders serving with Ayscue in 1652 had not only kept their ships well out of range of enemy guns, but had also (it was alleged) boasted afterwards to their royalist owners how they had strolled on deck drinking sack while his warships were being battered by the Dutch.[31] A change of policy was thus being

---

[27] *FDW* iii. 394. For examples of the new form of contract see *FDW* iv. 238–40; SP 18/49/5. The state now supplied powder and shot, and some guns; it retained the right to decide whether a ship had been lost honourably and the level of compensation.

[28] *FDW* iii. 168; Nickolls, *Original Letters*, 86.

[29] For problems before 1653 see SP 25/123, p. 199; Rawl. MS A 225, fo. 44ᵛ; BL Additional MS 9306, fo. 2; Bodl. Deposit MS C 169, fo. 82; Bodl. Tanner MS 56, fo. 174; for problems in 1653 see Rawl. MS A 461, fos. 2ᵛ–3; Rawl. MS A 227, fo. 61ᵛ; SP 46/119/179; SP 18/51/102; SP 18/52/107–8; *CSPD 1652–3*, 538.

[30] R. Badiley, *Capt. Badiley's Answer* (1653), 52, 72; idem, *Capt. Badiley's Reply* (1653), 1–2, 9. For their reluctance to fight or co-operate see T. A. Spalding, *A Life of Richard Badiley* (Westminster, 1899), chs. 8–16, and below, chs. 4, 5, 6. In 1650 the Navy Commissioners had been directed to treat only with well-affected owners in hiring ships for an expedition to reduce the American colonies: *CSPD 1650*, 502.

[31] HMC 29, *Portland*, i. 673.

forced on the Rump by political considerations as much as by the changing nature of war.

The new navy placed an immense burden on national resources. There was heavy strain on the dockyards, the ordnance office, and naval supplies, especially timber. Some of the building had to be dispersed to yards at Portsmouth, Southampton, and Shoreham in the south, Yarmouth, Woodbridge, Walberswick, and Maldon in the east, and Bristol and Lydney (utilizing timber from the Forest of Dean) in the west.[32] Demands on manpower were equally heavy. The summer guard planned for 1652, with the distant convoys already at sea, required a total of 10,024 seamen. A fleet survey of September 1653, in the midst of the Dutch war, recorded a figure of 19,254 men. The plans laid for the summer campaign of 1654 called for 30,000 men.[33] To put these figures in perspective we might note that Buckingham's expedition to the Île de Ré in 1627 had been manned by less than 4,000 sailors.[34] The demand for manpower remained high under the Protectorate. The summer guard of 1655 with the expeditions already dispatched to the Straits and the Caribbean required over 13,000 men.[35] The navy tried to improve conditions to attract volunteers, but there were never enough; only pressing on a large scale could supply such huge numbers.[36]

The last and greatest burden on the state's resources was financial. Expenditure, about £2–300,000 a year in the 1640s, rose dramatically under the Rump. The pursuit of Rupert in 1649–51 alone cost some £214,000. The summer guard for 1652, combined with squadrons already dispatched to the Straits, Virginia, and West Indies, required an outlay of £424,264.[37] During the Dutch war costs climbed higher still. The thirty frigates ordered in 1652 needed £300,000 to construct and set out.[38] Figures given later by Pepys

[32] R. G. Albion, *Forests and Sea Power* (Hamden, Conn., 1965); Anderson, *Lists*, 11–20; Pepys, *Cat.* i. 256–63; Oppenheim, 330–40, 362–8.

[33] *CJ* vii. 69–70; *FDW* i. 64–8; *FDW* vi. 49–53; Rawl. MS A 223, p. 130.

[34] G. E. Manwaring (ed.), *The Life and Works of Sir Henry Mainwaring* (NRS, 1920/2), i. 171–2.

[35] SP 25 I 75, pp. 412–13, 666; SP 18/94/60; Powell, *Blake*, 254; Penn, *Memorials*, ii. 17–18. The summer guard for 1658, when there was no major expedition, numbered 8,000 men, plus small forces already in the Straits and at Jamaica: PRO Adm. 3/273, fo. 172.

[36] See ch. 8.

[37] Rawl. MS A 223, p. 77; Bodl. Dep. MS C 170, fo. 300; *FDW* i. 70. On naval finance see Hammond, thesis, ch. 4; Cogar, thesis, chs. 2, part iii, 3, part vi.

[38] *CJ* vii. 222.

showed £1.41 millions spent on the navy in 1653 and £1.06 millions in 1654. A Treasury paper of February 1654 put the total sum due for the navy the previous year at a staggering £2.16 millions, almost matching the state's entire income for the same period.[39] The revenues traditionally used to finance the navy, mainly from customs, were totally inadequate; even in 1651 customs had provided only half the sum required.[40] During the Dutch war Parliament had to assign up to a third of the monthly assessment, its main tax, to the navy, instead of reserving it to the army as was usual. Cromwell was not far off the mark in claiming later that the war had 'cost this nation full as much as the taxes came unto'.[41] Under the Protectorate naval expenditure was somewhat lower, at half to three-quarters of a million pounds annually.[42] But state revenues also fell as the assessment was cut for political reasons, and naval administrators had to fall back on traditional sources which were still insufficient.[43] A Council order of 1655 earmarked all revenues for the navy except the monthly assessment,[44] but this too failed to solve the problem, and Admiralty papers in the late 1650s show mounting anxiety and desperation. By the last months of the interregnum the stores were totally depleted and contractors were refusing any new supplies until the state settled its old debts, while seamen and dockyard workers were unpaid and angry. There was a growing danger that the navy would simply disintegrate. It was estimated in March 1660 that some £1.2 millions would be needed by October to clear the navy's charge, and this debt was one of the most pressing problems confronting Charles II when he returned to England a few weeks later.[45]

The Commonwealth governments successfully built and deployed a magnificent navy but failed, like Charles I before them, to find a politically acceptable way of paying for it. Yet the question of whether naval expansion had been a wise policy would have seemed meaningless to them. In 1649 a strong navy was essential if

---

[39] Bodl. Carte MS 74, fo. 123. The state's total revenue was put at £2.5m.; the army's cost, at £1.5m., was well below that of the navy at this point.

[40] *CJ* vi. 580.

[41] *CJ* vii. 225; *A and O* ii. 653; Cromwell, *Writings*, iii. 438.

[42] Rawl. MS A 181, fo. 36; M. Ashley, *Financial and Commercial Policy under the Cromwellian Protectorate* (2nd edn., 1962), 48.

[43] Adm. 3/274, fo. 103ʳ⁻ᵛ; Ashley, *Financial Policy*, 57.

[44] *CSPD 1655*, 394.   [45] *CSPD 1659–60*, 383; below, ch. 10.

the new republic was to survive, and even in the later 1650s Cromwell did not feel secure enough to disband the force he had inherited. He plunged into war with Spain in the hope that the navy could pay for itself from captured treasure, while simultaneously undermining the power of Antichrist. Though his gamble failed, such grandiose designs had belonged to the world of dreams only a few years earlier.

Part I

2

The Revolt of 1648

DURING the civil war the navy was in the hands of experienced and respected leaders. The earl of Warwick, the Lord High Admiral, had organized and led many privateering expeditions, and William Batten, his vice-admiral, was a professional seaman who had been surveyor of the navy before the war.[1] Both were strong Puritans, Warwick being regarded as one of the main pillars of the Presbyterian party in the Lords, and together they moulded an officer corps reflecting this outlook.[2] When the Self-Denying Ordinance forced Warwick out of office in 1645 Batten stayed on as vice-admiral and took over command of the fleet.[3]

The end of the civil war in 1646 failed to bring the political settlement such moderates had sought. They grew increasingly afraid that militant Independents in the Commons and the army would instead sweep away the old constitutional order altogether. When Batten was sent to Tynemouth at the close of 1646, to foil a suspected plan to smuggle the king abroad, he came into close contact with the Scots Commissioners who held similar fears, and the episode no doubt deepened his sense of mistrust. Batten's views were probably reflected in a sermon which his chaplain, Samuel Kem, preached before the king on the need for moderation and reconciliation, a theme which pleased Charles but caused some disquiet in London.[4]

In the spring of 1647 the friction between moderates and radicals came to a head over Parliament's attempt to disband the New

[1] DNB; J. R. Powell, The Navy in the English Civil War (1962), passim; DCW 1–261.
[2] Clarendon, History, ii. 225 (Batten), iv. 245 (Warwick).
[3] S. R. Gardiner, History of the Great Civil War, 1642–1649 (1894), ii. 190; DCW 178, 194–6, 198–200; V. A. Rowe, Sir Henry Vane the Younger (1970), 125–8.
[4] DCW 264, 269–70; HMC 3, 4th Report, 274. For Kem see DNB; he had served as a major in the army, and years later was to command a privateer in the Second Dutch War: PRO HCA 25/9, 25/10.

Model Army, which was rightly seen as the major obstacle to a settlement with the king. (Warwick played an active part in this programme, visiting the army headquarters in April to urge the officers to accept the terms on offer.) The soldiers refused to disband until their grievances were met, and a full-scale mutiny ensued, soon absorbing elements of Leveller ideology, and many of the leading officers (including Cromwell) threw in their lot with the mutineers.[5] Batten was warned to look out for attempts to subvert the navy, and the army agitators did indeed publish an appeal to the seamen in July; but the army's radicalism appears to have made no headway in the fleet at this stage.[6]

In August the army occupied London and its political allies resumed their seats in Parliament, bringing charges of treason against their leading opponents. Six of those accused tried to escape abroad, leading to an incident which exposed the massive gulf dividing the army and navy. For when the vessel hired by the fleeing MPs was overhauled in the Channel and brought into the Downs Batten merely examined their passes and then allowed them to resume their journey, instead of sending them up to London.[7] This blatant affront convinced the newly dominant Independent group at Westminister that it was essential to place the navy in more reliable hands. On 9 September the Commons named several new Admiralty Commissioners, transforming the political complexion of the body; among the newcomers were the radical Independents Col. Thomas Rainborough and Henry Marten. The Commissioners then summoned the vice-admiral to explain his recent conduct.[8] They had before them a report that he had accused the army of planning to put the king to death, and even if his remarks had been distorted his general hostility to the army and its allies was clear. There is evidence too that he had written to the earl of Lauderdale offering naval assistance to the Scots should they try to restore the king by force, though the Commissioners appear to have been unaware of this. They had sufficient ammunition for their needs: when Batten appeared before them on 17 September they

[5] For contrasting accounts of this episode see e.g. Gardiner, *Civil War*, iii, chs. 47–50; M. Kishlansky, *The Rise of the New Model Army* (Cambridge, 1983), ch. 7; A. Woolrych, *Soldiers and Statesmen* (Oxford, 1987). For Warwick's role: J. Rushworth, *Historical Collections* (1659–1701), vi. 457, 496; Gardiner, *Civil War*, iii. 233.

[6] *DCW* 282; PRO Adm. 7/673, pp. 323, 330; Woolrych, *Soldiers*, 127, 129.

[7] *DCW* 284–7.   [8] *CJ* v. 297; Adm. 7/673, pp. 376, 379, 381; Rowe, *Vane*, 132.

threatened to bring charges unless he resigned his post, and he promptly did so rather than risk an inquiry into his activities.[9] A hundred naval officers had earlier declared their support for Batten's decision over the six MPs, a dramatic indication of his popularity, and his abrupt removal predictably aroused deep anger within the fleet.[10]

The earl of Warwick was conspicuously absent from the group of Commissioners who sat in judgement on Batten.[11] Prominent among those who did attend was the newly appointed Col. Rainborough, the only high-ranking army officer with experience in the parliamentary navy. Rainborough came from a prominent seafaring family; his father had commanded an expedition against the Moorish corsairs at Sallee in 1637 and he himself had commanded a warship in 1643 before transferring to service ashore.[12] He was therefore in many ways an obvious choice to succeed Batten: Independent leaders could be sure of his support as they drove a hard bargain with the king, and they would be relieved to have the one senior officer sympathetic to the Levellers removed to a safe distance. On 27 September the Commons nominated him vice-admiral and commander of the winter guard, and the Lords gave their approval (despite Warwick's dissent). But before taking up his new command Rainborough was involved in Leveller agitation at the army rendezvous at Ware, and the Lords thereupon voted to block his appointment.[13] This led to a long and damaging hiatus in the naval high command. When the king escaped to the Isle of Wight in November, clearly bent on reopening the war, the army officers closed ranks; Rainborough apologized for his past conduct and General Fairfax urged the Lords to reinstate him. They still refused. The Commons feared that without a politically reliable

[9] *DCW* 266–7, 287–90, 364–5.
[10] *A Declaration of the Representations of the Officers of the Navy* (1647), 5; *DCW* 365.   [11] *DCW* 289.
[12] *DNB; DCW* 70, 277; for his family background see W. R. Chaplin, 'William Rainsborough (1587–1642) and his Associates of the Trinity House', *MM* xxxi (1945), 178–97.
[13] *CJ* v. 318, 359, 366, 378, *LJ* ix. 459, 526; Rushworth, *Collections*, vii. 822; Clarendon, *History*, iv. 331; Woolrych, *Soldiers*, ch. 11. Cromwell had opposed the appointment, preferring his own protégé Richard Deane as a more amenable commander: *The Tower Letter-Book of Sir Lewis Dyve 1646–47*, ed. H. G. Tibbutt (Bedfordshire Historical Record Soc., xxxviii; 1958), 84–5, 89; Rowe, *Vane*, 132–3. Ironically he feared Rainborough would have too much personal support among the seamen, and might infect them with his Leveller views!

head the fleet might allow Charles to be spirited away to France or Scotland, and on 1 January 1648 they therefore directed Rainborough to take up his command in defiance of the Lords' veto. The momentous vote of No Further Addresses followed two days later.[14]

Once in place Rainborough threw himself energetically into his new work, calling for ships to be set out with haste to suppress Irish privateers and blocking a suspected design by the Dutch admiral Tromp to rescue the king.[15] Early in February the Commons agreed on a list of ships for the summer guard. The selection of commanders, however, dragged on well into the spring; it was a politically sensitive matter, complicated by divisions among the Admiralty Commissioners as well as in Parliament. Rainborough himself was reappointed only after further dispute. He was directed to observe his captains closely and dismiss any who appeared politically suspect, and two other senior army officers, Cols. Popham and Lidcott, were offered important naval commands to strengthen his position. Some appointments for the summer guard were not finalized until early in May, a delay that was to prove very damaging.[16]

The political situation was deteriorating rapidly. The continuing deadlock, with the general hatred of heavy taxes, military domination, and oppressive county committees, led to a series of disturbances in the spring of 1648. Fighting broke out in South Wales in March, and a few weeks later in May a serious upheaval followed in Kent. It began with a petition which called for a personal treaty between king and Parliament, the disbanding of the army, the lifting of taxes, and a return to traditional forms of local government; these aims had almost universal appeal, and the movement quickly became a general revolt. While the cavaliers naturally sought to exploit this eruption, it seems to have sprung spontaneously from a simple longing for normality, intensified by hatred of

---

[14] *CJ* v. 403, 405, 413, 417; *LJ* ix. 614–15, 616, 627; Rushworth, *Collections*, vii. 942, 944, 945, 948, 952; *DCW* 311–12; B. Whitelocke, *Memorials of the English Affairs* (Oxford, 1853), ii. 253, 256. Warwick dissented from the vote for No Further Addresses: *LJ* ix. 662.

[15] *DCW* 312–13, 314–15; Rushworth, *Collections*, vii. 989.

[16] *CJ* v. 458, 503–4, 545; Rushworth, *Collections*, vii. 989, 1067; BL Add. MS 9305, fos. 4ʳ⁻ᵛ, 5, 7, 28ᵛ–29, 43ᵛ, 47, 51ᵛ, 55, 60; *DCW* 312–14. In the event Popham and Lidcott did not serve until 1649. The ships they had been offered, the *Swallow* and *Satisfaction*, were both involved in the revolt.

Independent leaders both in the county and at Westminster.[17] The rebellion in Kent was the most dangerous episode of the 'Second Civil War', for the county was close to the capital and as it lay alongside the Thames the rebels could threaten the nation's major trade route; they were also well placed to receive support from abroad.

In the event the Kent revolt was short-lived. Fairfax marched into the county when the petitioners brushed aside an offer of indemnity, and on 1 June he stormed Maidstone. The rebels' morale collapsed: insurgents at Rochester and Dover fled before his troops arrived, and the main body surrendered at Canterbury on 9 June. But long before then disaffection had spread to the Channel fleet, which was based in the Downs, with serious and more lasting consequences.[18]

On 23 May the Navy Commissioner Peter Pett had sent an urgent warning from Chatham that parliamentary control in the area was on the point of collapse.[19] The Derby House Committee (Parliament's executive body) tried hard to contain the danger, directing Rainborough to station ships off the Medway to control movements to and from Chatham, and ordering the *Fellowship* and *Hector* to put to sea at once to avoid capture. It called too for stronger guards on the great *Sovereign* and *Prince*, lying in reserve at Chatham, and two senior and politically dependable commanders (Moulton and Hall) were given charge of them. Next day the Committee wrote to Trinity House, the association of shipmasters, urging its members to do all they could to keep the seamen loyal.[20] But these moves came too late to be effective and Pett found himself isolated at Chatham, his communications to London cut. The rebels seized Upnor Castle, controlling the Medway, and checked all ships attempting to pass. Capt. Jervoise of the *Fellowship* made no effort to put to sea and readily allowed the rebels to take over his ship.[21] Many of the senior dockyard officials at Chatham threw off their parliamentary allegiance; they were followed by many standing

[17] Gardiner, *Civil War*, vi, ch. 62; A. Everitt, *The Community of Kent and the Great Rebellion, 1640–1660* (Leicester, 1966), ch. 7.

[18] There are accounts of the naval revolt in Powell, *Navy*, chs. 10–12; *DCW* 299–407; D. E. Kennedy, 'The English Naval Revolt of 1648'. *EHR* lxxvii (1962); R. C. Anderson, 'The Royalists at Sea in 1648'. *MM* ix (1928), 34–46; Kennedy, thesis; Baumber, thesis.

[19] *DCW* 348; *CJ* v. 572; Rushworth, *Collections*, vii. 1127.

[20] *CSPD 1648–9*, 78–81; Add. MS 9305, fos. 72ᵛ, 75ᵛ.   [21] *DCW* 348–9.

officers of the ships in reserve there, among them the purser of the *Sovereign*, who also happened to be the mayor of Rochester. The rebels took control of the *Sovereign* and *Prince*, carrying away the powder and some of the guns.[22]

In the Downs there had been earlier signs of impending trouble. On 19 May an impostor landed at Deal claiming to be the Prince of Wales; though he was alone and almost destitute, sailors from the *Providence* accepted his claim and gave him money and relief, and some of the officers and men joined him at Sandwich, where he was able to establish himself in some style. The ship's captain, John Mildmay, expressed fears to Rainborough about the rest of his crew and was ordered to sail away north with the *Convertine* (also suspect) before the trouble spread any further—'if the men will be commanded to it'.[23]

Much worse was to follow. The Kent rebels occupied Sandwich on 23 May and their leaders soon received a visit from Samuel Kem, Batten's former chaplain, now minister at Deal and still active on his behalf. Kem offered to help spread the revolt to the fleet, and letters were quickly dispatched to every ship in the Downs, with copies of the Kent petition. On 27 May Kem found an opportunity to go aboard the flagship, the *Constant Reformation*, while Rainborough was ashore inspecting the defences of the small forts in the Downs. His arrival sparked off a mutiny.[24] Rainborough heard the clamour and hastened back to find his flagship in open revolt, along with the *Swallow*, *Roebuck*, and *Hind*. The mutineers refused to allow him back on board, and after delivering a volley of abuse and threats they bundled him and his family aboard a small vessel bound for London. They then took control of the remaining ships in the Downs, the *Satisfaction* and the *Pelican*, a hired merchantman. Any officers who remained loyal to Parliament were seized and imprisoned by their men. At first the mutineers appear to have had Batten in mind as leader, but when one sailor called for the earl of Warwick 'all the rest cried out presently, "a Warwick, a Warwick" '. They assured Capt. Penrose of the *Satisfaction* that they were not cavaliers and wanted to serve both king and Parliament, vowing to

---

[22] *DCW* 349–50; *CJ* v. 606–7.

[23] *DCW* 327–8, 329, 334; M. Carter, *A Most True and Exact Relation* (1650), 42–3, 46–7; *LJ* x. 288–90; *CSP* ii. 406.

[24] Carter, *True Relation*, 40, 51–3; *CSP* ii. 406; *DCW* 330–1; *Newes from Kent* ([1 June] 1648), 6.

'live and die' in that cause; Penrose refused to join them but agreed to take letters stating their position to Warwick and the Speaker of the Commons.[25] A number of gentlemen involved in the Kent rising came aboard and the mutineers readily endorsed their petition for a personal treaty and the disbanding of the army. Two of the visitors remained close by in Sandwich to liaise with the mariners.[26] On 28 May the mutineers sent a declaration justifying their actions to the Admiralty Commissioners in London.[27]

Parliament grasped at once the seriousness of the revolt. The Derby House Committee sent urgent letters to Rear-Admiral Bethel, commanding the squadron at Portsmouth, in an attempt to prevent the mutiny from spreading, and to Col. Hammond, the king's custodian in the Isle of Wight, to forestall any bid to rescue the king.[28] Rainborough's authority was clearly at an end. The City of London petitioned for Batten to be reinstated but Parliament had already reappointed Warwick as Lord High Admiral, on 29 May, and he sailed next morning for the Downs with authority to offer an indemnity if the mutineers agreed to submit. Before he reached the main rebel force, however, his little *Nicodemus* was intercepted by the larger *Hind*, and a rebel delegation came on board. Capt. Penrose and Capt. Harris of the *Swallow*, who were among this party, warned him that the position had grown worse. The mutineers would have accepted an indemnity until the previous evening, they explained, but then the two rebel leaders at Sandwich had come out and 'infused such dangerous principles into the seamen that they had wholly deserted their former resolutions, and were resolved not to admit his lordship aboard without his engagement with the Kentish gentlemen'. Lengthy negotiations ensued. Warwick repudiated the mutineers' declaration of 28 May and refused to meet the Kent leaders ashore, demanding instead the right to enter his flagship and take command of the fleet. But with no force at his disposal his bargaining power was nil; he could only appeal to the seamen's loyalty and repeat the offer of indemnity. The sailors spurned this, and some even threatened to open fire on the *Nicodemus*. Their leaders insisted that Warwick return to

[25] *DCW* 330–3, 335; Bodl. Clar. MS 31, fos. 90, 95; *The Kingdomes Weekly Intelligencer*, 23–30 May; *A Perfect Weekly Account*, 24–31 May.

[26] Carter, *True Relation*, 58–9, 66; *CSP* ii. 406.

[27] *DCW* 332–4; *Newes from Kent* ([17 June] 1648), 12–14.

[28] *DCW* 335–6; *CSPD 1648–9*, 85, 87.

London and report their demands, and he had to set out back for the capital with his mission a total failure.[29]

Fairfax's march into Kent naturally changed the situation. News of his advance soon brought the sailors and dockyard workers at Chatham back to their duty, and Pett was able to resume control of the ships in reserve; with a boatload of musketeers he also recaptured the *Fellowship* as she was preparing to escape to sea.[30] The army's advance also made a deep impression in the Downs. Opinion among the local population ashore swung rapidly against the cavaliers, who were now held to blame for the bloody retribution that was expected to follow.[31] Fairfax shrewdly tried to capitalize on the new mood by allowing a party of mutineers' wives to go down by ship to urge their husbands to submit.[32] Warwick heard of the army's success on his way back to London, and at once sent a tough letter warning the mutineers that only prompt submission could now avert the 'misery and ruin which will otherwise fall upon you'.[33] But, as they were fully aware, he had no naval forces to back up these strong words.

After reporting on his mission Warwick was next sent to assess the situation at Portsmouth, where he arrived on 4 June. He examined the four ships lying there and sent word that their crews appeared to be loyal.[34] Developments elsewhere were more alarming. The *Convertine* joined the mutineers, there were signs of disaffection among the ships at Harwich, and news arrived that the rebel force had left the Downs and appeared off Yarmouth. Warwick commented that if the northern squadron defected the one at Portsmouth would probably follow suit despite the assurances he had received.[35] The Derby House Committee sent two senior agents to Harwich to strengthen its hold there, and Warwick hastened back to London.[36] In the event the mutineers quickly returned to

[29] *DCW* 336–41 (quotation p. 337); *LJ* x. 299–300.

[30] *DCW* 350–1.

[31] R. L'Estrange, *L'Estrange his Vindication* (1649), sigs. D^v–D2.

[32] *Sir Thomas Payton* . . . (with) *A Letter from the Navy* (1648), 2; *A Perfect Weekly Account*, 7–14 June.

[33] *DCW* 342.

[34] *CSPD 1648–9*, 90, 91; *DCW* 344; Whitelocke, *Memorials*, ii. 328.

[35] *DCW* 344–5; *CSPD 1648–9*, 100, 101, 107; Add. MS 19367, fo. 3; Clar. MS 31, fo. 128^{r-v}; S. R. Gardiner (ed.), *The Hamilton Papers* (Camden Soc., 1880), 212.

[36] *DCW* 345–6; *CSPD 1648–9*, 107, 114; Add. MS 9300, fo. 87. The two agents were Robert Moulton and Capt. Alexander Bence, a Suffolk MP and Navy Commissioner.

the Downs, having achieved nothing at Yarmouth, and now talked of stopping shipping in the Thames. This would have been their most effective strategy, for a blockade would have made the merchant community intensify its pressure for a personal treaty; a royalist observer could remark with some justice, 'this city must go with the fleet, and neither can nor dare do other'. They also talked of a descent on the Isle of Wight to free the king.[37] But the swift collapse of the revolt in Kent had weakened their position and undermined their confidence, leaving them unsure what course to pursue.[38] A stalemate ensued, for Fairfax, though triumphant on land, had no force to send against them. On 10 June he renewed the offer of indemnity, which was spurned once more; the rebels resolved instead to put their ships at the disposal of the Prince of Wales, and sailed away for Holland.[39] The chance of a speedy, peaceful end to the mutiny was past.

There had been nothing comparable to the revolt of 1648 in English naval history. Within a few days of its outbreak the six ships which had mutinied in the Downs had been joined by the *Convertine*, and by the *Greyhound* and *Warwick* from the North Sea squadron. These last two quickly returned to Parliament but this success was offset by the desertion of the *Antelope* and *Crescent*, and in July the *Constant Warwick*, a powerful privateer often hired by the state, sailed to Holland to join the prince.[40] Though the ships Warwick had investigated at Portsmouth remained loyal, others returning to the port later brought further problems. The crews of the *Garland* (Rear-Admiral Bethel's flagship) and the *John* refused to serve against the mutineers, or indeed to serve at all until they were paid. Warwick had to swallow his pride lest the ships fall into rebel hands, and the men were paid off at Deptford with a whole company of cavalry in attendance.[41] The loyalty of many other ships was doubtful. At Harwich the *Tiger* and *Providence* were known to be mutinous, the *Fellowship*—once briefly in the mutineers' hands—was wholly unreliable, and

[37] *DCW* 346, 353; *Perfect Weekly Account* 7–14 June; 'The Reasons the Navy give for their resolution' (BL shelf-mark E 448 (3)); *Newes from Kent* ([17 June] 1648), 12–13; Gardiner, *Hamilton Papers*, 212.

[38] *CSPD 1648–9*, 100, 113.

[39] Rushworth, *Collections*, vii. 1149–50; *DCW* 343; *CSPD 1648–9*, 362.

[40] *DCW* 345, 346–7, 354; *CSPD 1648–9*, 124, 361. On the *Constant Warwick* see HMC 70, *Pepys*, 273, 279; *DCW* 366; A. W. Johns, 'The *Constant Warwick*', *MM* xviii (1932), 254–66.   [41] *DCW* 357, 360; *CSPD 1648–9*, 223, 367, 369.

there was trouble in the *Tenth Whelp*.[42] A correspondent at Portsmouth commented gloomily, 'I fear no commander will be safe in any ship'.[43] Of the total summer guard of thirty-nine ships, twelve were at some point in rebel hands, two more were so disorderly they had to be laid up, and a further four were known to be mutinous, making a total of eighteen. This was roughly half the summer guard, and well over half of the forces in the Channel and North Sea. Warwick initially had only nine scattered ships at his disposal, some of them unreliable, and weaker overall than the mutineers.[44] The revolt had spread to five of the seven second- and third-rates employed in the summer guard: only the *Bonadventure* and the *Lion*, both serving in the west, remained untouched. When the *Lion* returned to Portsmouth in June Sir George Ayscue and his officers sent a loyal message denouncing the 'scandal and foulness of the revolt'. This was almost the only good news from the navy that summer, and the Commons promptly published the letter and the names of its signatories—even the cook's, who had signed by a mark. A parliament which proclaimed the allegiance of an illiterate ship's cook was demonstrating mainly its own sense of insecurity.[45]

The activities of Irish privateers made it impossible for Warwick to draw off any ships from the Irish Sea. Though the Irish squadron was less affected than those in the Channel and North Sea it too was suspect. Even in 1647 the Admiralty had been worried about seamen in it who had served in royalist ships and had not taken the Covenant.[46] Fears grew in the spring of 1648 when the earl of Inchiquin, commander in Munster and the only Irish magnate loyal to Parliament, defected to the royalists. The head of the Irish squadron, Vice-Admiral Crowther, sent timely warning of this defection, for which Parliament was grateful.[47] But Inchiquin's close ties with the naval officers serving in the region, reinforced by his extensive shipping and commercial interests, inevitably raised doubts about their loyalty. There were reports that Rear-Admiral Penn and Capt. Swanley (Crowther's brother-in-law) had taken a force into Milford

[42] *DCW* 357, 362; *CSPD 1648–9*, 364, 370, 371.

[43] *The Fight at Sea* ([28 June] 1648), 3.

[44] For the summer guard of 1648 see *DCW* 313–14. Not all ships were available for service against the rebels: on 13 June Derby House listed nineteen it hoped to be able to use, and nine then in the mutineers' hands: *CSPD 1648–9*, 124.

[45] *A Letter sent to the Earl of Warwick from . . . the Lyon* ([7 July] 1648); *LJ* x. 355–6.

[46] Adm. 7/673, p. 260; *DCW* 359.

[47] *CJ* v. 529; *LJ* x. 189–90; *DCW* 322. For Inchiquin see *DNB*.

Haven to join the revolt in South Wales, and Parliament ordered Penn's arrest—though it sent him a letter of reassurance when the story proved false.[48] It took other precautions too. The *President* was laid up and her crew paid off after allegations against her captain, and the *Charles*, a hired ship belonging to Inchiquin, was sequestered.[49]

The speed and scale of the navy's revolt took contemporaries by surprise. Why had the loyalty it had shown throughout the civil war collapsed so suddenly? It would be natural to find grievances over pay and conditions, such as provoked the great naval mutinies of the late 1790s and lay behind the army revolt in 1647.[50] Yet contemporary accounts are notably silent on such matters. Admittedly men from the *John, Garland,* and *Fellowship* were angry over arrears of pay and threatened to smash down the Navy Commissioners' office and their houses too.[51] But these ships were only on the outer fringe of the troubles. The main revolt in the Downs, by contrast, was strongly political in nature. The sailors who had rallied to the impostor a few days earlier were not desperate for money; they had recently been paid and had cash to give him. Rainborough was right when he declared that 'the greatest motive to the disturbance of the seamen is that these parts are wholly for the king'.[52] The seamen's declaration of 28 May matched the Kent petition in calling for a personal treaty with the king, the disbanding of the army, and a return to traditional forms of government. Another statement, agreed by the companies of ten ships, condemned the extremism of the 'Independent party', the army's 'plundering the country, as if it were a conquered nation', the arbitrary powers of county committees, and the burden of taxation. Subsequent declarations complained that the 'army of sectaries' was determined to destroy the king.[53] It is hardly surprising that the seamen were attuned to the general mood ashore, for there was constant traffic between ship and shore when squadrons lay in the Downs, and a considerable number of the sailors were natives of the coastal towns of Kent.[54]

[48] *CJ* v. 530, 533; HMC 63, *Egmont*, i. 328–9, ii. 362; HMC 29, *Portland*, ii. 16; Gardiner, *Hamilton Papers*, 188; Add. MS 9305, fo. 57.
[49] *CSPD 1648–9*, 279, 280, 365; Add. MS 9305, fo. 56ʳ⁻ᵛ.
[50] For the mutinies of the 1790s see J. Dugan, *The Great Mutiny* (1966); G. E. Manwaring and B. Dobree, *The Floating Republic* (1966).
[51] Bodl. Tanner MS 56, fo. 258. Some of the men were eighteen months in arrears.
[52] *DCW* 330, 334.
[53] *DCW* 332–4, 338, 354–5, 364–6; *The Declaration of the Sea Commanders* ([7 Aug.] 1648); W. Batten, *The Sea-Mans Diall* ([17 Aug.] 1648).
[54] *DCW* 346–7.

As in all revolts it is difficult to disentangle the aspirations of the leaders from those of the led, but it is clear that from the outset the sailors were clamouring for a personal treaty and supporting the Kent petition.[55] The first leaders were thrown up from among the mutineers themselves and presumably represented the views of the ordinary seamen. Most were petty or warrant-officers. Thomas Lendall, their first head, was boatswain's mate of the flagship; he was joined and perhaps superseded by the boatswain himself, Andrew Mitchell.[56] Other leaders in the flagship included the gunner and carpenter, though the newly appointed lieutenant was active too. In the *Roebuck* the gunner Philip Marshall took the lead, while in the *Swallow* the master, gunner, and carpenter were to the fore.[57] Warrant-officers often stayed with the same ships for years, unlike captains and lieutenants, and they were obviously well placed to sway the men they directed day by day.

There were several specific grievances which brought naval and national concerns together. The fleet of 1648 was set out in the name of Parliament alone instead of king and Parliament, with obvious implications.[58] There was still deep resentment over Batten's removal the year before. 'How this wrought upon my brother-seamen,' Batten wrote later, 'I hope all my life I shall thankfully remember.' He and Warwick did not hide their disgust at Rainborough's appointment, and their feelings were widely shared.[59] Hostility to the new vice-admiral was certainly a major cause of the revolt. His unpopularity was well known even before the uprising in Kent, and the mutineers declared that his 'insufferable pride, ignorance and insolency' had 'alienated the hearts of the seamen'.[60] Rainborough may have been proud—one account claimed that he arrived to take up his post in a coach and four, attended by trumpeters and soldiers—but he was no ignorant

[55] Carter, *True Relation*, 51; Clarendon, *History*, iv. 332.

[56] For Lendall see *DCW* 331–2; *CSP* ii. 406. Mitchell seems to have played a larger role in subsequent negotiations: *DCW* 333, 347; *Newes from Kent* ([17 June] 1648), 12–14; *LJ* x. 300; Rushworth, *Collections*, vii. 1150.

[57] *DCW* 333, 337; Adm. 7/673, pp. 216, 217; R. C. Anderson, *Lists of Men-of-War, 1650–1700: Part 1, English Ships, 1649–1702* (2nd edn., no date), 16. Marshall and Mitchell later became commanders of royalist privateers. Charles Pullen, gunner of the *Hind*, became master of the *Hart* when she defected to the royalists: PRO HCA 25/9; *CSPD 1649–50*, 208, 247.

[58] *CJ* v. 75; Rushworth, *Collections*, vii. 989; *DCW* 334, 354–5.

[59] *DCW* 365; Clarendon, *History*, iv. 331.

[60] *DCW* 334; Clar. MS 31, fo. 67; Gardiner, *Hamilton Papers*, 188.

landsman, and the charge of insolency hardly tallies with his popularity among the common soldiers. One royalist account even says the mutineers 'did confess he had been a loving and courteous colonel to them' and vowed not to harm his person or belongings.[61] The real basis of their distrust was that they regarded him as 'a man not well affected to the king, Parliament and kingdom', 'a man of most destructive principles both in religion and policy, and a known enemy to the peace and ancient government of this kingdom'. His links with the Levellers were well known.[62] He was identified with the hated army, and the seamen felt he had been foisted upon them, a symbol of the Independents' determination to bring the navy to heel. It was said he had promised to be always 'conformable to the judgement and directions' of Cromwell and Ireton in his handling of the fleet.[63] Parliament's offer of other important commands to army officers led to fears of 'a design of introducing land-soldiers into every ship, to master and overawe the seamen'. Batten denounced this as contrary to ancient custom and called it 'the most ridiculous tyranny ever yet imagined'.[64]

Batten himself had helped to prepare the ground for revolt. After his fall he continued to negotiate with Scottish and other agents in London, and undertook to lead a force of 'borrowed or hired' warships to rescue the king. Royalist agents worked on the seamen in the Downs and at Portsmouth to build up support for him within the fleet. One of them claimed in April—before the Kent petition—that 'all the navy is discontented and wavering', and another alleged a few weeks later that many seamen were ready to defy their officers and bring their ships to join Batten once he had assembled a force in the king's name.[65] The revolt in Kent came as a surprise to royalist leaders abroad, and the naval mutiny broke out before Batten's plans were mature. Samuel Kem, his agent, could not ignore such an opportunity, though as the mutineers called for Warwick to lead them Batten chose not to reveal his hand. He was still a Navy Commissioner and in that capacity he followed Warwick to Portsmouth early in June, as directed; he helped to persuade the

[61] Carter, *True Relation*, 52–3; HMC 9, *Salisbury*, xxii. 409.
[62] *DCW* 333, 355. Ironically the Levellers suspected Rainborough of betraying their cause by accepting his post in the navy: *Letter-Book of Dyve*, 91.
[63] *LJ* x. 411. Given the friction between Rainborough and Cromwell and Ireton this report seems somewhat unlikely.
[64] *DCW* 334, 355, 366.
[65] *DCW* 302, 328, 343, 365–6; Clar. MS 31, fo. 67.

Admiral that it was safe to return to London, and then set out to subvert the seamen there, with considerable success.[66] But when the Derby House Committee summoned him back to London, after receiving word of his earlier activities, Batten decided it was time to make his escape; in mid-July he boarded the *Constant Warwick* (of which he was part-owner) at Leigh Road in the Thames, 'and by his malignancy poisoned the company and carried away the ship to the prince's fleet'.[67]

The commissioned officers of the fleet appear to have had a poor grasp of the situation in the spring, and little influence over their men. Rainborough thought that disaffection had been contained, and claimed that only two hours before the mutiny broke out his captains had assembled in the flagship and assured him that 'they knew not aboard any of them the least cause to suspect their men'.[68] He himself had had little chance to build up a fund of personal loyalty; his absence the previous autumn while Lords and Commons quarrelled over his appointment had weakened his standing and, as Fairfax remarked, had left the fleet in 'too loose a posture'.[69] Authority was weak in several other ships too. The *Antelope* had indeed been sent to sea without a captain, as the Lords and Commons vetoed each others' nominations. In many other cases the commissioned officers were very new to their ships and had yet to establish themselves.[70] They were shocked and bewildered by the revolt. When the *Satisfaction*'s new captain, Penrose, called on his men to stand by Parliament he found himself rebuffed.[71] Capt. Seaman too had to yield his *Pelican* to the mutineers. Coppin of the *Greyhound* pretended to go along with them and only saved his ship by putting to sea in haste while most of the crew were ashore; Mildmay of the *Providence* followed a similar course.[72] Capt. Man and his officers in the *Convertine*, less fortunate, were

[66] *DCW* 342–3, 348, 353; Add. MS 9300, fo. 87; *The Resolution of the Prince of Wales* ([31 July] 1648), 5.

[67] *DCW* 348, 352, 365–6, 392; *Mercurius Elencticus*, 7–14 June; *The Moderate Intelligencer*, 20–7 July; HMC 70, *Pepys*, 279; Anderson, 'Royalists in 1648', 39–40. Batten took Capt. Elias Jordan with him.

[68] *DCW* 330.

[69] *DCW* 296.

[70] *CJ* v. 537; *LJ* x. 155, 232. Rainborough complained from the Downs on 28 Apr. that there were no captains or lieutenants aboard the *Antelope*, *Swallow*, and *John*: *DCW* 324.

[71] *DCW* 331–2, 339, 341.

[72] *DCW* 334, 341, 346–7. Coppin's men took revenge by plundering his house at Deal, seizing goods worth £200: Bodl. Rawlinson MS A 224, fo. 68.

seized by the crew at Leigh Road and dumped ashore, and the same
fate befell Fearnes of the *Warwick* at Yarmouth.[73] As a group the
captains were instinctively hostile to mutiny, though many of them
probably sympathized with the call for a personal treaty. Only
three remained with the mutineers, whether by choice or compul-
sion, trying without much success to moderate their course. Of the
three, Leonard Harris of the *Swallow* appears to have been the most
sympathetic. Saltonstall of the *Hind* was probably responsible for
her return to Parliament in November, for the Commons quickly
gave him a new command. And Nixon of the *Roebuck* cannot have
shown much enthusiasm for the revolt, for he was replaced by a
cavalier soon after arriving in Holland; he had found his way back
to England by September, and Parliament judged that he too could
be trusted with a new commission.[74]

Once the mutineers sailed for Holland it was clear that only force
could end the revolt. Parliament set about assembling a new fleet for
the task, and also launched a propaganda campaign. A declaration
issued in July, based on a memorandum by Warwick and his
colleagues, set out a reasoned condemnation of the mutiny and
stressed the threat it posed to trade and prosperity. Parliament
renewed its offer of indemnity but warned that the mutineers would
be prosecuted as rebels and traitors if they failed to submit by a
specified date. To help man its new fleet it offered a gratuity of two
months' additional wages to all sailors willing to serve, payable once
the revolt was crushed, and it placed a total embargo on shipping in
the Thames to help Warwick with recruitment. It appreciated that
he would also be facing a delicate diplomatic position and, at his
request, appointed two Commissioners to liaise with the Dutch
authorities, Alexander Bence MP and Walter Strickland, its envoy
in the Netherlands.[75]

Preparations for Warwick's expedition went forward slowly. The
problems he faced were considerable. Many of the dockyard

[73] *DCW* 345; Rawl. MS A 224, fo. 77.

[74] *DCW* 333, 337, 341; *Newes from Kent* ([17 June]), 13–14; Add. MS 9300, fo.
108; *The Moderate*, 22–9 June. On 23 Dec. Nixon and Saltonstall signed the naval
declaration condemning the revolt: *The Navall Expedition of . . . Robert, Earl of
Warwick* (1649), 13. They were commanding the *Fellowship* and *John* respectively in
Mar. 1649: Clarke MS 4/4, 1649 (43); cf. Add. MS 9300, fo. 116.

[75] *DCW* 351; *CJ* v. 632–3, 635, 639, 642; *LJ* x. 379, 382–3, 397–8; *CSPD 1648–9*,
195, 201. Strickland took the place of Edward Popham, who had declined to serve.

craftsmen needed to fit the ships were still being detained in London over their suspected part in the revolt, and it was some time before he could secure permission for them to return home.[76] A more intractable problem was how to find enough 'cordial and well-affected' sailors to man the new fleet.[77] It was exacerbated by the fact that some of the seamen already in service were disorderly and unreliable: the *Fellowship*'s captain had been removed earlier, and after a further examination it was felt necessary to turn out the master and thirty-five of the crew too. There was even some disaffection in Warwick's new flagship, the *St George*.[78]

A major difficulty in manning the fleet was that Trinity House refused to help. When Warwick wrote to it for assistance in mid-June a group of officials responded by calling an unauthorized meeting, at which the proposed expedition was condemned. By a massive majority the meeting called instead for a personal treaty with the king as the proper way to resolve the crisis. The Younger Brothers of Trinity House sent a petition to this effect to the Master and Wardens, arguing that the use of force was impracticable because the seamen of England belonged 'as it were in a fraternity' and would refuse to fight each other, 'the desire of a personal treaty by the revolted ships being no other than is earnestly desired by the generality of all the seamen'. Responding to this pressure, the Master, Wardens, and Assistants presented a petition to Parliament on 29 June calling for a personal treaty, and this was accompanied by another to the same effect from some 468 shipmasters and mariners. The Lords, eager for a settlement on almost any terms, returned hearty thanks; the Commons, clearly embarrassed, responded with an argued defence of their plans.[79]

At the initial Trinity House meeting of 21 June only a dozen of those present had responded favourably to Warwick's appeal. A pamphleteer dismissed them as 'a few ignorant and simple fellows, . . . some of which can scarcely read, nor the best among them

[76] HMC 29, *Portland*, i. 482, 485; *DCW* 367; cf. Add. MS 4165, fo. 150.

[77] *DCW* 351; Add. MS 9300, fo. 95.

[78] *DCW* 352, 357–8, 361, 362; *CSPD 1648–9*, 370, 371.

[79] *DCW* 351; *LJ* x. 339–40, 351–2; *CJ* v. 603, 615–16; 'Mariners and seamen of ye Trinitie House, their resolution' (BL shelf-mark 669 f 12 (51)); *The Humble Tender and Declaration of many well-affected Mariners* ([23 June] 1648); *Mercurius Elencticus*, 21–8 June; *The Humble Petition and Desire of Commanders, Masters . . .* ([1 July] 1648); R. Badiley, *The Sea-men Undeceived* ([18 Aug.] 1648); Rushworth, *Collections*, vii. 1169; J. Kersey, *A Brief Narrative* (1677), 4–5; HMC 29, *Portland*, i. 469.

write their names without underlining'.[80] The only figure of real
note among them was Capt. Robert Moulton, a senior commander
during the civil war. Moulton set out at once to rally more support
and within a couple of weeks he was able to present a counter-
petition to Parliament, backing the proposed expedition and insisting that any settlement with the king must guarantee liberty and
religious reform. Predictably the Commons welcomed this petition,
while the Lords made only a cursory acknowledgement. A hostile
journalist claimed it represented no more than 'the very scum of the
sea', though the signatories included several men who were soon to
play a leading role in the Commonwealth navy, among them
Richard Badiley, William Goodson, William Wildey, Robert
Hackwell, and the young Christopher Myngs. Yet Moulton had
been able to find only sixty-two signatories, compared with the 468
who had signed the rival petition, and he conceded that some were
merely masters of barges, hoys, and other small craft. Plainly,
though radicals did exist within the seafaring community, they were
far inferior both in numbers and quality to those supporting a
personal treaty.[81] During the summer both groups tried to sway
opinion among the more substantial and literate mariners. William
Batten published two declarations justifying his change of sides,
denouncing Parliament's political extremism and its handling of the
navy.[82] In reply Richard Badiley warned of the dangers of letting
mutiny go unpunished, and argued that trade would be driven
elsewhere unless the revolt was quickly suppressed.[83]

The Commons deeply resented the hostile, obstructive attitude of
the merchants and shipmasters. It told those who complained that
trade was being disrupted by the prolonged crisis that they had only
themselves to blame.[84] 'Malignant' merchants were allegedly even
boycotting the few shipmasters helping with preparations for the
expedition. Warwick declared in exasperation that 'either the navy
is very ill served, or truly Parliament is betrayed in all things they

[80] *Lj* x. 340 (Richard Fearnes and William Wildey were among the group; two
signed by a mark, including the future naval captain Philip Goose); 'Mariners and
seamen'; *Mercurius Elencticus*, 21–8 June.
[81] *The Humble Declaration, Tender, and Petition of divers cordiall and well-
affected Marriners* ([6 July] 1648); *LJ* x. 363; *CJ* v. 624; Badiley, *Sea-men
Undeceived*, 6–8; *Mercurius Pragmaticus*, 4–11 June.
[82] *DCW* 346–6; Batten, *Sea-mans Diall* (dated from the Downs, 10 Aug.).
[83] Badiley, *Sea-men Undeceived*, esp. 3, 29. Badiley's moderate tone reflects in
part the radicals' weak position.
[84] *CJ* v. 665–6.

undertake'.[85] He intercepted one merchant ship trying to join the
rebel force, and the embargo on shipping was designed in part to
prevent others from doing the same. One master who had signed
the petition for a personal treaty was only permitted to sail after
entering a bond for £10,000 not to carry his ship to the mutineers,
and others had to give similar undertakings.[86] In the face of such
deep hostility from the seafaring community Warwick had no
choice but to resort to the press to man his fleet.[87]

For many weeks the initiative thus lay with the mutineers. Their
arrival at Helvoetsluys had greatly excited the exiled royalists, and
though it was doubtful how far the seamen could be trusted the
Prince of Wales could not ignore such an opportunity. He decided
to take command in person, and on 17 July he put to sea with his
new force, hoping to exploit the sympathy he knew to be
widespread in England.[88] At least four possible courses of action lay
before him. He could disrupt trade, and perhaps even blockade
London, in the hope that economic dislocation would force Parliament to agree terms with the king; he could attempt to rescue his
father from the Isle of Wight; he could try to seize a port and re-
kindle the civil war; or he could sail north to join the Scots, who
had already invaded England in the king's name. He was unlikely
to meet any opposition at sea: the Commons ordered Warwick to
fight the prince but its fleet was still far from ready.[89]

The royalist commanders decided to sail first to the Downs, to
assess the situation. Adverse winds drove them instead to
Yarmouth, where their arrival on 22 July produced some disturbances ashore in the prince's favour, but once it became clear that
parliamentary forces were firmly in control they resumed their
journey. The mutineers had published a declaration before they left
Holland, calling on the rest of the navy to join them, and the
royalist leaders issued another to the same effect once they reached

---

[85] *DCW* 356; *CSPD 1648–9*, 365; *To the Right Honourable the Commons . . . the
Humble Petition of divers well-affected Masters* (1648; presented on 11 Sept.).

[86] Tanner MS 57, fo. 183; *LJ* x. 432–3; *CSPD 1648–9*, 331.

[87] *Mercurius Pragmaticus*, 4–11 July; *The Parliament-kite*, 13–20 July; *Mercurius
Bellicus*, 19–26 July; *The Resolution of the Prince of Wales* (31 July 1648), 6; *LJ* x.
385; *CJ* v. 642–3.

[88] Anderson, 'Royalists in 1648', 38; Clarendon, *History*, iv. 337–40. An oath was
drawn up binding the sailors not to hand over the prince to Parliament: *The Oath
taken by the Seamen* ([15 July] 1648).

[89] *CSPV 1647–52*, 66; *CJ* v. 630; *LJ* x. 397, 401.

the Downs.[90] The fleet then began snapping up merchant shipping which, as intended, led London merchants and shipowners to redouble their clamour for a settlement. The prince was in ebullient mood and impudently offered to call off the attacks if Parliament sent him money and supplies.[91]

The royalists however failed to exploit their opportunities to the full, for they had problems of their own. There were major disagreements over tactics. When they left Holland the seamen had wanted to sail into the Thames to 'invite their brothers to come to them'; they were confident that many of Warwick's men would refuse to fight, and it was rumoured that three warships in the River were indeed planning to mutiny as soon as the prince appeared. Charles's council rejected the plan.[92] The sailors gave Batten a warm welcome when he arrived on 10 August, confident they now had a fighting seaman in their midst, and there was renewed talk of advancing into the Thames. But instead the fleet remained in the Downs, continuing its attacks on merchant shipping.[93] While this strategy did something to increase pressure in London for a settlement, it was much less effective than a total blockade: it antagonized sympathetic merchants and shipowners without producing the economic paralysis needed to transform the political situation. The foolish practice of seizing merchant ships and then releasing them on payment of a composition was counter-effective and inevitably led to rumours of private profiteering. An observer noted that Batten and Elias Jordan, who negotiated most of these deals, quickly ceased to be the sailors' favourites and were instead 'upbraided . . . to their faces with treason and corruption'. The seamen were outraged to see prizes sailing away unplundered, and the cavaliers resented making sacrifices to appease Presbyterian merchants they despised.[94] Batten faced further criticism over

---

[90] *DCW* 345–5, 378; *The Declaration of the Sea Commanders . . . now with Prince Charles* ([7 Aug.] 1648); Whitelocke, *Memorials*, ii. 367–8; *CSPD 1648–9*, 201, 208–9; *LJ* x. 399; Rushworth, *Collections*, vii. 1206–7; Gardiner, *Civil War*, iv. 171.

[91] Anderson, 'Royalists in 1648', 38–9; *LJ* x. 417–18, 426; *CJ* v. 665–6; *CSPV 1647–52*, 72–3; Clarendon, *History*, iv. 361–3; Whitelocke, *Memorials*, ii. 372, 375–6; *DCW* 378.

[92] *DCW* 378; Clar. MS 40, fo. 174ʳ⁻ᵛ.

[93] *DCW* 379; HMC 29, *Portland*, i. 494; Gardiner, *Hamilton Papers*, 237–8; Clar. MS 40, fo. 175; *The Resolution of the Prince of Wales* ([24 Aug.] 1648), 6.

[94] *DCW* 379; Clar. MS 40, fo. 175ᵛ; Clarendon, *History*, iv. 361–3, 411; *CSP* ii. 416.

supplies. His confidence that sympathetic merchants in London would send provisions proved unfounded, and the royalists remained dependent on irregular supplies from Holland.[95]

The other courses of action open to the rebels were explored only half-heartedly. An attempt in August to persuade Yarmouth to declare for the prince produced nothing.[96] Forays ashore in Kent also failed; a bid to relieve Deal Castle in August was beaten off with heavy losses, and the sailors were disheartened by the fact that Lendall, their first leader, was among those taken prisoner.[97] An attempt to free the king from the Isle of Wight might have succeeded in May, with the benefit of surprise, but now stood little chance. When the king sent a message late in August ordering such an attempt to be made, a cavalier on board noted that 'it was no more listened to, or regarded, than if a dog had been sent to them'.[98] The final option, going north to Scotland, was canvassed by the earl of Lauderdale, the Scots' Commissioner in attendance, but had no support from the prince's other advisers or from the seamen.[99]

The prince also faced a continuing problem over the command of his new force. The mutineers' own leaders had naturally been superseded when the ships reached Holland, 'vice-admiral' Lendall being rewarded with a commission as lieutenant of the flagship.[100] Charles himself became admiral in name as the sailors demanded a royal prince at their head, but the choice of Lord Willoughby of Parham as vice-admiral to command the fleet won little support. Willoughby was a former moderate parliamentarian who might reassure waverers in England, but he had no maritime experience to win the seamen's respect, and his political background made him unpopular with the cavaliers. The expedition was thus plagued throughout by acrimonious disputes. To strengthen the command Batten was knighted on his arrival and made rear-admiral, and his companion Elias Jordan became flag-captain to Willoughby, effectively taking over control of his ship. But these appointments too provoked controversy, for Prince Rupert and his friends scorned the newcomers as merely two more Presbyterian renegades. Rupert

[95] E. Warburton, *Memoirs of Prince Rupert* (1849), iii. 250.

[96] Rushworth, *Collections*, vii. 1224–5; Whitelocke, *Memorials*, ii. 378.

[97] *CJ* v. 672; Rushworth, *Collections*, vii. 1228; *DCW* 381. Deal surrendered to Parliament on 25 Aug.

[98] *CSP* ii. 416.

[99] *CSP* ii. 414–15; Gardiner, *Hamilton Papers*, 239, 243, 245.

[100] HMC 70, *Pepys*, 230.

was also waging feuds with the Scottish Commissioner Lauderdale and with other royalists, such as Culpeper, who favoured alliance with the Presbyterian Scots.[101]

The politicians were uncomfortably aware in the midst of these wrangles that the seamen had views of their own. Mutineers who had turned out one admiral and his captains could do the same again, and their behaviour showed plainly that they realized their power. One cavalier recalled later that the 'high mutinies of the seamen' had been so frequent and fierce that he and his friends wondered whether they were the sailors' prisoners rather than their leaders.[102] No one commented on the irony that sailors who had mutinied in the name of king and tradition should display an open contempt towards their lords and masters, face to face, that had rarely been paralleled.

By late August supplies and morale were low, and the royalist leaders decided to give up and return to Holland. This brought tensions to a head. For the seamen it would mean cutting themselves off from their families in England indefinitely, something far from their minds in May. They scorned the idea of going back to Holland without either fighting Warwick's force or trying to win it over. They protested loudly when the prince proposed to return to Holland before the rest of the fleet, to resupply his ship and go on to Scotland; they cursed Lauderdale and Culpeper as the authors of the plan, threatening to throw them both overboard, and forced Charles to abandon his design. It was left unclear whether they would now all sail directly for Holland or put into the Thames on the way, as the sailors demanded. On 29 August Charles's flagship set a course for Holland, but sailors on board several of the other ships defied their officers and steered away for the Thames, and the prince and his advisers had little choice but to submit to this 'very arrant mutiny' and follow. The royalists were very uneasy as they entered the Thames, fearing the seamen would decide to make their peace by handing them over to Parliament; they even made the sailors swear an oath not to 'deliver up his Highness unto any person whatsoever'. Charles recalled years later

---

[101] Clarendon, *History*, iv. 337–41, 360, 373–4; Gardiner, *Hamilton Papers*, 220, 222–3, 229, 237–8; *DCW* 367–7. Willoughby had been appointed by Prince James before Charles joined the royalist fleet. Batten had failed to catch up with the fleet earlier because it had been blown off course to Yarmouth: *DCW* 378.

[102] *CSP* ii. 414.

how Batten had been sweating with fear. Rupert suspected that Batten himself intended to betray them all, and threatened to shoot him if he attempted to do so.

Later in the day the cavaliers sighted Warwick's fleet and pursued it as it withdrew upriver. That night, as the two forces lay about a league apart, the prince sent a summons calling on Warwick to submit, which was naturally rejected. On the 30th bad weather conditions prevented further manœuvres. The commanders on both sides were reluctant to risk battle among the shoals and sandbanks, and next day the royalists fell downriver once more, watching to see if Warwick would follow and offer to engage. Warwick preferred to follow at a safe distance, showing no inclination to fight and anchoring when night fell. Charles continued under sail, and during the night his fleet passed through the Portsmouth squadron on its way to reinforce the Lord Admiral; some of the prince's sailors recognized the ships and some even opened fire on their own initiative, but Batten persuaded Charles to sail on. Next morning Warwick found the enemy gone and his own reinforcements at hand. Once it was clear the royalists had withdrawn to Holland he assembled his combined force in the Downs and awaited further orders.[103]

This inglorious episode left a sense of wasted opportunities on both sides. Warwick had had the enemy pinioned between his fleet and the Portsmouth squadron and had allowed it to escape, though he must have been relieved that his men had made no attempt to defect. There were no such consoling thoughts for the royalists, who reached Holland on 1 September 'full of anger, hatred and disdain', in the words of an observer aboard. 'I see no hope to reconcile our differences,' he added, 'nor to preserve this fleet.'[104] The commanders hurled recriminations of cowardice and incompetence at one another. The expedition had failed and supplies were spent.

The initiative thus passed back to Warwick and Parliament. The threat to London's commerce was over, the fleet was ready at last, and the seamen had remained obedient. A few weeks later Warwick sailed with a fleet of about twenty ships for Helvoetsluys, where the

[103] *DCW* 369–72, 376–82; Warburton, *Memoirs*, iii. 251–3; Clar. MS 31, fos. 233–4, MS 40, fos.145–6ᵛ; *CSP* ii. 414–16; *A Letter sent from aboard His Highness* ([25 Aug.] 1648), 2; Pepys, *Diary*, v. 169.
[104] *DCW* 382.

royalists had taken refuge, with orders 'to reduce them by force or otherwise as opportunity should offer'.[105] Arriving on 19 September he anchored within sight of the enemy force, then numbering about eighteen vessels, large and small. Warwick summoned Charles to submit, but the prince was away in The Hague and it was several days before a scornful reply was returned.[106] In the meantime Warwick took no action other than publishing Parliament's renewed offer of indemnity, and when Dutch officials forbade hostilities in a neutral port he promised to avoid violence except in self-defence. A few days later a powerful Dutch squadron under Tromp anchored between the two fleets to enforce the promise.[107] Warwick was quite prepared for a long stay. His mere presence was enough to prevent the royalists from disrupting commerce. Their ships were in no condition to fight, and he hoped the disillusioned seamen would either yield them up without bloodshed or desert. This was a quite likely prospect, as many of the royalist leaders were aware; the sailors were now lodged ashore, scattered among several different towns, drinking heavily and mutinous. They readily listened to Warwick's agents and pocketed the money that was handed out. Many declared truculently that they would settle with Parliament whenever they chose and some apparently decided to bring their ships over by night to join him, though these plans were foiled by Tromp's arrival.[108]

As the stalemate lengthened, however, the Derby House Committee grew restive, fearing Warwick was losing the initiative once more. It pointed out that the expedition was eating up money and provisions while the prince was at liberty to refit his ships and would probably be able to find Irishmen and Dunkirkers to man them even if his original sailors deserted. The Dutch authorities could never approve an attack, the Committee observed, but would probably have been glad if Warwick had seized the rebel fleet on his arrival and settled the matter.[109]

---

[105] *DCW* 375. For Warwick's fleet see *DCW* 374.
[106] *DCW* 382–3, 386; *LJ* x. 522–3; *Clarke Papers*, ii. 39–40. For details of the royalist forces see Anderson, 'Royalists in 1648', 41–2; Bodl. Firth MS ch. 8, fo. 99; Clar. MS 31, fo. 308.
[107] *DCW* 384–90.
[108] *DCW* 388–90; *Clarke Papers*, ii. 41–2; Whitelocke, *Memorials*, ii. 399, 403, 408; Warburton, *Memoirs*, iii. 261; Rushworth, *Collections*, vii. 1259; T. Carte, *A Collection of Original Letters and Papers, 1641–1660* (1739), i. 180; Clar. MS 31, fos. 295, 308ʳ⁻ᵛ.
[109] *DCW* 383–4, 387–8; HMC 53, *Montagu of Beaulieu*, 163.

Warwick's cautious strategy did eventually bear some fruit,
however, through the royalists' own internal divisions. Rupert was
ambitious for the supreme command and deliberately undermined
the authority of Batten (who had succeeded as vice-admiral in
September), stirring up the sailors to blame him for the shortages of
pay and provisions. More important, Rupert put forward a viable
plan for the fleet to operate from a base in Ireland, and was far more
committed to getting it back to sea. Finally, late in October,
Charles was persuaded to appoint him commander.[110] It was a
highly controversial move, for Rupert was a symbol of cavalier
intransigence at its worst. Batten and Jordan were embittered and
promptly left for Rotterdam; Batten refused to go back even on a
temporary basis, till Rupert could take up his post, complaining
that some of the seamen had vowed to kill him—stirred up, he may
have suspected, by Rupert's friends.[111] The fleet was thus left for the
moment without a head and the royalist councillor Edward Hyde
had to go down to restore what order he could, meeting the sailors'
angry demands for pay with fair words; 'we thought it not season-
able to be sharp with them,' he reported, 'as they might desert'. He
thought many of the officers were unreliable too, and called for a
purge as soon as possible.[112] Privately Hyde thought that Rupert's
appointment was provocative. He saw that it might have been the
only way to save the fleet from disintegration but felt it was essential for Prince James to join it too to provide a focus for loyalty
above the warring factions.[113]

Many of the ordinary seamen were hostile to Rupert, a foreigner
with a black reputation, and very few wanted to go to Ireland.
Rupert dealt brusquely with trouble-makers by threatening to
throw them overboard, and brought soldiers into the ships to keep
'the fickle and licentious seamen . . . in some sort of awe and obedience'.[114] Warwick's agents could now argue plausibly that with
Rupert at its head the revolted fleet was an obstacle to a compromise
peace, not a help. The new situation clearly improved the chances of

---

[110] HMC 70, *Pepys*, 292; Clarendon, *History*, iv. 416–17, 423; *DCW* 390–1.
[111] Firth MS c 8, fos. 82, 118, 121; Clar. MS 31, fos. 291, 308ᵛ, 322; Carte, *Original
Letters*, i. 189; *A Perfect Remonstrance and Narrative* ([1 Jan.] 1649), 5–6.
[112] Firth MS c 8, fos. 87, 96, 118, 119.
[113] Carte, *Original Letters*, i. 189; Firth MS c 8, fo. 87; Clarendon, *History*, iv.
423; Clar. MS 31, fo. 308; Warburton, *Memoirs*, iii. 279–80; cf. HMC 70,
Pepys, 274.
[114] Clarendon, *History*, iv. 423–5; Warburton, *Memoirs*, iii. 261–3; Carte,
Original Letters, i. 199.

winning over the mariners, and Robert Moulton, Warwick's flag-captain, even ventured to go aboard the enemy flagship to appeal to the men. (Rupert promptly arrested him, but the Dutch intervened to secure his release.) Sailors from the two forces continued to meet ashore in drinking bouts and brawls, and the rate of desertion increased. When the Dutch warships withdrew at the beginning of November events quickly moved towards a crisis, in an atmosphere thick with rumours of treachery. Warwick had begun discreet negotiations with Batten for the return of the *Constant Warwick*, of which both were co-owners, using the Dutch-born diplomat Isaac Dorislaus as his intermediary, and on the night of 5 November the ship slipped away and joined the parliamentary fleet. Warwick's force now moved closer, encouraged by reports that other ships were ready to follow suit. Despite Rupert's countermeasures the *Hind* too defected on 8 November. Rupert thereupon abandoned his plans to put to sea and decided to take his remaining ships through the sluice into the well-protected inner harbour, managing in this way to save seven of the larger ships and five small ones. The *Satisfaction*, however, ran ashore and surrendered—perhaps by design, for Hyde had judged its captain unreliable. The *Love*, a merchantman whose captain had also 'been tampered withall', submitted without a struggle, and another merchant ship and a ketch were captured. Warwick's patience had at last paid off, at least in part.[115] Hyde complained bitterly that Batten and Jordan had 'played the rogues with us', secretly preparing to betray the ships and using 'all their skill to corrupt both officers and men'. The pair did not wait to answer his allegations. Once the *Constant Warwick* was back in Warwick's hands they made their way quickly to The Hague to ask Charles for testimonials and passes for England. The prince amazingly complied, to Hyde's fury and astonishment. Walter Strickland, Parliament's agent at The Hague, felt similar anger over the indemnity they had received from Warwick, hinting that the Admiral had been more concerned to safeguard his property than to destroy the enemy. Batten had 'made a fleet revolt', Strickland commented sourly, 'and must be saved for a part of a ship'.[116]

---

[115] *DCW* 392–9; Warburton, *Memoirs*, iii. 263–5; HMC 70, *Pepys*, 238–9; Clar. MS 31, fo. 308ᵛ; *Perfect Remonstrance*, 6–7; Firth MS c 8, fos. 87, 118; PRO HCA 13/62, testimony of W. Jessop, 9 Feb. 1650.

[116] Warburton, *Memoirs*, iii. 279, 296; HMC 70, *Pepys*, 235, 285; *DCW* 405; *CJ* vi. 106. Batten and Jordan then set off for Calais; Batten's subsequent movements are

Warwick's success was none the less welcome news to the Derby House Committee, and it urged him to 'finish what remains of this work before the winter'.[117] This however was far from easy. Rupert had set up batteries ashore to protect his remaining ships, and any frontal assault against them by land would inevitably provoke a major row with the Dutch, which Warwick was anxious to avoid. The fact that the royalists had unloaded their guns and unrigged some of their ships persuaded him that they had given up any idea of putting to sea before the spring. The low morale, desertion, and disorder among them strengthened his conviction, and he judged it was therefore safe to lift the blockade. On 21 November he sailed for England with his entire fleet.[118] His reasoning may have been sound but he was greatly at fault in leaving no ships behind to watch the enemy. For Rupert immediately changed his plans once more: after a wild drinking spree to celebrate his luck he had his ships hastily refitted, and several of them were out at sea attacking commerce by the first days of January 1649. On 21 January he was able to lead out a squadron of eight ships and sail to Ireland unchallenged.[119]

The threat posed by the naval revolt of 1648 was thus by no means over at the close of the year, and Warwick had thrown away much of his success. There had been complaints about his slowness and excessive caution ever since his reappointment as Admiral, and also darker insinuations: his name had been linked with calls for a personal treaty in the spring, and suspicions lingered despite his denials. They were strengthened by the fact that his brother, the earl of Holland, was deeply implicated in the revolt ashore.[120] Though Warwick had been the inevitable choice as Admiral, many must have doubted his commitment. A sardonic journalist pointed out that while Warwick was leading a fleet against the prince his

not clear, but Jordan crossed back to England: HMC 3, *4th Report*, 274–5; *Mercurius Elencticus*, 19–26 Dec.; HCA 13/62, testimony of Jordan, 7 Jan. 1650.

[117] *DCW* 395; *LJ* x. 596; *CJ* vi. 79–80.

[118] *DCW* 396, 399; Firth MS c 8, fo. 96ʳ⁻ᵛ; *Perfect Remonstrance*, 7–8; *Perfect Occurrences*, 8–15 Dec.

[119] *DCW* 400–2, 405–6; Warburton, *Memoirs*, iii. 280–2; HMC 3, *4th Report*, 275; Carte, *Original Letters*, i. 199; R. C. Anderson, 'The Royalists at Sea in 1649', *MM* xiv (1928), 320–2. Two more of Rupert's ships were already at sea. There had been urgent discussions in England about sending another force to blockade Rupert, once his intentions were known, but nothing was done in time: *Perfect Occurrences*, 5–12, 12–19 Jan. 1649.

[120] *LJ* x. 264; *CJ* v. 563; Gardiner, *Hamilton Papers*, 171; HMC 53, *Montagu of Beaulieu*, 163.

sickly young grandson had been sent to the Isle of Wight to be healed by the royal touch.[121] Charles himself urged Warwick to change sides when he first arrived in Holland, offering a pardon and pointing out that his family could not hope to survive the revolution which now appeared imminent.[122] The lack of any action between the two fleets gave rise to rumours that the earl had indeed made his peace and planned to join the prince if Parliament's negotiations with the king broke down. Such rumours predictably surfaced again after the fleet's sudden return home.[123]

There is no evidence that Warwick ever thought of betraying Parliament, but his political misgivings may well help to explain his apparent lethargy. He had always hoped that a political settlement would save the two fleets from having to fight one another, and failing that he wanted to take no action that would damage the chances of a negotiated peace. His two advisers, Bence and Strickland, repeatedly pressed for firmer action, and both strongly criticized his decision to return to England.[124] Back home, Warwick had no appetite for the revolution some were now demanding and distanced himself from events, choosing not to resume his place in the Lords.[125]

On 6 December the army staged the bloodless coup known as Pride's Purge, by which moderates were barred from Parliament to prevent a settlement on terms the officers considered unsafe. The Rump—the remnant of the Long Parliament—broke off negotiations with the king and resolved to put him on trial. The nation, cowed by the army, remained sullenly passive.[126] But inevitably a new question mark hung over the navy. Many of its officers shared Warwick's hopes and fears, and a leading MP had already observed that if negotiations with the king were to fail its loyalty would be gravely in doubt.[127] If Parliament's actions in 1647–8 had provoked a revolt which had yet to be suppressed, how would the fleet react to a real revolution?

---

[121] *Mercurius Pragmaticus*, 4–11 June.

[122] *LJ* x. 522–3.

[123] *The Declaration and Resolution of Robert Earle of Warwick* ([30 Oct.] 1648), a forgery repudiated in *A Declaration of the Earle of Warwick* ([11 Nov.] 1648); Rushworth, *Collections*, vii. 1326, 1366; *The Resolution of his Excellency the Lord General Fairfax* (1648), 4–5; Whitelocke, *Memorials*, ii. 433; *A Perfect Diurnall*, 11–18 Dec.; cf. Carte, *Original Letters*, i. 187; Firth MS c 8, fo. 93.

[124] *DCW* 385, 396, 405; cf. 399.

[125] *LJ* x. 637; Rushworth, *Collections*, vii. 1326; below, ch. 3.

[126] D. Underdown, *Pride's Purge* (Oxford, 1971).

[127] *CSPD 1648–9*, 319.

3

The Navy New-Modelled

CHARLES I's execution on 30 January 1649 paved the way for the abolition of monarchy and the establishment of a Commonwealth. The regicides could ignore the general dismay at home, but the king's death had serious repercussions abroad, too, which could not be brushed aside. News of the execution had horrified governments throughout Europe, from Russia to Portugal. Not one was ready to recognize the new regime.[1] This posed an immediate threat to English overseas trade, and raised the alarming possibility of foreign intervention to help the Stuarts recover their throne—a threat all the more plausible since the signing of the Peace of Westphalia. In these circumstances the navy's role assumed a new and crucial signifi-cance: the revolution was the work of the army, but its defence would fall to the navy's lot. There was unwitting symbolism in the fact that Charles's executioner had been disguised as a sailor.[2]

Cavalier journalists naturally made the most of European outrage. One reported with satisfaction how 'even the Turk himself doth now hate Englishmen to the death', and they were delighted when the Russian tsar denounced the Rump as 'devils incarnate' and called for a Holy League to overthrow it. They made repeated claims that foreign help was on its way, one reporting that a great fleet was being assembled by eleven states, another dreaming of an armada a thousand strong.[3] No such armada was ever to materialize but the sense of outrage on the continent was real enough.

The Rump at first controlled little more than England and Wales.

[1] C. V. Wedgwood, 'European Reaction to the Death of Charles I', in C. H. Carter (ed.), *From the Renaissance to the Counter-Reformation* (1966), 401–19.

[2] R. W. Blencowe (ed.), *Sydney Papers* (1825), 60–1. Was this disguise meant to distract onlookers from the army's role?

[3] *A Great Victory obtained by Prince Charles* (1649), 6; *The Man in the Moon*, 25 July–2 Aug. 1649; ibid., 16–23 Jan. 1650; ibid., 8–23 May 1650; *Mercurius Elencticus*, 13–20 May 1650; *A Declaration of His Imperiall Majestie, the . . . Emperor of Russia* (1650); *The Royal Diurnall*, 4–11 Mar. 1650.

Scotland proclaimed its allegiance to the late king's son as Charles II, and almost the whole of Ireland was in royalist hands, along with the Scillies, most of the Channel Islands, and colonial settlements such as Virginia and Barbados. Charles was thus a king in more than name alone; he was indeed busy with plans to invade England and Wales using Ireland as a springboard, once the royalists' hold there was complete.[4] A strong and loyal navy was indispensable if the Rump was to assert its authority in all the crown's former dominions. And without a strong navy the Rump's own long-term survival would be in doubt.

Warwick's sudden return to the Downs in November 1648 had been unwelcome news to Parliament, and his position was clearly precarious. He was saved for the moment by the delicacy of the political situation: talks with Charles I on the Isle of Wight had reached a critical point when the army staged its coup on 6 December, and to sack Warwick now might well provoke another revolt, undoing all that had been achieved since the summer. The earl moreover took steps to strengthen his position by showing that the fleet's return had been a collective decision; the commanders still in the Downs declared that no other course had been practicable, and twenty-two captains who had served in the expedition published a vigorous defence of their proceedings and of their decision to return.[5]

In the face of this show of solidarity the new regime moved with caution. Shortly before Pride's Purge the army had written seeking the naval officers' support for its recent *Remonstrance,* in which it attacked the peace proposals and called for those responsible for the war to be punished. The navy made no immediate response to this, or to further appeals.[6] But a few days after the purge Warwick declared his continuing loyalty and repudiated stories of a secret agreement with the Prince of Wales.[7] This signalled his

[4] Gardiner, *CP* i. 18–22, 92; Clarendon, *History,* v. 3, 28, 31; J. Rushworth, *Historical Collections* (1659–1701), vii. 1366.

[5] *DCW* 400–5; *CJ* vi. 96, 106; Bodl. Clarendon MS 34, fo. 18; *The Navall Expedition of the . . . Earl of Warwick* (1649)—dated at the Downs on 23 Dec. 1648, though the signatures must have been collected earlier.

[6] *Clarke Papers,* ii. 62; *The Declaration and Engagement of the Commanders* (1648), 3.

[7] *The Resolution of his Excellency the Lord General Fairfax* (1648), 4–5; *The Remonstrance . . . of . . . Robert, E. of Warwick* ([14 Dec.] 1648); *Mercurius Elencticus,* 19–26 Dec.; cf. *DCW* 405.

acquiescence, and the Rump thereupon set out to woo him. On 18 December the Commons graciously accepted his protestations of loyalty and praised his 'good affections'. Fairfax, Cromwell, and a number of MPs went down to give him a belated welcome home and to ask for his co-operation, which he readily promised.[8] Over the next few critical weeks he took an active part in the deliberations of Parliament's Navy Committee, attending meetings during the final days of the king's trial and signing an official paper on the very day of the execution. The royalists mocked him as a shameless weathercock.[9]

During the few weeks since the purge it had become clear that the fleet contained at least a few genuine radicals. A letter from the flagship on 11 December claimed that many of the mariners now supported the army's stand, and gave the deliberately misleading impression that Warwick himself had done so.[10] On 24 December the four captains stationed in the Downs published a strong letter backing the army and calling for justice against delinquents. Robert Moulton and Richard Haddock (vice-admiral in Warwick's recent expedition) were among the signatories, and they claimed to have further support among captains now scattered on duties elsewhere. Haddock had already written privately to the army headquarters indicating his readiness to co-operate.[11] Warwick's commitment to the Rump was in reality, of course, far from whole-hearted. It was said that he had come up to London secretly on his return and only accepted the new regime on learning from his old friends that their position was hopeless. There was certainly some friction at his meeting with Cromwell over the treatment of the king; Warwick did not approve of putting him on trial, and was not even named to the High Court set up for the purpose. His views were well known and prompted rumours that he had threatened to turn the navy against the Rump if the trial went ahead.[12]

It is unlikely that the Rump ever intended to retain Warwick once

[8] Rushworth, *Collections*, vii. 1366; *The Declaration of his Highnesse the Prince of Wales* . . . (with) *New Propositions from the Navy* (15–21 Dec. 1648), 6; *Mercurius Pragmaticus*, 19–26 Dec.

[9] Bodl. Rawlinson MS A 224, fos. 1–13, 22.

[10] *Resolution of Fairfax*; *Remonstrance of Warwick*; *Declaration of the Prince of Wales*, 1–2, 6.

[11] *Declaration and Engagement*; *Navall Expedition*, 10–14; B. Whitelocke, *Memorials of the English Affairs* (Oxford, 1853), ii. 480–1; *Clarke Papers*, ii. 138–9.

[12] *Mercurius Elencticus*, 19–26 Dec.; *Declaration of the Prince of Wales*, 6; T. Carte, *A Collection of Original Letters and Papers, 1641–1660* (1739), i. 212.

its position was secured; it would hardly otherwise have brushed his pleas aside and proceeded with the trial and execution of his half-brother, the earl of Holland, for complicity in the 1648 rising.[13] Moreover the Admiral's age, ill-health, and apparent lethargy made him a doubtful asset quite apart from his political scruples. One account ascribed his return from Helvoetsluys to an attack of scurvy, and a wit mocked the decrepit commander 'whose crazy skin | Can scarce keep all his dry bones in'. Another observer thought London merchants would be very unwilling to advance money to set out a fleet under 'such an idle Admiral as can lie still, and suffer their shipping and goods to be taken from them by the Irish'.[14]

Though the Rump did not want to shift Warwick until the king's fate was settled, it took immediate steps to strengthen its hold over the navy. This was achieved by expanding the role of the parliamentary Navy Committee, traditionally concerned mainly with financial matters, to cover the entire range of naval affairs. The Committee was dominated after the purge by prominent radicals such as Miles Corbet, Valentine Walton, and Gregory Clement, all soon to be regicides, and their influence was such that contemporaries could even refer to the fleet as 'Miles Corbet's navy'. Several other notable radicals were added at this time, including Cromwell and his son-in-law Ireton, who took an active part.[15] The Committee was very willing to make use of Warwick's expertise but it proved equally ready to act without him.[16] And Warwick found his authority diminished in other ways too: when he invited his old colleague Henry Bethel to serve as rear-admiral of the winter guard the Commons promptly quashed the move, ordering him to appoint no one without their approval.[17]

It is possible that the army leaders had originally intended to reinstate Rainborough once the revolt was crushed, a solution ruled out by his death late in 1648 at the hands of cavalier assassins.[18] Despite that blow the idea of finding an army officer to command

[13] Gardiner, *CP* i. 11; *Perfect Occurrences*, 2–9 Mar. 1649.
[14] Clar. MS 34, fo. 19; *Mercurius Elencticus*, 26 Dec. 1648–2 Jan. 1649; *Mercurius Bellicus*, 11–18 July 1648.
[15] Rawl. MS A 224, *passim*; *CJ* vi, Dec. 1648–Mar. 1649; *Mercurius Pragmaticus*, 19–26 Dec. 1648.
[16] *CJ* vi. 117; cf. 99, 109, 112.
[17] *Perfect Occurrences*, 29 Dec. 1648–5 Jan. 1649; *CJ* vi. 109.
[18] Clarendon, *History*, iv. 404.

the navy remained attractive to a regime which depended on military backing for its very existence, and it clearly inspired the new arrangements which took shape in February 1649. On the 12th the Commons nominated Cols. Popham, Blake, and Deane to command the next summer guard. On the 23rd a brief Act deprived Warwick of his office as Lord High Admiral, without ceremony or thanks, and the following day another Act appointed the three colonels 'Admirals and Generals of the Fleet now at sea'.[19] The idea of a joint command had been mooted in 1645, when the office of Lord Admiral had previously lapsed, and it had additional appeal now that the fleet would have to be divided to deal with Rupert without leaving the Channel unguarded.[20] The three colonels had all proved their worth during the civil war, Blake indeed becoming something of a national hero after the siege of Lyme. They were reliable supporters of the new regime, though none seems to have possessed the ambition to carve an independent political career; Popham and Blake sat in the Rump, while Deane was a regicide and a close associate of Cromwell. Though they were best known as soldiers, Popham had commanded warships in the late 1630s, and Deane was a former shipmaster and had been considered a possible successor to Batten as vice-admiral in 1647. Blake had been active as a merchant in the 1630s and he too may have gone to sea on trading voyages to Spain and Holland.[21]

The new Generals at Sea inherited only part of Warwick's former powers. The Council of State—the Rump's executive body—retained ultimate authority over the navy in its own hands. This arrangement soon proved unsatisfactory, however, for the Council was unable to provide the close, day-by-day scrutiny such a large and complex organization required. Almost at once it delegated

---

[19] *CJ* vi. 138, 149–50; *A and O* ii. 13–14, 17; *CSPD 1649–50*, 13, 14.

[20] V. A. Rowe, *Sir Henry Vane the Younger* (1970), 127. (Warwick, Peregrine Pelham, and Alexander Bence had been proposed.)

[21] See *DNB* and M. Ashley, *Cromwell's Generals* (1954), ch. 7; C. H. Firth, 'Sailors of the Civil War, the Commonwealth and the Protectorate', *MM* xii (1926), 242–53. On Blake see Powell, *Blake*; C. D. Curtis, *Blake: General at Sea* (Taunton, 1934); R. Beardon, *Robert Blake* (1935). On Deane: J. B. Deane, *The Life of Richard Deane* (1870). On Popham: F. W. Popham, *A West Country Family: The Pophams from 1150* (Sevenoaks, 1976). Deane had been a friend of Rainborough, witnessing his will, and had earlier worked for his father: *The Tower Letter-Book of Sir Lewis Dyve*, ed. H. G. Tibbutt (Bedfordshire Historical Record Soc., xxxviii; 1958), 85. See also D. O. Shilton and R. Holworthy (eds.), *High Court of Admiralty Examinations, 1637–8* (1932), 245; P. White, *A Memorable Sea-Fight* (1649), 16.

various naval matter to small *ad hoc* committees, and on 12 March it established a permanent group to handle the administrative duties formerly belonging to the Admiral, such as general supervision of naval finances, the setting out and deployment of ships, and the selection of officers.[22] The Council's new Admiralty Committee had at first only three members. Easily the most important was Sir Henry Vane, a leading figure in the new regime, who had been Treasurer of the Navy since 1642 and had served as an Admiralty Commissioner from 1645 to 1648. Vane, more than any other individual, dominated the Rump's naval administration. Valentine Walton was another prominent Rumper, formerly a colonel in the New Model, and Cromwell's brother-in-law. Alderman Rowland Wilson, the third member, was a leading Independent merchant in the City, where his influence might be expected to help the Rump secure the loans and co-operation vital to the navy's smooth running.[23] Other members were added later, among the most active and important being the regicides Denis Bond, William Purefoy, Anthony Stapley, and Thomas Challenor. A new Council of State was elected each year, and a new Admiralty Committee was usually appointed shortly afterwards; six Committees existed in all between 1649 and the end of 1652, with a total of forty-seven members. Vane and Walton belonged to them all, and were among the most regular attenders at the daily meetings.[24] The system had obvious strengths, notably the ability of Vane and his colleagues to persuade the Council and Parliament to implement whatever decisions they thought necessary. But it had several flaws too. Continuity suffered from the rapid turnover of members, some of whom had no expertise in naval affairs and seldom attended. It was also slow and cumbersome: matters were referred from the Commons to the Council and thence to the Committee, which then had to report back for approval. In 1651 Vane himself called, without success, for a new body of permanent, professional administrators.[25] Measured by results however the system proved fully adequate for the needs of the time.

The replacement of Warwick was only the first step towards

[22] *CSPD 1649–50*, 34.
[23] See *DNB* and *BDBR* for all three, and Rowe, *Vane*, esp. ch. 7, for Vane and Walton.
[24] PRO SP 25/123, pp. 11–12 and *passim*. For an assessment see Rowe, *Vane*, ch. 7; Hammond, thesis, ch. 3; Cogar, thesis, ch. 2, part ii.
[25] Rowe, *Vane*, 173; *CJ* vi. 592.

creating a republican navy. It was common knowledge that the revolt in 1648 had found many sympathizers ashore within the navy's administrative machine and the dockyards, and the new regime regarded a sweeping purge and reorganization as essential.

On 16 January 1649 the Rump completed an Act 'touching the Regulating of the Officers of the Navy and Customs'. Drawing attention to 'manifest distempers', it appointed sixteen 'Regulators' to join the Navy Commissioners in investigating all branches of naval administration, as well as the officer corps, directing them to examine the political reliability, honesty, and efficiency of all concerned.[26] The new body was dominated by the Independent London merchants now prominent in the City's government, and became widely known as the Committee of Merchants. Its most eminent member was the regicide Alderman Thomas Andrewes, Lord Mayor in 1650. Also prominent was Maurice Thomson, a merchant and army contractor with interests in both the American and East Indies trades. Many of the members belonged, like him, to the 'colonial-interloping' group of merchants who flouted the East India Company's monopoly and generally held political views more radical than those of the merchant community as a whole; among them were William Pennoyer, Samuel Moyer, a Baptist and partner in Thomson's ventures in the East and in Africa, Richard Shute, Stephen Estwick, and James Russell. The committee also contained two experienced naval administrators in John Hollond, a Navy Commissioner during the civil war, and Richard Hutchinson, a former New England settler who was Vane's deputy (and later successor) as Navy Treasurer.[27]

The Regulators began by investigating the Navy Commissioners themselves—the senior officials responsible for the dockyards, the fitting out, hire, and manning of ships, and the payment of the seamen.[28] One Commissioner, the former vice-admiral William Batten, had clearly disqualified himself. Another, Richard

[26] *CJ* vi. 119; *A and O* i. 1257–60.

[27] For a general assessment see W. Reid, 'Commonwealth Supply Departments within the Tower, and the Committee of London Merchants', *The Guildhall Miscellany*, ii (1977), 319–52; Cogar, thesis, ch. 2, part vii. On colonial-interloping merchants see R. Brenner, 'The Civil War Politics of London's Merchant Community', *Past and Present*, lviii (1973), 76–82, 97–107. On Hollond see J. Hollond, *Two Discourses of the Navy*, ed. J. R. Tanner (NRS, 1896), pp. ix–lxxviii; on Hutchinson see G. Aylmer, *The State's Servants* (1973), 247–50.

[28] A. C. Dewar, 'The Naval Administration of the Interregnum, 1641–59', *MM* xii (1926), 417.

Crandley, was suspect too, for as Master of Trinity House he had been involved in the peace petitioning in 1648.[29] The others then in office were Peter Pett, of the shipbuilding dynasty at Chatham, Thomas Smith, a shipowner and secretary to Lord Admiral Northumberland before the civil war, and Roger Tweedy, an Elder Brother of Trinity House and a Commissioner since 1642.[30] The Regulators proposed to confirm Smith, Pett, and Tweedy, and replace Batten and Crandley with two of their own number, John Hollond and William Willoughby (a merchant and shipowner with New England ties who had given energetic support in 1648).[31] On 16 February the Commons approved most of these recommendations but vetoed Tweedy, who was thereupon replaced by another of the Regulators, Maurice Thomson's brother Robert.[32] Willoughby became resident Commissioner at Portsmouth till his death in 1651; when his successor, Robert Moulton, died the following year, the post went to Willoughby's son Francis.[33] Most of the group were to remain in office for many years, and the evidence indicates that they were loyal, hard-working, and efficient.[34]

Trinity House, the shipmasters' association, also came under investigation. It had traditionally acted as an unofficial branch of naval administration but in 1648 had displayed instead an 'imbosomed malignancy', as some petitioners had reminded the Rump. Following the Regulators' report the old governing body was swept away and replaced by a new committee, whose members included two of the Regulators themselves (Maurice Thomson and Samuel Moyer), one of the new Generals at Sea (Deane), and the Navy Commissioner Thomas Smith. Under its new leaders Trinity House

[29] Batten: *CSPD 1648–9*, 276; on Crandley see G. G. Harris, *The Trinity House of Deptford, 1514–1660* (1969), 39, 274; *CSPD 1629–31*, 152; SP 16/135/38; *LJ* x. 351–2; Dewar, 'Naval Administration', 423, 425.

[30] *A and O* i. 27, 29–30; Cogar, thesis, ch. 2, part iv. For Pett see *DNB; CJ* v. 329; for Smith: Chaplin, 'Bourne', 121; *CJ* v. 285; for Tweedy: Harris, *Trinity House*, 34, 39, 284; SP 16/135/38; *CSPD 1628–9*, 287, 302; *CSPD 1629–31*, 153.

[31] *CJ* vi. 144. On Willoughby see A. Everitt, *The Community of Kent and the Great Rebellion, 1640–1660* (Leicester, 1966), 110–11; Chaplin, 'Bourne', 52; *CSPD 1648–9*, 210, 275; Bodl. Rawlinson MS A 226, fo. 37; *CSPD 1656–7*, 209; *CJ* v. 649; PRO Adm. 7/647, p. 164; *A and O* i. 1057, 1256, ii. 123.

[32] *CJ* vi. 144, 269. For Thomson, who was not officially appointed until late July, see *BDRB*; Cogar, thesis, 46; Rawl. MS A 224, fo. 59.

[33] *CSPD 1651*, 131; *CJ* vii. 185–6; *FDW* ii. 267. On Francis Willoughby see Chaplin, 'Bourne', 69.

[34] I concur with the verdicts of Oppenheim, 347 ff.; Dewar, 'Naval Administration', 422; Harris, *Trinity House*, 42; and Aylmer, *State's Servants*, 40.

was to prove predictably loyal and co-operative.[35] The Regulators turned next to the Customs, devising a 'New Model' which the Rump approved in April. Control passed to a small syndicate of merchants (among them the Regulator Stephen Estwick), who were authorized to remove any officials they considered politically unsound or inefficient.[36] The investigation of naval personnel affected mainly warrant-officers of ships in reserve and dockyard officials. Anyone involved in the previous year's attempts to secure a personal treaty was automatically barred by a clause in the 'Regulating Act'; some withdrew on this account, and the Regulators identified and removed a number of others. Many of them begged to be reinstated, pleading they had done nothing more than sign a petition, and the Regulators did show mercy to many lesser offenders, aware that a large-scale purge in the dockyards would be counter-productive. For similar reasons they recommended leniency towards contrite boatswains, carpenters, and other warrant-officers, and the Rump left it to the Generals to pardon and reinstate as many as they wished.[37]

A verdict on the Regulators' 'new modelling' is not easy. Against the enthusiasm of a modern investigator we have the stinging attack of John Hollond, one of their own number.[38] Hollond said later that he had stayed only till he 'smelled and saw the design'. 'The welfare of the English navy', he alleged, 'was of no more concern to them than was the navy of the great Turk, unless it were to settle a brother and a friend in two or three of the best places thereof; but the customs was the morsel they gaped for.' All the other activities, and the display of virtue and godliness, were mere camouflage to hide their bid for this lucrative prize. Hollond also accused the new Customs syndicate of corruption, and of driving out competent officials simply to make room for friends.[39] His cynical view is supported by the fact that one of the new syndicate, Edmund Harvey MP, was later sent to the Tower charged with defrauding

[35] *CJ* vi. 150, 160, 290; Harris, *Trinity House*, 37–8, 229–30; *The Resolution and Remonstrance of the Navie* (1649), 6.

[36] *CJ* vi. 193–4; Aylmer, *State's Servants*, 16. For the phrase 'New Model' see *CJ* vi. 194; Rawl. MS A 224, fo. 7ᵛ.

[37] *A and O* i. 1257–8; BL Add. MS 4165, fo. 50; *CJ* vi. 169. 170; Rawl. MS A 224, fos. 12ᵛ, 19ᵛ–20, 26ᵛ, 70ᵛ; *CSPD 1649–50*, 527–8.

[38] Reid 'Supply Departments'; Hollond, *Discourses*, 120–4; Aylmer, *State's Servants*, 16, 84. Cogar, thesis, 74–88, gives a favourable assessment.

[39] Hollond, *Discourses*, 120–4 (quotation p. 120).

the state of over £30,000.[40] Hollond condemned the Navy Commissioners too, for pursuing their commercial activities while holding public office. Some were even supplying goods to the state, and the public interest inevitably suffered when officials and contractors were one and the same. The Regulators might also be charged, finally, with causing some administrative confusion, for their powers overlapped with those of the Navy Commissioners and the Commons' own Navy Committee.[41]

Hollond was a biased witness, however, and his sweeping condemnation should not be accepted at face value.[42] The Regulators took sensible measures to reduce corruption in the dockyards, raising salaries to reduce temptation and imposing stiffer penalties for embezzlement. On the same principle they secured higher salaries for the Navy Commissioners (£250 each, with £300 for Hollond as Surveyor), while prohibiting the traditional fees and perquisites.[43] On the other hand the charge of blurring public and private interests does carry weight. When Thomas Smith leased his ships to the navy, for example, he was entitled as a Commissioner to decide the rate of hire. Peter Pett was both a major naval shipbuilder and, as a Commissioner, responsible for placing contracts for new warships.[44] Similarly the Regulators William Pennoyer and Samuel Moyer leased ships to the navy, and Pennoyer also contracted to supply it with gunpowder.[45] It needs to be stressed though that the Rump's main concern was political, to see naval administration placed in safe hands, and in a regime resting on such a narrow base it was probably inevitable—and a price worth paying—that reliable officials and dependable suppliers would be drawn from the same small pool. The same overlap can be found in the Commons' Navy Committee: Col. Venn was a large-scale naval contractor and Cromwell himself supplied six hundred timber trees.[46] Judged by political criteria, the Regulators' work was undoubtedly successful. The Navy Commissioners and dockyard

[40] Aylmer, *State's Servants*, 161–2.
[41] Ibid. 16; *CJ* vi. 147, 169, 170; *CSPD 1649–50*, 34.
[42] Hollond, *Discourses*, pp. xxvii–xxviii.
[43] Reid, 'Supply Departments'; *CJ* vi. 148; Aylmer, *State's Servants*, 107.
[44] On Smith see *CSPD 1650*, 500; *CSPD 1651*, 507; *CSPD 1651–2*, 519; *CSPD 1658–9*, 39. On the Pett clan see Aylmer, *State's Servants*, 156–9; Cogar, thesis, 88–99; Hollond, *Discourses*, pp. xxiii–xxiv, 310.
[45] Rawl. MS A 224, fos. 92ᵛ, 98; *CSPD 1650*, 536; *CSPD 1651–2*, 115, 144, 175.
[46] Rawl. MS A 224, fos. 21, 22ᵛ, 48ᵛ, 60 (Venn), fo. 87 (Cromwell).

officials proved loyal and efficient too throughout the interregnum, and Trinity House gave valuable help with hiring ships, pressing men, providing technical expertise, and much besides.[47]

Reorganizing naval administration was only the prologue to the more important task of building up a powerful and politically dependable fleet. The Rump embarked at once on a major programme of naval rearmament, placing its first orders for new ships as early as March 1649. By the close of 1651 twenty new warships had been built and added to the fleet, and a further twenty-five had been acquired by purchase or capture. The navy had almost doubled in size.[48] The navy's new, republican character was emphasized from the outset. The Council ordered new flags to be supplied and the Commonwealth's arms to be engraved on the stern on every ship in place of the king's.[49] Early in 1650 several of the greatest ships were renamed, on ideological grounds. The *Charles* became the *Liberty,* to symbolize the change from royal tyranny to republican freedom (though some may have found it significant that she was wrecked soon afterwards). The *Henrietta Maria* too became her antithesis, in Parliament's eyes, as the *Paragon,* and the *Royal Prince* was renamed *Resolution.* The *Royal Sovereign* was known henceforth simply as the *Sovereign,* symbolizing England's command of the seas, though in 1652-3 she was sometimes called the *Commonwealth.*[50] Three new frigates built in 1650 were named the *(Valiant) Fairfax, (Faithful) Speaker,* and *President,* Fairfax and Speaker Lenthall themselves being among the dignitaries attending the launching ceremonies.[51] A cavalier wit suggested that *Perjury, Covenant-Breaker,* and *Pilate* would have been more appropriate names. Others speculated on when to expect

[47] On Trinity House see e.g. HMC 7, *8th Report,* i. 247-8; *CSPD 1650,* 39, *CSPD 1651,* 523; Rawl. MS A 225, fos. 31, 50ᵛ, 53ᵛ, 55ᵛ, 59, 61; Harris, *Trinity House,* 229-30.

[48] *CSPD 1649-50,* 59, 82. For details of naval expansion see R. C. Anderson, *Lists of Men-of-War, 1650-1700: Part I, English Ships, 1649-1702* (2nd edn., no date), 6-13.

[49] *CSPD 1649-50,* 11, 14.

[50] *CJ* vi. 340; Anderson, *Lists,* 5; cf. *CSPD 1649-50,* 482. On the *Commonwealth* see *The Declaration . . . of the Lord Admiral Vantrump* (1653), 8; *The Moderate Publisher,* 3-10 June 1653; *The Letters of John Paige, London Merchant, 1648-1658,* ed. G. F. Steckley (London Record Soc. xxi; 1984), 67.

[51] J. Nickolls (ed.), *Original Letters and Papers of State* (1743), 8; *CSPD 1650,* 545.

the *Faithful Cromwell* or *Noll-Nose*, and in 1651 the new *Worcester* did indeed commemorate Cromwell's 'crowning victory'.[52]

The reconstruction of the naval officer corps was a more complex task. As captains and lieutenants were commissioned for a particular ship and service and normally paid off at its conclusion it was much easier, in principle, to remodel the officer corps than in the army, where commissions were on a more permanent basis. The difficulty lay in knowing which officers could be safely re-employed, and where to find suitable replacements for those laid aside. The officers for the summer guard in 1649 were vetted very thoroughly. A draft list prepared during Warwick's last days in office was referred to the Regulators for scrutiny, the Rump itself made further changes, and the Generals were then authorized to make any additional alterations they felt necessary.[53] The final list showed a very considerable turnover in personnel since the army's irruption into politics in 1647. Of the forty-three commanders named for the summer guard of 1647, two-thirds (twenty-seven) were not recommissioned in 1649 or at any other time during the interregnum. The summer guard of 1648 had itself been carefully vetted following Batten's removal, but even so a quarter of its commanders were not re-employed.[54] Among these now dropped were several of Warwick's most senior associates, notably Bethel (formerly vice-admiral), Swanley and Crowther (flag-officers in the Irish Sea), John Man, and John Bowen sen. In most cases we do not know whether they were barred or had refused to serve the new regime. Some had probably withdrawn in disgust, just as Capt. John Stansby had refused to serve after 1647 because of political developments ashore. Capt. Robert Dare had gone still further, taking the *Constant Warwick* to Holland in 1648 and signing a contract leasing her to Prince Charles. But Bethel had apparently been willing to accept a new post at the close of 1648, and he and Crowther were probably laid aside because of their close association with the displaced Admiral.[55]

[52] *Mercurius Elencticus*, 22–9 Apr. 1650; ibid., 29 Apr.–6 May; *Mercurius Pragmaticus*, 30 Apr.–7 May; *Man in the Moon*, 24 Apr.–2 May.

[53] Rawl. MS A 224, fo. 32ᵛ; *Perfect Occurrences*, 29 Dec. 1648–5 Jan. 1649; *CJ* vi. 129, 136, 166, 181. For the summer guard of 1649 see Add. MS 9300, fo. 116; cf. Clarke MS 4/4, 1649 (43, 7).

[54] The summer guards of 1647 and 1648 are given in *DCW* 274–6, 313–14. Rainborough and T. Pacey were dead by 1649.

[55] SP 18/223/44 (Stansby); on Dare, who served in 1642–7, see HMC 70, *Pepys*, 273; *CJ* vi. 106; on Bethel see *Perfect Occurrences*, 29 Dec. 1648–5 Jan. 1649. Man

The new title 'General at Sea' symbolized a resolve to bring the navy politically into line with the army, a task for which the new commanders-in-chief were well equipped. In February 1649 some 'well-affected' naval and merchant officers called for close liaison henceforth between the army and navy, urging that 'there may always be some of the land officers at sea, and some of the sea officers at land'.[56] The Rump and army too may have envisaged some kind of continuing interchange between service afloat and ashore. In the late summer of 1649, for example, Cromwell invited Blake to become his major-general of foot in Ireland, though Blake politely declined.[57] Deane's career provides perhaps the best example of interchange. In 1650 his ships supplied the artillery used in the siege of Wexford and he seems to have taken a direct part in the operations ashore; the following year he became commander of the English army in Scotland, returning to the navy as General at Sea during the Dutch war. The career of George Monck, a later General, followed a somewhat similar pattern, and there are parallels too among other officers drawn from the army, such as Col. Leonard Lidcott and Jeremiah Smyth. There was to be an important military presence in the fleet throughout the 1650s, and in addition captains on the Scottish and Irish stations were directed to follow the orders of the military commanders ashore.[58]

In appointing senior commanders the Rump naturally turned to the small band of radicals already in the fleet. Robert Moulton was easily the most prominent of them and played a key part in the first weeks of the new regime. During the winter he commanded in the Downs, with Parliament and Council repeatedly praising his zeal and merits, and then served as vice-admiral under the new Generals. Moulton matches perfectly the 'colonial-interloping' model. He had emigrated to New England in 1629 and later collaborated with Warwick in privateering ventures as another co-owner of the *Constant Warwick*. In 1636 he was second in command of an

had signed a peace petition in 1648 *(The Humble Tender)*. On the exclusion of Warwick's friends see Clar. MS 47, fo. 12.

[56] *Resolution and Remonstrance*, 4.

[57] Powell, *Blake*, 85; Blake, *Letters*, 46. Blake did accept a temporary position commanding land forces in the south-west when the Scots invaded England in 1651.

[58] For Deane, Monck, and Smyth see *DNB*; see also below, ch. 6. Lidcott did serve in 1649, despite Anderson's doubts (R. C. Anderson, *List of English Naval Captains* (1964), 15; BL Loan MS 29/241, fo. 32; SP 25/123, fo. 161), but not in 1650 *(CSPD 1650*, 574). Few naval officers served with the army, though Capt. John Sherwin fought at Worcester (SP 18/107/89).

expedition to the Far East organized by Sir William Courteen, in defiance of the East India Company's monopoly. Moulton had served in the parliamentary navy from 1643, while his son looked after the family's shipping interests.[59] Another of the Rump's senior officers, Edward Hall, had also commanded a ship in Courteen's expedition and was a man of similar stamp. Hall's outspoken views on the monarchy had brought his naval career to an abrupt halt when they came to Parliament's notice in 1646, but he was now welcomed back as flag-captain in 1649, rear-admiral in 1650, and commander of a squadron in the Mediterranean in 1651.[60] Richard Haddock might have had a good command too but was apparently piqued at the greater favour shown to Moulton; the Rump's preference is understandable, for Haddock was already in his mid-sixties and his political commitment was less clear.[61] Command of the forces in the Irish Sea went to Sir George Ayscue, rear-admiral in the expedition to Holland and a kinsman by marriage of Sir Henry Vane.[62]

There were only a few reliable radicals among the senior captains. The Rump was reluctant to promote junior officers too fast, for they lacked experience of command in large ships and their political views were often doubtful. It preferred instead to recruit experienced merchant commanders who were known to be committed radicals. William Wildey, Richard Badiley, and Robert Dennis, for example, had been taking large ships to the Straits or the Americas for many years.[63] Robert Hackwell, admiral in the Irish Sea in the

[59] Whitelocke, *Memorials*, ii. 489; *CJ* vi. 109; *CSPD 1649–50*, 9–10. On Moulton see *DNB*; Chaplin, 'Bourne', 68; A. W. Johns, 'The *Constant Warwick*', *MM* xviii (1932), 255; *CSPD 1635–6*, 308; Sir W. Foster, *The English Factories in India* (Oxford, 1906–27), v. 331, vi. 7. He was born about 1592 (PRO HCA 13/58, fo. 89) at Landulph, Cornwall (J. and G. F. Matthews (eds.), *Abstracts of Probate Acts in the Prerogative Court of Canterbury, 1652–3* (1911), 340).

[60] Foster, *Factories*, iv. 169, 172, 250–3, 259, 264, 272; vi. 121, 223–4; E. B. Sainsbury (ed.), *A Calendar of the Court Minutes of the East India Company* (Oxford, 1907–38), i. 88, 256; *CSPD 1635–6*, 308; *CSPD 1636–7*, 528; Adm. 7/673, pp. 2, 32, 40–1; *CJ* v. 503, 537; *LJ* x. 155, 231, 232; Add. MS 9305, fo. 43ᵛ.

[61] Bodl. Tanner MS 57, fo. 546; Rawl. MS A 224, fos. 4ᵛ, 6ᵛ, 9; Add. MS 9300, fo. 116; *CSPD 1649–50*, 15.

[62] P. Le Fevre, 'Sir George Ayscue, Commonwealth and Restoration Admiral', *MM* lxviii (1982), 189–202; *CJ* vi. 154; Rowe, *Vane*, 12.

[63] Wildey: *DNB*; Chaplin, 'Bourne', 74–6; Adm. 7/673, p. 319; W. Okeley, *Eben-ezer* (1675), 25; HCA 13/52, fo. 204; PRO Calendar, C 54A, 12; *CJ* vi. 154. Badiley: *DNB*; T. A. Spalding, *A Life of Richard Badiley* (Westminster, 1899), 3; HCA 13/52, fo. 332ᵛ; W. Aspinwall (ed.), *A Volume . . . containing the Aspinwall Notarial Records from 1644 to 1651* (Boston, Mass., 1903), 47, 188. His brother

winter of 1649–50,had been sailing to the Levant, the East Indies, and America since the 1610s. John Harris, another such recruit, was beginning his new naval career at an age of more than sixty![64]

Men possessing the right combination of radicalism, ability, and experience were far from plentiful, and it sometimes required considerable effort to draw them into the navy. In 1649 Nehemiah Bourne was too entangled in commercial activities to accept a post, but when he returned from America early in 1650 Sir Henry Vane was determined not to miss him again. 'We will use our endeavours to take him off from his merchant affairs,' Vane wrote to the Generals; 'the man is without exception, and will do the state, and yourselves, both service and honour.' This time Vane succeeded. Bourne was in many ways an archetypal figure in the new officer corps. Born into an old maritime family he had settled in Massachusetts in the late 1630s and then, returning to England, had fought in the civil war as major in Rainborough's regiment, which had a strong New England flavour. He stayed on to play an important role in naval affairs throughout the 1650s.[65] John Lawson, also recruited in 1650, probably again by Vane, was to play a still more important part. Lawson had been bred in the hard school of colliers plying down the east coast. He was a skilful seaman, and his political record was sound; during the civil war he had commanded the hired *Covenant*, a small ship he part-owned, and had then served ashore for almost five years as a captain of foot.[66] There were relatively few such men, however, and some of them did not remain long before yielding to the pull of private business interests.[67] The Rump therefore also had to keep on many of the more junior commanders serving before 1649. Some of them were undoubtedly radicals: Owen Cox was later known as a Fifth Monarchist and George Dakins as a 'violent

---

William was among the new governing body of Trinity House: *CJ* vi. 290. Dennis: Chaplin, 'Bourne', 122; N. D. Davis, *Cavaliers and Roundheads of Barbados* (Georgetown, 1887), 46; J. H. Lefroy, *Memorials of the Discovery and Early Settlement of the Bermudas* (1877), i, 687; Shilton and Holworthy, *Admiralty Examinations*, 46; Rawl. MS C 416, fo. 30; HCA 13/52, fo. 389; Rawl. MS C 94, fos. 4, 7; *CJ* vi. 129.

[64] Harris: HCA 13/72, fo. 321; SP 25/123, p. 93; H. F. Waters, *Genealogical Gleanings* (Boston, Mass., 1901), 1250. Hackwell: Sainsbury, *Court Minutes*, iv. 167; Shilton and Holworthy, *Admiralty Examinations*, 37; SP 16/135/38; J. C. Hotten, *The Original Lists of . . . Emigrants . . . to the American Plantations, 1600–1700* (1874), 91–2; *CJ* vi. 129, 242.

[65] SP 25/123, fo. 226; Chaplin, 'Bourne', *passim*.

[66] *DNB*; *BDBR*; *FDW* iv. 45–6.   [67] See below, ch. 6.

Anabaptist'. Others were probably mere conformists. There was still room for a man such as Abraham Wheeler, who had been a captain since the late 1630s without leaving any trace of his views — if any — on the shifting political kaleidoscope.[68] But it was only in the solitary case of John Bowen jun. of the *Hind* that the Rump appears to have made a serious misjudgement. Late in 1649 Bowen was charged, *inter alia*, with declaring that he would have joined the mutiny the previous year if his ship had been in the Downs, and he allegedly welcomed former mutineers who fell into his hands, even offering them employment. He had attacked Parliament's shabby treatment of Batten and Warwick, and he accused the Rump, rather oddly, of favouring papists. He was promptly turned out.[69] It is of course possible that others shared his views, but if so they kept their thoughts to themselves.

The Rump was well aware that radicals formed only a small leaven in the seafaring lump, and it set out accordingly to find ways of binding the mass of worldly or traditionalist officers and sailors to its cause. The most obvious method was by improving conditions of service. In March 1649 it voted a substantial increase in officers' salaries, captains receiving a 50 per cent rise (from 6s. 8d. to 10s. a day in a third rate); many warrant-officers fared equally well, the pay of a gunner or carpenter in a third rate going up from 1s. 1d. to 1s. 8d. a day.[70] Ostensibly these increases were temporary gratuities, but they were renewed annually and then incorporated into a comprehensive new wage structure from the beginning of 1653.[71] Ordinary seamen's pay remained at 19s. a month, the rate established in 1643. This was roughly comparable to a foot-soldier's pay, but naval wages continued to lag behind those found in merchant ships, and the Rump preferred to woo the seamen by focusing on prize-money, which it rightly saw as a stronger inducement. A preliminary Act on prize was rushed through on 22 February,

---

[68] Cox: *BDBR*; B. S. Capp, *The Fifth Monarchy Men* (1972), 208, 213, 247. The Lords had blocked his appointment to the *Phoenix* in 1648, removing him to a smaller ship *(LJ* x. 503; *DCW* 313, 346). For Dakins see ch. 10, below. Even Wheeler seems to have had radical connections: below, ch. 9 n. 57.

[69] Clarke MS 4/4, 1649 (38); SP 25/123, p. 171; *CSPD 1649–50*, 434. He was sacked on the advice of the Regulators. For the Rump's alleged favour towards Catholics such as Kenelm Digby see Gardiner, *CP* i. 81–3. Bowen was probably related to his more senior namesake, whom the Rump had dropped.

[70] *CJ* vi. 173; *CSPD 1649–50*, 49.

[71] *CSPD 1649–50*, 289–90: *CSPD 1650*, 15, 415–16; *CJ* vi. 372; *CJ* vii. 11, 152; *FDW* iii. 283–5.

copies being sent down at once to the fleet, and a more considered measure filled out the details in April. Under the new arrangements a successful crew would receive half the value of a captured warship, the other half going for the relief of sick and wounded sailors, widows and dependants. An enemy warship sunk in action would be deemed a prize and valued according to the number of guns it had carried. Proceeds from the sale of captured merchantmen and their cargoes would be shared equally between the captors, the state, and the relief fund, while the tenths traditionally paid to the Lord Admiral were assigned for medals and gratuities to reward outstanding service. A new body of Prize Commissioners was established to run the system. On paper, if not always in practice, it was a vast improvement.[72]

A vigorous propaganda broadsheet set out to bolster these material inducements, calling on the seamen 'to engage cheerfully in England's honourable and just cause': 'Now my brave blades, my brethren and seamen, if ever, now is the time for you to stand to your tackle!' The enemy were 'sons of Belial, plunderers, murderers and Irish rebels,' in league with foreign papists; if they ever prevailed 'no people under the sun would be such slaves as you would be unto these cannibals'. Parliament by contrast—described with some hyperbole as 'the freest Parliament that ever England had'—cared deeply for their safety and freedom, 'watching night and day, that you may sleep'. 'God's gone before you, follow close, the chase will be successful, all's your own.'[73]

But the Rump was aware that persuasion might not be enough, and was ready with the stick as well as the carrot. The Act of 22 February authorized the pressing of sailors for the navy, threatening with prison any who resisted or ran away.[74] And in March the Rump enacted the first-ever 'Laws and Ordinances Martial' to regulate discipline on board ship. The new code, which laid down the death penalty in seven of its twenty clauses, was strongly coloured by the political insecurity of the time. Article 4, for example, dealt with attempts to stir up revolt, article 12 with carrying away a warship from the service of the state, and article 17 with 'words tending to the death' of the Generals or other senior officers.[75] As a further control the Generals were directed to impose

---

[72] *A and O* i. 74, II. 9–10, 18, 66–73; cf. Oppenheim, 292–3, 308–9; C. H. Firth, *Cromwell's Army* (1962 edn.), 184–5.

[73] *Arguments, Inviting all Faithful Marriners* ([16 Apr.] 1649).

[74] *A and O* ii. 12–13.

[75] *CJ* vi. 156–7.

an engagement on their officers and men, pledging allegiance to the state as now constituted without a king or House of Lords; the national Engagement, devised some months later, was also tendered to the mariners.[76]

Legal controls were tightened still more by another Act which imposed the death penalty for serious crimes committed at sea; it was made to apply retrospectively and so covered the mutiny and its sequel.[77] The Act was designed in part to demoralize sailors serving with Rupert, and to deter others tempted to join him. The cavaliers claimed that Parliament dared not enforce its law for fear of reprisals, but though captured officers generally remained in prison till they were exchanged or escaped, ordinary seamen had no sure protection.[78] In March 1649 Popham hanged two warrant-officers taken in the *Guinea* who had been involved in the revolt, and the following year Deane was directed to impose 'exemplary punishment' at the head of his fleet on the crew of a captured privateer.[79] But the articles of war and the Rump's savage laws were not enforced in any systematic way, for their purpose was largely deterrent. The Generals sometimes thought conciliation more appropriate. When the *Elizabeth hoy* deserted Rupert and submitted voluntarily in 1649 they promptly released her master and crew, in the hope that others would follow their example.[80]

Charles II hoped that many of the Rump's sailors would rally to his cause, and Rupert issued a declaration in March 1649 offering employment to all who would join him. One cavalier predicted that the seamen would soon drive out the new Generals as they had Rainborough.[81] In the event, however, the new-modelled navy remained loyal to the Commonwealth. Only one ship defected to the royalists (the little *Hart*, a sixth rate), and she was recaptured a few months later.[82] A disturbance in 1649 in the *Tiger* had at first

[76] *CSPD 1649–50*, 27; Blake, *Letters*, 39; *CJ* vi. 306–7; below, ch. 5; cf. *CJ* v. 652.
[77] *A and O* ii. 254–6.
[78] *Mercurius Pragmaticus*, 28 Aug.–4 Sept. and 17–24 Sept. 1649; *The Moderate*, 18–25 Sept.; *CSPD 1649–50*, 208, 247, 258, 544; *CSPD 1650*, 91, 95, 412; *CSPD 1651*, 517.
[79] Blake, *Letters*, 38; HMC 51, *Leyborne-Popham*, 13; SP 25/123, pp. 330–1.
[80] Blake, *Letters*, 20; *CSPD 1649–50*, 41, 48.
[81] *Mercurius Pragmaticus*, 24 Apr.–1 May 1649; *The Declaration of His Highness Prince Rupert* (1649), 8.
[82] *A Perfect Diurnall*, 19–26 Feb. 1649; *Mercurius Pragmaticus*, 13–20 Mar.; Clarke MS 4/4, 1649 (18); PRO Del. 2/117; *Perfect Occurrences*, 22–9 June; *CSPD 1649–50*, 206. The *Hart's* crew mutinied again in 1650, putting to sea whilst most of the officers were ashore, but this time they soon had second thoughts and returned voluntarily: *CSPD 1650*, 20, 23, 31, 32, 44.

appeared far more serious, for she was the new flagship of the North Sea squadron. Two Navy Commissioners hastened to Yarmouth to investigate, and other vessels blocked the harbour mouth to prevent her escaping to sea. But it soon became clear that the trouble was not political, having originated in a feud between the master and boatswain, and the company sent ashore a reassuring declaration of loyalty to the Rump to be posted in the market-place.[83]

Charles himself had undermined his cause by choosing Rupert as admiral, and the prince's subsequent behaviour did nothing to attract recruits. An eye witness remarked of his squadron in Holland that 'if hell be on earth, it is here,' and later reports suggest that the whiff of brimstone accompanied him wherever he went. Parliamentary propagandists attacked him as a bloodthirsty foreign pirate leading a disreputable band of papists, a near-madman who 'foams so beastly at the mouth'.[84] In April 1649 the Dutch admiral Tromp advised Charles to invite back Batten and Jordan to resume the command, which suggests that the Rump was already winning the propaganda war.[85] It would take more than words, though, to defeat the royalists at sea.

With Rupert's squadron already at sea and foreign governments openly hostile the Generals could not afford to wait for the results of the Rump's reforming measures to become clear. The new-modelled navy had to be put to the test without delay.

On 17 February 1649 the Council issued a daunting list of instructions. The Generals were to find and destroy Rupert's fleet and all other royalist shipping, prevent any invasion attempts from Europe, intercept supplies going to the royalists in Ireland, and assert English sovereignty of the seas—in addition to the traditional tasks of protecting trade and the fisheries.[86] They were responsible too, implicitly, for the honour and prestige of the new regime, and for persuading other governments to come to terms with it. These concerns clearly lay behind the Council's decision to set out two

[83] Clarke MS 4/4, 1649 (18, 20 21); *A Modest Narrative*, 11–18 Aug. 1649; *CSPD 1649–50*, 267–8, 285, 301–2, 433.
[84] *A Perfect Remonstrance and Narrative* (1649), 7; *A Perfect Diurnall*, 19–26 Mar. 1649; S. R. Gardiner (ed.), 'Prince Rupert at Lisbon' *(Camden Miscellany*, x; 1902), 18.
[85] *The Kingdomes Faithfull Scout*, 6–13 Apr. 1649.
[86] *CSPD 1649–50*, 23.

more of its greatest ships in the late summer, the *George* and *Unicorn*, while conceding that there was no operational need for them. 'It would add much to our reputation to let our enemies see that we are prepared', the Council explained, directing the ships to proceed down the Thames 'to be seen of all that come in and go out' and then cross to the Flemish coast to show the flag.[87]

The operations of the Rump's navy, though undramatic, were highly effective.[88] Contemporaries had no doubt about the importance of the struggle at sea: naval affairs took up a considerable part of the time of both Commons and Council, and pamphlets and newspapers gave extensive (if unreliable) coverage of every clash.

Rupert posed the most immediate threat. He had put to sea on 21 January 1649 and sailed to Ireland unhindered, steering deliberately close to the Downs to terrify the small parliamentary force there. On reaching Ireland he established a base at Kinsale, well placed for scouring the Channel approaches. The combined force of Rupert's squadron and the Irish privateers already active was about thirty vessels, posing a formidable challenge.[89] Royalists on the continent were delighted to hear how he was disrupting English trade and demoralizing the merchants. As one observed, 'It's hoped the reputation of so rich prizes taken by Prince Rupert will give his Majesty some credit here' — credit both political and financial.[90]

Coastal waters too were infested with royalist privateers, many operating from Dunkirk and Flemish ports. They inflicted heavy losses. In July 1649 the Irishman Thomas Plunket, a former parliamentarian, led an attack on a convoy off Newcastle, scattering the escorts and taking thirty or forty small prizes. In August the Council learned that eight merchantmen had been seized off Flamborough Head. September brought alarming reports of sixteen ships being fitted out at Dunkirk and Ostend to attack shipping in the Thames itself. An official remarked sadly that the Channel was now more dangerous than the waters off Algiers.[91] Sussex MPs

---

[87] Ibid. 253.

[88] For general accounts see Gardiner, *CP*, vols. i–ii; Powell, *Blake*, chs. 6–9; J. S. Corbett, *England in the Mediterranean* (1917), chs. 12–14; and, from the royalist angle, R. C. Anderson's articles in *MM* xiv (1928), xvii (1931), xxi (1935).

[89] R. C. Anderson, 'The Royalists at Sea in 1649', *MM* xiv (1928), 320–8; E. Warburton, *Memoirs of Prince Rupert (1849)*, iii. 281–8; Carte, *Original Letters*, i. 200, 201, 211; Clar. MS 37, fo. 74.   [90] Carte, *Original Letters*, i. 248, 279, 286.

[91] *The Moderate*, 3–10 July; *A Great Victory obtained by Prince Charles his Ships* (1649), 6; *CSPD 1648–9*, 278; *A Great Victory obtained at Sea* (1649), 3, HMC 51, *Leyborne–Popham*, 35.

complained of pirates lying off Beachy Head and disrupting the fisheries, while pirates off Barnstaple were seizing small vessels and then releasing them on payment of £50 to £60 apiece, a lucrative practice which flourished elsewhere too.[92] Privateers even seized ships carrying grain from Margate to the London markets, and the Council had to station a warship in the mouth of the Thames itself.[93] As Plunket's attack had shown, convoys themselves were not necessarily safe. On one occasion Capt. Robert Wyard, escorting a fleet of merchantmen, had to try to fend off attacks from six privateers at once.[94] Cavalier journalists were elated by these successes and reported (falsely) that the new Generals had been routed too, and Moulton taken captive.[95]

The Rump concentrated first on the threat from Rupert. Initially there were too few ships available for Moulton to mount an attack on Kinsale, though he moved his base to Plymouth to be closer. Sensibly the Council sent reinforcements as soon as ships became available, rather than waiting for the entire summer guard to be ready. The arrival of Popham in April with four more ships soon brought some successes, and Blake and Deane appeared in May with further reinforcements. On the 21st the three Generals arrived off Kinsale, and were delighted to find Rupert at his base. By blockading the harbour they were able to bring his depredations to an abrupt halt, and Popham returned home to report the good news. The Rump joyfully ordered a day of thanksgiving.[96] Blake and Deane responded to this with a characteristic blend of pious modesty and determination. They were the 'unworthiest instruments' of the Lord, they declared, needing the prayers rather than the thanks of mankind, but they vowed to pursue Rupert's forces 'whithersoever they shall go'. 'However it hath or shall please God to exercise us with varieties of providences, we shall not doubt . . . of good success, and a happy conclusion in the end.'[97] There were

[92] *CSPD 1649–50*, 179; *A Perfect Summary*, 9–16 Apr.; *The Kingdomes Weekly Intelligencer*, 3–10 July.

[93] Add. MS 18986, fo. 3; *CPSD 1649–50*, 378.

[94] Bodl. Dep. MS C 164, fos. 450–1; *CJ* vi. 454; *Severall Proceedings*, 8–15 Aug. 1650; *CSPD 1650*, 291, 327.

[95] *Mercurius Pragmaticus*, 6–13 Mar.; *Mercurius Elencticus*, 11–18 June; *Mercurius Pragmaticus*, 12–19 June (which claimed, most implausibly, that Blake and Popham were pining for the London brothels).

[96] Powell, *Blake*, 78–82; Anderson, 'Royalists in 1649', 326, 329–30; Carte, *Original Letters*, i. 226, 275–6; Blake, *Letters*, 41–2; Tanner MS 56, fos. 16ʳ⁻ᵛ, 20; *CJ* vi. 224–5.   [97] Blake, *Letters*, 42–3.

reasonable grounds for this confidence: Parliament had set out a strong summer guard of forty-nine state ships and eight hired merchantmen, later supplemented by royalist prizes, and had voted to keep this force at sea for eight months instead of the usual six.[98] But the Generals were also right to be cautious, for the strong fortifications at Kinsale ruled out a direct assault: though Rupert could not escape, they in turn could not reach him.[99] The Rump remembered the frustrating stalemate at Helvoetsluys, and feared he would simply resume his raids whenever short supplies or winter gales forced the Generals to lift the blockade. This would be politically humiliating, and the Council urged the Generals to do all they could to destroy Rupert's force rather than merely contain it. There might not be enough money, it warned, to set out so large a fleet another year.[100]

Rupert had problems too, however. He had to supply his needs through the sale of prizes, and this source dried up once the blockade was imposed. His sailors quickly became discontented and mutinous, especially those he had taken forcibly from captured merchantmen; there were reports that some had threatened to kill him, and he had to employ soldiers for self-protection.[101] Time was a pressing factor for Rupert as for his opponents: unless he could get back to sea quickly his squadron might disintegrate.

The stalemate was broken in the autumn. Cromwell had led an army to Ireland in August. The larger part of the English force, under Ireton, had planned to land near Kinsale in the south, to confront Rupert, though adverse winds had driven the fleet to Dublin. Even so Rupert's position came under threat by land as well as sea as the English marched south. Local military forces wavered as they approached, and when the garrison at Cork declared for Parliament on 17 October, nearby Kinsale was left highly exposed. By chance bad weather had driven Blake from his station a few days earlier, and Rupert hastily seized the opportunity to escape with the seven ships he had ready and manned. His goal now was Lisbon. John IV of Portugal warmly favoured the Stuart cause, and Rupert knew that at Lisbon he would be far away from

[98] Add. MS 9300, fo. 116; Clarke MS 4/4, 1649 (7); *CJ* vi. 224.

[99] Anderson, 'Royalists in 1649', 331.

[100] *CSPD 1649–50*, 150, 202–3.

[101] *The Impartial Intelligencer*, 11–18 Apr., 18–25 Apr., 13–20 June; *Joyfull Newes from the Princes Fleet* (1649), 3; *A Declaration of the Princes Navie* (1649), 1–3; Warburton, *Memoirs*, iii. 293–4.

parliamentary bases and well placed to intercept shipping homeward-bound from the Straits. His force, supplemented by prizes taken *en route*, was as strong as when he had left Holland at the beginning of the year.[102]

Once Rupert's whereabouts were known the Council resolved to send a fleet in pursuit, and Blake set sail with a strong force in March 1650.[103] He was determined not to imitate the caution Warwick had shown in Holland two years earlier. On arrival he wrote to King John hoping there would be no objection to an attack on the royalists, and next day—apparently without waiting for a reply—he sailed into the Tagus to launch an assault. Providence intervened, however, for the wind died away and the forts on the shore opened fire, forcing him to abandon his plan. He looked next for a diplomatic solution, sending his political agent, Charles Vane, to open negotiations. A few days later Vice-Admiral Moulton also went to urge the king to hand over Rupert's fleet or allow Blake to attack it, or, at least, to order both fleets to sea. John rejected all these proposals. A lengthy stalemate then ensued, punctuated by skirmishes between rival bands of sailors ashore and an abortive attempt by Rupert to booby-trap one of Blake's ships.[104] King John's response showed that Rupert could only be destroyed at the risk of war with Portugal. Accepting the risk, the Rump sent out Popham in May with strong reinforcements and new instructions authorizing the Generals to attack Rupert wherever he was, and to destroy any Portuguese ships trying to protect him. A few days before Popham's arrival Blake further strengthened his force by seizing nine English ships hired by the Portuguese as part of their outward-bound Brazil fleet.[105] As war now seemed inevitable the Portuguese reluctantly set about preparing their own forces. John and his ministers strongly favoured the Stuart cause but they were not eager to go to war for it; Portugal was a poor, small country, its independence still precarious, and already at war with Spain and the Dutch. It could hardly afford another entanglement, especially as it

[102] Anderson, 'Royalists in 1649', 331, 335–8; HMC 51, *Leyborne–Popham*, 26, 34–5; Warburton, *Memoirs*, iii. 299–301, 311–12.

[103] Powell, *Blake*, 88–90; *CSPD 1649–50*, 483–5; *Thurloe*, i. 134–6.

[104] Powell, *Blake*, 90–5; Blake, *Letters*, 74–86; Gardiner, 'Rupert at Lisbon'; R. C. Anderson, 'The Royalists at Sea in 1650', *MM* xvii (1931) 138–43; *A Perfect Diurnall*, 10–17 June 1650.

[105] *Thurloe*, i. 142–5; Powell, *Blake*, 95–6; Anderson, 'Royalists in 1650', 143–4; C. R. Boxer, 'Blake and the Brazil Fleets in 1650', *MM* xxxvi (1950), 219–20.

relied heavily on hired English shipping for its vital trade with Brazil. In the event naval operations therefore amounted to no more than shadow-boxing. Rupert twice tried to put to sea with his Portuguese allies but they showed no wish to fight, retiring to the safety of the Tagus as soon as the English approached. As stores ran low the Generals were forced to send many of their ships home, first the captured Brazil ships and then a further nine vessels under Popham. But at last, in September, Blake's perseverance had its reward: he met the homeward-bound Portuguese Brazil fleet and captured seven of its ships, sinking another, and scattering the rest. The prizes were taken to Cadiz for repairs and then sent home under Badiley. Blake himself intended to patrol off Lisbon a few weeks longer with his seven remaining ships until the onset of the winter storms.[106]

By the time Blake returned to the Tagus, however, Rupert had gone; his departure had been hastened by King John, convinced by the fate of the Brazil fleet that the price of supporting the Stuarts was too high. Rupert had sailed into the Straits with a squadron of six ships, and lost no time in resuming his attacks on merchant shipping. He captured two prizes without firing a shot by disguising his vessel as Blake's flagship, and burnt several other English vessels in Spanish harbours, ignoring the protests of the port authorities. But disaster then struck. Blake had followed through the Straits and caught up with the main royalist force early in November; the *Henry* (formerly *Roebuck*) surrendered without a fight, and the other five ships ran ashore and were quickly reduced to wrecks.[107] Rupert himself escaped, for he had left the others shortly before to pursue another prize. He found shelter for a time in Toulon and then slipped into the Atlantic, realizing that the Mediterranean was no longer safe. For a further two years he ranged down the African coast and across to the Caribbean, eventually returning to France early in 1653 with his one remaining ship. By then he had long since ceased to be a threat, for the Rump's seapower had driven him further and further away from the major shipping lanes, and his return passed almost unnoticed.[108] Blake by

---

[106] Anderson, 'Royalists in 1650', 149–57; Powell, *Blake*, 97–102; Boxer, 'Blake and the Brazil Fleets', 222–8; Blake, *Letters*, 63–5; NMM AGC/21/26.

[107] Anderson, 'Royalists in 1650', 157–67; Powell, *Blake*, 103–7; Blake, *Letters*, 65–70, 90–95; Warburton, *Memoirs*, iii. 315–24.

[108] Warburton, *Memoirs*, iii. 325–88, 532–46; R. C. Anderson, 'The Royalists at Sea in 1651–3', *MM* xxi (1935), 61–90.

contrast arrived home in February 1651 to a hero's welcome and a reward of £3,000 from the Commons.[109]

There were many royalist privateers operating independently of Rupert, and they too posed a serious threat to English commerce in the Rump's first months. But once Rupert was penned in at Kinsale the odds changed and the Rump's warships began to bring home a steady flow of prizes. The loss of Irish bases was a major blow to the royalists; the career of the notorious Plunket ended when he sailed into Cork in November 1649 unaware that it was now in parliamentary hands.[110] In August a squadron under Popham had begun to patrol off Dunkirk, and England's growing naval strength gave foreign shipowners pause for thought. Merchants at Dunkirk who had been intending to set out privateers in 1650 in Charles's name abandoned the idea when they learned the size of the Rump's summer guard.[111] Though some privateering continued it was reduced to manageable proportions. Privateers with foreign commanders and polyglot crews were often indistinguishable from pirates apart from the commission they sailed under, and reports of their outrageous behaviour did nothing to help Charles's cause. Two privateers captured by Capt. Peacock were manned by what he described contemptuously as 'eighty poor, tattered, lousy rogues of several nations'.[112] In June 1649 a boat party under Anthony Young had removed another threat by blowing up the warship *Antelope*, which Rupert had left behind at Helvoetsluys.[113] By the end of 1651 Charles's forces at sea were little more than the sweepings of the European waterfronts, and the navy's first task was largely completed.

The navy's second major role was to help consolidate the authority of the new regime. The years 1649–52 saw the dramatic assertion of the Rump's claim to all the lands traditionally subject to the crown, and the navy played an important part in this process. Ireland was the first target. Ayscue's squadron in the Irish Sea kept open the lifeline to Dublin and blocked the flow of arms to the royalists from

<hr/>

[109] *CJ* vi. 520–1, 534; Powell, *Blake*, 107.

[110] *A Briefe Relation*, 20–7 Nov. 1649.

[111] *CSPD 1649–50*, 290; C. H., *A Perfect Narrative of a Sea Fight* (1650), 5; NMM GOS/3.

[112] *The Moderate Intelligencer*, 2–10 May 1649. Cf. Adm. 7/674. fo. 62.

[113] *CSPD 1649–50*, 105, 206; *Perfect Occurrences*, 23–30 Mar. 1649; *The Impartiall Intelligencer*, 20–7 June; Spalding, *Badiley*, 29–30.

the continent; he also unloaded guns from his flagship in June 1649 to assist Dublin's beleaguered garrison. In August a vast armada of warships and transports commanded by Deane carried the army from Milford Haven to Ireland, and the reconquest began.[114] The navy gave what support it could. Deane helped with the siege of Wexford, for example, and in 1650 Penn blockaded Limerick, Waterford, and Galway; he also sailed up the Clare to destroy settlements along its banks and terrorize the local population — an operation he recounted to Cromwell with distasteful relish.[115] The invasion of Scotland in 1650 was launched overland, but food, ammunition, and equipment were transported north by sea under naval protection.[116] Where possible the navy provided direct assistance too. Hall's squadron bombarded Leith from the sea to cover the army's advance, and Deane provided small craft for armed reconnaissance. Capt. William Pestell even had a 60-ton pinnace dragged six miles overland to operate in Loch Ness, to the Highlanders' dismay.[117] The navy played a more central role in the recapture of the Scillies and Channel Islands. Both were important royalist privateering bases, and the problem became urgent in 1651 when the Dutch ordered Tromp to the Scillies, irritated by attacks on their own shipping. Blake was sent to make a pre-emptive strike, and the last stronghold there yielded to him on 3 June 1651. In October he led a force to attack the Channel Islands, the warships providing a heavy artillery bombardment and then covering the landing of the soldiers against stiff opposition. Both Jersey and Guernsey had been secured for Parliament by the end of the year. With the capture of the Isle of Man that autumn all the royalist privateering bases were at last eliminated.[118]

The main royalist stronghold in the New World was Barbados, where power had passed into the hands of cavalier refugees under a new Governor, Lord Willoughby, the former commander of the royalist fleet. Reports filtered back to England that parliamentary

---

[114] Tanner MS 56, fo. 66; *CPSD 1649–50*, 209–10; HMC 51, *Leyborne–Popham*, 34–5, 47; Cromwell, *Writings*, ii. 104, 108.

[115] Nickolls, *Original Letters*, 5–6.

[116] *CSPD 1650*, e.g. 548–54, 558–63; Gardiner, *CP* ii, ch. 12. Money for the soldiers' pay was also carried by sea; early in 1652 Peacock brought £80,000 to Leith and Taylor £60,000: Clarke MS 1/10, fos. 24, 77.

[117] *A Large Relation of the Fight at Leith* (1650); *Severall Proceedings*, 24 Apr.– 1 May 1651; *A Perfect Account*, 23–30 June 1652.

[118] Powell, *Blake*, chs. 8–9; *Severall Proceedings*, 2–9 Oct. 1651.

sympathizers were being driven from the island, and there was some concern that Rupert might try to establish himself there. Sir George Ayscue was therefore sent out in 1651 with a small force to mount a blockade, though he lacked the resources to challenge the 6,000 armed men set out by the colonists. News of Cromwell's victory at Worcester convinced the settlers that negotiation was the only realistic course open to them, and in January 1652 they accepted the generous terms Ayscue offered. The other West Indian islands submitted without resistance.[119] Virginia was subdued in March 1652 by another small force, though its commander, Robert Dennis, had perished in a shipwreck on the voyage out. Under his successor, Edmund Curtis, it went on to secure the submission of Maryland and so complete the reunion of the English settlements overseas.[120]

The navy's third major purpose was to uphold the authority of the new regime in the face of a hostile Europe. When the Rump fell in 1653 naval power had already done much to persuade other governments of the need to recognize the Commonwealth.

The operations off Portugal in 1650 were an early demonstration of the potential of the new gunboat diplomacy. Blake had forced John IV to abandon the Stuarts and dispatch an envoy to London, and the Rump felt confident enough to demand harsh terms, including a large sum of money to cover the cost of its fleet. When the dismayed envoy eventually gave way on all points he found that these were merely preconditions for talks, and that further concessions would be expected.[121] In the meantime naval pressure on Portugal continued. Ayscue touched there on his way to Barbados to 'put King John in a fright', and early in 1652 the Admiralty Committee suggested sending another fleet to force a complete submission to English terms.[122] The hapless Portuguese sent an ambassador in 1652 and articles were signed early the following year, bringing hostilities to a close. The Rump's further demands for free trade with Portuguese colonies and religious toleration for

---

[119] Davis, *Cavaliers and Roundheads, passim*; Gardiner, *CP* ii. 140–2; *A Perfect Diurnall*, 28 Oct.–4 Nov. 1650.

[120] Gardiner, *CP* ii. 142–3; *The Faithful Scout*, 14–21 May 1652; *The French Occurrences*, 17–24 May.

[121] *Mercurius Politicus*, 3–10 Oct. 1650; Gardiner, *CP* i. 312; E. Prestage, *The Diplomatic Relations of Portugal and England from 1640 to 1660* (Watford, 1925), 10–11.

[122] *A Perfect Account*, 28 Apr.–5 May 1652; Rawl. MS A 226. fo. 74ᵛ.

English merchants in Portugal were also incorporated in the treaty finally signed in 1654.[123] Portugal of course was a small nation dependent on foreign trade and therefore vulnerable to naval pressure. But the navy was also largely responsible for the fact that Spain, still a major European power, established sound working relations with the Rump with surprising speed. While deploring the king's death the Spaniards did not forget the Stuarts' close ties with the Bourbons, and when they saw the Rump turning its forces against the Portuguese and French they were ready to see their enemies' enemy as a useful friend. Spain was still hoping to reconquer Portugal and naturally welcomed Blake's operations off Lisbon, allowing him to refit and supply his fleet at Cadiz. Though reluctant to recognize the republic Philip IV displayed a benevolent neutrality, turning down the pleas of the royalist envoys Hyde and Cottington, and ordering their embassy to leave. Rupert's action in burning merchant shipping in Spanish harbours tipped the scales still further, and Spain was delighted when Blake destroyed most of the royalist force. Blake's flag-captain Charles Saltonstall observed, 'The Spaniards are now exceeding kind to us and the king of Spain hath made large expressions to our General how acceptable our service hath been unto him.' Blake's success, indeed, had major diplomatic repercussions: Philip decided that formal recognition was now inevitable, and in December 1650 a Spanish ambassador presented his credentials in London.[124] The cavaliers were naturally bitter, and Rupert's fury prompted wild rumours that he was even planning to attack the Plate fleet. Hyde too wrote scathingly that the Spaniards 'wish the king well, but dare not be known to do so, and abhor the rebels perfectly, yet court them with all submission'—notwithstanding the 'imperious and saucy' manner of the envoys.[125] A few months later the parliamentary commander Edward Hall could remark complacently, 'I believe in a short time the Spaniard, between fear and love, will grow respectful to us'. It was a statement of fact rather than a prediction.[126]

---

[123] Gardiner, *CP* ii. 243, iii. 78, 81–2, iv. 237–9; Prestage, *Diplomatic Relations*, 11–15. Letters of marque issued against Portuguese shipping were recalled on 2 Feb. 1653: HSA 25/10, order of Bradshaw (unnumbered bundle).

[124] Gardiner, *CP* i. 302–8; Clar. MS 39, fo. 80ᵛ; Anderson, 'Royalists in 1650', 161–3; *CSPV 1647–52*, 157, 160; Blake, *Letters*, 91.

[125] Gardiner, *CP* i. 309–12; Clar. MS 41, fos. 14–15, 65, 69; Warburton, *Memoirs*, iii. 324; *CSPV 1647–52*, 185; *A Perfect Account*, 17–24 Sept. 1651.

[126] *CSPD 1651*, 83.

France posed a far more difficult problem. Relations had been poor even before the king's execution, and the close blood-ties between Stuarts and Bourbons ensured that Charles's death had a greater impact there than elsewhere. An emotional edict, issued in Louis XIV's name, spoke of bloodthirsty regicides sending out emissaries 'like locusts' to stir up sedition in every land; it banned all trade with England and pledged France to finance a military force to help the Stuarts recover their throne.[127] The French also intensified the unofficial hostilities already existing at sea. Privateers commissioned by Charles II were allowed to operate freely from ports such as Dunkirk and Brest; Rupert too received some French reinforcements at Lisbon and later found protection at Toulon. By contrast English merchants in France faced harassment: a factor living in St Malo, for example, was imprisoned and ruined on account of his support for Parliament.[128] More important, French warships and privateers inflicted heavy losses on English commerce in the Mediterranean. In February 1649 the Levant Company complained to the Council that the French had sunk or taken eight ships worth (with their cargoes) some £300,000. By October 1650 at least another eighteen large ships had been lost, valued at half a million pounds. The French claimed they were merely seeking to prevent war materials from reaching Spain, but in practice they confiscated merchantmen whether or not the cargoes had been contraband. English shipmasters often put up stiff resistance before they were overwhelmed, and losses could be heavy. Newspapers in England gave full and emotive accounts of such actions and of alleged atrocities against the seamen taken prisoner.[129]

The Rump responded firmly. An Act of June 1649 enabled merchants to apply for letters of marque to recoup their losses, and in August the import of French goods was banned; there was talk too of an attack on Dunkirk.[130] In 1650 naval commanders were ordered to attack French shipping, naval as well as merchant, and clashes soon followed; in August, for example, John Mildmay

[127] *CJ* vi. 284; C. P. Korr, *Cromwell and the New Model Foreign Policy* (1975), 12–13; *A Declaration of the Most Christian King Louis the XIIIth [sic]* (1649).

[128] Anderson, 'Royalists in 1650', 147–8, 156, 158–60, 166; HCA 13/62, testimony of Jacob Reynolds, 12 Mar. 1650.

[129] Gardiner, *CP* i. 179–80, *306*; HCA 13/63, fos. 107 ff; 218 ff; H. Cary (ed.), *Memorials of the Great Civil War* (1842), ii. 264–5; *CSPD 1649–50*, 11–12; *A Briefe Relation*, 23–30 Apr. 1650 C. H., *Perfect Narrative*, 4–5; Dep. MS C 169, fos. 138–9ᵛ.

[130] *A and O* ii. 157, 239–40; *CSPD 1649–50*, 290–1; Clarke MS 4/4, 1649 (13).

attacked a mixed force of warships and merchantmen in the Atlantic, and the following month Lawson scattered a large fishing fleet from Newfoundland.[131] Later in the year the Rump organized a system of regular convoys to protect English shipping in the Straits, the first time cover had been provided there; a 15 per cent levy was imposed on Customs to cover the costs. The first convoy went out under Edward Hall in February 1651, and others soon followed under Henry Appleton and Richard Badiley.[132] Their squadrons also struck back at French commerce in the Straits, a blunt warning to France of the implications of the Rump's growing sea-power. Some of Cardinal Mazarin's agents urged him to recognize the new regime in England before France had to endure the same humiliations as the Portuguese.[133]

In 1651 Mazarin did attempt to open unofficial negotiations, only to find the Rump insisting on formal recognition as a precondition. He expected the outbreak of the Anglo-Dutch War in 1652 to soften its attitude, but in vain: the Rump ordered its forces to attack French as well as Dutch shipping.[134] Indeed English attitudes hardened as a result of French aid to the Dutch, with dramatic results. In the late summer of 1652 Dunkirk was on the point of surrendering to the besieging Spaniards, and the French dispatched a large fleet to relieve it by sea. The Rump ordered Blake to intercept it, and on 4 September he annihilated the French force, capturing seven of the eight warships and scattering the transports. The Governor of Dunkirk was left with no choice but to surrender the town. The Council brushed aside French protests with the bland remark that it was an act of reprisal not of war, offering to return the captured ships if the French would restore English prizes seized in recent years. The episode was a brutal demonstration of the Rump's new naval might. It persuaded Mazarin to swallow his pride and send an ambassador in December 1652, bringing formal recognition at last; though negotiations proceeded slowly the navy kept up steady pressure until a settlement was eventually concluded.[135]

---

[131] *Thurloe*, i. 142–5; *CSPD 1650*, 167, 184; *CJ* vi. 466. For Mildmay see *CSPD 1650*, 312–13; *Severall Proceedings*, 15–22 Aug. 1650; *A Briefe Relation*, 13–20 Aug.; for Lawson: *Mercurius Politicus*, 5–12 Sept.

[132] *A and O* ii. 444; Gardiner, *CP* i. 306; *FDW* i. 66–8.

[133] Korr, *New Model*, 19, 23.

[134] Ibid., chs. 3–5; *CSPV 1647–52*, *FDW* ii. 30.

[135] R. C. Anderson, 'Blake's Capture of the French Fleet before Calais on 4 September 1652', *MM* xlviii (1962), 192–207; Gardiner, *CP* ii. 190–1, 240–2;

The Rump's naval power quickly bred a new confidence and assertiveness in its leaders. Sir Henry Vane boasted at the end of 1650 that Blake's fleet had forced the Spaniards to send an ambassador and would soon be bringing 'great terror to the French'. 'The Portuguese likewise stands knocking at the door for audience,' he continued with obvious relish, 'and we pause upon it a little, that he may be sensible of his error in so rashly engaging against us . . . The French and Dutch will not sit out long.'[136] This haughty attitude is understandable: though the Rump could not make itself loved it was winning the grudging respect of its neighbours. The French and Dutch sat out longer than Vane expected but eventually came to terms with the Commonwealth. The Venetian republic too fell into line; living by trade it could not ignore the implications of the Rump's expansion into the Mediterranean. A Venetian diplomat observed in 1651 that the Rumpers were ignorant mechanics but possessed the finest navy in the world, and the Senate prudently voted to negotiate a formal recognition.[137]

Growing self-confidence is equally apparent in the behaviour of naval commanders, which frequently aroused angry comment.[138] Edward Hall provoked a diplomatic row by chasing two French ships inside the neutral Tuscan port of Leghorn, and then had the further gall to complain that his arrival had not been honoured by the proper salutes. The Grand Duke protested, and Hall faced an inquiry on his return home. But though the Rump assured the Duke that it wanted friendly relations it coolly observed that there were conflicting accounts of the incident and declared the matter closed, adding that English commanders would naturally expect to be saluted properly in future.[139]

In the few years since 1649 the alchemy of naval power had transformed the Rump's position and its attitude towards Europe. The navy it had built to protect the revolution had become in itself a major force shaping international relations. England's new might coincided with a period of weakness and instability in France and Spain, and for the first time in centuries the country found itself in the first rank of European states. It was an exhilarating position which England's rulers were determined to exploit to the full.

FDW iv. 261, 274, 277; CSPD 1652–3, 209. Korr is wrong in thinking (*New Model*, 67–8), that this pressure did not begin until the autumn.
[136] Nickolls, *Original Letters*, 41.
[137] *CSPV 1647–52*, 187, 213.   [138] Ibid. 164, 232–3.
[139] Ibid. 217. For Hall as a 'rash, insolent fellow' see Foster, *Factories*, vii. 3.

4

Gunboat Diplomacy and War, 1652–1660

THE aim of this chapter is to explore the navy's role in implementing foreign policy under the Commonwealth. To a considerable extent policy was shaped as well as implemented by the fleet, for political leaders were quick to grasp the potential of the force they had created. The dramatic consequences of that recognition are outlined below.

I. THE DUTCH WAR

The Rump's only full-scale foreign war, against the Dutch, was fought entirely at sea. The ideological ties linking the two Protestant republics were flimsy compared with the material interests that divided them. The Dutch held the lion's share of European maritime trade. They had driven the English from much of the Far East by methods fair and foul, and a bloody incident at Amboyna soured relations for decades. They tightened their grip on the Baltic by a treaty with Denmark in 1649 which freed their ships from tolls at the Sound. Their expansion in the Mediterranean was alarming the established English merchants, and Dutch interlopers were gaining the upper hand in trade with English plantations in the West Indies. Dutch maritime strength had originally been based on the massive herring fishery in the North Sea, and each year hundreds of fishing boats still followed the vast shoals from the Shetlands south to the Thames estuary. It is hardly surprising that the English resented this wealth culled from waters they saw as their own. James I had asserted England's right to license foreign fishing boats, and in 1635 Selden's *Mare Clausum* spelled out English claims to sovereignty over the neighbouring seas. The Ship Money fleets of

Charles I had been designed partly to enforce these claims, though in the event they had achieved little.[1]

These long-standing economic grievances assumed a new intensity after 1649. After making peace with Spain in 1648 the Dutch were able to pursue their commercial aims without distraction, whereas the new regime in England found its merchant shipping constantly threatened by hostile neighbours. A group of shipmasters had petitioned the Commons on this point even before the king's death, complaining that merchants were shifting all their goods in Dutch vessels for greater safety, and the trading companies made similar appeals in the months that followed. In response the Council set up a body to explore ways of restricting Dutch competition.[2]

Political rivalries were even more important. The problem arose from the close ties between the Stuart and Orange families: Charles I had married his daughter to William of Orange, who as William II was Stadholder from 1647. The Dutch gave shelter to the revolted fleet in 1648 and to Charles II's court-in-exile in 1649–50, refusing to recognize the new republic and taking little action when the Rump's agent was murdered by cavaliers. The Orangists had public opinion behind them and they dreamed of an alliance with France to restore the Stuarts by force. Yet opinion in the Netherlands was far from united. The merchant oligarchs who ruled Holland, the wealthiest province, were mainly concerned to protect commerce and sent their own agent to London. The States-General steered a middle course, sympathetic towards the Stuarts but anxious to avoid war.[3] William's sudden death in October 1650 left the Orangists without an effective head and transformed the situation. The merchant rulers of Holland quickly secured formal recognition of the Commonwealth and an English delegation led by St John and Strickland arrived early in 1651 to cement the new friendship. Despite the more auspicious climate, however, the negotiations

---

[1] C. Wilson, *Profit and Power* (1957), chs. 1–3; T. W. Fulton, *The Sovereignty of the Sea* (1911).

[2] *The humble Petition and Representation of divers well-affected Masters* (1648), BL 669 f 13 (17); PRO SP 25/123, pp. 106–7; Wilson, *Profit*, 54–6. English ships passing west through the Sound dropped from 130 to 22 between 1647 and 1651: R. W. K. Hinton, *The Eastland Trade and the Common Weal in the Seventeenth Century* (Cambridge, 1959), 228–9.

[3] Gardiner, *CP* i. 64–5, 318–20; P. Geyl, *Orange and Stuart, 1641–1672* (2nd edn., 1969), 46 ff.; Wilson, *Profit*, 14–15.

failed. The Dutch might want amicable relations but they shrank from English pressure for a close political and military alliance, which could easily jeopardize their trade by dragging them into future wars on England's behalf. Angry and offended, the Rump retaliated in October 1651: the Navigation Act struck a sharp blow to Dutch commerce by laying down that English imports must be carried only in English ships or those of the country of origin. The Act had the backing of influential trading and shipping interests but was clearly a response to the failure of St John's mission; the Dutch were its main targets and they hastily sent a delegation to England to seek its repeal.[4]

The Navigation Act by itself would probably not have led to war, for trade with England played only a subordinate part in Dutch commercial life. Much more important was the English claim to sovereignty of the seas. With its powerful navy the Rump could assert English claims far more effectively than ever before and it proceeded at once to do so, for political more than economic reasons. Behind the 'honour of the flag' lay more immediate concerns. Faced with rebellions in Ireland, Scotland, and across the Atlantic, and a state of semi-war with France, the Rump insisted on the right to stop and search merchant shipping and confiscate enemy goods found aboard. The Dutch insisted by contrast that 'the flag covers the goods'—that goods were protected if carried in neutral shipping. These positions were irreconcilable, and there were numerous violent clashes at sea over the issue. In July 1650, for example, Capt. John Stokes intercepted a large Dutch vessel heading for Scotland, and when its skipper refused to allow a search Stokes opened fire and battered it into submission. The skipper and most of his crew perished in the action, and the ship subsequently caught fire and sank.[5] Such incidents inflamed public opinion in both countries: the English saw the Dutch as abusing neutrality by carrying arms to rebels, and the Dutch condemned the slaughter of their innocent seamen. Orange and cavalier agents naturally exploited these clashes, on one occasion prominently displaying the bodies of twenty Dutch seamen to stir up anti-English feeling.[6]

[4] Gardiner, *CP* i. 320–30, ii. 146–50; L. A. Harper, *The English Navigation Laws* (New York, 1939); J. E. Farnell, 'The Navigation Act of 1651 . . .', *Economic History Review*, 2nd series, xvi (1963–4); M. Ashley, *Financial and Commercial Policy under the Cromwellian Protectorate* (2nd edn., 1962), 157 ff.

[5] *A Brief Relation*, 20 Aug.–10 Sept. 1650.

[6] *Continued Heads*, 4–11 May 1649.

There were clashes in more distant waters too, as when Hall's squadron intercepted Dutch shipping in the Straits early in 1651 and confiscated French and Portuguese goods found aboard. One of the main goals of the Dutch ambassadors sent to London later in the year was to secure the end of such practices. The envoys were very concerned too about the brutal harassment of Dutch seamen by English privateers. Torture was a speedy way of extracting false confessions that goods were French and so liable to confiscation, and eventually the Admiralty Court had to step in to condemn the evil practice.[7] There were even clashes between the two nations in the New World. When Ayscue arrived in Barbados in 1651 he promptly seized eleven Dutch ships trading there for contravening an Act of 1650—a forerunner of the Navigation Act—which barred other nations from the English colonies.[8] And as the navy expanded so did the definition of the 'British Seas' over which the English claimed to hold sovereignty. When three Dutch ships dipped their flags in brief salute to Penn's squadron off the mouth of the Straits in September 1651 he was far from gratified, summoning his captains at once to consider whether this was sufficient acknowledgement. There was a more serious incident early in 1652, when a frigate fired a broadside at three Dutch warships off the Barbary coast, to force them to strike sail.[9] A perceptive Venetian diplomat had already concluded that the Rump intended 'to lay claim to an absolute sovereignty' in the Atlantic as well as in home waters.[10]

By the close of 1651 there was widespread pressure in the Netherlands for war and revenge. An observer in The Hague reported that the government wanted peace but that merchants and shipmasters were clamouring for action, confident of easy victory and convinced that 'war is the time for them to make markets'; 'their fingers itch to be doing,' he added.[11] Public opinion in England was also hardening. Heavy-handed behaviour at sea had inevitably brought retaliation in kind, and there was growing resentment at the activities of Dutch privateers operating from French-held

---

[7] *Severall Proceedings*, 8–15 May 1651; Gardiner, *CP* ii. 169–70; *FDW* i. 49–51, 80–3.

[8] Gardiner, *CP* ii. 141; *The French Intelligencer*, 11–18 Feb. 1652. Ayscue's victims are variously numbered between 11 and 16.

[9] Penn, *Memorials*, i. 365; PRO Adm. 7/729, pp. 129–30; Wilson, *Profit*, 88–9; Clarke MS 1/10, fo. 61.

[10] *CSPV 1647–52*, 171.

[11] *A Perfect Diurnall*, 9–16 Feb. 1652; *Mercurius Politicus*, 6–13 Nov. 1651.

Dunkirk, some armed with commissions from Charles Stuart.[12] An angry pamphleteer told how an English privateering captain had been captured and flogged by the Dutch, while his crew were bound back to back and thrown overboard. (An official investigation found this account to be wildly distorted: the captives had been threatened but then released unharmed after a few weeks in gaol.) Memories of the Amboyna massacre were revived once more by a pamphlet which recited its history in lurid detail.[13] And jingoistic newspapers and almanacs threatened the Dutch with total destruction should they dare to challenge God's chosen people.[14]

By the end of 1651 the two nations were on the brink of war. The Dutch saw English naval searches as a threat to their national livelihood, and feared such pressures would grow year by year as the navy continued to expand. They had sent envoys to seek a negotiated settlement but there were signs that they were now ready to defend their position by force if the talks ended in failure. There were rumours in November that war was imminent, and the appearance of a Dutch fleet off Portsmouth in January 1652 aroused fears of invasion. Another squadron put into Pendennis about the same time, demanding the restitution of prizes held there, and its commander claimed to have orders to attack any ships interfering with free commerce. An English witness noted 'a far rougher temper in these Dutch captains than formerly'. In March the States-General resolved to set out an additional 150 warships to guarantee the freedom of trade.[15] Confrontation was now inevitable if the English continued to insist on their right to search. The breach came when Tromp met Blake off the Downs in May; he failed to lower his flag, Blake fired warning shots, and a fierce action quickly ensued.[16] Though the precise circumstances were disputed then and since, it was clearly the general policies of the two governments that had produced the collision, and even at this stage war could have been avoided if the political will had existed. Neither government was

---

[12] *Severall Proceedings*, 9–16 May 1650; *Bloudy Newes from Holland* (1652).

[13] *The French Intelligencer*, 30 Dec. 1651–6 Jan. 1652; SP 46/96/178–9; *Bloudy Newes from the East Indies* (1651).

[14] B. S. Capp, *Astrology and the Popular Press* (1979), 80–2; *The Dutch Spy*, 17–25 Mar. 1653.

[15] Gardiner, *CP* ii. 169–75; *FDW* i. 51–3; *Severall Proceedings*, 1–8 Jan. 1652; *A Perfect Diurnall*, 9–16 Feb. 1652; *The French Intelligencer*, 11–18 Feb. 1652; *A Declaration of the States of Holland* ([8 Mar.] 1652).

[16] Gardiner, *CP* ii. 176–9; *FDW* i. 169–298; Clarke MS 1/10, fos. 94–5.

seeking war, but neither was ready to make the concessions necessary to avoid it.

The course of the First Dutch War has been described in detail elsewhere, and only a résumé is needed here.[17] The Dutch had more seamen and more (if mostly smaller) ships. Geography however favoured the English, forcing Dutch merchant shipping to run a long gauntlet through the Channel. The fact that the Dutch economy rested almost wholly on its seaborne trade determined the strategic planning of both sides. Tromp's first responsibility was the protection of his convoys; he knew the only real security lay through the destruction of the English battle fleet, but throughout the war he and his colleagues had to combine offensive operations with the defence of trade. Blake's instructions also reflected the importance of Dutch commerce, directing him to seek out and destroy the enemy's East India and Baltic shipping and its North Sea fishing fleet.[18]

The campaigns of 1652 were indecisive, though English warships and privateers picked off prizes in large numbers. Ayscue was commanding in the Channel and destroyed a force of about forty merchant ships early in July, but he was lucky to escape when Tromp appeared with a much larger fleet. And when he attacked a Dutch convoy in August in the mouth of the Channel he was driven off by de Ruyter and forced to seek shelter in Plymouth. Meanwhile Blake had taken the main fleet north, as directed, and scattered the Dutch fishing fleet near the Orkneys, capturing its twelve escorts. His major objective was the homeward-bound Dutch East Indiamen, but by the time he located them Tromp had also arrived. A major action would have followed had not a severe storm battered both fleets, leaving the admirals reluctant to risk their ships further, and Tromp was able to take his East Indiamen home in safety. The flow of Dutch trade continued, large convoys from Spain and the Baltic reaching home unscathed. On the other hand Dutch attempts to take the offensive were unsuccessful; an attack on Blake's fleets off the Downs late in September backfired badly, for Blake's force was stronger and much better disciplined. The battle ended with twenty Dutch warships deserting their admirals

[17] For the course of the war see *FDW*, *passim*; Gardiner, *CP* ii, chs. 22–3, and iii, chs. 30–1; J. S. Corbett, *England in the Mediterranean* (1917), i, ch. 15; and, more briefly, Wilson, *Profit*, ch. 5.   [18] *FDW* i. 301–2.

and steering for home, leaving the rest with little choice but to follow.

Blake's victory off the Kentish Knock proved to be the only major English success of the year. In the Straits the two small English squadrons under Appleton and Badiley were defeated by a larger Dutch force and had to take shelter in Leghorn and Elba. In the north Denmark sided with the Dutch. The Danes seized twenty English merchant vessels laden with naval stores, and an expedition sent to negotiate their release returned empty-handed. English shipping was barred from the Baltic throughout the war, cutting off a vital source of naval supplies.[19] The gravest setback of the year was closer to home. Late in November Tromp put to sea with a force of eighty-five warships to escort a huge merchant fleet bound for Bordeaux; leaving his convoy off Dunkirk he stood over to the Downs to challenge Blake, commanding there with a force only half as large. Blake accepted the challenge, either over-confident after his recent victory or stung by criticism of his earlier caution.[20] The ensuing battle off Dungeness on 30 November took the form of the Kentish Knock in reverse, for twenty ships—roughly half Blake's force—stood aside from the action, leaving the odds hopeless. The English were badly mauled and had to retreat to the safety of Dover. Tromp proceeded with his convoy and then remained in the mouth of the Channel for over two months, snapping up English prizes with impunity.

The humiliating defeat at Dungeness alarmed the nation and demoralized the navy. Blake offered to resign, and a number of offending captains were arrested.[21] The Rump wisely declined Blake's offer but pressed ahead with a general reorganization of the navy, designed to strengthen the command and restore discipline and morale. A few days before Dungeness it had appointed Deane and Monck to serve as Generals alongside Blake, regarding a joint command as more appropriate in wartime. To help maintain order in battle the fleet was henceforth divided into squadrons, each under a junior flag-officer.[22] A comprehensive new disciplinary

---

[19] Gardiner, *CP* ii. 199, 213; *FDW* ii. 155–6, 376–7, 388; *The King of Denmark his Declaration* (1653); Bodl. Tanner MS 53, fo. 174ᵛ.
[20] For earlier criticism of Blake: *CSPV 1647–52*, 301; Bodl. Clarendon MS 47, fos. 178–80; *The Memoirs of Edmund Ludlow*, ed. C. H. Firth (Oxford, 1894), i. 325. On Dungeness see *FDW* iii. 1–266; Gardiner, *CP* ii. 203–10; Powell, *Blake*, ch. 14.
[21] Powell, *Blake*, 190–3.
[22] *CJ* vii. 222; Gardiner, *CP* ii. 214; *FDW* iii. 374–6; Clar. MS 47, fo. 182.

code strengthened the Generals' hold over their officers, and the officers' hold over their men; at the same time Parliament voted substantial improvements in the seamen's pay and conditions to raise morale.[23] The massive programme of naval shipbuilding already under way would reduce the need for hired merchantmen, which were proving inadequate in fleet actions and were partly to blame for the disaster at Dungeness.[24] There was also a hasty reorganization of naval administration to meet wartime needs. On 10 December the Rump swept away the Council's Admiralty Committee and established a new, more professional body of Admiralty Commissioners, only six in number and responsible directly to Parliament. Sir Henry Vane, who had long pressed for such a change, was the key figure among them, flanked by two of his parliamentary allies, Carew and Salwey; the other members were George Thomson, another MP, and two London merchants. Years later Thomson claimed that the new Commissioners had proved models of efficiency and responsibility, sitting 'daily both early and late', and though his opinion was hardly unbiased it seems to have been largely correct. The reorganization also tightened the radicals' grip on the Admiralty, evidenced by the even greater emphasis given henceforth to ideological criteria in the selection of officers.[25]

The outcome of the war was settled by the spring and summer campaigns of 1653. The English suffered a damaging set-back in the Straits in March, when Appleton's entire squadron was destroyed on attempting to break out of Leghorn; Badiley reached home safely but the navy could no longer offer any protection to merchant shipping in the area.[26] In the Narrow Seas, by contrast, the war moved steadily in England's favour. Blake, Deane, and Monck were at sea by February, and on the 18th off Portland they met Tromp returning from the west. The two fleets were roughly

---

[23] *FDW* iii. 283–9, 293–301, 318–19; see also ch. 8, below. A new disciplinary code had been planned for some time: *CSPD 1651–2*, 280, 415.

[24] Gardiner, *CP* ii. 199, 205; *CJ* vii. 186; above, ch. 1.

[25] *CJ* vii. 225, 227–8; V. A. Rowe, *Sir Henry Vane the Younger* (1970), 178–90; Hammond, thesis, 55–8; Cogar, thesis, 116–37; Clar. MS 47, fo. 182; see also below, ch. 6, sect. i. For Carew, Salwey, and Thomson see B. Worden, *The Rump Parliament* (Cambridge, 1974), A. Woolrych, *From Commonwealth to Protectorate* (Oxford, 1982), and *BDBR*. The other members were John Langley and James Russell.

[26] For the war in the Mediterranean see Corbett, *England in the Mediterranean*, i, ch. 15; T. A. Spalding, *A Life of Richard Badiley* (Westminster, 1899), chs. 7–18.

equal in size, but whereas the English were newly fitted and supplied, Tromp had been at sea since November, unable to replenish his ammunition since Dungeness and hampered now by the need to protect the large convoy he was escorting. The battle begun off Portland turned into a bitter, running fight ending off Beachy Head on the 20th. At the outset Blake's squadron was heavily outnumbered; his flagship was in the thick of the action, the captain and master both being killed and Blake himself severely wounded. But by the close victory clearly belonged to the English. Many of the Dutch ships ran out of powder and broke away to escape home, and the ordered withdrawal of the rest turned into a desperate flight. The Dutch lost about twenty warships, and about fifty of their merchantmen were taken prize. Human casualties were equally heavy. A witness gave a vivid description of captured warships being brought into Dover 'much dyed with blood, their masts and tackle being moiled with brains, hair, pieces of skulls; dreadful sights', and the Dutch also lost about 1,500 seamen taken prisoner. Though the English suffered heavy casualties too, they lost only one of their ships.[27]

Portland gave England command of the Channel, forcing Dutch shipping henceforth to use the long route round the north of Scotland. Tromp was determined to challenge the English again, and to this end he put to sea at the end of May with over a hundred ships, for once unhampered by the presence of merchantmen. On 2 June he met Deane and Monck, with about 113 ships, off the Gabbard shoal east of Harwich, and the ensuing action extended over four days. It began with a fierce cannonade which greatly favoured the stronger, more heavily armed English ships, and Blake's arrival with a further squadron during the course of the battle swung the odds still further against the Dutch. By the close they had lost about twenty warships sunk or captured, and suffered heavy casualties; a correspondent on the coast observed that 'the tide ever since brings in abundance of arms, and legs, and dismembered bodies, a sad spectacle to behold'. The English by contrast lost not a single ship and suffered only light damage and casualties (though General Deane had been killed on the first day), and their fleet was able to remain at sea.[28]

[27] *FDW* iv. 1–197 (quotation p. 111); Powell, *Blake*, ch. 16.
[28] *FDW* v. 1–146; Powell, *Blake*, ch. 17; *The Weekly Intelligencer*, 31 May–7 June 1653.

The victory off the Gabbard was decisive. For while Blake returned to England Monck and the fleet imposed a tight blockade of the enemy coast, bringing Dutch commerce almost to a standstill. There were fears of invasion, merchants broke in large numbers, and the people, reduced to poverty, were now clamouring for peace. After Portland two provinces, Holland and West Friesland, had approached the Rump to assess the prospects for talks, and the disaster at the Gabbard made the Dutch far more anxious to find an early settlement. De Witt, who was emerging as the foremost Dutch statesman, hastily sent commissioners to England to explore the prospects for peace, hopeful that the Rump's overthrow in April would have smoothed the path. The opposite proved to be the case, however, for England's new rulers knew little of foreign affairs and were inevitably preoccupied with domestic concerns. Some of them, puffed up by the recent victory, insisted on impossible terms, and even Cromwell, who had never favoured the war, clung to dreams of a union and a joint crusade against popery which the Dutch could never accept. Barebone's Parliament, assembling in July, also contained a militant war-party bent on making the most of victory, and there was talk of making the Dutch give up half their fisheries and surrender several towns to the English as places of security.[29] All this helped those in the Netherlands who argued that a great victory to reverse the Gabbard was the only way to secure a peace on reasonable terms. So, after making hasty repairs, Tromp slipped out to sea once more on 29 July and two days later the combined Dutch fleet confronted Monck off the Texel. It was the last and bloodiest battle of the war: Tromp himself was killed early on, and the Dutch lost about twenty-six warships and some 6,000 seamen dead, wounded, or captured. Though English losses were much lighter seven captains were among the dead, and the ships were so battered that Monck had to take most of his force home to refit. But late in August Lawson returned to the Texel to resume the blockade and Monck rejoined him a few days later. The Dutch had no wish for any further confrontation. Apart from leading out one convoy to the north the Dutch fleet did not venture out again. Monck was able to bring his fleet back to England, leaving small patrols to scour

<hr />

[29] *FDW* v. 147–50; Gardiner, *CP* ii. 238–9, iii. 39–45; Fulton, *Sovereignty*, ch. 11; Worden, *Rump*, 330; Woolrych, *Commonwealth*, 277–88; Wilson, *Profit*, 75–6.

the Channel while the main force made occasional short sweeps. The Channel remained largely closed to the Dutch throughout the winter, and smaller English squadrons harried their shipping in the North Sea too.[30]

During the winter lull both sides concentrated on preparing forces for the spring. In March 1654 Thurloe claimed England already had a hundred and forty ships at sea, 'in a better condition than they were in at any time since the war began'.[31] In the event peace terms were agreed just before the campaigning season began. Negotiations had dragged on throughout the winter, Cromwell long pressing for terms which were unacceptable and at times bizarre. At one point he suggested that the trade of the whole world should be divided between the two powers, Asia to the Dutch and the Americas to England, with the Dutch expected to help drive the Spaniards and Portuguese from the New World. The English demanded recognition of their sovereignty at sea, their right of search, and their ownership of the North Sea fisheries, and also demanded a limit on the number of warships the Dutch might set out in the Channel. But a more conciliatory spirit gradually prevailed, and in the event all these demands were dropped from the treaty signed at Westminster in April 1654.[32]

Many commentators both then and since have seen the treaty's terms as remarkably mild in the light of England's domination at sea. The merchant Slingsby Bethel later accused Cromwell of throwing away victory and making a 'damageable' peace. By contrast the royalist Clarendon judged it a triumph for Cromwell, containing 'all the advantages he could desire'.[33] These assessments were not in fact incompatible, for Bethel was judging by economic criteria and Clarendon by political. Cromwell himself put political interests first; indeed successive governments throughout the interregnum made the security of the new regime the bedrock of their foreign policy, much as Henry VII had done in somewhat similar

[30] *FDW* v. 145–429, vi, *passim*; Gardiner, *CP* iii. 45–8.
[31] *FDW* vi; Gardiner, *CP* iii. 59–60; S. von Bischoffshausen (ed.), *Die Politik des Protectors Oliver Cromwell* (Innsbruck, 1899), 172, 176.
[32] Gardiner, *CP* iii. 48–52; Woolrych, *Commonwealth*, 282–4, 322–5; Fulton, *Sovereignty*, ch. 11; for the text of the treaty see Cromwell, *Writings*, iii. 897–906.
[33] S. Bethel, *The World's Mistake in Oliver Cromwell* (1668), 3, 8; Clarendon, *History*, v. 291. For other criticism of the terms see M. Prestwich, 'Diplomacy and Trade in the Protectorate', *Journal of Modern History*, xxii (1950), 105–6; Wilson, *Profit*, 77; Battick, thesis, 84; Burton, *Diary*, iii. 164, 389–90, 440 474, 490; *CSPV* 1653–4, 210; S. Colliber, *Columna Rostrata* (1727), 137.

circumstances. With their excellent harbours and maritime strength the Dutch were best placed to assist a Stuart restoration, and the close links between the Orange and Stuart families were never forgotten. The treaty reflected this underlying concern, tackling political issues first; it stipulated that neither side was to help or shelter the enemies of the other, thus requiring the Dutch to abandon the Stuarts and bar royalist privateers from their harbours. A secret agreement with the province of Holland, on which Cromwell insisted, committed the Dutch to block for ever the appointment of any member of the Orange family to the office of Stadholder, an extraordinary promise for one state to make to another. Peace also brought Cromwell more immediate political advantages at home. The war had never been popular, and he later described it as 'occasioning a vast burden upon the people'. Heavy taxation, as he knew, bred political unpopularity, and the peace was intended in part to help secure the new Protectorate; the cheering crowds told him that he had judged the nation's mood correctly. A sour republican later remarked that by the peace 'England was conquered, instead of conquering Holland.'[34]

The arguments for prolonging the war were economic: one more successful campaign at sea might force the Dutch to make the drastic concessions they had so far resisted. But there would almost certainly have been a political price to pay, for the regents would probably not survive such a surrender. The defeats of 1653 had already prompted large-scale demonstrations in favour of the Orangists and Charles II, and the return of the Orange family would be a major blow for the Commonwealth. The vicious nickname 'Protector Werewolf', coined by a Dutch pamphleteer, was a reminder that an Orange regime might be prepared to turn the Stuarts' restoration into a war-issue, something the States-General had resolutely refused to do. Even on economic grounds the arguments for continuing the war were questionable. Any major concessions extracted from the Dutch over the right of search would strike at the very heart of their commerce and would only be honoured till they were ready for a further trial of strength. Thurloe explained that Cromwell had decided to offer the Dutch 'honourable' terms, knowing that 'a peace with them could not be otherwise lasting'. Moreover while some branches of English trade had undoubtedly flourished during the war, others had suffered heavily; English shipping had been totally excluded from the Baltic and badly hit in the Straits and Far East. Even the capture of an estimated 1,500 Dutch prizes had benefited the state and the captors rather than the trading community. Early in 1653 indeed a diplomat had reported that many London merchants were very relieved that a large Dutch convoy had escaped the English navy, having financial interests in it themselves.[35]

Cromwell's peace brought some real economic gains. The Baltic was reopened, and his subsequent treaty with Denmark contained a clause giving the English equality with the Dutch in the vital matter of tolls at the Sound. The owners of ships seized by Denmark in 1652 received compensation. The Dutch implicitly gave way over the Navigation Act, which was not mentioned in the treaty. Their obligation to strike the flag in salute was also enshrined in a treaty for the first time, though the original wording had been watered down. The crucial issue of the right of search was passed over in silence, but this settled it *de facto* in favour of England, whose navy clearly had the power to enforce it. The bloody demonstration of English naval supremacy in 1653 carried much more weight than any paper obligation could do. It was claimed later that the Dutch economy had suffered more during the short war with England than in the entire eighty years' struggle against Spain, and the Dutch government was understandably anxious to preserve peace in the later 1650s. Despite the treaty's silence Dutch merchantmen and warships proved ready, almost eager, to salute and submit to English searches in 1654. When several met an English squadron a few weeks after peace was signed the seamen 'not only lowered their sails, but let them fall upon the decks, and flinging up their caps, they fell a-dancing and capering'. Lawson observed with satisfaction how even the belligerent Dutch admiral de With was beginning 'to know his duty'.[36] The Dutch had failed totally in their major war-aim, to secure the right of their ships to trade freely everywhere

---

[35] *The Faithfull Scout*, 1–8 July 1653; Geyl, *Orange and Stuart*, 92, 97, 99, 105–7; Cromwell, *Writings*, iii. 170 n.; H. T. Colenbrander, *Bescheiden . . . omtrent de groote nederlandsche Zeeorlogen, 1652–1676* (The Hague, 1929), i. 15, 44, 68–9; Bischoffshausen, *Politik*, 152. Estimates of Dutch prizes ranged between 1,000 and 1,700: Harper, *Navigation Laws*, 326; Ludlow, *Memoirs*, i. 364; Colliber, *Columna*, 138.
[36] Cromwell, *Writings*, iii. 440–1, 900, 903–4, 925–30; Hinton, *Eastland Trade*, 229; *The Weekly Intelligencer*, 30 May–6 June 1654; Fulton, *Sovereignty*, 436–7.

unhindered by the English navy or the Navigation Act. Their diplomats tried repeatedly over the next few years to negotiate a revision of the treaty, in vain, and we find the Spaniards taunting them with the 'shameful terms' they had accepted from the English.[37]

II. FRANCE AND THE WAR WITH SPAIN

The peace with the Dutch opened a new phase in relations with the rest of Europe. The navy itself was now a major factor in moulding foreign policy. When Cromwell 'found 160 sail of brave ships well appointed swimming at sea' he was led to reflect that 'God has not brought us hither where we are but to consider the work that we may do in the world.' How could he best employ this naval might to benefit England and advance the Protestant cause?[38] Domestic political considerations were also involved. He could not lay the navy aside, for it remained essential to the security of the regime, but he recognized that its crippling cost was politically damaging. It was therefore necessary to find some way to make the navy pay for itself, or alternatively to engage in a new war which might create a patriotic mood and reconcile the nation to its expense.

Victory over the Dutch had created a sense of boundless confidence. One journalist thought the fleet was 'enough not only to daunt the Hollander, but peradventure the world'. Another speculated boldly about expeditions against the Turks, French, and Spaniards. 'Beware the Plate Fleet!' he advised the Spanish government with relish. 'Old injuries cannot be forgotten, Mr *Don*; long looked for comes at last.'[39] There was more than one view on how English interests might best be served, and the course of diplomacy in 1654 was complex and erratic. Cromwell seems to have been set on war against someone, but uncertain whether to make France or Spain his enemy. Relations with France were still sour. The

---

[37] C. H. Firth (ed.), 'Secretary Thurloe on the Relations of England and Holland', *EHR* xxi (1906), 322–3; *CSPV 1657–9*, 24. For a contemporary English view that the peace terms were humiliating to the Dutch in economic as well as political terms see S. M. Ffarington (ed.), *The Farington Papers* (Chetham Soc., 1856), 175.

[38] *Clarke Papers*, iii. 203, 207; R. Crabtree, 'The Idea of a Protestant Foreign Policy' in I. Roots (ed.), *Cromwell: A Profile* (1973); C. Hill, *God's Englishman* (1970), 155–68; Prestwich, 'Diplomacy and Trade', 103–21; Battick, thesis, ch. 3.

[39] *The Weekly Intelligencer*, 10–17 Jan. 1654; *The Faithfull Scout*, 14–21 July 1654.

undeclared war at sea had continued despite Mazarin's belated recognition of the Commonwealth, and there was no reason to doubt that French sympathies still lay with the Stuarts. But in a naval war France would offer few targets, possessing neither rich colonies nor merchant shipping on a large scale. By contrast war against Spain, a traditional enemy still regarded as the chief prop of the papal Antichrist, ought to be popular and would be easy to justify on religious grounds. Cromwell believed such a war could pay for itself through the capture of the Plate fleet and perhaps the silver mines themselves.

In the spring of 1654 Cromwell pursued parallel negotiations with France and Spain, enjoying their competition for his friendship as he explored the possibility of foreign subsidies for the navy. In May he provisionally accepted a Spanish offer to pay £300,000 a year towards the costs of an English naval and military attack on France; the following month he asked France for £400,000 a year to subsidize a war against Spain. But it soon became clear that France would not and Spain could not pay sums of this order, and this led him back to the idea of a war against Spain in the Caribbean, which might pay for itself. This policy had been urged by Pym, Eliot, Warwick, and other parliamentarians in the 1620s and was now being widely canvassed. A merchant observed in May that 'since the peace with Holland, most men cry up war with Spain, saying the fleet and army must be kept in employment and no place worth their attempting like unto the West Indies'. A debate in the Council on 20 July showed that Cromwell was set on this course and determined to sweep all objections aside.[40]

The military command of the 'Western Design', as it became known, was given to Col. Robert Venables and the fleet was entrusted to William Penn, now one of the Generals at Sea. Each was responsible for his own sphere, while decisions concerning the expedition as a whole were to be taken jointly with three Commissioners (one of whom, Edward Winslow, had sailed with the Pilgrim Fathers). Cromwell spelt out its objectives in his

[40] Gardiner, *CP* iii, ch. 33; Korr, *Cromwell and the New Model Foreign Policy* (1975), chs. 7–11; *Clarke Papers*, iii. 207–8; *The Letters of John Paige, London Merchant, 1648–1658* ed. G. F. Steckley (London Record Soc., xxi; 1984), 107. For earlier Puritan demands for such a policy see C. Russell, *Parliaments and English Politics, 1621–1629* (Oxford, 1979), 98, 188, 262, 293–4, 299–300; A. P. Newton, *The Colonizing Activities of the English Puritans* (2nd edn., Port Washington, NY, 1966); cf. C. Hill, *Puritanism and Revolution* (1962 edn.), ch. 4.

instructions to Venables, explaining that his first aim was to cut off the flow of treasure to Spain; he recommended an attack on Hispaniola as the most promising strategy, though the decision was left to the commanders on the spot. Ultimately Cromwell hoped to overrun the entire Spanish empire in the Americas, which would impoverish . Spain, enrich England, and strike a heavy blow against Catholicism itself. He had declared—or so it was alleged—that 'he intended not to desist till he came to the gates of Rome'.[41] Most of the soldiers and sailors taking part had far less grandiose ambitions. Their destination was widely guessed long before the expedition sailed, and newspapers reported the men's 'longing desire to have been with the Spanish Plate fleet' or in the treasure mines of Hispaniola.[42]

The Western Design was Cromwell's most ambitious venture and his greatest disaster. A fleet of thirty-eight ships left England late in December 1654 with 2,500 to 3,000 soldiers on board, and on its arrival in the West Indies about 5,500 new recruits were raised at Barbados and St Kitt's. In addition some 1,200 seamen were formed into a 'sea-regiment' for service ashore, so that Venables had in all a force of over 9,000 at his disposal. Its achievements were embarrassingly small. On 14 April 1655 most of the army landed about thirty miles west of San Domingo, in Hispaniola, and began its advance. By the time the troops approached the city on the 17th they were exhausted by dysentery and lack of water and food, and after some skirmishing Venables ordered a retreat. A second attack on 24–25 April ended in a humiliating rout by Spanish irregulars, whereupon morale and discipline collapsed. The officers were unable to bring their men to make a further attack, and the troops had to be re-embarked. The expedition then made its way to Jamaica, where the soldiers landed under fire on 10 May. The resistance was short-lived, but discipline and morale among the English remained low and the troops made little attempt to secure their position or lay the foundations of a permanent settlement. Disease reduced Venables's force by half within six months of its arrival in Jamaica, and most of the survivors desired nothing more than to go home. Any further operations by the army were out of the question. Penn decided that the presence of a large fleet was no longer necessary and sailed for

[41] Gardiner, *CP* iv. 120–6; Cromwell, *Writings*, iii. 531–6; *Clarke Papers*, iii. 203–8; *CSPV 1655–6*, 80.
[42] *Certain Passages*, 24 Aug.–1 Sept. 1654; *A Perfect Diurnall*, 21–8 Aug. 1654.

England on 25 June; Venables, who was very sick, followed a few days later.[43]

The failure at Hispaniola was rightly seen in England as a severe blow to Cromwell's personal standing and that of his regime. The capture of Jamaica brought little consolation: it had no riches of its own and was poorly placed for attacks on the Plate fleet. Cromwell angrily packed both Venables and Penn off to the Tower on their return. Venables himself apportioned blame liberally between General Desborough (the expedition's main organizer), the victuallers, his fellow Commissioners, his officers and men, and the navy. Some of his charges had force, though his own shortcomings as a commander are obvious too. The main blame must fall on the government itself, which had used the scourings of the army instead of experienced troops who might have provided a firm backbone for the West Indian recruits.

How far did the navy deserve its share of Venables's criticism? Relations between the two commanders were poor from the outset and Cromwell was aware of Penn's jealousy even before the expedition left England.[44] Venables's most serious charge was that the fleet overshot the proposed landing-place through negligence. The long, unforeseen march forced upon the army played a considerable part in the disaster, and Cromwell was later said to hold Penn to blame on this point. Possibly the guides were remiss, and Penn may have given insufficiently clear instructions. Penn himself claimed that local conditions had ruled out a landing at the place originally intended, and the evidence is inconclusive.[45] The charge of having refused earlier to land the army at San Domingo itself can be explained by an understandable reluctance to take the fleet into an uncharted harbour, where it might be grounded and destroyed by the Spanish guns ashore. In Penn's defence it can be said that once the troops had landed he had soundings taken and then repeatedly offered to send in ships to assist the army by firing at the fort and town. Venables turned down these offers, and did not mention

---

[43] Gardiner, *CP* iv, ch. 45; *The Narrative of General Venables*, ed. C. H. Firth (Camden Soc., 1900); S. A. G. Taylor, *The Western Design* (Kingston, Jamaica, 1965).

[44] Venables, *Narrative*, pp. xiii–xv; Cromwell, *Writings*, iii. 551.

[45] Venables, *Narrative*, pp. xv–xvi, 19–21, 24, 79–80, 82; Gardiner, *CP* iv. 133–4; *The Nicholas Papers*, ed. G. F. Warner (Camden Soc., 1886–1920), iii. 80; Penn, *Memorials*, ii. 81, 82, 110.

them in his apologia.[46] Penn was certainly more resolute than his partner and argued strongly for a further attempt against San Domingo; he was described as 'almost choked' with exasperation when the army leaders refused. He gave every assistance in the attack on Jamaica, leading the assault in person right up to the beach in the small *Martin* while the larger ships bombarded the forts.[47]

Penn was more clearly at fault in three other respects. First, he made no attempt to disguise his contempt for Venables and the soldiers and allowed his subordinates to abuse them openly, which inevitably undermined the expedition as a whole. Second, his return to England without orders amounted to desertion. His rather sheepish explanatory letter to Cromwell gave no satisfactory grounds, and his deputy and successor, Goodson, was unsympathetic on hearing of his consignment to the Tower.[48] Finally, as Thurloe explained, the government was furious that Penn had brought home the greater part of his fleet without making any attempt to capture the Plate ships, even 'after he understood where they were, and probably in his power'. Three weeks after sailing for England Penn had learned that part of the Silver fleet had arrived in Havana, and he assembled his captains to discuss the information. They decided an attack was impracticable, for it would mean beating back slowly against the wind and then assaulting a well-defended harbour with their depleted force. Penn was reported to have said angrily on his return that 'he was not to fight with impossibilities', but the government's chagrin that he had not tried to snatch victory from defeat is understandable. Though he was soon freed from the Tower after making an apology Cromwell never employed him again.[49]

Turning to the fleet as a whole, it is evident that morale and order remained better throughout than in the army. Many of the leading officers had previous experience of conditions in the Caribbean, an advantage the army officers lacked.[50] The sea-regiment led by Vice-Admiral Goodson, Benjamin Blake, and Edward Blagg—all Caribbean veterans—was exercised at every opportunity and observers

[46] Venables, *Narrative*, pp. xvi, 18, 22, 157, 159, 160; Penn, *Memorials*, i. 85, 87, 88, 92–6, 98; NMM WYN/10/2, 27 Apr. (Journal of William Poole).

[47] Venables, *Narrative*, 160–2; 'Richard Rooth's Sea Journal of the Western Design, 1654–5', ed. J. F. Battick, *Jamaica Journal*, v. (1971), 15; Penn, *Memorials*, ii, 94–5; *Thurloe*, iii. 755.   [48] Penn, *Memorials*, ii. 131–2; *Thurloe*, iv. 52.

[49] *Thurloe*, iv. 75; BL Sloane MS 3926, p. 36; Gardiner, *CP* iv. 143–4; *Nicholas Papers*, iii. 69; Venables, *Narrative*, 87; *CSPD 1655*, 396.

[50] See below, ch. 6, nn. 39–40.

agreed that it fought bravely and well, saving the expedition from still greater disaster.[51] When Robert Sedgwick arrived with reinforcements some months later he found the soldiers totally listless and idle, and remarked that it was the sailors alone who had brought the supplies ashore and built a storehouse to protect them from the weather.[52] The navy's role was of course subordinate, but it emerged with a certain degree of credit from this sorry affair.

The Protector had thought it possible that he might have war with Spain in the Americas while preserving peace in Europe. This was not an impossible dream.[53] Spain was already exhausted by its long war with France and lacked the energy and the resources for another conflict. Unable to mount a counter-offensive in the West Indies and reluctant to risk its European commerce, it might seek to limit its losses by negotiation. Philip IV's initial reaction was indeed measured: he did no more than place an embargo on English trade and seize English merchants and shipping in his ports.[54] Philip hoped the outcry from English merchants trading with Spain would persuade Cromwell to reverse his policy, especially as the attack on Hispaniola had failed. Cromwell however did not back down. Instead he published a declaration justifying the expedition and ordered a retaliatory embargo on Spanish trade, directing the navy to attack Spanish shipping everywhere. While not actively seeking war in Europe he seems to have viewed the prospect with equanimity; he had always regarded the Plate fleet as fair game, even in Spanish waters, and open war would allow him to revive his old ambitions against Dunkirk. Seeing him obdurate Philip took stronger measures, licensing privateers to operate from the Flemish ports. In March 1656 Spain formally declared war.[55]

In launching the Western Design Cromwell might seem to have committed himself to a *rapprochement* with France. In the event he displayed a remarkable insouciance, driving the French ambassador Bordeaux to complain that it was 'as if the power of the one and the other crown were not of any consideration unto him'. Another

[51] Penn, *Memorials*, ii. 73–5; Venables, *Narrative*, 29, 96, 97, 154, 158–9; WYN/10/2, 28 Apr.

[52] *CSP Col. 1675–6*, 102–3.

[53] Gardiner, *CP* iv. 122; Crabtree, 'Protestant Foreign Policy', 164–5; *Clarke Papers*, iii. 205.

[54] Gardiner, *CP* iv. 170–1. Blake's kinsman Sidrach was one of those arrested: *The Publick Intelligencer*, 22–9 Oct. 1655; *CSPD 1655–6*, 260.

[55] Gardiner, *CP* iv. 171–6; *CSPD 1655*, 405; Bischoffshausen, *Politik*, 199; Korr, *New Model*, 146.

diplomat reported that the English 'say plainly that they will force France to make peace with a dagger at her throat'.[56] The dagger was clearly the navy, and Cromwell was happy to prolong the state of semi-war at sea which had continued during and since the Anglo-Dutch conflict. In April 1654, for example, three frigates had inflicted heavy losses on a fleet of French whalers off St Malo, provoking fierce anti-English riots in the town. Mazarin commented wryly, 'I see that Mr Cromwell is not for us.'[57] English operations in the New World also upset the French. Early in 1654 a small force under Robert Sedgwick had set out intending to seize New Amsterdam (later New York); when this operation was forestalled by news of peace with the Dutch Sedgwick attacked the French instead, capturing three forts in Acadia (Nova Scotia). Cromwell stood by his action and the name *Accadia* was even given to a newly acquired warship.[58] Similarly in the Western Design Penn's instructions had directed him to attack French as well as Spanish shipping, and Penn left the same orders to his successor.[59]

A far more serious threat to the French was the fleet Blake led to the Mediterranean in October 1654. Though his instructions have not survived, Blake was clearly sent to check French depredations as well as subdue the Barbary corsairs. Cromwell had also been alarmed by a projected French invasion of Naples, designed to capitalize on local unrest; the French admiral Nieuchèse was preparing one squadron at Brest and planned to join another under the duke of Guise, fitting out at Toulon, for the assault. Cromwell asked for the use of Spanish ports, somewhat hypocritically, and Philip complied; though highly suspicious of Blake's intentions the Spaniards had no wish to provoke a conflict and were happy to see him challenging the French. Blake probably had orders to prevent the two French squadrons from combining and to block the invasion by whatever means proved necessary. In the event he achieved both objectives without bloodshed. Nieuchèse was already on his way south when he heard of Blake's approach, but promptly took shelter in Lisbon and remained there. Blake then passed through the Straits and pursued Guise to Naples, though by the time the fleet arrived Guise had called off the invasion and sailed for

---

[56] *Thurloe*, iii. 311–12; *CSPV 1655–6*, 8; Gardiner, *CP* iii. chs. 33–4; Korr, *New Model*, chs. 7–13.   [57] *Thurloe*, ii. 246; Gardiner, *CP* iii. 128; *CSPD 1654*, 93–4.
[58] Gardiner, *CP* iv. 161–2; *Thurloe*, ii. 259, 418–19, 425, 583–4.
[59] Penn, *Memorials*, ii. 23–7, 115.

home. There were conflicting reports on whether Blake had planned to fight him; some said he had boasted of his design to destroy Guise, and Bordeaux thought him sorry to have missed his prey. When the English did catch up with part of the French fleet at Leghorn a correspondent on board Blake's flagship affirmed their readiness to give battle if the French put to sea—though he thought this very unlikely, bragging that 'the grand uncircumcised Philistine the duke of Guise gave out at Castellamare [near Naples] that he would not fight us, for that we were brass without and steel within'. Blake was probably pleased to have gained his objectives by gunboat diplomacy rather than force, which might have brought open war with France. His mere presence, moreover, and the rumours that he was planning to land forces in Provence, had quickly brought a far more conciliatory attitude on the part of the French; Mazarin sent assurances that English merchantmen taken captive were now being scrupulously restored.[60]

The negotiations between England and France finally produced a treaty of friendship signed in October 1655, which ended at last the undeclared war at sea. There is no doubt that the navy's ability to harm or to advance French interests had been a major consideration in Mazarin's thinking. By an important secret clause the French agreed to expel Charles II and his brother James and give no further aid to the royalists. If the navy could not reach Charles himself, it could persuade his closest friends in Europe to abandon him.[61]

Cromwell doubtless enjoyed the alarm and speculation Blake's presence in the Straits had aroused throughout Europe. The duke of Tuscany feared the English had come to exact vengeance for the lack of protection shown them in 1652, and Badiley's return as vice-admiral of the fleet must have added to his concern. The duke hastily strengthened the defences of Leghorn, though in the event Blake brought professions of friendship from the Protector.[62] The pope was equally alarmed, being well aware of Cromwell's militant

[60] Powell, *Blake*, ch. 19; Gardiner, *CP* iv, ch. 46; Corbett, *Mediterranean*, i, ch. 16; *The Weekly Intelligencer*, 24–31 Oct. 1654, 21–8 Nov.; *A Message sent . . . to the Great Turk* (1654), 7; *A Perfect Account*, 19–27 Dec. 1654, 10–16 Jan. 1655; *The Faithfull Scout*, 9–16 Feb. 1655; *Thurloe*, ii. 391, 699, iii. 41, 103; R. Vaughan (ed.), *The Protectorate of Oliver Cromwell* (1839), i. 71, 87, 90–3, 97, 100, 108; *CSPV 1655–6, 5–6, 16.*

[61] Gardiner, *CP* iv. 191–3; Korr, *New Model*, ch. 13. See Cromwell, *Writings*, ii. 930–8 for the text of the treaty.

[62] *CSPV 1653–4*, 258; *CSPV 1655–6*, 6; Powell, *Blake*, 252, 257; Vaughan, *Protectorate*, i. 67, 75, 97, 108; Gardiner, *CP* iv. 148–50.

anti-Catholicism. Though defensive measures were ordered the citizens of Rome feared their city might be sacked, and some of the wealthier inhabitants retired to the countryside for greater safety. In Paris it was rumoured that Blake and Penn were planning to join forces and attack the papal states. Continental Protestants naturally took heart from such stories, and when the pope died in January 1655 some Swiss Protestants boldly declared that 'if they were so near Rome, and as well furnished as General Blake is, they would make the conclave choose a Calvinist'.[63] The Venetians had very mixed feelings. They hoped to see Blake turn his forces against the Barbary corsairs, but their ambassador in London reflected uneasily that if the English seized a naval base and established themselves in the Mediterranean they might prove even worse than the Turks.[64]

Cromwell had indeed directed Blake to proceed against the North African corsairs, in particular those of the Dey of Tunis, who were responsible for numerous attacks on English shipping. Blake arrived off Tunis in February 1655 to demand the release of English captives there and negotiate a treaty of friendship. When talks failed he went to reconnoitre the base at Porto Farina for a possible attack, and discovered nine warships lying at anchor there. They were protected by powerful forts ashore, which gave him pause for thought, but early on 4 April he boldly sailed into the harbour, battered the forts into silence from close range, and then sent boat parties to fire all the galleys. By 8 o'clock the operation was over and the English ships were warping out back to sea. The Dey of Tunis still refused to make peace, so the direct gains were limited (though the Dey of Algiers hastened to reach terms). But Blake's success in destroying an enemy force protected by batteries ashore was unprecedented in naval history, and this dramatic manifestation of English sea-power had a considerable impact throughout Europe. Blake himself, typically, was almost apologetic, uncertain whether his instructions covered such an attack and anxious about possible repercussions from the Ottoman government and the English Levant Company. Cromwell hastened to reassure him.[65]

    [63] *CSPV 1653–4*, 208; *CSPV 1655–6*, 3; G. Leti, *La Vie de Cromwell* (Amsterdam, 1746), ii. 314–5; Vaughan, *Protectorate*, i. 108, 109, 123, 129; W. Oldys and T. Park (eds.), *The Harleian Miscellany*, i. (1808), 564.

    [64] *CSPV 1653–4*, 207, 255; *CSPV 1655–6*, 13–14, 137; *CSPV 1657–9*, 268.

    [65] Powell, *Blake*, 258–66; Gardiner, *CP* iv. 152–9; Corbett, *Mediterranean*, i, ch. 17; Blake, *Letters*, 288–95, 300.

The Protector naturally kept his admiral informed about the changing political situation, and early in May Blake learned that Spain was now to be his enemy. Fresh orders arrived in the middle of the month directing him to make for Cadiz and intercept the returning Plate fleet, should it have eluded Penn. By early June he was in position and sent word that the Spanish fleet was expected within a month. Further orders from England authorized him to attack any Spanish force setting out for the West Indies or attempting to escort the Plate fleet into port. Nothing happened for several weeks until Blake learned early in August that a fleet had put to sea from Cadiz; he hastened in pursuit, caught up with the Spaniards on the 15th, and resolved to attack. For the next two days, though, weather conditions ruled out an engagement, and this gave him ample leisure to ponder the strange information he had picked up from a straggler: that the fleet was not bound for the Indies, had no orders to attack him, and knew nothing of the Plate fleet. Blake was always scrupulous not to exceed his orders and, perplexed by these mysterious 'checks of providence', decided on reflection that an attack would not be justified. Instead he retired to Lisbon to await new supplies, his provisions being almost exhausted; the victuallers from England failed to arrive, having been driven back by storms, and late in September he was therefore compelled to sail for home. The government did not conceal its disappointment, holding that he could and should have attacked the Spanish fleet, but Blake's reception was none the less fairly friendly. The expedition had secured important political objectives and had demonstrated to France and Europe as a whole the effectiveness of English sea-power even in distant waters.[66]

The outbreak of war with Spain in Europe changed the strategic position. The failure of the Western Design dissuaded Cromwell from further major operations in the Caribbean, and he decided it would be easier to intercept the Plate fleet off Spain. He was determined, however, to hold on to Jamaica and made vigorous efforts to entice planters to settle there. He was also still determined, he wrote, 'to strive with the Spaniard for the mastery of all those seas,' and he encouraged Penn's successor, Goodson, to search for Plate ships and attack the Spanish Main as well as protecting Jamaica from

[66] Powell, *Blake*, 265–72; Blake, *Letters*, 297–308; Gardiner, *CP* iv. 164–9; *Thurloe*, iii. 547; Cromwell, *Writings*, iii. 823–4; BL Lansdowne MS 821, fos. 24–5; *CSPV 1655–6*, 125–6.

counter-invasion.[67] Goodson was eager to put his twelve ships to good use, leading raids on the mainland and searching for the Plate ships at Cartagena. His force would have been too weak though to attack such a well-defended harbour, and even when reinforcements increased his fleet to about twenty his options remained limited. The problem, as he told Thurloe, lay in the shortage of men rather than ships; the toll of tropical disease meant that 'when you think you have a very considerable fleet abroad, you have rather a shadow than a substance'. In 1656 he made another sweep, looking into Cartagena, sacking Rio de la Hacha on the mainland, and patrolling off Havana during July and August in the hope of encountering the Plate ships—which had in fact sailed for Spain a few days before his arrival.[68] Goodson was also drawn into the running of the new colony. He had reluctantly agreed to serve as one of the Commissioners and by the middle of 1656 found himself the sole survivor. When a new military commander eventually arrived from England in December he gladly handed over responsibility and sailed for England a few weeks later, taking many of the larger ships with him.[69]

It was clear by now that Spain was not planning any serious attempt to recapture Jamaica, and the English naval force was accordingly scaled down and placed under the command of the military. The most important naval officer serving in the Caribbean in the late 1650s was Christopher Myngs, whose exploits quickly brought him both wealth and notoriety. Early in 1659 Myngs led 3,000 men in a raid on the Spanish Main, seizing plate, silver, and coin at Coro said to be worth £2–300,000, most of which he and his men allegedly purloined. He was packed home to England to stand trial for fraud, but a council of war found the evidence contradictory and sympathized with an officer who was clearly energetic and successful—qualities all too rare in the early history of Jamaica. Myngs was reinstated and was back in the Caribbean by the end of the year to resume his lucrative and swashbuckling career.[70]

The main war effort in 1656 was directed against Spain itself. A fleet of thirty-seven ships sailed at the end of March under the joint command of Blake and Edward Mountagu. There were political

[67] Gardiner, *CP* iv. 220–3; Cromwell, *Writings,* iii. 852–4, 857–60.
[68] *Thurloe,* iv. 52, 151–5, 159, 388–9, 451–8, 537–81, v. 340; SP 18/145/30; Firth, i. 50; *The Present State of Jamaica* (1683), 30–5.
[69] *Thurloe,* iv. 151–2, v. 771, vi. 25, 220; below, ch. 6.
[70] F. E. Dyer, 'Captain Christopher Myngs in the West Indies', *MM* xviii (1932), 168–87. *The Publick Intelligencer,* 27 June–4 July 1659.

reasons behind Mountagu's appointment as General and the Protector probably hoped too that his protégé's more pugnacious temperament would offset Blake's caution. It was doubtless intended that
Mountagu should lead any operations ashore.[71] The navy's likely
targets were once again the subject of anxious speculation throughout Europe. Would the English seize a base in the Mediterranean,
such as Majorca or Minorca? Or attack Italy, a prospect reported to
be putting the pope 'constantly on tenterhooks'?[72]

The expedition's real aim was to intercept the Plate fleet and
harry Spanish shipping. Cromwell also authorized the Generals to
attack Spain itself if suitable opportunities arose, and sent after them
a merchant ship, the *Cullen*, laden with thousands of pickaxes,
shovels, and other tools, with the promise of 3–4,000 troops if
required. In the event there were no operations ashore. Cadiz was
found to be too heavily fortified for an attack. The Generals also
considered an attempt on Gibraltar, but most of the officers
regarded their men as unsuitable for such an operation and when
Mountagu went to view the defences he estimated that 4–5,000 good
troops would be needed to seize and hold the place. Cromwell
favoured the project in principle but this report, coupled with news
that the *Cullen* had been captured by the enemy, persuaded him
that the operation was not practicable that year.[73]

The expedition was more successful in bringing Portugal to heel.
King John had refused to ratify the treaty agreed in 1654, balking
at a clause allowing English residents to practise their Protestant
faith, something anathema to both Church and people. The English
arrived off Lisbon in May and demanded the ratification of the
treaty within five days, using the threat of an attack on the Brazil
fleet—due at any moment—if the king refused. When John still
prevaricated Mountagu wanted to open hostilities at once; Blake on
the other hand urged patience, aware that a breach with Portugal
would mean losing Lisbon as a base for their operations against
Spain. His caution was soon vindicated. Fearing the English navy
even more than the wrath of the Catholic Church the king was

[71] Gardiner, *CP* iv. 228–9; Powell, *Blake*, 276–8; *CSPV 1655–6*, 178.

[72] *CSPV 1655–6*, 182, 198–9, 205; BL Add. MS 19770, fo. 34; Corbett,
Mediterranean, i. 286–7. The pope was still apprehensive two years later: *CSPV
1657–9*, 234.

[73] Powell, *Blake*, 278–81, 283–4; F. R. Harris, *The Life of Edward Mountagu*
(1912), i. 92–3; Gardiner, *CP* iv. 236–7; Corbett, *Mediterranean*, i, ch. 18; *Thurloe*
iv. 699, v. 67–70, 101–2, 133; *CSPD 1656–7*, 227.

brought to ratify the treaty at the end of May, which as Thurloe observed 'certainly he had otherwise never done'.[74] The news caused a momentary alarm in Madrid that the English and Portuguese would now launch a joint attack on the poorly defended capital, and a foreign diplomat there described Spanish ministers as 'shaking in their shoes'.[75]

In reality the English found it difficult to inflict any serious injury on the Spaniards. They could take few prizes for Spain had little merchant shipping of its own. Searching for contraband goods in neutral ships was time-consuming, laborious, and, as Mountagu commented, 'no pleasing employment; and when one has rummaged a ship, and finds nothing, it begets a great deal of ill-will'. The Spanish navy prudently remained in harbour. 'The Spaniard will neither fight nor trade,' an aggrieved Englishman later complained.[76] The Generals sent part of their fleet back to England and dispatched other ships to range the coasts of Galicia and Biscay; one task force attacked Málaga, firing nine Spanish ships and bombarding the city. Blake and Mountagu sailed over to the Barbary coast briefly to investigate the suitability of Oran or Tangier as a naval base in lieu of Gibraltar, leaving a squadron under Stayner to watch Cadiz.[77] The one great success of the year came some weeks later when Stayner sighted the Plate fleet which had eluded Goodson in the Caribbean. The seven massive galleons, making for Cadiz, were not alarmed by the relatively small English ships, mistaking them indeed for fishing craft, and they made no attempt to escape during the night. Next day, 8 September, Stayner launched his attack, capturing two great galleons and sinking two others. The news aroused great excitement in England. Rumour put the value of the captured bullion at up to a million pounds, enough, it was hoped, to pay for the entire war. When Mountagu returned home with part of the fleet late in October, however, the treasure was found to be worth only a quarter of that sum. The government believed most of it had been embezzled, Thurloe claiming that individual captains had helped themselves to £60,000 apiece and ordinary seamen £10,000, and complaining that 'this is so universal amongst seamen, and taken in the heat of the fight, that it is not possible to get it again nor any part of it'. No doubt many seamen

[74] Gardiner, *CP* iv. 237–40; Powell, *Blake*, 278, 281–3; *Thurloe*, v. 213–14.
[75] *CSPV 1655–6*, 209.
[76] *Thurloe*, v. 171, 216; Firth, i. 46–7; Blake, *Letters*, 432–8.
[77] Firth, i. 47–9; Powell, *Blake*, 284–6; Blake, *Letters*, 364, 440–7.

had seized their chance, but Thurloe appears to have plucked these figures from the air and the original estimates of Stayner's prize had probably been wildly inflated.[78]

Blake had remained off Spain to maintain the blockade through-out the winter—in itself another major innovation. He had kept some of the larger ships with him and Cromwell sent out reinforce-ments, for there was word of a Spanish fleet preparing at Cadiz and of another Plate fleet on its way. When news arrived in February 1657 that the Plate ships had been sighted, heading for the Canaries, Blake's captains urged him to send a squadron to intercept them and repeat Stayner's success. Blake refused, for his provisions were low and he was not prepared to risk his force by dividing it. The fleet remained on station. But when the victuallers arrived from England in March Blake felt able to take action at last, and learning from his scouts that the Spaniards at Cadiz were still not ready for sea he judged it safe to sail for the Canaries, taking almost his whole force with him. He found the sixteen ships of the Plate fleet lying at Santa Cruz, protected by the forts; the silver had been unloaded and the Spaniards were confident that the ships were invulnerable. As at Porto Farina it proved otherwise. On 20 April Stayner led twelve frigates into the harbour in line astern and brought them alongside the Spanish galleons, Blake following with the remaining ships to engage the shore batteries. The entire Spanish fleet was destroyed. The English escaped to sea without losing a single ship and with only fifty casualties, though the action had been much fiercer than these figures suggest; Stayner's own ship, the *Speaker,* was so battered that all her masts collapsed and she was barely kept afloat. The English had not been able to reach the Spanish bullion but it now had to lie uselessly at Santa Cruz, severely impeding Spain's war effort in Flanders and leading its invasion of Portugal to peter out. Blake himself was now called home at last. He had long been chronically sick, apparently living for months on broths and jellies alone, and did not survive the homeward voyage. He died on 7 August as his ship entered Plymouth Sound, and was buried in Westminster Abbey with well-earned pomp and ceremony—of which he would almost certainly have disapproved.[79]

[78] Firth, i. 49–57; Powell, *Blake*, 287–91; Blake, *Letters*, 447–52.

[79] Firth, i, ch. 8; Powell, *Blake*, ch. 21; Blake, *Letters*, 385–92, 452–60; C. H. Firth (ed.), 'A Narrative of the Battle of Santa Cruz', in *The Naval Miscellany*, ii (NRS xl; 1912), 125–36. There was talk of sending another expedition to the Canaries to seize the treasure, but this failed to materialize: *CSPV 1657–9*, 64–5.

Stokes had remained behind with half the fleet to maintain the blockade of Spain, which he did for the rest of the year. In January 1658 he sent part of his force back to England and took his ten remaining ships into the Straits. One squadron under Whetstone patrolled between Zante and Malta, while Stokes made his way to Porto Farina and concluded a new treaty with the Dey of Tunis. In May five ships under Whetstone went to serve with the French in a joint operation against Spain, though in the event the project was abandoned. The main English force continued its work protecting trade, searching neutral ships for contraband goods, and hunting down privateers; early in 1659 it passed back into the Atlantic and spent several weeks patrolling off Cadiz in the hope of intercepting the Plate ships. Stokes had to face numerous difficulties during his lengthy stay in the Straits. His squadron had much less leverage than Blake's massive fleet and received little assistance from the duke of Tuscany at Leghorn. The ships were now foul, their officers and men were eager to return home, and friction broke out among the senior commanders. Even so the squadron gave valuable protection to merchantmen and had some notable successes, such as the capture of the famous pirate Papachino. Stokes was eventually recalled in June 1659 and arrived home in September, some three and a half years after leaving England. A new force set out in October under Jonas Poole to take over the protection of shipping in the Straits, and England's naval presence there thus survived to the very end of the interregnum.[80]

From the middle of 1657 the focus of naval operations moved nearer England. Cromwell had concluded a treaty with Mazarin in March committing England and France to a joint campaign in Flanders, with the promise of Mardyke and Dunkirk if it succeeded. He had long been interested in Dunkirk as a base for intervening in continental affairs and as a bridle on the Dutch; equally important, its possession would make it much easier to block royalist invasion attempts from the Spanish Netherlands and would perhaps in time help to weaken Spain's hold in Flanders. It would be of immense

---

[80] Corbett, *Mediterranean*, i. 291–7; Davies, 211–12; *Thurloe*, vii. 75–7, 141–2, 144–5, 152–3, 189, 202–3, 209–10, 212, 234, 306, 580–1, 583, 587–8, 654; *CSPD 1657–8*, 145–6, 185, 307–10; *CSPD 1658–9*, 3, 72, 92, 135, 221, 330–2, 377; *CSPD 1659–60*, 201, 203–4; Bodl. Rawlinson MS C 381; Adm. 2/1731, fo. 89; BL Add. MS 1433.

value too in dislodging the Flemish privateers who were inflicting heavy losses on English commerce. The French attacked and captured Mardyke in September. Though Mountagu's fleet played only a minor part in the operation a squadron under Goodson then took up station offshore, its seamen helping to strengthen Mardyke's defences, and the ships bombarded Spanish positions to help drive back a counter-attack.[81]

The navy had a far more central role a few months later in foiling a projected invasion. The war had persuaded Spain to promise 6,000 troops to assist a royalist landing in the winter—the only season when they might elude the English navy during the Channel crossing. Troops assembled in Flanders and ships were hired in Holland to transport them. Nothing more could be done until the Channel was clear, and it was not until the end of January that storms and ice finally drove Sparling's squadron from its station, giving the royalists their chance. But before the Dutch transports could embark the troops Goodson had arrived to resume the blockade, and on 28 February he intercepted the five Dutch freighters on their way to Ostend, capturing three and driving the others ashore. His action effectively ended royalist dreams for another year.[82] Goodson was less fortunate though in May, when he gave naval assistance to an unofficial attempt to seize Ostend, devised by the French general D'Aumont. The plan misfired disastrously. Thurloe was deeply shocked that Goodson should have taken part without authorization, though the episode is further proof of the navy's enterprising new spirit; a generation earlier the Stuarts had worried about admirals falling short of their instructions, not exceeding them.[83]

In 1658 Mountagu and Goodson assisted the Anglo-French assault on Dunkirk by bombarding its seaward defences. The town surrendered on 24 June and was duly handed over to the English.[84] While the fleet still lay offshore Mazarin visited Mountagu on board the *Naseby*, which greatly impressed him, and they discussed ideas for further joint operations, such as an attack on the Spanish Indies

---

[81] Firth, i. 269–71, 282–7, 299; Harris, *Mountagu*, i. 103–5; *CSPD 1657–8*, 143. For Cromwell's thinking on Dunkirk see Bischoffshausen, *Politik*, 204–7.

[82] Gardiner, *CP* iv. 234; Firth, i. 299–301, ii. 66; *Thurloe*, vii. 38; HMC 4, *5th Report*, 166.

[83] *Thurloe*, vii. 109, 113, 128; Firth, i. 183–4; *Clarke Papers*, iii. 148–9.

[84] Firth, i. 184–201.

fleet then preparing at Cartagena. Such ideas were still in the air, and when a new fleet was set out under Goodson late in 1658 many believed, both in England and Europe, that it was being sent to attack Hispaniola or intercept the Plate fleet.[85] Mountagu (and Monck) wanted to seize Tangier and in 1659 Lawson too urged the need for a Mediterranean base to free England from dependence on the unreliable Tuscans. Charles Longland, the agent at Leghorn, also wanted a permanent naval presence in the Straits and pressed the government to swap Dunkirk for Oran when peace came to be made.[86]

In the event there were to be no further major operations against Spain. Cromwell's death in September 1658 removed the driving force behind the war, and the peace between France and Spain the following year ruled out further joint operations. The weaker regimes which succeeded Cromwell faced a deepening political and financial crisis, and found it harder to ignore the widespread opposition the war had aroused at home.

Much of the English merchant community strongly resented the Spanish war. There seems little doubt that it greatly diminished the volume and still more the profitability of trade between England and Spain; though goods might be carried in Dutch ships with false bills of lading it was said to cost £2–500 per ship to bribe the Spanish customs officials. The seizure of Spanish Plate ships was much less welcome to merchants than to the government. The Venetian ambassador reported that many merchants were delighted when a Plate fleet reached Spain safely early in 1656, shortly before Blake's arrival, for American bullion was used to pay off commercial debts throughout Europe and its capture would have hit merchants everywhere.[87] Cromwell's hope that privateering would provide a substitute for the closure of Spanish ports proved ill-founded, there being little Spanish shipping to attack. Any gains were more than outweighed by the heavy losses inflicted by Flemish privateers.

---

[85] Harris, *Mountagu*, i. 111–13; *Clarke Papers*, iii. 171; Clar. MS 59, fos. 202–3; *Thurloe*, vii. 534–5; HMC 4, *5th Report*, 171; *CSPV 1657–9*, 233, 250–60, 265–6.

[86] *Thurloe*, vi. 505, vii. 209–10, 810; Add. MS 18986, fo. 317. Longland had earlier urged the government to foment a rising in Naples—as the French had attempted—as more likely to weaken Spanish power than operations in the Caribbean: *Thurloe*, v. 93.

[87] Prestwich, 'Diplomacy and Trade', 108–11; Gardiner, *CP* iv. 170–1, 215; Davies, 198; *CSPV 1655–6*, 198; Bethel, *World's Mistake*, 8–9; *The Petition of the Marchants trading to . . . Spain* (1659), BL 669 f 21(18). For a reassessment of the economic effects of the war see Crabtree, 'Protestant Foreign Policy', 172–8.

Eighty-two privateers were licensed at Brussels in 1656 by the Spanish authorities, more than double the previous year's figure, and English ships were their main targets: 150 were captured in that year alone, colliers and fishing craft being the most common victims.[88] Demands for help poured into Whitehall. Petitioners from East Anglia complained in 1656 that a third of the local fishing fleet had already been lost, and the East Anglian ports were, understandably, strongly opposed to the war.[89] Estimates of the total number of ships lost range between 1,200 and 2,000, and though many of them were small their loss was a severe blow to the English merchant marine.[90]

At first attempts to protect English commerce had little success. Convoys were slow and unpredictable and many shipmasters preferred to sail alone and take their chance. Escorting warships were often unable to overhaul the privateers, which were kept clean and well-tallowed, and some even fell prey to the more heavily manned enemy vessels. Moreover, small privateers learned to hide close inshore where warships were unable to follow, and others successfully disguised themselves as fishing craft.[91] But from the summer of 1656 the situation gradually improved. In June the Council arranged for a squadron to patrol off the Flemish coast, the following spring the navy was able to impose an almost total blockade of Dunkirk and Ostend, and Dunkirk's capture in 1658 removed the major privateering base. As a result of these steps the number of English prizes carried into Flemish ports was halved in 1657–8. The problem was never completely solved, though. Some privateers still contrived to operate from Ostend and many others transferred to new bases on Spain's Atlantic coast, and when the Franco-Spanish war came to an end in 1659 they redoubled their attacks on English shipping, causing losses to soar once more.[92]

War with Spain inevitably brought renewed friction with the

[88] R. Baetens, 'The Organization and Effects of Flemish Privateering in the Seventeenth Century', *Acta Historiae Neerlandicae*, ix (1976), 54, 69; *CSPD 1655–6*, 519.

[89] SP 18/128/35, 44; *CSPD 1655–6*, 534, 539; *CSPD 1656–7*, 219, 232, 271.

[90] Crabtree, 'Protestant Foreign Policy', 169–70.

[91] The *Cat*, *Parrot*, and *Nonsuch ketch* were captured, and the *Greyhound* lost. Firth, i. 42–3; *CSPD 1655–6*, 528.

[92] *Thurloe*, v. 101–2; Firth, i. 44; Baetens, 'Flemish Privateering', 69; *CSPD 1655–6*, 345; *CSPD 1656–7*, 337, 348–9. It was stated in May 1657 that England had lost 20 ships in one week, and that 70 privateers were lying at Dunkirk: HMC 4, *5th Report*, 152.

Dutch, partly through their involvement in Flemish privateering. There were frequent complaints that the privateers obtained their ships, seamen, and capital in the Netherlands and disposed of their booty there. A Spanish privateer captured in the Straits was found to be Dutch-built with a Dutch captain and twenty-nine Dutchmen among its crew.[93] The English viewed Dutch protestations of neutrality with understandable cynicism. General Mountagu described the Netherlands as a 'nest to shelter rogues', arguing that open war would be preferable to the existing situation. 'Better an open than a close enemy', an MP agreed.[94] The major bone of contention was still the English demand to search neutral shipping for contraband goods. As memories of the last war began to fade the Dutch submitted to searches only when they felt too weak to refuse, and Thurloe noted in 1656, 'Our ships of war and theirs scarce ever meet in the Channel but they have some scuffle or other.' When the English did force their way on board a merchantman they generally found it carried false papers as protection in such a situation. An MP complained, 'If we are too weak [to overpower their ships], then they are Spanish; if too strong, Dutch.'[95] Neither Cromwell nor de Witt wanted war, but as in 1652 each side was reluctant to back down. In 1656 William Whitehorne, commanding in the Downs, was ordered to intercept a large convoy escorted by de Ruyter and if possible seize the silver it was thought to be carrying. The Admiralty voiced the pious hope that the Dutch warships would not interfere, adding vaguely, 'The Lord direct you to that which may be pleasing to him.' De Ruyter in fact had orders not to allow a search and a major confrontation was only averted by Whitehorne's common-sense decision that to attack with his small squadron would be mere folly. In the event Cromwell and de Witt succeeded in preserving a precarious peace, Cromwell intervening on several occasions to free Dutch ships brought in by his captains. But he never conceded the Dutch claim of *mare liberum* and he made it clear in 1657 that he would block any attempt to transport the bullion stranded at Santa Cruz in Dutch ships.[96]

[93] e.g. *CSPD 1655–6*, 358, 542; *CSPV 1655–6*, 104; *CSPD 1656–7*, 348–9, 368; Adm. 2/1729, fo. 215; Adm. 2/1730, fos. 80, 81ᵛ; Burton, *Diary*, iii. 461–2; *CSPD 1658–9*, 323–4, 334, 425.

[94] Firth, ii. 280–1; Burton, *Diary*, iii. 393.

[95] Firth, i. 45–6; Burton, *Diary*, iii. 462.

[96] Wilson, *Profit*, ch. 6; Adm. 2/1729, fo. 40ᵛ; Firth, i. 45–6. Monck, typically, concluded that Whitehorne was a coward: *Thurloe*, vii. 388.

There were several further grounds for dispute. The Dutch rightly saw the English occupation of Mardyke and Dunkirk as a potential threat to their position. There was friction too over saluting the flag, the confiscation of goods in Dutch ships for contravening the Navigation Act, and the seizure of ships and cargoes in the Caribbean: Penn seized sixteen Dutch ships at Barbados in 1655 for breaching the act of 1650 which barred foreign traders from English colonies, and others were taken at St Kitt's and later by Myngs. The Dutch in turn harassed the English wherever they were the stronger, particularly in the East Indies and on the North Sea fishing grounds. Their commitment to *mare liberum* was always selective, based on self-interest rather than principle.[97] The long-standing Dutch quarrel with Portugal developed into open war in 1657 and this too had serious implications, for English shipping and capital played a considerable part in the Portuguese Brazil trade. The Dutch blockade of Lisbon and de Ruyter's attack on the Brazil fleet in November 1657 underlined the threat to English interests, and Cromwell hastily offered to mediate in the dispute.[98]

The Dutch were widely held to blame for the frustrations of the Spanish war. An MP remarked, 'The Spaniard trades not. We can get nothing of him. The Dutch is at the bottom of all this business.' Another called it 'a Dutch war, under the Spaniard's name'. Many expected open war to follow, a prospect some welcomed, and there were rumours that an English fleet set out in 1657 was designed for use against them.[99] There was deep suspicion of Dutch intentions, the Admiralty warning commanders to 'be watchful and circumspect' in case of sudden attack. Many captains were already wary: Stokes, off Cadiz, thought the main aim of the Dutch 'was to strengthen the Spaniard and his interest', and from the Downs Whitehorne voiced fears that seventy Dutch warships preparing for sea might 'intend perfidiously to affront this commonwealth' by a

[97] Harper, *Navigation Laws*, 50–2, 304–5; Wilson, *Profit*, 86–8; *CSPV 1655–6*, 245–7; *Nicholas Papers*, iv. 26–7; *CSPD 1657–8*, 188–9; *A Perfect Account*, 27 Dec. 1654–3 Jan. 1655; *CSPV 1657–9*, 23–4, 122, 126, 214; Firth, 'Thurloe on Relations', 326–7; Bischoffshausen, *Politik*, 220–1; *Thurloe*, vii. 757–61: Firth, ii. 236–8; Fulton, *Sovereignty*, 438–9. On the Caribbean see Venables, *Narrative*, 145; WYN/10/2, 30–1 Jan., 6 Apr. 1655; BL Sloane MS 3926, fo. 8; *Thurloe*, iii. 142, 754.

[98] Firth, ii. 235–6; C. R. Boxer, *The Dutch Seaborne Empire, 1600–1800* (1977), 85–9; HMC 4, *5th Report*, 149, 173; Firth, 'Thurloe on Relations', 326.

[99] Burton, *Diary*, iii. 461, 464; Firth, i. 333–7, ii. 235–9; *CSPD 1657–8*, 261; *Thurloe*, vi. 146, vii. 284–5, 513; 'The Journal of John Weale', ed. J. R. Powell, in *The Naval Miscellany*, iv (NRS, 1952), 152; *CCSP*, iii. 344; *CSPV 1657–9*, 235.

surprise attack. It was reported too that the mood of the Dutch people was once more belligerently anti-English.[100]

In his more abrasive moments Cromwell vowed that he was ready to fight the Dutch and Spaniards together, but neither he nor de Witt really wanted war and they were able to smooth over clashes at sea by tactful diplomacy. After Cromwell's death there was talk of peace with Spain, especially after the fall of the Protectorate in May 1659; the restored Rump felt no commitment to Cromwell's war and Philip IV indicated that his quarrel had been only with 'the great pirate at sea Oliver Cromwell'.[101] There was to be no peace till after the Restoration, but the war was clearly winding down. This ought to have eased relations between England and the Dutch; instead the two nations drifted even closer to war. The peace terms of 1654 came under fierce attack from opponents of the Protectorate in Richard Cromwell's Parliament.[102] Even more important, jealousies of the Dutch stirred up by the Spanish war were exacerbated by a growing crisis in the Baltic. It was here that the Commonwealth navy was to play its last part on the international stage.

III. THE BALTIC CRISIS

English governments throughout the 1650s were anxious about free trade in the Baltic, a vital source of naval stores such as masts, spars, pitch, tar, and hemp. Denmark controlled access, levying a toll on every ship that passed through the Sound. The Dutch, who had long dominated Baltic trade, negotiated privileged terms in 1649 and aroused fears that they would soon establish a total monopoly, enabling them to charge whatever prices they liked or cut off supplies altogether. The Anglo-Dutch war, which had closed the Baltic to the English, naturally strengthened such fears.[103] There had been serious problems in refitting the fleet, and attempts to develop

[100] *CSPV 1655–6*, 167; *CSPD 1656–7*, 249, 307; *CSPD 1657–8*, 145–6; Adm. 2/1730, fos. 64ᵛ, 71, 204; Korr, *New Model*, 187–9.

[101] HMC 4, *5th Report*, 148; *The Weekly Post*, 17–24 May 1659; *CSPV 1657–9*, 271, 274; Davies, 200.

[102] Burton, *Diary*, iii. 390, 393, 440, 474, 490.

[103] R. G. Albion, *Forests and Sea Power* (Hamden, Conn., 1965), esp. ch. 4; Hinton, *Eastland Trade;* Wilson, *Profit*, 51–2. Ball's expedition to the Baltic in 1652 was the first of some 20 dispatched over the next 150 years to protect access to naval stores.

alternative sources in North America had brought only marginal relief; the navy had to muddle through with stores carried in neutral shipping or obtained by compulsory purchase as chance offered.[104] Access was restored in 1654, and Cromwell secured a guarantee that in future English traders would enjoy parity with the Dutch in the matter of tolls. A determination to prevent the Danes and Dutch from ever again being able to close the Baltic was a central plank of Cromwell's foreign policy.[105]

The best protection for English interests in the north appeared to lie in friendship with Sweden, Denmark's traditional enemy. Friendly ties were established with Queen Christina and continued under her successor, Charles X, though they were sometimes strained when his aggressive policies threatened to drag England into unwanted wars. Cromwell was resolved to protect England's position but he recognized that the Dutch could never allow Sweden to dominate the region. He therefore ignored Swedish requests for help against Poland in 1655–6, and did nothing to stop the Dutch sending a fleet to make Charles agree to peace on reasonable terms.[106] Charles begged for help again in 1657 when the Danes reopened the war, offering fortified bases in Denmark as bait as well as privileges for English traders, but as the war rapidly turned in Sweden's favour Cromwell merely offered friendly mediation. The Protector was determined though to hold the Dutch in check, and when a Dutch squadron was (wrongly) reported heading for the Baltic late in 1657 he promptly sent Mountagu in pursuit. Early in 1658 Denmark was forced to make a peace at Roskilde ceding the province of Scania on the north shore of the Sound, which reduced the Danish stranglehold on the Sound. The English agent Philip Meadowe had played a leading part in the negotiations and the outcome was very satisfactory for England. But the peace was short-lived, for in August Charles laid siege to Copenhagen and blockaded it by sea; Denmark's very survival appeared to be at stake, and the Dutch felt their own economic security to be in danger. The crisis entered a new phase with the two great maritime powers very much to the fore.[107]

---

[104] Albion, *Forests*, 200–11; M. Roberts, 'Cromwell and the Baltic', *EHR* lxxvi (1961), 414–15.

[105] Gardiner, *CP* iii. 76; Roberts, 'Baltic', *passim*.

[106] Gardiner, *CP* iii. 73–6, iv. 194–213; Roberts, 'Baltic', 402–24; Firth, i. 302–12; Wilson, *Profit*, 81–2.

[107] Roberts, 'Baltic', 424–43; Firth, i. 312–41, ii. 224–36, 281–90.

In the autumn of 1658 the Dutch responded to events in the north by sending a strong fleet under Opdam, who soon defeated the Swedes and lifted the blockade of Copenhagen. In turn the new Protector Richard Cromwell dispatched Goodson in November with a fleet of twenty ships to protect English interests. Goodson had thought it too late in the season for such an expedition and his fleet was driven back twice by storms, forcing the plan to be abandoned for the winter. 'The good will of the Lord must be submitted to,' the Admiralty Commissioners observed gloomily. As his fleet was only half the size of the Dutch his options would in any case have been limited; it was presumably sent as a political gesture, and Thurloe and others maintained that it had indeed dissuaded the Dutch from sending a second fleet to the Baltic.[108]

England also signalled its concern by allowing the Swedes to recruit English seamen into their navy. English privateers were already serving with Swedish commissions, and Sweden was now permitted to enlist officers and men to serve in the navy itself under the former admiral, Sir George Ayscue. The English government gave every assistance, ignoring Danish protests; the Admiralty for example released David Young from his post as master of the *Lichfield* so that he would be free to accept a Swedish commission. Over a dozen officers (including the former captain Owen Cox) joined the Swedes, along with nearly 400 seamen, and they were offered a passage in Goodson's ill-fated expedition.[109]

The English and Dutch were both resolved to send new forces to the Baltic in the spring.[110] Though both sides genuinely aimed at mediation they were determined to protect their own national interests, each realizing, as a modern scholar has remarked, that 'the contest of the peacemakers was more important than that of the belligerents'. This was very evident in a Commons debate in February 1659, when Thurloe warned of the dangerous consequences should the English be excluded from the Baltic as

---

[108] SP 18/183/99–101, 137, 146; *CSPD 1658–9*, 231; Adm. 2/1730, fos. 270ᵛ, 277; *Thurloe*, vii. 581; *Clarke Papers*, iii. 172; R. Manley, *The History of the Late Warrs in Denmark* (1670), 41–5, 138–9; Sandwich, *Journal*, pp. xiv–xv, xvii; Davies, 195–6; *CSPV 1657–9*, 276–7. For a list of the ships and captains in Goodson's expedition see BL Harleian MS 1247, fo. 38ᵛ.

[109] *CSPD 1658–9*, 245, 250–1; *Thurloe*, vii. 412, 467, 495, 509; *The Publick Intelligencer*, 8–15 Nov. 1658; Sandwich, *Journal*, pp. xv–xvii. On Young see *CSPD 1657–8*, 545 (and cf. 243); Adm. 2/1730, fo. 254ᵛ.

[110] Adm. 2/1731, fo. 56; *Thurloe*, vii. 616, 628; Davies, 203.

in 1652–4. 'If we had to do only with the Dane and the Swede, the thing were not very considerable,' another speaker observed, 'but the Dutch are most in our eye, and we most in theirs.'[111]

At the end of March Mountagu set out for the Baltic with a new fleet of forty ships, with Goodson and Stayner as his deputies. His instructions were complex. He was to mediate for peace on the terms agreed at Roskilde, and to warn the Swedes that England would give no help if they proved obstructive. If on the other hand it was the Danes who made difficulties he was to help the Swedes blockade Copenhagen, loan ships to their navy, and bar the transport of troops from Brandenburg (an ally of the Danes). As far as possible he was to co-operate with the Dutch, but he was ordered to prevent reinforcements from joining Opdam, by force if necessary.[112] It was obviously a very fragile situation, and he urged the English envoy to cut through the 'usual dull, formal gravities' of diplomacy and secure an agreement before the two mediators came to blows. As the talks dragged on, however, he came to suspect that the Swedes were trying to push England into a military alliance and that the Danes and Dutch were merely prevaricating while their forces assembled. Word arrived in May that de Ruyter was at last approaching with a fleet of forty warships, and that Opdam was planning to sail through the Belt to meet it. A council of war on 16 May resolved to block this conjunction.[113] The very next day however brought dramatic news from England that Richard Cromwell's government had collapsed, and fresh orders directed Mountagu not to fight except in self-defence. The belligerent mood among some of his officers is suggested by the fact that Capt. Simmonds, who brought the letters from England, later swore that had he known their contents 'he would have sunk both ship and letters'. A few days later news came that England, the Dutch, and France had agreed at The Hague on fresh endeavours for peace, and that English and Dutch commissioners would be coming to the Baltic to mediate.[114]

[111] Albion, *Forests*, 172–4; Davies, 197–9; Burton, *Diary*, iii. 376–403, 437–47, 450–93 (quotation p. 440); *Clarke Papers*, iii. 183–4.
[112] Sandwich, *Journal*, pp. xviii-xix, 3–10, 283–5; Harl. MS 1247, fo. 39^{r-v}; Davies, 203; *Thurloe*, vii. 644–5, 651–3.
[113] Sandwich, *Journal*, 17–19, 24–6, 29–30.
[114] Ibid., pp. xxii, 30–2; *Thurloe*, vii. 666; Davies, 203–4; *The Last of the Astrologers: Mr William Lilly's History of his Life and Times*, ed. K. M. Briggs (1974), 73.

Mountagu's position was now very difficult. As a firm Cromwellian he hated the newly restored Rump, which in turn viewed him with deep suspicion.[115] His new orders gave him little scope for helping Sweden, as he explained to Charles X. He did what he could, arranging a temporary truce with the Dutch admirals to defer the conjunction of their fleets; he also rescued a Swedish squadron being pursued by Opdam by a threatening manœuvre which distracted the Dutch from their prey. Charles was very appreciative, sending a present to Mountagu and 200 oxen and other provisions for his fleet.[116]

Ayscue's party, which had gone out with Mountagu's expedition, gave the Swedes more active help. Ayscue was received with honour by the king and was commanding a force in the Sound by July, though he personally achieved little.[117] Owen Cox was more fortunate. In July 1659 he set out with seven ships against a Danish–Dutch force preparing to ferry troops to the island of Funen, as a first step towards the relief of Copenhagen. The mission was a dramatic success: he captured or destroyed all the enemy warships and fired about thirty transports, taking prisoner a thousand Brandenburg and Imperial troops. The following day Cox fired another twenty transports further along the coast and returned to Sweden in triumph, having ended the threat of a Danish counter-invasion that summer. The king was delighted and gave him a thousand ducats, a gold chain, and the royal portrait set in diamonds, as well as promoting him vice-admiral with noble status.[118]

Relations between the English and Dutch forces remained tense. The Dutch remembered the Rump's belligerence a few years earlier; the English were conscious of being heavily outnumbered, and aware that the political confusion at home provided the Dutch with

[115] See ch. 10, below.
[116] Harris, *Mountagu*, i. 128–30, 141–2; Sandwich, *Journal*, pp. xxiii–xxv, 35–7; *Clarke Papers*, iv. 29–30.
[117] Add. MS 18986, fo. 228; Sandwich, *Journal*, 40; *Mercurius Politicus*, 24–31 Mar. 1659; *The Publick Intelligencer*, 25 Apr.–2 May, 2–9 May, 16–23 May, 30 May–6 June 1659; R. C. Anderson. 'Ayscue and Cox in Sweden', *MM* xlvii (1961), 298–300. Over a dozen captains and lieutenants serving under Ayscue in 1659 are listed in Harl. MS 1247, fo. 47; several, including David Young, had formerly served Parliament.
[118] Manley, *Late Warrs*, 56–7; R. C. Anderson, *Naval Wars in the Baltic* (1910), 96; idem, 'Ayscue and Cox'; *The Loyall Scout*, 26 Aug.–2 Sept. 1659; *The Weekly Post*, 30 Aug.–6 Sept.; *Clarke Papers*, iv. 30.

an ideal opportunity for revenge. The Rump was in fact committed to peace, as became clear when its commissioners arrived in July. Progress however was painfully slow, and Mountagu eventually suggested implementing one of the agreements made at The Hague, by which surplus ships would return home leaving two fleets of equal size to keep the peace; such a move would end the Dutch preponderance as well as conserving his supplies. His suspicion of the Dutch deepened when they refused to send any ships away without further authorization, and he decided that in this situation it would be better to send home the entire English fleet. Algernon Sidney, the most forceful of the English commissioners, bitterly resisted this proposal. There were political rivalries between the two men, and they differed too in their assessment of the other parties. Mountagu distrusted the Dutch and argued that Sidney's plan to keep back fifteen warships in the Sound would leave them at the mercy of the Dutch fleet, which numbered almost eighty. Mountagu furthermore continued to favour the Swedes, whereas Sidney leaned towards Denmark, either seeing Charles X as the chief obstacle to peace or regarding the Swedish alliance as an unwelcome legacy of the Cromwellian past. The agreement at The Hague authorized the two fleets to combine to force peace on whichever king was recalcitrant, and Mountagu strongly suspected that Sidney and the Dutch would pin blame on Charles and use English warships to attack Sweden, reversing Cromwell's policy. Sidney commented tartly that 'the king of Sweden was otherwise looked upon in England than in the late Protector's days'. There was further dispute over the fleet's dwindling supplies, which Mountagu said made a speedy return essential. He finally over-rode Sidney's protests and ordered the fleet to weigh anchor on 24 August and sail for England, arriving home on 6 September to a cold welcome.[119] If Mountagu had hoped to intervene in domestic politics he was disappointed, but his return did rule out the fleet's being turned against the Swedes, a prospect he detested. Charles X, very conscious of this danger, regarded the fleet's departure as an act of kindness and sent a magnificent jewel for Mountagu and gold chains and medals for the other English commanders—in gratitude for potential injuries averted as well as for services rendered.[120]

[119] Sandwich, *Journal*, 41–67, 286–8; Harris, *Mountagu*, 145–54, 156–7; *Thurloe*, vii. 731, 733–4; *Clarke Papers*, iv. 29–30; Davies, 204–7.
[120] Sandwich, *Journal*, 45; Harris, *Mountagu*, 154.

With Mountagu gone the Dutch were supreme, leaving the Swedes (and Ayscue) no option but to remain in port.[121] In November the Dutch helped Denmark recapture Funen. De Ruyter overwintered with part of his fleet and there was talk of further Dutch operations in the spring. The English by contrast played no further part. On Mountagu's return the Rump had resolved to send another force back to the Sound, but the idea was soon abandoned.[122]

England's intervention in the Baltic is sometimes seen as a fiasco.[123] In the event the northern war ended on terms very satisfactory to the English, for Charles X died early in 1660 and his successor made a peace preserving the essentials of Roskilde. This outcome was largely through chance, of course, but the Dutch probably accepted it because they realized the English would not long submit to any peace that threatened to exclude them from the Baltic. Mountagu had pointed out that English interests were the same whatever government was in power. In sending first Goodson and then Mountagu England had shown its determination to defend these interests, and though the domestic upheavals of 1659–60 blurred the message the Dutch did not forget it.[124]

Cromwell's foreign policy has always been controversial. He has been accused of ignoring England's economic interests and the emerging balance of power in Europe in order to pursue anachronistic and chimerical crusades. In his defence it has been argued that it was reasonable for him to see English interests as consistent with Protestant ideals.[125] More relevant here is the charge that he wasted the potential of the splendid navy he inherited.[126] He was undoubtedly disappointed that it brought no more tangible gain than Jamaica. But the fleet's primary purpose was always to guarantee the security of the regime abroad, as the army did at

---

[121] *The Publick Intelligencer*, 12–19 Sept. 1659; *The Weekly Intelligencer*, 27 Sept.–4 Oct.; *A Particular Advice*, 11–14 Oct.; Sandwich, *Journal*, p. xxviii; Ayscue remained in Sweden till after Charles X's death in Feb. 1660: B. Whitelocke, *Memorials of the English Affairs* (Oxford, 1853), iv. 402; Adm. 3/274, fo. 173; *CSPD 1659–60*, 382.

[122] *CJ* vii. 733; *CSPD 1659–60*, 163–4, 167; *CSPV 1659–61*, 73.

[123] Prestwich, 'Diplomacy and Trade', 115–16.

[124] Sandwich, *Journal*, 62; Albion, *Forests*, 175; Davies, 207.

[125] Prestwich, 'Diplomacy and Trade', 105, 121; Battick, thesis, *passim*; Crabtree, 'Protestant Foreign Policy'; Roberts, 'Baltic'.

[126] Battick, thesis, 84, 297.

home, and by this criterion it was highly successful. It isolated the Stuarts and brought the Commonwealth a prestige English kings had rarely known. It has been suggested earlier that Cromwell was more perceptive than some of his critics in bringing the unpopular Dutch war to an end. Prolonging it offered few advantages, and any major economic concessions squeezed from the Dutch were likely to be outweighed by the consequences of de Witt's overthrow, which would probably follow. Politically harsh, economically moderate, the peace reflected Cromwell's priorities. The Dutch abandoned the Stuarts and even agreed to bar the Orange family from office to meet his anxieties. They accepted their failure to outlaw English searches at sea and remove the Navigation Act. Naval victories alone could not win commercial supremacy, for England still lacked the necessary merchant shipping and financial expertise. In subsequent years Cromwell worked to preserve peace; perhaps he preferred, as a contemporary believed, to see the Dutch 'moulder by degrees' with the navy giving England an edge in peaceful competition. If so, it was a sound approach.[127]

In purely economic terms England would have benefited most by remaining neutral in the later 1650s. The war with Spain allowed the Dutch to recapture most of the ground they had lost. But Cromwell did not give priority to economic criteria; the security of the Commonwealth remained his chief concern, and he saw war against France or Spain as the best way of guaranteeing that they would not combine against him. Such a war also offered the chance of making the navy pay for itself, which would enable him to reduce taxes and strengthen his position at home. Though he was confident that providence had led him to this position he did not consciously sacrifice secular interests to religious: in his eyes God's will was to be sought where religion and national self-interest converged. Given Cromwell's need to wage war he was right to judge that Spain offered better prospects than France, though he badly underestimated the difficulties. The failure of the Western Design was by no means inevitable; with better military planning and a more resolute commander the attack on Hispaniola might have succeeded, with potentially far-reaching consequences. A rumour that Penn had indeed captured San Domingo prompted the Venetian secretary to ponder the implications, and with mounting concern he imagined Plate fleets cut off, Spain growing feeble without its vital supply of

[127] *Nicholas Papers*, iii. 89.

bullion, and the papacy itself eventually coming under attack.[128] This was unduly alarmist but Cromwell was indeed playing for high stakes, and a second expedition, learning from the mistakes of the first, might been more successful. Instead he adopted a new strategy of attacking the Plate fleet in European waters, which did bring some measure of success. Further attempts would almost certainly have followed but for Cromwell's death and the sudden emergence of a crisis in the north, which diverted attention and resources elsewhere.[129]

The naval wars of the 1650s are ultimately more significant for what they portended than for what they achieved. Whatever their wisdom, they marked the dawn of a new age of naval might, colonial expansion, and gunboat diplomacy—the unforeseen consequences of the Commonwealth's sense of insecurity in the years after 1649.

[128] *CSPV 1655–6*, 80.
[129] *CSPV 1657–9*, 233, 265–6, *CSPV 1659–61*, 4–5.

5

Politics and the Navy, 1649–1658

I N the last chapter we looked ahead to survey the role of the navy in England's sudden emergence as a Great Power. We must now turn back to explore the equally important relationship between the navy and domestic politics.

The navy's response to political events ashore was inevitably coloured by the fact that it was engaged in wars open or undeclared throughout the interregnum. Officers away at sea were poorly informed and poorly placed to organize collective action, and they faced strong pressures to bury any discontent in the interests of patriotism and national security. Nevertheless ties between the navy and political developments ashore remained very close. Foreign policy was closely linked to domestic issues, and the allegiance of the navy remained essential to the Commonwealth's survival. Cavaliers, and later republicans too, tried repeatedly to stir up mutinies in the fleet, hoping to link them to risings ashore as in 1648. The seamen had perennial grievances over pay which agitators might seek to exploit. The officers too had grounds for dissatisfaction. First, the army's sudden dissolution of the Rump in 1653 left them serving new, unwelcome masters. Second, the abrupt reversals of foreign policy created problems for the idealists among them. Were they to accept every new change of course without demur, becoming in effect mere mercenaries? It was only in the final months of the interregnum that the navy made a direct challenge to the regime ashore, but there was an undercurrent of dissent throughout the period. The navy was never the docile, apolitical force sometimes assumed.[1]

The remodelled navy was ordered to sea in 1649 before there had been any real chance to test its political reliability. Royalists claimed

[1] See chs. 3, 4, above and 10, below.

scornfully that its morale was low, and expected the seamen to mutiny and drive out the leaders newly foisted upon them. Some alleged that Popham might be won over by bribes and that the Rump, in desperation, was trying to coax Warwick back once more. A journalist gleefully reported that eight warships had defected to the royalists in March alone.[2] All these stories were false but Blake and Deane quickly became aware of dissatisfaction among the mariners. When they arrived in the Downs late in April they found some of the men unwilling to put to sea; though the grievances they aired were professional, the king's execution and Warwick's abrupt removal had also doubtless undermined morale, and enemies of the new regime certainly tried to fish in these troubled waters. Some rapid concessions on prize money helped to restore order, and after a rousing sermon by Cromwell's chaplain Hugh Peter the sailors vowed to 'live and die with the Admirals' against the enemies of the Commonwealth.[3] The incident was nevertheless a worrying reminder of the previous year's troubles. The Generals promptly drew up an engagement of loyalty to the new regime, 'the better to discover the mariners' affections', and copies were also sent to Popham's squadron in the west and to ships stationed in the North Sea. The seamen took the oath without demur.[4] Later in the year the Rump's national Engagement was also put to the mariners, who were now asked to give their home addresses 'as a further tie upon them', and this seems to have been enforced systematically for some time; in March 1651 for example, Capt. Woolters of the hired *Mayflower* sent up two rolls listing the names and addresses of his crew, adding that they had subscribed very cheerfully.[5] The sailors' loyalty was never taken for granted. The Council instructed Blake to keep a close watch on his men when Charles Stuart marched into England in 1651, and the Rump was quick to send the fleet word of victories such as Dunbar and Worcester, partly no doubt to convince waverers that its authority was unshakeable.[6]

[2] Bodl. Clarendon MS 37, fo. 12; *CSPD 1650*, 7; *Mercurius Pragmaticus*, 27 Mar.–3 Apl. 1649; *Mercurius Elencticus*, 11–18 June 1649; above, ch. 3 n. 81.
[3] R. P. Stearns, *The Strenuous Puritan: Hugh Peter, 1598–1660* (Urbana 1952), 344–5; Powell, *Blake*, 80; Blake, *Letters*, 29–31; *Continued Heads*, 20–7 Apr. 1649.
[4] Blake, *Letters*, 39; *CSPD 1649–50*, 27; above, ch. 3 n. 76.
[5] *CJ* vi. 306–7; Clarke MS 4/4, 1649 (33); *Severall Proceedings*, 29 May–5 June 1651.
[6] e.g. *CSPD 1650*, 330; *CSPD 1651*, 357, 410, 419.

Whatever the seamen's private feelings, royalist hopes were sadly disappointed. In the whole of the interregnum only one small ship, the *Hart*, was to mutiny and join the Stuart cause.[7] The Rump's mariners proved very willing to fight against Rupert, and at Lisbon in 1650 it was his men who tried to desert to Blake, not vice versa.[8] The navy's new leaders had of course been chosen for their whole-hearted commitment to the new regime. Blake pursued Rupert with a fervour that went far beyond mere professional diligence. 'I should have accounted it my greatest outward happiness', he told the Council, to have secured 'the total destruction of that piratical crew'. At Cadiz he publicly declared that the world was tired of monarchy, that France was already following England's example, and that in Spain too monarchy would be rooted out within a decade—a prophecy the Spanish king did not appreciate.[9] Though he declined Cromwell's invitation to serve as major-general of the foot in Ireland in 1649 he offered his prayers 'for your army and undertaking' and interpreted victories in Ireland as proof that 'God is still working for us.'[10] William Penn was equally militant. He was delighted to hear of Charles's defeat at Worcester and called a day of thanksgiving, firing off thirty-one guns in celebration. His view of Rupert was much like Blake's: 'The Lord forgive the bloody wretch, and convert him, if he belongeth unto him,' he prayed, 'otherwise, if his Holiness please, suddenly destroy him.'[11]

Many other officers showed equally committed support for the new Commonwealth. In February 1649 several signed a *Remonstrance* thanking the army for bringing back liberty after 'a long, insolent, arbitrary tyranny' and praising the Commons as 'true patriots'.[12] Others used highly emotive phrases in describing the royalists they met at sea—a 'papist pirate', 'sons of Beulah', 'an ungodly crew of revolters'. In October 1649 Capt. Nathaniel Fearnes praised the king's execution as a 'gallant act', which God had clearly vindicated in the Rump's subsequent successes by land and sea. In 1650 Capt. Robert Wyard fought a long, running battle

[7] *Mercurius Pragmaticus*, 27 Mar.–3 Apr.1649; ch. 3 n. 82, above.
[8] Blake, *Letters*, 79.
[9] Ibid. 44, 54, 68, 70; *CSP* iii. 27; *CSPV 1647–52*, 169–70.
[10] Blake, *Letters*, 46, 47, 49; HMC 51, *Leyborne–Popham*, 35; Powell, *Blake*, 85.
[11] Penn, *Memorials*, i. 368, 380–1.
[12] *The Resolution or Remonstrance of the Navie* (1649), 1, 5; signatories included Haddock, Jordan, Dakins, and Fearnes.

against six royalist privateers who had attacked him with the cry
'For King Charles the Second, you Round-headed dogs'. 'We
fought the Lord's battle,' Wyard later informed the Council, 'and
the Lord of Hosts did appear for me in preserving me and all my
men out of the hand of wicked and unreasonable men.' Cromwell's
victory at Worcester prompted a euphoric tribute from Capt.
William Rowse, who saw the ruin of the Stuarts as the threshold of
Christ's kingdom on earth.[13]

Though not all officers were radicals or zealots, only one captain
voiced political doubts loudly enough for the Rump to take notice.[14]
The mariners' well-documented lust for plunder was not incompatible with strongly held political or religious views; plundering
foreign papists had indeed always been a feature of one brand of
Puritan militancy. A pamphlet on the exploits of Capt. John
Greene, a well-known privateer, displays a vigorous if crude political radicalism as well as a predictable thirst for booty. It mocks the
French king's royal title, derides his subjects as 'proud Franciscans',
and declares in robust doggerel:

> Hi ho the matter is great
> now seamen fight
> for their birthright.[15]

Political radicalism stopped short however of support for the
Leveller movement, which seems to have made little impact on the
navy. The *Remonstrance* of February 1649 showed interesting signs
of Leveller influence, notably in the demand for naval offices to be
filled by annual elections and for 'agents' to monitor the conduct of
those chosen. But much of the document was concerned with
conditions of service and it would be rash to assume that those who
signed necessarily supported all its more radical proposals.[16] Leveller agents appear to have been involved in the disturbances in the
Downs in April 1649, which coincided with the outbreak of new
mutinies in the army. One newspaper reported that some of the
agitators arrested in the Downs had also been involved in Leveller
attempts to subvert the army.[17] In 1650 Charles Thoroughgood,

[13] Clarke MS 4/4, 1649 (11), 1650 (14); *A Modest Narrative*, 14–21 July 1649;
Severall Proceedings, 2–9 Nov. 1649; ibid. 8–15 Aug. 1650; Bodl. Dep. MS C 164,
fos. 450–1, *Severall Proceedings*, 6–13 Nov. 1651.

[14] See above, ch. 3 n. 69.

[15] *An Exact Relation of 2 Bloudy Fights at Sea* (1650), 1, 2, 4. Though the pamphlet
is anonymous the author appears to follow Greene's own views very closely.

[16] *Resolution of the Navie*, 4, 7.

[17] *Continued Heads*, 20–7 Apr. 1649; Stearns, *Strenuous Puritan*, 344–5, 347–51.

Blake's flag-captain in the fleet off Portugal, sent his 'kind respects', to the Leveller leader John Lilburne, though nothing more is known of the links between them.[18] The Council was aware of a possible danger from the radicals and was determined to check it. Blake and Popham had a vessel searched in 1649 for seditious works by Lilburne, and ordered a search of warehouses along the Thames for pamphlets describing his trial.[19] In 1650 the Council vetoed a naval commission for Major William Rainborough, who had Leveller and Ranter affiliations and was the brother of the former vice-admiral. When Rainborough offered his services again during the Dutch war, with fervent assurances of his zeal and conformity, he was turned down once more.[20]

The Rump was generally more concerned, rightly, about royalist sentiment in the navy. Though Charles's invasion from Scotland in 1651 had failed to shake the fleet's loyalty, the Dutch war of 1652–4 provided another and greater test. The cavaliers welcomed the war, hoping that defeat at sea would undermine the Rump and that the Dutch could be brought to declare for the Stuarts, as Orange party leaders were known to wish. The Dutch admiral Tromp favoured the Stuart cause, and it was said that Dutch ships had even been seen with Stuart colours.[21] The royalists were eager to play a direct part in Dutch naval operations. Charles offered to take personal command of a squadron, declaring his belief that English warships would defect to his side, and gave his blessing to an abortive plan to take control of the *Garland*, an English warship captured by the Dutch. The royalists also hoped that Rupert would be allowed to lead a squadron of privateers operating from Dutch harbours. When the Dutch blocked all these proposals Charles explored the possibility of taking command of a Danish force instead and using it to launch an invasion of England, though the Danes proved similarly unresponsive.[22] The royalists considered simpler wrecking tactics, too: an agent reported from London that there were men

[18] Blake, *Letters*, 84. In 1651 he was questioned over scandalous remarks about the Navy Commissioners which allegedly reflected on the government: BL Add. MS 9306, fo. 36; Bodl. Rawlinson MS A 225, fo. 71.

[19] *CSPD 1649–50*, 558. The master of one of the ships searched was Robert Robinson, perhaps a kinsman of the naval captain.

[20] *CSPD 1650*, 11; NMM AGC/12/1. On Rainborough see *BDBR*.

[21] *Another Bloudy Fight at Sea* ([30 July] 1652); *CSP* iii. 152, 156; *A Declaration of ... Van Tromp* (1652); *The Weekly Intelligencer*, 10–17 Aug. 1652; P. Geyl, *Orange and Stuart, 1641–1672* (2nd edn., 1969), 100.

[22] Clarendon, *History*, v. 257–9; *CSP* iii. 135, 141, 159, 164; *CCSP* ii. 140, 147, 157, 185, 199, 216; Geyl, *Orange and Stuart*, 104; HMC 58, *Bath*, ii. 107.

willing to enlist in the English navy for suitable rewards and destroy ships by arson.[23]

It was widely recognized in England that the Rump's enemies would seek to exploit the war. Alarming rumours circulated during its early stages: that seven hundred English seamen had gone aboard the Dutch fleet, that Sir John Carteret, once head of the privateers in Jersey, was at sea with a large squadron, that Sir William Batten, a prominent figure in the 1648 revolt, had returned to Holland to offer his services. Even John Lilburne, now in exile, was rumoured to be fitting out a privateer against England for the royalists.[24]

There were inevitably some worries too about the officer corps, now massively swollen to meet the needs of the wartime navy. The inconclusive victory off the Kentish Knock in September 1652 led to talk of deliberate negligence; the Venetian secretary in London remarked that the Rump could not trust 'all those who profess to be well affected, as in the present straits they are liable to change sides'. After the defeat at Dungeness Blake demanded an inquiry into why some of his officers had held back, and several of the Council's Admiralty Committee hastened down to investigate.[25] An intelligencer, commenting on the defeat, called for a thorough purge: 'I pray when you begin to new model that you will new model to purpose', he urged, to sweep away 'those wasps and drones who serve not but for filthy lucre'.[26] Though this assessment was unduly harsh the Admiralty stepped up the vetting of officers, both senior and junior, and gave even more weight to ideological criteria in new appointments.[27] Nothing politically incriminating was found against the officers suspended after Dungeness, but further inquiries did unearth several disaffected captains serving in the fleet. Philip Marshall of the hired *John and Elizabeth* had been in the 1648 mutiny and had later commanded a ship in Rupert's squadron, as had John Golding, captain of a Dutch prize taken over by the navy. Francis Harditch of the *Arms of Holland* was also thought to be

[23] Clar. MS 45, fo. 439ᵛ.

[24] *French Occurrences*, 5–12 and 19–26 July 1652; *Bloudy Newes from Holland* ([17 Mar.] 1652), 8; *Several Informations . . . concerning . . . Lilburne* ([13 July] 1653). Lilburne in fact defended the English cause and left Dutch territory: P. Gregg, *Free-Born John* (1961), 312–13. The story may have originated in the fact that his brother Anthony was commanding a privateer (though *against* the Dutch).

[25] *CSPV 1647–52*, 302; *FDW* iii. 92, 96–9; cf. *CSP* iii. 135; *CSPV 1653–4*, 33.

[26] Bodl. Tanner MS 53, fo. 174ᵛ.

[27] See ch. 6, below.

politically unreliable. All three were turned out.[28] Similar inquiries
were made into the loyalty of warrant officers. John Poortmans, an
Admiralty official and radical, quizzed officers of ships at
Gravesend and Chatham in January 1653 and reported that the
boatswain of the *Sussex* was a 'cavalier and a profane man', the
boatswain of the *Kentish* had been a mutineer in 1648, and the cook
of the *Convertine* was a 'very profane and wicked man, and a
perfect enemy to the commonwealth'; all must be removed. He
wanted to sack the *Vanguard*'s gunner too, but it transpired that the
suggested replacement had himself been 'turned out for the Kentish
insurrection', which underlined the scale of the navy's problem.[29]

The reliability of officers in hired merchantmen was especially
doubtful. Most shipowners did not support the Rump, and the
same was true of many of the officers they employed. Political
animosity sometimes contributed to their notorious reluctance to
commit their ships to battle, and it greatly hindered Richard
Badiley's efforts to press English merchant ships and crews at
Leghorn in 1652. One master, he reported, drank a toast to 'the
confusion of the state of England' with such a hearty flourish that
he inadvertently 'heaved his hat overboard', and another struck a
captain who spoke up for Parliament. Though they were all in
danger from the Dutch squadron blockading the port they mocked
Badiley with the taunt that it was the Rump's problem, not theirs.[30]

The temper of the ordinary seamen remained an unknown
quantity. Badiley was far from sure how his men would behave if
Rupert were to appear in the Straits, as was rumoured.[31] Edward
Hyde boasted that the Dutch owed their victory at Dungeness to
Charles Stuart, 'the mariners for his sake refusing to fight'.[32] Even
Blake and Monck feared a plot behind the disturbances which broke
out a few weeks later over pay.[33] In the Rump's new disciplinary
code, introduced at the close of 1652, no fewer than nine articles
dealt explicitly with political offences such as helping or defecting to
the enemy, and sheltering rebels.[34] One intractable problem was

---

[28] PRO SP 18/46/8; SP 18/48/81; Rawl. MS A 227, fo. 32ᵛ. After his removal
Golding sought letters of marque against the Dutch, but in 1656 he did defect to the
royalists: *CSPD 1653–4*, 10, 142, 226; below, n. 139.
[29] SP 18/46/7, 8; *FDW* iii. 382; below, ch. 6.
[30] R. Badiley, *Capt. Badiley's Reply* (1653), 1–2, 9; idem, *Capt. Badiley's Answer*
(1653), 13, 52.   [31] Badiley, *Answer*, 7.
[33] NMM AGC/B/8.   [32] *CSP* iii. 135.   [34] *FDW* iii. 293–301.

that the navy was forced to press seamen on a massive scale, which inevitably sucked in royalist sympathizers. A group pressed at Plymouth included a former lieutenant in the king's army, who soon persuaded the rest to run away.[35] The further the press reached out, the greater the danger: over one-third of a group brought from Jersey in 1653 was found to have served under Rupert. Sailors pressed in Scotland in the same year were carefully divided among the fleet with no more than six allowed to serve together.[36]

The royalists continued to believe throughout the war that most seamen were cavaliers at heart, waiting only for an opportunity to reveal their true loyalties. It was said after the Texel, in July 1653, that English sailors had asked Dutch prisoners why they did not hang out the king's colours, 'for then they would fight with, not against them'.[37] But in the event there were no desertions whatever from the English fleet to the other side. The fact that the Dutch steadfastly refused to declare for the Stuart cause greatly reduced the danger, and once blood was spilled patriotic feelings swept all else aside. And both officers and men, whatever their political leanings, relished the unprecedented opportunities for plunder and prize-money the war brought in its wake.

The Dutch war coincided with dramatic political upheavals at home and these provided a further test for the navy's loyalty. For over four years the Admiralty had worked to mould an officer corps loyal to Parliament, only to see the Rump abruptly swept away on 20 April 1653 by Cromwell's military coup. How would the navy react?

The coup had an immediate and dramatic impact on naval administration. At the close of 1652 Parliament had set up a new body of Admiralty Commissioners, most of them naturally staunch supporters of the Rump. Sir Henry Vane, the most important of them, had been singled out for attack by Cromwell and promptly left London, severing his connections with the navy.[38] Richard Salwey and John Carew complained in a dispirited letter that they were the only Commissioners still active, and only Carew

---

[35] SP 18/37/75.
[36] *CSPD 1652–3*, 565; Rawl. MS A 227, fos. 61, 69.
[37] *CCSP* ii. 135, 157, 185, 236; *Thurloe* i. 331.
[38] V. A. Rowe, *Sir Henry Vane the Younger* (1970), ch. 8; SP 18/35/145; Rawl. MS A 227, fo. 70; ch. 4 n. 25, above.

welcomed the change; Salwey was assiduously courted, being named to the new Council of State and later to Barebone's Parliament, but he played no part in either, denounced the coup to Cromwell's face, and gradually withdrew from Admiralty work. George Thomson and James Russell were both dismissed in May after petitioning for the Rump's restoration. Thomson felt passionately about the coup: years later he recalled with grisly relish how General Deane's 'right hand was shot through his body in the next fight' after he had signed a paper accepting the new regime. The remaining Commissioner, John Langley, was away sick. For a brief period the entire administrative machine was close to breakdown, and the Navy Commissioners admitted in embarrassment that they did not even know the fleet's whereabouts. Deane inquired drily 'whether in the great revolution there be anybody takes care of us and of the naval affairs'.[39]

News of the army's action caused some dismay in the fleet too; 'Come, let's all be mad together', a leading officer is said to have exclaimed. Cromwell wrote at once to Deane and Monck, who were with the main force at Portsmouth. Deane's initial reaction suggests his confusion at the 'strange and various acts of providence'. 'I praise my God my trust is in him,' he wrote, 'and am not much solicitous though the world be turned upside down.' Rear-Admiral Lawson, whose links were with Vane rather than Cromwell, clung to the hope that God would somehow 'bring glory to himself and good to his people by all these revolutions'.[40] The two Generals met thirty-five of their senior officers on 22 April to consider the situation, at the end of which they all signed a carefully worded declaration explaining that they felt themselves called by the nation 'for the defence of the same against the enemies thereof at sea' and would be loyal to their trust. The Generals sent word of their proceedings to Penn, then commanding a squadron off Harwich, and Cromwell wrote to him too; Penn and his

[39] SP 18/35/145; *FDW* iv. 368, 382–3; Rawl. MS A 227, fos. 70 ff. On Salwey see *The Memoirs of Edmund Ludlow*, ed. C. H. Firth (Oxford, 1894), i. 351, 358; A. Woolrych, *From Commonwealth to Protectorate* (Oxford, 1982), 156, 198. On Thomson: *DNB*; Clarke Papers, iii. 6; Clar. MS 47, fo. 183ᵛ. On Russell: *Clarke Papers*, iii. 7. On Langley: Woolrych, *Commonwealth*, 127. See also Cogar, thesis, 141–2.

[40] C. Hill, *The World Turned Upside Down* (1972), 227 n.; SP 18/35/143, 157; *FDW* iv. 368–9. For Lawson's relation to Vane see *FDW* iv. 45.

colleagues similarly resolved to press on and expressed their readiness to accept the new government.[41] The navy's acquiescence had been rapid but hardly enthusiastic; it had given no positive support whatever to the army's action. The phrasing of the declaration suggests rather a formula carefully devised to paper over the cracks in the interests of national security. The new rulers probably felt sure of Deane, a confidant of Cromwell who was likely to follow him whatever his doubts. Leading Rumpers had given out that they had a great friend in Monck, but Cromwell held talks with him a few days before the coup and found he felt no particular commitment to the Parliament; they could be sure of him too. But the two Generals had only recently joined the fleet and their influence over the other officers was uncertain. Monck indeed seems to have aroused some resentment as a landsman foisted upon them by the army; 'The whole navy displays a mutinous spirit and a disinclination to obey Colonel Monck,' the Venetian secretary had reported a few weeks earlier.[42] The studiously neutral declaration from the fleet was probably the most that could be secured. There were no public expressions of approval even by the most radical officers, as had followed Pride's Purge. When an army pamphleteer urged the navy to welcome the coup and help the soldiers in choosing a new government he found no response whatever.[43]

General Blake did not sign the declaration of 22 April, for when the Rump fell he was ashore, sick. Royalist agents reported that he was 'highly discontented', being 'much for the Parliament', and had been turned out of office; on 6 May one wrote that he was still 'not yet cured, nor satisfied'.[44] It is quite likely that Blake's initial reaction was dismay; he was a loyal Parliamentarian, and did not share his partners' intimacy with the army Grandees. But there is no firm evidence to corroborate the rumours, and if he had doubts he quickly silenced them. Whether or not he ever spoke the words attributed to him by his first biographer, ' 'Tis not for us to mind state affairs, but to keep foreigners from fooling us,' they appear to represent the conclusion he reached. His wounds and sickness

---

[41] *A Declaration of the Generals at Sea* (1653), BL 669 f 16 (92); *FDW* iv. 369; *Mercurius Politicus*, 28 Apr.–5 May 1653.

[42] T. Gumble, *The Life of General Monck* (1671), 73; *CSPV 1653–4*, 16. Deane and Monck had been named Generals on 26 Nov. 1652: *CJ* vii. 222.

[43] J. Spittlehouse, *The Army Vindicated* (1653), 10–12.

[44] Clar. MS 45, fos. 335, 356, 366; Gardiner, *CP* ii. 270 and n.

provided him with a perfect excuse for quitting, had he so wished; instead his arrival at Westminster on 27 April suggests he had already decided to remain in harness. By the second week in May he was busy once more on Admiralty affairs.[45]

There was however a small group, most of them officials, who warmly welcomed the new regime. Some believed it would prosecute the war more effectively.[46] Others welcomed the change for its own sake. The Fifth Monarchists, who had been demanding the fall of the Rump for months, spoke confidently of their 'friends in the fleet'. They had friends in naval administration too, notably the Admiralty Commissioner John Carew and John Poortmans, who had taken over the important post of Secretary to the Generals at Sea. Poortmans was delighted by the coup. 'My heart rejoices within me to hear it,' he declared, adding that God would destroy any person or power trying to keep Christ from his throne.[47] Robert Blackborne, the influential secretary to the Admiralty Commissioners since the end of 1652, was almost as enthusiastic and looked on the Rump's fall as 'the dawning of the day of redemption'. Blackborne seems to have given the first news of the coup to Lawson and probably others, and his firm backing for it may well have helped to settle their doubts.[48]

Though the summer of 1653 was the crucial phase of the war there were many in the fleet eagerly following political developments ashore. Poortmans, serving with the Generals in the *Resolution*, was delighted to receive a list of those nominated to the new representative. He was very pleased with an account of the opening of Barebone's Parliament, as it became known, from 'his assured brother in the faith' Richard Creed, an Admiralty clerk and another of the godly fraternity; he wrote in reply that he rejoiced 'to hear of such a heavenly frame among them, I hope their fruits will be answerable'. As the fleet lay off the Texel in July he reported that 'All that fear the Lord here are much in expectation what will be done by the new representatives, they have our prayers for them

---

[45] Clarendon, *History*, v. 288; J. Oldmixon, *The History and Life of Robert Blake, Esq.* (1740), 72; *A Perfect Diurnall*, 25 Apr.–2 May, 16–23 May 1653; Blake, *Letters*, 212; Clar. MS 45, fos. 382, 401; *FDW* v. 67–8.

[46] *CSPV 1653–4*, 75.

[47] *Severall Proceedings*, 10–17 Feb. 1653; SP 18/35/142, 156. The previous holder of the post, Drue Sparrow (Deane's brother-in-law), had been killed at Portland.

[48] SP 18/35/156–7.

that God will direct them for to do that which may be most for his glory and the good of the Commonwealth, and that they may not tread in the steps of those who have gone before them.' He thanked Blackborne for the news he had sent, 'both in print and otherwise', but lamented that it 'hardly satisfies our gaping expectations at present'.[49] There is no evidence on how the fleet responded to the brief and turbulent history of Barebone's Parliament, though in September a writer in the *Amity* could still interpret the sinking of a Dutch warship as proof of divine support. The surviving correspondence of the Generals reveals nothing of their views, and though Blake and Monck eventually took their seats in the assembly they played a negligible part in its proceedings.[50]

Early in its career Barebone's Parliament established a new and radical body of Admiralty Commissioners. John Carew and Langley continued in place. They were joined by the Fifth Monarchist Col. Nathaniel Rich, the Baptist (and later Quaker) Dennis Hollister, Lt.-Col. Salmon, Lt.-Col. Kelsey, Governor of Dover Castle, and Major William Burton, a Yarmouth merchant and shipowner; the war had already drawn the last two into naval administration. The assembly also nominated Major-General Desborough, a co-opted member and Cromwell's brother-in-law.[51] The new Commissioners proved energetic, but they were to lose their grip on naval administration even before the fall of Barebone's Parliament. The new Council of State elected on 1 November showed a marked swing away from the radicals, and a similar shift is apparent in the new set of Admiralty Commissioners approved on 3 December. The Fifth Monarchists Carew and Rich were dropped, along with Hollister, Langley, and Salmon; Carew had asked not to be reappointed, probably a sign of growing disillusion with the assembly. Only Burton and Kelsey survived, both having a local influence which was hard to replace, plus Desborough who now became an ex-officio member as a land-based General at Sea. The new recruits included Col. Philip Jones, a prominent Cromwellian soon to be an important figure in the Protectorate, and other moderates such as Col. John Clarke, John Stone, and Edward

[49] *FDW* v. 195-6, 303; SP 18/38/30.
[50] *An Exact and True Relation of the Great and Mighty Engagement* (1653), 1-2; *CJ* vii. 328, 332.
[51] *CJ* vii. 285, 289, 292; *A and O* ii. 708. On the new Commissioners see *BDBR*; Woolrych, *Commonwealth*, 189-90, 420-1 (Hollister), and 196, 412-13 (Burton); B. S. Capp, *The Fifth Monarchy Men* (1972), 260 and *passim* (Rich).

Horseman.[52] The new Commissioners were to display none of their predecessors' ideological fervour in the selection of officers. As officials they proved active, capable, and reliable, but they carried little political weight, and this shortcoming was to have serious consequences in the years to come.

The spirit of the Protectorate thus captured the Admiralty even before it was inaugurated. John Poortmans was quick to see the significance of the change. He did not know the new Commissioners, he told Blackborne, and feared the worst: if they 'be not as full of the holy spirit and wisdom as those excluded, then I may say that our masters have not walked according to the rule in their choices'. If godly men were laid aside, he went on, it was likely that the Lord would withdraw his blessing.[53]

The resignation of the assembly on 12 December did not perturb the new Commissioners—though it interrupted business for a week and they had to apologize to Monck for not answering five of his letters from the fleet. Blake was in Whitehall at the time and sent a bland account to Monck and Penn (appointed a fellow General on 2 December): 'It having pleased the Lord who is the wise-disposer of all things so to order it that the Parliament have this morning dissolved in such a manner as was without any great noise.' Monck asked Thurloe for some official account 'to make use of' among his officers and men, and once the Commissioners were reinstalled they sent Kelsey to explain the circumstances.[54] The assembly's fall seems to have made little impact on the fleet. Some commanders appear to have welcomed the change: four serving in the north-east wrote to the Protector early in January 1654 expressing their pleasure over the new government, and their men's support for it. Blake and Penn too sent professions of loyalty when they received new commissions from him later in the month.[55]

The establishment of the Protectorate did nevertheless arouse

---

[52] *CJ* vii. 362; *A and O* ii. 812. For Jones see Woolrych, *Commonwealth*, 107, 174, 420–1; A. H. Dodd, *Studies in Stuart Wales* (Cardiff, 1952), 149–71; for Clarke see Woolrych, *Commonwealth*, 181–2, 199, 343, 382, 414–15; for Stone see G. Aylmer, *The State's Servants* (1973), 241, 406–7; for Horseman see Woolrych, *Commonwealth*, 175, 385, 420–1.

[53] SP 18/42/13.

[54] Rawl. MS A 461, fos. 28, 29ᵛ (Blake's letter, fo. 28, was in the name of all the Admiralty Commissioners, but bears only his initials); SP 18/62/101; *Articles of High Crimes . . . exhibited against Lt. Col. Kelsey* (1659), 1.

[55] SP 18/78/48 (one of the signatories was James Abelson, one of Lawson's disaffected group in 1656); SP 18/78/170.

some misgivings within the fleet. Poortmans's dissatisfaction grew and he left the navy in the autumn, though his friend Blackborne remained in place, helping to reassure waverers; Capt. John Stokes turned to him for 'satisfaction concerning the grand case of Protectorship', which Blackborne duly supplied.[56] Some officers appear to have suspended judgement. A declaration in the name of the Generals and several commanders addressed the new Protector early in 1654 in a curious blend of flattery, exhortation, and veiled warning. It hailed Cromwell as an instrument of divine providence, bringing peace to a distracted nation, spoke of his 'great affection and yearning bowels after the weal of God's people', and urged him to have a 'special eye of favour unto them, above all others, in regard they are near and dear' to Christ. If he did so, it went on, he would have the blessing of the godly and of God himself; but if not, not, was the unspoken corollary. The document did not appear in print and its status is unclear; it probably did not have the Generals' blessing and was more likely the work of Vice-Admiral Lawson's circle. Lawson described himself as 'dull and indisposed' during the opening weeks of 1654, and he may have been cast down by political developments as well as by his own and his wife's illness. On first reaching a flag-position he had vowed 'to serve the designs of God . . . and the honest interest of England', and he was to become a notable thorn in the Protector's side.[57]

All these political changes took place against the background of the Dutch war, and in the face of a national emergency it was natural for the navy to swallow its doubts: patriotism dictated acquiescence. Yet paradoxically the war itself posed a threat to naval unity, for it proved highly divisive, creating sharp disagreements in the Rump and Barebone's Parliaments, in the army, and among commercial interests and radical sectarian groups. Sir Henry Vane, the leading figure in naval administration at its outbreak, was himself a prominent critic.[58] Would these divisions surface in the

---

[56] *CSPD 1653–4*, 412; *CSPD 1654*, 319; SP 18/79/54.

[57] 'A Declaration with the humble Addresses of the Generals and several commanders', BL Add. MS 9300, fo. 73ʳ⁻ᵛ (no signatories are given). For printed versions see *Certain Passages*, 27 Jan.–3 Feb. 1654, *The Perfect Diurnall*, 30 Jan.–6 Feb.; *The Weekly Intelligencer*, 31 Jan–8 Feb.; *A Perfect Account*, 1–8 Feb. For Lawson's vow see SP 18/48/57; for his illness: SP 18/79/191.

[58] B. Worden, *The Rump Parliament* (Cambridge, 1974), 299–306, 313–14, 330–1; Woolrych, *Commonwealth*, 277–88, 322–5; Rowe, *Vane*, 144–8.

navy too? Might the seamen challenge the policy of going to war against fellow Protestants?

On the whole the navy supported the war. Many officers, as we have seen, had long resented Dutch behaviour at sea, and it was friction at sea that nudged the two governments towards war before either had determined a clear policy. The numerous clashes over the flag and over rights of search generated a sense of justified grievance on both sides, which at times took on an ideological hue. A scuffle in the Channel in March 1652, for example, began with a Dutch skipper shouting that 'though they never cut off a king's head, they were the ancientest states'; the English commander, less of a scholar, retorted, 'I'll have some of *your* heads before I leave you,' as indeed he did.[59] Most officers were more than willing to assert England's claims. Anthony Young regarded it as deliberate provocation when a Dutch warship refused to strike sail to him, and he opened fire; 'I do believe I gave him his bellyful of it,' he reported with evident satisfaction.[60] Blake's momentous encounter with Tromp a few days later reveals a similar sense of righteous indignation. Tromp, annoyed over recent incidents, appears to have had no intention of striking sail as custom demanded, and Blake's warning shots provoked a pitched battle. Blake had no doubt that if war broke out 'the righteous God' would punish the Dutch, 'they being the first in the breach, and seeking an occasion to quarrel'. Tromp's specious claim a few days later that his intentions had been peaceful merely infuriated Blake further. 'I do not think fit to return any other answer,' he replied, 'but that I presume you will find the Parliament sensible of these great injuries and of the loss of the innocent blood of their countrymen.'[61] Rear-Admiral Bourne, whose squadron was also involved in the action, noted that 'we had a strong God on our side who would judge between the nations' and punish the Dutch for breaking the peace.[62]

[59] *Bloudy Newes from Holland* ([17 Mar.] 1652), 3–5; *French Occurrences,* 17–24 May 1652 (italics added). Another officer remarked later that the Dutch 'call themselves the Elder States, but I am sure the Commonwealth of England prove the better Gentlemen': *The Weekly Intelligencer,* 12–19 Oct. 1652.

[60] *FDW* i. 178–83.

[61] *FDW* i. 194–5, 216–18; T. W. Fulton, *The Sovereignty of the Sea* (1911), 772, gives the original text of Blake's letter to Tromp. The version printed in *FDW* i. 257–8 and Blake, *Letters,* 162–3, has been translated back from a Dutch translation. For a discussion of the incident see *FDW* i. 170–6.

[62] *FDW* i. 252 n., 256.

From the start Blake was thus, in Gardiner's phrase, 'the incarnation of the war-spirit'.[63] He claimed the fleet as a whole shared his view, and it is not surprising that once fighting began most of the officers rallied against an enemy they believed to have deliberately provoked war.[64] When the Rump fell rumours circulated in London that the fleet was determined to have 'another bout' with the Dutch, whether or not the new government wanted to continue the struggle.[65] Officers repeatedly expressed their satisfaction at bringing low 'the pride and arrogance of that insulting enemy'. One described the battle off Portland as divine retribution for the 'haughty conceits' of the Dutch: 'They might have gone from us, but their pride brought them down to us; they thought we durst not stay them one broadside . . . thus are men caught in the devices and imaginations of their own hearts.'[66] Blake's fierce patriotism was widely shared. When Rear-Admiral Packe's leg was shattered in battle, for example, he was reported as saying 'that he hopes God will strengthen him to venture his other leg for his country against the Dutch'.[67]

Among religious radicals ashore there was a current of thought which saw the war as an apocalyptic crusade rather than a merely patriotic struggle. Such a feeling was expressed shortly after Portland by Major-General Harrison, soon to be a prominent member of Barebone's Parliament and already the hero of the Fifth Monarchy firebrands. Should not the godly, he demanded, 'run after Christ to sea whereon he hath begun to set his right foot?'[68] Some leading officers in the fleet held similar views. Even the Generals described their victories as furthering God's cause; Blake, Deane, and Monck wrote to the Speaker after the victory at Portland hoping it would promote 'the preservation and interest of God's people'. Vice-Admiral Penn too believed the war was for 'the good of God's people'.[69] Richard Lyons, flag-captain to the Generals at the Gabbard, believed the victory showed how God 'will

---

[63] Gardiner, *CP* ii. 202; Blake, *Letters*, 165; *FDW* iii. 93.

[64] *FDW* i. 307–8.

[65] Clar. MS 45, fo. 365ʳ⁻ᵛ.

[66] *FDW* ii. 268, iv. 171–2, v. 373, vi. 215.

[67] *FDW* ii. 121. In the event Packe died of his wounds.

[68] Quoted by Worden, *Rump*, 304; see n. 56 above and Capp, *Fifth Monarchy*, 152–4.

[69] *FDW* iv. 169. They also hoped it would advance 'those rights and liberties which God and nature hath afforded us'; were they trying to pressurize the Rump? For Penn see *FDW* ii. 242.

make a difference henceforward 'twixt Israel and Egyptians'.[70] John Lawson, who had been intending to retire from the navy, described how the outbreak of the war changed his plans: 'I could not satisfy my conscience to leave at this time,' he wrote, 'being very well satisfied that this service is in order to the design of God in the exaltation of Jesus Christ, and therefore with much cheerfulness shall spend myself in this cause where the glory of God and the good of his people is so much concerned.[71] Capt. Edmund Thompson of Yarmouth went still further, selling his own ship to serve in the navy 'for the cause of God and the good of this nation'. He described the victory off the Texel in the language of religious rhapsody: 'It was the day of the Lord and we will rejoice in it, and tell it to our children and let them tell it to generations to come, so that the goodness of the Lord may never be forgotten by us nor them'; the English 'though sinful men [were] yet instruments in the hands of God to carrying on his own work'.[72]

The same spirit is evident within the Admiralty. The Commissioners thanked God for his mercy at Portland and exulted after the Texel that 'the harvest grows ripe'.[73] Nehemiah Bourne, who became a Navy Commissioner at the close of 1652, expected God to bear 'witness against those who have lifted up themselves against him and his interest', and the navy agent at Plymouth, Henry Hatsell, took a similar view.[74] So did Robert Blackborne, describing the war as 'the great work of God now in the wheel'; his friend John Poortmans wanted to force the Dutch to accept a peace guaranteeing 'the exaltation of our Lord Christ, who must now be king though the heathen rage'. 'The time of Antichrist's glory is now expired,' he explained, 'and as he hath had a time to rise and grow, so now must the people of the Lord have their time, whose kingdom shall never fail.'[75]

Yet support for the Dutch war was never universal. Some officers had been unsure of its justification at the very outset. Penn wrote to Cromwell in June 1652, 'I find the most, and indeed those that are best principled and most conscientious of our commanders do

---

[70] *The Moderate Publisher*, 3–10 June 1653. This part of the letter is not given in Penn, *Memorials*, i. 496–8, or *FDW* v. 82–5.
[71] *FDW* iv. 46.
[72] SP 18/103/1; *FDW* v. 352–3; cf. *FDW* ii. 272.
[73] Rawl. MS A 227, fos. 40ᵛ–41, 100, 122.
[74] *FDW* v. 77, vi. 186 (Bourne); *FDW* iv. 103.
[75] *FDW* iv. 230, v. 106–7 (see also ibid., v. 51, 89–90, 196, 304).

much desire some information of the justness of our quarrel with the Hollander, which they do not in the least doubt of; yet I find them somewhat troubled and dejected for their ignorance in that point.'[76] It is clear that they resented being treated as mere mercenaries, expected to turn their guns against any target without question or explanation. A few weeks later, in September, Sir George Ayscue left his command and came up to London, taking no further part in the war. As flag-officer commanding in the Channel his action caused a considerable stir. His motives remain obscure. He claimed to be in poor health, but contemporaries were probably right to see this plea as a mere pretext. He may simply have wished to return to civilian life, for on returning from Barbados he had found his estate in Surrey badly damaged by projectors trying to make the River Wey navigable. Ayscue also had grounds for thinking his services poorly rewarded; he had been ordered against the Dutch without being paid for his Barbados voyage, possibly because some Rumpers regarded the terms he had offered as too generous. Only in November, after his resignation, did the Rump make an order for his arrears, voting the following month to grant him £500 a year and lands worth £300 a year in Ireland as compensation for his losses over the Wey navigation. Cromwell remarked later that 'his services have been considerable for the state; and I doubt he hath not been answered with suitable respect'.[77] But it is quite possible too that Ayscue had doubts about the justice of the war. The Independent minister Hugh Peter sent him a letter shortly before his resignation, urging him not to fight against fellow Protestants, and though Ayscue promptly reported this approach it may be significant that Peter had chosen him for his appeal. Certainly Ayscue's letters during the war show none of the religious fervour or patriotic zeal displayed by many others.[78] Whatever his motives, a doubt hung over his name for the rest of the decade.

Neither Ayscue nor any other officer openly criticized the war and we have only tantalising hints that doubts existed. One

[76] J. Nickolls (ed.), *Original Letters and Papers of State* (1743), 87.

[77] *FDW* ii. 265 and n.–266 n.; *CSPV 1647–52*, 283; *CSPV 1653–4*, 16; *CJ* vii. 160, 236; Bodl. Dep. MS C 159, fos. 124–6; Rawl. MS A 226, fo. 237; P. Le Fevre, 'Sir George Ayscue, Commonwealth and Restoration Admiral', *MM* lxviii (1982), 196; Cromwell, *Writings*, iii. 89.

[78] Stearns, *Strenuous Puritan*, 389; Gardiner, *CP* ii. 188, 194; *FDW* ii. 266 n. According to one account Peter told Ayscue he had already won over Blake; if he made any such claim it was highly misleading: Clarke MS 1/12, fo. 17'.

wonders how the captains visiting the prophetess Anna Trapnel in November 1652 reacted as they listened to her gruesome vision of 'ships burning, bones and flesh sticking upon the sides of the ships, the sails battered, and the masts broken'.[79] When the Rump appointed a day of thanksgiving for the victory at Portland a royalist news-writer reported that 'several of our captains which were in the fight went out of town to avoid going to the church'.[80] Some officers were certainly eager for peace by the summer of 1653. One ended his description of the Gabbard with a fervent plea for the war to end: 'O what is more wished or would be more welcome than peace? What is better or sweeter than peace? What is more splendid and beautiful than peace?' Capt. Joseph Cubitt's account of the Texel ended similarly: 'I pray God make this mercy a further blessing unto us in the procuring a good peace betwixt us both, who have been so long friends formerly and so useful one to the other, and that our nation be not lifted up with successes lest we be humbled by them: [and . . .] that brotherly love may continue.'[81]

There were negotiations for peace during the autumn and winter of 1653–4, but as they dragged on with little sign of progress the navy was obliged to press ahead with preparations for another campaign. There was much discussion over what was likely to happen.[82] Officers at sea, waiting hungrily for newspapers and news of any kind, were irritated at how little information they received. John Poortmans wrote on 1 April 1654 that 'though the Generals [Blake and Penn] are not much in words, yet they think it somewhat strange that there should be so little intercourse'. 'Several commanders in the fleet,' he added, 'are much unsatisfied, that they are kept in so much ignorance, and that they are looked upon as mercenaries, which they do disown.'[83] At the end of the war, as at its outset, the more principled officers resented being taken for granted. The problem was to recur.

Blake and Penn were among those hoping for peace, and there was probably widespread relief when it was concluded.[84] There were few expressions of satisfaction, though, in the weeks that

---

[79] A. Trapnel, *The Cry of a Stone* (1654), 7. She was, however, predicting an English victory!

[80] *FDW* iv. 352–3.

[81] *A Declaration of the Further Proceedings of the English Fleet* (1653), 5; *FDW* v. 369.

[82] SP 46/115, fo. 264; SP 18/78/202.

[83] SP 18/69/1; cf. SP 18/78/189.

[84] Blake, *Letters*, 252, 263.

followed. Some officers no doubt felt their massive victories had been wasted. General Monck, who had already left to take up his new post as Commander-in-Chief in Scotland, was said to have regarded the settlement 'as a thing infamous and dishonourable to the nation', believing that Cromwell had thrown away the fruits of victory when the Dutch were on the point of collapse.[85] Those who had seen the war as a crusade must have been dismayed by Cromwell's Laodicean peace, and their disillusion probably contributed to the undercurrents of discontent visible in the navy throughout the Protectorate.

Though the navy was at the very centre of Cromwell's grandiose international designs as Protector, it always remained primarily a weapon of party. The names given to new warships continued to commemorate parliamentary triumphs. The *Marston Moor, Langport, Basing,* and others recalled the First Civil War, the *Colchester, Preston,* and *Fagons* the Second; the *Tredagh* and *Wexford* were reminders of Cromwell's victories in Ireland, and the *Dunbar* and *Worcester* glorified his final successes on the mainland. The *Worcester* was at first known as the *Protector,* and the greatest ship of the period, the *Naseby,* bore an effigy of Cromwell on horseback. The last major warship launched in his lifetime, the *Richard,* was named after his son and successor. As their names indicate, the ships were glorifying Cromwell as much as the parliamentary cause; it is striking too that they celebrated military rather than naval triumphs. Only the *Portland* echoed the victories of the Dutch war, and there were none honouring Blake's achievements at Porto Farina or Santa Cruz. The subordination of the navy in an essentially military regime was manifest.[86]

Though the fleet had submitted peacefully to the Protectorate its commitment was uncertain. At the end of the Dutch war many officers returned to private life; no doubt most simply wished to resume their normal peacetime activities, but others may have left— or been laid aside—for political reasons. It was alleged later that Capt. John Best, a protégé of Lawson, had withdrawn in 1654 out of dislike for the new regime and returned later only because his

[85] T. Skinner, *The Life of General Monck* (1723), 59; Gumble, *Monck,* 74; M. Ashley, *General Monck* (1977), 109.
[86] R. C. Anderson, *Lists of Men-of-War, 1650–1700: Part 1, English Ships, 1649–1702* (2nd edn., no date), 17–20; NMM CAD/D/3.

business interests had failed. Owen Cox, a radical officer with many years' service, also left the navy at this point and when he too fell into poverty and begged to return his request was ignored. A former naval lieutenant was arrested in 1655 after denouncing Cromwell for betraying the parliamentary cause.[87] More serious from the government's point of view was the possibility that other officers harbouring similar views might have clung on to their posts. Lt. Nathaniel Rockwell, a former officer under Harrison, was questioned in January 1654 after boasting of his part in the army's revolt in 1647 and spreading damaging stories about Cromwell, Lambert, and Monck. Another such case came to light in May. The Baptist chaplain of the *Gainsborough*, Samuel Bradley, returned from a visit to London and began to inveigh against the new regime, sounding, according to the clerk of the cheque, like a missionary sent by the Fifth Monarchists. 'Lord, what is become of the praying officers in the army?' Bradley demanded, within earshot of the ship's senior officers. 'The world has stopped their mouths; the world had choked them. They pretended they were pulling down Babylon, but behold they are setting it up.' The clerk informed the Admiralty and a court martial subsequently dismissed the chaplain. But a few weeks later the clerk was begging for protection from his captain, Robert Taylor, now victimizing him for Bradley's dismissal. Taylor was not employed again.[88]

More serious trouble appeared in the early autumn, at the time of the first Protectorate Parliament. The former Leveller John Wildman had drawn up a petition denouncing the new regime as a tyranny and calling for a free parliament to restore liberty and justice. He was hoping to win support in the army and encourage Cromwell's opponents in the new assembly, and though the government suppressed the petition when only three colonels had signed, a copy soon appeared in print. Wildman also set out to exploit his links with the navy. He owed his election as MP for Scarborough in part to the backing of Vice-Admiral Lawson, a native of the town and long-standing member of its council. Lawson was present at a meeting between Wildman and the three colonels in September and tried to fan unrest in the navy, hoping to

[87] SP 18/158/105; NMM ADL/Z/8; SP 18/145/105; SP 25 I 92, fo. 401; *CSPD 1655*, 154.
[88] Rockwell: SP 46/97/77, A–B; A. Woolrych, *Soldiers and Statesmen* (Oxford, 1987), 281 n., 282 n. Bradley and Taylor: SP 18/71/80; SP 18/84/127.

link it with the opposition ashore.[89] He was well placed for such a venture, commanding the Channel forces with little supervision from the Generals: Blake was at Plymouth from the end of August and sailed for the Straits early in October, while Penn was ashore busy with preparations for the Western Design. There were genuine grievances in the navy which Lawson might hope to exploit. In August Blake's officers had demanded the prize-money due to them from the Dutch war before they left for foreign service, threatening to appeal to the Protector himself if they did not receive immediate satisfaction.[90] Seamen in Penn's fleet at Spithead drew up a more alarming petition in October, their complaints over conditions of service raising broader constitutional issues. It was 'thralldom and bondage', they declared, for seamen to be pressed into the navy by force; they called on Parliament to stand up for the liberties of free-born Englishmen and cited army declarations from the 1640s to support their case. The appeal to Parliament as champions of freedom was perhaps intended to strengthen the hands of Cromwell's opponents in the House, and could certainly be used to that end. On 17 October Lawson held a council of war at Spithead (in Penn's absence) and persuaded his colleagues to approve the seamen's right to petition and to endorse their demands. The text of the petition and details of the council's discussion appeared widely in the press. The seamen's action was a threat to the Western Design, and their stand on pressing could jeopardize the Protector's entire naval strategy. Penn and Desborough hastened to Portsmouth to investigate, and the Admiralty Commissioner Thomas Kelsey came down to help. Though they managed to quieten the seamen by a lavish distribution of money, the Venetian envoy reported that the fleet 'certainly prefers Parliament to the Protector' and thought the men might refuse to sail until their grievances were met in full.[91] In the event the crisis passed and Penn was able to leave for the Caribbean at the end of December.

[89] Gardiner, *CP* iii. 211–14; M. Ashley, *John Wildman, Plotter and Postmaster* (1947), 86–8; B. Taft, 'The Humble Petition of Several Colonels of the Army: Causes, Character, and Results of Military Opposition to Cromwell's Protectorate', *Huntington Library Quarterly*, xlii (1978–9), 20, 25.

[90] BL Add. MS 18986, fo. 176; Add. MS 22546, fo. 185.

[91] Gardiner, *CP* iii. 214–17; *To His Highness the Lord Protector: the Humble Petition of the Sea-Men* ([4 Nov.] 1654), BL 669 f 19 (33); *Swiftsure. At a Council of War held aboard, the 17 of October, 1654*, BL 669 f 19 (32); SP 18/89/92; SP 18/90/6; *CSPV 1653–4*, 278–9, 281. Details of the petition and the council of war were widely reported: *The Weekly Post*, 31 Oct.–7 Nov.; *The Faithful Scout*, 3–10 Nov.; *A Perfect Account*, 1–8 Nov.; *The Weekly Intelligencer*, 7–14 Nov.

Dissent ashore had not ended with the arrest of the three colonels. The ex-Leveller Edward Sexby toured the country with copies of Wildman's petition, seeking further support among army and civilian republicans. The conspirators also made contact with Monck's army in Scotland and it was there that they found most response. Papers circulated condemning the Protectorate as a new bondage and calling for the restoration of England's lost liberty. A plan gradually took shape for the soldiers to seize Monck, march into England with the sympathetic Major-General Robert Overton at their head, and re-establish parliamentary rule. Monck got wind of the plot, however; Overton was arrested and shipped off to the Tower, and the conspiracy collapsed.[92] How far the navy was involved in all this is uncertain. Lawson had met Sexby at Deal and had further meetings with him and Wildman in London, and they appear to have cherished hopes of securing a port such as Hull. An agent named Dallington was landed from the *Constant Warwick* near Harwich to 'find how the country stood', and gave assurances that the fleet was fully behind the republican petition. Lawson was later said to have promised that his squadron would support the Scottish army if it captured Monck and crossed into England.[93] The collapse of the Scottish conspiracy inevitably shattered plans for agitation in the south: Wildman and Dallington were soon arrested, and Sexby fled abroad. Lawson was questioned but no firm evidence was found against him and, remarkably, he retained his sensitive command in the Channel. His reprieve was a tribute to his popularity among the seamen, now reinforced by his support for their petition, and it suggests that the government was not altogether sure of its hold over them.[94]

The rumblings in Lawson's squadron found echoes in the fleets serving overseas. Blake was still at Plymouth when Parliament met, and he arranged for his fleet to observe the national day of prayer on 13 September 1654, to 'cast in our mite into the treasury of prayer'. Though he appears to have done his best to instil respect for the new regime subversive ideas circulated among some of his officers. Lt. Samford of the *Entrance* boasted that three-quarters of the fleet opposed the Protectorate and would turn their guns against

[92] Gardiner, *CP* iii. 226–32; Ashley, *Wildman*, 88–94; Rawl. MS A 34, pp. 49–52.
[93] *Thurloe*, iii. 35, 146–8, 185, vi. 829–30.
[94] Gardiner, *CR* iii. 216–17. Poortmans may have been linked with the unrest; a former colleague referred to his 'sad fall': *CSPD 1654*, 319; SP 18/106/119.

Cromwell, defying Blake, if the opportunity arose. Samford, allegedly a former cavalier, was described as an Anabaptist preacher, and his captain, Anthony Tucker, was said to hold similar views. How far Samford's claims rested on fact is impossible to establish, though Lawson certainly had friends among Blake's commanders. In the event the *Entrance* was paid off, and neither Samford nor Tucker was employed again.[95] Blake's own loyalty is not in doubt. When news reached him of the disputes between Cromwell and the Parliament he sided with the Protector, perhaps understandably in the light of Parliament's bid to reduce the strength of the armed forces. He welcomed its dissolution in January 1655. 'I cannot but wonder', he wrote, 'that there should yet remain so strong a spirit of prejudice and animosity in the minds of men, who profess themselves most affectionate patriots, as to postpone the necessary ways and means for preservation of the Commonwealth, especially in such a time of concurrence of the mischievous plots and designs both of old and new enemies.'[96]

Penn's expedition to the West Indies encountered more serious difficulties. An informant wrote from Barbados that the fleet contained many 'Anabaptists' who 'justify Admiral Lawson's late actings, that he was questioned for'. Richard Newbery of the *Portland*, one of the most senior captains, was busy spreading disaffection among the soldiers and sailors. Newbery was a militant Anabaptist, he added, had seditious papers from his church in England in his possession, and might be engaged in some subversive design.[97] A more immediate problem was the contempt the sailors showed for the army, especially after its humiliation at Hispaniola. Rear-Admiral Dakins taunted the soldiers with their earlier bravado, inviting the Spaniards to 'come and cut off these army rogues, that we may no more be troubled with them', and his lieutenant wished the soldiers overboard and gone. Many officers talked of sailing away and leaving the army to its fate. The military commanders feared they might even carry out such a plan, and insisted on the sea-regiment being the last to re-embark as a guarantee against the navy's desertion. The attacks originated in interservice rivalry but some also revealed hostility to the regime at

---

[95] Blake, *Letters*, 282–3; SP 18/76/41. (Among Blake's captains were Hill and Abelson, for whom see nn. 114–16, below.)

[96] Blake, *Letters*, 291.

[97] *Thurloe*, iii. 157–8.

home. An army correspondent complained that the Anabaptists were abusing both the army and 'the power we act under'.[98] Even Penn blamed the fiasco on 'sin at home in England, as well as here'.[99] When he sailed for home the militant Newbery chose to go with him, although his ship had been assigned to the squadron remaining behind, and three other commanders—Dakins, Crispin, and Storey—followed suit. Dakins and Crispin never served under Cromwell again, and both were soon to become involved in Lawson's political scheming.[100]

Cromwell's establishment as Protector and his peace with the Dutch had dealt a severe blow to royalist hopes. Royalist privateers were no longer able to operate out of Dutch harbours, and several made their own peace and returned home.[101] Some cavaliers decided that sabotage was now the only way to undermine the Commonwealth's power at sea. A sailor in the *Elizabeth* boasted in May 1654 that five hundred royalists had enlisted in the navy with the aim of blowing up its ships, and declared roundly that he hoped to see Cromwell's throat cut and '10,000 more of Grandees' meet the same fate. There was no action, though, to match these bold words. The one banal success of cavalier saboteurs was to creep into the dockyard at Woolwich and hack off the nose of Cromwell's effigy on the prow of the *Naseby*.[102]

In the winter of 1654–5 cavalier plotters laid plans for a series of risings designed to topple the Protectorate.[103] They were apparently hoping to exploit unrest in the navy too, and one claimed that naval officers had offered to seize Portsmouth or the Isle of Wight if the cavaliers appeared in arms in those parts. The royalists were well aware of Lawson's discontent too, and Charles wrote to him

---

[98] *Thurloe*, iii. 507; *The Narrative of General Venables*, ed. C. H. Firth (Camden Soc., 1900), 32, 35.

[99] Venables, *Narrative*, 160, 161; Penn, *Memorials*, ii. 94. Penn himself was not attacking the government, and was indeed worried that the fiasco would undermine its authority. His immediate targets were presumably Desborough and the other planners.

[100] Penn, *Memorials*, ii. 108.

[101] *CSPD 1655*, 49, 58, 68; *CSPD 1658–9*, 74. The notorious Richard Beach later claimed he had been offered senior commands under Blake: *CSPD 1666–7*, 395. More likely there were contacts over a pardon.

[102] SP 18/73/18; B. Whitelocke, *A Journal of the Swedish Embassy* (1772), ii. 343–4; *The Faithfull Scout*, 12–19 Jan. 1655.

[103] Gardiner, *CP* iii. 270–95; D. Underdown, *Royalist Conspiracy in England, 1649–1660* (New Haven, 1960), ch. 7; A. Woolrych, *Penruddock's Rising* (1955).

secretly in February 1655 promising a pardon and reward if he changed sides.[104] All the cavalier schemes failed dismally, however. On land only Penruddock's rising in Wiltshire materialized, and it was quickly suppressed. The royalists were moreover wrong to assume that dislike of Cromwell within the fleet implied any wish to serve the Stuarts. Lawson, commanding in the Downs, warned all ships to look out for cavaliers, 'wicked and unreasonable men whose very mercies are cruelties'. God might use them as a rod to punish his sinful people, he reflected, but once 'the dross is scoured off' they would be cast aside, and he saw Penruddock's defeat as 'another signal testimony of God's displeasure against that wicked interest'.[105] Capt. Nicholas Heaton felt much the same, though he was wryly amused to hear they had seized two judges at Salisbury; the lawyers 'that heretofore played their game on all sides,' he remarked, 'begin to bear their part in the suffering; the Lord . . . can catch the wise in their own craftiness'.[106] Senior naval officers at Portsmouth set out boats each night to forestall any attempt by the 'foolish mad men', as John Bourne described them. Others spoke in similar terms of the cavaliers' 'hellish inventions'. One officer ridiculed poor, misguided souls who could still hunger for 'an old thing, called a king'. An officer in Lawson's flagship was confident that the ordinary seamen too condemned the cavaliers. 'I verily believe that most of our mariners would be very glad to fight them, were there any at sea,' he wrote, 'being sensible of their having caused the shedding of so much blood in the late war.'[107]

Despite their failure in 1655 the royalists did not abandon their designs on the navy; indeed the fiasco was proof that risings were futile without military support from abroad, and it was impossible to transport soldiers to England without securing at least the acquiescence of the fleet. Secretary Nicholas clung to a fanciful hope that part of Blake's force would declare for the king on its way back from the Straits, and claimed that Blake himself was afraid to set foot in England lest he be sent to the Tower like Penn.[108] Better-informed royalists turned to the possibility of exploiting republican

---

[104] *CSP* iii. 265; Clar. MS 49, fo. 347. The offer over Portsmouth may be the origin of Clarendon's improbable story that Penn had made overtures to the king before sailing for the Caribbean: Clarendon, *History*, v. 347, vi. 5; Gardiner, *CP* iii. 216 n.

[105] SP 18/95/28, 88.

[106] SP 18/97/62.

[107] SP 18/95/19, 33, 48, 49, 51, 64; SP 18/96/9; SP 18/106/48.

[108] *CSPD 1655*, 365, 388.

dissent in the fleet. Sexby had escaped to the continent when the republican conspiracy collapsed, and was now convinced that the enemies of the Protectorate must pool their resources. He placed this proposal before royalist advisers in the early summer of 1655, promising that conspirators in England could organize a rising, seize a port, and hold it till troops arrived from the continent. As a sweetener Sexby said he would be willing to see the king restored, provided he was willing to rule with annual parliaments as laid down in the Levellers' *Agreement of the People*. He claimed to have support from the republicans, sections of the army, 'a great part of the navy', and some seaports, and showed letters from Lawson, Wildman, and others as evidence, hinting that Lawson might even bring ships over to Dunkirk and place them at Charles's disposal. If Lawson was really prepared to do this he had shifted his position very dramatically. This is just possible, for he was later described as totally under the influence of Sexby and Wildman. Sexby may have told him they would merely use the royalists to restore a republic, or he may have argued that a democratic monarchy would be preferable to Cromwell's military tyranny. But it sounds improbable. It is far more likely that Sexby concealed his plans for royalist and Spanish support; according to a royalist negotiator he refused even to mention his dealings with the king to his republican friends. One of his servants testified later that the naval conspirators had simply aimed 'to make a disturbance in England' coinciding with risings ashore, which they presumably believed to be a purely republican venture. Cromwell himself believed the republican dissidents in 1655–6 were unaware of the web Sexby was trying to weave abroad.[109] Charles and his advisers were very interested in using Sexby but they preferred not to commit themselves, and in any case they had neither money nor soldiers to offer him. They urged him to press forward on his own account, and he therefore moved on to Spain to seek the backing of Philip IV. The Spaniards toyed with a variety of bizarre schemes; if Charles became a Catholic, some claimed, the pope himself would fund Sexby and all Cromwell's opponents—including the Fifth Monarchy Men! The king was far more cautious, promising only that money would be made available once a rising was under way in England.[110]

[109] Gardiner, *CP* iv. 223–5; Ashley, *Wildman*, 95–8; *CSP* iii. 272–3, 277, 286, 315–17, 331; *CCSP* iii. 40, 51; *Thurloe*, vi. 831–3; Cromwell, *Writings*, iv. 268.
[110] Gardiner, *CP* iv. 225–6; *CCSP* iii. 92; *CSP* iii. 281.

Lawson was commanding in the Channel while these talks were in progress. The government had some idea of his disaffection but was also uncomfortably aware of his popularity among the seamen. These two considerations explain why late in January 1656 he was appointed vice-admiral of the fleet preparing against Spain: he would be safely removed from his sensitive post without being able to pose as a martyr.[111] Blake was to lead the expedition, sharing the command with Edward Mountagu, a much younger man without naval experience who was now appointed a General at Sea. This move aroused much speculation. To some extent operational needs explain it: Cromwell hoped there would be attacks on the Spanish mainland and Blake was too old and sick to lead them in person. But political considerations were important too, for Cromwell wanted someone with more political subtlety than Blake to watch over Lawson and check his influence. Mountagu's appointment solved a further worry, for should Blake die during the course of the expedition—as he did—Lawson could obviously not be allowed to take over the supreme command. Ludlow's claim, however—that Mountagu was intended to spy on his partner—is absurd.[112]

Trouble broke out even before the fleet left England. On 11 February 1656, while it was still preparing at Portsmouth, Lawson suddenly resigned his command, giving out that he would not go to sea without knowing the object of the expedition. This was plausible: we have seen earlier resentment in the navy at being treated as a mercenary force. It is likely though that his resignation was also linked with the thwarting of the plans he was laying with Sexby. Sailing with Blake he would have no independent command, and there was little time to work on the other officers before the fleet sailed; an informant later reported him as lamenting that 'the ships were not come up according to expectation'. Lawson was not arrested and received his pay in full. He was good at covering his tracks and the government had no wish to turn him into a martyr.[113]

Blake and Mountagu were still in the Downs when Lawson resigned, and only when they reached Portsmouth about 29 February did they learn that he still had friends in the fleet who were equally dissatisfied. Capt. Lyons of the *Taunton* resigned on 1 March and William Hill of the *Speaker* said he intended to follow

[111] *CSPD 1655–6*, 138, 141; Powell, *Blake*, 275.
[112] *CSPD 1656–7*, 17; Ludlow, *Memoirs*, ii. 37; above, ch. 4.
[113] *Thurloe*, vi. 833; Gardiner, *CP* iv. 230–1 and n.; HMC 4, *5th Report*, 149.

suit. They were both arrested, and Desborough and Commissioner Kelsey hastened down to Portsmouth to assist the investigations. Capt. James Abelson of the *Mermaid* also resigned, on 7 March, having been questioned earlier as another of Lawson's circle, and a day or two later the Generals sacked the *Resolution*'s lieutenant for speaking in defence of Lawson. Thurloe hoped the removal of these ringleaders would cow any others who might harbour discontents.[114]

Under questioning the dissidents explained their conduct in a variety of ways, stressing personal problems and professional grievances. Hill said that his health could not stand a hot climate and that his wife opposed his going; Abelson too claimed his wife 'could not bear his absence upon so long a voyage'. Lyons and Hill both said they were dissatisfied with the state's provision for dependants, especially for mariners who died in service. Lyons said Lawson had told him he would be justified in laying down his commission at any time on these grounds. These concerns were probably genuine, and Abelson's wife was known to be seriously ill.[115] But the Generals, probing further, soon uncovered political discontents too. Lyons said he was 'not satisfied in the design we were about; neither against whom he should go, nor where'. Hill was more explicit. He would be willing to fight the Spaniards if they were threatening England, he explained, but he would not fight them in the south or in the Caribbean when the English were unjustified aggressors. Mountagu asked if he had read the government's formal apologia, 'which he said he had very often with consideration, yet thereby found no satisfaction'. Hill said further that he had served with Blake in the expedition of 1654–5 and had deeply resented Cromwell's order for it to seize the Plate fleet. It is clear that at least some officers refused to accept the Protector as the sole arbiter of national interests and true patriotism. Mountagu suspected there was dissatisfaction of a still deeper kind, challenging Hill to admit that 'dislike of the authorities at home must be at the bottom,' but Hill denied this.[116]

Though Lawson's resignation may have been no more than a

---

[114] Blake, *Letters*, 339, 393–7; *Thurloe*, iv. 582; SP 18/136/60, 77, 95; T. Carte, *A Collection of Original Letters and Papers, 1641–1660* (1739), ii. 81, 88, 90–2, 94–5.

[115] Blake, *Letters*, 393–6; *Thurloe*, iv. 582. For Abelson's sick wife see SP 18/133/112.

[116] Blake, *Letters*, 394–5. Hill's views may have helped dissuade Blake from attacking the Spanish fleet off Cadiz in 1655.

gesture of despair, it is at least possible that he and Sexby hoped to trigger a spate of resignations and paralyse the expedition. If they could also arouse the seamen to protest over conditions they might create a situation which could then be exploited by republicans ashore. The government firmly believed that political intrigue lay behind the unrest. Hatsell, the navy agent at Plymouth, thought Lawson 'strongly biased by those that wish not well to the present public transactions'. Thurloe was convinced from the intelligence he gathered that 'the finger of Job, viz. Spain, is in all this business'. He saw the troubles as rooted in an unholy alliance between Sexby, Charles Stuart, and Spain, with money being sent over from Flanders to subvert the mariners before the expedition sailed. The conspirators even had a treasurer, he declared, a seaman closely linked to Lawson and his friends. (This may point to Edward Hall, formerly a vice-admiral under the Rump; Sexby had lodged at his house in Rotherhithe, and some £750 sent to Hall from Flanders fell into the government's hands.) Lord Broghill, commenting on information sent by Thurloe, expressed shock that Lyons and Hill should 'try to sell their country as much as in them lies for a little money'.[117]

The government remained jittery about the troubles at Portsmouth until the fleet was safely on its way. The Admiralty was worried, for example, that the failure of Commissioner Willoughby to warn it of the unrest there might have been deliberate, a suggestion he strongly denied. Moreover in the midst of the crisis an alarming letter arrived from John Bourne, designated rear-admiral of the expeditionary force, complaining that his services had been poorly rewarded and owning to 'doubtful and dark thoughts' on whether to remain in the navy. When Bourne arrived in Portsmouth and grasped the situation, however, he quickly dissociated himself from Lawson's group and pledged his loyalty.[118] There was a further alarm over Richard Badiley, the man chosen to replace Lawson as vice-admiral. Desborough received word that Badiley had 'been tampered with at London, and a little stumbled', and wanted to have him questioned as soon as he arrived at Portsmouth to find 'what temper he is in'. In the event Badiley proved loyal,

---

[117] SP 18/134/34; *Thurloe*, iv. 597; Carte, *Original Letters*, ii. 88, 103; Cromwell, *Writings*, iv. 268–9. Hall admitted receiving money from Antwerp but pleaded ignorance of any design: Cromwell, *Writings*, iv. 173; cf. *Thurloe*, vi. 830.

[118] SP 18/136/60 (Willoughby); SP 18/135/70; SP 18/136/87 (Bourne).

though he may have been out of temper, for his enemies had contrived to have him arrested for debt on the way and the Council of State had to intervene to secure his release; whether this was a private matter or a further spoiling tactic by the dissidents, we do not know.[119] Royalists reported that Cromwell was 'most odious now among the seamen', following Lawson's resignation, adding that Badiley did not have his predecessor's popularity.[120] But the fleet was able to sail at last on 15 March, and it made its way to Spain without incident.

Lawson continued to scheme against the Protectorate, and was a leading figure in the group trying to build an alliance between Commonwealthsmen (republicans) and Fifth Monarchists in the spring and summer of 1656. His former naval colleagues Dakins (rear-admiral in the Caribbean), Lyons, and Crispin were also involved, with Col. Okey representing dissidents in the army and the preacher Thomas Venner acting as spokesman for the more militant Fifth Monarchists. John Poortmans, once an Admiralty official and now a Fifth Monarchist preacher, provided a natural link between the different groups. One of the subjects they discussed was how to influence the forthcoming parliamentary elections. Late in July however the government broke up the meetings and arrested Lawson, Okey, and Col. Rich, a leading Fifth Monarchist (and former Admiralty Commissioner) who had joined them; among the others taken for questioning were Lyons, Poortmans, and Venner.[121] The most direct attempt to influence the elections and subvert the armed forces was a pamphlet entitled *England's Remembrancers*, which may well have emanated from this group and certainly circulated at Venner's meeting-house. Its author denounced Cromwell as a despot and called on the people to choose MPs who would rescue the nation's 'gasping liberties' from total extinction. One section of the pamphlet lamented the sad plight of the honest seamen, 'the wall and bulwark of our nation against foreigners', now 'barbarously forced from their wives and children to serve the ambitious and fruitless design of one man'—'witness Jamaica'.[122] This seems to have been intended to stir up the seamen as well as arouse sympathy for them. Several packets of printed

---

[119] *Thurloe*, iv. 582; *CSP 1655–6*, 211.

[120] SP 18/125/4; Carte, *Original Letters*, ii. 90–2.

[121] *Thurloe*, v. 317, vi. 185–6; Carte, *Original Letters*, ii. 111–12; *CSPD 1656–7*, 581; Gardiner, *CP* iv. 259–61; Firth, i. 208–10; Capp, *Fifth Monarchy*, 114–15.

[122] The pamphlet is reprinted in *Thurloe*, v. 268–71; Gardiner, *CP* iv. 261–3.

papers, probably the *Remembrancers,* were sent aboard the squadron in the Downs in August, addressed to Capts. Smyth,
Whitehorne, Clarke, and Heaton. Smyth called it a 'villainous
pamphlet' and promptly sent a copy to the Admiralty Commissioners, warning the magistrates at Dover and Deal and arranging for
the post to be carefully watched.[123] In September merchant ships
carrying supplies to the fleet off Spain also brought thousands of
subversive papers, probably the *Remembrancers* once more, and
many were distributed without the Generals' knowledge. Once
they were alerted they seized the remainder, but they remarked of
those already circulated that they 'thought best to let them pass in
silence', which suggests some lingering doubts about their men.[124]
When Mountagu returned to Portsmouth in the autumn the government was concerned that Lyons, Poortmans, and other dissidents
might try again to 'infuse evil principles into the fleet', and sent
orders for them to be closely watched and arrested at the first sign
of trouble.[125]

There were other echoes of republican feeling in the navy that
summer. A writer in the *Selby,* for example, cruising off Havana,
wrote a letter of sympathy to Major-General Overton, who was
still languishing in the Tower for his part in the Scottish conspiracy
eighteen months before.[126] More important were the allegations
against Capt. John Best, commander of the *Adventure* on the
north-eastern coast. A long-running dispute within the company
ended with a series of charges brought against him by the warrant-
officers. They accused him of saying, *inter alia,* that Cromwell was
guilty of crimes ten times worse than those for which Charles I had
lost his head. He had associated with disaffected republicans such as
Mrs Overton, who was now back in Hull—where her husband had
been Governor—probably trying to subvert the garrison. He
possessed a copy of a pamphlet expounding Fifth-Monarchist and
republican views, and allegedly used it to undermine his officers'
loyalty. He was also said to have criticized the war with Spain,
declaring that the government cared not how many lives were lost in
its greed for Spanish treasure. His behaviour was as rash as his
words. He had seized the gunner of the Scarborough garrison after
a quarrel, and when the lieutenant of the castle came to demand the
man's release Best seized him too and clapped him in irons, declaring that sailors were not to be servants to the soldiery. These

---

[123] SP 18/129/150.   [124] Blake, *Letters,* 420.
[125] *CSPD 1656–7,* 149.   [126] *Thurloe,* v. 367.

charges led to a court martial in September. The feuds within the ship's company made much of the evidence unreliable, and Best was eventually acquitted after protesting his loyalty to the state and his support for the war; but he admitted having the seditious pamphlet in his possession and seizing the army officers at Scarborough, and he was never employed again. Even if the political charges against him were grossly distorted it is clear at the very least that the company was well informed of republican activities and arguments.[127]

As General Blake's life drew to a close in 1657 there was much discussion over who might take his place. 'Many are competent to fill it', one observer remarked, 'but Cromwell cannot entirely trust them'; there was even speculation that the aged earl of Warwick might be brought out of retirement.[128] In the event no one was appointed and the inexperienced Mountagu was left as sole General at Sea. The government continued its close watch on dissidents. No one could be certain of Lawson's surviving influence in the fleet, and one royalist reported that he had a hold over the new vice-admiral, Goodson; another described Goodson as a 'high Anabaptist' and 'discontented'.[129] Lawson was arrested again briefly in April 1657 at the time of Venner's attempted Fifth Monarchist rising, and Sexby was finally captured in July on a secret visit to England. Poortmans too was arrested again early in 1658 and held until after Cromwell's death.[130]

The navy's loyalty to Cromwell in the later 1650s was bound up in part with its views on the Spanish war, which was rightly seen as Cromwell's personal policy. Some officers regarded the war as cynical and immoral. Others were disillusioned by the bloody failure at Hispaniola or grew bored and resentful at the tedious months spent patrolling off the Spanish coast in 1656–7. Even Goodson, one of the most energetic, had concluded by 1657 that Spain was an unrewarding enemy, comparing the Plate fleet to 'a lottery, where many blanks are drawn before it's got'. Flanders, he added, had long been a drain on Spanish resources and might prove the same for England.[131] The war however also had numerous champions within the fleet, though they seem to have felt less

[127] SP 18/129/91; SP 18/141/207; SP 18/142/16; SP 18/145/104–5; SP 18/158/105; Gardiner, *CP* iv. 260. See ch. 7 below for the feud in Best's ship.

[128] *CSPV 1657–9*, 63, 102; *CSPD 1657–8*, 87.

[129] Firth, i. 33–6, 113–16, 219–29; *CSP* iii. 331; Clar. MS 57, fo 149ᵛ.

[130] Firth, i. 217, 232–3, ii. 35; Capp, *Fifth Monarchy*, 118, 120–1.

[131] Blake, *Letters*, 412–13, 432, 436–7; *Clarke Papers*, iii. 12.

excitement than during the earlier struggle against the Dutch. Some were swayed by jingoism and the hope of plunder.[132] Others shared Cromwell's instinctive loathing for the traditional foe. The Venetian envoy spoke of Blake's 'implacable and unreasoning hatred' of Spain, and Capt. Robert Plumleigh attacked the Spaniards as an 'Antichristian brood whose fall draweth nigh'. Capt. Robert Robinson saw Stayner's capture of the Plate ships as a seal of divine approval for a 'just and necessary' war.[133] Once it became known that the Stuarts and Spaniards were planning a joint invasion from Flanders attitudes were inevitably coloured by fears of a royalist restoration. The Admiralty Commissioners welcomed Stayner's success partly because it curbed 'the insolency of the malignant party' at home and would put an end to the levies Charles was raising abroad with Spanish money. Similarly in 1658 John Stokes welcomed the capture of Dunkirk because it 'put an end to the vain hopes of Charles Stuart, and that party'.[134]

The royalists continued to claim throughout the Protectorate that they enjoyed widespread support in the navy. This seems to have been no more than wishful thinking, at least as regards the officers. Only one commander was ever accused of royalist sympathies, in 1654, and he was at once defended by numerous witnesses who deposed that the charge had sprung merely from malice. A cavalier claimed in 1656 that Capt. Sacheverell had been well-disposed towards the king and might have brought over his ship; but as Sacheverell had just been killed in action the claim could hardly be verified and had no practical significance.[135] At various times in 1657 and 1658 the royalists cherished foolish and vain hopes that Blake, Stokes, or Stayner might respond to a personal approach.[136] It is rather more likely that Ayscue gradually came to favour the Stuarts, but he had left the navy long ago and had no influence in it.[137] During the Spanish war the royalists cherished hopes that ships would sail into Flemish or Spanish ports and declare for Charles

---

[132] e.g. SP 18/133/35.

[133] *CSPV 1657-9*, 102; SP 18/146/150; SP 18/145/104; SP 18/146/90.

[134] PRO Adm. 2/1729, fos. 142ᵛ-143; *Thurloe*, vii. 189.

[135] SP 18/71/51, 108-9 (Capt T. Elliott); SP 18/128/106.

[136] CCSP iii. 267-8, 282-3, 344, iv. 107; Clar. MS 59, fos. 86ᵛ, 186.

[137] *CSPD 1655-6*, 123; CCSP iii. 119. Ayscue is said to have refused to serve under Cromwell: *CSPV 1657-9*, 102; *FDW* ii. 266 n. He may have been swayed by his royalist stepson, John Boys of Hoad Court, Kent: *CSPD 1655-6*, 166; *The Visitation of Kent, 1663-8*, ed. Sir G. Armytage (HS liv; 1906), 23; *Lincolnshire Pedigrees*, ed. A. R. Maddison (HS l; 1902), i. 62.

II.[138] When John Golding brought his ship into Ostend at the end of 1656 they remarked cheerfully that it would be 'a good leading card to the rest of his rough tribe'. Golding commanded a privateer, however, not a naval vessel, and his defection had no political significance for he had earlier served under Rupert; moreover a royalist *émigré* promptly had him arrested for debt, which can hardly have encouraged other waverers.[139] Cavalier dreams proved to be as ill-founded as during the Dutch war, and not a single naval officer followed Golding's example. A royalist attempt to appeal directly to the ordinary seamen proved equally unproductive. Edward Cotterell enlisted in the *Merlin* at the end of 1656 with the aim of stirring up the company to seize her in the king's name; when he approached the ship's cook, however, the man denounced him to the captain and Cotterell was sent back to England in irons.[140] It was natural that the cavaliers should have distrusted Sexby and his republican friends, but they had represented the only real chance of breaking Cromwell's grip on the navy. Once Lawson and his allies had been ousted the cavaliers had to base their invasion plans on the forlorn hope of escaping the fleet in the Channel.[141]

Cromwell's death on 3 September 1658 did not shake the government's hold over the fleet. On the 6th the Admiralty Commissioners wrote to John Bourne, commanding in the Downs, to inform him of Richard Cromwell's peaceful accession. Bourne was pleased that the smooth transition had frustrated the cavaliers' designs, 'very great evidence that the Lord has not forsaken the nation,' and assured them that his captains had readily accepted the new Protector.[142] General Mountagu, then in London, drew up a declaration of loyalty to Richard, and early in October he led a deputation of naval officers to present it to the Protector at Whitehall. They professed confidence that Richard would 'carry on the glorious work of liberty and reformation' begun by his father, and pledged their loyalty to government by a Single Person and two Houses of Parliament, repudiating both the republicans and the royalists, that 'profane and enraged party'. Richard was delighted by this public

[138] *CSPD 1657–8*, 325–6; *Thurloe*, vii. 234; *CCSP* iii. 254.
[139] *CCSP* iii. 242–3, 255; *CSPD 1656–7*, 229, 288–9.
[140] SP 18/131/42; *CSPD 1656–7*, 490, 497; *CSPD 1657–8*, 494, 515. Cotterell was to hold several commissions between 1661 and 1672 but was not rated highly: Pepys, *Cat.* i. 399; Coventry MS 99, fo. 91.
[141] Firth, i. 300–1, ii. 65–7.
[142] Adm. 2/1730, fo. 236; SP 18/182/96.

display of support and promised the navy his especial care.[143] Several other commanders wrote independently from sea paying similar tribute to Oliver ('that famous and worthy instrument of God's glory,' one called him) and pledging allegiance to his son.[144]

The government took particular care over Stokes's force in the Straits, perhaps aware that the Spaniards and royalists were considering an approach to him now that Cromwell was dead. The Admiralty wrote stressing that Richard had been accepted at once by the Council, the army, and the home fleet, and urged Stokes to make good use of these points. Mountagu also wrote, enclosing a copy of his declaration and asking Stokes's officers to sign and return it; this they did, and their address was presented to Richard in due course.[145] There was, however, one small hiccup. Robert Saunders of the *Torrington*, one of the most senior captains, refused to sign, protesting that the declaration did not bear Mountagu's signature. He eventually gave way but the episode appears to have intensified a personal grudge against Stokes and shortly afterwards, while commanding a small group away from the main force, Saunders summoned the other captains and vented his suspicion that Stokes was guilty of 'revolting'. What he meant by that is obscure, but Saunders thereupon deserted his station and took his ship back to England without orders, apparently by the advice of his Anabaptist lieutenant, William Phipps. The ship's unexpected arrival in England caused surprise and some concern. Mountagu examined the captain and reported that he 'told so idle and bad a story' that he was judged to be 'something distracted, and foully in fault'. A court martial cashiered him and sentenced him to indefinite imprisonment.[146]

Richard's ready acceptance by the navy, with the exception of one 'distracted' individual, was a triumph. The new Protector could

---

[143] *The Publick Intelligencer*, 27 Sept.–4 Oct. 1658; *CSPD 1658–9*, 184; *A True Catalogue . . . of . . . where, and by whom, Richard Cromwell was Proclaimed Lord Protector* (1659), 25.

[144] SP 18/182/93, 98, 99; *CSPD 1658–9*, 443, 446.

[145] Adm. 2/1730, fos. 240, 244; *CSPD 1658–9*, 139, 141; Clar. MS 58, fos. 332, 335; Clar. MS 59, fo. 32; Bodl. Carte MS 73, fo. 207; *The Publick Intelligencer*, 25 Oct.–1 Nov. 1658; *Mercurius Politicus*, 28 Oct.–4 Nov. 1658. Warrant- as well as commissioned officers were asked to sign. For Spanish and royalist interest in Stokes at this time see Clar. MS 59, fos. 86ᵛ, 186.

[146] SP 18/83/111; Adm. 2/1730, fo. 268; *CSPD 1658–9*, 193, 196, 200, 211, 507. On Phipps see SP 18/201/41; Coventry MS 98, fo. 66ᵛ. For the disputes in Stokes's squadron see also ch. 6, below.

reflect that no previous change of regime during the interregnum had brought such an emphatic pledge of support. It was a clear indication of the ascendancy Mountagu now enjoyed in the navy, which was to have crucial significance a year and a half later. But the calm was deceptive. In the navy, as in the nation at large, the months ahead were to witness greater political confusion and strife than in the whole of the Commonwealth's history so far.

Part II

6

Naval Officers: A Social Profile

THIS chapter is concerned with the background and recruitment of
naval officers, and the pattern of their careers in the state's service.
At the top were the commissioned officers, the captains and lieutenants responsible for the general government of a ship and its
conduct in action. Altogether about 375 men were commissioned as
captains of state-owned warships in this period.[1] The captain was
often the sole commissioned officer aboard; lieutenants were carried
only in the larger ships (the first three rates, and fourth-rates from
the end of 1652), and no ship, however great, was allowed more
than one.[2] About three hundred have been identified serving during
the Commonwealth. A further hundred and fifty commissioned
officers belonged to the navy in a much more limited sense, serving
exclusively in hired merchantmen; they were often appointed by the
owners, and are largely omitted from the following analysis.[3]

I. COMMISSIONED OFFICERS: SELECTION

Under the Rump the Council of State was responsible for senior
naval appointments, most of the work being handled by its
Admiralty Committee. Twice a year the Council scrutinized lists of
commanders nominated for the summer and winter guards, and
presented the names to Parliament for approval. The Admiralty
Committee turned to the Generals at Sea for guidance, and it was
they who prepared the draft lists.[4] The Council's own role was by
no means a formality. In 1650 it rejected three men nominated for

---

[1] For a listing (though incomplete) see R. C. Anderson, *List of English Naval
Captains* (1964).
[2] Bodl. Rawlinson MS A 226, fo. 117; *FDW* iii. 285, 372.
[3] On the captains of hired merchantmen see ch. 1, above.
[4] *A and O* ii. 13–14; Rawl. MS A 225, fos. 40ᵛ, 70ᵛ, 99; *CSPD 1650*, 11.

the summer guard (including Rainborough's brother William), and the following year it rejected two outright and ordered further inquiries into the suitability of three others.[5] On a few occasions it took the initiative, as in 1650 when it put forward the name of Henry Appleton, a merchant commander, for a senior appointment, asking the Generals for their comments.[6]

The system worked satisfactorily until the outbreak of war with the Dutch, which disrupted the usual process of consultation. Blake was inevitably needed at sea, as the only General still in place, and made scathing remarks after Dungeness about officers who had been installed without his approval.[7] A general reorganization of naval administration followed in the wake of that defeat. A small, standing body of Admiralty Commissioners took over from the Council's Committee, with the Generals (now once more three in number) as ex-officio members.[8] The Council itself played a much smaller role henceforth. On receiving a draft list of the summer guard early in 1653 the Councillors blandly observed that they were familiar with some of the names 'and not doubting but the Commissioners have enquired and satisfied themselves concerning the abilities of the rest, do approve of all'.[9] The new structure continued under the Protectorate. The Commissioners drew up lists with the help of their secretary and the Generals and presented them to the Council for formal approval.[10] It was only with the return of the Rump in 1659 that Council and Parliament again played a central role.[11]

The selection of officers was governed by a wide variety of considerations. Ideological criteria were more important, predictably, than ever before or since. Political reliability was the key issue in remodelling the officer corps after the king's death, as we have seen earlier. It was equally important in 1659–60: the recall of Lawson and his friends following the collapse of the Protectorate was a deliberate attempt by the restored Rump to strengthen its position within the fleet. A few months later the restored Long Parliament recalled Mountagu with the equally specific aim of

[5] *CSPD 1650*, 8, 11; *CSPD 1651*, 73, 77; Rawl. MS A 225, fo. 75.
[6] *CSPD 1650*, 392.
[7] *CSPV 1647–52*, 322.
[8] V. A. Rowe, *Sir Henry Vane the Younger* (1970), ch. 8; above, ch. 4 n. 25.
[9] *FDW* iii. 424.
[10] e.g. PRO SP 25 I 75, pp. 412–13, 666–7; SP 18/76/39; SP 18/126/4.
[11] See ch. 10, below.

undoing Lawson's influence.[12] Even in quieter times political commitment was never overlooked. When the shipmaster Henry Land sought a commission in 1656, for example, his sponsors were careful to stress that he 'did ever bear a real affection to this state and present government'.[13]

Religious zeal was an equally important consideration, for the first and only time in the navy's history. It was especially evident in 1653, when the leading Commissioners included Sir Henry Vane, a man of deep (if obscure) religiosity, and John Carew, a prominent Fifth Monarchist. In some Admiralty lists compiled early that year nominees were even grouped into distinct categories of the 'godly' and the merely 'civil'. A deputation of army officers waited on the Commissioners in January, to urge 'that godly, able persons may be preferred to command in the fleet, and if such they wanted the army could nominate several to them'. This message was warmly received.[14] The Commissioners also placed considerable weight on the views of senior commanders belonging to the radical Puritan fraternity. Blackborne, the Admiralty secretary, was later to recall how such captains 'would with a sigh and casting up the eye say "Such a man fears the Lord" — or "I hope such a man hath the spirit of God."' Blackborne was himself a key figure in this fraternity and played an active part in the process.[15] Many petitioners supplied testimonials vouching for their godly life and zeal, some from prominent radical ministers.[16] In 1653 John Woolters was supported by the entire congregation of his gathered church at Sandwich, who testified that he was 'God-fearing, faithful, and skilful for a command at sea'. The order in which they placed these attributes is striking and was almost certainly deliberate, for they went on to declare that God intended in these latter days 'to make use of his own children to manage and bring about his great work for him', laying aside men of the world as broken reeds.[17] In such a climate more moderate or worldly men may well have suffered. One Tobias Sackler was kept waiting many years for his first command merely

---

[12] See chs. 3, above, and 10, below.

[13] SP 18/176/95.

[14] SP 18/48/78–80; Clarke MS 1/12, fo. 104ᵛ; cf. *Severall Proceedings*, 1–8 Dec. 1653; see also ch. 9, below.

[15] Pepys, *Diary*, iv. 375. Blackborne's cynical tone is explained by the fact that many Puritan officers failed to resist the Restoration, which convinced him they had always been hypocrites.

[16] See below, ch. 9 n. 14.

[17] SP 18/32/68a.

because he was 'soberly principled' and 'not an Anabaptist'—or so General Monck, his patron and kinsman, was later to claim. In 1653 there had been rumours that Monck himself was to be laid aside as too worldly for such a position.[18]

In many other respects, though, the Admiralty continued to apply traditional criteria. As in every period it needed officers who would be resolute in action and able to maintain discipline and harmony among the seamen. A record of courage in battle weighed heavily with the Commissioners. Michael Packe was the sort of 'stout' officer they admired. When his leg was 'shot off' in an action against the Dutch in August 1652 he vowed defiantly to return to the war if he survived; in the event his wound proved fatal but the Council rewarded his patriotic gesture by naming his brother to the vacant command.[19] General Monck, who had little interest in ideology, laid particular stress on fighting spirit. When he urged a remodelling of the officer corps late in 1658 he strongly recommended officers he personally knew to have 'given eminent proofs of their courage', and branded the current commander in the Downs 'a coward and unfit for employment'.[20]

Petitioners naturally drew attention to their fighting record, sometimes using bizarre means. Daniel Baker, for example, offered to send the Admiralty 'sundry great bones' taken out of his leg after a wound as irrefutable proof of his valour. The Commissioners, suitably impressed, gave him a commission in recognition of his sufferings.[21] Francis Cranwell sent a petition in heroic verse, in the hope that a display of martial spirit would atone for his admitted shortcomings in other respects. He had served against the Scots, he reminded them, and 'With thundering cannon made them fly | From town and castle to mountains high'. Given another ship he would make the Spaniards quail too: 'Then, Spanish admiral, stand you clear, | For Cranwell means a chain of gold to wear.'[22] Cranwell was right to suppose that a martial reputation might outweigh other failings. When Capt. John Jefferies was found guilty of fraud in

---

[18] SP 18/223/113; *CCSP* ii. 262. Sackler was a kinsman of Monck's wife: Coventry MS 98, fo. 52.

[19] *FDW* ii. 106–7, 121, 173; *CSPD 1651–2*, 378. Packe's funeral was attended by 'many thousand people': *A Perfect Account*, 6–13 Oct. 1652.

[20] *Thurloe*, vii. 388. The commander in the Downs, Whitehorne, had shown sense rather than cowardice: see ch. 4 n. 96, above.

[21] SP 18/103/124; PRO Adm. 2/1730, fo. 87ᵛ.

[22] SP 18/133/35.

1656, for example, he escaped with a small fine and a reprimand because the Admiralty was reluctant to lose such 'an active and a stout fighting man' in the midst of a war.[23] Bravery was still more important in the selection of lieutenants, who were essentially fighting officers with few specific responsibilities in the running of the ship. Admiralty notes compiled at the height of the Dutch war make the point well: John Penry was judged 'an active stout man, but little skill at sea: fit for a lieutenant', and John Bowry 'a raw seaman but civil and stout, fit for a lieutenant'.[24]

Broader qualities of leadership were also taken into account, especially in senior appointments. It was on such grounds that Robert Coytmor, a senior official, criticized a proposal to give command of a squadron to Anthony Young. 'I hold Young to be a very honest man,' he observed, 'yet not fit for such a command.' Young was not appointed and indeed, though a brave and respected captain, never reached a flag-position. Coytmor recommended instead an experienced merchant seaman, Richard Badiley, who accepted the post and quickly proved his worth. Officers needed to be responsible as well as brave, and Coytmor bluntly dismissed the former privateer Richard Ingle as one of the irresponsible 'mad captains' the navy would be better without. Ingle was soon laid aside.[25]

Another part of a captain's duties was to oversee his warrant-officers and check their accounts. This called for some measure of clerical and administrative skill, and officers of humble origin knew they had to convince the Admiralty of their competence in this respect. A testimonial for Isaac White stated that he was 'sober and diligent in his business and can write well', and Daniel Baker was careful to stress his skill with the pen as well as his honourable wounds. The bluff Francis Cranwell felt his career had suffered because he was 'no penman' (and no poet, we may add), complaining that the Admiralty valued bureaucratic skills more than valour.[26]

The importance of social criteria in the interregnum is much harder to assess. The period is generally seen, rightly, as the great age of 'tarpaulin' captains—professional seamen of non-gentle

---

[23] SP 18/125/19. Jefferies had been cleared of more serious charges.
[24] SP 18/46/16.
[25] Clarke MS 4/4, 1649 (18, 20). Coytmor was co-Secretary to the Admiralty Committee; for a good assessment of his influence see G. Aylmer, *The State's Servants* (1973), 265–6.
[26] SP 18/125/3; SP 18/103/124; SP 18/202/28.

birth. But the old preference for officers of higher birth did not vanish altogether, and (other things being equal) Commonwealth governments still probably preferred men with gentry backgrounds. This should not surprise us, for the Rump was a body of landed gentlemen with conservative social views and the Protectorate was even more traditional in outlook. Nathaniel Boteler had argued before the civil war that only a gentleman-captain could have 'the civility of carriage and behaviour, which is natural to the place he holds and the company he is to keep'.[27] His point has some force. Senior captains, for example, were often called upon to carry English and foreign diplomats, and sometimes had to engage in diplomacy themselves. A degree of ease in polite society was obviously an advantage in such circumstances.[28] Boteler was also convinced that a gentleman-captain possessed a more natural authority and so more effective control over his men. A plebeian captain flouted the general convention that government was the province of gentlemen. Behind this lay a widespread assumption that military honour and political commitment existed only among men of 'good' birth. Thus Monck urged Richard Cromwell to choose men with 'good estates and interests', warning him that low-born captains might prove 'apt to betray or sell' their ships in wartime. A generation later Pepys too asserted that a gentleman was 'more sensible of honour than a man of meaner birth', even while conceding that naval history offered little to support such a view.[29]

Tarpaulin captains flourished in the 1650s partly because politically-sound naval officers of good birth were scarce. The 'russet-coated captains' had risen in the army in the 1640s for much the same reasons. Cromwell himself held traditional values. 'Better plain men than none', he had observed in 1643, but where there was a choice a gentleman was preferable.[30] This remained true of his attitude to the navy a decade later. His protégé Mountagu had the

[27] *Boteler's Dialogues*, ed. W. G. Perrin (NRS, 1929), 7.

[28] For example Blake sent Moulton to negotiate with the king of Portugal, and Andrew Ball was sent to the Sound to secure the release of shipping detained by the Danes: Blake, *Letters*, 82–3; *FDW* ii. 155–6, 364–5; cf. F. R. Harris, *The Life of Edward Mountagu* (1912), i. 111–13.

[29] *Thurloe*, vii. 388; *The Tangier Papers of Samuel Pepys*, ed. E. Chappell (NRS, 1935), 122.

[30] Cromwell, *Writings*, i. 256, 262. Social conservatism may explain why the Rump failed to make Lawson a General in 1659, which would have strengthened his position, and its own, against Mountagu.

highest birth of all the Generals. It was no secret under the Protectorate that good birth was still an advantage, and one official was careful to introduce his own protégé as 'a pretty artist, with a good landed estate'.[31] Cromwell's nephew, Thomas Whetstone, alarmed fellow-officers in the Straits in 1658 by declaring that in future the Protector intended to 'make no more use of seamen but have gentlemen to command his ships'.[32] Though this was untrue Cromwell did encourage young gentlemen-volunteers to go to sea to fit themselves for senior appointments, anticipating Restoration practice. He intervened personally in one case to ensure that two young gentlemen sailing with Blake were suitably provided with servants and good accommodation. Such intervention was perhaps necessary, for these privileged youngsters were not always welcome: one patron complained that his young kinsman had been treated outrageously in Badiley's flagship, being made to live as an ordinary seaman and share the common victuals, and denied leave to go ashore.[33]

But if traditional social prejudices survived they carried much less weight in the 1650s than in most periods. Not only ideology but seamanship and experience too had assumed a new importance. A generation earlier it was observed that a captain was 'chosen for his warlike spirit' alone, with the master expected to provide the necessary expertise in seamanship. The Commonwealth, by contrast, wanted captains to be qualified in both respects.[34] The importance now placed on professional skill and experience is evident at every level. Many of the escorts protecting Yarmouth fishing boats in the North Sea and off Iceland were assigned to mariners from Yarmouth itself. In the north-east William Nesfield of Scarborough was selected to patrol the coast specifically for his local knowledge.[35] Similarly we find James Cadman of Rye and Ambrose

---

[31] SP 18/125/3. The official was Hatsell and his protégé Richard Penhallow, for whose family see *The Visitation of Cornwall, 1620*, ed. J. L. Vivian (HS ix; 1874), 166–7.

[32] Bodl. Carte MS 73, fo. 205ʳ⁻ᵛ; BL Add. MS 9304, fo. 170.

[33] Adm. 2/1729, fos. 184, 185; SP 46/117, fo. 305; SP 18/136/136. For Badiley's victim, Sandes Temple, see further ch. 11, below.

[34] *Naval Tracts of Sir William Monson*, ed. M. Oppenheim (NRS, 1902–14), iv. 152; cf. iii. 433–5, iv. 14.

[35] Yarmouth examples include Robert Mackey and Robert Wyard. Nesfield: Clarke MS 4/4, 1649 (17); SP 25/123, fo. 153; *CSPD 1649–50*, 407. Francis Allen and Anthony Lilburne also lived and served in the north-east.

Smith of Arundel being chosen to protect the Sussex coast, and James Coppin of Margate patrolling the Thames estuary.[36] The same stress on experience is evident in the planning of more distant operations. Robert Plumleigh, sent with the fishing fleet to Newfoundland, belonged to a family which was itself engaged in this trade. Two of the first convoys to the Straits were sent out under Badiley and Appleton, both Mediterranean veterans. And Robert Dennis, who led the expedition to subdue Virginia, was himself a former Virginian trader.[37] The principle was applied still more thoroughly in choosing captains for the Western Design. William Goodson, the vice-admiral, had sailed in the Caribbean in the 1630s and spent some time at Cartagena on the mainland. Benjamin Blake had lived in the region for several years as a soldier and planter.[38] Edward Blagg, one of the most senior captains, had been trading to the West Indies for fifteen years. Giles Shelley too was a Caribbean veteran.[39] Penn was indeed taking with him, as was remarked, 'most of the ablest commanders for the West Indies coast that [he] could get in England'.[40]

II. THE ANATOMY OF THE OFFICER CORPS

The Rump was mainly responsible for shaping the interregnum officer corps, first through the remodelling after the king's execution and then through the rapid expansion of the fleet on the outbreak of the Dutch war. Cromwell's role as Protector was relatively minor. Some 230 captains were first appointed in the years 1649–53, compared with 89 in the period 1654–60. Only 54 captains had formerly commanded warships in the parliamentary fleets of 1642–8, and only two had served at this level before the civil war.[41]

---

[36] Add. MS 18986, fo. 235; *Severall Proceedings*, 24 Apr.–1 May 1651 (Cadman); Adm. 2/1731, fo. 98ᵛ; C. H. Ridge, *Index to Administrations in the Prerogative Court of Canterbury, 1655–60* (1949), iii. 40 (Smith); Add MS 18986, fo. 3 (Coppin).

[37] Add. MS 18986, fo. 174; below, nn. 109, 202. For Appleton see *A Perfect Diurnall*, 31 Dec. 1649–7 Jan. 1650; for Badiley and Dennis see ch. 3 n. 63.

[38] *Thurloe*, iv. 453; PRO HCA 13/66, 9 Nov. 1652 (Goodson); *Thurloe*, v. 368; *CSPD 1650*, 499 (Blake).

[39] *Thurloe*, ii. 250, 543, iii. 11; *CSP Col.*, i. 474; HMC 31, *Loder–Symonds*, 385.

[40] *The Letters of John Paige, London Merchant, 1648–1658*, ed. G. F. Steckley (London Record Soc., xxi; 1984), 119.

[41] The figures are based on Anderson's listings, revised and expanded. Captains of hired merchantmen are only included if they went on to command state-owned

Keith Thomas has pointed out that in many fields the revolution allowed men to reach high positions much earlier than in normal times.[42] The navy did not conform to this pattern. The mean age of a newly appointed captain in the interregnum as a whole was about 36, rather higher than in later periods. The six Generals at Sea averaged about 41 on appointment. The youngest, Mountagu, was only 31 but he owed his place to favour at the Protector's court, hardly a revolutionary factor.[43] One general explanation lies in the Rump's practice of recruiting experienced merchant shipmasters into the navy. The Rump, nervous and insecure in 1649, needed senior commanders who combined political commitment, experience, and authority. The navy it inherited contained very few such men and to fill many of the most important posts it turned to outsiders, men known to hold the right political and religious views. Many of them were already advancing towards middle age or beyond. Goodson was 44, Reed of the *Sovereign* and Wildey both 47, Hackwell well into his fifties, Harris over 60. Richard Haddock came back as vice-admiral in 1652 at the age of 70.[44] The other explanation lies in the unusually high proportion of captains promoted in the 1650s from among the warrant-officers: such men, often from humble backgrounds and lacking influential patrons, generally took years longer to reach the top.[45] It should be added though that the averages conceal wide variations, and that the pattern changed over time. Once the Commonwealth was well established younger men came increasingly to the fore, helped by the rapid expansion of the fleet during the Dutch war. Samuel Howett and Michael Packe were flag-officers at 32, Badiley and John Bourne at a year older. Many officers secured commands in their mid-twenties: Robert Robinson at 23, Whetstone at 24, Bunn

warships. The two men who had been captains before 1642 are Wheeler and Lambert. Gen. Popham had also served as a captain in the late 1630s.

[42] K. Thomas, *Age and Authority in Early Modern England* (1976), 10.

[43] Based on a sample of 92. Ages are mostly derived from depositions in the Admiralty Court, and are approximate. For the Restoration period see Davies, thesis, 54.

[44] HCA 13/66, 9 Nov. 1652 (Goodson); D. O. Shilton and R. Holworthy (eds.), *High Court of Admiralty Examinations, 1637–8* (1932), 150; HCA 13/65, 5 Feb. 1652 (Reed); HCA 13/52, fo. 204 (Wildey); HCA 13/72, fo. 321 (Harris); HCA 13/58, fo. 524, 13/61, fo. 397 (Haddock). Hackwell had been a master's mate in the East Indies in the late 1610s, and was a Younger Brother of Trinity House by 1629: E. B. Sainsbury (ed.), *A Calendar of the Court Minutes of the East India Company* (Oxford, 1907–38), iv. 167; SP 16/135/38.

[45] See section iii, below; cf. N. A. M. Rodger, *The Wooden World: An Anatomy of the Georgian Navy* (1986), 264.

and Sansum at 25, the younger Haddock at 26, and Myngs at 28. In the right circumstances promotion could be rapid.

The commissioned officers of the period fall into three main groups. First come the shipmasters recruited from the merchant service. There were over a hundred captains in this group, and several other former shipmasters can be found serving as lieutenants.[46] The prominence of this group contrasts sharply with the pattern of the 1630s, and still more so with the Restoration and Hanoverian navies.[47] All but a handful of these former shipmasters entered the navy between 1649 and 1653. The Protectorate navy, more settled and no longer expanding, rarely needed to look outside its own ranks to fill vacancies.

The shipmasters themselves can be divided into two broad types. The more senior men were invited, even begged by the Rump to serve the new Commonwealth, and during the Dutch war there was a systematic campaign to entice 'the best and ablest commanders that could be heard of' into the service.[48] Some of them were drawn in gradually, serving first in hired merchantmen (often ships they part-owned), and then, if they had performed well, being invited to command one of the navy's own vessels. No les than forty captains served first in hired merchant ships, among them prominent flag-officers such as Lawson, Goodson, and John Bourne. The second type of shipmaster was less affluent or secure, and had turned to the navy for reasons of his own, explored further below.

Senior recruits were given some of the very best ships. Nicholas Reed's first and only naval appointment was as captain of the *Sovereign,* the greatest ship in the fleet. Though a newcomer to the navy Reed had lengthy experience commanding large merchantmen to the Straits, and had once led a flotilla of English merchant ships pressed into service by the Turks.[49] Similarly Peter Strong was given

---

[46] I have identified 109 captains of this type, and there may have been others. Ex-masters serving as naval lieutenants include Robert Lord (HCA 13/69, 7 Aug. 1654) and John Purvis of Yarmouth, a shipowner and former privateer killed in 1652 while serving as lieutenant to Blake; he was described as 'a man of great estate'. (*CSPD 1651*, 507; H. Swinden, *The History and Antiquities of Great Yarmouth* (Norwich, 1772), 558; *FDW* ii. 274; *CSPD 1652-3*, 485; *The Faithfull Scout,* 1–8 Oct. 1652.)

[47] D. E. Kennedy, 'Naval Captains at the Outbreak of the English Civil War', *MM* xlvi (1960), 183–8, 191–3; Davies, thesis, ch. 2; Rodger, *Wooden World,* 264–5.

[48] SP 18/46/12–18, 47; SP 18/48/78–80, 127; Bodl. Clarendon MS 47, fo. 181ᵛ; see also ch. 3, above.

[49] Sainsbury, *Court Minutes,* ii. 191, 358, iv. 122–4, v. 223–4; Rawl. MS C 416, fos. 59ᵛ, 61; *CSPV 1647–52,* 111, 112–13, 122; SP 25/123, p. 163.

three senior commands in quick succession in 1653, though his only previous naval service had been ten years earlier in a hired merchantman he part-owned. But he too had wide experience outside the navy and had commanded ships to both West and East Indies; he was now in his late forties and came recommended as godly and able. Strong probably held advanced political views too, for his partners included the radical merchants Gregory Clement, MP and regicide, and Maurice Thomson.[50]

While the recruits came from every branch of commerce there is a striking predominance of American traders among the more senior of them. At least thirty captains belonged to this group, including the flag-officers Nehemiah and John Bourne, and William Goodson. The Bournes' close associate Thomas Graves, another senior recruit, had once settled in Boston.[51] Mark Harrison and John Littlejohn had been active in the Newfoundland fisheries.[52] So had the Witheridge brothers, carrying fish to Spain and the Mediterranean, bringing southern wares to England, and then taking a third cargo back to New England, where one of the brothers had settled. By 1650 the Witheridges had switched to the Lisbon-Brazil trade, a reminder that New England was only one of several American connections.[53] There were many former Caribbean traders too, some already mentioned. Peter Strong and Robert Dennis had been regular visitors at Barbados since the colony was founded, Nicholas Foster had been a settler there, and Charles Saltonstall had been trading in the Caribbean since the 1620s for both Dutch and English masters.[54]

---

[50] HCA 13/58, fo. 579ᵛ; SP 18/46/16; SP 18/48/78; SP 18/55/130; Rawl. MS C 94, fo. 10ᵛ; BL Sloane MS 3231, fo. 53ᵛ; Sainsbury, *Court Minutes*, iv. 75, 213; W. Aspinwall (ed.), *A Volume . . . containing the Aspinwall Notarial Records from 1644 to 1651* (Boston, Mass., 1903), 11; *CSPD 1653-4*, 534.

[51] Chaplin, 'Bourne', *passim* (for John Bourne see esp. 142–50, and for Graves 41, 46–8, 54–5, 85); J. R. Powell, 'John Bourne, sometime Vice-Admiral', *MM* lxii (1976), 109–17.

[52] Aspinwall, *Notarial Records*, 218; HCA 13/62, 20 Dec. 1648; HCA 13/64, 14 Feb. 1651.

[53] Aspinwall, *Notarial Records*, 79, 397, 400, 402; HCA 13/64, 24 Jan. 1651; HCA 13/66, 9 Nov. 1652; PRO RG 4/4414, fo. 5. Cf. B. Bailyn, *The New England Merchants in the Seventeenth Century* (Cambridge, Mass., 1955), 76–86. Philip Gethings also traded in Newfoundland fish to Spain: HCA 13/62, 15 Aug. 1649.

[54] C. Saltonstall, *The Navigator* (1642), esp. 57–9; E. G. R. Taylor, *The Mathematical Practitioners of Tudor and Stuart England* (Cambridge, 1954), 211; N. Foster, *A Briefe Relation of the late Horrid Rebellion acted in the Island of Barbadas* (1650); see also above, n. 50 (Strong) and ch. 3 n. 63 (Dennis).

The importance of the American traders is not hard to explain. Returning New Englanders played a large part in many spheres of the Commonwealth's life and were well represented in the higher echelons of naval administration. Vane was a former Governor of Massachusetts. His deputy and successor as Treasurer, Richard Hutchinson, was another former colonist, as were several of the Navy Commissioners. Vane was an active broker in recruiting old associates, and his colleagues doubtless used their own connections in the same way.[55] There was often an ideological affinity between them, for shipmasters trading with the Americas tended to be more radical in outlook than those specializing in other distant markets, as did the merchants who employed them.[56] The explanation lies partly in the relative freedom of American trade, and partly in the mixed tradition of Puritan emigration and anti-Spanish privateering in the New World. Several officers had links with the Providence Island Company, which had fused Puritan zeal and privateering, and Saltonstall had taken part in the privateering venture mounted in the Caribbean by the earl of Warwick in 1643.[57]

Recruits from other long-distance trades played a much smaller role. Former masters in the Levant and East Indies trades had been a key element in the parliamentary navy of the 1640s, but very few of them served under the Commonwealth. Moulton and Hall, two exceptions, had both been interlopers rather than servants of the East India Company, and Moulton also had strong American ties. Hackwell, Wildey, and Reed were also drawn into the navy but none of them remained long. Richard Badiley was the most important recruit from the Mediterranean trades; a strong Puritan faith and business ties with the Bournes' circle may explain his greater commitment to the navy.[58] Not all recruits were drawn from the

---

[55] W. L. Sachse, 'The Migration of New Englanders to England', *American Historical Review*, lv (1947–8), 251–78. The Navy Commissioners Francis Willoughby, Bourne, and Hopkins were New Englanders. Hugh Peter also helped to recruit fellow returnees: SP 18/103/41; Aspinwall, *Notarial Records*, 265, 276–7 (Blofield); Add. MS 9300, fo. 123 (Walter Wood). Blofield and Wood both enjoyed backing from Cromwell, perhaps through Peter's agency.

[56] R. Brenner, 'The Civil War Politics of London's Merchant Community', *Past and Present*, lviii (1973).

[57] Among them William Rowse, Nicholas Parker, and John Edwin: *CSPD 1651–2*, 494; *CSP Col.*, i. 126, 184, 235, 280, 299, 304, 324; for Saltonstall see 'The Voyage of Captain William Jackson, 1642–1645', ed. V. T. Harlow, *Camden Miscellany*, xiii (1923), 11; *DNB*.

[58] Among such officers in the 1640s were Swanley, Trenchfield, Andrews, and Blith; for their careers see Sir W. Foster, *The English Factories in India* (Oxford, 1906–27); Sainsbury, *Court Minutes*; Baumber, thesis; idem, 'An East India

deep-sea trades. Many experts believed that the colliers plying along the east coast provided the toughest and best school of seamanship, and among its graduates in the navy were the flag-officers John Lawson of Scarborough and James Peacock of Ipswich.[59]

The personal influence of senior officials helps to explain the striking geographical pattern of recruitment. Most of their contacts were naturally with merchants and mariners in and around London, which in any case handled the bulk of England's sea-borne trade. Most provincial recruits came from the south-east and east, which reflects both the pattern of civil war allegiances and the main theatre of operations during the Dutch war. Ports with a resident Commissioner or agent, such as Yarmouth, Plymouth, and Dover, supplied many more officers than those little used by the navy, such as Bristol or Liverpool.[60] Yarmouth's links with the interregnum navy were particularly close. Its MP, Miles Corbet, was very active in naval administration in the first months of the Rump. During the Dutch war a prominent local merchant, William Burton, served as an Admiralty Commissioner in the town as well as representing it in Barebone's Parliament. Yarmouth supplied at least ten captains to the interregnum navy, as well as many lesser officers; Robert Coleman, who was typical of the group, had the backing of both Corbet and Burton.[61] The neighbouring port of Lowestoft, by contrast, was not used by the navy and appears to have supplied none. It had supported the king in the civil war, partly through rivalry with Yarmouth, and its best-known mariner, Thomas Allin, became a privateering captain under Rupert.[62] Plymouth, like Yarmouth, had an energetic, resident Admiralty official. Henry Hatsell was both a zealous parliamentarian (and MP during the Protectorate) and an important figure in the town's commercial life,

Captain: The early Career of Capt. Richard Swanley', *MM* liii (1967), 265–79; Kennedy, 'Naval Captains', 194–7. On Hackwell and Wildey see ch. 3 nn. 63–4; Hackwell had visited Japan in 1613.

[59] Add. MS 11602, fo. 126; *Boteler's Dialogues*, 49; R. Davis, *The Rise of the Shipping Industry in the Seventeenth and Eighteenth Centuries* (1962), 114–15. For Lawson and Peacock see *DNB*.

[60] Portsmouth also had a resident Commissioner, but I have identified only a few officers from the town: Dornford, Hodges, Reeves (from Gosport), and Baskett (from the Isle of Wight).

[61] For Coleman see Rawl. MS A 207, fo. 21ᵛ; SP 18/150/68; below, ch. 9. Other captains from Yarmouth were Ames, Goodson, Gosling, Mackey, Mould, Michael and Henry Packe (?), Purvis, Joseph Saunders (?), Edmund Smith, Edmund Thompson, Wheeler, Wilgress, Wyard. The Yarmouth corporation favoured close links with the navy: *FDW* iii. 346–9.

[62] E. Gillingwater, *An Historical Account of Lowestoft* (1791), esp. 156–7.

and he took considerable pains to draw good local men into the navy.[63]

Personal connections were not the only 'pull' factor at work. Pay and prize-money helped to attract many other shipmasters. The captain of a third-rate earned £14 a month, and even the commander of a sixth-rate £7; an officer serving as rear- or vice-admiral received twenty or thirty shillings a day. These figures compared very favourably with the pay of a merchant shipmaster, which stood at £6 a month for London ships trading abroad. Moreover the Dutch war offered the possibility of instant riches through the capture of prizes. A merchant complained in the spring of 1653 that 'Both masters and seamen are much altered within this six months; having much encouragement in the state's service, [they] care not for merchant voyages.' They were particularly swayed, he noted, by the prospect of plunder.[64] A shipmaster who had been serving for wages alone might well feel the navy had far more to offer.

The navy's financial 'pulling power' was none the less limited. Pay was often far in arrears, and captains serving abroad might have to meet heavy expenses and end substantially out of pocket. On paper Goodson was earning 30s. a day as vice-admiral in the Caribbean; in reality he had to watch his arrears and expenses steadily mounting. Eventually he appealed to Thurloe, complaining that he had served the state 'for naught, but spent out of my own estate between four and five hundred pounds'. Not until February 1658 did the Admiralty order his salary to be paid, for a period stretching back over three and a half years.[65] Similarly John Bourne begged in 1655 for at least part of what he was due. His service, he observed drily, had brought him heavy responsibilities and painful wounds 'but no great alteration in my small estate'. Many others complained in similar terms.[66] Prize-money too was unpredictable. Officers dreamed of instant wealth and many no doubt profited handsomely during the Dutch war. But not all were lucky, and the wheels of the Prize Office ground slowly and erratically. Jacob Reynolds, for example, complained in 1654 that he had captured fifteen prizes

---

[63] SP 18/45/90; cf. SP 18/29/49; SP 18/46/13; SP 18/46/61.

[64] *FDW* iii. 285; Davis, *Shipping Industry*, 138–9; *Letters of Paige*, 89. For the pay of flag-officers, ranging from 7s. 6d. to 30s a day, see BL Add. MS 22546, fo. 143; *FDW* iii. 376, 436; SP 25 I 75, p. 411. The Generals were paid £3 a day.

[65] *Thurloe*, iv. 458; *CSPD 1657–8*, 525. For the problems of Mary Goodson see Rawl. MS A 187, fo. 404; *CSPD 1655*, 559; *CSPD 1655–6*, 317, 375, 565.

[66] SP 18/97/91, 91a; SP 18/135/70.

worth £20,000 and had yet to receive a penny. Prizes and plunder were a smaller inducement in the later 1650s, once it became clear how few targets Spain offered. Stayner's success against the Plate ships disguises the fact that the state's total net revenue from other prizes in the period from 1655 to 1659 was a trifling £8,000.[67] Prizes moreover could sometimes be a mixed blessing. Many ships carried false papers so that ownership was often in doubt, and a captain might subsequently face an action by the owners alleging plunder or fraud. The plaintive letter sent from a London gaol in 1658 by Robert Coleman shows that indemnity could be a sensitive issue in the navy as well as the army. He had been arrested, he explained, in a private suit brought over prizes captured years earlier, and his fate posed a threat to all naval officers. Were they to be left to suffer at law at the hands of their 'conquered enemies' for actions in wartime carried out in pursuit of their orders? If so, he reflected, 'our end of war is but the beginning of trouble', for there would soon be as many legal actions as there were shipowners.[68]

The navy's financial attractiveness varied according to the status of the shipmaster. Overall naval service probably offered little to masters with a stake of their own in ships and cargoes, especially as they were usually given great ships in the main battle-fleets where they stood little chance of intercepting prizes. Those who stayed on in the navy almost certainly did so more from patriotic or ideological commitment than for financial advantage. By contrast the navy must have appeared very attractive indeed to the lower ranks of shipmasters, who were serving for wages alone and had no guarantee of regular employment.

Many lesser shipmasters, however, were pushed into the navy rather than exercising a free and considered choice. The almost continuous warfare of the period spelt ruin to many seafarers. Jeffrey Dare, for example, described how the Dutch had seized his ship coming from Barbados. He lost £400, he explained, 'his whole estate', and he turned to the navy as the only way of providing for his family. Many other victims reasoned similarly. Sometimes the

---

[67] NMM ADL/Z/8 (12); M. Ashley, *Financial and Commercial Policy under the Cromwellian Protectorate* (2nd edn., 1962), 84–5; for Stayner see Firth, i. 56–7; Powell, *Blake*, 290.

[68] SP 18/195/57. In another case Capt. John Smith was prosecuted by the Prize Goods Commissioners for taking silk from the captain's cabin of a prize; the Admiralty had to intervene to explain that he was allowed such goods by the 'custom of the sea': Adm. 2/1730, fo. 267.

local authorities approached the Admiralty on their behalf: the magistrates of Hull recommended Francis Allen, for example, and the mayor of Newcastle explained how John Wetwang had been ruined by the loss of his ship.[69] There was an almost constant flow of petitions, for the Rump had many enemies and each quarrel produced its crop of innocent victims. John and Edward Witheridge were ruined when the Portuguese seized their ships at Lisbon in 1650 in the course of the dispute over Rupert. John had a three-quarters share in his vessel and lost about £2,500. When the brothers reached home both accepted commands in the navy and remained in its service.[70] Peter Butler was ruined by the Spaniards, who seized his ship at Santo Domingo when it was driven there by a storm. There were many similar cases.[71] Of course not every victim was offered a commission. The Admiralty vetted petitioners very carefully, anxious lest they should try to recoup their losses by embezzling public property. When Hugh Peter wrote on behalf of one public-spirited shipmaster he took care to explain that the man 'comes not in an indigent way, but out of a real desire to serve'.[72]

Other mariners were pushed into the navy through the closure of the trade routes which had provided their livelihoods. During the Dutch war the Baltic was closed to English shipping, a particularly heavy blow to the masters of ships held in the Sound. Though the Danes eventually freed the men they faced ruin without their ships, and the Admiralty helped by employing several of the victims.[73] It was the disruption of English trade in the Mediterranean that drove Jonas Poole into the navy. His ship was pressed into naval service at Leghorn to strengthen the English squadron, and though it eventually reached home safely its cargo was left behind and perished. The owners held him responsible and sued him. Spurned by his old employers, Poole was glad to accept an invitation to serve

[69] *FDW* iii. 400–2; SP 25/123, p. 121; SP 18/48/63; SP 18/46/14, 47.

[70] HCA 13/64, 8 Jan. 1651; HCA 13/66, 9 Nov. 1652; Rawl. MS A 225, fos. 45, 47ᵛ, 89, 138ʳ⁻ᵛ; Bodl. Dep. MS C 170, fos. 224–5; *Mercurius Politicus*, 17–24 Oct. 1650. John was killed in 1652; Edward served throughout the 1650s.

[71] HCA 13/67, 17 Aug. 1653; HCA 13/70, 24 Nov. 1655; *CSP Col.*, i. 432. Other former victims include Shelley, captured by the French (SP 18/94/77), Tarleton, captured by both royalists and French (SP 18/58/92), and Mootham, enslaved by the Moors of Algiers (Pepys, *Diary*, ii. 34).   [72] Add. MS 9300, fo. 123.

[73] The ships and masters held in the Sound are listed in *Thurloe*, ii. 402; Edward Nixon of Newcastle and George Acklam and Robert Drew of Hull received commands; others became masters in the navy: see n. 230, below.

with his kinsman William Penn.[74] Similarly the later war with Spain served to push Eustace Smith into the navy. Smith, a veteran Spanish trader, was at Cadiz when he learned that war was imminent; seeing his old livelihood gone he sailed at once to find Blake and offer his services.[75]

The second major group of officers comprises men who had risen within the navy itself. Under the Protectorate internal promotion was far more common than recruitment from outside. Of the eighty-nine captains first appointed between 1654 and 1660 only four transferred directly from a merchant command, and none was given one of the larger ships.[76] The navy could now replenish itself from its own resources.

Future officers in this group can often be glimpsed on the way up, serving as gunners, boatswains, carpenters, or petty officers.[77] As in later generations the lieutenant's place was often the final stepping-stone to a command, but many masters too went on to become captains and by no means all had served as lieutenants.[78] The officers in this group had generally gone to sea at an early age, learning their craft as servants to a captain or warrant-officer. Some came from naval families and had probably spent most of their working lives in the navy. Roger Cuttance served throughout the civil wars, though he did not obtain a command until 1651. Anthony Young's career can be traced back much further. Young had sailed as a ship's boy in Buckingham's expedition to the Île de Ré in 1627, at the age of ten, and served under Sir John Pennington in the 1630s; he went on to become a gunner's mate and then gunner before securing his first command in 1645. A namesake, a naval gunner under Charles I, may have been his father and perhaps

---

[74] *CSPD 1654*, 319; SP 18/182/56–7; Adm. 3/273, fo. 201; T. A. Spalding, *A Life of Richard Badiley* (Westminster, 1899), chs. 10–12; *CSPV 1647–52*, 323–4, 326–7; *CSPV 1653–4*, 13–14. Poole had £500 reimbursed in 1658. He was married to Penn's sister (Pepys, *Diary*, ii. 112).

[75] *Thurloe*, iii. 694; Blake, *Letters*, 307. On a previous voyage to Spain in 1649 Smith had been captured by Rupert; the ship (which he part-owned) was worth, with its cargo, £4,100 (HCA 13/66, 7 Jan. 1653; Blake, *Letters*, 80, 84). He served in the Dutch war in a hired ship.

[76] Butler, Henfield, Marsh, Robert Martin.

[77] Hodges, Noades, and Whitehorne were ex-gunners; John Wager, Ashford, and Baker ex-boatswains; Clay and Pickering ex-carpenters; Evans and Middleton ex-pursers; Jowles an ex-mate. William Pestell had been armourer under Sir John Pennington in 1632–5; NMM JOD 1/2, fos. 5, 35, 58, 79.

[78] At least 42 captains had served as lieutenants, and at least 20 as naval masters.

taught him his trade.[79] Similarly the future captain Richard Country appears in 1635 as boatswain's boy in the *Vanguard,* serving under the boatswain John Country, probably his father. At the start of the civil war Richard was still in the same ship, one rung higher as boatswain's grommet. Jacob Reynolds and Charles Wager appear in the 1640s as boatswain's mates.[80] Capt. Nicolas Heaton was said to have risen within the navy from the modest position of trumpeter's mate.[81] Even an ordinary seaman taken by the press could go far if he showed real ability. Anthony Mellidge was pressed as a youth in the late 1640s; ten years later he was commanding a fourth-rate.[82]

The two groups discussed so far were professional seamen. The third, by contrast, consisted of landsmen—army officers transferring to service afloat. The practice of appointing high-ranking soldiers to command fleets was very old. What was new in the interregnum was the scale of the military presence, ranging from admirals to warrant officers and below. At the higher levels army recruits were perhaps taking the place of the gentleman-captain, for they shared some of his attributes: they too were thought to possess superior fighting qualities, and a few enjoyed the support of powerful patrons ashore.

Five of the six Generals who served at sea under the Commonwealth had been army colonels; only Penn had a wholly maritime background. (General Desborough, who did not serve afloat, was another soldier.) When Blake was thought likely to die of his wounds in 1653 Col. Pride was talked of as a probable successor. The pre-eminence of the military even prompted a rumour that year that Cromwell was planning to make himself Lord Admiral and go to sea in the *Sovereign.*[83] The Generals' military background did have some relevance to their new profession. The warship had by now evolved into a floating artillery platform, so Deane's experience as an artillery officer was of particular value. All the Generals brought with them hard-won skills in deploying fighting units and

[79] Cuttance: C. H. Mayo (ed.), *The Minute Book of the Dorset Standing Committee, 23rd Sept., 1646 to 8th May, 1650* (Exeter, 1902), 262. Young: Adm. 7/729, pp. 251–2; Adm. 7/730, fo. 198ᵛ; NMMJOD 1/2, fo. 35; Add, MS 9301, fo. 113ᵛ; *CSPD 1643–4,* 558. Robt. Storey had a namesake (and father?) who was a master-gunner in 1634: Add. MS 9301, fo. 113ᵛ.

[80] JOD 1/2, fo. 128; Add. MS 9299, fo. 105 (Country); Adm. 7/673, p. 465 (Reynolds); *FDW* i. 6 (Wager). Reynolds was perhaps a son of Israel Reynolds, a naval boatswain in the 1630s.

[81] *FDW* i. 23.   [82] A. Mellidge, *A True Relation* [1657], 1–4.

[83] *FDW* v. 291; *Several Informations . . . concerning . . . John Lilburne* (1653), 8.

maintaining order in battle. Professional seamen had plenty of experience fighting pirates and privateers but the Dutch war was the first time the navy had been called on to fight a fleet action since Elizabethan times.

The military presence and the fact that so many ships were named after battles ashore strongly influenced the navy's contemporary image. Popham, Blake, and Deane were often referred to in Admiralty records by their old military titles, and one journalist referred to Popham's 'brigade' instead of his squadron. Nehemiah Bourne and Edward Blagg both chose to be known by their military titles as majors.[84] Penn was occasionally described as 'Colonel' and John Stokes as 'General', though neither had a military background; Andrew Ball, another professional seaman, was praised as a 'noble and approved soldier'.[85]

The Generals were only the conspicuous tip of the military iceberg. Some of their old colleagues followed them to sea. Major Jeremiah Smyth joined his colleague and patron Monck, though as a former mariner he is hard to categorize. He entered the navy as a captain and was soon commanding the squadron in the Downs.[86] Most army recruits, lacking any experience at sea, came in as lieutenants or *reformados* (ex-officers serving in the ranks). The lieutenant was primarily a fighting officer and a lack of seamanship mattered little if he could lead a boarding party and inspire his men; if he proved himself he might look for a command of his own after a couple of years. Thomas Adams, Blake's former lieutenant at the sieges of Lyme and Taunton, illustrates the pattern well. He served first as a reformado to gain experience and then as lieutenant in the flagship, going on to become commander of a Dutch prize and finally, on Blake's recommendation, captain of a newly built frigate.[87]

Naval officers' pay lagged somewhat behind that of their army

---

[84] For Bourne see e.g. *FDW* vi. 216, 233; for Blagg see e.g. SP 18/100/151. Blagg had served in the Plymouth garrison during the civil war (SP 18/100/151), and later in the sea-regiment at Hispaniola.

[85] *A Perfect Diurnall*, 5–12 Aug. 1651; *FDW* iv. 125; *Thurloe*, vi. 679; *FDW* iv. 101.

[86] *DNB*. Smyth was briefly captain of a privateer set out in 1647 by the future regicide MP Col. John Moore: Adm. 6/673, p. 243. For his earlier years as a merchant seaman see Adm. 7/729, p. 128; F. W. Brooks (ed.), *The First Order Book of the Hull Trinity House, 1632–1665* (Yorks. Arch. Soc., cv; 1942), 49.

[87] *FDW* i. 11, v. 381; Blake, *Letters*, 196; *Terrible and Bloudy Newes from Sea* [6 Aug.] 1652, 8; SP 18/83/90; Powell, *Blake*, 254, 277. Adams died in 1658.

colleagues: only in the largest ships (first to third rates) did a naval commander earn more than an army captain. The captain of a fourth-rate received 7s. 8d. a day, compared to an infantry captain's 8s. and a cavalry captain's 10s., even though the naval officer commanded more men and held a far more responsible position. A senior navy captain was arguably closer to a major in terms of responsibility, but even in a first-rate his daily pay (15s.) was some way below a major's (21s.). A naval lieutenant, paid from 2s. 6d. to 3s. a day, was also well behind his army equivalent (4s. in the infantry, 5s. 4d. or more in the cavalry).[88] There were nevertheless several considerations which might draw army officers into the navy, even if they had no influential patron there. Its rapid expansion offered good prospects for promotion, especially during the Dutch war. It was, predictably, the years 1652–3 which saw the largest influx. John Cuttle, a typical recruit, had been serving in the army from the outbreak of the civil war but he became a naval lieutenant in 1653 and remained in the service, eventually gaining a command. The navy provided free board and lodging and the difference in pay was offset by the chance of a rich prize. In any case many army recruits, perhaps most, had been NCOs (or even less) rather than commissioned officers, with correspondingly lower pay. Capt. Benjamin Sacheverell had been a mere trooper in the Dorset local forces in the civil war. Similarly William Phipps had been only a trooper in Cromwell's horse regiment in the New Model before switching to the navy; he was made a lieutenant in due course and served in this position throughout the later 1650s, with higher pay than he would have received in the army.[89]

In other cases army officers were pushed into the navy by circumstances. When the Western and Northern armies were disbanded in 1646–7 there were many young ex-officers with no civilian livelihood to resume. Several former army officers were already serving as naval lieutenants by 1648, such as Robert Haytubb and Stephen Rose.[90] The New Model itself shrank during the 1650s, reducing jobs and opportunities, and much of what remained was stationed permanently in Scotland and Ireland, offering only a spartan and inglorious existence far from home. Some

---

[88] C. H. Firth, *Cromwell's Army* (1962 edn.), 42–3, 186–7; *FDW* iii. 285.

[89] Sacheverell: Mayo, *Minute Book*, 235. Capt. David Dove had been a gunner in the Weymouth garrison: ibid. 232–3. Phipps: SP 18/53/88–9; SP 18/225/7. For army officers' pay see Firth, *Cromwell's Army*, 186–7.

[90] SP 18/64/49; SP 18/80/47. Rose had been an army captain.

NCOs were pushed into the navy in a still more literal sense, arriving among the thousands of soldiers sent to help man the fleet during the Dutch war. One Gregory Tom, who came with a party from Col. Ingoldsby's regiment, felt sufficiently qualified after two summers at sea to apply for a lieutenant's place.[91]

If we compare the officers of the interregnum with those of other periods it is clear that the pendulum had swung a long way back towards the tarpaulins. The navy of the 1650s contained very few of the gentleman-captains prominent in the 1630s and none of the aristocratic captains, appointed on the strength of court connections, to be found after the Restoration. At the end of the century Richard Gibson listed twenty men who had risen from cabin-boy to admiral, and it is striking that no fewer than fourteen had achieved their first commands under the Commonwealth.[92] It was not a wholly 'tarpaulin navy', of course. The Generals themselves were well-born: Popham, who had served under Charles I, belonged to a substantial landed family, and Mountagu's family had entered the peerage under James I.[93] Monck and Deane too both came from landed families, though as younger sons they had had to make their own way.[94] Blake's background was mercantile but he had acquired a gentleman's education at Oxford. (He even tried for a college Fellowship, and was wont in later years to bemuse his naval colleagues with Latin witticisms.) He had acquired a gentleman's tastes too, furnishing his quarters with royal tapestries from Somerset House—till Cromwell commandeered them.[95] Even Penn, younger son of a younger son, had gentry forebears.[96] Sir George Ayscue, one of the most senior flag-officers, also came from a long-established landed family. His father had held a minor post at the

[91] SP 18/61/110–11. Tom served as an army captain under Venables in the West Indies, and settled in Jamaica: *The Narrative of General Venables*, ed. C. H. Firth (Camden Soc., 1900), 117 and n. For NCOs sent to the navy during the Dutch war see also SP 18/55/31; *FDW* iii. 424.

[92] 'Extracts from a Commissioner's Notebook', in *The Naval Miscellany*, ii, ed. Sir J. Knox Laughton (NRS xl; 1912), 160–1. For a survey of the gentleman-tarpaulin controversy see N. Elias, 'Studies in the Genesis of the Naval Profession', *British Journal of Sociology*, i (1950), 291–309.

[93] *DNB*; Harris, *Mountagu*, ch. 1. Mountagu said in 1660 that he would rather marry his daughter to a bankrupt gentleman than to the richest merchant: Pepys, *Diary*, i. 269.

[94] *DNB*: M. Ashley, *General Monck* (1977), 2–5; J. B. Deane, *The Life of Richard Deane* (1870), 48.

[95] J. Oldmixon, *The History and Life of Robert Blake, Esq.* (1740), 4, 114; *CSPD 1654*, 291.   [96] *DNB*.

court of Charles I, and Ayscue himself lived in considerable style on his Surrey estate.[97]

But if the preference for men of gentle birth was far from dead the gentleman-captain, however widely defined, played only a minor part in the interregnum navy. Under Charles I many captains had been younger sons of gentry origin, going to sea at an early age to make a career, and this type of officer was to become predominant by the eighteenth century.[98] In the Commonwealth navy there were relatively few such men. Only about twenty captains can be linked with the landed gentry, and the links were often tenuous. Moulton, Lane, Smyth, Plumleigh, and many others belonged to junior branches already firmly rooted in maritime trade.[99] Badiley belonged to the junior branch of a fairly modest Staffordshire family.[100] Charles Saltonstall was connected with a better-known landed family, but he remarked that his kinsfolk ashore would long since have forgotten his very existence.[101] John Wetwang's family, though established in Northumberland since the thirteenth century, was now in decline and had never been rich. Wetwang himself belonged to a junior branch engaged in trade on such a modest scale that the capture of his ship by the Dutch had spelt ruin.[102] Francis Penrose, a minor Cornish gentleman, was similarly pushed into the navy by personal disaster, for the cavaliers overran his estate early in the civil war and left him destitute.[103] Richard Rooth was brought

[97] *DNB; Lincolnshire Pedigrees*, ed. A. R. Maddison (HS l; 1902), i. 62. Ayscue leased the small manor of Hamm Court in 1634 for £18 p.a.: P. Le Fevre, 'Sir George Ayscue, Commonwealth and Restoration Admiral', *MM* lxviii (1982), 189. Apart from naval pay, his income appears to have been mainly from commercial ventures.

[98] Kennedy, 'Naval Captains', 191–3; thesis, ch. 2; Rodger, *Wooden World*, ch. 7.

[99] Moulton was born at Landulph, Cornwall, and was probably related to the Devon family: J. and G. F. Matthews (eds.), *Abstracts of Probate Acts in the Prerogative Court of Canterbury, 1652–3* (1911), 340; *The Visitation of the County of Devon, 1620*, ed. F. T. Colby (HS vi; 1872), 196; Lane was of Beccles, probably related to the Lanes of Ipswich: J. and G. F. Matthews (eds.), *Abstracts of Probate Acts . . . 1653–4* (1914), 139; Add. MS 19139, fos. 42ᵛ–43, 45; *A Visitation of Suffolk, 1664–8*, ed. H. Reynolds (HS lxi; 1910), 149; Smyth was from Hull, but probably related to the Smyths of Kent (and previously Suffolk): *DNB; The Visitation of Kent, 1619–21*, ed. R. Hovendon (HS xlii; 1898), 48; for Plumleigh see nn. 109, 202, below.

[100] *The Diary of Henry Townshend*, ed. J. W. Willis Bund (Worcestershire Arch. Soc., i; 1920), 32; *Staffordshire Pedigrees, 1680–1700*, ed. Sir G. J. Armytage and W. H. Rylands (HS lxiii; 1912), 13.   [101] Saltonstall, *Navigator*, sig. Aᵛ.

[102] E. Bateson, *A History of Northumberland* (1893–5), ii. 186–9, 191.

[103] *CSPD 1644*, 551; *Vis. of Cornwall*, 170; D. Gilbert, *The Parochial History of Cornwall* (1838), ii. 25–30.

up in the household of the famous cavalier Ormonde, but this connection must have been more hindrance than help; Rooth owed his rise in the navy to his tarpaulin kinsman Penn.[104]

The 'tarpaulin' officer dominated the navy of the 1650s. The term was often used very loosely, though, and to be useful it needs to be defined more closely. Even if restricted to professional seamen of non-gentle birth it still spans the vast gulf separating the ordinary, penniless sailor from the rich shipmaster commanding a great East Indiaman. Most of the navy's senior captains were indeed born into seafaring families, but they were often families of some substance. Monck's call had been for good estates *or interests*, and many had sizeable family interest in shipping and trade. Nicholas Reed, captain of the *Sovereign*, provides the most dramatic example. Reed was a professional seaman, and thus a tarpaulin; but he was a rich shipowner too, able to acquire an estate at Stokes Hall, Suffolk, and lift his family into the ranks of the landed gentry.[105] The gap between gentleman and tarpaulin might thus be less significant than differences within the ranks of the tarpaulins themselves. Many other senior captains came from well-established families. Nehemiah and John Bourne's father owned a shipyard at Wapping, which Nehemiah continued to run.[106] Richard Haddock went to sea in his mid-teens but had little in common with the other ship's boys, for his father was master and co-owner of the vessel and his grandfather was a senior parliamentary commander.[107] William Goodson, a shipowner, had been able to buy an estate of 500 acres in the Fens, probably from trading profits made before he entered the navy.[108] Many other officers belonged to families prominent in the provincial seaports. Thomas Teddiman's father had been mayor of Dover. Joseph Cubitt was mayor of Dartmouth both before and after his time in the navy. Robert Plumleigh belonged to another notable family there, and could count a former mayor and one of Charles I's admirals among his kinsmen.[109] Seth Hawley was to be

---

[104] Coventry MS 98, fo. 52ᵛ; G. E. C[okayne], *The Complete Peerage* (1910–59), i. 225; the Rooths held lands in Kilkenny.

[105] *Vis. of Suffolk*, 137; SP 18/90/130; H. F. Waters, *Genealogical Gleanings in England* (Boston, Mass., 1901), 1354–5. Reed styled himself 'esquire' in his will.

[106] Chaplin, 'Bourne', esp. 31–2, 72–3, 93, 101, 111.

[107] HCA 13/62, 7 Mar. 1650; cf. *Correspondence of the Family of Haddock*, ed. E. M. Thompson (Camden Soc., 1883).

[108] *Thurloe*, iv. 458.

[109] S. P. H. Statham, *The History of . . . Dover* (1899), 168; *DNB* (Teddiman); SP 18/46/13; SP 18/148/116; E. Windeatt, 'The Borough of . . . Dartmouth', *Transactions of the Devonshire Arch. Soc.*, xliv (1912), 668 (Cubitt); *Vis. of Devon*,

mayor of King's Lynn, as his grandfather had been before him. Edward Tarleton belonged to a respectable Lancashire family and became mayor of Liverpool after the Restoration.[110] There were certainly other officers who came from much humbler backgrounds. Myngs's father, for example, was still alive and working as a shoemaker, and John Harman's brother worked as an upholsterer in London.[111] Most of the warrant-officers promoted in the mid- and late 1650s were similarly of modest birth. Even so it is clear that many captains, especially in the larger ships, were men of substance. An ignorant landsman might lump all 'tarpaulins' together; the Admiralty and mariners themselves knew better.

How fair then was the general view that tarpaulin officers were a rough and uneducated breed? An early Stuart official spoke contemptuously of 'mechanick men that have been bred up from swabbers', and some did behave as boorishly as he would have expected.[112] Even respectable officers were defensive about their lack of polish. William Penn apologized for his 'rude and uncult' style, and Giles Shelley for his simple 'sea-breeding'. But Shelley's fluency of phrase and elegant script convey a very different message from the words themselves. His 'rudeness', like Penn's, was a very relative matter, and his apology shows merely that he was conscious of lacking a gentleman's style (despite—or perhaps because of— possible ties with a Sussex gentry family).[113] Tarpaulins varied as much in education and behaviour as in social and economic background. Capt. Nicholas Foster impressed Ambassador White-locke with his civility and polish. Lt. Nathaniel Browne was able to sprinkle a letter of application with Latin tags. Nehemiah Bourne had been intended for Oxford. Several officers published tracts, on religion as well as navigation and travel; Saltonstall's manual on navigation, an authoritative work, was based on wide

211; P. Russell, *Dartmouth: A History* (1950) 106–7, 110, 133. For the naval career of Sir Richard Plumleigh see *CSPD 1627–37*.

[110] 'A Calendar of the Freemen of Lynn, 1282–1836', *Norfolk Arch. Soc.*, supp. vol. (1913) 110, 122, 128, 181; C. J. Palmer, *The Perlustration of Great Yarmouth* (Yarmouth, 1872–5), iii. 39, 399 (Hawley); *Familiae Minorum Gentium*, ed. J. W. Clay (HS xxxvii–xl; 1894–5), i. 131–3 (Tarleton).

[111] Pepys, *Diary*, vii. 166 (though even Myngs had some distant landed connections: *DNB*); *Le Neve's Pedigrees of the Knights*, ed. G. W. Marshall (HS viii; 1873), 3.

[112] Oppenheim, 226; Monson, *Tracts*, iii. 434–5; Clarke MS 4/4, 1649 (38).

[113] Penn, *Memorials*, i. 163; Adm. 7/674, p. 57; cf. Heaton: 'I am no scribe but a seaman': *CSPD 1654*, 303–4.

reading as well as long practical experience.[114] We thus need to distinguish once more between the various groups which made up the seafaring world. The 'sea-breeding' of many a shipmaster set him far apart from the mind and manner of the ordinary sailor. To be successful he had to learn not only navigation but how to deal with merchants, owners, and suppliers at home and abroad. He might acquire linguistic skills too: Capt. Robert Wilkinson had learned Spanish, French, and Dutch in the course of his seagoing career. Capt. Mark Harrison spoke Dutch, Spanish, and Portuguese, and could understand French. Edward Coxere tells us that despite his parents' modest circumstances they sent him to live in France at the age of fourteen to learn the language, appreciating how much it would help his future career. From the outset he thus belonged to a different world from his unskilled, uneducated shipmates.[115] Competent literacy was virtually a prerequisite for a naval commission. Only three captains were unable to sign their names and none of them advanced far.[116] Though the education of a tarpaulin officer was likely to have been mainly practical it would be a serious mistake to brush it aside.

III. PROMOTION AND PATRONAGE

It is generally accepted that most officers in the seventeenth century did not think in terms of a 'naval career' but moved in and out of the navy as circumstances changed. None the less the constant warfare of the 1650s, requiring large fleets to be set out each year by the state, helped to give the officer corps a more permanent character than ever before. There seems to have been a growing sense of professional identity among its members, and notions of precedence began to take shape based on length of service within it. When the Dutch war made rapid expansion necessary the Admiralty resolved that naval officers who had already served well should 'be preferred into better ships before others, and that such [outsiders] as shall be recommended for employment be placed in their rooms, an orderly

[114] *Thurloe*, i, 602; SP 128/108/2; Chaplin, 'Bourne', 32; Saltonstall, *Navigator*. For religious writings see ch. 9.

[115] HCA 13/64, 3 May 1651; HCA 13/70, 5 Feb. 1655; E. Coxere, *Adventures by Sea*, ed. E. H. W. Meyerstein (Oxford, 1945), 3–4.

[116] Pittock, King, Goose; cf. Rodger, *Wooden World*, 262. Dutch captains may have been rather less literate: *FDW* iv. 338.

course to be had in all removes'.[117] Though this resolve was often ignored, the thinking behind it is suggestive. There was deep resentment among senior captains in 1653 when Anthony Earning was suddenly promoted from a hired merchantman to a powerful new third-rate, and all the Generals were caught up in the ensuing row. Blake and Desborough admitted making a mistake: they had thought the new ship was smaller, and to restore calm they had to promise equally good ships to aggrieved officers such as Stayner and Cuttance.[118] On another occasion Lawson gave a very frosty reply when he was approached about a merchant shipmaster being considered for a fourth-rate: the person was wholly unsuitable, he wrote, 'having never borne any office in a man of war'. The proposal was quietly dropped.[119]

A commissioned officer in the seventeenth century did not hold a permanent rank, and had no guarantee that he would be employed again at the same level—or at all. Opportunities for promotion were fewer after the Dutch war, so some officers who had risen rapidly found themselves unable to climb any higher. Anthony Earning, after his sudden elevation, remained in his new ship for the next six years. Henry Packe, after succeeding his brother in the *Amity*, remained there from 1652 to 1659.[120] More junior men who had won commissions during the war often had to drop back later to lower positions. Richard Suffield, for example, had secured the command of a Dutch prize early in 1653 despite being 'judged questionable' by the Admiralty; he had no chance of a commission in the smaller post-war navy and had to settle for a master's place.[121] Former lieutenants sometimes served as warrant-officers or reformados. It would thus be quite wrong to think of an officer as steadily climbing a 'career ladder'; in some cases a game of snakes and ladders would be a more appropriate image. Edward Tarleton's erratic progress makes the point well: Tarleton dropped from captain to midshipman when his vessel was wrecked, rose to be captain of another ship, dropped again to a reformado's place when this too was lost at sea, and rose once more as far as lieutenant. The

[117] Rawl. MS A 226, fo. 224.

[118] SP 18/60/4, 5; *CSPD 1653–4, 516*; SP 18/62/129; Rawl. MS A 461, fo. 31ᵛ.

[119] SP 18/86/12.

[120] Anderson, *List of Captains*, 10, 17.

[121] *CSPD 1652–3*, 42, 513; SP 18/46/16; SP 18/79/55; SP 18/79/12; Adm. 3/273, fo. 68. Similarly Capt. Joyne dropped to a lieutenant's place after the war, and Crapnel, Harditch, and Jones served as masters.

Admiralty understandably refused to give a third ship to a man so accident-prone.[122]

Promotion could be very rapid for a man of obvious ability. William Whitehorne rose from ship's gunner to become Commander-in-Chief in the Downs in the space of four years.[123] But as in most professions an officer's rise was likely to be slow and unpredictable if he depended on merit alone. It took Thomas Trafford eleven years to rise from corporal to lieutenant (in 1653), and a further thirteen to become a captain. Tobias Mihill had served sixteen years as midshipman, mate, and lieutenant when he applied (in vain) for a command. Men from artisan backgrounds usually took much longer to work their way up than those from well-to-do families or with influential friends. William Pickering, a former ship's carpenter, was already in his mid-fifties when he was first made captain.[124]

Luck played an important role. Many a lieutenant had his first taste of command in a prize his ship had captured; in the early 1650s prizes were often added to the navy, so he might then have a good chance to prove his worth.[125] Others were rewarded for conspicuous bravery in action.[126] Many vacancies arose unpredictably through death, sickness, or dismissal, every such personal tragedy creating a welcome opportunity for another.

Patronage too remained central to the pattern of promotion. In the 1650s it was mostly exercised by the senior officers serving afloat. A contemporary recalled, for example, that Penn's 'interest was always very great, so as the captains of his fleet in the Straits [1650–2] had great and speedy preferment'. Four of his seven captains on that expedition later became flag-officers and two others flag-captains.[127] On a lesser scale every captain was a patron, each

[122] SP 18/58/92; *CSPD 1655*, 529, 530, 553; SP 18/122/93; Adm. 3/273, fo. 247ᵛ; Carte MS 73, fo. 222.

[123] *CSPD 1652–3*, 516, 519; *CSPD 1657–8*, 524.

[124] SP 46/114, fo. 70; Add. MS 9300, fos. 292ᵛ–293; Pepys, *Cat.* i. 415 (Trafford); SP 46/117, fo. 158; 18/122/55 (Mihill); HCA 13/65, 20 Mar. 1652; SP 18/28/31; Blake, *Letters*, 325 (Pickering). For the duties of a ship's corporal see *Boteler's Dialogues*, 32.

[125] e.g. Richard Country, John Grimsditch, Benjamin Blake, Edward Moorcock.

[126] e.g. Anthony Rively (Adm. 2/1730, fo. 244ᵛ), and Thomas Wright, who lost a leg while commanding a hired merchantman and was then made captain of a state ship (*FDW* i. 343–4, vi. 51).

[127] Penn, *Memorials*, ii. 616; *FDW* i. 67. His captains were Lawson, Howett, Ben. Blake, and Jordan, all flag-officers; Ball and Mildmay, flag-captains, both killed in 1653; and Robert Saunders.

with his own circle of clients and dependants. He had a completely free hand in choosing petty officers and could often influence the choice of his lieutenant and warrant-officers.[128] Captains naturally suggested men they knew and trusted, often someone already serving on board. The captain of the *Ruby* thus proposed as lieutenant a man 'who hath been with me a long time, I knowing him to be a very able honest man for the place', and Blagg put forward a man he 'had good experience of, in several engagements'. Capt. Robert Blake wanted one of his volunteers, an ex-boatswain; the man's brother, the previous lieutenant, was doubtless responsible for bringing him to Blake's notice.[129]

Patronage was sometimes ideological in character. Several of Lawson's protégés, for example, shared his hostility to the Protectorate.[130] Anthony Mellidge was aware how much he owed to the religious radicalism he shared with successive captains, recalling how Nehemiah Bourne 'loved me, and would have preferred me in the service', and how he had then been 'beloved' by Capt. Heaton, his commander in the *Sapphire*; when Heaton fell sick Mellidge was made acting commander, though he had been serving only as master's mate.[131] In other cases there were ties of friendship between people from the same neighbourhood. Nicholas Reed, from near Ipswich, no doubt helped his neighbour Lionel Lane of Beccles to succeed him in the *Sovereign*. Lane in turn was the patron of his neighbours Nathaniel Browne of Woodbridge (who became his lieutenant) and Thomas Elliott of Aldeburgh.[132] Similarly Goodson and his protégé Christopher Myngs both had roots in Norfolk, and Myngs later advanced the future admiral Sir John Narbrough, who had been born in the very same parish and first went to sea under him; in turn yet another boy from the parish, the future admiral Sir Cloudesley Shovell, began *his* career under Narbrough.[133]

In many cases, predictably, there were ties of blood between patron and dependant. Blake was the eldest of eleven children, and many of his kindred followed him into the navy. His brother

---

[128] *FDW* iii. 285. There were many nominees for commands in 1653, but few for lieutenancies: SP 18/46/47. Lt. Haytubb, a former army officer, complained that the pay was inadequate to support his family: SP 18/64/49.
[129] SP 18/46/82; SP 18/82/92; SP 18/84/80.
[130] e.g. Abelson, Dakins, and Best.
[131] Mellidge, *True Relation*, 3; SP 18/114/34.
[132] *Vis. of Suffolk*, 137; HMC 39, *Eliot Hodgkin*, 50; SP 18/79/44; SP 18/105/126; SP 18/108/2; SP 18/64/133.
[133] *FDW* i. 12–13; F. E. Dyer, *The Life of Sir John Narbrough* (1931), 8–9.

Benjamin, nephews Robert and Samuel, and cousin William became captains. William's son Thomas was a naval officer too, and Sidrach (or Shadrach) Blake, Benjamin's father-in-law, was commander of a hired merchantman. Another Robert Blake was a purser, his warrant signed by the Admiral himself; when the man asked for another job an official in the Navy remarked: 'I conceive [it] will not be denied him, he being a kinsman to General Blake.'[134] Penn too was zealous in advancing his relations. On his expedition to the Caribbean he took his brother-in-law Jonas Poole as captain of the flagship, another relation (Richard Rooth) as its lieutenant, and a third as boatswain. Several of Poole's sons also went along, and Penn gave one of them (William) a lucrative post as Collector of Prize Goods, as well as advancing Rooth to a vacant command. Penn was later able to help William Poole and Rooth to successful careers in the Restoration navy.[135] Nehemiah Bourne was another energetic nepotist. His younger brother John followed him as flag-officer, and Nehemiah lobbied hard to win their brother-in-law Anthony Earning a good command. Bartholomew Bourne, almost certainly another relation, was lieutenant under John in the Dutch war.[136] The other Generals were less assiduous in advancing their kin, though Deane may have been related to Capts. Grimsditch and Mildmay, and Monck was possibly related by marriage to his protégé Smyth.[137]

Ordinary captains naturally behaved like their superiors. Anthony Young obtained a new command for his kinsman Thomas Wilkes when his ship was lost in the Indies.[138] Plumleigh said bluntly that the man he wanted (and got) as his lieutenant 'being a relative is valued at a higher rate'.[139] Captains were able quite frequently to instal a close relation as lieutenant. Young's lieutenant in the *Worcester* in 1652, for example, was his brother Joseph; when Young was turned out Joseph lost his place too, for the incoming captain contrived to have his own brother appointed in his stead.[140]

[134] C. D. Curtis, *Blake: General at Sea* (Taunton, 1934), 176–7; Blake, *Letters*, 343–4, 368; NMM ADL/Z/8 (13; cf. 4, 8).

[135] Penn, *Memorials*, ii. 18, 616; SP 18/182/57i; Cromwell, *Writings*, iii. 575; 'Richard Rooth's Sea Journal of the Western Design, 1654–5', ed. J. F. Battick, *Jamaica Journal*, v (1971) 8; Venables, *Narrative*, 51; Pepys, *Cat.* i. 394–5. Rooth had earlier served with Penn as a volunteer in 1650.

[136] SP 18/60/4; *CSPD 1653–4*, 516; SP 18/78/73. Bartholomew was killed at Portland in 1653.

[137] Deane, *Deane*, 57, 425, 578; Clar. MS 71, fo. 243 (which states that Smyth was married to Monck's sister).

[138] SP 18/116/9.   [139] *CSPD 1658–9*, 535.   [140] SP 18/122/121.

Stayner and Newbery also had brothers serving with them, while John Lambert had his son as lieutenant.[141] The Admiralty often turned down requests for such arrangements in the later 1650s but the practice proved hard to eradicate.

Serving officers were not the only patrons. Any civilian with influential contacts might seek to use them on behalf of a needy relation, and how far this could go is indicated by a letter to Mountagu begging a lieutenancy for the writer's wife's aunt's half-brother![142] MPs inherited at least some of the influence courtiers had once enjoyed. In 1648 the Independent MP Robert Reynolds (later Solicitor-General) helped Thomas Sparling to his first command.[143] Under the Rump Henry Appleton probably owed his appointment to his contacts with Speaker Lenthall and Fairfax, and the MPs John Lisle and William Purefoy also intervened on behalf of kinsmen in the navy.[144] And it doubtless helped Capt. Robert Vessey to have the Admiralty Commissioner and MP Thomas Kelsey as his brother-in-law.[145]

Inevitably the army, as a key element in the new political establishment, also played a considerable part in naval patronage. The powerful support of Major-General Harrison secured a lieutenant's place in 1653 for Edmund Nightingale, described as godly, able, and 'very valiant'.[146] Some military leaders obtained commissions for their own kinsmen, and we find lieutenants with such names as Alured, Axtell, Ludlow, and Pride. Philip Ludlow, a younger brother of the future Major-General, was made lieutenant of Rainborough's flagship in 1648 while still only nineteen. Two years later he was flag-lieutenant to Popham, and was given charge of the Brazil ships being sent home from Portugal. His death during the voyage cut short what promised to be a rapid advance, and his burial in Westminster Abbey made it plain that he was not regarded as any ordinary lieutenant.[147]

Army commanders in Scotland and Ireland exercised particularly

[141] *A Perfect Account*, 6–13 Oct. 1652; SP 18/146/19.
[142] SP 18/224/1.
[143] Add. MS 9305, fo. 42.
[144] *A Perfect Diurnall*, 31 Dec. 1649–7 Jan. 1650. (For Lenthall as patron see also SP 18/176/22.) Add. MS 9305, fo. 25ᵛ; Clarke MS 4/4, 1649 (18, 29); *CSPD 1651–2*, 367.
[145] SP 18/139/87.
[146] SP 18/46/47.
[147] On Ludlow see *The Memoirs of Edmund Ludlow*, ed. C. H. Firth (Oxford, 1894), i. 236; HCA 13/61, fo. 117ᵛ; NMM AGC/21/26, fo. 2ʳ⁻ᵛ.

strong influence. They helped to direct naval operations in those parts, and they had some forces under their own immediate control. Three Dutch prizes were sent to Deane in Scotland in 1652, for example, for him to use as he saw fit.[148] Col. Alured, Governor of Ayr, bought a ship for its garrison to use in reducing the Scottish islands and suppressing privateers, and the captain he appointed, Tarleton, later secured a more regular naval command.[149] Ireland offers parallel cases. Nathaniel Cobham, a military officer attached to the Ordnance Office, served as master-gunner in Cromwell's army there in 1649; General Ireton gave him a ship to use against Irish strongholds in the south-west, and he was rewarded for his good service with command of a new frigate.[150] The next commander in Ireland, Fleetwood, also set out a ship to assist military operations, and in due course the Admiralty added it to the navy's establishment.[151]

Though the system of naval patronage might look indefensible to modern eyes, it has received a vigorous and effective defence in N. A. M. Rodger's recent book on the Hanoverian navy. Rodger argues in part from results: the navy's impressive record shows beyond doubt that the system worked. It was natural and desirable for senior officers to advance deserving subordinates and they were unlikely to recommend the incompetent for, as he points out, this would damage their credit and might one day even place their own lives at risk.[152] A patronage system of some kind was inevitable, given the nature of seventeenth-century society, and one exercised mainly by the senior officers in the fleet, as in the 1650s, was the most satisfactory. In general patrons appear to have acted responsibly. Blake advanced his kinsmen but scrupulously chose not to intervene when his brother Benjamin ran into trouble with the authorities. Richard Gibson, who noted how Penn advanced his protégés, noted too that subsequently 'his favourites kept their places, being founded upon merit'.[153] The interregnum navy probably came as near to providing a career open to talent as was possible in that age.

---

[148] *French Occurrences*, 2–9 Aug. 1652.

[149] SP 18/55/21, 22, 29; SP 18/58/93. Tarleton also had the support of the Scottish C.-in-C., Robert Lilburne.

[150] *CSPD 1649–50*, 187, 536; *CSPD 1651*, 547; *CSPD 1651–2*, 525; *CSPD 1652–3*, 615; SP 18/38/118.   [151] SP 18/137/111–12.

[152] Rodger, *Wooden World*, 273–302.

[153] For Ben. Blake see below, n. 183; Penn, *Memorials*, ii. 616.

But the navy's success should not blind us to the drawbacks inherent in the system, however responsibly it was operated. Some discontent existed at the time. In the wake of Dungeness a critic demanded 'What can be expected when captains are put into ships through favour, not through desert?' The navy, he complained, was still full of 'wasps and drones' serving merely for 'filthy lucre'. Criticism was mainly voiced, of course, by those without effective patrons. Francis Cranwell wrote bitterly to the Admiralty Commissioners in 1659, 'I see it is neither desert nor ability, but favour which carries the game.' Tried seamen like himself were laid aside, he claimed, while senior posts went to well-connected, inexperienced newcomers. 'All your commanders have not been masters before they were commanders', he observed tartly, 'but leaped more in one year than I have done in ten.'[154] Capt. William Godfrey was indignant at being laid aside after eighteen years's service to make room for a man who had served only one year but enjoyed the influential backing of General Fleetwood.[155] Another officer, lamenting that he had 'no friends to procure his preferment', appealed to Monck in rhyme:

> Some deserve ere they desire, and yet do lack when they require;
> Some desire and never deserve, and get the gain—the other shall starve.

He should have known that Monck was not the man to be softened by verse.[156]

It might be argued that a good officer would always attract a patron, and that complaints came only from the incompetent. But there is evidence that able men too could be ignored if they lacked influential friends. John Wetwang begged the Commissioners in 1654 for promotion from the tiny *Wren*. 'I have very few friends to move for me', he explained, and as he lived and served 'out of the way' (on the north-east coast) he was slow to hear of vacancies. His request for a new frigate is endorsed 'disposed of long since', which underlines his point; dissatisfied, he left the navy. Yet Wetwang's ability is not in doubt: he returned in the Second Dutch War and went on to a distinguished career, rewarded with a knighthood.[157]

---

[154] Bodl. Tanner MS 53, fo. 174ᵛ; SP 18/202/28.

[155] SP 18/176/22. He was replaced by Peter Butler.

[156] SP 18/61/24. This was William Sanders, probably identical with Richard Gibson's kinsman who later served as master of the *Brier* (*FDW* i. 28).

[157] SP 18/81/19; *DNB*; Pepys, *Cat.* i. 421–2. Wetwang lived at Dunstans, Co. Durham.

Even William Penn had felt forgotten serving in the Irish Sea in 1646, calling it a 'dull and fruitless employment [to be] chained on this coast' and begging to serve directly under Batten, where he might earn the admiral's favour.[158] The major flaws in the system were nepotism and the large part played by chance. Promotion depended first on good luck in finding a patron, and then on that patron surviving and retaining his influence. The death of an influential man blighted the prospects of his clients at every level. Nathaniel Browne wrote plaintively in 1655 that all his patrons were either dead or serving far away, and as a stranger to the new Admiralty Commissioners he had no means 'whereby I can expect any future employment'—especially living in a 'remote habitation' (Woodbridge, Suffolk).[159] There were many such upsets. One master ambitious for a command had pinned all his hopes on the Navy Commissioner Robert Moulton, his 'near kinsman (and best friend under the Almighty)'. Moulton's sudden death blasted his hopes for ever.[160] Political reversals could be equally devastating. Major-General Harrison and John Carew were powerful figures in 1653 when they helped Nathaniel Rockwell to a lieutenancy, but their influence vanished when Cromwell became Protector, and Rockwell's career advanced no further.[161] Capt. Robert Coleman's career was blighted by the death or downfall of all his patrons. He served in the Dutch war with Deane, Penn, Lawson, and Lane, all influential men, and had been promised promotion to a better ship. But by 1656 they were all dead or out of office, as he glumly observed, and his promotion had failed to materialize.[162]

Patronage by influential political figures ashore carried much greater dangers: feuding between rival factions, the promotion of officers regardless of ability by politicians who did not have to live with the consequences, and the risk of an officer capitalizing on influential connections to subvert the authority of his superiors. The 1650s were largely free from irresponsible political appointments, but the one major exception illustrates vividly the dangers they could pose.

[158] Penn, *Memorials*, i. 221.
[159] SP 18/105/126; SP 18/108/2, 64; SP 18/109/48. Browne was particularly hit by the death of his neighbour Lionel Lane. As often Blackborne came to the rescue and helped him to a command.
[160] SP 18/28/151.
[161] SP 18/48/127; Add. MS 18986, fo. 62; SP 46/97/71, 77.
[162] SP 18/138/28.

The culprit was the Protector himself. Cromwell championed several relations serving in the navy, the most notable being his young nephew Thomas Whetstone, the son of his sister Catherine and Roger Whetstone of Whittlesea. The older Whetstone had been a professional soldier, serving in the Netherlands; Thomas was born abroad about 1631, and was later naturalized by Act of Parliament.[163] In 1654 he sailed in Penn's flagship in the West Indies expedition. Cromwell commended him to the admiral's care, writing to Penn later that he 'took it as granted you would make my nephew Whitstone [*sic*] your lieutenant'; he was indignant when Penn kept his own cousin Rooth in the post, and angrily demanded the removal of the admiral's kinsman to make room for his own. Penn, no mean nepotist himself, found a better solution: he made room for Whetstone as lieutenant by advancing Rooth to a command which fell vacant, and on the voyage home he was able to give Whetstone a command of his own in the little *Golden Cock*.[164] Back in England Whetstone's career advanced apace. In 1656 he became captain of the fourth-rate *Phoenix*, being picked out for the honour of carrying diplomats abroad; in 1657 he took command of the third-rate *Fairfax* 'by His Highness' special order', and went out to join the fleet off Spain. When most of the fleet came home later in the year he became second-in-command of the force remaining out under Stokes. And in 1658, when part of this force was summoned home, the Admiralty named him commander of the returning squadron simply out of respect to his Highness'.[165]

There was nothing in Whetstone's record to justify this rapid rise. The Admiralty had indeed been exasperated by his conduct. William Burton called him a 'saucy jack' and the Commissioners received many complaints of his absenteeism and neglect. When his ship was stationed at Plymouth in 1656 they ordered him to the Downs instead where they could watch him more closely; without

---

[163] On Whetstone's background see M. Noble, *Memoirs of the Protectoral House of Cromwell* (Birmingham, 1784), ii. 262–4; J. Waylen, *The House of Cromwell* (1897), 186; *CJ* vii. 453, 466. Cromwell also championed George Smithsby (Cromwell, *Writings*, iii. 516) and Lt. William Steward, a kinsman of his mother, who served under Penn and Stokes (ibid. ii. 621; Add. MS 9300, fo. 289); John Steward, lieutenant to Whetstone in 1658, may also have been a kinsman.

[164] Cromwell, *Writings*, iii. 516, 575; NMM WYN/18, fos. 28, 89; 'Rooth's Journal', 6; *Certain Passages*, 7–14 Sept. 1655.

[165] M. L. Baumber, 'The Protector's Nephew. An Account of . . . Thomas Whetstone in . . . 1657–1659', *MM* lii (1966), 233–5; Adm. 2/1730, fos. 93ʳ, 255.

such close supervision, they told him bluntly, they knew there was 'little or no service to be expected' from him. Whetstone evaded the order, pleading a sudden illness.[166] Either no one dared bring his record to Cromwell's attention or the Protector brushed it aside, for he was then promoted to the *Fairfax* instead of being turned out. The whole affair shows the regime in a very unflattering light. Whetstone's subsequent behaviour in the Mediterranean was predictably poor. His master and lieutenant both quitted in disgust, the latter declaring that in all his years at sea he had never seen such 'exceeding insolence' from so 'young and raw' a captain. Relations with Stokes and the other captains were no better. Whetstone's imperious manner and extravagant lifestyle irritated his colleagues, while he in turn wrote to England complaining that he was not shown proper respect. It was his version which carried weight in Whitehall: Thurloe assured him that captains who were disrespectful to a kinsman of the Protector were failing in their duty and would suffer accordingly.[167] The whiff of courtly ways was very much back in evidence. By this time Whetstone was openly flouting Stokes's orders and obviously trying to supplant him. Stokes, afraid of offending Whitehall, dared not act. But once news arrived that Cromwell was dead, Stokes promptly arrested his deputy and shipped him home to England. Whetstone now faced a formidable list of twenty-nine charges, including drunkenness, disobedience, gambling, frequenting brothels, cowardice, failing to maintain order, and disorderly behaviour, and he was also accused, for good measure, of provoking a diplomatic row with Portugal. Yet Stokes was still afraid his former deputy might use his connections to turn the tables. Ambassador Lockhart, Cromwell's son-in-law and envoy to France, indeed dismissed the allegations and blamed Stokes for dealing so roughly with a relation of the Protector. Mountagu and the Admiralty, however, stood by Stokes, and Whetstone's naval career came to an abrupt end.[168] Whetstone's case, it should be stressed, was unique in the 1650s. It stands as a dramatic reminder of the pitfalls of patronage and nepotism when exercised irresponsibly by politicians ashore.

[166] SP 18/144/26; Adm. 2/1729, fos. 133ᵛ, 142.

[167] SP 46/118, fo. 104; Baumber, 'Protector's Nephew', 233–44; *Thurloe*, vii. 285–6.

[168] Rawl. MS C 381, *passim*; Add. MS 9304, fos. 169–75; *CSPD 1658–9*, 156, 161; *The Nicholas Papers*, ed. G. F. Warner (Camden Soc., 1886–1920), iv. 104; Baumber, 'Protector's Nephew', 233–46.

IV. AUTHORITY

Even without political interference the structure of naval command under the Commonwealth might seem almost deliberately designed to create warring factions. Authority was shared between several Generals at Sea, each with his own clients and dependants. That no such factions emerged owed much to the good sense of the Generals themselves, who worked together successfully despite differences of outlook and temperament. Two of the initial trio, Blake and Popham, were old colleagues, and Deane soon established a good relationship with them.[169] The joint command ended in 1651 but worked smoothly again when it was renewed in the Dutch war. The new General, Monck, a former royalist, sailed in the same flagship as the regicide Deane and paid respectful tribute when his partner was killed in action.[170] A cavalier claimed that Monck 'gaped after the absolute command' when Blake went ashore sick, but the evidence for this is very weak. Far from wanting sole command Monck had pressed earlier for a third General to take Deane's place, and years later, on hearing of Blake's death, spoke of his former partner as an 'old friend'.[171] The final experiment in joint command was the expedition of Blake and Mountagu to Spain in 1656. Blake was rumoured to have complained at being saddled with such a 'worthless fellow', and there was persistent gossip in London of friction between them, which probably had at least some foundation. Mountagu was twenty years younger than his partner, totally inexperienced, and eager for action; Blake, a reserved, cautious man and chronically ill, must have found the situation difficult. Even so the two learned to work together, and when Mountagu returned home Blake's letters to him were friendly and trusting.[172]

Commanders-in-chief frequently consulted their captains, as directed, to decide tactics or discuss routine matters such as the state of provisions. What do these meetings reveal about the nature and extent of the Generals' authority? Did the councils debate matters freely, or merely give formal endorsement to the Generals' wishes? There is considerable evidence that the Generals were able to

---

[169] Ch. 3, above; Clarke MS 4/4, e.g. 1649 (24, 29), 1650 (9).   [170] *FDW* v. 72.

[171] *FDW* v. 73, 311; *Thurloe*, vi. 467. The colleague Monck wanted was admittedly his ally Penn, who was eventually appointed in Dec. 1653 (*FDW* vi. 189).

[172] *CSPD 1656-7*, 17; ch. 5 n. 112, above; for evidence of good relations between them see Blake, *Letters*, 375-6, 381-2; Powell, *Blake*, 283, 291.

dominate the proceedings when they so wished. Mountagu had certainly resolved to take his fleet home from the Baltic in 1659 before he called the council which ostensibly took that decision.[173] Blake too usually had his own way, and could even persuade his colleagues to fall into line when he changed his mind. He summoned two councils on 3 December 1652, for example, calling the second to reverse the decision taken by the first—which it duly did. Similarly when his fleet met a Spanish force off Cadiz in 1655 he persuaded his colleagues to accept his 'second thoughts' and rescind their earlier decision to attack.[174]

But at other times there seems to have been more open debate, with the Generals genuinely anxious to hear their officers' views. Blake held several councils in the Tagus in 1650 to discuss how to dislodge Rupert without provoking war with Portugal. In 1655 he and his officers discussed whether it would be right to attack Tunis when the Moors proved defiant. There was debate too in 1656, off Spain, when he found there was no enemy fleet to engage. A council was summoned to consider other courses of action; Mountagu thought it would opt to attack Cadiz but he added, 'This is but my single opinion: what we may be directed to when we meet, is impossible for me to write.' In the event his forecast proved correct, for the captains expressed a 'general dread of the [West] Indian voyage', the main alternative.[175]

The aim of a council was to reach consensus on the course to be pursued. There is only one recorded case of officers voting on opposite sides, and on that occasion none of the Generals was present.[176] But heated debate was not unknown. One clash allegedly occurred in 1652 during Blake's voyage north in search of the Dutch East Indies fleet. Meeting with no success, he eventually proposed to abandon the quest. His captains were very reluctant to lose such a prize and some angrily demanded to have their dissent recorded in the minutes; to restore harmony Blake withdrew his proposal and agreed to continue the search. Or so it is said: the story comes from an official who was not present and wrote it down over ten years later, in a highly prejudiced account.[177] There was another alleged

---

[173] Harris, *Mountagu*, i. 152–4; Sandwich, *Journal*, 44–5; ch. 4, above.

[174] Blake, *Letters*, 186–7, 307–8; cf. ch. 4 n. 66, above.

[175] Blake, *Letters*, 74–6, 82–3, 359–60, 400, 404. A royalist claimed that the Generals planned to send a force to the West Indies, but that the captains flatly refused to go: SP 18/128/106.

[176] See ch. 5 n. 91.   [177] Clar. MS 47, fo. 180.

dispute over the attack on Santa Cruz in 1657. When word arrived that Plate ships were heading for the Canaries the junior flag-officers, Bourne and Stayner, urged Blake to despatch a squadron to intercept them. They had the backing of many other captains, but Blake angrily refused. They pressed him again on hearing that the Plate ships had arrived at Santa Cruz, again to no avail. Their frustration was natural, and Stayner's account gives the impression of an over-cautious, tetchy commander ignoring the sound advice of his subordinates. But Stayner's partisan account of the episode, the only source for this clash, was written after the Restoration for the eyes of Charles II, and he was clearly trying to claim all the credit for himself. Blake had sound reasons for his initial caution. Once he felt it was safe to go ahead he consulted his captains thoroughly in planning the attack, calling no fewer than three councils to discuss it.[178] It would not be surprising if adventurous subordinates sometimes felt frustrated by Blake's caution, especially if he failed to take them sufficiently into his confidence.[179] Chronic ill-health cannot have helped his temper; at the time of Santa Cruz he was a dying man. It is clear however that no one dared challenge a General's authority, however resentful he felt. Stayner recalled indeed that at one council none of the captains dared speak at all, fearing to offend Blake still further. Even when harmony failed, authority did not falter.

Commanders of smaller squadrons serving far from home did not enjoy the same standing or the same automatic obedience. Factional disputes in the interregnum navy are to be found at this lower level, away from the Generals. There were three serious episodes in which order broke down, in each case the second-in-command defying the authority of his commander.

The first and most serious was in the Straits in 1652–3.[180] At the start of the Dutch war there were two English squadrons serving in the area, both much weaker than the Dutch forces in the region. Appleton's squadron was blockaded in Leghorn, while Badiley's took shelter at Porto Longone in Elba. The English realized they were trapped and abandoned—'sent abroad for destruction', as Badiley put it—and morale and discipline quickly deteriorated.

---

[178] Powell, *Blake*, 297 ff.; Blake, *Letters*, 386, 459; C. H. Firth (ed.), 'A Narrative of the Battle of Santa Cruz', in *The Naval Miscellany*, ii. 127–32; cf. ch. 4 n. 79.

[179] For Blake's reserve see *CSPV 1655–6*, 10, 19, 29.

[180] For what follows see Spalding, *Badiley*, chs. 7–18, and *DNB* under Appleton and Badiley.

Badiley made the point graphically by reporting how a Christian Turk at Leghorn had reverted to Islam in horror at the debauchery of the English sailors ashore.[181]

The situation at Leghorn was exacerbated by the lack of trust between Appleton and some of his captains, especially the most senior of them, Owen Cox. Appleton had little naval experience and was not a forceful leader. His plaintive remark that 'no man can govern more ships than himself is aboard of' suggests he was not the ideal man to be commanding a squadron. Cox had far more energy and experience and felt no respect for his superior. Appleton complained that he was 'intolerably proud, never owning me in anything he did', and tried to remove him; Cox refused to quit and was confirmed in his place by Badiley, who had now received overall command from London.[182] Appleton's relations with Badiley, now *his* superior, were equally poor. The situation became critical when the Tuscans tired of their unwanted guests, and Badiley devised a plan to end the stalemate. He would sail from Elba towards Leghorn and Appleton would slip out during the night to meet him, enabling the English forces to combine before they had to face the Dutch. The plan itself was sound, but the breakdown of authority and co-operation led to disaster. Appleton spent the crucial night arguing with his captains and missed his chance. When Badiley appeared next day and the Dutch sailed out to challenge him, Appleton followed behind much too closely; seeing their opportunity, the Dutch turned back and crushed him before Badiley was near enough to help. All but one of the English ships at Leghorn were sunk or captured, and Badiley had to make his escape and lead his own demoralized force back to England.

The affair was not yet over. Appleton made his way home overland and published a fierce attack on Badiley and Cox, claiming they had held back deliberately to allow his force to be destroyed. Badiley published a detailed reply and Appleton issued a further rejoinder. A parliamentary committee was set up to examine the charges, and rumours spread that Badiley was to be disgraced or even executed. In the event the inquiry vindicated him fully, whereas Appleton was never employed again. The English position in the Straits may have been untenable, but the breakdown of order had guaranteed disaster.

---

[181] Spalding, *Badiley*, 135, 274.
[182] SP 46/96/211; R. Badiley, *Capt. Badiley's Answer* (1653), 54; *CSPD 1651–2*, 465–6.

There was a further serious clash some years later at Jamaica. Goodson, Penn's successor, found his authority challenged by his vice-admiral, Benjamin Blake. Whereas Goodson had been reluctantly drawn into the running of the new colony Blake wanted to be out at sea, searching for prizes and plundering Spanish settlements. He drew up several papers abusing the army and calling for action; many of the naval officers were indifferent to the colony's survival, and by 'frequent feasting and entertaining only to that purpose [he] seduced a great party in the fleet'. Resentful and alarmed, Goodson brought charges against him in June 1656 and made him lay down his commission and return to England. He described Blake as 'a person of such a turbulent spirit, and so opposite to me in most of my commands' that co-operation was impossible; Blake's own account quotes Goodson as saying 'he would ruin me, or I should ruin him'. Back home Blake attempted to clear his name, citing several captains who would testify on his behalf. Goodson begged to be recalled too, to defend himself, but the government sent assurances that it upheld his action and would continue to give him its trust.[183]

The third breakdown of authority occurred in the squadron under John Stokes, who took over the forces remaining off Spain in 1657. Two of his captains simply ignored orders about the station they were to keep, and then sailed home with a prize without bothering to inform him.[184] Later, in the Straits, he met with open defiance from his deputy Whetstone, as we have seen. And the man suggested by the Admiralty to replace Whetstone as deputy took his part instead and then deserted, bringing his ship back to England without orders.[185]

Badiley, Goodson, and Stokes were very able and experienced officers. The problems they encountered, admittedly in very difficult circumstances, make the Generals' success in maintaining order all the more impressive. Authority could never be taken for granted. If only a General could secure total obedience the government's policy of having several in harness together was well-advised.

---

[183] Add. MS 18986, fos. 202, 241ᵛ–242; *Thurloe*, iv. 151–2, v. 154, 367–8, 771; vi. 220; A. P. Watts, *Une Histoire des Colonies Anglaises aux Antilles* (Paris, 1924), 293–5.

[184] Blake, *Letters*, 460–2; Adm. 2/1730, fos. 49ᵛ–50.

[185] Adm. 2/1730, fo. 268; *CSPD 1658–9*, 161, 190, 193; SP 18/183/111; Add. MS 9304, fo. 163ʳ⁻ᵛ; ch. 5 n. 146, above.

V. TURNOVER

One of the most striking characteristics of the officer corps was its high rate of turnover. Many things could cut short an officer's career. There was almost constant war at sea, and casualties were heavy: the year 1653 saw three major sea-battles, each on a scale previously unknown in English history. There was little protection in a wooden sailing ship fighting at close quarters, pounded by cannon-balls and swept by small-arms fire and flying splinters; a captain standing on the quarter deck was as vulnerable as any of his men, and more so than most. Some thirty-six captains of warships and hired merchantmen were killed in action during the interregnum, possibly more than in the whole of the navy's previous history. Most of them perished during the Dutch war, including General Deane (struck down, it was reported, 'as he stood flourishing his sword at the head of the ship'), three other flag-officers, and two flag-captains.[186] Parliament awarded the victims' families prompt and fairly generous compensation, ranging between £400 and £1,200, partly to reassure other officers that their families were safe, however great the dangers they faced themselves.[187] Another thirty-eight captains died in service or very shortly thereafter. Misadventure accounted for some: three drowned in boat accidents and another died of injuries from a fall on board.[188] Many of the deaths ostensibly from 'natural' causes were undoubtedly linked with old injuries. Blake himself never recovered fully from his wound in 1653, and Samuel Hawkes's colleagues testified that his death in the West Indies in 1656 was from the lingering effects of wounds suffered during the Dutch war.[189] Many other officers fell victim to the rapid spread of disease in cramped and unhealthy conditions. The captain and lieutenant of one ship in the Caribbean died on successive days; the ship's surgeon, far from being able to save them, succumbed himself the day after.[190]

Though some officers remained in the navy after losing a hand,

[186] The flag-officers were Graves, Packe, and Peacock, the flag-captains Ball and Mildmay. For Deane see *A Declaration of the Further Proceedings of the English Fleet* (1653), 8. Another 20 Commonwealth captains were killed after 1660, mostly in the later Dutch wars. For losses in the Seven Years' War (17) see Rodger, *Wooden World*, 256. [187] *CJ* vii. 279; Hammond, thesis, 228–9.

[188] Fearnes, Noades, and Evans drowned; Odey died after a fall.

[189] SP 46/98/19; *CSPD 1652–3*, 491; SP 18/64/46–7; SP 46/97/151.

[190] 'Rooth's Journal', 8.

arm, or leg, injury inevitably forced many to retire.[191] Some never recovered.[192] Those who survived had to rebuild their lives, usually with some financial assistance from the Admiralty. When John Coppin left the navy in 1652 with a shattered leg he received £400 in compensation and was allowed to buy a Dutch prize at a reduced rate to re-establish himself in civilian life.[193] No such option was open to Lt. John Weale, who retired with a gratuity of £100 after being blinded in both eyes; he later eked out a living as a fencing-master—a doubly hazardous profession in the circumstances![194]

Most officers left the navy in less traumatic circumstances. A few moved into naval administration ashore: Bourne and Moulton became Navy Commissioners, Charles Thoroughgood and William Hill Masters Attendant at Portsmouth and Chatham respectively. William Crispin, a captain in the West Indies expedition, became a contractor arranging supplies for the new colony at Jamaica.[195] Some officers went back to military service, including a few who rejoined the army in Jamaica.[196] Several others resigned or were purged for ideological reasons, notably Lawson and his friends and the Quaker converts Baker and Mellidge.[197]

A much larger and more important group left the navy to return to trade. Many of them part-owned ships and had shares in other ventures; though ready to help the state in an emergency they always regarded trade as their primary concern. Thus leading shipmasters such as Hackwell and Wildey, recruited in 1649, and Reed and Strong, recruited during the Dutch war, served for only a few months.[198] Similarly Joseph Cubitt left the navy as soon as the Dutch war ended, declaring that his private affairs required his

---

[191] Wright lost a leg, Rively and Cuttle the use of an arm, Mills the use of a leg and an arm, Terry a hand, etc.

[192] e.g. William Brandley: *FDW* i. 385; *CSPD 1653–4*, 402, 459; SP 46/97/151b, d; *CSPD 1655–6*, 93.

[193] *CSPD 1652–3*, 102, 484; SP 18/57/95; *CSPD 1654*, 28. Coppin returned to the navy in 1656.

[194] 'The Journal of John Weale', ed. J. R. Powell, in *The Naval Miscellany*, iv (NRS, 1952), 87; Adm. 3/273, fo. 254.

[195] For Thoroughgood and Hill see *CSPD 1653–4*, 554; SP 18/218/154; Adm. 3/274, fo. 100; for Crispin see 'Rooth's Journal', 19 (where 'Kelsey' should read 'Kirby'); HMC 29, *Portland*, ii. 94; Add. MS 18986, fo. 209; *CSPD 1655–6*, 405, 479, 542.

[196] Lidcott, Smyth, and Cobham returned to the army; Haytubb served with the army in Jamaica for two years: 'Rooth's Journal', 20; *CSP Col.*, i. 454.

[197] For Baker see ch. 9, below.

[198] Hackwell and Wildey served only in 1649–50, Reed in 1652, Strong in 1653.

presence; when the Admiralty tried to tempt him back he was willing to serve only in a shore-based capacity where he could look after his business interests. William Burton of Yarmouth had felt too enmeshed in commercial operations to serve at all, turning down one of the best ships in the fleet in 1653. He explained that he dared not 'leave his credit and estate to so great a hazard', though he too was ready to accept an administrative post ashore.[199]

Senior officers trying to keep up their commercial interests inevitably faced serious difficulties. Some families, such as the Moultons and Haddocks, solved the problem by having some members looking after their business affairs while others served the state.[200] This kind of arrangement was not possible for all. Joseph Jordan, serving as rear-admiral with Blake in 1655, felt obliged to throw up his commission and return home to attend to 'some extraordinary business'.[201] Robert Plumleigh remained in the navy ('the Lord having given me a public spirit, to serve my generation'), but in 1656 he had to beg for home leave to look after his family's interests. Most of his estate, he explained, was tied up in trading ventures to the Newfoundland fisheries. His partners had failed to provide any accounts and his family had written that they would be cheated of their due unless he came to investigate in person; he had spent only two weeks with them, he added, in the course of three years.[202] William Goodson had similar worries while stationed at Jamaica. Most of his estate, he wrote to Thurloe, was 'scattered abroad in the world by adventures and parts of shipping', and his family's livelihood was at risk unless he could attend to it in person.[203]

The fact that many senior officers retained their former commercial interests created problems for the Admiralty. For it could not simply assume that they would always be willing and available to serve; rather it had to pull constantly against the ties drawing them back into civilian life. Even flag-officers might not feel committed to the navy. At the close of 1653, for example, the Admiralty approached Lionel Lane very diffidently to say that a good ship

[199] SP 18/116/142; SP 18/136/131; *CSPD 1652–3*, 540; SP 18/46/14.
[200] Robert Moulton jun. left the navy in 1652, the year his father died—to look after the family's business interests? William Haddock, son of Richard sen. and father of Richard jun. (both flag-officers), remained in commerce.
[201] SP 18/113/9; Blake, *Letters*, 311.
[202] SP 18/133/127; SP 18/134/41, 56; Stowe MS 427, fo. 15; Adm. 2/1730, fo. 66ᵛ.
[203] *Thurloe*, iv. 458.

would be available if he felt inclined to serve again. Similarly when Goodson's ship was paid off in 1658 Mountagu urged the Commissioners to find him another command very quickly so 'that he may not engage himself in commercial ventures'. And when Jonas Poole returned to England sooner than expected in 1659 the Commissioners were most apologetic that they could not at once offer him another ship befitting his status.[204] The Admiralty thus had to negotiate with the most senior commanders on almost equal terms. It did its best to keep their goodwill, trying, for example, to reconcile the conflicting pressures they faced. When Sir Richard Stayner sought permission to go to London on business the Commissioners observed that 'if his occasions be so urgent, we cannot but give way'.[205] Similarly General Popham intervened to help Badiley, his rear-admiral, when he was threatened by an expensive lawsuit, arranging legal protection for Badiley while he was at sea so that he would not have to choose between his private concerns and the service of the state.[206] Senior officers could even negotiate over where they would serve. Thus when Edward Blagg said he was reluctant to go back to the West Indies, because his wife disliked the idea, he was offered another posting. Similarly Robert Saunders claimed he was not free to return to the Caribbean 'by reason of some engagements that lie upon him', and again the Admiralty offered an alternative.[207] Such freedom existed, of course, only for senior commanders the Admiralty was anxious to retain. When Edmund Curle complained about a posting to Iceland, 'apprehending that climate to be prejudicial' to his health, he was told bluntly that he must accept it or resign.[208]

Most officers were not in a position to bargain with the Admiralty. Many of those who returned to civilian life did so by necessity not choice, having failed to obtain further employment. Competition for places was inevitably intense in the smaller fleets set out after the peace with the Dutch. In addition over fifty captains (plus a considerable number of lieutenants) were sacked or deliberately laid aside for misconduct. Some of them were removed by court martial, though it was a difficult and laborious task to

---

[204] Rawl. MS A 461, fo. 32ᵛ; Add. MS 9304, fos. 144, 146; Adm. 2/1731, fo. 56.
[205] Adm. 2/1731, fo. 49ᵛ; cf. Adm. 2/1730, fos. 66ʳ⁻ᵛ, 116ᵛ.
[206] Clarke MS 4/4, 1651 (23).
[207] SP 18/114/119; SP 18/115/1, 104; Adm. 2/1730, fos. 86ᵛ, 87ᵛ.
[208] Adm. 2/1729, fo. 217.

assemble all the captains, evidence, and witnesses required.[209] Sometimes the Council itself removed offenders. Very often the Admiralty weeded out unsatisfactory officers by simply refusing to employ them again, exploiting the system of short-term commissions. Faced with allegations of serious misconduct it would often suspend the officer while the matter was investigated. These inquiries frequently petered out without leading to a formal trial, but if the charges appeared well-founded the accused was not restored to his post and would not be re-employed. The procedure might be indefensible but it was not necessarily unfair in practice. So it would seem, at least, from the case of five captains removed and sent for trial by the Council after Dungeness. Preliminary investigations apparently showed the charges of cowardice to be ill-founded; the accused were never formally cleared, for the cases never reached court, but four of the five were soon employed again.[210]

The great majority of officers laid aside were charged with mundane failings such as absenteeism, drunkenness, embezzlement, or failing to maintain proper discipline.[211] There was a bitter proverbial saying among the sea-officers that seven years' good service counted for nothing against one hour's alleged misconduct. When the Commissioners found Capt. Leonard Harris drunk in the street at Chatham early in 1653 they sacked him on the spot—though circumstances soon forced them to offer him another command! One can imagine their chagrin.[212] For much of the period the Admiralty clearly held the upper hand. Even during the Dutch war it usually had some freedom of manœuvre, for the increased demand for officers was partly balanced by an increased supply of applicants. During the Spanish war the navy was less attractive in

[209] For examples of captains removed by court martial see Robert Saunders (above), John Vessey (Add. MS 9304, fo. 154ʳ⁻ᵛ; Adm. 2/1730, fo. 227ᵛ); and John Clarke (SP 18/100/101; *Thurloe*, iii. 682). A court martial in 1653 allowed John Day to choose between a fine and a discharge, but he was not employed again (*FDW* v. 429); cf. Oppenheim, 353–4. For the problems of mounting a court martial see Rodger, *Wooden World*, 222.

[210] Young, Taylor, Blake, Chapman, and Saltonstall: see *FDW* iii. 7, 163–4, 173–4, 267–8, 364, 406, 412, 418, 437, 445. For earlier allegations of cowardice by Blake against Taylor see Clarke MS 1/10, fo. 104ᵛ.

[211] But Tarleton, Francis Kirby, Sherwin, and Cranwell were blamed for wrecks, Horne for surrending his ship, and Appleton for the disaster at Leghorn in 1653.

[212] D. Pell, *Nec Inter Vivos, Nec Inter Mortuos* (1659), 23; Rawl. MS A 227, fo. 29; *FDW* iii. 442.

terms of prizes and plunder, but the depressed state of trade and the ravages of privateers meant that prospects were poor in the mercantile sector too. The readiness of some former captains to remain in the navy as lieutenants, masters, or even reformados is very suggestive. And other officers who had left voluntarily were soon back at the Admiralty's door. William Coppin pleaded his 'many losses at sea by shipping' and 'the badness of the time'; Owen Cox explained that he had six children and no means of supporting them. Capt. Simmonds, who had left at his wife's request, was even willing to come back as a purser.[213]

The longer an officer served in the navy the harder he found it to return to merchandizing unless he had shares in a merchant vessel. The large fleets set out annually in the 1640s and 1650s provided steady employment and made many officers virtually dependent on the state. If they were then dropped they faced ruin, or at least a drastic fall in their standard of living. Very often they begged the Admiralty to take them back. Jacob Reynolds was laid aside in 1654, 'to his unutterable grief', after ten years in the navy; his family, he claimed, would now be 'exposed to hardship and extremity'. William Cockraine pleaded that he had 'lost acquaintance among owners and merchants'. Roger Jones, dropped after fifteen years' service, said that after being away from trade so long 'an employment in that behalf is not (in these sad times) easily obtained'. 'I cannot say my actions have been exempted from human frailties', he admitted, with charming delicacy, but he begged to be forgiven.[214] Men who had entered the navy after suffering some personal disaster were of course even more dependent. Jeffrey Dare's whole estate had been tied up in his ship, which had fallen victim to the Dutch. He could not hope to sail as a master again, he explained, because he lacked the capital to buy a share in another ship, and all the merchants he had once known were now either 'dead or gone'.[215]

The Admiralty discriminated carefully in such cases. It tried to find new commands for men who had performed well and sternly ignored pleas from those who had proved unfit. Where malpractice was suspected but unproven it was ready to leave the petitioner

[213] NMM ADL/Z/8 (19); SP 25 I 92, fo. 401; SP 18/133/34.
[214] ADL/Z/8 (12); SP 18/122/18; *CSPD 1654*, 63; SP 18/136/179; cf. *CSPD 1654*, 16; *CSPD 1656–7*, 501.
[215] SP 18/193/100.

dangling for months or even years. He might be left unpaid as well as unemployed, for a captain received his wages only when the ship's accounts were passed, and this could be delayed almost indefinitely. Such was the fate of Francis Parke, described as a 'notorious plunderer'. Parke pleaded in 1657 that he had been forced to live as a prisoner in his own house, knowing he would be arrested for debt if he ventured out. If he were promised further employment, he wrote, he could make a composition with his creditors. A year later he complained that he had been 'rendered less able to subsist than when first I entered the service'; even so he had to wait yet another year before the Admiralty finally relented.[216]

The relationship between the Admiralty and the commissioned officers rested in delicate equilibrium. The Commissioners dared not behave as autocrats: they had to coax senior commanders to remain in the service, and they could not afford to dismiss *every* officer who infringed regulations. At the same time officers knew they risked dismissal and unemployment if they overstepped the mark, and knew there were many others ready to take their place. As we shall see, the pattern of checks and balances which resulted was in many ways comparable to the situation on board each ship between a captain and his crew.

VI. THE WARRANT-OFFICERS

The warrant-officers can be described more briefly, for they differed little in many respects from their counterparts in other periods.[217] These men, masters, gunners, boatswains, and the like, were responsible for the handling of the ship. Each had his sphere of expertise and responsibility, and his team of assistants.

In a merchant vessel the master was the commander (as he still is), and a naval master too was expected to be able to take over as captain in an emergency.[218] But the posts carried very different responsibilities and were filled by different criteria. The master had charge of the ship's navigation, and it was he who bore the blame if

[216] SP 18/122/134; SP 18/173/43; SP 18/195/88; Add. MS 9310, fo. 48ʳ.
[217] M. Lewis, *England's Sea-Officers* (1939), ch. 13. For 17th-cent. accounts of their duties see *Boteler's Dialogues*, 14–32; Monson, *Tracts*, iv. 22–65.
[218] See e.g. Adm. 2/1730, fos. 142, 257.

it was lost at sea. When the *Laurel* was wrecked in 1657 only the master was court-martialled. When the *Expedition* ran aground in good weather and a calm sea the master and pilot were sent for trial, whereas the captain was merely reprimanded.[219] The criteria employed in choosing masters were primarily technical skill, experience, and steadiness of character. John Malinge of Wapping was recommended as an 'ancient able master, of good life and judged godly'—for this was in 1653—and 'a good coaster', i.e. skilled in coastal navigation.[220] A master needed to be familiar with the area where the ship was to serve. One captain was asked to check that his master knew the coasts and harbours of Ireland, where he was to be stationed. When Robert Dennis found his master knew nothing of Virginia, where he was bound, he asked at once for a replacement.[221] Masters themselves sometimes asked to be released if they lacked appropriate expertise. One said he was totally ignorant of the Caribbean and begged to serve in the Channel instead. Another was dismayed to find his ship appointed to the French coast 'contrary to my expectations when I first came on board. I cannot speak myself able, my ability being altogether for the nor'ard, where I expected our station would have been'.[222]

The Council of State and Parliament did not normally concern themselves with the appointment of masters or other warrant-officers. The Admiralty lacked the resources to vet them thoroughly, and relied heavily on advice from the Generals and senior captains, and from the Navy Commissioners. When a spate of petitions arrived in 1651 for places in four new frigates the Admiralty Committee simply referred the matter to the Navy Commissioners, telling them to sift through the applicants and choose the best.[223] The agent at Plymouth, Hatsell, often selected masters for ships stationed there and sometimes received blank warrants from London to fill in as he thought fit.[224] The Admiralty was more closely involved, however, in appointments to the greater ships, and when a master was needed in 1652 for the *Sovereign* the Council itself attended to the matter. The ship was a symbol of

[219] Adm. 2/1730, fos. 82ᵛ, 257ᵛ–258, 262.

[220] SP 18/46/17.

[221] Rawl. MS A 225, fo. 153; Adm. 2/1729, fo. 176.

[222] SP 18/83/17, a; SP 18/111/69. Similarly Samuel James resigned his place because he was not familiar with the Straits: SP 18/176/63.

[223] Rawl. MS A 225, fo. 138.

[224] e.g. Adm. 2/1730, fo. 256.

national prestige, and the Council directed that twenty 'very able seamen' be specially recruited to assist the master for her greater security, ten of them to be paid as masters themselves.[225]

Finding suitable masters for the very largest ships was not easy. Merchant seamen with appropriate experience were relatively few, and those willing to serve looked to do so as captains, not subordinates. In a crisis the Admiralty called on the Masters Attendant (the officials responsible for ship movements within the dockyards), who were always experienced shipmasters. Thomas Arkinstall, for example, Master Attendant at Chatham, went to sea as master of the *Sovereign* and several other great ships. But there were only a few such men, and they were not always available. In 1658 Arkinstall pleaded ill-health, and the Master Attendant at Portsmouth, Thoroughgood, flatly refused to serve under officers he regarded as his inferiors (for he was himself a former naval captain).[226] Faced with this chronic shortage the Admiralty was sometimes forced to employ former commanders who had been turned out for misconduct. Thus John Littlejohn was made master of one of the great second-rates in 1657 only a few weeks after being sacked for deserting his station. The Admiralty clearly felt he possessed professional skills and experience it could ill afford to lose, even though he lacked the judgement necessary in a captain.[227] Capt. John Clarke, dismissed for embezzlement and neglect, was also promptly made master of another ship. Similarly Capt. George Crapnel, who resigned in 1655 rather than face a court martial, subsequently became master of a third-rate—though he was later turned out of this post too and labelled 'not deserving of any public trust'.[228]

While former shipmasters naturally preferred to serve as captains, with far higher pay and status, there were many who were willing to accept a master's place. Mostly they were former part-owners 'impoverished by the casualties of the seas', as one was described, or men who had served for wages alone and had no security of employment.[229] To such men it seemed better to be a master in the navy than drop to a mate's place, or something less, in a merchant

[225] SP 18/28/54.

[226] Add. MS 9300, fo. 289; Adm. 2/1730, fos. 62, 64; *CSPD 1656-7*, 571.

[227] Adm. 2/1730, fos. 49ᵛ, 56ᵛ-57ᵛ, 64; Adm. 3/273, fo. 66ᵛ.

[228] Clarke: *Thurloe*, iii. 682; SP 18/100/101; WYN/18/4, fo. 84. Crapnel: 'Weale's Journal', 119; Add. MS 9305, fo. 142ᵛ; Adm. 2/1730, fo. 80.

[229] *CSPD 1656-7*, 555. For naval masters' wages see *FDW* iii. 285; they were generally less than in foreign-going merchant ships: Davis, *Shipping Industry*, 138.

ship. Some had lost all by shipwreck. Several had been masters of
ships impounded by the Danes at Copenhagen in 1652. The
Admiralty may have felt morally obliged to offer Edward Dunning
a job, for his ship had been accidentally rammed and sunk by one of
its warships.[230] Many had been ruined by enemy action: one had
been captured twice in a single year, and another had sunk so far
into debt and destitution that he was afraid of being pressed as a
common seaman. Such men often remained in the navy for years,
knowing they had few prospects elsewhere.[231]

Shipmasters who were somewhat better placed might move in
and out of the navy as circumstances changed. The career of Robert
Thorpe, originally a Hull shipmaster trading to the Baltic and the
Netherlands, offers a good case history of this type. Thorpe served
in the navy in 1650 as master of the *Swiftsure* but left after quarrelling with his captain. He was pushed back into the navy when the
Dutch war cut off his usual livelihood, this time securing a
command of his own. He then went back to commerce for a time,
but on the outbreak of war with Spain he obtained letters of marque
to recoup old losses at the hands of the Dunkirkers; when he lost his
licence for plundering neutral shipping he turned back to the navy a
third time. In 1659 he was serving as master of the *Indian*. Thorpe's
course was perhaps more erratic than most, but it illustrates well the
factors which could push mariners to and fro.[232]

The other leading warrant-officers were the gunners, boatswains,
and carpenters. They held important executive positions in the ship
and were responsible for large and valuable stores; a checklist of
boatswain's stores in 1655, for example, ran to over 250 items.[233]
These were the standing officers, who served on a continuous basis.
Many remained in their ships for years and regarded themselves as
permanent fixtures. Ned Ward later described the gunner as 'a little
king in his own conceit,' treating the gunroom as his hereditary
estate. When Jonas Palmer informed the Admiralty that he had been

[230] SP 18/122/80–3; SP 46/97/80; Adm. 3/273, fo. 93ᵛ. Masters who had been held
in the Sound include William Bixby, Solomon Clarke, and Edward Nixon;
cf. *Thurloe*, ii. 402.

[231] *CSPD 1653–4*, 168, 538; *CSPD 1652–3*, 504.

[232] Brooks, *First Order Book*, 18, 23, 54, 56, 98; *CSPD 1650*, 498; SP 25/123,
fo. 490; Rawl. MS A 225, fos. 113ᵛ–114; SP 18/30/92–4; *CSPD 1655–6*, 162, 187;
SP 25 I 92, fo. 570; HCA 25/227, fos. 11ᵛ, 13; *CSPD 1656–7*, 101–2; Adm. 3/274,
fos. 51, 96.

[233] NMM ADL/D/13. A single ship would not carry every item.

carpenter in the *Adventure* under four captains 'besides this that we have now' we can almost hear his sniff of resentment at the newcomer who had dared to disrupt his comfortable routine.[234] Some standing officers would eventually move on to better ships, and a minority would rise to higher posts as masters or commissioned officers. There was no retirement age in the navy and some warrant-officers were indeed Ancient Mariners: one gunner was finally eased out at the age of seventy-three and another septuagenarian was still at his post despite the fact that his eyesight and hearing were failing. He was unwilling to retire for naval service carried no pension, and he asked permission instead to serve his place through a deputy.[235] The luckiest veterans were those holding sinecure places as warrant-officers in ships in ordinary (i.e. laid up in reserve); Charles I's navy contained one such boatswain still serving—at least on paper—at the age of a hundred![236]

The standing officers were unusual in the degree of tenure they enjoyed. Masters and inferior officers such as mates and quartermasters had no such security, and moved up, down, and sideways as chance decreed. The professional mariner, whether in the navy or the merchant marine, had to be adaptable and keep all his options open. One former mate, displaying typical flexibility, stressed his readiness to serve whether as master, lieutenant, gunner, or boatswain.[237] In bad times a mariner had to settle for whatever he could find, regardless of the drop in pay and status.

Under the Commonwealth ideology became important in the selection of warrant- as well as commissioned officers. Indeed, a standardized letter authorizing a warrant, signed by Deane in 1650, placed it first, beginning: 'Whereas I am well satisfied of the fidelity of *John Jordan* to the present government of this Commonwealth, as also of his abilities to execute the office of *carpenter* . . .'[238] No one forgot that it was warrant- and petty officers who had led the 1648 mutiny. Two men petitioning years later for posts as carpenter and cook emphasized that they had been among the few sailors in the ships involved to have remained faithful. Another carpenter produced evidence in 1653 to show that he was 'very really affected to the Parliament and the present government'. Even a cook's mate

[234] SP 18/129/91.
[235] SP 18/62/85; SP 18/176/90.
[236] *Boteler's Dialogues*, 9 n.
[237] SP 18/174/46.   [238] NMM AGC/3/1.

thought it prudent to produce a testimonial emphasizing his political zeal and fidelity.[239] Evidence of Puritan faith naturally weighed in an applicant's favour, and it was not unusual for warrant-officers to bring certificates from radical ministers to that effect; one carpenter came armed with a testimonial from Cromwell's own chaplain, Hugh Peter.[240]

Warrant-officers were mostly drawn from the pool of experienced mariners carried aboard every ship. Some of these were petty officers—gunner's or boatswain's mates and the like—who were appointed by the captain.[241] Others, rated higher, were serving as midshipmen. In this period midshipmen were experienced seamen able to navigate the ship and take over as gunners or boatswains if required. An official defined them as 'the most choice and able mariners that were out of employment and such as were fit for command if occasion required it'.[242] As this implies, former warrant- and even commissioned officers were to be found among them. So were former army officers hoping now for advancement in the navy, though many must have been technically unqualified.[243] Those who had served as army gunners had the best prospects, and a considerable number of them went on to obtain comparable posts in the navy. A gunner recommended by Cromwell in 1653 had formerly served in the Artillery Train, and when the Admiralty wanted a gunner to serve at sea in the *Sovereign* it was to the Ordnance Office that it turned.[244]

The other warrant-officers had less in common than those discussed so far. The cook's office had steadily declined in importance over the centuries, and was now very often held by old or crippled seamen unable to take on more active employment. It later became official policy to reserve it for such men. One cook appointed in the 1650s was a former slave in Algiers who had suffered a gunshot wound in the head during the Dutch war; nothing was said, perhaps tactfully, of his skill in the galley.[245]

[239] Rawl. MS A 225, fo. 109ᵛ; Add. MS 9306, fo. 43ᵛ; SP 18/55/128; SP 18/176/49–50.
[240] SP 18/55/12–13; SP 46/117, fo. 123; SP 18/46/12, 47.
[241] For petty officers and their wages see *FDW* ii. 285.
[242] *FDW* iii. 285, 417; *CSPD 1655–6*, 56–7; WYN/12/2; Clar. MS 47, fo. 182.
[243] e.g. Rawl. MS A 461, fo. 26; *CSPD 1653–4*, 539; NMM ADL/Z/8 (8).
[244] SP 18/92/3; Rawl. MS A 227, fo. 112ᵛ; *CSPD 1653–4*, 487. For an ex-army carpenter see *CSPD 1653–4*, 538, and for a cook who had been a private soldier see SP 46/114, fos. 79, 82.
[245] *CSPD 1659–60*, 537; Lewis, *Sea-Officers*, 239.

The purser's office was far more important. He was responsible for obtaining and overseeing the ship's provisions and for keeping its books. He had care of valuable stores and large sums of money (to purchase supplementary provisions), and had to produce sureties of several hundred pounds as a safeguard against fraud.[246] In 1653 the post was briefly suppressed and its duties shared between a clerk of the cheque and a steward; the change was designed to increase efficiency and prevent fraud, but pursers naturally saw it as demotion and the experiment presumably failed, for it was abandoned after two years.[247]

Pursers required distinctive skills, apparent in the criteria used in selecting them. Thurloe for example recommended one petitioner as 'a good accountant'. An official jotted against another man's name: 'if an accountant, then meet for a clerk of the cheque; if not, then gunner or master's mate'.[248] Clerical skills were naturally essential. Some of the other warrant-officers on board might be technically illiterate—unable to sign their names (though they were almost certainly able to read); even a man as senior as Thomas Brotheridge, master of the *James* and *Triumph*, both second-rates, was illiterate in this sense.[249] An illiterate purser, by contrast, was a contradiction in terms.

It was generally agreed that a purser's pay and allowances fell short of his expenses. The place offered considerable opportunities to the sharp-witted, however, and it was much sought after. Pepys found the *Naseby*'s purser living at home very 'plentifully and finely', with good food and wine in abundance, and his daughter ready to entertain guests at the virginals; yet the man had begun life as servant to a tavern-keeper.[250] In career terms the office was by no means a blind alley. Some pursers went on to obtain commissions: John Poyntz, for example, who had served fourteen years at sea in other capacities, went on to become a captain.[251] A number of

---

[246] Lewis, *Sea-Officers*, 242–52; *Boteler's Dialogues*, 13–14. Sureties were usually £200–600.

[247] *FDW* iii. 373–4, 406; *CSPD 1652–3*, 515, 607; *CSPD 1653–4*, 547 (misdated); *CSPD 1655*, 543. The experimental arrangements survived in some ships till the Restoration: Adm. 106/2, fo. 105.

[248] SP 18/46/14, 47; cf. *FDW* iii. 373.

[249] Rawl. MS A 187, fo. 398ʳ⁻ᵛ.

[250] J. Hollond, *Two Discourses of the Navy*, ed. J. R. Tanner (NRS, 1896), 163 and n.; Pepys, *Diary*, i. 301, 312–13, x. 310.

[251] SP 18/46/47. Borough, Crispin, Evans, I. White and Pyend (after 1660) became captains; Richard Bradford a lieutenant.

pursers were drawn from the merchant service, one explaining frankly that trade was slack and that he had few friends to help him to employment.[252] But as the place required no maritime skills it also attracted many landsmen, mostly tradesmen who had fallen on hard times. Typical applicants include a London haberdasher with a failing business, a Leicester man who had been ruined by the sack of the town in 1645, and a scrivener who was 'finding little to do in his shop'.[253] Such petitioners were often in financial difficulties, but the need to provide substantial bonds meant that pursers were likely to be higher in social status than other warrant-officers. In 1648 the purser of the *Sovereign* (then in ordinary) was also serving as mayor of Rochester.[254] Whereas boatswains and carpenters rarely had any patron other than a former commander, many aspiring pursers were recommended by substantial merchants or even prominent political and military figures, such as Lord Grey of Groby, Broghill, Thurloe, Nathaniel Fiennes, Cols. Walton and Pride, and Sir James Harrington.[255] Col. Rich successfully pressed the suit of his kinsman Jeremiah, who had served under him in the army and was later to become well known as the inventor of a popular system of shorthand.[256] The army was once more an important source of recruits. Some had been aiming for higher things. Richard Bull, an army officer for many years, went to sea as a reformado during the Dutch war and accepted a steward's place—which he thought 'something below his quality'—only because he had failed to win a commission. John Weale, more successful, was soon made a lieutenant.[257] Others appear to have been attracted more by the prospect of a comfortable life and the financial perks of the place. The army of the 1650s contained many men, now advancing in years, who had no civilian trade to resume and might well prefer a comfortable berth as purser, clerk, or steward to the rigours of service in Scotland and Ireland. This was surely the reasoning of one Nettles, who sought a steward's place in 1653. Nettles had joined

[252] *CSPD 1658–9*, 512.
[253] *CSPD 1653–4*, 478, 539; SP 18/108/27; Rawl. MS A 187, fos. 439, 441; Rawl. MS A 184, fos. 72–3.
[254] *CJ* v. 606.
[255] SP 18/46/47; *CSPD 1658–9*, 527; Carte MS 73, fo. 148.
[256] *Severall Proceedings*, 4–11 Dec. 1651; SP 18/84/3, 133; A. T. Wright, *Jeremiah Rich: Semiographer of the Commonwealth* (1911).
[257] SP 18/59/34; cf. SP 18/105/58; Weale had been recommended to Desborough by Capt. Roger Alsop, his army commander: SP 18/85/68. The purser Thomas Sacheverell was a former army trooper: Mayo, *Minute Book*, 229.

the army as a young man and served for ten years, taking part 'in all the considerable fights'; he had no trade to pick up and presumably turned to the navy for a reasonably secure future. We may be sure he was not drawn by hopes of further adventure, for he admitted ingenuously that during his army career he had been taken prisoner no less than seven times![258]

The one remaining warrant-officer to be considered is the surgeon.[259] He generally acted as physician too, carrying a supply of julep, liquorice, cordials, and pills, and was allowed a sum of between £3 and £10 to stock his medicine chest.[260] The surgeon naturally required specialist expertise, and he was very rarely a seaman.[261] His importance was obvious in the cramped, unhealthy conditions of life at sea, especially in wartime. One ship which lacked a surgeon even left its station and returned to port in search of one, the crew presumably being reluctant to stay out without medical provision.[262]

The calibre of naval surgeons had often been abysmal in Tudor times, and improvements had been slow and patchy. The Company of Barber-Surgeons was required to provide recruits for the navy, by pressing if necessary, and many of those supplied were poorly qualified and resentful. The interregnum witnessed a concerted effort to improve medical provision and standards. The package of reforms introduced at the end of 1652 included widespread improvements in the care of the sick and wounded. Every surgeon was now allowed a mate, even in the little sixth-rates, and the surgeon's pay was raised to £2. 10s. a month, which, with the 2d. deducted monthly from the wages of every seaman, would bring it in a large ship to the level of a gunner's or boatswain's, or even higher.[263]

It has been claimed that the Commonwealth's reforms ended the old abuses of ignorance and malpractice.[264] This is too optimistic: complaints remained widespread and were often clearly justified.

---

[258] SP 18/48/30; cf. SP 18/86/4.

[259] On the surgeon see J. J. Keevil, *Medicine and the Navy, 1200–1900* (1957–8), esp. ii. 1–79; Lewis, *Sea-Officers*, 253–9.

[260] SP 18/57/182; Add. MS 9300, fo. 299ᵛ.

[261] But for a surgeon begging a command see SP 46/117, fo. 93; he claimed 27 years at sea had made him 'somewhat intelligent' in maritime affairs!

[262] Adm. 7/674/20.

[263] *FDW* iii. 285; cf. Blake, *Letters*, 21. See ch. 7, below, for other reforms. The surgeon's previous pay had been £1. 10s.

[264] Keevil, *Medicine*, ii. 34.

Some surgeons were young and raw, such as the youth in the *Francis* prize who had five years of his apprenticeship still to serve.[265] Others were horribly incompetent: the 'unskilful' drunkard of the *Falcon* was reported to have gratuitously hacked off a patient's leg.[266] Some deserted at the first opportunity.[267] Several were court-martialled and turned out for offences such as fraud, drunkenness, and insubordination.[268] The authorities, if not the patients, were also concerned that so many fell woefully short of the Puritan, parliamentary ideal. One official begged in 1653 for surgeons who were not atheistical, and there were royalist sympathizers still in place at the end of the decade.[269]

Nevertheless some progress was certainly achieved, and there were now many good surgeons to set alongside the drunken and incompetent. Quite often a captain asked for his surgeon to be reappointed, or transferred with him if he was moving to another ship. Blake and Popham commended the public spirit shown by one officer who had supplied his medical chest from his own pocket.[270] Perhaps the real significance of that incident is that he was able as well as willing to do so: the pay was now high enough to attract some men of substance, at least in the larger ships. The surgeon who lost £150 in medical supplies, equipment, books, and cash when his ship was wrecked in 1657 clearly did not belong to the pauperized dregs of the profession.[271] Blake's own surgeon, John Haslock, was an Oxford graduate and an able and respected practitioner, later chosen to embalm Cromwell's body.[272] James Pearse, a former army surgeon who served in the *Naseby* under Mountagu, rose in his patron's wake to become surgeon to the Royal Household and Master of the Barber-Surgeons.[273] The surgeon of a flagship might well consider the post a very promising step in his career.

---

[265] *CSPD 1659–60*, 3.

[266] *CSPD 1653–4*, 557.

[267] *CSPD 1656–7*, 466, 468; Adm. 2/1729, fo. 172.

[268] SP 18/85/9; *CSPD 1656–7*, 428, 468, 512, 540, 552; *CSPD 1657–8*, 387; SP 18/195/28.

[269] Add. MS 18986, fo. 104; *CSPD 1650*, 16, 24–5, 35; *CSPD 1659–60*, 182.

[270] NMM REC/1, fo. 71; SP 18/118/147; Blake, *Letters*, 59–60.

[271] SP 18/168/49–50; cf. a surgeon who had spent £54 on medical supplies, despite wages far in arrears: *CSPD 1654*, 509.

[272] Keevil, *Medicine*, ii. 35–6, 48–50; Blake, *Letters*, 111; J. Foster, *Alumni Oxonienses . . . 1500–1714* (Oxford, 1891–2), ii. 670.

[273] Pepys, *Diary*, x. 310–11 and sources there cited.

Warrant-officers were thus spread across a wide spectrum in terms of social background and standing. Some had experience of command themselves and a few, mainly pursers and recruits from the army, had influential connections ashore. All held responsible positions, and a sensible commander regarded them as colleagues, not servants. Even a staunch champion of the gentleman-captain, writing before the civil war, urged that they be treated with respect and consideration.[274] For it was the warrant-officers who determined how effective the ship would be in action, and the standards and morale of the company as a whole depended on their wholehearted co-operation.

[274] *Boteler's Dialogues*, 33.

7

The Floating Commonwealth

A LARGE warship with a crew of two or three hundred men formed a community the size of many villages ashore. The navy as a whole, with over 20,000 men at sea at its peak, was more populous than all but the greatest cities in England. The aim of the present chapter is to explore the social characteristics of what one commander called the 'floating commonwealth'.[1]

The traditional image of life in a warship is of brutal discipline and appalling conditions. 'No man will be a sailor who has contrivance enough to get himself into a jail', Dr Johnson observed, 'for being in a ship is being in a jail, with the chance of being drowned.' It was by no means an original view; a Jacobean admiral had similarly described a ship as a 'running prison', and an official under Charles I conceded that sailors were 'used like dogs' and would as soon be hanged.[2] But such a picture of unrelieved gloom is misleading, and in recent years several naval historians have cast doubt upon it. N. A. M. Rodger, in his study of the mid-eighteenth-century navy, dismisses it altogether and paints instead a scene of general harmony and content.[3] It will be argued here that the evidence we have on social relationships within the interregnum navy does not really accord with either view. Indeed no single image could convey the very diverse patterns which emerge. Conventions of behaviour were still very loose, and the social order on board each ship depended on a whole constellation of variables.

---

[1] The phrase was used by Capt. John Sherwin: BL Add. MS 22546, fo. 160. For manning levels see e.g. *FDW* i. 64–8, v. 16–20. The *Resolution* carried 550 men in May 1653.

[2] *Boswell's Life of Johnson*, ed. R. W. Chapman (1953), 246–7; G. W. Manwaring (ed.), *The Life and Works of Sir Henry Mainwaring* (NRS, 1920/2), ii. 18, 189.

[3] N. A. M. Rodger, *The Wooden World: An Anatomy of the Georgian Navy* (1986), ch. 6. For more cautious revisionism see D. A. Baugh, *British Naval Administration in the Age of Walpole* (Princeton, 1965); J. Ehrman, *The Navy in the War of William III, 1689–1697* (Cambridge, 1953); Davies, thesis.

I. THE SHIP'S COMMUNITY

A ship's 'company' was, ideally, much more than the aggregate of its officers and men; as the term suggests, it could be a real community bonded together by the perils of the sea. Every mariner knew that once under sail the lives of all on board depended on co-operation and trust, and a good captain fostered these qualities by granting easy access to his men and taking care of their needs. Volunteers naturally wanted to serve in ships where they would find such a sense of community, and often sought out captains they already knew and respected, either personally or by repute. Charles Shadwell's play, *The Fair Quaker of Deal*, dates from half a century later but it shows well the startling familiarity which could exist between naval officers and their men. Commodore Flip makes a point of getting drunk with each mess every week, confident that in return the seamen will serve him all the more readily; 'My joculous-ness with 'em makes 'em fight for me', he explains. Shadwell does not sentimentalize the relationship, and depicts the commodore as a man of rough and capricious ways. But Flip has spent his whole life at sea, serving in every post from cook's boy upwards, and has remained close to the ordinary seamen, familiar with their ways, their jokes, and their needs; 'I love a sailor', he says simply.[4] Of course not every ship's company enjoyed a spirit of community. Some captains abused their authority, some warrant-officers were bloody-minded towards their superiors and overbearing towards those below them, and some of the sailors—especially those seized by the press—were deeply resentful and eager to escape. But the communal spirit was probably more widespread in the navy of the 1640s and 1650s than in most periods, for a high proportion of commissioned officers were professional mariners from seafaring families, familiar with the ways and the world of the ordinary seaman. During the interregnum there was little place for the ignor-ant gentleman-officer, who in the proceeding generation had often alienated his company by flouting the seamen's communal ethos—if indeed he had even been aware of it. Whenever a 'decayed, forlorn gentleman' came on board, a mariner had complained bitterly in

[4] C. Shadwell, *The Fair Quaker of Deal* (1710), 4. Shadwell does not suggest that all commanders behaved thus: Flip is presented as one of several contrasting stereotypes.

1627, the 'first title that he layeth claim to is: "This is my ship, my boat, my men". And so likewise "mine" of everything [that] pertaineth to the ship'—an attitude which appeared 'improper and vainglorious to an understanding seaman'.[5]

A company living together in relative harmony leaves less evidence for posterity than one with a tyrannical captain or truculent crew, and what does survive is likely, by its very nature, to be undramatic. But there is more than enough to establish that a genuine sense of community did exist in many interregnum warships.

The senior officers displayed a paternalistic concern for their men, very unlike the attitude shown by most of their predecessors in the 1620s. Many were appalled, for example, by the heavy casualties suffered in the Dutch war. Shortly after the bloody action off Portland the commanders petitioned for the relief of widows, orphans, and crippled seamen, urging far more generous terms than the government was ever willing to concede.[6] The Generals themselves were quick to bring the men's needs to the attention of the Admiralty. In the early summer of 1653 Blake and Monck reported 'great complaints of stinking beer and salt beer, which occasions sickness in those ships where it is very much,' and other complaints about meat, mouldy bread and a shortage of hammocks.[7] A few weeks later Monck took personal action to relieve the plight of sick and wounded sailors lodged in Southwold and adjacent towns, whose inhabitants were complaining about the heavy cost of caring for them. As the state had no ready cash available Monck and a local captain who was known and trusted engaged themselves for the repayment of all expenses, to ensure that care of the sick would continue.[8]

There are numerous examples of individual captains bringing their sailors' needs to the Admiralty's notice, sometimes forcefully. Many sympathized deeply with their men's grievances over lack of pay, food, or clothing, and pressed the Commissioners for relief.[9] If their requests were ignored they sometimes spoke out very freely.

---

[5] 'The Earl of Warwick's Voyage of 1627', ed. N. P. Bard, in *The Naval Miscellany*, v (NRS, 1984), 65; cf. Oppenheim, 196.

[6] *FDW* iv. 211–15. A widow with three dependent children would receive a pension equal to her husband's full wage. The petition was signed by Peacock, Lane, and Howett in the name of all. Cf. Oppenheim, 222, 233.

[7] NMM AGC/B/7.   [8] *FDW* v. 269.   [9] See ch. 8, below.

John Sherwin's *Primrose* was stationed out of the way in the Irish Sea and the needs of her men were repeatedly brushed aside. When the ship was ordered late in 1652 to remain out over winter Sherwin's fury erupted. How did the Council expect 'a company of sick, naked men' to stay out without either pay or clothing? Those responsible for the order, he told the Navy Commissioners bluntly, must be a 'company of barking whelps that minds their own prey more than the welfare of their dam, that values not the frigate so long as their self-interest is promoted'.[10] Very often officers took action themselves if the state failed to provide relief, handing out tickets or money on their own authority. Peter Strong declared his ship's beer so foul that he would pour it overboard rather than make the crew drink it. He bought canvas to make hammocks for soldiers serving with him so they would not have to sleep on bare boards. Jonathan Taylor bought fresh food for some of his men who were sick, explaining that he found it 'painful to see them tied to salt in their condition'.[11]

The balance between paternalism and calculation in such incidents is hard to determine, and perhaps unimportant. Captains knew that sick and resentful sailors would perform poorly, and might desert or disobey. Sherwin had warned the Council on a previous occasion that his men were on the verge of mutiny, and the Admiralty had hurriedly supplied pay and clothing to ward off the danger. When Robert Clarke's men refused to put to sea in 1653 he handed out tickets 'for quietness' sake'.[12] But it would be wrong to explain everything in terms of self-interest. There are many letters, like Sherwin's, which convey a strong sense of moral outrage at the sufferings of the men. Any officer who had tried to create a sense of community among his seamen was inevitably troubled by their wants, and anxious to do whatever he could to relieve them.

It is evident that many captains succeeded in creating an atmosphere of mutual trust and harmony. When they moved to another ship they often asked to take some of their old officers and men with them. Lawson wanted *all* his chief officers to go with him into the *George* in 1653. Francis Kirby took his lieutenant along when he moved from the *Bear* to the *Mathias,* and his successor brought his own lieutenant with him into the *Bear.* The Admiralty

[10] PRO SP 18/28/141.
[11] *CSPD 1652–3,* 589, 590; cf. Oppenheim, 236.
[12] Bodl. Rawlinson MS A 225, fos. 124ᵛ–125; SP 18/55/2.

generally welcomed such arrangements, 'conceiving it may be for
the advantage of the service'.[13] It is still more striking that ordinary
sailors quite often asked to go with their captain. When the *Lily*
sank in 1653 seventeen survivors, ranging from master to ordinary
seaman, asked to serve with the captain again. When the *Pelican* was
destroyed by fire her crew too wanted to remain with their
commander.[14] Some forty sailors accompanied Robert Robinson
when he moved to a new command in 1655. And if only twenty
went with William Whitehorne it was not, he explained, through
lack of volunteers but rather that he did not want to leave an empty
ship for his successor.[15]

The sense of community can sometimes be confirmed by other
kinds of evidence. A ship's company might rally, for example, to
defend the reputation of a captain under attack. When Charles
Thoroughgood of the *Worcester* was dismissed for cowardice and
neglect in 1652 the lieutenant, master, and forty-seven other officers
and men called for a council of war to clear their captain from the
'false aspersion of some envious tongues'. Similarly the lieutenant
and ninety-seven of the crew of the *Providence* testified to the
innocence of their own captain, John Pearce, who had been turned
out on the same grounds.[16] Scattered evidence of a more trivial kind
provides further confirmation. The boatswain who directed a letter
'To his loving commander', and added 'with my love to your wife',
was clearly a friendly colleague, not a trembling vassal.[17] Commissioned and warrant-officers often ate together and spent leisure time
ashore together. Richard Gibson and John Weale both mention the
friendly welcome they found, as warrant-officers, from more senior
officers in other ships. When Weale himself obtained a commission
he hospitably invited the gunner, boatswain, carpenter, and purser
to dinner.[18] Some captains even appear to have used Christian names
in addressing their subordinates.[19]

[13] *CSPD 1652–3*, 546; NMM WYN/18, pp. 44, 53; SP 18/90/63; Add. MS 9300,
fo. 290ᵛ; Rawl. MS A 227, fo. 110ᵛ.
[14] SP 18/60/68–9; SP 18/134/12–16.   [15] SP 18/116/1; SP 18/141/174.
[16] *FDW* i. 249–50; SP 18/41/91–5. Pearce's lieutenant, also named John Pearce and
perhaps his son, may have applied pressure.
[17] SP 18/58/82. The commander was Philip Gethings.
[18] *FDW* i. 11; 'The Journal of John Weale', ed. J. R. Powell, in *The Naval
Miscellany*, iv (NRS, 1952), 89, 104.
[19] T. Lurting, *The Fighting Sailor turned Peaceable Christian* (1801), 18.
Warwick, addressing a ship's company in 1627, called them 'Gentlemen' and referred
to the captain as 'Dick' ('Warwick's Voyage', 26); cf. R. Badiley, *Capt. Badiley's
Answer* (1653), 91.

Captains were not the only officers to inspire loyalty and affection. The officers and the men of the *Greyhound* said in 1656 that they were sad 'our loving commander Captain Edmund Thompson is to leave us . . . which doth much grieve us to part from so honest a gentleman'. But if it had to be so, they went on, they would like the master to take his place, for he too was a man they knew and trusted.[20] When the captain of the *Great President* died in 1656, fifty-five of the officers and crew signed a petition asking for the master to succeed him, as a 'deserving and knowing' man.[21] Lt. John Cuttle of the *Mayflower* enjoyed similar respect. He had taken charge when the captain was killed in action, and directed the fight for the rest of the day despite his own wounds. When the Generals appointed an outsider as captain twelve of the ship's surviving officers sent a strong letter asserting Cuttle's right to the succession 'by the law of arms and all other right'.[22]

The constant struggle against the elements helped to bind officers and men together in a sense of community; so of course did the pursuit of prize-money. In many cases these bonds were strengthened by other links, such as ties of blood. A number of captains installed a brother or son as lieutenant, and other kinsmen might be serving as warrant- or petty officers or midshipmen. Penn's flagship in 1654 might almost be seen as a rare English example of an extended family household.[23] Similar practices obtained in merchantmen. In 1652 the hired ship *Prosperous* had John Barker as captain, his son as master, and his son-in-law probably as mate.[24] Warrant-officers, who were allowed a servant, sometimes brought a son to gain a free practical education.[25] The formal hierarchy of a ship's company could thus be blurred and softened by the existence of family ties within it.

Sailors who volunteered very often did so to serve with a particular captain, someone they had sailed with before, quite often from their own home town. Warrant-officers too could draw men with them into the navy, or rather into their particular ship. There might thus be several groups within a single company bound together by

---

[20] SP 18/64/34 (misdated 1653 in *CSPD*); SP 18/134/116.
[21] NMM ADL/A/9. [22] SP 18/61/9.
[23] Ch. 6, part iii, above. Cornelius had a brother-in-law as master (SP 18/112/16); Nutton had a son-in-law as mate (*CSPD 1658–9*, 559); for other examples see Rawl. MS A 226, fo. 154ᵛ (Pacey); SP 18/81/200 (Southwood).
[24] SP 18/64/6.
[25] e.g. N. Gettonsby (Rawl. MS A 207, fo. 91ᵛ), H. Reeves (SP 18/55/119), both masters; ch. 6 nn. 79–80 above.

old acquaintance and mutal trust. Most volunteers had familiar faces around them.[26] Some companies indeed had a pronounced local character. Coppin and most of the *Greyhound*'s crew were from Deal. Heaton and many of the *Sapphire*'s men were from Plymouth. Lambert Cornelius of the *Cornelian* and many of his men were from Weymouth.[27] In a few cases this pattern can be traced back to the ship's own origins. The *Portsmouth* was built in the town's dockyard and one of her first captains, Robert Dornford, had been master-gunner of the garrison. A local newspaper correspondent referred to it proudly as 'our frigate'.[28] The *Yarmouth* too was named after the town where she was built, and her first captain, Robert Mackey, was a local shipmaster and a member of the town council. The clerk of the cheque was also a local man, and there were no doubt others among the crew.[29] Ties of blood, friendship, and locality reinforced one another.

How far the communal spirit extended varied from ship to ship, depending on size, the proportion of volunteers in the crew, and the temperament of the captain and other officers. As the captain was often the only commissioned officer on board he was obliged to work with the warrant-officers as close colleagues. Many captains were themselves former warrant-officers, and they in turn had mostly risen from the ranks of midshipmen, petty officers, and volunteers. A warship's company was in many ways a seamless web.

The account so far has focused on harmony and community. But several other, more jarring elements have to be fitted into the picture. First, in most companies there was a fundamental division between volunteers and pressed men. Most ships had to resort to the press to meet their manning requirements, and the lengths to

---

[26] See ch. 8 below.

[27] *DCW* 346; Rawl. MS A 224, fo. 68; *FDW* i. 23–4; *CSPD 1655*, 524. (The *Cornelian* was a former Brest privateer and was not named after Cornelius, though his appointment to her was perhaps prompted by the similarity of names.)

[28] J. Rushworth, *Historical Collections* (1659–1701), vii. 1388–9; *A Perfect Diurnall,* 27 May–3 June 1650.

[29] For Mackey see *A Calendar of the Freemen of Great Yarmouth, 1429–1800* (Norfolk Arch. Soc., 1910), 77; A. S. Brown (ed.), 'Baptisms and Deaths recorded in the Church Book of the Great Yarmouth Independent Church, 1643–1705', in *A Miscellany* (Norfolk Record Soc., xxii; 1951), 39. For the clerk see Rawl. MS A 184, fos. 72–3.

which sailors went to escape it suggest the deep resentment that must have existed among those who failed. One reason indeed why a captain needed a core of reliable, co-operative volunteers was to provide him with an effective press-gang to complete his crew.[30] Second, the naval seaman often had deeply felt and justified grievances over pay, food, and clothing. These matters, largely outside the captain's control, are discussed further in the next chapter.

Another discordant element was the ferocious disciplinary code in whose shadow the seamen had to live. It was tightened in 1649, and again after the demoralizing defeat at Dungeness; no less than twenty-five offences could carry the death penalty under the Articles of War established, with unconscious black humour, on Christmas Day 1652. A copy was posted in each ship in the steerage and read out at intervals to the crew.[31] The political situation at the time does much to explain their ferocity, but contemporaries throughout the century argued that sailors were a tough and violent breed and that discipline had to be correspondingly harsh. Seamen 'are of all men the most uncivil and barbarous', said the Jacobean commander Henry Mainwaring. Edward Barlow agreed, remarking later in the century after a lifetime at sea that many were 'of that lazy, idle temper, that let them alone and they never care for anything they should do, and when they do anything it is with a grumbling, unwilling mind, so that they must be forced and drove to it'. Even one of the most enlightened Restoration commanders thought it 'folly to say that good words only without blows will wholly command an English seaman'.[32] Contemporaries were probably right to believe that a tough regime was necessary when large numbers of young men, many of them resentful and often bored, were living cheek by jowl. An official with the fleet in May 1653 reported that though courts martial were being held every other day there was no apparent improvement in general behaviour. 'They are the rudest generation of men I ever saw', he observed with disgust.[33]

[30] e.g. SP 18/141/12. For the press see ch. 8, below.
[31] *FDW* iii. 293-301; ch. 3 n. 75, above. For its public reading see e.g. Penn, *Memorials*, ii. 65.
[32] *Life of Mainwaring*, ii. 42; *Barlow's Journal of his Life at Sea*, ed. B. Lubbock (1934), 452; *The Tangier Papers of Samuel Pepys*, ed. E. Chappell (NRS, 1935), 173.
[33] SP 18/51/16.

The savagery of the disciplinary code is none the less misleading. The code served mainly as a deterrent: in the whole period from 1649 to 1660 there is only one definite instance of a sailor hanged for an offence committed on board ship. Several other sailors who had been condemned were reprieved.[34] Courts martial repeatedly ignored the mandatory death penalty laid down for crimes such as desertion. John Weale, who notes the sole execution, mentions only three other severe punishments imposed in the course of Blake's last two expeditions: in each case the offender was whipped from ship to ship, one for striking his commander, another for theft, and the third for fighting and drunkenness.[35] Drunkenness was a very common offence, but it was only in aggravated circumstances that it was punished so harshly. A persistent drunkard might be turned out of his place, as happened to the *Maidstone*'s lieutenant in 1655. A quartermaster drunk on watch, a serious offence, was whipped and reduced to the ranks, and a boatswain who was frequently drunk and abusive was ducked and turned ashore.[36] Individual captains dealt with minor offences (including most cases of drunkenness), and had a range of traditional punishments at their disposal. An offender might be put in the bilboes (in irons), struck on the forehead with the boatswain's whistle, or gagged with a notice pinned to his chest describing his crime. For a more serious offence he might be ducked, discharged, or whipped. But a heavy flogging could only be imposed by a higher court martial, attended by all the available captains and often with a flag-officer presiding, and such sentences were much rarer and less severe than in later generations.[37]

Naval discipline, if hardly mild, was thus much less brutal than

---

[34] 'Weale's Journal', 143. Weale does not specify the crime. The Venetian secretary said in Feb. 1653 that Blake had executed a seaman for refusing to serve and threatening to fire his ship, but there is no evidence to confirm this (*CSPV 1653–4*, 25). For reprieves see Penn, *Memorials*, i. 332; below, ch. 8 nn. 129, 140.

[35] 'Weale's Journal', 98.

[36] Ibid. 105; Rawl. MS C 381, p. 16; SP 18/42/80, part ii.

[37] SP 18/77/87, part iii; *Boteler's Dialogues*, ed. W. G. Perrin (NRS, 1929), 16–19; Oppenheim, 188, 239. A century later captains were allowed to order twelve lashes on their own authority, and often exceeded this number, while courts martial imposed savage sentences of up to 1,000 lashes: Rodger, *Wooden World*, 218–29. By contrast when Capt. Strutt sentenced an offender in 1658 to nine strokes (for three offences), with the approval of a flag-officer, the victim lodged a complaint alleging cruelty (*CSPD 1657–8*, 512).

the code allowed. Even Mainwaring had stressed that harshness by itself was no solution: a captain had to rule 'both in fear and love' to be effective, and most officers appear to have shared his view.[38] A brisk paternalism was more often the order of the day. Discipline in the interregnum navy was not only less harsh than the legend, it was milder than in the New Model Army. There were many more executions and heavy floggings in the army; in the garrison at Dundee alone military courts condemned two men to death and imposed sentences of between thirty and sixty lashes on half a dozen occasions in the course of a mere five months in 1651 to 1652.[39] Naval discipline was also no tougher than in many merchant vessels, for civilian shipmasters had a virtually free hand over their men. Naval captains by contrast had to act in conjunction with the warrant-officers and sentence according to the will of the majority, which provided some protection against arbitrary behaviour. They were not allowed to impose any sentence involving loss of life or limb, and if they acted unreasonably the victim could appeal to a higher authority for redress.[40]

Some interregnum captains undoubtedly did behave in a harsh and unreasonable manner, abusing their authority—as of course remained the case down the centuries. What seems to have been characteristic of the 1650s was the readiness of the victims to complain to the Admiralty, and of the Admiralty to take their part.[41] An account of the voyage of the *Adventure* to Iceland in 1652, on fishery protection duty, provides a particularly vivid example. Once the ship was at sea, it was alleged, Capt. Robert Wyard informed the crew that 'he had martial law, to hang whom he pleased, if they did not obey his word for a law, for, saith he, I have as much power as the General, and now I have got you from under the Flag I'll make you observe my words for a law'. The chaplain preached obsequiously that the captain must be obeyed as

---

[38] *Life of Mainwaring*, ii. 46; cf. Pepys, *Tangier Papers*, 173.

[39] C. H. Firth, *Cromwell's Army* (1962 edn.), ch. 12; Clarke MS 1/9.

[40] *FDW* vi. 193–5; *Boteler's Dialogues*, 18; E. Coxere, *Adventures by Sea*, ed. E. H. W. Meyerstein (Oxford, 1945), 20–2, 36; R. Davis, *The Rise of the English Shipping Industry in the Seventeenth and Eighteenth Centuries* (1962), 154; Oppenheim, 244.

[41] This procedure was still possible a hundred years later (Rodger, *Wooden World*, 229–35), but appears to have been far more prevalent during the interregnum than at any other time.

'a king in his throne'—not the ideal image to use in a new republic. During the voyage Wyard

> was ever beating and abusing the seamen, breaking some men's heads and arms and kicking some in the mouth, and cocked his fowling pieces at the boatswain, and threw a crossbar shot at him, like to have killed him in his cabin, beating others with horsewhips and canes, and calling men rogues, rascals, whores, birds, whoresons and the like, so that men lived all that voyage more like slaves than the state's servants.

But this last phrase makes it clear that sailors did not expect to be treated thus, and once the ship returned home many of them marched off to London to press charges against the captain. The Admiralty took the allegations seriously, and despite Wyard's protestations an inquiry found in favour of the men. Even during the Dutch war he remained out of employment, damned in the Admiralty's files as 'a man of a riotous, corrupt life, a drone, a coward, and a base, self-seeking fellow'.[42]

There were several other captains of the same type. John Bowen, in drink, beat his pilot and threatened his coxswain with a pistol. Edward Grove threatened to throw his carpenter overboard, along with his warrant. John Lightfoot frequently struck his men, allegedly urging the boatswain to break their arms and legs and kill them.[43] Still more outrageous was the conduct of John Vessey, who on going out to his ship one day after a heavy drinking bout ashore drew his cutlass and slashed at the boat-crew, forcing several men to leap into the sea in panic.[44] But again the seamen knew that redress was possible. In each of these cases the victims brought complaints, and in three out of four the captain was turned out. The most bizarre case of all underlines the point. One day in the autumn of 1652 Capt. Peter Warren of the little *Merlin*, in a state of drunken bravado, ordered his men to attack a Dutch flagship. A spokesman for the crew pointed out that this would be suicidal, whereupon Warren flew into a rage and shot him in the back, killing him. The company refused to be cowed; they secured the captain and brought the ship home to England, and Warren was put on trial for murder and hanged.[45]

Allegations of violence are often difficult to assess. The evidence,

[42] SP 46/96/217–26, 232; SP 18/46/14.
[43] Clarke MS 4/4, 1649 (38); SP 18/174/188; SP 18/137/29.
[44] Add. MS 9304, fo. 154.
[45] *FDW* ii. 262, 266, iii. 37; *The Speech of Captain Henry* [sic] *Warren at the Place of Execution* (1652); *French Occurrences*, 11–18 Oct. 1652; *A Perfect Account*, 13–20 Oct. 1652.

though copious, is frequently contradictory and inconclusive. Once men decided to bring charges against their captain, for whatever reason, they usually threw in everything they could think of—fraud, drunkenness, cowardice, sedition, and blasphemy, as well as cruelty. The captain generally denied all and made a series of counter-accusations. Often the charges, on both sides, were exaggerated or wholly untrue. The *Nantwich*'s cook accused Capt. Jefferies of 'tyrannical usage' and massive fraud, but a court martial discovered only minor misdemeanours and drew attention to the cook's provocative behaviour, noting that he had given his captain 'abusive language and did (as is affirmed) run both his fists in his face'.[46] In many cases the evidence was evenly balanced.[47] Courts martial were often confused, and sometimes concluded—probably rightly—that there was blame on all sides.

Whatever the facts in individual cases, it is clear that officers and men with a sense of grievance were ready and able to complain to the Admiralty. The Commissioners treated such charges seriously, displaying a sensible and balanced attitude. While they naturally wanted to uphold a captain's authority, they were equally anxious to promote harmony. Their pragmatism is clear, for example, in their reaction to a complaint from the *Newcastle* in 1658. The men complained that the 'imperious and insulting carriage of the captain towards all his company is so much that they are discouraged thereby from doing their duties or continuing any longer in the service'. Behind this careful phraseology lay the threat of mutiny or mass desertion; even so the Commissioners, after investigating, sided with the crew. Brushing aside Capt. Curtis's attempts to justify himself, they gave him a stern warning and some sensible advice: 'It is necessary you should bear a command, and we would not weaken your hands in it, though our advice be, that you would do it with that prudence and good temper of spirit as may not needlessly exasperate the ship's company, and make the service burdensome to them.' They had a similar message for Capt. John Parker, telling him more brusquely to cease the 'abusive and absurd carriage' which had provoked his men.[48]

The balance of authority between a captain and his crew in the mid-seventeenth-century navy was complex and delicate. The sailors knew they could bring charges against a captain with a

[46] SP 18/122/109; SP 18/125/19; SP 18/135/49, 90.
[47] e.g. Rawl. MS A 187, fos. 239–48.
[48] PRO Adm. 2/1730, fos. 242ᵛ, 248ᵛ; Adm. 2/1729, fo. 146ᵛ.

reasonable chance of success, and in these circumstances a sensible officer trod with care. In some cases sailors openly declared they intended to lodge a complaint, and anxious officers occasionally wrote to put their own side of the story first.[49] The position of a warrant-officer, who could not be dismissed by a captain solely on his own authority, was particularly strong. Some undoubtedly abused their relative independence. The idle, drunken, and quarrelsome boatswain of the *Lizard* allegedly ignored frequent warnings to mend his ways, and 'when the captain went on shore on one side, he would go ashore on the other without leave, and continue there drinking and carousing for three or four nights'. Capt. Gethings complained with feeling of a boorish master who had been drunk for a week, 'drinking of strong waters in his round-house by himself and never looks after the ship at all'.[50] Most captains had to contend with such officers at some point.

The captain's position was however much stronger than this might suggest. The Admiralty did not want to undermine discipline, and would only take action against a commander if the evidence appeared compelling. Moreover it took considerable courage on the part of ordinary seamen to challenge their commander. He could often intimidate them, either physically or by refusing to sign their pay tickets on some bogus ground. The officers of the *Rosebush* reported that her whole company resented the conduct of Capt. Valentine Tatnel but that 'fear of punishment and losing of their pay maketh many of them silent'.[51] Even a warrant-officer was open to intimidation. He did not enjoy absolute security and knew that by defying his captain he would be putting his own position at risk. The captain might ask the Admiralty to remove him, or refuse to sign his accounts at the end of the voyage, in which case his wages would be withheld indefinitely. A court martial found that Capt. James Strutt had coerced seven of his officers into backing false allegations against the master. Another captain threatened to have his officers turned out if they failed to vote the 'right' way in a court martial.[52] Such factors help to explain why discontent often festered for months before leading to a formal accusation, and no doubt in many cases tensions never came to the

[49] e.g. SP 18/137/29; SP 18/86/19; Adm. 2/1732, fo. 98.
[50] *CSPD 1657–8*, 408; Clarke MS 4/4, 1651 (10).
[51] SP 18/85/38.
[52] Sp 18/173/40–1; SP 18/174/18, 60; SP 18/157/17.

Admiralty's notice. Some junior officers were clearly very nervous when they pressed charges. The ex-steward of the *Worcester* accused Capt. Robert Nixon of fraud in 1657, but was so terrified that he turned to Cromwell himself for protection. Nixon was a very powerful man, he informed the Lord Protector, and was threatening 'great and grievous actions' against him and his witnesses; if the captain had him arrested he would be unable to find bail and would be ruined.[53]

With the scales finely balanced, much depended on the character of the participants. A captain had to earn respect, rather than assuming unquestioning obedience. It seems beyond doubt that the regulations governing behaviour at sea were widely ignored, and that each company worked out its own rough-and-ready pattern of social relations. The Admiralty appears to have been quite happy with this situation provided that the ship functioned efficiently and neither captain nor crew overstepped the mark.[54]

In most respects interregnum practice seems preferable to the rigid discipline and brutality which were to provoke the great mutinies of 1797. It did carry risks, however. One flaw was that the Admiralty's readiness to hear complaints could encourage false accusations motivated by ambition or malice. Lt. Henry Barrow, who denounced his captain in 1654, was said to have remarked that 'if he could inform against any man to better himself or to get his place, he would do it'.[55] Capt. Thomas Fleet reported that when he refused to sign his steward's books, because they were fraudulent, the man 'threatened he would pick a hole in my coat before the term of the voyage be ended'.[56] The officers who alleged fraud in the *Hopewell* pink in 1655 were blatantly jockeying for the vacant command, and the Admiralty wisely appointed an outsider.[57]

Another and more serious danger was that a ship could be virtually paralysed if a harsh or over-zealous captain encountered a

---

[53] SP 18/102/190; SP 18/157/17, parts i–vii. If Nixon really had defrauded the state of £100,000, as alleged, the steward had good reason to doubt his chances in a prolonged legal battle.

[54] Even in the more professional navy of a hundred years later, it has been argued, an officer still only 'hoped to persuade' his men and could not simply 'expect to command': Rodger, *Wooden World*, 206.

[55] SP 18/77/87, part i; cf. Peter Bowen, who in 1653 denounced the captain of the *Nightingale* as a coward and asked for his job: *CSPD 1652–3*, 193

[56] SP 18/86/19.

[57] SP 18/109/84; SP 18/111/54, 147–9; SP 18/112/16, 17.

group of bloody-minded subordinates. Feuding within a ship's company was a considerable problem in the 1650s. The best-documented and (one hopes) most extreme instance was the running battle aboard the *Adventure* in 1656.[58] Some forty-three of the crew deposed that Capt. Best was a drunken and incompetent bully, and the warrant-officers brought many further charges. Best pleaded his innocence. He was being maligned, he claimed, because he had imposed strict discipline and had tried to bring his unsatisfactory subordinates up to scratch. He damned the boatswain as a 'slut', the carpenter as wholly useless ('he being a drinking man'), and the gunner as incompetent. When the ship went into action one day Best allegedly turned to him and said, 'Gunner hit, be sure, for I think you never hit ship in your life.' The gunner and his friends, for their part, scorned the captain as a coward who only altered the trim of the sails during a chase to make sure that the enemy remained safely out of reach. The sailors would set up a derisive chant, 'A man of war ahead, a man of war ahead'—derisive because they knew 'ahead' it would safely remain. Best, though strict, was plainly unable to control his officers. They defiantly stayed ashore when the ship was in port, allowing some of the pressed men to seize their chance and desert. The Admiralty was outraged when it learned of this state of affairs, and Best eventually faced a court martial. It found that the vast array of charges against him sprang from malice, and had been provoked by the severe regime he had tried to impose. He took this careful formula to mean he was fully vindicated, but the Admiralty never entrusted him with another command. The real verdict has to be that the collision of an intemperate captain with truculent subordinates effectively destroyed the ship's military usefulness for a period of several months.

There were a number of similar episodes in other ships. Quarrels in the *Phoenix* in 1655 rendered her useless too. Lawson held a court martial, which recommended that the master be dismissed, but feared there would continue to be 'parties in the ship by reason the contest hath been betwixt two such officers', and advised that she be called in.[59] A feud between the captain and master of the *Portland* in 1656 was so divisive that the commander in the Downs dared not send her to sea, keeping her under his own guns 'for fear

⁵⁸ SP 18/42/93–4 (misdated in *CSPD*); SP 18/129/91; SP 18/138/142; SP 18/141/147, 207; SP 18/145/104, 107; SP 18/146/18, 28–9; SP 18/150/165; SP 18/158/105–7; SP 18/162/40; Adm. 2/1729, fos. 42ᵛ, 81ᵛ.					⁵⁹ SP 18/104/97.

of a greater evil'.[60] Similar hatreds existed on board the *Pearl*.
Sixteen of the crew denounced Capt. John Smith, who deposed in
reply that he had overheard them plotting to murder him; he added
that he carried a loaded pistol at all times to defend himself, and
asked for troops to be sent on board to protect him. An inquiry
concluded that the charges against him were false but had been
provoked by his strictness.[61]

Attempts to impose stricter discipline appear to have been a
frequent source of feuds. Officers who possessed Puritan aspirations for higher standards of honesty and obedience but lacked the
requisite qualities of leadership may have been especially likely to
encounter problems.[62] As we have seen, junior officers and seamen
were unlikely to submit passively if they felt the captain was going
beyond the unwritten codes of behaviour. But feuds could have
many other causes too. Blatant favouritism was one of them. A clerk
in the *Sophia*, for example, complained that Capt. Robert Kirby
applied double standards over discipline, being ready to 'wink at the
vicious courses of those who are his own favourites'. He treated
volunteers worse than pressed men, and had given tickets for seven
months' pay to his favourites and only one month's to the rest.
Similarly officers in the *Islip* complained that Capt. Tarleton was
harassing the master with a design to oust him and install one of his
own favourites, a man they described as drunken, blasphemous,
and licentious.[63]

Other feuds were caused by a captain's sins of omission rather
than commission. Some commanders were not forceful enough to
impose peace on quarrelsome subordinates. The newly appointed
captain of the *Forester* found the master and boatswain 'frequently
fighting and quarrelling each with other', and proved quite unable
to stop them.[64] Clay of the *Sapphire* found his company so torn by
rivalries that he dared not put to sea.[65] Quarrels were particularly
likely to arise if captains spent too long ashore, a common failing.

---

[60] SP 18/174/37; SP 18/175/56–7, 163–70, 184–5; SP 18/205/56 (misdated in
CSPD); Adm. 2/1730, fos. 139ᵛ, 144. The captain (H. Powell) and master were both
replaced.

[61] SP 18/148/39; SP 18/149/14, 47–8, 178.

[62] This seems to have been a factor in the case of Best and the *Adventure*. See also
SP 18/118/120; SP 18/78/191; below, ch. 9.

[63] SP 46/97/49B; SP 18/88/65.

[64] Adm. 2/1730, fos. 89, 105ᵛ–107ᵛ.

[65] *CSPD 1656–7*, 538, 540, 542.

Many captains were glad of any 'excuse to lie loitering in London', Popham complained in 1649, and Capt. Godfrey was described as 'very much addicted to the shore wheresoever he comes'.[66] Similarly Valentine Tatnel spent a pleasant fortnight at home leaving his ship to look after itself when he was stationed at Dover, where he lived.[67] Order and discipline inevitably suffered in such circumstances. A weak, lax, or absent captain not only undermined the efficiency of his ship; he also threatened the well-being of his men, for he was leaving them unprotected from bullies, petty thieves, and slackers. Several commanders were indeed charged by their men with failing to keep proper order. One captain was said to have taken no action over a fight in which a sailor had been stabbed, and another had allegedly spent less than ten weeks on board his ship in the ten months he had held the command.[68] For the honest seaman, anarchy was an evil to be feared as much as tyranny.

Despite the seamen's many quarrels and complaints, outright mutiny was very rare. Mutiny was a desperate step, and those who took it knew they were cutting themselves off from their homes and families, and risking death. Faced with a bullying captain it was much wiser to dodge the blows, and perhaps bring charges against him later. Though contemporaries frequently spoke of mutinies and mutinous behaviour, they were generally using these terms very loosely. Most such cases involved rash, disorderly actions by a boorish individual, often under the influence of drink. A boatswain's mate in the *President*, for example, faced a court martial in 1656 for 'mutiny while drunk', and another court heard how the *Indian*'s boatswain, a 'drowsy, idle fellow' when sober, had nearly 'split the captain's head with an axe' after a bout of heavy drinking.[69] Such incidents, however alarming, are far removed from mutiny in the sense of collective defiance aimed at seizing control. Mutinies of this kind were rare indeed. The mutinies of the *Hart* in 1649 and the *Oxford* ten years later were both political in origin.[70] In the vast

---

[66] *CSPD 1649–50*, 223; SP 18/59/42.

[67] SP 18/85/37–8. Merchant skippers were no better. It was noted a few years earlier that a shipmaster in his home port would think it quite sufficient to lock the hold overnight and take the key home, leaving only 'a boy or two on board to look after the vessel'. (PRO HCA 13/58, fo. 538).

[68] Clarke MS 4/4, 1649 (37); SP 18/174/188; cf. Rodger, *Wooden World*, 227–9.

[69] SP 18/141/58; SP 18/117/68; see also e.g. SP 25/123, pp. 191, 489; Adm. 2/1730, fo. 243'.

[70] See ch. 3 n. 82 and ch. 10 n. 77.

majority of disturbances the sailors' target was not their officers but the authorities ashore. This was so when the *Tiger* mutinied in 1649. Discontent had swelled while Capt. Peacock was ashore enjoying the comforts of home; it came to a head when the ship put to sea, and the crew forced Peacock to return to port. The men had no quarrel with their captain: their aim was simply to press demands over pay.[71] The Admiralty might well feel that naval discipline needed to be tightened, for on several other occasions too under the Rump sailors persuaded their officers to bring a ship home in order to press claims for pay. When Newbery brought the *Dolphin* home in 1649 he had no explanation to offer but that his men had wanted him to do so. An official thought him 'an honest, careful man in his employment but not to be of that spirit and judgement which a commander ought to have, and that he had little or no command over his men'. The ships involved in these incidents were mostly hired merchantmen, and their commanders seem to have required little persuasion.[72] The great majority of disorders broke out in ships already in harbour, or among sailors ashore; they were in effect strikes aimed at the Admiralty rather than mutinies against the officers, and belong more properly to the next chapter.

The period did however witness a few mutinies of a very different kind, when seamen flatly refused to fight against hopeless odds. One occurred in the Straits in 1652, when Badiley's squadron clashed with a much stronger Dutch force. When the two sides drew apart at the end of the day the men insisted on surrendering if the Dutch attacked again next morning. Badiley tried in vain to revive their fighting spirit, and another officer urged that Parliament would be dishonoured if they yielded up one of its best frigates. The men were unmoved. 'We'll fight no more', one replied, pointing out with irrefutable logic that 'the state hath better ships, but we have no more lives.' Fortunately the next morning saw a flat calm, and the action was not resumed.[73] In another incident, several years later, Capt. Horne surrendered the small *Parrot* without firing a shot when it was attacked by four Flemish privateers in the Channel. After his release he deposed that the entire crew had refused to fight in such a hopeless situation.[74]

---

[71] Clarke MS 4/4, 1649, (18, 20).
[72] e.g. *CSPD 1649–50*, 301–2, 319–20; Clarke MS 4/4, 1649 (37).
[73] Badiley, *Answer*, 24–5, 91.
[74] SP 18/158/62–3; Adm. 2/1730, fos. 80, 138ᵛ. Horne was not employed again.

The harmonious 'floating commonwealth' was thus always menaced by the 'chaos of confusion', as Capt. Sherwin termed it.[75] Officers who tried to impose very strict discipline risked provoking resentment that might lead on to feuds and disorder, while easy-going officers might find the men abusing their liberty by feuding among themselves, jeopardizing the running of the ship. It is worth noting that most of those who encountered problems were in relatively small ships, nearly always serving away from the main fleets. Defiance was no doubt easier when there was no admiral at hand to uphold authority, or to curb a captain's abuse of it. There was also less distance in a small ship between a captain and his crew, either socially or physically, which made it harder for him to assert his authority. Living together in close proximity was more likely, with poor officers, to breed friction and contempt than create harmony and intimacy. None the less the dramatic evidence of complaints, feuds, and mutinous behaviour should not obscure the fact that the great majority of commanders encountered no serious disciplinary problems.[76] Most of the larger ships, and most ships serving in the main fleets, appear to have run smoothly. A reasonable degree of harmony was the norm, whether it was created by good government or a judicious give and take between the commander and his company.

II. PUBLIC AND PRIVATE INTEREST

In general the Admiralty welcomed a communal spirit, as likely to raise morale and improve efficiency. But solidarity could also bring problems when it was directed against the state rather than the enemy, and this was quite often the case. If Admiralty orders threatened communal self-interest a company might seek ways to evade them. A tradition passed down about Nicholas Heaton and the *Sapphire* illustrates the point well. The ship was usually based in Plymouth, where Heaton and many of his men lived, and an order directing them to another station when their refit was complete was definitely 'not to their liking'; with the connivance of a local

---

[75] Add. MS 22546, fo. 160.

[76] About one-fifth appear to have been the subject of allegations at some point, though a considerable number of these were merely frivolous; others of course may have escaped notice by successfully intimidating their men.

Admiralty official they therefore set out to thwart it. The company worked feverishly round the clock, loading stores and powder and setting a new mainmast, rigging, and shrouds, and the ship was able to sail within forty-eight hours; the official then notified London, as arranged, that he could not pass on the order because the *Sapphire* was already at sea.[77]

There were other, less innocent ways in which a company could foil the Admiralty's wishes. When Capt. Curle reported in 1657 that his ship was too leaky to sail for Iceland the Commissioners were very suspicious, for it had recently been refitted. They sent him a stiff reply: 'We wish your company have not made her unserviceable on purpose, out of the dislike they had to the voyage'.[78] They were suspicious too a few months later when the *Fame* returned to port after losing her mainmast. 'We suspect it was a wilful and mischievous act of some of your company to disable the frigate, on purpose of coming into port', they told Capt. Wright. Their suspicion grew with the arrival of a petition from the seamen demanding pay, 'which we are apt to think could not be carried on by the whole company without your privity'. Though Wright pleaded his innocence the Admiralty's attitude is suggestive.[79] On other occasions, as we have seen, captains had agreed to return home without order so the men could press a pay claim.[80]

The capture of a prize might similarly unite a ship's company against the state. The state recognised that plunder was a powerful motivating drive, and the prize regulations of 1652 allowed officers and men to pillage goods—but only those found on or above the gun deck. A lot depended on the officer in command to enforce this restriction, for it was virtually impossible for a court ashore, sitting weeks or months later, to establish where booty had been located. Some undoubtedly looked the other way while their men rifled goods that legally belonged to the state. It was said that Heaton 'gave his company more liberty to plunder than other captains', which helps to explain why the *Sapphire* became celebrated for the number of her prizes and was always well manned with volunteers. The state may not have derived much benefit from her triumphs.[81]

---

[77] *FDW* i. 23–4.
[78] Adm. 2/1730, fo. 46ʾ; Adm. 2/1729, fos. 217, 222.
[79] Adm. 2/1730, fos. 147, 149ʾ; *CSPD 1657–8*, 510.
[80] See n. 72, above.
[81] *FDW* i. 21–3, iii. 276, 295; see also ch. 8, below.

A prize could also unite a company against other crews. Where several ships were involved in a capture there might be rival claims, and every member of the company had an interest in its being credited to his own ship rather than another. Under the Rump several disputes went as far as the Council of State.[82] Rival claimants might even come to blows. In 1653 John Wetwang in the *Sparrow* and Edward Mould in the hired *Concord* chased two Dutch vessels in the North Sea; Wetwang captured one, put a prize-crew on board, and sailed away to pursue the other. While he was gone Mould sent his own men to take over the prize, turned Wetwang's men ashore, and towed the ship into Lynn as his own trophy. Wetwang and his company were naturally outraged. A dispute over prizes may also have lain behind a squalid incident at Harwich in 1649, when Capt. Philip Holland was assaulted on the quayside by Capt. John Bowen and his boat-crew. Holland, though badly beaten, left his rival with an embarrassing injury from a bite under the nose.[83]

The state suffered further through the embezzlement of warships' own stores and tackle. This, and several other widespread malpractices, benefited particular individuals rather the company as a whole, but it was suspected that many captains and other officers joined in concealing it. The Navy Commissioners complained in 1655 that captains almost never sent information about such practices, 'which we are apt to think if they were diligent and faithful in their places they might be able (at least sometimes) to attain'.[84] Again, some chose not to look too closely. A customs official at Newcastle complained in 1653 that the *Brier*'s men were selling ropes, casks of beef and peas, and barrels of gunpowder from the ship, 'which some here conceive . . . the captain was not ignorant of'.[85] General Monck noted that many ships ran up suspiciously large bills because captains did not bother to check their warrant-officers' stores or accounts. As warnings had no effect he urged the Admiralty 'to shorten one or two of their pay, which will make the rest look after their business'. An official observed that other

[82] *CSPD 1649–50*, 69, 71, 204, 249–50; SP 25/123, pp. 29–33 (Willoughby v. Peacock); SP 25/123, pp. 426, 448–9; *A Brief Relation*, 13–20 Apr. 1650; *An Exact Relation* ([26 Aug.] 1650); HCA 13/65, 20 Mar.–6 Apr. 1652; *CSPD 1650*, 310, 212–13 (Mildmay v. Henley v. Green).

[83] SP 18/52/49; Clarke MS 4/4, 1649 (38).

[84] SP 18/117/74, 109.

[85] *FDW* iii. 419–20. (The captain was Robert Sansum.)

officers generally kept silent 'lest they should be accounted informers', feeling more loyalty to their companions than to the state.[86]

Another common practice was the misuse of warships for private trading. It was customary for merchant shipmasters and some of their men to carry a private 'adventure', and similar attitudes were carried into the navy. A pamphleteer in 1649, setting out a programme of naval reform, had indeed urged that officers and men should have a formal right to carry goods free of duty, and he won the support of a vice-admiral and twenty-five senior officers.[87] Though the state never endorsed the proposal many officers behaved as if it had, and it was hard for the Admiralty to restrain men who felt they were acting by the custom of the sea.[88] Private enterprise was especially blatant in the Irish Sea, where there was little supervision. John Sherwin for example was said to carry a 'multitude of passengers', pocketing the fees. Robert Vessey's men refused to allow a customs officer on board and threw him into the sea as they rowed him back to shore. The bedraggled victim complained to London but there was little to be done: the Customs Commissioners lamented that such treatment had 'of late become a general distemper'.[89] Captains serving on fishery protection off Iceland were also notorious offenders. Rowland Bevan brought home eighty-three packs of merchandise and so much timber that the ship was left dangerously low in the water and quite unable to fight an enemy.[90] Robery Wyard too left the fishing boats to fend for themselves while he went 'to truck and exchange his commodities with the inhabitants, staying sometimes a month in a harbour, chiefly minding his own profit'. He turned his own ship into a fishing boat, landing 10,000 cod, and filled it with horses, timber, and other goods for the voyage home.[91]

Finally each of the ship's officers could exploit his post for private gain. Captains, who inevitably had the greatest opportunities, were again among the worst offenders. One of their most profitable devices was to demand money from merchant ships under convoy, ignoring the Admiralty's strict prohibition.[92] Few shipmasters

---

[86] Add. MS 9300, fo. 351; cf. *CSPD 1666–7*, 159; *CSPD 1667*, 346.

[87] *The Resolution and Remonstrance of the Navie* (1649), 9.

[88] e.g. Adm. 2/1729, fos. 46ᵛ, 51; Adm. 2/1730, fos. 271ᵛ–272; *CSPD 1659–60*, 519.   [89] *CSPD 1658–9*, 209; SP 18/111/131; SP 18/128/83, part i.

[90] SP 18/184/90; SP 18/223/169.   [91] SP 46/96/220.

[92] For the prohibition see *FDW* iii. 300; it was frequently repeated. The penalty for this offence was to be cashiered.

would dare to argue and some were not given the chance: John Bowen allegedly opened fire on one ship whose master was slow to offer a gratuity.[93] Many commanders were also personally involved in the plunder of prizes. The Prize Commissioners were overwhelmed by the flood of captures during the Dutch war, and even in the Downs captains found it quite easy to dispose of prize goods ashore.[94] Further afield it was easier still. William Pestell sold prize goods and ships at Leith for his own profit, tarrying so long in June 1653 that the locals thought the English must have lost control of the sea.[95] Commanders in the Irish Sea could sell prizes and their cargoes at Dublin or Milford.[96] Or they could release a prize at sea after extorting bribes from the owners, as Robert Clarke was said to have done. The Council of State ordered him to put in bail of £6,000 while allegations against him were examined, but as so often proceedings petered out for lack of evidence.[97] Captains who did plunder prizes would naturally destroy the relevant bills of lading to cover their tracks, and it was then hard for investigations to make much progress. The Prize Commissioners could do little without the Admiralty's full co-operation, and though the Admiralty Commissioners were sympathetic they were naturally reluctant to keep officers and witnesses ashore in wartime when every ship and sailor was urgently needed at sea.[98]

An enterprising captain might also cheat the state by keeping false books, for the cumbersome system of wages almost invited fraud. He could keep men on the books who were in fact dead, runaways, or discharged; he could sell the victuals they would have consumed, bringing a further windfall; he could enter boys and servants as able seamen, pocketing the difference in wages; and he could accept bribes to discharge men. He could even claim pay for seamen who had never served, pretending they had died or run. Philip Holland told the young Pepys how to 'make some advantage' by this device when he went to sea in 1660, urging him 'to have five or six [fictitious] servants entered aboard as dead men, and I to give them what

[93] Clarke MS 4/4, 1649 (38). Valentine Tatnel was said to have taken money and wines from merchant ships and then abandoned them when a hostile privateer approached: SP 18/85/37.

[94] e.g. SP 18/194/40; Rawl. MS A 184, fo. 351.

[95] *CSPD 1652–3*, 424, 503.   [96] *CSPD 1652–3*, 599.

[97] *CSPD 1650*, 124–5, 238; *CSPD 1651*, 260; Rawl. MS A 226, fo. 39. Clarke pleaded his innocence and later claimed to be a paragon of honesty: SP 46/117, fo. 167.   [98] *CSPD 1654*, 37; SP 18/137/29; Barlow, *Journal*, 135.

wages I pleased, and so their pay to be mine'. Pepys prudently does not say whether he followed the tip.[99]

At least seventy interregnum captains, mostly serving away from the main fleets, were accused of plunder and fraud. If, as suggested earlier, many companies developed a sense of communal solidarity, how did so many offenders come to the state's attention? The answer lies mainly in the fact that, as we have seen, other companies were riven by personal feuds and factions. Seamen pressing charges against an unpopular commander made use of all the ammunition they could find. They were particularly likely to charge him with fraud if they felt that *they*, rather than the state, had been the victims. A greedy captain who cheated his men or refused to allow them a reasonable share of plunder was courting danger. He had broken the code of communal solidarity first. Double standards over prizes were especially provocative, because the seamen rightly saw plunder as the one great bonus the navy could offer them. Francis Parke appears to have been such a man. Prize officials regarded him as a notorious plunderer, remarking that 'they thought the Devil was in that captain, to sell all and bring nothing but the bare hulls'; foolishly, he allowed nothing for his company.[100] Thomas Sparling was another. He claimed self-righteously to have protected prize goods from his rapacious sailors, hinting that some reward would be appropriate, but several members of the crew described how he and his favourites had made repeated visits to the prizes, breaking into the holds and removing large quantities of tobacco, sugar, silk, and other goods for themselves.[101]

Captains who sold their own ship's stores for personal gain aroused even fiercer resentment. Alexander Farley, who was denounced on this score by his men, sounds a very determined profiteer indeed and had allegedly boasted that 'he would kill his father for money, and that he would pull his father's soul out for money, that a man's money was his soul'. The Admiralty Commissioners, deeply shocked, brushed aside his attempts to explain and

[99] Pepys, *Diary*, i. 82–3. For other cases see Adm. 2/1730, fo. 242'; *CSPD 1655*, 516; SP 18/125/19; SP 18/59/77; SP 18/142/29; SP 18/184/90; SP 18/174/188; SP 18/216/19; SP 18/223/169.
[100] SP 18/122/134; though see SP 18/109/48 for a defence of Parke.
[101] SP 18/111/49, 68.

did not employ him again.[102] Valentine Tatnel similarly disposed of brandy sent by the General for the company as a whole, seized prize goods the men thought rightfully theirs, and sold some of the ship's provisions while the steward was away sick. When his crew informed the Admiralty he could offer little defence and was cashiered.[103] Selling the ship's stores was a doubly dangerous course for a captain to follow, for it put his senior officers at risk. 'If a captain may do what he pleases, and sell what provisions he will out of the ship, how shall a purser be able to live to bring in a punctual account?' one asked plaintively.[104] If his accounts did not tally they would not be passed, and he might face ruin. In such circumstances an officer was almost bound to press charges in self-protection.

The captain was by no means the sole offender, of course. An official remarked in 1655 that there were few really honest gunners, boatswains, or stewards, and officials throughout the century would have agreed.[105] This situation gave the captain some degree of protection, for if his subordinates pressed charges they knew he was likely to retaliate in kind, and they might end by destroying one another. Some captains reached a tacit understanding with their warrant-officers, each conniving at the irregularities practised by the other. And in the face of provocation by the state—through non-payment of wages and prize-money—even honest commanders might not want to look too closely into the peccadilloes of their subordinates.

For gunners the easiest fraud was to dispose of powder and shot left over at the end of a voyage and mark it down in the accounts as expended. The scale of this practice was revealed by a spectacular case in 1655, concerning one Henry Dunning, a Thames hoyman and probably a former naval gunner. At first Dunning admitted only to receiving three or four barrels of powder, but under prolonged grilling by Major-General Desborough and other Commissioners a vast pattern of fraud emerged. The three or four barrels had grown to over five hundred before the interrogators switched to another line of questioning, demanding details of suppliers and purchasers. 'Alas, shall I undo a thousand families', Dunning wailed, hastily claiming to have forgotten all their names.

[102] SP 18/142/29–34.
[103] SP 18/85/37.
[104] SP 18/29/87.
[105] SP 18/95/39.

Under pressure his memory revived and he listed seventeen warships from which he had bought powder, naming several of the gunners involved. He had driven a brisk trade, buying at £2. 10s. a barrel and selling to outward-bound merchantmen at £3 or £3. 10s.; his hoy, sailed by only two men and a boy, had attracted little attention. Further investigations exposed other hoymen following the same trade, often striking their deals ashore in Thames-side alehouses. Minor officials who stumbled across their path were bought off. One official had confiscated a cable from Dunning and then returned it for a £30 bribe. Another had seized some embezzled shot, but as the hoyman had 'cried and kept a great stir' they repaired to an alehouse in Wapping where the hoyman handed over £19 to recover his goods.[106]

Though one of the receivers in this racket was said to have amassed an estate of £5,000, the gunners themselves were described as poor men.[107] It was indeed the poverty of seamen, and the age-old nature of their practices, that made fraud impossible to eradicate. Even when they were detected and punished they were unlikely to change their ways. The behaviour of the gunner Richard Leake illustrates the point. Leake had been dismissed after the Dunning case, but was given another chance two years later. He promised to behave impeccably in future, yet within a matter of days he was detected in 'his old trade of thievery', caught 'in the very act of stealing and conveying away six barrels of powder'. It transpired that he had also forged his captain's signature to cover his tracks.[108] Leake was perhaps a more flagrant and unlucky offender than most, but the Admiralty was well aware that to sack every dishonest gunner would mean committing itself to unilateral disarmament.

The state did what it could to tighten control. In 1653 the Admiralty ordered gunners to give security, to be forfeited if they submitted dishonest accounts. There were however cogent reasons why this arrangement was impracticable, as Monck pointed out; his

---

[106] SP 18/105/50; SP 18/108/67–71; SP 18/98/42. One of Dunning's former contacts was Butler Noades, ex-gunner of the *George* and later a captain; he was dead by 1655. For a Henry Dunning, naval gunner, see Add. MS 9301, fo. 114.

[107] SP 18/98/42, 109.

[108] SP 18/105/50; *CSPD 1656–7*, 545, 550, 569, 577; Adm. 2/1730, fos. 64, 82ᵛ. Leake was none the less an able gunner. His son, who trained under him, became Master-Gunner of England under Charles II, and a grandson was knighted and became an admiral of the fleet: see *DNB*, Richard Leake and Sir John Leake.

own suggestion, typically, was to hang convicted embezzlers to deter the rest.[109] Under the Articles of 1652 embezzlers could indeed be sentenced to death, though in practice this appears never to have been done. Captains were not prepared to see men die for petty fraud when, in some cases, their own hands were not clean and when the state itself often failed miserably to discharge its financial obligations to the mariners. The usual penalty was a fine (of between £10 and £30) and discharge, sometimes with a ducking. The courts sometimes also imposed ritual humiliation as a further deterrent to others. One gunner was sentenced to be taken round the fleet tied to a boat's mast, with drums beating; a paper fixed to his chest, describing his crime and punishment, was to be read out at the side of every ship. Similarly a master's mate was put in irons, ducked three times, and then carted through the streets of Portsmouth with drums beating.[110] Periodically there were major drives against embezzlement, focusing on the dockyards as well as ships. A search at Rochester in 1655 unearthed some 300 tons of embezzled stores, which indicates the scale of the problem.[111] Another investigation exposed an extensive network of corruption at Woolwich in 1658, and savage punishments were imposed on several of the ringleaders. One boatswain was sentenced to thirty-nine lashes and transportation to Jamaica, a dockyard worker was flogged and had part of his ear cut off for perjury, and other offenders were fined or cashiered.[112]

Of all the ship's offenders it was the purser (or his equivalent) who was most notorious for dishonesty. Contemporaries accepted that an honest purser did not, and perhaps could not, exist. The expense of the place far exceeded its allowances so that, as Pepys remarked, 'a purser without professed cheating is a professed loser, twice as much as he gets'.[113] Pursers naturally hoped for 'easy,

[109] *FDW* vi. 185. For similar orders about other warrant-officers see e.g. *FDW* iii. 25.

[110] *FDW* iii. 295; HMC 39, *Eliot Hodgkin*, 298–9; SP 18/164/87–8. For a punishment involving 'rough music' as ritual humiliation see 'Warwick's Voyage', 80.

[111] *CSPD 1655*, 563.

[112] Adm. 2/1730, fos. 217ᵛ, 222ᵛ, 226, 228ᵛ; SP 46/118, fos. 46, 134; Add. MS 9304, fos. 158–60; *CSPD 1657–8*, 428, 430, 431, 433-4, 439. See also G. Aylmer, *The State's Servants* (1973), 160. Thirty-nine lashes would not have been considered harsh a century later: see n. 37, above.

[113] Pepys, *Diary*, vi. 306; M. Lewis, *England's Sea-Officers* (1939), 242–5; Oppenheim, 284, 356; J. Hollond, *Two Discourses of the Navy*, ed. J. R. Tanner (NRS, 1896), 163. Some years later Pepys described Richard Gibson, who had served in the 1650s, as 'a purser extraordinary, being sober, ingenuous and honest': *The Further Correspondence of Samuel Pepys*, ed. J. R. Tanner (1929), 69.

heedless commanders' (in Ned Ward's phrase) who could be ignored or hoodwinked.[114] Or they worked in collusion with the captain, and often with the victuallers too. In such cases the state could do little. Seamen who dared to complain to the captain might risk a beating.[115]

A fraudulent purser ran into difficulties only when he exceeded the generous limits tolerated by custom, or quarrelled with his captain. Both errors were in fact fairly common. The purser of the *Gillyflower*, for example, failed to load sufficient provisions when the ship sailed for the Baltic, forcing the crew to live on bread, pease, and water for over a week. On their return the men naturally complained to the purser (who had prudently remained behind), whereupon he allegedly replied that 'he scorned their guts, he told them he cared not so he could get five or six hundred pounds a year out of their bellies'.[116] Not surprisingly resentment occasionally exploded into violence. The *Elias*'s men beat up their hated steward in 1655 when the ship returned to port.[117] Usually it was the captain who took action. Honest captains wanted to curb fraud, and even a lax commander could not let the functioning of his ship be undermined.[118]

Petty officers and seamen had far fewer opportunities for fraud and embezzlement than their superiors. For them plunder was the only real chance to supplement their wages, and a rich prize was their perpetual dream. Edward Coxere's appetite in 1656 was sharpened by his sufferings as a prisoner of the Moors, but his outlook was typical: 'I being poor and wanted both money and clothes, I had hopes to recruit myself from the first Spaniard I could meet with at sea.' And so he did.[119] As this suggests, it is misleading to think of plunder solely in terms of valuables, for it was more often a way for sailors to provide themselves with basic necessities. An inventory of goods seized from another ship lists pots and pans, breeches, shirts, stockings, waistcoats, handkerchiefs and a pillow. Sailors half-dressed in rags were sometimes accused of 'tearing the men's shirts from off their backs'.[120]

---

[114] E. Ward, *The Wooden World* (2nd edn., 1708), 59. For deceived captains see e.g. *CSPD 1656–7*, 405, 528.
[115] SP 46/121, fos. 9, 13; Lewis, *Sea-Officers*, 243–7; Barlow, *Journal*; 54; cf. J. Baltharpe, *The Straights Voyage*, ed. J. R. Bromley (1959) for the seaman's dream of seeing the purser and steward hanged .   [116] SP 18/48/81.
[117] SP 18/117/16.   [118] *CSPD 1650*, 209.   [119] Coxere, *Adventures*, 67-9.
[120] SP 18/110/31; Penn, *Memorials*, ii. 69. Plunder of such articles was allowed under the naval code.

Stories of plunder are legion. The most notorious episode was the looting of the Plate ships seized by Stayner in 1656, though the full details never emerged.[121] In the West Indies Myngs's sailors allegedly broke into the hold of a prize in 1659 and fought each other over the spoils, plundering goods worth £10–15,000.[122] On several occasions during the Dutch war the men were so determined to strip a battered prize that they ignored orders to come away and were drowned when it sank beneath their feet.[123] Nor were enemy ships the only targets. A press-gang from the ill-named *Amity* boarded an Ipswich coaster in 1657, broke into the master's cabin, and stole money and clothing. Sailors from another warship, which had accidentally collided with a merchantman, promptly clambered aboard the stricken vessel to plunder it. And when the *Antelope* ran aground in 1652 some of the crew began pillaging their own ship instead of trying to save her.[124]

The crew bringing home a prize had the best opportunity for plunder. A court martial in 1651 heard how one prize-crew had systematically divided its cargo into shares and embezzled it.[125] A prize-crew from Heaton's *Sapphire,* blown off course to the Scillies, seized the opportunity to sell part of the cargo there, disposing of most of the rest when they reached Plymouth.[126] Prize officials had to contend with local residents eager to buy plundered goods, and were ill-advised to interfere unless they were well protected. An official who was beaten up at Plymouth in 1654 found no redress, for the local constables, being friends of the traffickers, ignored the incident.[127] Nehemiah Bourne complained at Dover in 1652 that an illicit trade went on there 'under the noses of prize officers,' the townsfolk regarding it as 'no wrong to the state but free to them'. Bourne of course had other ideas and prodded the mayor into conducting a thorough search of the town, with dramatic results.

---

[121] Firth, i. 56–7 and sources cited there. Cf. the looting of bullion from a Spanish prize captured by Mackey: Adm. 2/1730, fo. 57.

[122] *Weekly Intelligencer,* 28 June–5 July 1659; *Publick Intelligencer,* 27 June–4 July 1659; F. E. Dyer, 'Captain Christopher Myngs in the West Indies', *MM* xviii (1932), 181–2.

[123] *Severall Proceedings,* 10–17 June 1652; *A Perfect Account,* 6–13 Oct. 1652. (Stayner's brother was one of the victims.)

[124] Adm. 2/1730, fo. 61ᵛ; SP 46/97/80; Rawl. MS A 207. fo. 80.

[125] Rawl. MS A 226, fos. 31ᵛ–32ᵛ.

[126] H. E. Nott and E. Ralph (eds.), *The Deposition Books of Bristol,* ii, *1650–1654,* (Bristol Rec. Soc., xii; 1948), 146.

[127] SP 18/88/59–64.

Such zeal, he remarked, seemed 'very strange to this sharking people'.[128]

The code of 1652 left the penalties for plunder at the courts' discretion. The sentences handed down were surprisingly mild. In one case the ringleader lost his wages and was imprisoned briefly, while his fellows merely forfeited the prize-money they would have been due but for their 'misdemeanour', as it was termed.[129] It was impossible to stamp out plunder while the state remained so slow to pay wages and prize-money. Captains could hardly restrain their men, an official conceded, when 'the gunnage and tonnage that was promised [by the prize arrangements established in 1652] hath not been paid them'.[130] Had they succeeded, against all the odds, they would have destroyed much of the seamen's fighting spirit at a stroke.

The evidence certainly demonstrates that the Puritan Revolution failed to kill the Old Adam—which should hardly surprise us. None of these malpractices was new, however; standards of honesty had been notoriously low under Elizabeth and the early Stuarts. Fraud indeed remained commonplace throughout the age of sail. Restoration captains too had a sharp eye for profit and often turned a blind eye to the petty frauds of their subordinates. As Sir William Coventry wearily remarked, 'men will do what is easiest for themselves, most complaisant to those they live with, and most in fashion'. None of the Commonwealth captains, so far as we know, matched the cheek of the Restoration captains who entered the ship's dog in the pay books under the name of 'Mr Bromley'![131]

It is very unlikely that standards in the 1650s were lower than in other periods. If more prizes were plundered this was largely because far more prizes were taken than ever before. And if there were more allegations of fraud, the officer corps itself was much larger. Fraud was also more likely to be detected, partly because the Admiralty was receptive to complaints from the seamen, and partly

---

[128] *FDW* iv. 145–6. Bourne pointed out that not only the state suffered: the 10–15 sailors who formed the typical prize-crew were profiting at the expense of the rest of the company which had captured the prize.

[129] *FDW* iii. 294–5; Rawl. MS A 226, fos. 31ᵛ–32ᵛ.

[130] SP 18/126/52. James, as Lord High Admiral, later made the same point: *Samuel Pepys's Naval Minutes*, ed. J. R. Tanner (NRS, 1926), 34.

[131] Oppenheim, 146, 158–9, 194, 284–6 (for malpractice in earlier periods); *CSPD 1667*, 346; Pepys, *Cat.* iv. 135.

because some of the senior commanders were men of unusually strict principles. Blake kept a notoriously tight rein on his officers. Penn too was stern. When English sailors plundered two merchant ships at Barbados in 1655 Penn called their action a 'great scandal and dishonour to the fleet'. He blamed their captain for setting a bad example and told him bluntly: '' 'Tis you, undoubtedly, must make satisfaction for the whole, to the utmost farthing.'[132] On the same expedition he had one captain (Tickle) cashiered for issuing false tickets, and another (John Clarke) turned out for receiving embezzled goods from the *Red Horse* pink; its master was sentenced to thirty lashes, a very severe sentence for this period.[133]

It is quite likely that the incidence of fraud was *lower* than usual. Officers serving with the fleet probably had less licence. Given the number of deeply religious captains it is also reasonable to suppose rather higher general standards of professional conduct. Allegations against senior, Puritan commanders are conspicuously lacking.[134] The state was probably right to believe that godly captains were more honest, and most of the larger ships were in the hands of men carefully selected for their trustworthiness. William Hill was 'a known opposer of all vice in the navy', and Thomas Graves was described as a man 'of perfect trust'. Such officers naturally tried to impose their own standards on their crews. Robert Plumleigh, another of the godly, was outraged when a carefully selected prize-crew from his ship embezzled some of the prize's stores; he promptly clapped the ringleaders in irons and sent them for court martial.[135] We hear too of an honest lieutenant bringing home intact a valuable Dutch East India prize, despite his 'company of as wild seamen as ever breathed'.[136]

Most of the captains accused of fraud in the 1650s were commanding small ships in the Irish Sea, or serving on convoys and

---

[132] Penn, *Memorials*, ii. 69; WYN/10/2, 26 Feb. 1655. The captain was Robert Saunders. For later, partisan claims that Penn had been an unscrupulous profiteer see Pepys, *Diary*, viii. 229.

[133] SP 18/100/148; 'Richard Rooth's Sea Journal of the Western Design, 1654–5', ed. J. F. Battick, *Jamaica Journal*, v (1971), 20 (Tickle); SP 18/100/101; SP 18/111/9; BL Sloane MS 3926, fo. 37 (Clarke). Capt. Lightfoot was also court-martialled over the *Red Horse* affair.

[134] See ch. 9. Stayner's part in the plunder of the Plate ships is not known; he is a dubious Puritan, and was not at that time a flag-officer. For the view that the incidence of fraud in the 1650s was relatively low see also Oppenheim, 355.

[135] SP 18/55/130; SP 18/146/150.   [136] *CSPD 1654*, 122.

coastal protection. These ships were notoriously neglected by the Admiralty, and their crews were under the greatest temptation to fend for themselves. The officers were in most cases relatively poor men, dependent on pay which was far in arrears, and resentful over prize-money held back or diverted. Capt. Henry Powell, who allegedly sold an anchor to a Flemish ship in the Channel, was a former shipmaster ruined by Rupert's privateers. It was impossible, he complained, to live on the state's wages.[137] James Cadman, convicted of embezzling goods worth £150, was sentenced to pay back only £80 on the grounds of his extreme poverty.[138] Many officers remained poor even after many years of service. Those laid aside often claimed to be facing destitution.[139] William Coppin begged a place as a Poor Knight of Windsor, pleading old age and poverty. Richard Country, after a lifetime in the navy, begged a gunner's place in a ship in ordinary so that he could at last retire from the sea: not the action of a rich man.[140] If such men had dabbled in fraud its scale must have been trivial. Though doubtless some became rich through prizes and plunder, the image of naval officers growing fat at the expense of the state and innocent civilians is in most cases misleading. The officers had at least as many justified grievances against the state as vice versa.

III. THE QUALITY OF LIFE

Admiralty records inevitably tell us little about the nature of everyday life at sea, and we have to rely on accidental scraps of information and the comments of a few contemporary observers. The life was undoubtedly hard. Edward Barlow endorsed the old saying that 'whosoever putteth his child to get his living at sea had better a great deal bind him prentice to a hangman'. But we should be cautious before generalizing from petitions and protests, for the seaman's life was not one of unrelieved suffering. The Quaker evangelist William Caton provided a very different perspective when he denounced the sailor's ways, 'your mirth and your

[137] SP 18/174/37; SP 18/205/56; HCA 13/68. fo. 51ᵛ.
[138] Add. MS 9305, fo. 109; Add. MS 18986, fo. 235.
[139] See ch. 6 nn. 213–15, above. Even Sir John Harman, a senior flag-officer after the Restoration, died poor: *CSPD 1673–5*, 208; Pepys, *Further Correspondence*, 278–9.　　　[140] SP 18/176/13; Pepys, *Cat.* iii. 311–12; cf. NMM ADL/Z/8 (19).

melody, your jesting and your folly, your laughter and your vanity, your pastime and your singing'.[141]

The naval seaman judged his lot by what he could reasonably expect elsewhere, in a merchant ship, or as a labourer or poor artisan ashore. Discipline in the navy was usually no worse than in merchantmen. Though wages were lower there were fewer stoppages, and in several other respects conditions were superior: warships were more heavily manned, for example, reducing the burden of work for each individual.[142] The food was probably better too. The diet laid down—hot meals with beef, pork, or fish every day—was far beyond the reach of most labourers ashore, even if the standard of the food actually supplied often fell short of what was prescribed.[143] The seaman was in any case inured to hard fare. According to a contemporary he had 'an invincible stomach, which ostrich-like could well near digest iron'; it was indeed proverbial that 'nothing will poison a sailor'. Faced with rotten provisions the seaman often found relief in sardonic humour. There was, for example, a proverbial formula for brewing ship's beer: 'Take a peck of malt and heave it overboard at London Bridge and let it wash or swim down the river of Thames as low as Gravesend, and then take it up again.'[144] Long experience taught him to be resourceful. In one ship where an incompetent purser had failed to supply platters the men nonchalantly ate peas out of their hats![145] If provisions ran low they might supplement them by using short-allowance money to buy food ashore. Booty from a prize might also provide a remedy. Coxere tells how his friend and messmate spent money from a Spanish prize to buy fresh provisions, so that henceforth they 'had good victuals and good drink often'. If all else failed they could raise money from food and drink by buying clothes on credit from the purser and selling them ashore.[146] This meant sacrificing future wages, but it was fully in keeping with the sailor's philosophy of life.

[141] Barlow, *Journal*, 90; cf. 60; W. Caton, *The Sea-mens Invitation* (1659), 14. For sailors 'playing or jesting with [one] another in the cookroom' in 1627 see 'Warwick's Voyage', 80.

[142] Barlow, *Journal*, 83, 89, 426; Oppenheim, 243–4; Rodger, *Wooden World*, 63–4, 116–17; on discipline see above.

[143] C. Lloyd, *The British Seaman, 1200–1860: A Social Survey* (1970 edn.), 85–6; Oppenheim, 324–7; Rodger, *Wooden World*, 84–7, 116–17; Hammond, thesis, ch. 8; for complaints about food see below, ch. 8.

[144] Lloyd, *British Seaman*, 67; Barlow, *Journal*, 127; Oppenheim, 236.

[145] This was some years later: *CSPD 1667–8*, 410. Ned Ward commented that the sailor knew no more of a fork than did a horse: Ward, *Wooden World*, 103.

[146] Coxere, *Adventures*, 68–9; Barlow, *Journal*, 54, 68–9, 151–2; SP 18/187/123.

It was generally agreed that sailors lived for the moment. Most of them were young, single, and carefree. Moreover a life of perpetual uncertainty and danger almost inevitably produced a short-term, feckless outlook, as Pepys was to remark.[147] Several of their catch-phrases reflect such a philosophy: 'A merry life and a short', 'Longest liver takes all', 'Never let us want when we have it [sc. money] and when we have it not too.' They quickly ran up debts ashore to alehouse-keepers, landladies, and friends, which ate up much of their wages. As long as they had money in their pockets they spent freely. Ned Ward observed later that sailors might squander a whole year's pay in a single week, or even in one day's gaming.[148]

Mariners had some time to relax on board ship between watches, and much more when in harbour. At sea they spent most of it in their quarters, swapping old jokes, stories, and oaths with their comrades.[149] Whenever possible they supplemented the gallon of beer allowed them daily with something stronger. Though the sale of liquor was prohibited some captains connived at the practice or even sold it themselves, and many pursers carried on a private trade.[150] Tobacco was the natural accompaniment of drink. Smoking carried obvious risks in a wooden sailing ship, and was banned below decks and in private cabins; even so carelessness led to an explosion in the *Foresight* and to a fire which destroyed the *Paragon* in 1655, with the loss of a hundred lives.[151] Fishing was another common pastime. Occasionally we also hear of mariners 'carving toys and fancies'; a sailor in the *Richard*, for example, built and rigged a model ship which his captain presented to Mountagu.[152] We know too that sailors in the West Indies in 1655 went swimming for relaxation, though we hear of it only because

[147] *Pepys's Naval Minutes*, 255; for the age-structure see Rodger, *Wooden World*, 78, 360–3. There are no figures for the 1650s but the pattern was probably similar.

[148] Barlow, *Journal*, 160; Ward, *Wooden World*, 100–1; cf. J. Taylor, *Faire and fowle Weather* (1615), sigs. B3ᵛ–B4.

[149] Ward, *Wooden World*, 98; Shadwell, *Fair Quaker*, 4.

[150] Ward, *Wooden World*, 99. For the prohibition of liquor see *FDW* vi. 198, but for its unauthorized sale see e.g. SP 46/96/220; SP 18/77/87, part i. Cf. a steward in 1654 who gave 'his mind more to being a tapster than a steward, in selling of tobacco and strong water': SP 46/120, fo. 255.

[151] *FDW* vi. 298; *The Faithful Post*, 8–15 July 1653; *Thurloe*, iv. 8; B. Whitelocke, *A Journal of the Swedish Embassy* (1772), i. 110. A tub of water was provided for the ash. For earlier restrictions see 'Warwick's Voyage', 85; Oppenheim, 239.

[152] Whitelocke, *Journal*, ii. 362; Pepys, *Diary*, i. 169; Barlow, *Journal*, 49; SP 18/176/1.

two unlucky boys were attacked and killed by a shark.[153] John Weale tells how a captain in the Straits allowed a performing bear to be brought on board to amuse the company.[154] There were sometimes games on deck, too. When Bulstrode Whitelocke was on his way to Sweden as ambassador in 1653 he spent a lot of time talking with the mariners and watching them play. He even joined in the horseplay himself, 'affording them now and then a douse in the neck, or a kick in jest, . . . which demeanours,' he adds rather primly, 'please those kind of people'.[155] There may also have been dancing in some ships, as there certainly was in other periods: a Restoration sailor describes sailors dancing the 'hay' on the forecastle, while the less proficient clumsily hopped about.[156] There was certainly singing, sometimes rowdy and drunken. Coxere commented on the seamen's scandalous practice of going straight from the evening psalm to sing 'vain, idle songs with ungodly words and actions' in their quarters.[157] Inevitably there were quarrels too among bored men living in overcrowded conditions. Ward observed that the sailor 'loves his honour like roast-beef, and is ready to spend his blood upon any fair quarrelsome occasion'. Scuffles were common, and fights among the ship's boys appear to have been accepted as normal.[158] Despite their rough manners however the seamen were also capable of acts of striking generosity. In 1655 for example Blake's men voted to contribute a dollar each from their short-allowance money to ransom Dutch slaves at Algiers, a gesture particularly impressive only eighteen months after the end of the bloody Anglo-Dutch war.[159]

Officers found relaxation at sea mostly around the dinner table.[160] Flag-officers sometimes entertained their captains: Blake was host to Ayscue and his officers when they returned from the Caribbean in 1652, and Penn dined his captains while the fleet lay at Barbados early in 1655.[161] Whenever ships were anchored close together there

---

[153] WYN/10/2, 6 Mar. 1655.　　　　　　[154] 'Weale's Journal', 131.
[155] Whitelocke, *Journal*, i. 137; Pepys, *Diary*, i. 14, 166, 169.
[156] Baltharpe, *Straight Voyage*, 22; Pepys, *Tangier Papers*, 8, 11.
[157] Coxere, *Adventures*, 88 (though this was in a merchantman). See also *FDW* iii. 165; SP 18/118/120, 142; n. 141, above; Baltharpe, *Straights Voyage*, 38.
[158] Ward, *Wooden World*, 104; Clarke MS 4/4, 1649 (38); SP 18/147/141.
[159] Blake, *Letters*, 314; cf. Barlow, *Journal*, 153.
[160] 'Weale's Journal', *passim*; Pepys, *Diary*, i. 167, 217, 262, ii. 17.
[161] *Severall Proceedings*, 17–24 June 1652; WYN/10/2, 20 Feb. 1655. For their part captains occasionally sent presents to flag-officers under whom they had served; Stokes sent a Barbary horse and cup of 'unicorn horn' (ivory) to Mountagu in 1657: Bodl. Carte MS 73, fo. 142.

was constant traffic between them, visitors sometimes staying overnight. Weale's journal records one such occasion when the captains assembled to sample some beer newly arrived from England, a nostalgic reminder of home.[162] Music provided another form of relaxation. We hear of the *Merlin*'s mate taking his viol and cittern to play with the captain of the *Gift*. Capt. Sparling kept a harpist aboard.[163] On the eve of the Restoration Mountagu even assembled an impromptu band in the flagship, using the lieutenant's cittern and pressing candlesticks into service as cymbals. Pepys describes him singing a satirical ballad too, as well as playing ninepins on deck and relaxing over cards.[164] The atmosphere in the spring of 1660 was of course exceptional, and it is hard to imagine Blake or Deane ever indulging in such frivolities. A panegyrist writing shortly after Blake's death observed sternly that 'No chamber-music squeaking in the night, | Nor noise of viols did him much delight'; the General had preferred the 'bass' of roaring cannon and the 'treble' of bullets whistling by.[165]

Reading would seem a natural pastime for officers at sea, though surprisingly little evidence has survived about it. The Admiralty Commissioners often enclosed newspapers when writing to senior commanders, and it is likely that they circulated fairly widely. John Poortmans wrote asking for 'good store of news books' when he was serving with the fleet in 1653.[166] The following year the officers of the *Pearl* asked the editor of the *Faithfull Scout* to supply half a dozen copies of each edition in return for regular news from sea. The editor responded favourably and published flattering accounts of the ship's exploits, drawing fanciful and gratifying comparisons between its captain (Sacheverell) and heroes of antiquity such as Julius Caesar.[167] Some of the chaplains had small libraries on board and probably lent books to the officers, as one is known to have done in the 1640s. Some officers had bibles and probably other

[162] 'Weale's Journal', 142 and *passim*.

[163] SP 18/77/87, part iii (the *Gift*'s captain was Samuel Dickenson); Pepys, *Diary*, i. 119, 153.

[164] Pepys, *Diary*, i. 114, 118, 166, 169. In 1655 Edward Nixon, a master, was accused by Capt. Adams of singing an obscene song on Poplar dock on the sabbath: SP 18/118/120.

[165] G. Harrison, *An Elegie on the Death of . . . Robert Blake* (1657), BL 669 f 20 (21).

[166] e.g. Clarke MS 4/4, 1650 (1); Adm. 2/1729, fo. 142ᵛ; Adm. 2/1730, fos. 103ᵛ–104; SP 18/78/189; FDW v. 195–6, 303.

[167] *The Faithfull Scout*, 7–15 July, 21–8 July 1654; *The Weekly Post*, 25 July–1 Aug. Cf. *A Great and Glorious Victory obtained by the English against the French* (1654), on the exploits of Sacheverell and Foster, based on this correspondence.

religious works, and at least a few possessed almanacs. The only other publications we hear of on board, besides nautical manuals, are occasional subversive pamphlets and Quaker tracts.[168] The restrictions of life at sea made officers anxious for leave ashore whenever possible. When Lt. John Weale's ship called at Plymouth in 1656 he hired horses to visit his relations in Cornwall. He also visited a cock-fight (despite his Puritan leanings) and went 'a-walking in the hills' with his captain. Like many others Weale used leave abroad to see something of foreign customs, visiting Catholic services and processions, a Jewish synagogue, and an Italian carnival. Mountagu went to see a bullfight when he was in Portugal in 1661.[169] Officers also took the opportunity to buy exotic trophies to bring home as presents. Capt. Sacheverell bought presents for his wife, and a Turkey carpet and silk quilt for his sister (who was married to an Admiralty Commissioner). At a humbler level Weale bought some pictures at Alicante for a modest two and a half dollars.[170]

Ordinary seamen were equally eager to go ashore at every opportunity, and when ships were in harbour captains found it very hard to keep them on board. Freedom to visit the shore was a valued privilege, and the key difference between volunteers and pressed men. Most captains appear to have been generous in granting leave, signalling the time to return by lowering a topsail, beating drums, or firing a gun. Volunteers would not normally desert, though they were sometimes dilatory in coming back.[171] Refusing leave was guaranteed to create bad feeling, and there was even a brief mutiny in the *Worcester* at the end of 1652 over this issue. Some of her men tried to slip ashore without permission, declaring they would rather

---

[168] A. C. Miller, 'John Syms, Puritan Naval Chaplain', *MM* lx (1974), 153, 161; Add. MS 35297, fos. 1ᵛ, 179ᵛ–183ᵛ. One possibly bookish lieutenant, aptly named Milton, referred to a study in his house (*CSPD 1658–9*, 414). For Quaker tracts: Adm. 2/1730, fo. 53ᵛ. Capt. Robert Knox took at least two religious works with him on a voyage to India in 1658: Lewis Bayly's *The Practice of Pietie* (1st pub. 1612) and Richard Rogers's *The Practice of Christianitie* (1st pub. 1618). Knox had commanded a hired ship during the First Dutch War. R. Knox, 'Nineteene Years Captivity in the Kingdom of Conde Uda, in the Highlands of Ceylon' (1681), in E. Arber, *An English Garner*, i (1877), 350.

[169] 'Weale's Journal', 96, 99, 100, 124, 128, 130; Sandwich, *Journal*, 100–1. Barlow also went to see the bull-baiting in Lisbon in 1661, in which some of the English sailors took part. Though no Puritan or sentimentalist he thought it 'small sport in my judgment, and more like butchery' (*Journal*, 65).

[170] SP 18/110/37; 'Weale's Journal', 115.

[171] SP 18/96/50; *Thurloe*, iv. 598; SP 18/92/36; *FDW* v. 270.

serve the Turks than be kept slaves on board, and when they were prevented there was a scuffle and threats of violence. One man vowed wildly to blow up the ship and send her whole company to the devil.[172]

Sailors ashore were notoriously boisterous. A group caricatured in Shadwell's *Fair Quaker* debate whether to amuse themselves by assaulting the mayor and corporation, drowning the constable, ravishing every woman they meet, or smashing all the windows in the town.[173] The alehouse was their usual destination, and they spent freely till their money and wits were gone. Fights and brawls were commonplace, and sometimes led to serious injuries: one sailor, for example, had his upper lip bitten off in a fight with his boatswain, and another drunken seaman stabbed a shipmate to death. Tensions which had built up during long weeks at sea could easily explode once the men set foot ashore.[174] Naval administrators were deeply concerned at the 'mad, savage spirit' of drunken sailors. Pett at Chatham complained that seamen would not go aboard as long as they had any money or credit to buy a drink. Bourne campaigned to have alehouses suppressed, and Hatsell reported that one bowl of the 'abominable strong drink' sold at Plymouth rendered a sailor 'half out of his wits'. He blamed the brewers for the violent brawls that resulted, and wanted to have them pressed and transported to Jamaica.[175]

A ship's crew was a one-sex society and experienced all the conse-quential problems and pressures.[176] Many of the officers and some of the men were married, and a long voyage kept them away from their families for months or even years. The emotional wrench could be severe. At the start of a long voyage there was sometimes a prolonged leave-taking; when the *Jersey* left Portsmouth for the Straits in 1656, for example, several officers' wives remained on board till the ship was off Cowes.[177] While they were away senior officers did what they could to maintain contact with their wives. A captain writing to the Admiralty from sea would sometimes enclose

---

[172] NMM HSR/A/27.

[173] Shadwell, *Fair Quaker*, 38. But for sailors ashore going into a field merely 'to play', perhaps at football, see SP 18/81/153.

[174] *CSPD 1657–8*, 537; NMM AGC/1/39; SP 18/69/8.

[175] SP 18/60/107; SP 18/57/104; *CSPD 1653–4*, 2; SP 18/96/50; *FDW* iii. 439; Rawl. MS A 461, fo. 12.

[176] For sex and marriage in the Hanoverian navy see Rodger, *Wooden World*, 75–81.

[177] 'Weale's Journal', 128.

a letter to his wife, asking for it to be forwarded. John Bourne, flag-captain at the Gabbard, snatched a moment as the two fleets closed once more to dash off a reassuring note to his wife. Popham too wrote often and affectionately to his wife, and she replied — though it was hard for wives to write unless they knew the ship's itinerary.[178] How far more junior officers kept in touch we do not know. Weale sent several private letters from the Straits, and was overjoyed to hear from loved ones in England; a delightfully laconic entry in his journal records a red-letter day when 'The General called a council of war and I received a letter from Mrs A. S.'.[179] Weale however was a fairly well-educated man, like many pursers; skill with the pen was much less common among other warrant- and petty officers, and few letters exist from them. One exception, a clumsy, moving letter from a quartermaster at Jamaica, shows all too clearly his painful struggle against limited schooling and tropical disease to set down a last message to the 'loving wife' he would never see again.[180] Most seamen and almost all their wives were unable to write, and most of them had to make do with memories and dreams.[181]

Prolonged separations placed heavy strains on the marriage bond, both emotional and financial. Even the wife of the flag-officer commanding at Jamaica, Mary Goodson, ran into financial difficulties during his long absence, as well as worrying about his health and safety. She, however, had well-placed friends close to the Admiralty whom she could badger for the latest news and for some of the pay due to her husband.[182] Ordinary seamen's wives faced far greater problems. Coxere tells how he returned to sea only seven weeks after his marriage and was gone eight months before coming home to find himself a father; his wife was so overcome that she 'could hardly speak to me, for she knew not before whether I was

---

[178] SP 18/110/37; *Two Letters from the Fleet* ([4 June] 1653); Clarke MS 4/4, e.g. 1649 (2, 6), 1650 (3), 1649 (9, 37.) Coytmor acted as intermediary in forwarding letters between Popham and his wife. In 1672 Richard Haddock sent his wife details of the ship's itinerary so that she could write to him: BL Egerton MS 2521, fo. 23.

[179] 'Weale's Journal', 110, 145. Cf. a letter from an officer (the purser?) in the *Pearl* to his wife, commenting that she must be surprised not to have heard from him before: *Faithfull Scout*, 5–12 Aug. 1653.

[180] SP 46/117, fo. 325.

[181] For the literacy rate among sailors see D. Cressy, *Literacy and the Social Order* (Cambridge, 1980), 131–5; cf. 'Weale's Journal', 109. It was said to be common in the early 1700s for ordinary sailors to write to their wives, who would write back with the help of an amanuensis: Ward, *Wooden World*, 97, 101. I have found no evidence for this in the 1650s.

[182] Rawl. MS A 187, fo. 404; *CSPD 1655–6*, 516.

dead or alive'. She was to face such fears many times. Coxere's next voyage kept him away seven months, and his third no less than nineteen, and his wife was forced to open a shop to support herself and the family while he was gone. Other wives earned a pittance by spinning or making stockings or children's clothes.[183]

The problems facing all mariners' wives help to explain the striking fact (given the patriarchal conventions of the age) that on several occasions wives were able to persuade officers not to go on a voyage likely to prove particularly dangerous or long. When Edward Blagg came home from the disease-ridden new colony at Jamaica in 1655 his wife was dismayed to learn that his ship had been directed to return there. With nine children to support her anxiety is understandable. Blagg said he was not unwilling to go but 'tender of grieving my nearest relations thereby'. Mrs Blagg begged the navy agent at Plymouth to secure her husband's transfer, and Hatsell informed the Admiralty that she was indeed 'passionately affected with his absence'. Her campaign was victorious: Blagg enjoyed some home-leave and was then given another ship, appointed to sail with Blake on a healthier expedition to the south.[184] Paradoxically when two of Blake's other captains dropped out they cited their wives' dissatisfaction; one said his wife 'could not bear his absence on so long a voyage'. Both men had grievances of their own too, but it is clear that a wife's feelings could carry weight, and there are other instances in the merchant service to prove the point.[185]

When a ship was stationed in home waters it was much easier to maintain family ties, especially for the commanders. Perhaps too easy: the Admiralty was naturally irritated by captains who stayed at home when they should have been looking after their ships. It disapproved still more of officers who invited their wives on board. After Capt. Harrison's wife went down to his ship in 1649 nothing was heard from him for a whole month; 'If you permit your captains to have their wives on board, the state will suffer much damage', an official complained to Popham.[186] In 1655 John Best

---

[183] Coxere, *Adventures*, 33–4, 51–2, 67, 80; C. Saltonstall, *The Navigator* (1642), sig. A2ᵛ; SP 18/81/195; W. Mountford, *The Launching of the Mary* (Oxford, 1933; written in 1632), 79, 100, 108.

[184] SP 18/115/1, 104.

[185] *Thurloe*, iv. 582, 589–90; above, ch. 5 nn. 115–16. See also *CSPD 1652–3*, 265; *The Letters of John Paige, London Merchant, 1648–1658*, ed. G. F. Steckley (London Record Soc. xxi; 1984), 50–1; SP 18/133/34.

[186] Clarke MS 4/4, 1649 (18); SP 18/85/37.

took his ship into Bridlington and spent two days fetching his wife from Hull 'on purpose to see Scotland', whither the ship was bound. Jeremy Country was accused of engaging an enemy in a half-hearted manner out of concern for his wife, who was then on board. In defence he pleaded rather ungallantly that he 'had not a thought of her' during the entire action.[187] Only a handful of wives are recorded at sea but their presence was probably not uncommon in ships away from the main fleets.[188] An officer in the *Merlin* kept his wife, sister, and two children on board for several months, and the captain neither reported it nor tried to remove them.[189] Short visits by sailors' wives to ships at anchor appear to have been quite acceptable, though again we hear of them only in unusual circumstances.[190]

But a life of perpetual journeying and uncertainty meant that for many sailors the marriage bond was weak and easily broken. The seaman's attitude to marriage was indeed proverbially casual, and was summed up neatly in a Restoration ballad entitled *The Mariner's Delight, or the Seaman's Seven Wives*. In 1656 Capt. Thomas Wright was puzzled to find that two members of his company apparently had five wives between them.[191] 'Beastly sailors' wives', as an unkind contemporary called them, could be as casual as their menfolk. Susan Cane, married to a cook's mate, was denied relief because she had not lived with her husband and was 'a woman of loose life, frequents evil company'.[192] Marriage could be hastily entered into, on both sides, and as easily abandoned. Infidelity was certainly regarded as commonplace among seamen's wives. Some women found casual liaisons preferable to the life of hard toil and poverty they faced otherwise when their husbands were away at sea. Poverty and uncertainty drove some into prostitution; sailors' wives ran several of the brothels in Wapping. The temptations

---

[187] SP 18/42/93; SP 18/202/45.
[188] Adm. 2/1729, fo. 119; below, n. 201; cf. Barlow, *Journal*, 133. Female passengers were also carried from time to time.   [189] Rawl. MS A 187, fo. 242.
[190] e.g. a Dover woman drowned with her child going back to the shore after visiting her husband (*CSPD 1656–7*, 562), and the wife of a deserter who went on board the *Merlin* to ask for her husband's ticket—which she was given! (Rawl. MS A 187, fo. 242). See also SP 46/97/49B.
[191] *The Roxburghe Ballads*, ed. W. Chappell and J. W. Ebsworth (1871–99), vii. 490 (c.1681); SP 18/140/48.
[192] HMC 63, *Egmont*, 508; SP 18/81/195. See also the two pretended wives of a seaman killed in the *Arms of Holland*, one of whom already had another consort; SP 18/146/173–6.

facing women with husbands away at sea were well known. In 1655 reports circulated that one woman had felt driven to covenant with the Devil for maintenance after the money left by her husband had been spent; the story ended in grisly style with the Devil eventually appearing to claim his due and tearing her limb from limb.[193]

A casual attitude to marriage was inevitably shared by some of the officers. Edward Barlow noted that the master's mate of the *Naseby* 'laid [it] not very hard to heart' in 1659 when he heard of his wife's death, and used his next leave to find a replacement, mainly it would seem to guarantee comfortable quarters ashore. A widow with a cook-shop in Whitechapel provided the perfect solution.[194] Bigamy was not unknown. A clerk of the cheque was found to have one wife in London and another in Scotland. The bigamous boatswain of the *Sorlings* explained that he had felt free to marry again because he had not seen his first wife for several years and did not know if she were still alive.[195] The best illustration of how fragile marital ties could be is the tragi-comedy of Nicholas Foster, captain of the *Phoenix* in the mid-1650s. Foster had first married in 1639, going back to sea a few weeks later. Soon afterwards he was shipwrecked and stranded penniless in Holland; he found new employment there which took him eventually to Barbados, where he settled. According to his own later account he married again after hearing that his first wife was either dead or remarried; she however said she had remarried only on learning that he had done so. In 1650 Foster returned to England; his second wife, following behind, was drowned on the passage. Finding his first wife still alive he asked her to live with him once more, and she agreed partly because her new husband was away on a lengthy voyage to the East Indies. She was living with Foster in the *Phoenix* when a further twist brought the whole affair to the Admiralty's notice. For Foster had allegedly been planning a third marriage, to a young woman in Dover, until

[193] J. Martin, 'The Seaman's Folly' (c.1681), in *Roxburghe Ballads*, vii. 555–6; Mountford, *Launching*, esp. 40, 58; [J. Birkenhead], *Bibliotheca Parliamenti* (1653), 4; R. Ashton, 'Popular Entertainment and Social Control in Later Elizabethan and Early Stuart London', *The London Journal*, ix (1983), 14; Ward, *Wooden World*, 96; 'A Farewell to Graves-end', (c.1680), in *Roxburghe Ballads*, vii. 505–6; L Price, 'Strange and wonderfull news', in H. E. Rollins (ed.), *Cavalier and Puritan: Ballads and Broadsides Illustrating the Period of the Great Rebellion, 1640–1660* (New York, 1923), 372–8.

[194] Barlow, *Journal*, 35, 39.

[195] *CSPD 1656–7*, 479; Adm. 2/1729, fo. 178; SP 18/92/43; SP 18/132/15. Cf. *CSPD 1671–2*, 324.

his master and carpenter went to the girl's home and revealed his picaresque history. The balance between casual opportunism, misfortune, and muddle in Foster's story is hard to establish, but the tendency of the mariner (and his wife) to live for the moment is clear enough.[196]

Most seamen in the seventeenth century, especially the young and single, took an opportunist attitude to sex. A Quaker evangelist declared that no one could exceed the sailor in 'licentiousness and lasciviousness'.[197] Female company was a major goal of sailors going ashore, and with their free spending and tales of foreign adventure they found little difficulty in attracting the opposite sex. They frequented brothels too, both in England and overseas. A character in Shadwell's play observes that it was slothful for sailors to be landed two hours and not yet among the women. Some, he adds, could not even wait till they got ashore: 'There's many a lad in the navy gets a clap before the ship's moored.' It was indeed common practice for women to go out to ships as soon as they arrived in port, and there were said to be many English women among the prostitutes waiting to greet sailors in the Mediterranean ports.[198]

Whether commanders in the 1650s allowed such free access and casual promiscuity on board we do not know. Some appear to have been lax. One allegedly turned a blind eye when his steward 'kept a

---

[196] SP 18/94/93–4; SP 18/101/75. Foster (interestingly, one of the godly), said he returned to his first wife out of a sense of duty. The kindest reading of the evidence would be that he initiated the third match on learning that his second wife was dead and before discovering that his first wife was still alive. For captains' marital problems after the Restoration see Pepys, *Cat.* iv. 305, 309, 524, 526–7. Foster's complex marital status was not unique. Some years earlier Richard Farnham, the prophet, had married an admiring female disciple whose husband was away at sea. When the husband returned to England he had her committed to Newgate for bigamy but relented and took her back as his wife; when he went back to sea, however, she returned to her 'new' husband: *False Prophets Discovered* (1642), sigs. A2ʳ–A3. Cf. the story of a sailor away three years and presumed lost who returned to find his wife had remarried and produced two children; the first husband then married her again to save her from disgrace. J. W[ade], 'Vinegar and Mustard or Worm-wood Lectures' (1673), 11–12, in C. Hindley (ed.), *The Old Book Collector's Miscellany*, iii (1873).

[197] Caton, *Sea-mens Invitation*, 4; cf. J. Durant, *The Christian's Compass* (1658), sig. A2.

[198] 'Upon the Great Ship' (c.1637), in C. H. Firth (ed.), *Naval Songs and Ballads*, (NRS, 1908), 38–9; Ward, *Wooden World*, 35, 42, 48, 62; Barlow, *Journal*, 63, 163–4, 193; Baltharpe, *Straights Voyage*, 37, 39; Shadwell, *Fair Quaker*, 15, 17; Coxere, *Adventures*, 46; *Mercurius Elencticus (for King Charles II)*, 7–14 May 1650; *Roxburghe Ballads*, vii. 505–6. For 18th-century naval promiscuity on an epic scale see Rodger, *Wooden World*, 255; cf. 75–80.

woman in the boatswain's store-room all night, . . . he having first made her husband drunk upon the deck'. Another was accused of permitting adultery to reign supreme in his ship. The lieutenant and clerk of the *Gift*, close friends, were said to have shared the favours of the clerk's wife, both ashore and on board.[199] Wives were allowed to visit their husbands when the ship was in harbour, and the officer with designs on a sailor's handsome wife was sometimes a problem in fact as well as fiction. A long-running feud in the *Grantham* began when the boatswain's wife visited him before the voyage began. Capt. Lightfoot invited her to dine privately with him in his cabin, prompting the jealous boatswain to ask her bluntly whether she 'came hither for his use or his captain's'. Thereafter there was bitter hostility between the two officers, and eventually each brought charges against the other.[200] Ordinary seamen were certainly still eager to grasp every sexual opportunity, as a farcical incident in 1653 revealed. The *Sovereign* was then lying in reserve at Portsmouth, and her men were delighted to receive a visit one day from two 'sweet creatures, . . . gallantly garnished, and daintily dressed up'. The men readily obeyed the coxswain's order to hand the 'gentlewomen' on to the deck, saluting them with kisses which the women 'took in as good part, as if it had been their trade' (as the sailors doubtless hoped it was). But then, alas, 'some of the youngest sparks, proud of such a prize, from billing fell to feeling' and found to their dismay that the visitors were in fact men— smooth-skinned young cavaliers, concealing incendiary devices beneath their clothes with which they had planned to set the ship on fire.[201]

The evidence from the 1650s is too sketchy to establish what was normal practice. Though some officers were lax it is likely that many others tried harder than in most periods to ensure that visiting 'wives' really were such. Puritan officers and chaplains would certainly not have shared Parson Teonge's indulgence over the orgiastic scenes he witnessed in a Restoration warship on its last night in England, with tipsy men and women shedding all inhibitions on the gun-deck. A chaplain serving in the Straits in the 1650s

---

[199] Rawl. MS A 187, fo. 452; SP 46/97/49B; SP 18/77/87, part i.
[200] SP 18/137/29. For an earlier feud with similar origins see 'Warwick's Voyage', 23.
[201] *The Moderate Publisher*, 3–10 June 1653. The visitors were arrested. The editor promised to follow up the story but was distracted by news of the Gabbard.

urged commanders to keep their men away from the local brothels, though it would have been hard to enforce any such rule. Lawson even opposed paying sailors short-allowance money there, on the grounds that they would spend it ashore on prostitutes.[202] Courts martial during the interregnum sometimes punished sexual offenders very harshly. In 1653 a carpenter's mate convicted of 'uncleanness with women' and drunkenness was sentenced to ten lashes at the side of each flagship, and a discharge. The Admiralty welcomed such severity; when the Commissioners heard of a 'most lewd' purser boasting of his sexual exploits they demanded a full and urgent investigation.[203] Puritan local authorities sometimes helped too: the magistrates at Plymouth tried to stamp out the practice of women going out to ships in the harbour by threatening to have them ducked and put in the stocks.[204] The laxity recorded in some ships serving on isolated stations may thus have been very untypical of conditions in the Commonwealth navy as a whole.

One other sexual practice remains to be considered: homosexuality. The surviving evidence suggests that it was rare and generally unacceptable, despite a recent claim to the contrary; contemporary moralists and character-writers, who have much to say about seamen's promiscuity, do not mention it.[205] The few recorded cases demonstrate how hard it was in small, crowded ships for homosexuals to remain undetected. When a seaman in the hired *Peregrine* took the boy in the next hammock into his own one night a sailor in the hammock below quickly became suspicious, called for a light, and reported the incident. The captain, a firm Puritan, referred the case for trial by the High Court of Admiralty.[206] In 1654 a

---

[202] *The Diary of Henry Teonge, 1675–1679*, ed. G. E. Manwaring (1927), 29; D. Pell, *Nec Inter Vivos, Nec Inter Mortuos* (1659), sig. c 6; Pepys, *Cat.* iii. 181. In 1627 Warwick laid down the death penalty for rape by seamen ashore, whether of 'heathen' or European women: 'Warwick's Voyage', 89.

[203] SP 18/42/80, part ii; Adm. 2/1730, fo. 174.

[204] R. N. Worth (ed.), *Calendar of the Plymouth Municipal Records* (Plymouth, 1893), 68.

[205] B. R. Burg, *Sodomy and the Perception of Evil* (1983). Ward however does suggest that some boatswains gained sexual gratification from flogging their victims (*Wooden World*, 77). Sodomy may have been more common among pirates, who provide most of Burg's evidence; cf. the 'filthy sins of sodomy' among the crew of a Jacobean pirate, 'The Seaman's Song of Captain Ward' (1609), in Firth, *Naval Songs and Ballads*, 26. See also Rodger, *Wooden World*, 80–1. In addition to the cases cited in the text, the chaplain Edward Ferrar appears to have had homosexual leanings: A. Wood, *Life and Times*, ed. A. Clark (Oxford, 1891–1900), i. 370 n.

[206] HCA 1/8/5–7. The boy himself had not objected.

newspaper reported that two youths had been sent up from the fleet for trial at the Old Bailey for 'most horrid buggery with each other', which some 'young godly youths' on board had made known to the officers.[207] The offenders were presumably sent ashore because the navy's code did not specify the punishment for such an act, whereas under statute law it had long been—at least on paper—a capital offence; the captains clearly wanted a severe sentence, though no one appears to have been hanged.[208] Only senior officers enjoying some privacy and protected by their station had any hope of remaining undetected. Two well-documented cases concerned ship's masters, who of course had their own cabins. Thomas Rownen, master of the *Great Charity,* was sent for trial in 1653 on charges of buggery against two 16-year-old boys in the company. He had chosen his moments with some care: two incidents occurred when the captain was ashore, and another at 6 o'clock one winter morning, when Rownen summoned a boy to his cabin, plied him with brandy, locked the door, and blew out the candle. All this came to light only when he began to pester one of the boys so incessantly that the lad reported him, saying he had grown 'a-weary of my life and afraid to be alone'.[209] The master of the *Amity* also found his partners (or victims) among the ship's boys; one of them happened to be the son of a mate, which may have brought about the master's downfall.[210] It may be significant that the boys had not complained straight away, and there were probably other cases which did not come to the authorities' notice. But all the evidence suggests that homosexual practices were rare. There is no reason to question the contemporary image of the sailor as a lusty heterosexual.

[207] *Severall Proceedings*, 10–17 Aug. 1654. The report mentions another recent, similar case.

[208] Mark Hawkins, the defendant in the *Peregrine* case, occurs as a ship's cook in 1659: SP 18/199/60. According to the newspapers there were no executions following the Old Bailey trials in 1654.

[209] SP 18/60/39–40; *CSPD 1653–4*, 521; Rawl. MS A 461, fo. 19ᵛ. Rownen died in prison before trial.

[210] *CSPD 1658–9*, 513. A new master was appointed (Adm. 3/274, fo. 64ᵛ), but the fate of the old one is unknown.

8

Manning the Fleet

MANNING was one of the greatest problems the Admiralty faced throughout the interregnum. This chapter investigates how seamen were recruited, and equally important, how they were were retained despite the state's frequent failure to pay or feed them properly.

I. VOLUNTEERS AND THE PRESS

Well over 17,000 men were on board the English fleet at the Gabbard in June 1653, and many others were serving elsewhere. The Admiralty made provision for 30,000 seamen for the summer guard for 1654 if the war continued.[1] These huge figures represented a very high proportion of the seafaring population. Early in Charles I's reign an official had estimated that England possessed only 18–20,000 seamen, and though numbers certainly increased during the intervening quarter-century many sailors were at sea at any given moment and so unavailable. In 1652 some 5–6,000 were said to be employed by the Dutch, who offered better pay and conditions.[2] Not surprisingly the Commonwealth found it very hard to recruit seamen in sufficient numbers, and undermanning was a critical problem throughout the Dutch war. It proved almost impossible to replace the heavy casualties suffered at Portland in February 1653.[3] Several Dutch prizes the Admiralty wanted to add to the fleet had to

---

[1] *FDW* iv. 16–20; NMM REC/1, p. 73; Bodl. Rawlinson MS A 223, p. 130; see ch. 1, above.

[2] Oppenheim, 242, 244–5; C. Lloyd, *The British Seaman, 1200–1860: A Social Survey* (1970 edn.), 49–50, 72–3; *CSPV 1647–52*, 245; C. Saltonstall, *The Navigator* (1642), 3–4.

[3] See chs. 2–4, above; for shortages after Portland see *FDW* iv. 218, 234–5, 284, 299; Rawl. MS A 227, fo. 54.

lie idle because the 6–800 extra sailors needed to man them could not be found. The great *Sovereign* also lay idle at Portsmouth throughout the summer because, as the Commissioners admitted, 'we cannot hope to get men enough to man her where she is, nor from all the western parts'. General Monck, setting out with the winter guard in December, feared he would 'be forced to sail with 20, 30 and 40 men short to each ship'.[4] Though the Dutch also faced problems they could draw on a much larger body of trained seamen.

The navy preferred its ships to be manned by volunteers, who were valued far more highly than pressed men, and it was seen as essential to have at least a core of them in every company. To help attract volunteers the Long Parliament had increased seamen's wages in 1643 from 15s. to 19s. a (lunar) month. Early in 1649 the Rump awarded a substantial increase to warrant- and petty officers, with a further rise at the end of December 1652. To attract experienced mariners it established in 1652 a new category of 'able seamen'—defined as men 'fit for helm, lead, top, and yards'— whose pay was set at 24s. a month. At just over 10d. a day this matched the wage of a soldier or farm labourer, and the seaman also received free board and lodging. He was to wait another century and a half for his next increase.[5] But even with this increase wage-levels remained well below those to be found in merchant ships and privateers, which were often pushed up to 30–40s. a month during the Dutch and Spanish wars by the pressure of supply and demand. Capt. Giles Shelley wrote from Yarmouth in 1654, 'I dare not venture a man ashore, they give such great rates in merchants' ships, vizt. 40 shillings *per mensem* and more, insomuch the very volunteers will be enticed away, yea to the losing of five or six months' pay'. General Monck wanted to have shipowners barred from paying higher wages than the state's, but this would have been impossible to enforce; as merchant owners could not press men they had to offer higher wages or go out of business. The state could never compete, though it wisely left sailors' pay well alone when soldiers' wages were reduced in 1655.[6]

---

[4] Rawl. MS A 227, fo. 112; *FDW* vi. 190.
[5] *A and O* i. 73–4; *CJ* vi. 173; *FDW* iii. 284–5. The pay of ordinary seamen remained at 19s.
[6] R. Davis, *The Rise of the English Shipping Industry in the Seventeenth and Eighteenth Centuries* (1962), esp. 135, 152; E. Coxere, *Adventures by Sea*, ed.

Prize-money was the key element in attracting volunteers. The Long Parliament had improved the terms on offer and early in 1649 the Rump made further important changes covering enemy warships (captured or sunk) as well as merchantmen. The complex administrative system broke down in the Dutch war so Parliament established a new, simpler method of valuation at the close of 1652. At the same time, and perhaps equally important, it gave sailors the formal right to plunder ships taken in fight, keeping anything they found on or above the gundeck.[7] After the war there was some doubt as to whether these new arrangements still applied. When officers in the West Indies pressed Penn he assured them that they did, though he then had to write hastily to England to ask if this were really so. The Council stood by his promises and the 1652 regulations remained in force for the rest of the decade.[8]

Volunteers did come forward in considerable numbers. About two hundred men volunteered at Dover on the outbreak of the Dutch war, apparently prompted by patriotic zeal. About half the two hundred men recruited at Yarmouth in February 1653 were volunteers, and over half the 130 men enlisted at Dover in 1656.[9] The Admiralty also sent out circular letters in 1653 to owners and masters, recognizing the great influence they wielded in every seafaring community, urging them to encourage local seamen to volunteer.[10] It is clear that in many cases volunteers were not 'joining the navy' as such but enlisting to sail with a particular officer, often a former merchant skipper they had served with in peacetime. Valentine Tatnel, who belonged to a well-known seafaring family in Dover, was said to have a fine record 'in enticing of divers other voluntary, able, and experienced seamen and mariners to join with him in the public service'.[11] Sometimes indeed the Admiralty

E. H. W. Meyerstein (Oxford, 1945), 20; PRO SP 18/90/81; *FDW* vi. 190. For soldiers' pay see C. H. Firth, *Cromwell's Army* (1962 edn.), ch. 8; the army was able to rely wholly on volunteers from 1651 (ibid. 37).

[7] *A and O* ii. 9–11, 72–3; *FDW* iii. 286–7; Oppenheim, 292–3, 308–9. From Jan. 1653 a crew would receive 10s. per ton for every ship it captured (whether warship or merchantman), plus £6. 13s. 4d. for each gun it had carried; sinking a warship would bring a bounty of 10s. a gun. For earlier arrangements see Oppenheim, 165–6. Cf. ch. 6 n. 64, above.

[8] Penn, *Memorials*, ii. 73; *CSPD 1655*, 206; *CSPD 1655–6*, 11, 171; see also *CSPD 1655*, 45.

[9] *FDW* i. 371; *CSPD 1652–3*, 527; *CSPD 1655–6*, 475; SP 18/116/133; see also *CSPD 1656–7*, 405. [10] Rawl. MS A 227, fos. 19, 32ᵛ.

[11] SP 18/56/176; Coxere, *Adventures*, 5. See also ch. 7 nn. 26–9, above.

appointed officers partly on the strength of their ability to bring men with them into the navy. In 1652 the shipmaster Edward Blagg of Plymouth was given the command of a Dutch prize being fitted out there after an official reported that this would be 'a principal means for supply of men, which if strangers command will hardly be obtained'. Volunteers drawn by such personal ties naturally helped to give a company greater cohesion and effectiveness. The Admiralty valued them so highly that when another group of Plymouth sailors wanted to serve with Blagg in 1659 it readily provided transport to carry them over three hundred miles to Gravesend, where his ship was then lying. In similar fashion it provided transport for a party of seamen from the Weymouth area who had volunteered to serve with Capt. Cuttance, formerly a shipmaster in the town.[12]

While personal loyalties and patriotism were important it was undoubtedly the prospect of prize-money and plunder that did most to draw men into the navy. A merchant complained early in 1653 that the easy plunder of Dutch vessels in home waters had taken away the appetite of shipmasters and seamen for long trading voyages.[13] Even in the later 1650s popular captains in good, fast ships could quite often man them wholly with volunteers.[14] It was much less easy to find volunteers for the great ships of the battle fleets, where the prospects of prizes and plunder were poor. As a sop the Admiralty offered a bonus of an extra month's pay to every seaman who had served against the Dutch in 1652 and was willing to re-enlist for 1653, and it made a similar offer the following year.[15] But any attempt to dictate where volunteers should serve met with strong resistance. Capt. Edmund Curtis complained that he had few volunteers, for his ship (the *Guinea*) sailed heavily and was a poor prospect. 'Those which are able seamen will go in what ship they please,' he wrote, 'let the Commissioner do what he will to them'. Volunteers took a whole range of circumstances into account in making their choice. When a large party arrived to join the *Fairfax* in 1651 they found that many of her company were landsmen,

[12] SP 18/29/49; PRO Adm. 2/1731, fo. 56ᵛ; Adm. 2/1731, fo. 61ᵛ; see also Rawl. MS A 227, fos. 32ᵛ, 57ᵛ; SP 18/30/93; *FDW* iii. 86.

[13] *The Letters of John Paige, London Merchant, 1648–1658*, ed. G. F. Steckley (London Record Soc. xxi, 1984), 89.

[14] e.g. SP 18/116/121; *FDW* i. 21; Adm. 2/1730, fo. 196; Oppenheim, 319.

[15] *FDW* iii. 287; *An Order by the Admiralty Commissioners* (16 Jan. 1654) (BL 669 f 17 (74)).

soldiers, and mere boys, and they promptly went off to seek better ships, declaring they were not prepared to do others' work for them.[16]

The relative freedom of the volunteer led many seamen to come forward rather than take the risk of being pressed. As volunteers they could choose their own ship and commander, the two key factors determining the quality of life and the prospects of prize money and plunder. They were also free to relax ashore when in harbour, whereas pressed men were kept on board to stop them deserting. The contrast between the two groups was spelt out clearly after a recruiting drive in 1656: the volunteers, it was said, had gone to Portsmouth to choose their ships, and were to have liberty to pass between ship and shore as they wished, whereas the pressed men were to be 'kept as prisoners on board'.[17] Some sailors undoubtedly volunteered only because they thought it was impossible to escape the press and preferred to serve on their own terms. Edward Coxere was among those to take this course. He escaped a press-gang which boarded his merchant ship in the Thames in 1653 and contrived to reach home safely, only to find the press out in such force that he dared not leave the house, and he and his brother grew so miserable living virtually as prisoners that eventually they volunteered for a warship lying in the harbour. The story of Luke Harbottle is rather similar. Harbottle was among a group of newly pressed men in 1654 who escaped by overpowering their guards; though delighted to be free he none the less enlisted in the navy the very next day in another ship. If it was impossible to evade naval service he wanted to make sure of enjoying the privileges of a volunteer.[18] Such men were obviously 'volunteers' only in the most formal sense.

Volunteers, however loosely defined, were never sufficient for the navy's needs in this period, or indeed throughout the age of sail. Wages were uncompetitive, and both pay and prize-money were

[16] *FDW* iii. 400; SP 18/29/57.

[17] SP 18/133/96. Pressed men too were aware how much depended on which ship they were sent to, and sometimes tried to influence the decision. Officials complained in 1653 that they were 'so refractory and so resolved to go all in frigates [rather than the great ships of the battle fleets] that they hide themselves after they are pressed, in expectation till a frigate be ready': *FDW* iv. 39.

[18] Coxere, *Adventures*, 22–5; Rawl. MS A 187, fos. 445ᵛ–446. Harbottle's luck soon ran out: before reporting to his new ship he was spotted in the street by the officer who had earlier pressed him, and arrested; see also n. 47 below.

often far in arrears. Many men tempted by the thought of plunder preferred to serve in privateers, where voyages were shorter and the dangers less; a privateer, after all, could choose its adversaries and stay clear of bloody fleet actions.[19] How much fear deterred seamen from the navy we cannot tell, but it is reasonable to suppose that not all were born with hearts of oak and the unprecedented carnage of 1653 must have daunted many. A royalist agent reported after the first great battle of that year that the seamen 'absent themselves all they can, the late fight having shrewdly bruised their minds as well as their bodies'.[20] In the later 1650s there were also many sailors willing to serve in home waters who were terrified of being sent to the tropics. Very few were willing to serve in the Caribbean once news filtered back of the mortality rates there—so few indeed that when Christopher Myngs said he had enlisted some volunteers for Jamaica in 1655 the Admiralty immediately assumed he must have been offering bribes.[21] Overall most sailors, most of the time, felt that the drawbacks of naval service far outweighed its advantages.

Impressment therefore had to remain at the centre of the navy's manning policy. Authorized by a series of ordinances in the 1640s, the press was given a statutory basis by the Rump early in 1649, and further Acts and ordinances renewed these powers in subsequent years. All sailors were made liable to impressment except those holding senior posts in a merchant ship, and anyone evading or resisting it faced three months' gaol. Press-warrants usually specified that recruits must be over fifteen and under fifty, to bar the common practice of sending boys and old men, and this provision was incorporated in the Press Act of 1659. How critical the manpower problem remained is shown by a clause in the 1659 Act imposing the death penalty for resisting the press or failing to report.[22]

The navy's requirements followed a fairly regular pattern. Each spring thousands of men were needed for the summer guard, and there were several hectic weeks of recruiting and pressing. The state often laid an embargo on outward-bound merchant shipping, which had to lie idle until the navy's needs were met—or until the merchants' clamour forced the government to lift the ban. The

---

[19] *FDW* iii. 158-9, iv. 163; cf. below, nn. 115-16.
[20] *FDW* iv. 233.
[21] e.g. SP 18/84/83; for Myngs (who denied the charge) see SP 18/116/133.
[22] *A and O* ii. 12-13, 354-5, 578-80, 858, 1287-9; *CJ* vii. 269.

work of pressing was delegated to the magistrates in coastal towns and the Vice-Admirals of the coastal shires, who were empowered to call on other local officials to assist them. A press in Devon in 1655 shows the system at work. The Vice-Admiral wrote to the high constable of each hundred, and he in turn directed petty constables to leave a note at every seaman's house summoning him to the local market town on a specified day. Each constable was also ordered to attend in person, bringing a list of all the seamen of his parish. A newly pressed sailor received a shilling, a ticket stating where and when he was to report, and conduct money at 1½d. a mile to meet his expenses getting there. The local authorities could recoup their expenses later from the Navy Office on Tower Hill.[23] The largest concentration of seamen was of course in London, and the Council often sought help from Trinity House in pressing them. In 1653, for example, seamen were directed to assemble at its headquarters at Deptford, where officials would list them and direct them to the navy's warships.[24] Similarly the Watermen's Company, which supervised boats and barges in the Thames, was responsible for pressing the men who worked them.[25]

In London the press was highly effective. A royalist agent reported in March 1653 that the Thames had been 'so fleeced' that not one able man remained. Another spoke of 'whole churchfuls' being pressed at Ratcliff.[26] Outside London, however, the press faced enormous difficulties. The elaborate press in Devon, described above, achieved pitifully little. About a thousand seamen should have assembled at Newton Abbot but less than a hundred turned up, many of them old and infirm. The navy agent in attendance was able to press a mere twenty-eight—a typical experience, he noted glumly. He added that even these were likely to run off and join the Newfoundland fishing fleet unless they could be kept under constant supervision.[27] Similarly when Blake called on Rye to supply sixty able seamen in 1656 the magistrates apologized that only eleven could be found: some men were away at sea, some had

---

[23] e.g. *FDW* i. 225–7; NMM REC/1, p. 72.

[24] *FDW* iii. 410, vi. 38–9, 129; SP 18/46/68. Cf. G. G. Harris, *The Trinity House of Deptford, 1514–1660* (1969), 217, 219–221. It was suggested that the Newcastle Trinity House might press in the Tyne: *CSPD 1652–3*, 550.

[25] BL Add. MS 9300, fo. 224; *FDW* iii. 128–9, 145, 410–11, iv. 39, 130. Pressed watermen often failed to attend, and in general were poorly regarded: e.g. SP 18/133/3, 4, 27; *CSPD 1656–7*, 575.

[26] *FDW* iv. 233–4, v. 115.   [27] *CSPD 1655–6*, 157: SP 18/122/125.

already been conscripted, and others had fled at the first rumour of a press. It was a familar story.[28] Another difficulty was that parish constables were often afraid to carry out their orders. At Aldeburgh we hear that the constables, 'being poor men, were loath to displease and gave the men notice, so that no seamen were found'. Some constables were persuaded through fear or bribery to leave seamen alone and allow those who had already been pressed to escape. In Devon there were said to be many parishes 'where the sailors bear more sway than the constables and all other inhabitants besides, which is the reason why so few have been apprehended'. At Dartmouth the seamen kept together in large numbers and the constables dared not approach them. Though the Council authorized JPs to press the constables themselves if they were negligent such threats did nothing to change the underlying social realities.[29]

A more serious problem was that many provincial magistrates offered little or no co-operation. The press brought national and local interests into direct conflict and the latter usually prevailed, for impressment dealt a blow to the economic life of the entire local community. The seamen and their families suffered most, but owners and shipmasters were hit too as they found their labour force drained off by the state. Capt. Thomas Cheneys complained in 1653, for example, that so few sailors were left around Aldeburgh 'that our colliers have not any men to man them if they be minded for Newcastle'. During the Spanish war too, many magistrates had to watch local shipping fall prey to Flemish privateers, and they felt no inclination to help an unpopular government wage an unwanted war. The fact that they were expected to lay out ready cash for press and conduct money, which could be recouped from London only with much time and effort, naturally hardened their attitude.[30]

Some magistrates deliberately failed to press a single man. Others seized the opportunity to get rid of undesirables in the local

---

[28] Blake, *Letters*, 335–6; HMC 31, *Rye*, 227; *FDW* i. 139, iii. 416, 450–1; Adm. 7/674/10; *CSPD 1651–2*, 210. For magistrates who did their best to co-operate see also e.g. *FDW* iv. 138–9, v. 406.

[29] *CSPD 1652–3*, 497: SP 18/135/28, 40; SP 18/134/35; *FDW* i. 188. On bribery see SP 18/60/63; SP 46/119, fo. 83; Lloyd, *British Seaman*, 54; *A and O* ii. 355, 579, 1289.

[30] *CSPD 1652–3*, 588; *CSPD 1653–4*, 558; SP 18/124/18; SP 18/135/40; SP 18/136/46; *FDW* iv. 53. For Ipswich magistrates and the press see A. Everitt, *Suffolk and the Great Rebellion, 1640–1660* (Suffolk Records Soc., iii; 1960), 117–21.

community, following a hallowed tradition. Justices in Sussex sent the navy a group comprising 'a tinker, a Quaker, two glass carriers, a hatter, a chairmaker, and a tanner, with his little boy of seven years old'.[31] One levy contained millers, bakers, butchers, and tailors who 'never saw salt water before', and another included a sickly man pressed at the age of seventy.[32] Captains pointed out repeatedly and angrily that landsmen and even watermen were of little use. One officer said he had not dared to board a crippled Dutch vessel because his crew was so inexperienced: 'I had not above twelve men that knew anything at all', he explained. Similarly William Pickering complained he had not three men in his crew who knew how to furl a sail or pull an oar.[33]

The state therefore often turned to its own military and naval officials, both to galvanize the efforts of civilian magistrates and to act directly. In London Col. Barkstead, Lieutenant of the Tower, became a key figure in organizing the press, the state's bargemaster helping at a humbler level. At Hull the military governor, Col. Robert Overton, gave energetic assistance. In Scotland even customs officials were drawn in.[34] The commitment of the navy's own officials, such as Bourne at Harwich, Hatsell at Plymouth, and Burton at Yarmouth, did much to compensate for the sloth of civilian magistrates. John Poortmans, secretary to the Generals, also showed impressive zeal. Arriving at Gravesend in February 1653, at the height of the manpower crisis, Poortmans threw himself into the work at once, brushing aside doubts as to his authority to do so. He directed two thorough sweeps of the town, searched all ships coming downriver on the ebb-tide, and planned a third search of the town at midnight. Nehemiah Bourne arrived a few days later and scoured the town yet again under cover of darkness.[35]

Much of the burden of impressment nevertheless fell on press-parties sent out from a particular warship to supply its own needs. The officers had a vested interest in securing good recruits, but they

[31] *FDW* iii. 400, iv. 103; SP 46/119, fo. 83; SP 18/135/68–9. In 1667 Watermen's Hall pressed boys so young that a sardonic official remarked that they needed nurses to tend them: *CSPD 1667–8*, 364.

[32] *CSPD 1652–3*, 594; *CSPD 1653–4*, 551; cf. *FDW* iii. 400.

[33] *Severall Proceedings*, 13–20 Oct. 1653; SP 18/136/106.

[34] Rawl. MS A 461, fos. 4ᵛ, 17ᵛ; NMM REC/1, p. 76 (Barkstead); Adm. 3/273, fo. 65 (bargemaster); Rawl. MS A 227, fo. 82 (Overton); Rawl. MS A 227, fo. 61 (Scotland).

[35] For the Gravesend operation see *FDW* iv. 42–3, 54–6, 58–9, 86–7.

still had to match the ingenuity of seamen determined to escape them. Sailors with local knowledge could dodge through back lanes and narrow alleys in a game of hide-and-seek that was often played with deadly determination: sailors at Yarmouth in 1656 said they would rather be hanged than pressed for the West Indies. In Cornwall and Devon, it was reported, seamen would leave their homes and 'lie out in boats, some forty or fifty together for a week outright, boys and women carrying provisions to them'. Others took to the plough and spade, working inland as farm labourers to avoid the press.[36]

The navy's press-gangs also had to contend with obstruction from the local magistrates who were supposed to be helping them. Capt. Robert Mackey believed there were a hundred seaman available when he arrived in Southwold in January 1656, but deliberate procrastination by the bailiff and constables gave ample time for them all to flee or go into hiding. In two days Mackey found only one man to press. He returned later with a troop of horse but the officials were again so dilatory that many of the seamen escaped. It was alleged that mayors and constables in the southern counties deliberately spread word when a press was imminent, and one Cornish JP openly challenged the press, claiming that impressment was illegal.[37]

Even when the press found victims it might still have to face an angry crowd determined to rescue them. Robert Plumleigh had pressed only one sailor at Deal in 1655 when a mob attacked and stoned his men, driving them back to their boat. Plumleigh was badly injured in both eyes by flying stones and feared he would lose his sight. Was there no better way to man a ship? he asked plaintively.[38] Magistrates sometimes showed little haste to restore order in such incidents. The bailiffs of Ipswich allegedly allowed a mob to assault a press-gang in 1659 and free its victims, making no attempt to arrest the offenders.[39] The most striking combination of popular violence and magisterial ambivalence is found in the Channel Islands, where Capt. Robert Sansum arrived to press men in 1656. At Guernsey an angry crowd assembled and the bailiffs called a

---

[36] SP 18/124/18; Add. MS 18986, fo. 82; *CSPD 1652–3*, 277.
[37] SP 18/134/95–8; *CSPD 1655–6*, 158, 172, 215; SP 18/132/67; *FDW* v. 333.
[38] SP 18/104/23, 29; cf. SP 18/132/131. In 1667 a lieutenant was killed by a mob while trying to press men: *CSPD 1666–7*, 509.
[39] Adm. 2/1731, fo. 59ʳ.

special meeting of the island's court, which ruled that impressment was in breach of local privilege. The crowd disarmed Sansum's men and freed the seamen they had pressed, and the commander of the military garrison advised him to leave at once. In Jersey he fared still worse. An armed mob of two hundred forced his men to take shelter in a house, where they remained under siege till the governor sent a party of horse to rescue them; the soldiers had to open fire to disperse the crowd, killing one and wounding several. Sansum eventually left the islands with a modest haul of fifty new men, a triumph of perseverance over common sense.[40]

Complaints by press-gangs have to be placed alongside complaints about their own behaviour. The atmosphere during a press was always tense, with violence never far away. When a lieutenant complained in 1656 that a mob at Aldeburgh had stoned and disarmed his party, the bailiff retorted that a naval seaman had provoked the trouble by striking a civilian with his sword. The press inevitably aroused resentment, especially when it seized landsmen to make up numbers, and direct action was often the community's only hope of redress.[41]

A sailor taken by the press still had two last chances of freedom. First, he or his family might appeal for his release on compassionate grounds. Capt. Richard Newbery allowed women to come on board in May 1657 to plead for their newly pressed husbands to be discharged. Such appeals were sometimes successful. Even during the Dutch war the master of the *Victory* discharged a waterman who explained that he had an aged father wholly dependent on his earnings. Capt. Bartholomew Yates, a soft-hearted or timid man, said he had pressed fifty keelmen at Newcastle but 'was forced to discharge them on account of the mighty clamour of their wives'. Such clamour was commonplace. When Hatsell pressed 300 men at Plymouth in 1653 he reported that their 'wives and angry folks come to me, and some cry and others frown, which is more trouble to me than all my other business'—though Hatsell was made of sterner stuff and refused to release any.[42] Elizabeth Wenman of Whitechapel resorted to stronger weapons than tears when her husband was pressed, with tragic consequences. She had recognized the pressmaster and allegedly took revenge by bewitching his wife

[40] SP 18/124/42.
[41] *CSPD 1655–6*, 158, 451; cf. ibid. 173, 475.
[42] *CSPD 1656–7*, 570; *CSPD 1652–3*, 353; Adm. 7/674/19.

and children, inflicting grievous pains, lameness, and blindness. The victim sought medical help (both conventional and magical) till at last, distracted, she turned to the famous astrologer William Lilly, who diagnosed witchcraft. A search of Wenman's house produced incriminating pictures of the victims pierced by holes at the very places where their pains were sharpest. She was duly tried at the Old Bailey, sentenced to death, and apparently hanged.[43]

A pressed man's other chance of freedom was by absconding. Men were often given conduct money and left to make their own way to the fleet, sometimes a journey of many miles, and predictably many failed to arrive. Many of the sailors enlisted at Trinity House in 1653 promptly disappeared, some hiding in the city and others heading for the Suffolk ports to enlist in colliers. Of thirty men pressed by a captain early in 1656 less than six proceeded to Portsmouth as directed.[44] Officials were told to keep notes of the name, age, and appearance of every man they pressed to help identify runaways, but the scale of the problem was too vast for this to be very effective.[45] The only sure solution was to keep pressed men under constant guard until they could be delivered to the navy, and this was increasingly done. Many of the men pressed in London in 1653 were held in the Tower and then taken down river by barge to the fleet.[46] Even then really determined men could sometimes beat the system. One evening in March 1654, for example, Lt. Thomas Gwynne of the *Victory* put a group of pressed men into a hoy to be carried down from the Tower to his ship in Tilbury Hope, but *en route* they seized their chance by rushing up from the hold and overpowering the guards, cutting the throat of one, and then escaped by running the hoy ashore.[47]

Many officers preferred to press at sea where there were fewer chances for sailors to hide or escape and no danger from hostile crowds.[48] Normally the navy was only allowed to take men from homeward-bound ships nearing harbour, for pressing from outward-bound ships left them undermanned and vulnerable to enemies and bad weather. In an emergency however this restriction

[43] *The Grand Politique Post*, 17–24 Jan. 1654; *The Weekly Intelligencer*, 17–24 Jan. 1654. The case appears to have been unnoticed hitherto.
[44] *FDW* iii. 158, 306, iv. 38–9; *CSPD 1655–6*, 466.
[45] e.g. *FDW* i. 226.
[46] *FDW* iv. 352; *CSPD 1655–6*, 157.
[47] Rawl. MS A 187, fo. 448; *CSPD 1654*, 124–5.
[48] e.g. SP 18/136/46.

might be lifted, and early in the Dutch war the navy had leave to take up to a quarter of the crews of outward-bound ships in the Downs.[49] Colliers, whose seamen were reputed the best, were always a favourite target. A fleet of colliers entering the Thames estuary in April 1653 found the formidable Commissioner Bourne waiting in the *London*. Bourne fired forty or fifty shots to make the more 'insolent' skippers drop anchor and then combed the ships for recruits, 'digging for them where they have burrowed themselves'. Boats that managed to slip by found other warships lying in wait higher up the river.[50] The colliers' men knew that escorting warships would probably board them as they neared harbour, and a battle of wits often ensued: the colliers often tried to slip away, some landing most of their men at Harwich or Leigh in Essex to be picked up again on the return journey. Sometimes they gave young sailors bogus posts as gunner or boatswain to make them ineligible for the press.[51]

Press-gangs were of course as unwelcome at sea as on land. A group of shipmasters told a naval captain in 1654 that 'they had rather meet with a Turks' man-of-war than with any of the state's ships'; one master drew his cutlass and threatened to kill anyone who laid hands on his men. Violent clashes sometimes occurred.[52] Not all masters, however, tried to protect their men, and some welcomed the opportunity to pocket wages due to sailors who had been pressed near the end of a voyage.[53] In the last resort a sailor had to depend on his own wits alone, as Edward Coxere's memoirs show; at various times Coxere borrowed landsman's clothes to disguise himself, pretended to be a foreigner unable to speak English, lied freely, and was ready to use force to break free when all his subterfuges failed.[54]

Popular sympathies lay then, as now, with the victims of the press, and it is easy to identify with the dismay they must often have

[49] *FDW* i. 186, 187, 191, iii. 409; Rawl. MS A 461, fo. 1; Adm. 2/1731, fo. 52ᵛ. Men had sometimes been pressed from outward-bound ships before, without authorization: *CSPD 1651-2*, 218.

[50] *FDW* iv. 348–9.

[51] Add. MS 18986, fo. 72; *FDW* iii. 166, 393, iv. 290, 357, 385; *CSPD 1654*, 113; *CSPSD 1656-7*, 575.

[52] SP 18/89/50; SP 18/86/50; *Certain Passages*, 18–24 Aug. 1654.

[53] SP 18/132/115; cf. *Barlow's Journal of his Life at Sea*, ed. B. Lubbock (1934), 146.

[54] Coxere, *Adventures*, 22–5, 27–8.

felt.[55] But impressment has to be seen in the context of a national shortage of trained seamen, when the navy had no other way to man its fleet. Some attempt was made (if not very consistently) to see the system operated fairly. When circumstances permitted the press took single rather than married men.[56] The Council issued protections to a number of individuals who could show they had elderly relations dependent upon them. Similarly the Admiralty Commissioners were ready to consider appeals on behalf of men already pressed if there were special family circumstances. One man explained that his wife was dying and that he had four small children to care for, and another pleaded that his son-in-law was too short-sighted to be of any use to the navy. One father secured his son's release on the grounds that he had already lost both his other sons in the navy's service.[57] The Commissioners also intervened when serious abuses of the system came to their notice. They ordered the arrest of a press-gang which had used gratuitous violence, rebuked over-zealous officials who had pressed merchant officers (who were exempt by law), ordering the victims to be released, and investigated incidents where the press had been used as an excuse to plunder or pay off private scores.[58] On the other hand they did not release the numerous landsmen who were taken, although press-warrants only covered sailors: the desperate shortage of trained seamen forced them to connive at this widespread and dubious practice.

There is no doubt that many of the naval officers involved in the press disliked it intensely, while conceding its necessity. Robert Mackey made no secret of his distaste when he was sent to press near his home town of Yarmouth in 1655. He was now hated by his neighbours, he complained, though once he had been a popular figure in the community, and he added that he would much rather have given £20 to the poor. Another officer employed to press near

---

[55] One journalist enjoyed telling the exploit of a man pressed into the *Church* who quipped 'that he had never been in a church before since the reign of the late king, neither would he ever come into any during the time of this', whereupon he leaped overboard and swam to freedom: *The Weekly Post*, 24 Apr.–1 May 1655.

[56] *FDW* v. 310; cf. J. Baltharpe, *The Straights Voyage*, ed. J. R. Bromley (1959), 12.

[57] SP 18/86/77; *FDW* iii. 445, iv. 51, 141; SP 18/150/114.

[58] SP 18/132/6; Rawl. MS A 227, fos. 89, 93ᵛ; Adm. 2/1730, fo. 61ᵛ; *CSPD 1657–8*, 446, 451; Adm. 2/1730, fo. 121ᵛ.

his home begged to serve at sea instead.[59] Even more striking is the officers' response to the seamen's petition of 1654, which denounced impressment as 'inconsistent with the principles of freedom and liberty'. The officers debated this view at a council of war and voted by 21 to 4 to endorse it, the flag-officers Lawson and Dakins leading the radical majority. Several years later, in 1659, Lawson called for impressment to be abolished, except for the immediate defence of the nation.[60] Of course victims of the press did not necessarily benefit from the scruples of their officers. But many captains appear to have discharged landsmen whenever possible. On one occasion Plumleigh discharged thirty pressed men out of a group of sixty-eight. One captain denounced those who pressed landsmen as 'manstealers'. Some were willing too, as we saw, to listen sympathetically to sailors or their wives who had special family problems.[61] Officers who disliked the system could at least try to operate it humanely.

The chronic shortage of seamen led the Commonwealth to employ large numbers of soldiers in its fleets, mostly during the Dutch war. They were sometimes carried for service ashore, as in the combined operations in the Channel Islands in 1651-2 and the Caribbean in 1654-5. 'Seamen are not for land service unless it be for sudden plunder', Mountagu observed, stating a view that was generally held; 'they are then valiant much, but not to be ruled and kept in any government on shore'.[62] There was talk of a landing on the Dutch coast after the Gabbard, and spades, pickaxes, and other implements were taken aboard. Similarly Blake's expedition in 1656 had an attack on Gibraltar among its possible objectives, and the Council directed 2,000 soldiers to go with it.[63] Soldiers were also needed for actions at sea fought at close quarters, when their role was to provide small-arms fire and lead or repel boarding-parties; soldiers joining the fleet in June 1652 brought with them half-pikes,

---

[59] SP 18/135/21; SP 18/136/24.

[60] *Swiftsure. At a Council of War held aboard, the 17 of October, 1654*, and *To his Highness the Lord Protector: the Humble Petition of the Sea-men* (1654) (BL 669 f 19 (32-3)); see also ch. 5, above: *A Declaration of Vice-Admiral John Lawson* (13 Dec. 1659).

[61] SP 18/139/100; *CSPD 1653-4*, 543; *CSPD 1655-6*, 497.

[62] Blake, *Letters*, 404. Goodson reported that sailors employed at Mardyke in 1657 soon began to complain at having to serve ashore: *CSPD 1657-8*, 143.

[63] *FDW* v. 197, 208; *CSPD 1655-6*, 65, 119, 192, 466. Army lieutenants were sent to command them: Clarke MS 1/15, fo. 158ᵛ.

pistols, short swords, and muskets.[64] In theory then soldiers were supernumeraries carried when a fleet action or a foreign landing was anticipated. In practice they were also needed during the Dutch war to help work the ships. Unlike other landsmen they already possessed at least some discipline and skill with weapons. The Council directed that they were 'to perform as far as they are able all service as seamen, and to be ordered in the like capacity as the rest'. Like the others they were paid by the Navy Treasurer.[65]

The Generals and the Admiralty Commissioners decided that soldiers and other landsmen might form up to a third of a ship's complement. In the event the proportion might be higher still. Deane and Monck complained in May 1653 that in 'the fleet here we have more landsmen than seamen, so that we are not able to manage our ships as we ought, and yet we want men'. The soldiers serving afloat during the Dutch war probably numbered in all at least three or four thousand.[66] The Council assigned large numbers of troops to the navy from an early date and regularly offered more. In January 1653 it drafted men disbanded from regiments in Scotland, and a few weeks later agreed that 1,200 men should be drawn from the regiments of Cromwell and Ingoldsby. Five hundred soldiers went on board some hired merchants ships in April, and Bourne shipped a further 700 at Leigh Road in June. A thousand were assigned to Blake and Penn early in 1654, and 400 had already gone on board when the approach of peace halted the operation.[67]

Soldiers helped to swell numbers but were not altogether satisfactory. Many arrived without bedding or spare clothes and soon fell sick, spreading disease among the rest of the crew. Blake and Monck turned down an offer of more troops in January 1653 as 'of little advantage to the service, they being unprovided of all conveniences and not able (as we have found by experience) to brook this winter weather'.[68] The Generals never accepted that soldiers were adequate substitutes. When the Council offered to send four or five thousand more in March, Deane and Monck countered with proposals designed to attract more seamen into the navy instead.

[64] *Faithfull Scout*, 11–18 June 1652.
[65] *FDW* iii. 424, 432. The soldier was paid 18s. a month, 1s. less than an ordinary seaman.
[66] Rawl. MS A 227, fo. 14ʳ·ᵛ; *FDW* iv. 390; Oppenheim, 314–15.
[67] *FDW* i. 185, 369–70, ii. 120, iii. 398–9, 423–4; iv. 175, 216, 236–7, 325–7, v. 79; *The Perfect Diurnall*, 6–13 Mar. 1654; *FDW* vi. 247.
[68] *FDW* v. 187, 196–7; Blake, *Letters*, 195.

They also wanted to pay soldiers a mere 13*s*. or 14*s*. a month (the wages of a 'grommet' or youth), which shows their low opinion of their value, and use the money thus saved to pay the best able seamen more by rating them as midshipmen.[69] The Generals were willing to accept more soldiers only as a last resort, and even then only 'the choicest and ablest'.[70] Army officers of course did not usually part with their best men, and some of those they sent were raw recruits. Capt. William Kendall of the *Success* complained with feeling about fifty men who 'came under the notion of soldiers, but they are not, for they are boys and old decrepit men, and some fitter for hospitals than to be sent upon present service, for I have exercised them already and I cannot find six in the fifty which is able to fire a musket'.[71]

Relations between sailors and soldiers were often poor. This was partly through inter-service rivalry but mainly reflected anger over the widespread use of troops in pressing seamen, capturing deserters, and keeping order ashore. An official conceded in 1653 that using soldiers in the press 'breeds much heart-burning between seamen and soldiers'.[72] Similarly calling in troops to restore order was a step which could easily backfire; when the *Tiger* mutinied at Yarmouth in 1649 it was decided that sending in troops would merely inflame the situation. Several years later there was the 'beginning of an ugly mutiny' at Harwich when Bourne used soldiers to drive some drunken, disorderly sailors back to their ships.[73] Soldiers arriving to serve afloat might thus find a cold welcome. Some even deserted because of the treatment they received, and the authorities had to insist there should be no discrimination against them.[74] Inevitably the soldiers sometimes replied in kind.

Rivalry between the two services recurs throughout the period, exacerbated by a sense of grievance on both sides. A brawl at Gravesend in 1653 ended disastrously with a soldier shooting and killing the armourer of the *Phoenix*.[75] Soldiers and sailors taking

[69] *FDW* iv. 253–4.
[70] *FDW* iv. 390; cf. v. 314, 329.
[71] *FDW* iv. 253, v. 376.
[72] *FDW* v. 277.
[73] Clarke MS 4/4, 1649 (20); *FDW* v. 295.
[74] Rawl. MS A 227, fos. 54–5.
[75] *Faithfull Scout*, 28 Oct.–4 Nov. 1653; Rawl. MS A 227, fo. 111; *The Moderate Publisher*, 23–30 Dec. 1653; cf. *Certain Passages*, 18–24 Aug. 1654.

part in combined operations were also quick to blame each other for any failures. When the attack on the Scillies in 1651 suffered an early setback a number of seamen made contemptuous jibes about the army's cowardice; one army officer was stung into publishing a fierce rebuttal, in which he denounced several naval officers by name.[76] The expedition to the Caribbean in 1654–5 saw far more serious rivalry, the feuding between Generals Penn and Venables being matched by abuse and sometimes violence among the rank and file.[77] Soldiers were an indispensable part of the interregnum navy, but contemporaries were well aware of the problems they could bring.

II. THE SEAMEN'S GRIEVANCES

Manning a ship involved far more than finding a crew: there was also the perpetual problem of holding on to the men and keeping them reasonably co-operative and healthy. As in former times the seaman had many well-founded grievances, mainly over provisions and pay.[78]

The quality of provisions was a perennial source of discontent. The state tried to ensure that victualling was carried out responsibly but the food and drink supplied were in practice often poor. The navy's expansion made unprecedented demands on the system, and the victuallers were forced to subcontract large numbers of brewers and other suppliers over whom they had little control. Their budget was also extremely tight—at 8*d*. (later 9*d*.) a day per man—which meant that low standards and abuses were inevitable. Foul beer and rotten meat quickly undermined a company's morale, bringing sickness and death in their wake, and they provoked numerous protests.[79] In 1653 an official at the Deptford yard denounced the 'stinking victuals' which had brought death and disease to many of the seamen. 'Shall not their blood be required at the hands of those that, for gain, undertake the victualling . . . ?' he demanded. 'Certainly the great God of heaven and earth will make inquisition for blood if men do not'.[80] When several of Robert Plumleigh's men

---

[76] Blake, *Letters*, 125–7.

[77] Ch. 4, above. On one occasion soldiers beat up a boat-crew waiting on the beach at Jamaica: Penn, *Memorials*, ii. 105–6.

[78] Oppenheim, *passim*.

[79] Oppenheim, 324–8; Hammond, thesis, ch. 8.   [80] *FDW* v. 276.

died suddenly in the *Reserve* in 1658 he found that the ship's beer was to blame; one of the casks had even contained offal, which had rendered the beer highly toxic. The Admiralty (to its credit) was appalled and ordered a full inquiry to trace the victualler responsible. On several occasions entire companies were incapacitated by food poisoning, leaving their ships immobilized.[81] It would not have comforted the victims to know that standards overall had substantially improved; the 1650s witnessed nothing comparable to the thousands of deaths through foul provisions which had marked Elizabeth's war with Spain and the naval expeditions of the late 1620s.[82]

Shortage of clothing was another common grievance. There was no naval uniform in this period, and pressed men often brought few clothes with them; after several months at sea they might be reduced to rags. Every winter many sickened from cold and exposure. In 1658 the crew of the *Bramble* lamented—in their spokesman's eloquent words—that after a hard winter at sea with nothing 'to cover our nakedness' they had become 'a spectacle of woe and a looking-glass of calamity'.[83] Their plight was common. Though some clothing was generally kept on board to be sold to the men on credit the system often functioned poorly. The suppliers, or slop-sellers, were private contractors concerned mainly with profits and they charged high prices for shoddy goods. Away from the Channel ports spare clothing was often wholly unavailable.[84] If a ship was leaky and rotten the seamen suffered still more, for clothes and bedding that were perpetually sodden greatly increased the risk of sickness.[85]

Pay and prize-money were still more general and deep-rooted sources of discontent. The prize-money system established at the end of 1652 did not end complaints, partly because the cash was distributed only when the ship was paid off, which made long delays inevitable. The huge numbers of prizes taken during the Dutch war overwhelmed the Admiralty Court, leading to further delays. William Kendall of the *Success* complained in April 1654

[81] Adm. 2/1730, fo. 252. See also *CSPD 1649–50*, 298; Adm. 2/1730, fo. 155ᵛ; Adm. 2/1731, fo. 55; SP 18/145/30; *CSPD 1657–8*, 184, 187.

[82] Oppenheim, 136–9, 187–8, 222–4, 230–2, 237. On the Armada campaign see also M. Lewis, *The Spanish Armada* (1960), 184–5, 198–201; J. J. Keevil, *Medicine and the Navy 1200–1900* (1957–8), i. 74–6.   [83] Add. MS 18986, fo. 286.

[84] Oppenheim, 138–9, 285–6, 329; Lloyd, *British Seaman*, 57, 89–90; *CSPD 1656–7*, 391; *CSPD 1657–8*, 384.   [85] e.g. SP 18/118/88.

that a prize his men had captured fourteen months earlier had yet to be condemned, hinting darkly at deliberate time-wasting and corruption.[86] The administrators were in fact far from idle. John Poortmans was directed to distribute prize-money in the fleet in December 1653, and his accounts show that he paid out some £25,000. Even so the system was clearly inefficient and over-burdened. Officers of the fleet in the Downs complained in August 1654 that a third of the sums due from the Dutch war were still outstanding, and demanded to be paid before they left for service overseas.[87] The situation failed to improve in the later 1650s. Although fewer prizes were taken during the Spanish war and the administrative load was much less, the government regarded prize funds as a useful cash reserve which could be diverted to meet more pressing needs; they were used in 1655, for example, to help pay off Blake's fleet on its return from the Straits.[88]

The seamen had two legitimate grievances over pay: the method of payment, and the fact that wages were often long overdue. When a sailor was discharged he received a ticket stating the wages due, signed by the captain and clerk, and had to present it at the Navy Office in London to be checked and countersigned before he could receive the money from the Navy Treasurer's officials. This centralized procedure, though cumbersome, allowed the Admiralty to control expenditure and avoided the risks in sending large sums of money around the country. Its drawback was that seamen were often left with pieces of paper they were unable to cash because they were far from London or because the Navy Office lacked sufficient funds. They were sometimes kept waiting so long by the Treasurer's office that they ran up expenses amounting to more than their wages were worth.

The massive expansion of the navy during the Dutch war brought enormous problems in paying the seamen when the summer guards were called in. Fear of large-scale disorders led the Admiralty to reverse its normal practice and pay off large squadrons in cash (as far as it could) at Portsmouth or Harwich, safely distant from the capital.[89] Even so there were widespread disturbances at the end of

[86] *FDW* iii. 286–7; *CSPD 1653–4*, 242; SP 18/147/88; Add. MS 18986, fo. 122ᵛ.
[87] SP 18/134/34; *FDW* vi. 184, 190; Blake, *Letters*, 264; Add. MS 18986, fo. 176.
[88] *CSPD 1655*, 372; cf. *CSPD 1654*, 37; Oppenheim, 317.
[89] *FDW* iii. 395–6, 438, vi. 168–9, 173, 176; *CSPD 1652–3*, 510; *Thurloe*, iv. 79–80; Rawl. MS A 227, fos. 7, 8ʳ–ᵛ, 10ᵛ–11.

1652 and more serious rioting followed in London in the autumn of
1653.[90] The Protectorate tried hard to pay off returning fleets
without delay, borrowing from London financiers and even taking
personal loans from members of the Council to make up the
balance. In 1655 the Admiralty calculated that £120,000 was needed
to pay off Blake's fleet and reported that the Navy Treasury was
almost bare. Yet the money was found somehow: the Council had
learned that the sailors of a large fleet were too many and dangerous
to be ignored.[91]

Men serving in smaller squadrons or in ships operating singly had
far less leverage and suffered accordingly. The seamen's petition of
1654 complained that wages were often held back for ten or twenty
months, and demanded that in future they be paid at intervals of not
more than six.[92] The worsening financial situation meant that these
demands were not met. Indeed the Admiralty brushed aside
petitions from companies owed a mere six months' wages, remarking blandly on one occasion that bachelors had no pressing need for
money and that married men were mostly officers 'and so not
probably to be in want'.[93] In the late 1650s the position grew still
worse. A list drawn up in June 1658 showed that the great ships
were paid off fairly promptly when the summer guard was called in
but that others had to wait very much longer. Some sixty-five ships
on the list were owed a year's pay or more; twenty-one of them
were over two years in arrears and one, the *Brier*, no less than four.
In the last months of the interregnum the position came close to
breakdown. The officers and men of the *Wolf* had been waiting for
their pay ever since the vessel was first fitted out fifty-one months
before.[94]

Even when money was available the navy often held back part of
the wages due. Once sailors were discharged and paid they wanted
several weeks to relax ashore before going back to sea, and they
might then choose a merchant vessel. Paying only part of the wages
due was an obvious way to bind them to the navy's service. The
Admiralty also revived the practice of transferring men directly

⁹⁰ *FDW* iii. 175, 308, 317–18; see further below, section iii.
⁹¹ *CSPD 1655*, 370–2, 382; Clarke MS 1/15, fo. 136.
⁹² *Humble Petition of the Sea-men* (BL 669 f 19 (33)).
⁹³ Adm. 2/1729, fo. 126; Adm. 2/1730, fo. 148.
⁹⁴ Adm. 3/273, fos. 208–9; Adm. 3/274, fo. 109⁼; see also ch. 10, below.

from ships coming in to others going out, often giving them no opportunity to cash the tickets they had received.[95]

These practices aroused deep resentment. The Navy Commissioners had observed back in 1648 that the seamen's 'nature is such that they will be paid for one voyage before they begin another'— reasonably enough—and warned that any other course was dangerously provocative. Their warning was timely. Monck and Deane wrote from Portsmouth in the spring of 1653 that destitute seamen were following them through the streets clamouring to have their tickets paid and complaining that 'a little bit of paper is soon lost'.[96] The families of married seamen suffered still more. The men at least received free food and lodging but their families had no such protection, and the credit they usually enjoyed was jeopardized when their menfolk were transferred to other ships without pay at the end of a voyage.

Seamen with tickets they could not cash often swapped them locally for goods and services, on whatever terms they could get. A brisk trade soon developed. Landlords accepted tickets in return for food and lodging, and shopkeepers for clothing; the Navy Commissioners complained in 1658 that they were being presented every day by tradesmen and alehouse-keepers who had taken them as payment for debts or drink.[97] This trade, which went back to Charles I's reign, was to continue for generations. Much of the evidence from the 1650s relates to Plymouth and Liverpool, where the problems seem to have been most acute. Edward Patterson of Plymouth charged a commission of 3s. in the pound, claiming that he was left with only a small profit once he had met the costs of a journey to London to cash the tickets. Patterson had the approval of General Blake, and could rightly argue that there was strong demand for his services and that sailors would otherwise have to go to London themselves at far greater expense. Even so the navy agent in the town, Hatsell, thought dealers were charging too much and asked to have tickets cashed in Plymouth, which would have killed the trade at a stroke. The Admiralty ignored this proposal and merely banned Patterson from trafficking; this of course solved

[95] e.g. *CSPD 1653–4*, 497, 508,

[96] Add. MS 9300, fos. 110–11; *FDW* iv. 284, 305–6.

[97] Rawl. MS A 184, fo. 339; *CSPD 1657–8*, 334. See also Lloyd, *British Seaman*, 63; Oppenheim, 228, 287.

nothing, for other dealers moved in charging fees of 50 per cent, and Patterson soon resumed his trade with encouragement from the mayor and other local magistrates. He was, as Hatsell had explained, a necessary evil.[98] Fees charged by dealers in later generations were to be considerably higher.

Admiralty officials were not as indifferent to the sufferings of the men as this catalogue of woes might suggest. They intervened, as we saw, to check the worst abuses of the press, investigated complaints over victualling, and usually refunded money—eventually—which captains had been forced to spend from their own pockets. They also did what they could to assist with the supply of clothing, endorsing the arrangements devised by local officials and commanders. They made special arrangements for the Western Design, asking Vice-Admiral Goodson to assemble a stock of clothing worth almost £5,000 instead of leaving provision to the hit-and-miss arrangements of slop-sellers and pursers.[99] They even intervened on occasion to help individuals in distress, such as the sailor's wife who turned to them in despair when her landlady refused further credit and threatened her with eviction.[100] Officials in the 1650s felt the same compassion that Pepys was to confide to his diary a few years later in similar cicumstances. What the Admiralty lacked was resources, not compassion. It lacked the financial resources to provide regular pay, good provisions, and adequate clothing. And it lacked sufficient manpower to exercise close and regular supervision of minor officials and subcontractors. Torn between human sympathy and financial pressures over which it had no control, it had to harden its heart to keep the navy operational.

Officials serving away from London were less aware of the financial constraints and leaned far more towards the sailors. Willoughby, for example, the Navy Commissioner at Portsmouth, was sometimes prepared to place the seamen's needs before the convenience of the Admiralty. When the *Hampshire* arrived home from the Straits in 1655, after being away two years, her men were desperately short of money and clothing and many had families in

---

[98] SP 18/90/38; Blake, *Letters*, 107; SP 18/124/24; SP 18/134/120. For Liverpool see e.g. SP 46/121, fo. 9.

[99] Rawl. MS A 225, fos. 124ᵛ–125; *CSPD 1655–6*, 413; Rawl. MS A 187, fos. 431ᵛ–432; SP 18/89/3.

[100] SP 18/146/10; Adm. 2/1729, fo. 139ᵛ. Thomasine Salmon had promised to pay the rent when her husband returned from sea and was paid; it was now a year in arrears. The startled landlady was summoned before the Navy Commissioners and told to reach an accommodation with her lodger.

distress; Willoughby urged the Admiralty to give them wages and leave rather than transfer them to another ship, and declared that he was quite ready to trust their promise to return later.[101]

Naval officers sided still more openly with the men, knowing their plight at first hand. This was true even of the Generals. Deane and Monck, writing from Portsmouth in the spring of 1653, were highly critical of the Admiralty's policy of transferring sailors from one ship to another, and expressed outrage that they were often sent back to sea without being able to cash their tickets. 'We think it is neither reason nor conscience to compel men to go who must perish for want of clothes, having formerly lost them in the service, nor yet when their families are ready to starve, as they tell us, and have money due from the state and their tickets signed and their captains satisfied they will not run away'.[102] The Generals also appreciated the real hardship that distant expeditions meant for the dependants of married seamen. On the expedition to the Straits in 1654–5 Blake authorized each of his captains to issue up to twenty tickets to men with families in need, to be sent back and cashed by relations in London. And knowing that officials might prove obstructive he directed that all such tickets should be cashed without delay, 'notwithstanding any order to the contrary'. Penn adopted similar measures while he was in the Caribbean, and they were continued by his successors there with the state's approval.[103]

Most captains tried to help their men by bringing grievances to the Admiralty's notice. There is a vast correspondence dealing with foul provisions and the seamen's desperate need for pay and clothing, with the officers appealing to the Admiralty's sense of compassion and sometimes warning too that without relief their men were likely to desert or mutiny. The Commissioners did what they could to balance the demands of natural justice and financial stringency. One partial solution was to give captains a supply of tickets to be handed out to men still serving who could prove they had families in real need—though some captains then showed themselves far too liberal for the Admiralty's taste.[104]

If appeals to the Admiralty were ignored a captain might take personal action to provide a remedy. When sailors had tickets they could not cash he might depute a trusted seaman to go up to

[101] SP 18/118/134.
[102] *FDW* iv. 284, 305–7.
[103] Blake, *Letters*, 303; Penn, *Memorials*, ii. 67; *CSPD 1655–6*, 452.
[104] *CSPD 1657–8*, 513, 546; ibid., 545, for a captain fooled by a bogus claimant. For a reprimand to an over-generous captain see Adm. 2/1730, fo. 148.

London to collect the money due to them all.[105] Anthony Archer, serving in the Irish Sea, advanced part of his men's wages out of his own pocket. Nutton of the *Satisfaction*, based at Liverpool, devised elaborate arrangements to secure clothing which his men desperately needed for the winter.[106] With regard to prize-money officers shared a vested interest with their men in having it paid promptly.[107] Faced with administrative delays they countered by increasingly bypassing official channels. Philip Gethings kept back sugar, tobacco, and other goods from a prize, and when this came to light he requested that they be formally assigned to his men as a reward in kind. Capt. Cornelius did the same.[108] Many captains also appear to have turned a blind eye to plunder by their men, in the absence of the prize-money rightfully theirs. Myngs decided to ignore the rules after losing some prizes he had taken in the West Indies through the slow and (he thought) unjust proceedings of the Admiralty Court in England, and henceforth allowed his men free rein.[109] It is easy to see why sailors usually blamed the Admiralty, not their officers, for the hardships they had to endure.

III. DESERTION AND MUTINY

If captains refused to help, or their appeals were ignored, dissatisfied seamen naturally looked for remedies lying in their own hands. The most obvious was desertion. Though statistics are few, desertion on a very considerable scale plagued the navy throughout the period. The clerk of the *Satisfaction* reported in 1654 that her men were 'continually coming and going, choosing rather to lose a little time than serve long'. The muster-book of the *Bear* shows that 149 men were present in November 1654 while no less than 184 had run away during the course of the summer. Musters early in 1656 showed 148 runaways from the *Worcester*, 65 from the *Plymouth*, and 40 from the *Bridgewater*.[110]

---

[105] e.g. *CSPD 1656–7*, 525; SP 18/58/121; SP 18/113/33.

[106] SP 18/79/20–1; Rawl. MS A 187, fo. 431ʳ⁻ᵛ.

[107] e.g. Adm. 7/674/51; SP 18/85/86; see also ch. 7, part ii.

[108] SP 18/113/37; SP 18/109/84.

[109] F. E. Dyer, 'Captain Christopher Myngs in the West Indies', *MM* xviii (1932), 178–82.

[110] *CSPD 1654*, 261; SP 18/90/63; SP 18/132/139; see N. A. M. Rodger, *The Wooden World: An Anatomy of the Georgian Navy* (1986), 188–204 for a perceptive discussion of desertion.

Sailors were opportunist by nature, and many were always on the look-out for a chance to run. A sailor named Abel Outlaw seized his chance when his ship had to put in for repairs, persuading several others to go with him; he had 'a name agreeing to his condition', the captain noted sourly. The gunner of the *Advice* deserted, ironically, when he was sent ashore to lead a press gang, and the rest of his party followed suit.[111] Sailors were naturally most likely to run when they had just been paid. Though the practice of holding back part of their wages deterred some, as was intended, others were willing to sacrifice even several months' pay. The crew of the *Nonsuch ketch* provided a vivid if extreme illustration of the point: two or three days after receiving part of their wages, a correspondent on board reported in 1654, 'the most part of our officers with some of our common men took the boat in the night from the stern and went ashore at Deal'. They did not return, though they were forfeiting another four months' pay. Henceforth Blake had to transfer most of the ketch's men into his flagship whenever she put into harbour.[112] Such cases show that volunteers too could be unreliable, especially if they were inflamed by drink or a sense of grievance. When a ship was in harbour they would often spend their time ashore drinking heavily in local alehouses, and then 'march away in their mad fits' on the spur of the moment. Some of them were merely stragglers and returned a few days later when their money was spent, but others went home or enlisted in privateers or merchantmen. The Navy Commissioners put the blame on the 'excessive number of base tippling houses' which had debauched them.[113]

The shortage of trained seamen meant that deserters could easily find work elsewhere, and even volunteers were sometimes tempted away by the high wages available in merchant ships. Colliers, which lost many men to press-gangs, were always ready to welcome deserters.[114] Privateers too lured men away, offering them the prospect of plunder as well as good pay. The navy strongly resented their poaching, and friction between them reached a climax after the defeat at Dungeness when the Council, desperate to maintain some form of offensive at sea, rashly gave privateers the right to press

[111] SP 18/62/115; SP 18/38/121.
[112] SP 18/88/43; cf. *CSPD 1654*, 587.
[113] SP 18/96/50; SP 18/141/61; *FDW* vi. 83; cf. ch. 7, part iii.
[114] Blake, *Letters*, 254–5; SP 18/90/82; SP 18/79/186; SP 18/86/50.

merchant seamen. This brought them into direct competition with the navy, and the consequences were so disastrous that the Council was soon forced to restore the navy's monopoly, even authorizing it now to press the privateers' own men.[115] Feelings ran high on both sides. A year later Capt. Sacheverell complained from the Downs that 'privateers still infest these parts, and do much disservice to the Commonwealth in enticing our seamen and raising mutinies and violence on our men, when at any time we send our officers to press men for the state'. Hatsell, the agent at Plymouth, retaliated by authorizing officers to go aboard privateers and retrieve deserters, though this of course was easier said than done: one naval captain found his way blocked by an angry officer threatening to shoot him.[116]

The scale of desertion and the desperate shortage of skilled mariners saved runaways from harsh treatment if they were recaptured. The navy totally ignored the mandatory death penalty laid down in its Articles of War. Recaptured men were merely returned to their own ship or another, forfeiting any pay they were due, and there the matter ended. Applying the full severity of the law in every case would have produced a bloodbath; it was simpler and much less provocative to replenish crews by pressing new men. We find more rigorous treatment only when there were special circumstances, mainly in squadrons serving far from home where it was not possible to press more men. Thus four sailors belonging to Stokes's squadron in the Mediterranean were flogged in 1658 when they tried to run off and join a privateer.[117] A deserter at Deal in 1655 was also punished severely, being ducked three times and given ten lashes on each of the ships in the Downs, but as he had flatly refused to go back aboard he was probably being punished for mutiny rather than desertion.[118]

Naval officers devoted much time and effort to the task of holding on to their men. Constant vigilance was required to stop pressed men slipping ashore in the ship's boat. Giles Shelley remarked wearily at Yarmouth in 1654 that he and his officers 'must watch ourselves from off of our legs, to preserve the boat from being stole away from the stern'.[119] A corporal on watch who shot a

[115] *FDW* iii. 96, iv. 56, 65, 231.
[116] *FDW* vi. 253; SP 18/96/50; *CSPD 1653–4*, 6.   [117] Rawl. MS C 381, p. 24.
[118] *FDW* iii. 297; SP 18/38/121; *A Perfect Account*, 22–9 Aug. 1655.
[119] SP 18/84/83; SP 18/90/82. Blake stressed the need to keep boats firmly chained when not in use: NMM UPC/1, fo. 2.

deserter trying to escape this way was acquitted by a court martial on the grounds that he was merely doing his duty.[120] In 1655 Thomas Bunn requested two files of troops, to help with pressing and to stop men he had already taken aboard from deserting. Every ship, he suggested, should carry soldiers for this purpose. Soldiers were sometimes used to strengthen the watch in harbour, though even they could not prevent men leaping overboard and swimming ashore.[121] Some ships therefore came into port only when it was absolutely unavoidable, and they sometimes tallowed at sea. During the Dutch war Edmund Chapman of the *Golden Cock* thought it quite impossible to keep men on board in harbour and chose to remain out even when the enemy fleet was close by.[122]

The Admiralty too did all it could to check desertion. Its policy of paying wages only in part was one response to the problem, and officials constantly sought other ways to solve it. When Commissioner Pett found a new site for tallowing on a small island near Sheerness he stressed that it added 'much to the comfort of the place that the seamen could not get away'.[123] An observer at Portsmouth in 1653 noted that when the seamen went back to their ships to be paid they were 'kept on board, and not suffered to go on shore again to fetch their clothes, and to take their leave of their friends' lest they desert.[124] Similarly the sailors of the *Marston Moor* were forbidden to go ashore when they arrived home from Jamaica in 1655, for the ship was due to return there and they had vowed to be hanged before they would go back. An official who came to pay them on board was told they would then all desert, so he went away again taking the money with him.[125]

The government made its own contribution by deploying troops on a large scale during the Dutch war to round up sailors who had run. Soldiers lay in wait on the main roads between Portsmouth and London to intercept them and return them to the fleet. Such measures were very effective, though they soured relations between

[120] SP 18/174/60; *CSPD 1657–8*, 440.

[121] SP 18/58/82; SP 18/109/94.

[122] *CSPD 1652–3*, 592.

[123] SP 18/141/148–9; SP 18/147/2.

[124] *FDW* vi. 176.

[125] The last blow proved too much: 150 men abandoned the ship and set off for London to complain. Though many lost heart and turned back, the new captain (Myngs) found the crew so 'base' and uncooperative that he insisted on a new one before sailing. SP 18/114/119; SP 18/115/83, 143; SP 18/116/15, 133; Dyer, 'Myngs', 173–5.

sailors and soldiers yet further. Local magistrates were also directed to set guards on roads leading to London from Kent, Essex and East Anglia.[126]

Sailors who were unable or unwilling to desert might organize a petition for redress of their grievances. This was quite acceptable provided it was organized with the captain's knowledge and consent and forwarded through him.[127] But the authorities responded sharply if the sailors went over his head, for any petition concealed from those in authority had a whiff of sedition, however deferentially it was phrased. The men of the *Bramble* were most apologetic about asking for their wages in 1658, 'knowing your Honours' thoughts are employed about more sublime matters', but the Commissioners still scolded the captain for failing to discover and suppress their petition and they ignored its contents.[128] A 'round robin' discovered in Mountagu's fleet in 1657 was treated very seriously indeed, four ringleaders being sentenced to death by a court martial. Cromwell himself was said to regard it as 'a very mutinous attempt', and he made the four cast lots for their lives, though the loser was eventually reprieved.[129]

The sailors' ultimate weapon was mutiny. Mutiny at sea directed against the ship's officers was very rare.[130] Far more common were disorders in harbour, directed against the authorities ashore. Most are best seen as strikes: the men simply refused to go back aboard their ships or put to sea until their grievances were righted. More serious disorders broke out when large numbers of seamen were left without pay or with tickets they were unable to cash, as had happened earlier in the late 1620s. The first new trouble of this kind came in 1648, from men discharged in the aftermath of the revolt: two of the Navy Commissioners reported that the unruly seamen 'not only threaten our persons, but the pulling down our offices and our own houses', and begged for protection.[131]

---

[126] *FDW* iv. 218, v. 259, vi. 169; Rawl. MS A 227, fos. 11ᵛ, 53.

[127] e.g. SP 18/137/111–2; SP 18/140/12.

[128] Add. MS 18986, fo. 286; Adm. 2/1730, fo. 277; cf. NMM REC/1, fos. 74–5; *CSPD 1651–2*, 504, 511.

[129] Adm. 2/1730, fos. 110, 116. Its contents are unknown. The large-scale petitioning in 1654 probably began with the approval of officers such as Lawson. The council of war forwarded the petitions to the Generals rather than directly to Cromwell, so observing the proprieties; see ch. 5, above.

[130] See ch. 7, part i, above.

[131] Bodl. Tanner MS 56, fo. 258.

The Dutch war strained naval finances to breaking-point and produced trouble on a much larger scale. Disorders broke out in numerous ships when the fleet came in at the close of 1652; many of them were hired merchantmen, whose crews suspected the owners of fraud when they found they were being paid for only part of their service. The *London*'s men defied their officers and went ashore at Gravesend, carrying their sea-chests with them, and fifty of the *Reformation*'s crew marched to Whitehall to put their demands in person.[132] With huge numbers of men back from sea and clamouring for wages the situation was obviously ripe for trouble. The unrest continued for several weeks, becoming so widespread that even the phlegmatic Blake and Monck feared there might be a plot behind it.[133] There were similar disorders at Portsmouth. Several ships were strike-bound, the men refusing to stir till they had their wages in full, and it was reported that one of their leaders 'hath broke the pay-house windows and threatened to pull down the house'.[134] Capt. Thomas Thoroughgood of the hired *Crescent* penned a graphic account of the mood there. His men thought the owners were cheating them of part of their pay and 'swore they would have it all or else the ship should lie here and rot', Thoroughgood reported, 'and they are grown to such a height that they will not be at my command, but do what they please'. When he went below decks one night to stop their 'singing and roaring' they declared 'they would not be under my command, so I struck one of them, and the rest put out the candle and took hold of me as though they would have torn me to pieces, so that I am almost beside myself, not knowing what to do'.[135] There was trouble at Bristol too and at Plymouth, where the mayor himself had allegedly advised sailors not to go aboard their ships till they were paid.[136] It was alarm at the extent of these disorders, coming on top of the defeat at Dungeness, that prompted the Rump to push through its far-reaching package of reforms at the end of 1652.

Trouble occurred on a still larger scale in the autumn of 1653 when the fleet came in after a long and bloody campaign. At Chatham Commissioner Pett ordered the seamen to refit their ships

[132] *FDW* iii. 382; Tanner MS 53, fos. 150–1; NMM REC/1, fos. 74–5; NMM HSR/A/27.
[133] NMM AGC/B/ 8.
[134] *FDW* iii. 311–12, 337, 366.
[135] *FDW* iii. 164–5, 279.
[136] *CSPD 1652–3*, 305, 572; SP 18/37/75.

before they were paid; they flatly refused, suspecting—reasonably enough—that they would be sent back to sea with neither wages nor leave. Two hundred men from the *Unicorn* marched on Pett's office on 5 October and refused to go back on board till they were paid in full, and other companies were equally mutinous. Pett pleaded with them in vain; the sailors 'cried one and all for London' and made off.[137] Over the next three weeks thousands more angry seamen poured into the city, and on 26–7 October rioting broke out at Tower Hill and elsewhere. On the first day the men eventually dispersed when Cromwell and Monck met them and promised their wages. Next day however the rioting was worse, a large, armed mob advancing on Whitehall with drums beating. This time the sailors found their path barred by Cromwell's Lifeguard and a substantial body of troops, and an ugly fray ensued. The Council issued a proclamation the same day threatening savage reprisals if the rioting continued, and on the 28th Parliament rushed through an additional article of war (with retrospective force) imposing the death penalty for riots ashore. One ringleader was later hanged on Tower Hill for drawing his sword on Monck, and another was whipped beneath the gallows with a halter round his neck.[138]

There was trouble too at other bases, notably Harwich and Portsmouth. At Harwich Bourne reported angry sailors from the *Assurance* and *Mermaid* roaming the streets demanding money and clothes, and large bands of them marched into the countryside smashing down gates and stiles. The atmosphere in the town remained tense for several weeks.[139] At Portsmouth the crew of the *Portland*, armed with pistols and other weapons, took over part of the ship in defiance of their officers, laying hands on the captain and assaulting the master. A court martial subsequently condemned six ringleaders to death, and though they were later reprieved their punishment was savage: three had their right hands nailed to the mainmast for several hours with halters round their necks, while the others suffered thirty lashes apiece. Copies of the sentence were sent to the other ships at Portsmouth for all 'to read and take warning by'.[140] This was the harshest treatment of mutineers

---

[137] *FDW* vi. 107–8; *CSPD 1653–4*, 191–2.

[138] Gardiner, *CP* iii. 58–9; *Weekly Intelligencer*, 25 Oct.–1 Nov. 1653; *Severall Proceedings*, 25 Oct.–1 Nov.; *Moderate Publisher*, 28 Oct.–3 Nov.; *CSPD 1653–4*, 219; *FDW* vi. 133–4; *Thurloe*, i. 576–7.

[139] *FDW* vi. 129, 168–9, 176.

[140] SP 18/42/80, part ii; SP 18/61/6.

throughout the period. Nerves were on edge, and the court no doubt felt that seamen who had seized their ship and manhandled their officers had committed a much graver offence than sailors who were 'on strike' ashore.

The seamen's riots of 1653 were the worst since the late 1620s, when large numbers of unpaid and riotous sailors returning from expeditions against France and Spain had similarly poured into London; more recently seamen had joined in the rioting of 1641 and 1642 which had helped to destroy the king's control of his capital.[141] The Protectorate was determined to prevent any recurrence of such threats to public order and generally succeeded in paying off the main fleets as soon as they returned to port. Though disorders still broke out occasionally in individual ships over lack of wages they were relatively small in scale.[142] Money for the navy was still chronically short but the Protectorate had learned how to minimize the consequences.

Lack of pay, however, was not the only cause of strikes and disorders. Rotten provisions could also trigger action, and the seamen's anger sometimes erupted into violence against the victuallers they held to blame. At Milford in 1656 the crew of the *Basing* stormed ashore vowing to demolish the victualling-house. Two years later part of a victualling-house at Rochester was smashed down by a band of seamen from the *Maidstone* and several other ships, no doubt a highly satisfactory way of releasing their feelings.[143] Lack of clothing was another common contributory factor. On a very few occasions sailors went on strike because they felt their ship itself posed a threat to life and health. In 1654 the crew of the *Truelove* flatly refused to put to sea unless another ship sailed in company, claiming their own was so rotten and leaky she was certain to sink.[144]

Many captains clearly sympathized with the sufferings of their men and played a mediating role when trouble broke out. While

---

[141] For the late 1620s see R. Lockyer, *Buckingham: The Life and Political Career of George Villiers, First Duke of Buckingham, 1592–1628* (1984 edn.), 340, 342–44, 361–2, 420–1, 447–8, 452–3. K. J. Lindley, 'Riot Prevention and Control in Early Stuart London', *Transactions of the Royal Historical Soc.*, 5th ser., xxxiii (1983), 112–13.

[142] SP 18/139/81–2; *CSPD 1657–8*, 531, 533–4.

[143] SP 18/141/33: SP 18/183/86, 94; Adm. 2/1730, fos. 261, 264.

[144] For the *Truelove* see Rawl. MS A 184, fo. 406. For other disputes over rotten clothing or ships see *CSPD 1657–8*, 531, 533; *CSPD 1659–60*, 122; Adm. 7/674/95; SP 46/119, fo. 108; *CSPD 1650*, 209.

trying to restore order they laid stress on the seamen's justified grievances, hoping that these mitigating circumstances would avert retribution. Capt. Penrose of the *Maidstone* clearly understood what had provoked his men to demolish the victualling-house at Rochester. He told the Admiralty he was not able to name any of the ringleaders and chose instead to emphasize the justice of the seamen's complaints: the food supplied had been 'full of maggots, and so rotten that no dog would eat it', and the victualler had threatened to send worse if they dared to complain.[145] When Gabriel Saunders's men staged a similar attack at Harwich he too stressed how they had been provoked by loathsome provisions and by the victuallers' contemptuous indifference.[146] The authorities sometimes suspected officers indeed of conniving at mutiny. Very occasionally there is evidence to justify their suspicions. A court martial in 1659 sacked the lieutenant of the *Guinea* for urging his sailors not to take the ship to sea; he had told them whimsically that she let in so much water she was more suitable for ducks than men! The clerk of the *Sophia* was alleged to have stood on the forecastle as the men hauled in the anchor, calling them fools to sail till they had their pay.[147] But such cases were exceptional; captains had no wish to subvert discipline, however much they sympathized with the plight of their men.

On the whole the authorities too responded to 'mutinies' and strikes with moderation. When crews refused to put to sea or made their captains return early the Commissioners merely detained the ringleaders for a few days, withholding their wages, and paid off the rest. The Navy Commissioners most directly involved with disturbances during the Dutch war always tried first to restore order by peaceful persuasion. If this failed they steered a middle course, offering concessions while mounting a limited display of force to encourage the mutineers to accept. Thus at Portsmouth when the *President*'s men refused to go to sea till they were paid, at the close of 1652, Willoughby promised to have money waiting for them on their next return; when they rejected this offer he allowed them to remain in harbour, arranging for the ship to be refitted while they waited for their wages to arrive. He faced more serious trouble when the pay took place, and had to use both carrot and stick to restore order, discharging the more 'unstable spirits' and arresting a

[145] SP 18/183/86; Adm. 2/1730, fos. 261, 264.
[146] *CSPD 1656–7*, 551; *CSPD 1657–8*, 531.
[147] *CSPD 1659–60*, 122; Rawl. MS A 184, fo. 359ʳ⁻ᵛ.

number of trouble-makers. Interestingly, he chose not to inform the Admiralty Commissioners in London of this disturbance, and when they heard by another source he commented, 'I thought it more convenient to bury it than otherwise'. He admitted releasing the prisoners after a few days, and argued that moderation was the best way to win the seamen's co-operation: 'Your Honours know that they are men of turbulent spirit, and must sometimes be dealt withal with as much tenderness as may be.'[148] The other Navy Commissioners adopted a very similar approach. Bourne used 'fair persuasive language with promises' when he encountered mutinous sailors in the streets of Harwich in October 1653, and eventually restored order by briefly imprisoning four leading dissidents and paying off the rest. (Some of the money was paid out, prudently, only when the men were back on board and at sea once more.)[149] Though Bourne often became infuriated at the unruliness of the seamen, branding them as 'wicked wretches', 'below the beasts that perish', he never pressed for severe penalties and regarded a brief imprisonment of ringleaders as punishment enough.[150]

There were two main reasons for this general moderation. First, the officials in the front line clearly sympathized with the seamen's plight. Hatsell at Plymouth explained in January 1653 that the mutinous sailors of the *Expedition* were owed two years' pay and were reduced to rags; many also had families in want. They had assured him that as soon as they were paid they would nevertheless readily serve again, and he accepted that they had good cause to complain. Bourne too was critical of the Admiralty, pointing out the folly of keeping seamen hanging about ashore unpaid while tempers frayed. Willoughby observed that in such circumstances they inevitably ran up large bills for drink and lodgings which they might then be unable to pay, a sure recipe for trouble.[151] Second, common sense also suggested restraint. An official confronting a crowd of angry seamen knew that he was dangerously exposed and that fair words served better than empty threats. Bourne once explained that he had been 'more mild than otherwise I should' because he lacked the force needed for any firmer course.[152] At Plymouth the corporation itself had thought it wise to appease the

[148] *FDW* iii. 301, 311-2, 438-9.
[149] *FDW* vi. 128-30, 168-9, 172-3.
[150] *FDW* v. 295, vi. 174.
[151] *FDW* iii. 377, 438, vi. 129-30. A strike at Portsmouth in 1658 was blamed on landladies who wanted their rent and persuaded seamen not to go back to their ships till their wages were paid: *CSPD 1657-8*, 536.   [152] *FDW* iii. 366, vi. 101.

mutinous seamen of Ayscue's squadron, back from Barbados in 1652, by giving them money to buy drink.[153]

Officials were determined though not to undermine their authority by giving way completely. Pett offered some concessions to mutineers at Chatham in October 1653, but he thought it would be dangerous and dishonourable to concede their demands in full and wrote urgently to London for a troop of horse to be sent down. His ideal was to have some soldiers available at all times to strengthen his authority and round up deserters.[154] Similarly at Harwich Bourne sometimes called in soldiers from the nearby Landguard Fort and cavalry from Colchester. He thought it essential to have troops within easy reach, and threatened to resign when it was proposed to abandon a small fort in Harwich itself, manned by the Landguard garrison. Without soldiers, he pleaded, 'there will be no living here, or keeping up any face of authority'.[155]

Though officials liked to have soldiers close by they preferred to restore order by persuasion and compromise, combining partial redress with a limited show of force. They knew the hardships which had driven the seamen to protest, and chose to ignore the ferocious disciplinary code they could have invoked. A naval mutiny or strike in the mid-seventeenth century had many parallels with a contemporary food riot.[156] Both were designed primarily to trigger action on the part of the competent authorities, by bringing the gravity of the situation to their attention. In many cases rioters and mutineers succeeded in this aim: the authorities, alerted to the scale of the problem, provided relief to head off greater unrest, imposing some (often quite mild) punishment on a few ringleaders to preserve the proprieties. It was, of course, a risky strategy: if the agitators went too far they were seen not as demonstrators but as enemies of the state, and retribution could be fierce. But the naval authorities usually responded with sense and discretion. The abiding impression is of moderation, with mutineers and officials tacitly agreeing to ignore the formal conventions and proceed by a far more flexible, unwritten code of their own.

[153] R. N. Worth (ed.), *Calendar of Plymouth Municipal Records* (Plymouth, 1893), 164.

[154] *FDW* vi. 107–8; SP 18/60/107. Troops had been sent to Chatham to keep order at the pay there the previous January: Rawl. MS A 227, fo. 7.

[155] *FDW* vi. 83, 86–7, 100–1, 103, 129.

[156] J. Walter and K. Wrightson, 'Dearth and the Social Order in Early Modern England', *Past and Present*, lxxi (1976).

9

Saints Afloat? Religion in the Fleet

In most periods religion has a very marginal place in naval history. A recent, thorough study of the Hanoverian navy omits the subject, on the grounds that the sources provide virtually no material.[1] The sources for the 1650s, by contrast, leave no doubt whatever that under the Commonwealth religion played a central and probably unparalleled part in naval life.

I. THE OFFICER CORPS

Many of the leaders of the new officer corps created after 1649 were men of strong and radical religious outlook.[2] At the very highest level, two of the first three Generals at Sea (Blake and Deane) were firm Puritans. Blake, a very early opponent of the Laudians, had offered to stand at a by-election in Bridgwater in 1642 mainly to help Puritan MPs expel the bishops from Parliament. Popham's views are little known but were probably close to those of Blake, his long-standing associate. Though Penn and Mountagu are best known to us through Pepys's *Diary* as worldly figures of the Restoration age their earlier careers give a very different impression. Penn's journals and correspondence make it much easier to see how he came to win Cromwell's affection: they reveal a man much given to pious reflections, who called frequent prayer meetings 'to seek the Lord' and enforced the sabbath strictly. His journal of a voyage to the Straits in 1650 begins with the words: 'I humbly implore the Lord for his direction, protection, preservation, and that I may act nothing but what may tend to his glory, the good of his people, and the eternal comfort of my own soul, when this world shall be no

[1] N. A. M. Rodger, *The Wooden World: An Anatomy of the Georgian Navy* (1986), 11–12.
[2] See chs. 3, 6, above.

more. In God's name and strength, not in my own, I humbly desire to proceed.' Blackborne recalled after the Restoration that it had been Penn's 'pretence of sanctity that brought him into play. Lawson and Poortmans and the Fifth Monarchy Men, among whom he was a great brother, importuned that he might be General.' Though this account was coloured by bias and exaggeration it almost certainly had a kernel of truth.[3] Mountagu's earlier reputation was also that of a religious radical. He had been known in the 1640s as a supporter of sectaries and lay preaching, and while this side of his character was fading by the mid-1650s some echoes remained.[4] Of the six Generals who served afloat only Monck was largely secular in spirit. Significantly he thought it prudent in 1653 to adopt the religious rhetoric of his radical colleagues, making good use of their Fifth Monarchist secretary, John Poortmans; even so there were rumours that he would be laid aside as too worldly.[5] A similar pattern can be found among the lesser flag-officers. Lawson's religious radicalism was well known. Richard Badiley belonged to the Independent church at Stepney, and wrote at some length on religious matters.[6] William Goodson had been a follower of the Puritan minister William Bridge at Yarmouth; Bridge fled to The Netherlands in the 1630s to escape Laudian persecution and Goodson settled there too, perhaps for the same reason. By the late 1640s he belonged to a separatist church in Wapping. Nehemiah and John Bourne had been among Puritan emigrants to Massachusetts. Even Stayner had been picked out by Blake for promotion as a 'godly and valiant man'; and so on.[7]

[3] J. Oldmixon, *The History and Life of Robert Blake, Esq.* (1740), 6; J. H. Bettey (ed.), *Calendar of the Correspondence of the Smyth Family of Ashton Court, 1548–1642* (British Record Soc., xxxv; 1982), 168. For Penn's journal see NMM WYN/4/5; see also Penn, *Memorials, passim*. For Blackborne's comments see Pepys, *Diary*, iv. 375.

[4] *A Second Narrative of the Late Parliament* (1658), 6 (2nd pagination); see also his effusion on providence in Sept. 1656: *Thurloe*, v. 433.

[5] Compare Monck's letter of 31 July 1653 in *FDW* v. 347–50 with Poortmans's letters, published as *A True Relation of the Late Great Fight* ([4 Aug.] 1653). Poortmans probably drafted Monck's letters. See also *FDW* v. 302, vi. 220. For the rumour about Monck: *CCSP* ii. 262. His chaplain later claimed that Monck '(though without ostentation) was truly religious': T. Gumble, *The Life of General Monck* (1671), 184.

[6] R. Badiley, *The Sea-men Undeceived* (1648), esp. 34, where he cites his substantial (unpublished?) religious writings. He joined the Stepney gathered church in 1653: Stepney Church Book (see below, list of sources), fo. 2ᵛ.

[7] Goodson: 'Baptisms and Deaths recorded in the Church Book of the Great Yarmouth Independent Church, 1643–1705', in *A Miscellany* (Norfolk Record Soc.,

Puritanism in the fleet had parallels in the administration ashore. In the first weeks after Pride's Purge naval affairs were dominated by the Rumper Miles Corbet, another follower of Bridge at Yarmouth. Religious radicals such as Walton and Vane were prominent among the Admiralty Commissioners appointed early in 1649, and Vane and Carew were leading members of the new body of Commissioners established late in 1652. Barebone's Parliament added others of the same type, including the Fifth Monarchist Nathaniel Rich and the Independents Desborough, Burton, and Kelsey; another recruit, the Baptist Dennis Hollister, subsequently became a Quaker.[8] The more radical figures dropped out when Cromwell became Protector, but Kelsey remained in office and the New Englander Edward Hopkins was among his colleagues. The Navy Commissioners, the workhorses of the administration, included several Puritan New Englanders, probably recruited through Vane—Willoughby, Hopkins, Bourne, and Hutchinson, the Treasurer.[9] At a slightly lower level, Robert Blackborne, secretary to the Admiralty Commissioners, acted as friend, guide, and spiritual counsellor to numerous officers and officials.[10]

The dockyards show a similar pattern. The Chatham yard remained a centre of religious radicalism for many years, despite fierce struggles between rival preachers and their partisans. A conventicle there was led after the Restoration by the Master Attendant of the yard, the Baptist Thomas Arkinstall.[11] The Master Attendant at Portsmouth was an 'Anabaptist', the master shipwright at Harwich, Robert Grassingham, was a leading Quaker by the late 1650s, and the influential navy agent at Plymouth, Hatsell, was a zealous Puritan who counted Blackborne as his 'dear friend'.[12] The list could be greatly extended.

Senior appointments in the navy reflected the wishes of the flag-officers and Admiralty Commissioners, who naturally favoured

xxii; 1951), 10–11; PRO SP 18/89/14; D. Brown, *Two Conferences* (1650), 1, 9. Stayner: Blake, *Letters*, 239 (where for *Forester* read *Foresight*). For the Bournes and other senior religious radicals see above, chs. 3, 6.

[8] See chs. 3–5, above. Desborough belonged (later at least) to John Owen's congregation.   [9] For Hopkins see Chaplin, 'Bourne', 70.
[10] G. Aylmer, *The State's Servants* (1973), 266–7.
[11] For Chatham see below; for Arkinstall see 'The Baptist Licences of 1672', *Transactions of the Baptist Historical Soc.*, iii. (1912–13), 173.
[12] For the Master Attendant (Thoroughgood at Portsmouth) and Grassingham see Bodl. Carte MS 73, fo. 403'; B. Reay, *The Quakers and the English Revolution* (1985), 105; for Hatsell and Blackborne see e.g. PRO Adm. 7/674/21.

men with views akin to their own. Between 1649 and the end of 1653 religious commitment was a very important criterion in selecting officers. The period when the radicals were most firmly in control of the Admiralty (December 1652–December 1653) coincided with the rapid expansion of the fleet in the Dutch war, and the flood of appointments made at this time influenced the character of the officer corps to the very end of the interregnum.[13] Prominent Independent ministers took it upon themselves to press the claims of godly mariners they knew, with considerable success. Among the most active were Hugh Peter, a New Englander and one of Cromwell's chaplains, William Greenhill of Stepney, Thomas Brookes of St Margaret's, Westminster (formerly chaplain to Vice-Admiral Rainborough), and William Bridge of Great Yarmouth, who in 1653 was indeed asked by the Admiralty to recruit godly shipmasters into the navy.[14]

The natural outcome of these influences was the growth of a substantial Puritan bloc among the officers. Using a wide variety of sources we can identify about a hundred captains of this type, over a quarter of the total; there may well have been others, for in many cases no evidence has survived concerning officers' religious opinions. It is of course a crude statistic, taking no account of the varying nature, intensity, or duration of religious commitment. But it confirms the Puritans' importance, especially as they are most prominent among senior commanders and flag-officers — partly through better documentation and partly through the favour and promotion they received.[15] The parallels with the officer corps of the New Model Army are obvious.

Religious enthusiasts in the navy had a clear sense of fraternity in a common cause. When Lawson was promoted rear-admiral in March 1653, for example, Blackborne wrote to him seeking a closer acquaintance; Lawson replied that he too was eager to establish 'that union which ought to be amongst the members of that body, whereof Jesus Christ is the head'. At a humbler level Deane wrote on behalf of an officer who was anxious to serve as lieutenant, but only in a ship 'whereof a godly man is captain'.[16] Occasionally

---

[13] Ch. 6, above.

[14] All are in *DNB*; for the invitation to Bridge see Bodl. Rawlinson MS A 227, fo. 56ᵛ. Brookes had preached Rainborough's funeral sermon in 1648.

[15] This estimate is based on letters, testimonials, church membership records, and some wills. The records are too sketchy to permit any estimate for junior officers, though most captains had of course risen from their ranks.

[16] SP 18/48/141; SP 18/55/20.

ambition or clashes of temperament overwhelmed the ties of faith, as in the feud between the Independents Goodson and Benjamin Blake in the West Indies, but the prevailing impression is of solidarity.[17] General Deane expressed satisfaction at the list of commanders selected for the summer guard of 1653, 'knowing most of them as godly men'.[18] Their sense of fraternity found expression in numerous 'Days for seeking the Lord'. Penn held a day of prayer in his flagship when setting out for the Straits in 1650, with four chaplains leading the prayers and all the captains in attendance. After a similar occasion he noted, 'blessed for ever be his great and glorious name, we found much comfort'. When they were homeward-bound he and his captains resolved to spend another day 'in praising the Lord for his great mercies, and to implore him for the continuance of them'.[19] He followed the same practice in the Caribbean in 1654–5, though presumably with rather less comfort. On a day appointed to seek the Lord's presence on the homeward voyage the *Paragon* caught fire and sank with heavy loss of life, confirming the sense that God had been signally absent throughout the ill-fated expedition.[20] Blake held similar days of fasting and seeking God. When Admiralty Commissioners arrived from London for urgent consultations late in 1652, following the defeat at Dungeness, they had to wait patiently till evening, when the religious exercises would end.[21] Blake summoned his officers to seek God's presence and blessing before the attacks on Porto Farina and Santa Cruz, and on other occasions too.[22] The most intriguing prayer-meeting took place in his flagship one evening early in 1653 when he was searching the Channel for the Dutch fleet, anxious lest it slip by in the fog. The company 'asked God to tell us where they [sc. the Dutch] were, and the answer was made out of those words in the 2 Chron. xx. 16, which then was the chapter spoken out of; and no sooner did daylight dawn, but betwixt us and the shore we saw the enemy's fleet'. The victory off Portland followed. It was not of course the scriptural text ('Tomorrow go ye down against them: behold they

[17] For the feud see ch. 6, sect. iv; for their church affiliations see nn. 7 above, 54, 58 below.
[18] *CSPD 1652–3*, 297; the captains serving that summer are listed in *FDW* v. 16–20.
[19] Penn, *Memorials*, i. 318, 339, 369, 388.
[20] BL Sloane MS 3926, pp. 35, 37; Penn, *Memorials*, ii. 127–8; WYN/10/2, 9 Feb., 9 Mar., 13 July 1655; 'Richard Rooth's Sea Journal of the Western Design, 1654–5', ed. J. F. Battick, *Jamaica Journal*, v (1971), 5, 9, 20.
[21] Rawl. MS A 227, fo. 20.
[22] Blake, *Letters*, 320, 386; *The Publick Intelligencer*, 25 May–1 June 1657.

come up by the cliff of Ziz') which had guided the English to the right place, but the apparent speedy fulfilment of God's promise and the great victory must have seemed dramatic proof that the Lord was indeed with them.[23]

The navy, like the army, contained a considerable number of preaching officers. A chaplain of conservative views complained that 'preaching seamen, and preaching sea-captains' were signs of a 'mad age' (along with female preachers and 'women politicians').[24] Edward Mauditt of the *Lion* served simultaneously as lieutenant and chaplain in 1651–2. Capt. Robert Coleman led the ship's services himself if the chaplain was away.[25] Some captains had the confidence to engage in religious polemic. Robert Dornford published two lively tracts on Christian faith and life, in which he defended the separatists while denouncing Ranter excesses. Thomas Penrose of the *Bristol*, a Baptist, was able to unleash a battery of scriptural citations against a petty officer who had converted to Quakerism.[26] Many officers were indeed steeped in scripture, as their correspondence reveals. Only in this period, perhaps, would a commander describe a storm at sea by telling the Admiralty that he had 'experienced the words of the 26th and 27th verses of the 107th Psalm to the letter'.[27]

What kind of faith did these officers possess? Its most striking feature was a conviction that they were serving God's cause and were merely the instruments of divine providence. In 1650 Charles Saltonstall marvelled how Rupert's squadron had been destroyed when most of the parliamentary force had already returned home, leaving 'little of the arm of flesh amongst us'. 'Thus hath God owned us in the midst of our implacable enemies,' he wrote, 'so that the terror of God is amongst them, five chaseth a hundred and ten a thousand, which is marvellous in our eyes'.[28] Nicholas Heaton, a highly successful captain during the Spanish war, observed to Blackborne: 'You know, I know, all men know: often instruments

[23] *FDW* iv. 94, 164.

[24] D. Pell, *Nec Inter Vivos, Nec Inter Mortuos* (1659), sig. d.

[25] *CSPD 1651–2*, 120, 220, 411; Rawl. MS A 226, fo. 14. Mauditt was probably the former lieutenant/chaplain preaching at Deptford in 1655: *The Diary of John Evelyn*, ed. E. S. de Beer (Oxford, 1955), iii. 147. For Coleman see SP 18/150/68.

[26] R. Dornford, *Gospel-Light and Gospel-Life* (1652), esp. 57, 69–80; idem, *Gospel Mysterie* (1652), 50–2. Dornford adds a few details to the story of the pseudo-messiah John Robins and his disciple Joshua Garment. For Penrose see T. Lurting, *The Fighting Sailor, turned Peaceable Christian* (1801), 11 ff.

[27] *CSPD 1654*, 585.   [28] Blake, *Letters*, 91.

by thousands fall, yet God's design shall go on'.[29] Blake and Deane
reported victories much as Cromwell had done in the 1640s, with
euphoria tempered by a sense of human weakness. Shortly before
Portland they wrote to Parliament: 'We dare not in this great
business to promise anything for or to ourselves, because it is God
alone who giveth courage and conduct.'[30]

While victory was naturally seen as proof of divine favour the
doctrine of providence was much more than a crude rationalization
of success. Blake, like Cromwell, was often wracked by uncertainty
and turned to providence for guidance. At Porto Farina in 1655 he
was unsure whether an attack was prudent or even covered by his
instructions. He gave the eventual order partly on impulse,
incensed by the Moors' provocation, but he turned to providence to
justify it. God had provided perfect weather conditions during the
operation, after which a long spell of stormy weather ensued; 'the
Lord afforded that nick of time, in which it was done. And now,
seeing it hath pleased God so signally to justify us therein, I hope
his Highness will not be offended by it'. When he encountered a
Spanish fleet the following year, however, the strange twists of
providence convinced him that this time the Lord did not wish to
see battle joined; once more he explained his reasoning and hoped
Cromwell would understand.[31]

Providence was a less comfortable faith in times of adversity. We
find Blake ruminating on 'divers mixed providences, and strange
dispensations, never to be forgotten by us'.[32] Lawson pondered the
meaning of the English defeat by the Dutch in the Straits, conclud-
ing that even 'the most cross providence' must be a secret blessing:
if 'mercies were not mixed with some bitter pills' men would grow
careless of God's power and will.[33] John Bourne had to confront the
problem directly in 1654 when storms battered his ship on its way
to Newfoundland and forced him to limp home. He confided his
doubts at length to Secretary Blackborne, 'as to one of whom I have
heard much of godliness and Christian experience'. 'My spirit is
very much cast down', he admitted, for he feared God had rejected
him as an unworthy instrument. After more soul-searching he

[29] SP 18/111/92.

[30] Blake, *Letters*, 203. For Cromwell and providence see C. Hill, *God's
Englishman* (1970), ch. 9; B. Worden, 'Providence and Politics in Cromwellian
England', *Past and Present*, cix (1985), 55–99; see also K. V. Thomas, *Religion and
the Decline of Magic* (1971), ch. 4.

[31] Blake, *Letters*, 294–5, 307, 309.   [32] Ibid. 287.   [33] SP 18/34/113.

wrote again a few days later. In times of adversity 'it is not so easy a
matter to live the life of faith', he confessed ruefully, but it was a
'very poor and base kind of spirit, when believers cannot trust God
no further than they see him'. He resolved—like Cromwell and
Milton—to serve God as best he might, however inscrutable the
divine purpose might be; his own fate as a minor instrument was of
no account. Setting out with Blake against Spain in 1656 he
described himself in deprecating terms as 'a poor sinful worm,
unworthy altogether to be employed in the meanest and lowest part
of God's work'; what mattered was the work itself which, he
added, 'I am confident is the Lord's'.[34]

For many God's work had an apocalyptic character. When the
Rump was driven out in 1653 Deane hoped that 'Christ alone may
be exalted, which is the end of all these terrible shakings'.[35] Many
saw the wars against the Dutch and Spaniards as heralds of Christ's
approaching kingdom and signs of Babylon's impending fall.[36] An
elegy on Deane mentioned the hope that he would have knocked at
the gates of Rome had he lived. An elegy on Blake, by one of his
officers, listed among the admiral's many virtues that 'he was a
zealous hater of the scarlet whore'.[37] There are numerous examples
of anti-Catholic bigotry scattered among the navy papers. Capt.
Henry Fenn casually referred to the pope as 'his abominableness'.
John Weale described priests leading a procession through the
streets of Alicante as 'deceivers, ravening wolves', and on a later
occasion he and friends provoked trouble at a mass in Lisbon by
their disrespectful behaviour.[38] The persecution of the Waldensians
by the Catholic Duke of Savoy in 1655, which prompted Milton's
famous sonnet, also aroused concern in the fleet. John Bourne,
commanding the squadron in the Downs, called a day of fasting and
organized a collection for the relief of the victims.[39]

One of the signs widely believed to herald the coming of Christ
was the conversion and return of the Jews, and some radicals
thought the navy had a part to play in this process. The preacher

---

[34] BL Add. MS 18986, fos. 178–9; SP 18/87/52; Add. MS 19367, fo. 12.

[35] *FDW* iv. 368–9.

[36] See ch. 5, above.

[37] J. R., *An Elegie upon the Death of . . . Deane* (1653) (BL 669 f 17 (21));
G. Harrison, *An Elegie on the Death of . . . Blake* (1657) (BL 669 f 20 (61)).

[38] *CSPD 1658–9*, 301; 'The Journal of John Weale', ed. J. R. Powell, in *The Naval
Miscellany*, iv (NRS, 1952) 96, 124.

[39] SP 18/97/87–8.

Christopher Feake declared in 1653: 'We shall carry the Gospel with our navy up and down to the Gentiles, and afterward we shall gather home the Jews . . . the ships of Tharsis shall do it'.[40] The previous year the captain, chaplain, and several officers of the *Phoenix* had visited a synagogue at Leghorn and discussed the Jews' conversion with an English-speaking worshipper who predicted the fall of Antichrist and the coming of the Messiah within ten years. The officers sent home a report of their encounter which appeared in the newspapers, with the Jew's request that his people should be allowed to settle in England once more.[41] Lt. Weale and his friends also visited the synagogue, some years later.[42] A rumour in Amsterdam late in 1654, that the Generals at Sea had petitioned Cromwell for the return of the Jews to England, was thus by no means absurd even if it lacked foundation.[43] The Protector established a commission to investigate the issue and a lively public debate ensued. The Navy Commissioner at Portsmouth, Francis Willoughby, discussed the matter at some length with Secretary Blackborne, and felt so strongly about the Jews that they took precedence over official business in his letters.[44]

The Puritan officers were strict sabbatarians, as we would expect. Penn circulated stern instructions against the profanation of the sabbath when his fleet was at Barbados late in 1654. He forbade sailors to go ashore, even when they claimed to be going to a religious service; they were told to visit another ship if there was no minister in their own. The journal kept by Richard Rooth during the expedition contains the recurring entry, 'Being Lord's day, nothing was done', which suggests that the sabbath was indeed strictly observed.[45] Richard Badiley, commanding a squadron in the Straits, was shocked to hear that English merchant seamen had profaned the sabbath by taking part in an Italian carnival, dressed in women's clothes, and even more scandalized that their commander had gone ashore to watch them. When their ship was destroyed by

[40] D. S. Katz, *Philo-Semitism and the Readmission of the Jews to England, 1603–1655* (Oxford, 1982); for Feake see L. F. Brown, *The Political Activities of the Baptists and Fifth Monarchy Men* (1911), 24 n.
[41] *Severall Proceedings*, 29 Apr.–6 May 1652; H. Jessey, *A Narrative of the late Proceeds [sic] at White-hall* (1656), 11; Katz, *Philo-Semitism*, 188.
[42] 'Weale's Journal', 99.
[43] Katz, *Philo-Semitism*, 191–2.
[44] *CSPD 1655–6*, 51, 57–8.
[45] Penn, *Memorials*, ii. 64; 'Rooth's Journal', *passim*.

fire soon afterwards Badiley had no hesitation in discerning the hand of divine retribution.[46]

Evidence for the religious characteristics discussed so far is plentiful, but it is often hard to go much beyond this in defining the officers' creed. They were mostly men of limited education bred to a life of action rather than contemplation, and their faith has to be painted with broad brush-strokes. We find Blake, Lawson, and others occasionally speaking of God's free grace (saving grace given unconditionally), and Anthony Young refusing to give his evidence at a court martial on oath, a scruple common among radical Puritans.[47] Some officers undoubtedly held more heterodox ideas. Lt. Samford of the *Entrance* caused outrage by denying the resurrection, implying that Christ was only mortal, and Capt. Richard Newbery was similarly accused of propagating anti-Trinitarian views.[48] Others were drawn towards a more spiritualizing faith. General Deane was said to have admired the ideas of Jacob Boehme, the sixteenth-century German mystic whose works were very influential in the 1640s and 1650s. A scandalized chaplain claimed that some commanders ignored the Lord's day, holding that every day was a sabbath.[49]

It is impossible to pin denominational labels on the Generals and many of the other leading officers. Like Cromwell, they seem to have held a broad, undenominational Puritanism, believing that the godly could and should work together. Some affirmed their belief in toleration, at least among Protestants. Deane was said to stand for the principle that *in sacris nec cogere nec cogi*. Nehemiah Bourne had signed a petition for the relief of Anabaptists before leaving New England. Lawson too called for religious freedom, and he also signed a petition seeking mercy for the gaoled Quaker leader, James Nayler, mutilated by parliamentary order for alleged blasphemy.[50] Many officers were content to worship in their parish churches,

---

[46] R. Badiley, *Capt. Badiley's Reply* (1653), 6.

[47] Blake, *Letters*, 280; *FDW* iv. 46; Dornford, *Gospel-Light*, 7; Add. MS 9304, fo. 204; cf. C. Hill, *Society and Puritanism* (1966 edn.), 399–408.

[48] SP 18/76/41; *Thurloe*, iii. 159.

[49] Gumble, *Monck*, 60; Pell, *Nec Inter Vivos*, 54.

[50] J. B. Deane, *The Life of Richard Deane* (1870) 536; C. H. Firth, 'Sailors of the Civil War, the Commonwealth and the Protectorate', *MM* xii (1926), 255; *A Declaration of Vice-Admiral Lawson* (13 Dec. 1659); SP 18/131/45. Other signatories included ministers such as Joshua Sprigge and William Sedgwick, the navy official Methuselah Turner, and John Stokes and William Phipps, perhaps the naval officers of those names.

provided there was a suitable (preferably Independent) minister, while supporting toleration for those with tender consciences. This was the position of Capt. Robert Dornford, who defended the rights of separatists but chided them for being too narrow-minded and exclusive. Lawson was often described as an 'Anabaptist' and his chaplain for almost four years was a separatist preacher from Wapping, but there is no real evidence that he ever belonged to a gathered congregation; though he wanted to see tithes abolished he was ready to accept a national ministry supported by some other means.[51] Many of the leading naval officers of the late 1640s and 1650s attended the church at Stepney, where the Independent William Greenhill served first as lecturer and then minister. The flag-officers Dennis, Hackwell, and Crowther appear as vestrymen, and Swanley and Wildey (and several captains) served as churchwardens.[52] Penn went ashore in Cornwall in 1650 to hear the radical Independent Hugh Peter preach at a lecture, which may indicate that he too favoured a non-separating Independency at this period.[53]

The officer corps did none the less contain many who belonged to gathered congregations, particularly the church at Stepney founded by Greenhill in 1644 and drawn mainly from members of his public congregation. A remarkable number of senior officers joined it, including Vice-Admiral Badiley and Capts. Lyons, Strong, Earning, and Thomson. Benjamin Blake was elected deacon in 1658. Edward Witheridge, a member of the church at Boston, Massachusetts, also attached himself to the Stepney congregation. Many other officers appear in its marriage and baptismal registers, among them George Dakins, Richard Potter, Francis Parke, and the Navy Treasurer Hutchinson. Nehemiah Bourne too figures in the church's records in 1650 taking part in a debate, though probably as a visitor.[54] With such a membership the Stepney church—public and private—could bring considerable influence to bear on naval appointments. One beneficiary was Daniel Baker, a master's mate

[51] Dornford, *Gospel-Mysterie*, 50–2; *Declaration of Lawson*. For Lawson's chaplain, Claudius Brussells, see n. 115 below.

[52] G. W. Hill and W. H. Frere, *Memorials of Stepney Parish* (Guildford, 1890–1), *passim*. Maurice Thomson served as churchwarden: p. 189.

[53] Penn, *Memorials*, i. 319.

[54] Stepney Church Book, fos. 1–4ᵛ, 192, 193ᵛ; PRO RG 4/4414, fo. 5 (Witheridge). Capts. Pestell, Higgenson, and Baker also belonged, and the wives of Hackwell, Rively, Robt. Clarke, and Hide.

whose family faced ruin when he was badly wounded at Portland; many members of the gathered church and the public congregation rallied to his support, among them Greenhill, the merchants Maurice Thomson and John Limbrey, and a bevy of captains. When he recovered Baker was given his own command, a promotion he owed to the godly fraternity as well as his own undoubted merits.[55]

At Great Yarmouth the situation was very similar. William Bridge held a position in the parish church and also led a gathered congregation, among whose members were Miles Corbet, Yarmouth's MP in the Rump, and William Burton, an important figure in naval administration.[56] The gathered church had close ties with the fleet: the commanders Robert Mackey, Joseph Ames, and Edmund Thompson became members, as did the wives of William Goodson and Robert Coleman. Rebecca Wheeler, wife of another Yarmouth captain, had been known in the 1630s as an associate of Hugh Peter. It is not surprising to find the congregation meeting after Dungeness to seek God's blessing on the navy.[57]

Most early gathered congregations are poorly documented, and only scraps survive to supplement the findings at Stepney and Yarmouth. William Goodson belonged to the fiercely separatist church of Duppa and Chidley after his move to London.[58] Members of the Tatnel and Teddiman clans, both prominent in the interregnum navy, had been among the early separatists of Dover. We learn that Capt. John Woolters belonged to the Congregational church at Sandwich from a letter it sent supporting his request for a commission in 1653. Woolters also sought help from Andrew Ball, the Generals' flag-captain, addressing him as a 'dear brother in the fellowship of the Gospel'—another glimpse of the Puritan nexus in action.[59] After the Restoration, and probably earlier, Robert

---

[55] SP 18/57/200–1. Baker was formally admitted to the gathered church in 1654: Church Book, fo. 3.

[56] Dr Williams's Library, London, MS 38–208, Records of the Congregational Church at Great Yarmouth, fos. 42, 65; G. Lyon Turner, *Original Records of Early Nonconformity* (1911–14), ii. 896; G. Nuttall, *Visible Saints* (1957), 12, 20.

[57] Records of . . . Gt. Yarmouth, fos. 20, 30, 34, 40, 86; SP 18/150/68; J. Browne, *History of Congregationalism in Norfolk and Suffolk* (1877), 229, 422–3; above, n. 7.

[58] Brown, *Two Conferences*, 1, 9; M. Tolmie, *The Triumph of the Saints* (1977), 21–2.

[59] *FDW* iii. 420–2; SP 18/32/68a. For the Tatnels and Teddimans see 'The Trendall Papers', *Transactions of the Congregational Historical Soc.*, i (1901–4), 196–7; Valentine Tatnel wanted the Baptist Samuel Bradley as chaplain in 1656: SP 18/148/37.

Plumleigh belonged to the Congregational church at Dartmouth, while at Plymouth Edward Blagg was a follower of the pastor, Abraham Cheare.[60] There were several Baptists too among the senior commanders, notably Michael Packe, a flag-officer, John Mildmay, flag-captain in 1652–3 (both killed in the Dutch war), Thomas Penrose, and John Harman (a senior flag-officer after the Restoration). Capt. Edward Moorcock was a preacher and a prominent figure among the General Baptists for over a generation.[61] There was some Fifth Monarchist support too. The preacher John Rogers held a general meeting in 1653 at which he called on God to bless 'our friends in the fleet'. The following year saw Capt. Robert Taylor encouraging his outspoken Fifth Monarchist chaplain, and Capt. Owen Cox was labelled a Fifth Monarchist after the Restoration. The naval administrators John Poortmans and his brother were leading figures in a Fifth Monarchy Baptist congregation in London.[62]

The Quakers, spreading rapidly from the mid-1650s, could count two naval commanders among their converts. One was Daniel Baker of the Stepney church, who shocked the Admiralty by throwing up his command in 1657 to devote himself to the Quaker cause. Baker became a prominent evangelist, travelling to the Mediterranean and the Americas; many years later he was captured and held slave by the Algerian corsairs, and we catch a glimpse of his indomitable spirit from his attempt to establish a Quaker meeting in Algiers.[63] The other notable convert was Anthony Mellidge, who was acting commander of the *Sapphire* when he was won over from the Baptists. He too resigned his post and became an

[60] Lyon Turner, *Original Records*, i. 208; H. M. Nicholson (ed.), *Authentic Records relating to the Christian Church . . . in Plymouth* (1870), 28.

[61] R. Deane, *A Copy of a Brief Treatise* (1693), 10–11; Lurting, *Fighting Sailor*, 11, 20 (Penrose). For Moorcock see A. Taylor, *The History of the English General Baptists* (1818), i. 271–2; T. Crosby, *The History of the English Baptists* (1738–40), iii. 109–13; *BDBR*. Many other captains were loosely described as 'Anabaptist', but this is not proof of Baptist church membership. Richard Newbery may have been a Baptist: see *Thurloe*, iii. 159 (though he must be distinguished from the General Baptist minister of that name).

[62] B. S. Capp, *The Fifth Monarchy Men* (1972), 81, 208, 213, 258–9; for Taylor see ch. 5 n. 88, above.

[63] Adm. 2/1730, fo. 87ʳ; *CSPD 1657–8*, 410; Stepney Church Book, fo. 193ʳᵛ. For Baker's Quaker career see his pamphlets; W. C. Braithwaite, *The Beginnings of Quakerism* (1923), 429–33; *Extracts from State Papers Relating to Friends*, ed. N. Penney (1910–13), 46, 59–61; K. L. Carroll, 'Quaker Slaves in Algiers, 1679–1688', *Journal of the Friends' Historical Soc.*, liv (1982), 303, 306, 310.

active evangelist, suffering imprisonment for his new faith (like Baker) even before the Restoration.[64] Another captain was known to have a Quaker wife, and the Friends won further proselytes among the warrant-officers and seamen.[65]

The Quakers aroused hostility in the navy as elsewhere.[66] Hatsell at Plymouth ascribed their rise to the workings of Satan. A captain taking two Quaker evangelists to France changed his mind when he heard them haranguing his crew, and brought them back to England as dangerous trouble-makers.[67] Some officers however were more sympathetic. Lawson, as we have seen, sought mercy for the Quaker leader James Nayler.[68] And though the Quaker seaman Thomas Lurting makes much of his sufferings at the hands of profane commanders a rather different picture emerges when we read his colourful account more closely. Thus he describes the rage of Capt. Penrose (a Baptist), but concedes that Penrose later became 'very kind and respectful' and considerate to all the Quakers on board. After the Restoration Lurting was pressed into a ship under the former Cromwellian commander Jeremiah Smyth, whom he calls 'very loose and wicked' and a 'very furious man'. Yet by Lurting's own account Smyth was willing to give him posts where he would not have to break his pacifist principles, such as cooper or surgeon's mate, and when he refused them Smyth eventually agreed to discharge him.[69]

It is hard to see how a very able naval historian could believe there was little sign of 'Puritan fervour or even of ordinary religious feeling' in the Commonwealth navy.[70] The evidence to the contrary is overwhelming. Nevertheless the Puritans were no more than an energetic and vocal minority, as they always recognized. We find a Puritan officer in the *Laurel* lamenting in 1653 that he 'lived prisoner-like' in the ship, finding no one aboard except the minister with whom to share 'the melody of experienced saints'.[71] Some of the godly themselves proved unable to resist the perennial temptations of life at sea, drink and embezzlement. A few became

---

[64] A. Mellidge, *A True Relation* [1657]; *Extracts from State Papers*, 46, 59–60.

[65] Capt. P. Mootham's wife: Coventry MS 98, fo. 68; see also nn. 163–4 below, and ch. 11.

[66] Reay, *Quakers*, chs. 3–4.

[67] SP 18/97/83; SP 18/154/102; Adm. 2/1730, fo. 53ᵛ.

[68] SP 18/131/45.

[69] Lurting, *Fighting Sailor*, 11–29. For Smyth's interest in religion see SP 18/147/162.

[70] Oppenheim, 355.

[71] SP 18/35/159.

renegades. Capt. William Pestell, for example, was an early member of the gathered church at Stepney but also the very first to be expelled; after the Restoration he became a government spy informing on conventiclers.[72] Some of the supposed 'godly' were no doubt merely time-servers. One chaplain spoke scornfully of officers who cultivated the outward appearance of piety, seeing it as the best way to preferment 'as the times go'.[73] And the Admiralty always had to appoint a considerable number of officers who made little pretence to religion, for the 'godly' were never sufficient to supply the whole fleet. These men, whatever their professional skills, were likely to be indifferent or hostile to Puritan ideals, and some of them were indeed denounced by Puritan (or malicious) subordinates as blasphemous and profane.[74] The advancement of godly officers was not enough, by itself, to create a fully Puritan navy. A massive evangelical campaign was also needed, to reform the unregenerate and reach out to the mass of common seamen. This was the task assigned to the chaplains.

II. THE MINISTRY AT SEA

The Commonwealth was eager to have good ministers spreading the Gospel at sea. Evangelism lay at the heart of the Puritan impulse, of course, and the Admiralty was aware too of the material benefits that might accrue from higher standards of honesty and reliability.[75]

The first of the Articles of War established in 1652 demanded 'that Almighty God be solemnly and reverently served in the respective ships, all profaneness and irreligiousness avoided, preaching and praying and other religious duties be exercised and duly frequented, and the Lord's day religiously observed'.[76] Short daily services, at the setting of the watch, had long been a customary part of life at sea. (Many years later Ned Ward described memorably how the seaman's day generally began with 'the dreadful doomsday sound of the boatswain: "Get up, all hands to prayer,

---

[72] Stepney Church Book, fos. 1, 192. He was admitted in 1644 and expelled in 1650; a request in 1653 to be readmitted was turned down. See also Capp, *Fifth Monarchy*, 205, 207; ch. 11, below.

[73] Pell, *Nec Inter Vivos*, 22.

[74] See further chs. 6–7, above.

[75] See e.g. the comment that a god-fearing, honest Master Attendant at Chatham would save the state thousands of pounds each year: SP 18/55/85, 130.

[76] *FDW* iii. 293.

and be damned."') Services were taken by the ship's minister, if it
had one; otherwise one of the officers supplied his place. During the
interregnum the service might include prayers (probably extempore), a psalm, and a reading from scripture, sometimes with an
exposition of the passage.[77] On the sabbath there would often be a
sermon by the chaplain, and sometimes a minister from another
ship would be invited to preach. The episcopalian Thomas Fuller
said there were sermons twice a week, though he thought the Lord's
Supper had not been celebrated anywhere in the fleet for several
years.[78] The chaplains also led prayers before a battle, attended the
wounded and dying, and—all too often—conducted funerals. At
sea the dead were 'heaved overboard', in the common phrase of the
period, with little ceremony. Funerals ashore could be quite
elaborate affairs: all the commanders of Penn's fleet attended Capt.
White's funeral at Barbados early in 1655, and the minister of the
flagship preached a sermon; a guard of 150 seamen fired three
volleys in the dead man's honour while the flagship and White's
own fired salutes. Two days later the joint funeral of a boatswain
and surgeon was attended by all the boatswains and surgeons of the
fleet.[79] Some chaplains also performed more secular tasks: Francis
Nelson, for example, sent the Admiralty a short journal of his ship's
movements. Others made themselves moral guardians and reported
misconduct by the officers. One denounced his captain for selling a
prize privately; another, apparently acting as spokesman for the
company, brought detailed charges of corruption against his captain
and accused him of cheating the crew.[80]

Though there had been chaplains in the navy long before the civil
war the interregnum saw a massive increase in their numbers. Some
175 chaplains can be identified for the years 1649–60, and this figure

[77] G. Taylor, *The Sea Chaplains* (Oxford, 1978), 65 and *passim*; Oppenheim, 239;
E. Ward, *The Wooden World* (2nd edn., 1708), 102. For details of services see
Clarke MS 4/4, 1649 (37); B. Whitelocke, *A Journal of the Swedish Embassy* (1772),
i. 110; SP 18/147/162. Mountagu's chaplain in 1660, Ibbott, defended extempore
prayer: Pepys, *Diary*, i. 105. The boatswain was responsible for attendance:
J. Smith, *The Sea-Man's Grammar* (1652), 61; Lurting, *Fighting Sailor*, 5. The traditional penalty for absenteeism could be 24 hours in irons: Oppenheim, 239. For
merchant practice see e.g. E. Coxere, *Adventures by Sea*, ed. E. H. W. Meyerstein
(Oxford, 1945), 88.
[78] T. Fuller, *The Worthies of England*, ed. J. Freeman (1952; 1st pub. 1662), 257;
Weale notes two sermons one Sunday in 1655, one by a visitor: 'Weale's Journal', 99.
[79] 'Rooth's Journal', 8. It was thought unlucky to keep a corpse aboard.
[80] SP 18/137/67; SP 18/83/11; SP 18/122/134. See also Add. MS 18986, fo. 251.

is far from complete. Goodson's squadron to the Baltic in 1658 comprised twenty-nine ships, and twenty-two of them carried chaplains.[81] The figures are very impressive given the daunting hazards of life at sea for a minister. Though he was regarded as an officer and usually allowed a servant, his pay was modest. He received the ordinary seaman's wage (19s. a month) plus a groat (4d.) deducted from the monthly pay of each sailor; the Admiralty estimated that in a ship of average size this would produce an income of about £40 a year.[82] But it was not a regular salary, for the chaplain had no continuity of service. At the end of a voyage he was discharged and had to provide for himself until he could find another place, and, like other seamen, he often found it hard to obtain the wages he was due. John Harrison, for example, petitioned repeatedly, pleading that he had received nothing for most of his five years at sea and had lost £400 in the state's service. Many chaplains were clearly impoverished, and their wives and families suffered severely.[83] Constant Courtney wrote in 1659, after several years at sea, that a short illness had left him totally destitute; Courtney, like many others, needed an impress—money on credit, set against the wages he would earn—before he could take up his next post.[84] Lack of money was not the only problem. The very nature of life at sea appalled some ministers who were unable or unwilling to adapt to their new surroundings. Instead of books and educated discourse they found perpetual noise and confusion; one wrote with feeling of the constant din of drums, trumpets, and guns, and the appalling rowdiness of the seamen: 'ranting roisters and ear-deafing [sic] sails and cordage are evermore roaring about one'.[85] The life was dangerous as well as uncomfortable. Several chaplains were killed or maimed, at least one went down with his

---

[81] There is an incomplete list in Taylor, *Sea Chaplains*, 488–9. For Goodson's squadron see Add. MS 18986, fo. 291. I have identified 20 serving in Penn's fleet in 1654–5 (mostly from the Wynne MSS).

[82] There was a suggestion—not implemented—under the Rump that chaplains should have a fixed salary according to the rate of the ship: Rawl. MS A 207, fos. 23ᵛ, 34; Add. MS 9300, fo. 182ʳ⁻ᵛ; cf. *FDW* iii. 284. For the estimated average see *CSPD 1655–5*, 65; the figure may be too high. Very occasionally the chaplain had more than one servant (e.g. SP 46/97/40).

[83] *CSPD 1658–9* , 419; SP 46/117, fo. 280; SP 18/144/113; NMM ADL/Z/8 (11); SP 46/121, fo. 188; SP 46/121, fo. 170; *CSPD 1658–9*, 501.

[84] Adm. 3/274, fos. 87, 92. Courtney was given £6; the usual advance was £10: Rawl. MS A 224, *passim*; cf. Blake, *Letters*, 280.

[85] Pell, *Nec Inter Vivos*, sig. a5.

ship, some were deafened by the noise of the guns, and many others fell victim to disease and fevers. At least eighteen died in harness during the 1650s, proof of the naval chaplain's hard and dangerous life.[86]

The dockyards at Chatham and Portsmouth had their own resident chaplains. These were sensitive positions, and the government took a close interest in them. At Portsmouth Thomas Bragge, an Independent minister in the town, succeeded to the post in 1656 on the death of the previous occupant and remained in office until the Restoration.[87] The Chatham post had a much stormier history. The minister there was removed for complicity in the Kent revolt, and the Council replaced him with a reliable Independent, William Adderley. Adderley's political soundness was the more important as the parish minister at Chatham, a Presbyterian, had refused the Engagement and preached against the new republic till he was dismissed in 1650, whereupon Adderley took over his duties too.[88] But the following year Adderley made the fatal mistake of quarrelling with the Pett family, which dominated the yard as a private fiefdom. He sent a petition to the Council denouncing the Petts as corrupt; they brought counter-charges, and a fierce and prolonged row ensued.[89] Adderley was eventually forced out in the first months of the Protectorate, apparently through the Petts' influence, and was replaced by Lawrence Wise, who had already been preaching at Chatham.[90] Wise held the post till the fall of the Protectorate, when Sir Henry Vane reinstated Adderley, a sound republican. Wise did not give up easily: soon after the king's return he begged Mountagu to help him win back the post, signalling his readiness to accept the monarchy. The Stuarts naturally removed Adderley once more but they chose a more committed Anglican to succeed him.[91]

---

[86] e.g. Ashby and Morris were killed (*CSPD 1652–3*, 485, 556), Hampson died from wounds (SP 46/115, fos. 6–7; *CSPD 1653–4*, 153), Gilbert was drowned in a wreck (SP 46/97/40–3).

[87] *CSPD 1649–50*, 557; *CSPD 1655–6*, 451. Bragge was turned out at the Restoration: Adm. 2/1732, fo. 77. For his career see A. G. Matthews, *Calamy Revised* (Oxford, 1934), 70–1.

[88] *CSPD 1649–50*, 320, 520; *CSPD 1650*, 250, 257; *CSPD 1651–2*, 62; Matthews, *Calamy Revised* (Oxford, 1934), 70–1.

[89] *CSPD 1651–2*, 41–2, 57–8, 60–2, 65, 70, 128, 169–70; Aylmer, *State's Servants*, 157–9; Cogar, thesis, 88–99.

[90] SP 18/80/136; Add. MS 9308, fo. 90; *CSPD 1653–4*, 580; SP 18/57/179. On Wise see Matthews, *Calamy Rev.* 539–40.

[91] Adm. 3/274, fo. 102; Carte MS 73, fos. 402ᵛ, 481.

The Council of State was rarely involved in the selection of chaplains, though it tried to find one for the *Sovereign* in 1652. And in 1655 the Council of Ireland directed Joseph Scot, a Fellow of Trinity College, Dublin, to serve as chaplain in the *Primrose*, which was stationed in the Irish Sea.[92] The Admiralty played a much more active part, but it lacked sufficient resources for the task and often had to admit failure, directing individual captains to nominate suitable candidates.[93] Throughout the interregnum the responsibility for finding chaplains thus rested primarily with the commanders. Their methods of recruitment were inevitably informal. A captain whose ship was paying off might recommend his chaplain to a colleague. Many officers turned to Puritan ministers in London for help and advice. Capt. Whitehorne suggested in 1654 that Hugh Peter might be able to recommend a suitable New Englander.[94] Unbeneficed ministers sometimes presented themselves for employment, directly or through a sponsor.[95] While some captains were apparently ready to accept the first man they could find others devoted considerable effort to the task of selection. Benjamin Blake wanted a 'profitable, plain preacher'. Whitehorne picked a chaplain in 1655 only after investigating his preaching ability, moral character, and political soundness. A writer recalled years later the care many had taken to choose ministers who 'were pious and diligent, whose conversation as well as doctrine impressed the seamen with thoughts that there was more in religion than mere form, and who took care to see them read their bibles'.[96] The captain did not necessarily act alone. In the *Satisfaction*, for example, the selection was made in a democratic fashion. Some of the company told friends in London that they needed a minister, and one John Lane was sent down to fill the place; Lane officiated informally for some days and won general approval, whereupon the captain (Tatnel) and about twenty of his company wrote to the Admiralty in the name of the whole crew asking for his formal appointment.[97]

[92] *FDW* ii. 101, 105. on Scot see *CSPD 1655–6*, 279; Add. MS 9309, fo. 56ʳ; T. C. Barnard, *Cromwellian Ireland* (Oxford, 1975), 192 n., 203.

[93] e.g. Adm. 2/1729, fo. 222; Adm. 2/1730, fo. 83ʳ; SP 18/104/40.

[94] SP 18/147/29–31; SP 18/88/12; SP 18/123/59; SP 18/147/217; Add. MS 18986, fo. 144.

[95] e.g. SP 18/116/87; *CSPD 1658–9*, 503.

[96] 'An Inquiry into the Causes of our Naval Miscarriages', in *The Harleian Miscellany*, ed. W. Oldys and T. Park, i. (1808), 569; Add. MS 18986, fo. 144; SP 18/104/40.

[97] SP 18/149/216–7.

What sort of men became chaplains? They were a very heterogeneous body, containing men of Presbyterian as well as Independent and Baptist views, and others who were conformists or uncommitted. A few had served in the Established Church before 1642, and at least sixteen conformed after the Restoration. Many more however lost their posts on the king's return (and some other former chaplains were ejected from livings ashore), and remained nonconformists to the end of their lives.[98] In part this diversity reflects the diverse views found within the officer corps itself, though it also owes something to the fact that officers sometimes had to take anyone who offered his services, regardless of his suitability. It is noticeable that many chaplains came from maritime communities from Cornwall to East Anglia, where going to sea was a natural way of making a living; an unemployed minister, or one serving an underpaid cure, was very likely to take a chaplaincy if a visiting captain had one to offer. None of the naval chaplains had the eminence of some of their army equivalents. A military regiment was much larger than a warship's company, and offered higher pay and status; the life was easier too and much less dangerous.[99] The typical naval chaplain was a lowlier figure than most army chaplains, the majority of whom were beneficed ministers. Many naval chaplains are so obscure that we know nothing more than their names. Those who can be identified fall into three main groups: first, young university graduates; second, Puritan ministers displaced by the upheavals of the time; and third, lay preachers, some belonging to gathered churches ashore and others drawn from the navy itself.

About fifty chaplains had attended a university, with Cambridge leading Oxford by a ratio of about four to one. What stands out in this group is its youthfulness. For most university men a naval chaplaincy seems to have been the equivalent of a first curacy, a first step on the professional ladder. Francis Nelson and Daniel Pell were appointed at twenty-two. Nicholas Trevythvan similarly went to sea only one year after graduating BA at Cambridge, armed with

[98] Served before 1642: D. Harcourt, R. Hebblethwaite, N. Lane, E. Riggs. Conformed after 1660: H. Badcock, B. Bird, W. Castrey, N. Church, J. Cole, C. Courtney (?), H. Eedes, E Ferrar, D. Harcourt, R. Howes, E. Ibbott, N. Lane, F. Nelson, D. Pell, J. Turner, J. Vincent, R. Whichcote.

[99] Laurence, thesis, *passim*. Army chaplains were paid at over three times the rate of naval equivalents. For men who served as both: T. Bragge, T. Palmer, A. Tucker, J. Chiswell, W. Pearson, J. Roe, S. and W. Wright.

a certificate from the Master and Fellows of his college.[100] Even the largest and most important ships often had chaplains who seem remarkably young. In 1652 the *Sovereign*, the largest ship and so most lucrative chaplaincy in the navy, was served by a man of twenty-two. Ayscue's flagship in the Irish Sea in 1648 had a chaplain, one Michael Iles, who was still an undergraduate. He served with Ayscue again on the expedition to Barbados in 1651–2, staying on as chaplain to the new Governor there; he was by now a BA, and the Admiralty asked Trinity College, Cambridge, to hold his fellowship open till his return.[101] Some of these men were no doubt partly attracted by the prospect of travel and adventure. John Vincent, for example, had turned down several offers of employment ashore, and it was remarked that he 'would serve as well with a sword in his hand as the Word in his mouth'.[102]

A second group of chaplains were Puritan ministers whose careers had been disrupted by the religious upheavals of the mid-century. A few were returned migrants from New England, such as Nathaniel Norcross and George Moxon: Moxon asked for a naval post in 1653, the year he returned to England, perhaps because he had yet to re-establish himself. Nathaniel Mather, another returnee, was recommended as a naval chaplain in 1659 when he was forced out of his living at Barnstaple.[103] Nicholas Manley had also fled from Laudian persecution in the 1630s, finding refuge in the Netherlands; as a Yarmouth man and an associate of William Bridge the navy must have seemed a natural way of picking up his career in England.[104] Many of these men were naturally much older than the first group. Daniel Harcourt was in his fifties when he first became a naval chaplain; he has been a minister in Ireland till the 1641 revolt

---

[100] Pell: SP 18/133/146; J. and J. A. Venn, *Alumni Cantabrigienses . . . from the Earliest Times to 1751* (Cambridge, 1922–7), iii. 336; Nelson: *CSPD 1655–6*, 496; J. Foster, *Alumni Oxonienses . . . 1500–1714* (Oxford, 1891–2), iii. 1056. Trevythvan: *CSPD 1659–60*, 10, 529; Venn, *Al. Cantab.* iv. 264.

[101] The *Sovereign* (Rd. Mayo): *FDW* ii. 105; *DNB*; Matthews, *Calamy Rev.* 347. Iles: *A Letter sent to the Earl of Warwick* (1648), 6; Rawl. MS A 226, fo. 177; Venn, *Al. Cantab.* ii. 447.

[102] *CSPD 1655–6*, 130; Venn, *Al. Cantab.* iv. 303.

[103] Norcross: WYN/18, p. 7; 'Rooth's Journal', 8; Matthews, *Calamy Rev.* 366–7. Moxon: Matthews, *Calamy Rev.* 359; *DNB*. (He could be father or son; probably the latter.) Mather: *CSPD 1658–9*, 552; A. Woolrych, *From Commonwealth to Protectorate* (Oxford, 1982), 202 and n.

[104] SP 18/89/14; Add. MS 9305, fo. 110. Manley belonged to a separatist group in Yarmouth which merged with Bridge's congregation in 1659: *Records of . . . Gt. Yarmouth*, fo. 105.

and had then served as one of the commissioners investigating the massacres, publishing a chilling account of his findings.[105] The most picaresque career was that of Eleazar Gilbert, a Scots Presbyterian. Gilbert had become pastor to an Anglo-Scottish merchant community in Vilna in Poland in 1638, and published the story of his tribulations at the hands of Jesuits and Polish boyars. He followed this in 1645 with a vitriolic survey of the situation in Britain, cast in apocalyptic terms, in which he denounced the king as little more than a 'downright Roman Catholic' and Laudianism as 'loathsome spittle'. Gilbert seems to have acted as a regimental chaplain in the Scottish army, but transferred to the English navy following Cromwell's conquest of Scotland; in 1652 he was chaplain in the *John* in the expedition to reduce Virginia, and perished when the ship foundered in a storm on the voyage out.[106] Some naval chaplains had been casualties of the civil war itself. Cavaliers had driven John Syms from his curacy in Devon, forcing him to seek shelter in Plymouth; when a ship in need of a chaplain happened to call there he naturally offered his services. Robert Hebblethwaite arrived by a more circuitous route. He was intruded as vicar of Great Snoring, Norfolk, in 1643 but had to wage a protracted struggle against the supporters of the man he had replaced, a battle he eventually lost. His enemies had him removed and gaoled in Newgate on a charge of seditious language against the king, but with the establishment of the republic Hebblethwaite's sufferings and radical views became an asset, and they helped him to secure the post of minister in the *Garland* in 1649.[107]

Very few chaplains thought of the navy as providing a permanent career: for some it was a first step on the professional ladder, for others a useful stopgap. The more able and lucky in both groups

[105] D. Harcourt, *The Clergies Lamentation* (1644); idem, *A New Remonstrance from Ireland* (1643); Foster, *Al. Oxon.* ii. 646. For his service as chaplain in 1654–60: WYN/18, pp. 74, 76: SP 46/98/19d: Adm.2/1732, fo. 68.

[106] E. Gilbert, *Newses from Poland* (1641); idem, *The Prelatical Cavalier Catechized* (1645); SP 46/97/40–3; *Catalogue of the Graduates of the University of Edinburgh* (Edinburgh, 1868), 32; A. F. Mitchell and J. Christie (eds.), *The Records of the General Assembly of the Church of Scotland in 1646 and 1647* (Edinburgh, 1892), 7.

[107] A. Miller, 'John Syms, Puritan Naval Chaplain', *MM* lx (1974), 153; R. Hebblethwaite, *The Humble Petition of Robert Hebblethwaite . . .* (1647); J .C. Jeaffreson (ed.), *Middlesex County Records* (1886–92), iii. 186; *Perfect Occurrences*, 13–20 Apr. 1649; Rawl. MS A 224, fo. 31; A. G. Matthews, *Walker Revised* (Oxford, 1948), 268.

generally soon found positions ashore. Richard Mayo, chaplain of the *Sovereign* at twenty-two, went on to become curate and then vicar of Kingston-on-Thames; Francis Nelson, a chaplain in 1656, secured a living in Hampshire in 1657; John Westley (grandfather of the Methodist leader) was a naval chaplain in 1657 and vicar of Whitchurch, Dorset, by the following year.[108] Norcross, Moxon, and Manley, who all served in the navy after returning from overseas, also obtained livings ashore.[109] Several chaplains later worked in Ireland: Daniel How, a chaplain in 1657, was at Ennis the following year, and his former colleague John Marriott is found preaching in 'destitute places' in County Waterford.[110] Service in Ireland could represent a modest step forward in career terms. Thus Heretage Badcock was a naval chaplain in 1656 soon after leaving Cambridge, held a post in Ireland from 1657 till the Restoration, and then conformed and found a living in Bedfordshire.[111] But service in the remoter parts of Ireland was itself a very lowly rung of the clerical ladder, and could be as unrewarding in every sense as the navy. Joseph Binckes was a naval chaplain in the Dutch war and then became preacher at Tirawley, Co. Mayo, in 1656, but he was glad to serve again in the fleet when the chance arose.[112] Ministers who were less able or more unlucky might serve in the navy more or less continously. Constant Courtney and John Froud served throughout the Protectorate; perhaps they lacked the connections to secure a position ashore, and they were certainly too impoverished to be able to spend long looking for one.[113]

The third category of chaplains comprised men outside the public ministry: the lay preachers. Some were drawn from gathered churches with naval connections. For example, Josias Nicholls and

---

[108] Mayo and Nelson: nn. 100–1, above, and (for Nelson) Matthews, *Walker Rev.* 179. Westley: *CSPD 1657–8*, 474; Matthews, *Calamy Rev.* 521.

[109] Matthews, *Calamy Rev.* 359, 367; Matthews, *Walker Rev.* 274.

[110] How: *CSPD 1656–7*, 506; S. D. Seymour, *The Puritans in Ireland, 1647–1661* (Oxford, 1912; repr. 1969), 214. Marriott: *CSPD 1657–8*, 387; Adm. 3/273, fo. 72; Seymour, *Puritans in Ireland*, 216.

[111] *CSPD 1655–6*, 449; Seymour, *Puritans in Ireland*, 181, 207; Venn, *Al. Cantab.* i. 66.

[112] *CSPD 1653–4*, 528; SP 18/132/167; SP 18/223/138; Seymour *Puritans in Ireland*, 207; BL Stowe MS 427, fo. 16; Adm. 3/274, fo. 180ᵛ. Francis Nelson may have been an itinerant preacher in Ireland *before* serving in the navy: Seymour, *Puritans in Ireland*, 217.

[113] Courtney: Adm. 2/1729, fo. 109ᵛ; *CSPD 1656–7*, 408; *CSPD 1657–8*, 428; Adm. 3/273, fo. 255ᵛ; *CSPD 1658–9*, 572. Froud: SP 18/83/11; Adm. 2/1729, fo. 218; SP 18/195/105, 122; Adm. 3/273, fo. 237.

Arthur and James Norwood belonged to the Canterbury congregation of John Durant, who had begun his own ministry as a naval chaplain in the 1640s.[114] Claudius Brussells was put forward by a gathered church in Wapping following an approach from a captain; Brussells went on to serve under the radical commanders Lawson, Harman, and Goodson. Samuel Bradley, who served in 1654, was an active Baptist preacher in London.[115] William Starbuck, as a last example, was a veteran conventicler who had been gaoled under Laud and had later published doggerel verses to celebrate the downfall of his 'Jesuitical' persecutor.[116]

A further group of lay preachers was recruited from the navy itself. When a ship had no minister his duties were performed by one of the officers: thus William Borough acted as clerk of the cheque and minister in the *Bear* in the West Indies, and Simon Prior as minister and gunner of the *Fame* (a nice example of 'muscular Christianity' in action).[117] In some cases such men discovered a vocation and went on to become official chaplains, giving up their previous positions. The best-documented instance is Robert Rose, who served in the army in the 1640s, then became a naval steward, and acted as minister of the *Mary prize* during the Dutch war. He then became a soldier once more, serving in the garrison at Deal Castle and preaching regularly to the troops there, before returning to the navy in 1656 as chaplain of the *Pembroke*. Her captain, John Grove, had asked for him as a personal friend 'and one that will be very profitable amongst us in the making known of the truth of Jesus'.[118] Ralph Rountree probably followed a similar course: he held several chaplaincies in the 1650s and said he had served in the parliamentary forces by land and sea 'from the first distractions in England'.[119]

[114] PRO RG 4/2426, fo. 9; SP 18/133/94; SP 18/135/107; J. Durant, *The Christian's Compass* (1658), sig. A2.
[115] Brussells: NMM ADL/Z/8 (21). Bradley: SP 18/71/80; SP 18/147/38.
[116] W. Starbuck, *A Spiritual Cordial* (1644); idem, *A Spirituall Song of Comfort* (1644); idem, *A Brief Exposition* (1645); Adm. 3/274, fo. 62. He had served as curate at Bledlow, Bucks., in 1648: Matthews, *Walker Rev.* 76.
[117] Borough: SP 18/115/43–6; *CSPD 1659–60*, 511. Prior: Add. MS 9309, fo. 59ᵛ; SP 46/118/78; SP 18/202/41. See too Richard Boswood, clerk of the cheque and chaplain: Adm. 7/673, p. 52; Rawl. MS A 224, fo. 38; Clarke MS 4/4, 1650 (1). Surgeons sometimes filled the role: Add. MS 9306, fo. 25ʳ⁻ᵛ.
[118] SP 46/117, fos. 261–7; Add. MS 9305, fo. 146ᵛ; SP 18/116/149; *CSPD 1657–8*, 465; Adm. 3/273, fo. 188; SP 18/57/179.
[119] SP 18/92/38; SP 18/133/129; WYN/18, fo. 63. Pepys called him 'a simple mechanick': *Diary*, ii. 118.

The practice of recruiting chaplains by these somewhat haphazard means brought a predictable diversity of character, quality, and suitability. Many chaplains were highly regarded by their commanders. Ambassador Whitelocke too was highly impressed by the elderly seaman he found officiating as chaplain in the *Phoenix*, which was taking him to Sweden in 1653. The minister prayed and expounded each day, and preached a 'very honest and good sermon' on the sabbath. 'Though the man might want a cassock and silk girdle', Whitelocke reflected, his 'modesty, sobriety, meekness, good sense, and pious words' were clear evidence of spiritual gifts bestowed by God.[120] But when a man was appointed merely because he happened to be available the results could be highly unsatisfactory. Robert Leonard of the *Constant Warwick* was allegedly so drunk one day ashore that he had to be hoisted back over the ship's side with the tackles, and several others were similarly accused of repeated drunkenness. The captain of the *Nightingale* turned out his chaplain, George Brookes, as drunken, abusive, and quarrelsome, and the ship's previous commander confirmed that he too had found Brookes 'very idle and continually drunk'.[121] Other ministers were charged with a wide variety of misdemeanours: one deserted without warning, another never set foot in the ship though he was entered in its books for months, and a third, William Knowles, was sent for court martial on a charge of forging the signature of General Monck.[122] Some ministers were unsuitable on grounds of temperament. The preaching of Simon Prior allegedly produced 'a confusion rather than a reformation' and the captain tried (in vain) to silence him.[123] At least one chaplain used his place to preach political subversion.[124] Others vented dangerous heresies. Daniel Pell complained about the many false teachers introduced by 'schismatical sea-captains under the notion of chaplains, who never had any true call'. He was shocked by the

---

[120] Whitelocke, *Journal*, i. 130, 133. The chaplain, John Pearsall or Percall, later served with Goodson in the Caribbean: WYN/18, pp. 29, 76.

[121] SP 18/150/9–11. See also SP 18/118/142; Adm. 2/1729, fo. 197. For Brookes see M. Halhead and T. Salthouse, *The Wounds of an Enemie* (1656), 3, 30–1, 45–6.

[122] SP 18/149/170; SP 18/125/19; *CSPD 1653–4*, 414. Knowles must have been acquitted, or the charges dropped, for he remained in service. The affair perhaps arose out of a quarrel with his captain, Parke, whom he later denounced for embezzlement: SP 18/122/134. Whitelocke found him 'a confident young man' (*Journal*, ii. 354).

[123] SP 18/202/41, part i.

[124] Samuel Bradley: see ch. 5, above.

resulting plethora of 'crown-crazed fellows' who repudiated the divinity of Christ, the immortality of the soul, and the truth of the scriptures; some, he said, denied the existence of God, heaven, and hell. [125] Waldo of the *Sampson*, who sounds like a Ranter, was the sort of chaplain Pell had in mind: an official who examined him said he denied the Resurrection, was 'loose in his life and conversation', and had since gone off to London to seek a better job on the strength of a forged certificate. One chaplain may even have been a former disciple of the Ranter pseudo-messiah, William Franklin. [126]

There was no guarantee of course that even an educated and orthodox minister would make a good chaplain. To be effective he needed to adapt his style to the capacity of his audience. John Durant, for example, sprinkled his sermons with nautical images and anecdotes, illustrating the dangers of spiritual sloth by the tale of a sailor who fell asleep in the shrouds during a service and toppled overboard. Some chaplains failed to make the necessary adjustments. The Admiralty itself expressed concern that their 'high flown' and 'quaint language . . . (which some call learning)' was leaving the ordinary seaman in total darkness. [127] Some university men, for their part, were clearly appalled by the rough breed they had to serve. 'The Lord knows I took little contentment in the sea amongst that pack of rude and disorderly, swearing and profane wretches that go in it,' Daniel Pell admitted frankly, in the preface to a book he compiled on his experiences; by the time it appeared he had found a far more congenial berth as chaplain to Lady Hungerford in the Strand. [128] The Quaker evangelist William Caton claimed that ministers served in the navy only when they could find nothing better, and were more interested in the sailors' groats than their souls, forever seeking transfers to ships with larger crews and higher salaries. [129] His tirade was grossly exaggerated, but it was

---

[125] Pell, *Nec Inter Vivos*, sig. c8ᵛ, p. 42.

[126] *CSPD 1654*, 251. Was the Ed. Spradborough, chaplain of the *Leopard* in 1652, the same man as the Baptist clothworker of Andover who had been a prominent supporter of Franklin in 1650? Or perhaps a relation? A namesake was intruded as minister at Andover at some point. See R. Badiley, *Capt. Badiley's Answer* (1653), 71, 99; H. Ellis, *Pseudochristus* (1650), 22, 34, 43–5, 61; J. Friedman, *Blasphemy, Immorality, and Anarchy: The Ranters and the English Revolution* (1987), 161–6; Matthews, *Walker Rev.* 181.

[127] Durant, *Christian's Compass*, 78–9; SP 18/102/75, part i.

[128] Pell, *Nec Inter Vivos*, sigs. bᵛ, b2. Pell was none the less respected by his former captain and lieutenant, Simmonds and Weale.

[129] W. Caton, *The Sea-mens Invitation* (1659), 10.

evident that a considerable number of chaplains were far from ideal. During the course of the interregnum the state took several steps to improve the quality of religious provision. The first was an appeal to prominent Independent and Baptist ministers to supplement the chaplains' efforts. John Carew and his fellow Admiralty Commissioners issued a circular letter in the summer of 1653 bewailing the ignorance of the seamen and the impossibility of finding enough good men to serve at sea; they appealed to other ministers to visit warships whenever they could spare time, stressing how the 'interest of Christ' was 'wrapped up' in the navy's welfare. The recipients of this appeal mostly shared Carew's millenarian outlook; they included Morgan Llwyd, Vavasor Powell, Jenkin Jones, Henry Jessey, Christopher Feake, John Simpson, John Pendarvis, George Cockayn, and Lawrence Wise.[130] Jessey and Simpson did go out to the fleet at Sole Bay in August, after the victory off the Texel; they preached in the flagship at a day of thanksgiving 'with great attention of the seamen', and probably visited other ships. Carew also gratefully accepted an offer by two Suffolk Congregationalists, Benjamin Stoneham and Frederick Woodall, to spend some time with the ships at Harwich.[131] Many of those on Carew's list were to become outspoken critics of the Protectorate, and it must have been a relief to the government later in the 1650s that no more of them appear to have responded to the call.

The Protectorate too wanted to improve standards, but its priorities were different: its first concern was to suppress dangerous or unorthodox preaching. Early in 1654, in line with national policy, it directed that no chaplain was to be admitted henceforth unless he had a warrant from the Admiralty Commissioners or the Generals; chaplains already in place were to be expelled by 1 May unless they obtained a warrant by that date.[132] It was still usually left to captains to find suitable candidates but prospective chaplains

---

[130] SP 46/115, fo. 344. Was Gen. Harrison involved in this initiative? The others invited were Ambrose Mostyn, Thomas Ewens, Francis Syms, Richard Goodgroom, John Roberts. Pendarvis had been a naval chaplain in the *Eighth Whelp* in 1644: PRO HCA 13/59, fo. 253.

[131] *FDW* v. 411; Rawl. MS A 227, fo. 126ᵣ⁻ᵛ. For Stoneham and Woodall see Capp, *Fifth Monarchy*, 264, 269; Nuttall, *Visible Saints*, 18–19, 148.

[132] SP 18/80/138; SP 18/82/94. The Generals did issue many warrants themselves, mainly on expeditions overseas: Penn, *Memorials*, ii. 67; WYN/18, *passim*; SP 18/174/123.

now had to undergo a formal examination, which made it much easier to spot undesirables. The Admiralty was concerned about political as well as religious orthodoxy. It blocked the appointment of Samuel Bradley, for example, who had been dismissed from a previous ship for political subversion.[133] It also blocked the attempts of Samuel Oates, a former army chaplain, to secure a naval post. Oates had been removed from the army for his share in the 'Overton plot' in 1654, and the Admiralty Commissioners turned him away when he approached them in 1657. Oates then made his way to the Downs and persuaded Stayner to receive him on board as chaplain, but the Admiralty indignantly refused Stayner's request for a warrant.[134]

The task of vetting candidates was generally delegated to the Triers (Commissioners for the Approbation of Ministers), the body responsible for vetting in the Cromwellian church as a whole. Prominent Independents such as Caryl, Venning, and Cromwell's chaplain John Row handled much of the work. The Triers were directed to examine the candidate and 'sift into him, and as well by searching discourse as otherwise to inform yourselves as fully as may be of his grace and ability for that weighty calling'.[135] One candidate was so daunted by this ordeal that his sponsors begged for him to be excused.[136] In practice the system of control was no more than patchy. In the West Country there were no Triers available, so when a captain at Plymouth found a man willing to serve, the Admiralty had to ask the local navy agent (Hatsell) to examine him. James Norwood of Canterbury, who was taken into Robert Blake's ship in 1657, was not even aware that an Admiralty warrant was needed.[137] Throughout the 1650s there were many chaplains who had not been examined and had no warrant, usually because there had been no opportunity to obtain one. The Admiralty generally overlooked the omission if they behaved satisfactorily.[138] Overall the system was fairly effective in keeping out men with dangerous opinions, but it did nothing of course to improve the calibre of the men coming forward. The Triers recognized as much. They even

[133] SP 18/147/38; SP 18/148/37; SP 18/149/216–17.
[134] Adm. 2/1730, fos. 83ᵛ, 85. For the plot see ch. 5, above.
[135] e.g. Adm. 2/1729, fo. 205ᵛ; Adm. 2/1730, fo. 47.
[136] SP 18/92/34. This was Robotham, a cousin of the army chaplain John Robotham.
[137] Adm. 2/1730, fo. 273ᵛ; *CSPD 1658–9*, 490, 492; SP 18/133/94.
[138] eg. Adm. 3/273, fos 89ᵛ, 137ᵛ 144; Adm. 2/1729, fo. 109ᵛ.

awarded a certificate to a candidate whose abilities they described witheringly as 'mean and weak', in the hope that by diligence he might none the less prove useful.[139]

In December 1655 the Council took steps to attract at least some recruits of a higher calibre. It authorized the appointment of up to twenty chaplains at an improved salary of £100 a year to accompany Blake and Mountagu on their forthcoming expedition. This had some success: among those who came forward were Thomas Palmer, a prominent Independent, who served in the flagship, and Edward Ferrar, who served with the vice-admiral (and thirty years later was to become Master of University College, Oxford).[140] In 1657 Mountagu brought along his own protégé, John Turner, who held a living in the General's gift, which he naturally retained.[141] But the Commissioners confessed that it remained hard to attract suitable men, even for the best ships in the fleet.[142] While the interregnum saw some improvement in the quality of chaplains, as well as much greater numbers, achievements lagged well behind aspirations.

III. RELIGION AND THE SEAMAN

What impact did the evangelical efforts of Puritan officers and chaplains have on the navy as a whole? The situation varied, of course, from ship to ship. Some, as we have seen, had zealous ministers and Puritan officers bound together by mutual respect. Others (usually smaller ships) had no chaplain at all, and remained as benighted as the worst of 'the dark corners of the land'. It was reported in 1657 that there had been no religious service whatever in the little *Roe ketch* in the course of nine months.[143] Chaplains who had to serve with unsympathetic officers faced an uphill task. The chaplain of the *Laurel* decided to leave in 1653 after finding that with no support at all from the captain he could achieve nothing.

---

[139] SP 18/131/85.

[140] *CSPD 1655–6*, 65; SP 46/117, fo. 207. For Palmer see *CSPD 1655–6*, 454; Matthews, *Calamy Rev.* 380; for Ferrar see *CSPD 1655–6*, 449; Add. MS 9305, fo. 189ᵛ; Foster, *Al. Oxon.* ii. 485. During the 1650s Ferrar favoured the Independents, but after the Restoration preached bloodthirsty and vindictive sermons against them: A. Wood, *Life and Times*, ed. A. Clark (Oxford, 1891–1900), i. 370.

[141] *CSPD 1657–8*, 139, 399, 527; Pepys, *Diary*, i. 295; Venn, *Al. Cantab.* iv. 275.

[142] Adm. 2/1730, fo. 83ᵛ.   [143] SP 18/174/188; SP 18/175/200–1.

The *Sophia*'s captain had similarly allowed the ship's surgeon and his friends to be drunk during service-time on the sabbath, ignoring the chaplain's complaints. Capt. Robert Wyard referred openly to his chaplain as an 'old doting fool' and cut him short if he thought the service was going on too long.[144] Several commanders set out to sabotage the efforts of their ministers. John Bowen—'a profane blasphemer, cursing and swearing'—allegedly prevented any reading from scripture on weekdays and tried to pare the Sunday services to a bare minimum.[145] Conflict between a Puritan chaplain and anti-Puritan officers could have dramatic consequences. A few years previously the *Providence* had been virtually paralysed by bitter rivalry within the company between the supporters of John Syms, the chaplain, and Capt. John Ellison.[146] There might be similar feuding where a Puritan captain and chaplain battled together against hostile and disruptive warrant-officers, as in John Best's strife-ridden *Adventure*. The chaplain complained that her gunner was a profane and foul-mouthed man who stayed away from services and had stirred up the seamen against him when he was reproved for swearing.[147] A profane officer in another ship scandalized the godly by drinking a health to the devil, claiming flippantly when challenged that it was in honour of 'John Devell, a friend of his'.[148]

Some chaplains found themselves in a different but equally difficult situation, confronting officers whose religious outlook was far more radical than their own. Francis Perkins's teaching in the *Torrington* did not satisfy the ship's Baptist lieutenant, William Phipps, who joined with the surgeon to lead a party against him; when Perkins attacked them in his sermons they boycotted the services and persuaded most of the crew to do likewise, in a bizarre alliance of separatists and the profane. The captain did nothing to help, and when a new captain arrived who was himself a Baptist the chaplain abandoned the struggle and asked for a discharge.[149] In the *Duchess* it was the warrant-officers who proved disruptive, the gunner claiming to be 'above ordinances'. They stayed on deck talking and laughing during services, and the ordinary sailors

[144] SP18/35/159; SP 46/97/49; SP 46/96/220.
[145] Clarke MS 4/4, 1649 (38).
[146] Miller, 'John Syms', 157–62.
[147] SP 18/42/94. The chaplain was our old friend Daniel Pell.
[148] SP 18/195/130.
[149] SP 18/201/41. The new captain was Harman.

became resentful, asking, 'If our master will not go, why should we go?' The boatswain, responsible for the men's attendance, was among those who refused to be present.[150]

Puritan evangelism in the navy was thus hindered by internal divisions as well as open resistance. Moreover the sheer scale of the task, plus the rapid turnover in many ships' companies, ensured that progress would be slow and limited at best. Some observers claimed there was no progress at all. The Quaker William Caton said he could find no difference in religious and moral terms between ships with chaplains and those without; all sailors, he declared, were by nature ignorant, drunken, profane, and heedless, 'more like beasts than men'.[151] Daniel Pell, a diligent but embittered chaplain, also thought most sailors and many officers were beyond redemption. If fines for swearing were levied according to the rules laid down, he observed, the sailors would soon have cursed beyond the value of their entire wages and indeed beyond the value of the ship itself. 'There is such swearing in the sea,' he complained, 'as if both hell, the damned and all the devils in it were let loose.' Frustration and outrage led him to an astonishing outburst: 'Were I a commander, if fair means and sweet persuasions would not prevail, I would hang them up at the mainyard'.[152] The one consolation to be found in the sailors' massive indifference to religious instruction was that it immunized them against heresy and sedition. The crew of the *Gainsborough*, it was reported, had been exposed to the chaplain's dangerous Fifth Monarchist propaganda, but were protected by their 'careless supinity and extraordinary inadvertency' during his sermons. Apathy had its uses.[153]

As we might expect, the average seaman did not become a Puritan. But the negative assessments of Caton and Pell do not represent the whole truth, for seamen were not totally devoid of religious awareness. Most seem to have wanted a minister on board. Nine officers of the *Fame* reported that the company was suffering 'great necessities' through the lack of one. Capt. Simmonds of the *Jersey* wrote similarly, 'we are in affliction to go unprovided of a chaplain', and another commander stressed that a minister was essential for men who 'must look death in the face'.[154] This last

---

[150] Clarke MS 4/1, box 2 (unnumbered: letter of Capt. E. Smith, Jan. 1654).
[151] Caton, *Sea-mens Invitation*, 7, 11.
[152] Pell, *Nec Inter Vivos*, sigs. a7–a8.
[153] SP 18/71/80.   [154] SP 18/147/31; SP 18/133/146; SP 18/136/57.

point recurs often and was clearly crucial. Most of the sailors with Whitelocke were terrified when their ship ran aground by night in the North Sea, on the way home from Sweden; after she floated clear next day, to general amazement, he noted that many of them came to join in the service of thanksgiving he arranged. Mariners could hardly fail to think of the life beyond when there was 'but a plank between them and death', wrote the future vice-admiral Richard Badiley in 1648, in a tract intended to exonerate them from the common charge of irreligion. Many of them, he said, wore crosses round the neck or wrist 'to put [them] in mind of Christ and his passion' and though as a Puritan he conceded that such practices might be offensive to some, he argued tolerantly that they served a useful purpose and were not contrary to scripture.[155] Though it was proverbial that the sailors' concern with religion tended to vanish once a danger was past, some chaplains made an undoubted impact on their hearers. John Syms, serving in the 1640s, lent religious books to members of the company whose interest he had awakened.[156] Capt. Jeremiah Smyth described effusively how his chaplain, Walter Hawksworth, had made a deep impression on many of the company by his daily 'praying, expounding and opening the truth'.[157] Puritan officers and chaplains also worked together to raise the moral standards of the seamen. A Somerset man who served three years in Blake's flagship recalled later that he had never heard an oath sworn there or indeed throughout the fleet. Making every allowance for exaggeration it seems probable that officers such as Blake did succeed in creating a moral climate in the ships they commanded very different from that of the Stuart navy, though the changes no doubt sprang from fear as much as conviction: Penn reinforced the preachers' words by decreeing a fine of five shillings or twenty lashes for anyone found guilty of blasphemy or drunkenness.[158]

There are also indications that the radical religious beliefs found among the commissioned officers took some root among their subordinates. A boatswain with Puritan scruples, giving evidence, said he would 'not take an oath for to gain the whole world'.[159] A former clerk of the cheque published a work expounding free

[155] Whitelocke, *Journal*, ii. 363–74; Badiley, *The Sea-men Undeceived*, 34.
[156] Miller, 'John Syms', 161; Add. MS 35297, fo. 1ᵛ.
[157] SP 18/147/162.   [158] Oldmixon, *Blake*, 113; Penn, *Memorials*, ii. 64.
[159] SP 18/118/120; see also ch. 6, part vi.

grace.[160] A number of warrant-officers were members of gathered churches. The Stepney congregation included ordinary mariners as well as eminent commanders, and the gunner of the *Primrose* produced testimonials from the eminent lay pastors William Kiffin and Samuel Highland.[161] Even after the purges which paved the way for the Restoration royal officials found 'Anabaptist' boatswains, gunners, carpenters, and cooks scattered widely in the fleet.[162] Quakerism too made some headway among the lower ranks. A perplexed captain reported in 1656 that his gunner had remained shut in his cabin for two months, refusing to fire the guns lest blood be spilled! Another Quaker convert, Richard Knowlman, gunner of the *Assistance*, similarly refused to carry out his duties, and dropped the use of 'flattering titles of honour' in addressing his superiors. Both men were turned out.[163] We have one account of the Quakers' spread from their own viewpoint, in the autobiography of Thomas Lurting, who had been pressed into the navy at fourteen. He was serving as boatswain's mate of the *Bristol* in the Straits when he first encountered Quaker ideas, introduced by a soldier serving on board. A small group of Friends gradually formed among the seamen, growing to number twelve men and two boys (one of them the chaplain's young servant); they held private religious meetings and stayed away from the ship's services. Lurting adopted pacifist views, and the whole group decided to leave the navy at the end of the voyage. They were uncomfortably aware that in the meantime they risked death under the Articles of War if they refused to fight, and the captain indeed vowed to run his sword through anyone who disobeyed his orders. But they stood by their principles and prepared for the worst when an enemy was sighted and the ship cleared for action; fortunately the 'enemy' turned out to be a friendly Genoese.[164] The number of Quakers in the navy seems never to have been large, and most soon withdrew or were expelled. Even so they provide further proof that religious radicalism had some appeal at every level.[165]

[160] A. T. Wright, *Jeremiah Rich: Semiographer of the Commonwealth* (1911), 27–37, 41–3, 66; above, ch. 6 n. 256.

[161] SP 18/62/85–6; *CSPD 1658–9*, 559; Stepney Church Book, fos 1–4ᵛ; PRO RG 4/4414, pp. 4–7; Rawl. MS A 184, fo. 63.

[162] Coventry MS 98, fos 66ᵛ–83ᵛ; see also ch. 11.

[163] SP 18/146/144; SP 18/154/58; Braithwaite, *Beginnings*, 520–1.

[164] Lurting, *Fighting Sailor*, 1–25; Braithwaite, *Beginnings*, 521–2.

[165] Adm. 2/1730, fo. 87ʳ⁻ᵛ. See also ch. 11.

The perils of life at sea made sailors notoriously superstitious in the eyes of contemporaries.[166] This applies equally to the navy, although Admiralty records naturally have little to say on the subject. Christian doctrines had to compete with a variety of other beliefs. Lurting, the Quaker convert, tells us that he was able to take over an empty cabin in the *Bristol* because several occupants had died in quick succession and the other seamen believed it was troubled by an evil spirit; Lurting had no such fears and used it for Quaker assemblies.[167] The seamen were also swayed by omens. Even Deane is said to have taken it as a sign of imminent death when he found, on the eve of battle, that rats had eaten away part of his doublet. The shipmaster James Butler took an apparition of armies fighting in the sky to portend the death of his brother Gregory, who was serving as a Commissioner in the expedition to Hispaniola. The Restoration chaplain, Henry Teonge, recorded the direful omen of a death-watch beetle, and seems to have adopted much of the seamen's lore rather than trying to eradicate it. (We might note that Charles II took it as a good omen when a swarm of bees settled on one of his warships in 1662, and ordered them not to be disturbed.)[168]

Many sailors continued to believe firmly that witchcraft was sometimes to blame for storms and shipwrecks—as in *Macbeth*.[169] An officer whose ship was held up by cross-winds at Pevensey Bay

---

[166] Thomas, *Religion*, 649; G. E. Manwaring (ed.), *The Life and Works of Sir Henry Mainwaring* (NRS, 1920/2), ii. 163; J. Aubrey, *Remaines of Gentilisme*, in *Three Prose Works*, ed. J. Buchanan-Brown (1972), 256-7; P. Burke, *Popular Culture in Early Modern Europe* (1979 edn.), 45-6. On 15 Dec. 1987 *The Guardian* reported an exorcism service to cast out a spirit haunting a Bridlington trawler, the *Pickering*, whose skipper and crew were refusing to go to sea. The local DHSS office had called in the exorcist in the hope of saving the unemployment benefits being paid to the seamen; he was apparently successful, and was thanked by the trawler's owners.

[167] Lurting, *Fighting Sailor*, 18. For St Elmo's Fire as an evil spirit see J. Josselyn, *An Account of Two Voyages to New-England* (1674), 5.

[168] Gumble, *Monck*, 58-9; *Memoirs of the Life of Mr Ambrose Barnes*, ed. W. H. D. Longstaffe (Surtees Soc., 1867), 59-60; *The Diary of Henry Teonge, 1675-1679*, ed. G. E. Manwaring (1927), 170 (and cf. 30, 148, 205, 223, 224); Evelyn, *Diary*, iii. 322. See also *The Life of Marmaduke Rawdon of York*, ed. R. Davies (Camden Soc., 1863), 63-4.

[169] Thomas, *Religion*, 541, 560; *CSPD 1667-8*, 4; Josselyn, *Account*, 182. The witch in *Macbeth*, I. iii uses her arts to torment a mariner after his wife refused a request for food, closely following the general pattern of witchcraft accusations. There are many cases of witchcraft and shipwreck in C. L. Ewen, *Witch Hunting and Witch Trials* (1929) and idem, *Witchcraft and Demonianism* (1933).

in 1656 told the Navy Commissioners that witchcraft was the likely cause, and that a malicious old woman of the town (the likely witch) was prophesying that it would be unable to move for three months.[170] During the Second Dutch War a Cornish woman claimed to have bewitched the English fleet.[171] The journals of Edward Barlow, who joined the navy in 1659, record much lore of this nature. When his ship was hit by adverse winds off Algiers in 1661 the crew blamed the Moors' 'witches and soothsayers'; 'how true it is I cannot tell', Barlow commented. There was a more dramatic episode some years later, following a visit to Bergen in Norway. The shipmaster refused to settle debts his men had run up ashore and the ship sailed amidst the curses of the local landladies; the master feared they had bewitched his vessel, especially when a black cat was mysteriously found aboard, and surely enough it was wrecked on the Goodwin sands on the voyage home. This disaster left the sceptical Barlow deeply troubled. In more distant waters he had no hesitation in blaming storms and freak winds on the natives' 'black conjurors' or the devil they worshipped.[172]

Many mariners were also devotees of astrology. William Lilly, the leading practitioner of the mid-seventeenth century, had numerous ordinary seamen, junior and senior officers, and their wives and families among his clientele. Capt. Owen Cox was a regular visitor. Ordinary sailors and their wives were mostly concerned to know if a ship would return home safely, and Capt. Godfrey of the *Marmaduke* similarly came to ask about his imminent voyage to the Caribbean.[173] Other clients wanted to know about their career prospects. When Capt. John Clarke was in trouble his wife asked if he would lose his command—as he did. Another captain enquired if he would win the command of the *Gainsborough*. Lilly was even consulted by a naval chaplain, anxious to know if he would be employed again, and one of Lilly's almanacs was among the books another chaplain lent to his shipmates.[174]

[170] *CSPD 1656–7*, 424.   [171] *CSPD 1671*, 105.
[172] *Barlow's Journal of his Life at Sea*, ed. B. Lubbock (1934), 55, 190–1, 257–61, 471; cf. *Diary of Teonge*, 47.
[173] Thomas, *Religion*, 309–10, 319 n.; Bodl. Ash. MS 184, 427. For Cox see also J. Gadbury, *Nauticum Astrologicum* (1691), 79–80, and for Godfrey see Ash. MS 427, fo. 121. Capt. Simmonds was another of Lilly's acquaintances: *The Last of the Astrologers: Mr William Lilly's History of his Life and Times*, ed. K. M. Briggs (1974), 73.
[174] Ash. MS 427, fos. 75, 158ᵛ, 197ʳ⁻ᵛ; Add. MS 35297, fo. 183ᵛ. A naval official in Mar. 1673 reported a fierce storm as predicted in Gadbury's almanac (*CSPD 1673*,

There were very few mariners, however, with the expertise to make their own astrological calculations. The best-known of them was Jeremy Roche, who served in the Straits in 1659 and became lieutenant to Sir Frescheville Holles (another champion of astrology) in the Second Dutch War; Holles may well have chosen him on the strength of their common interest. Roche's journal contains numerous calculations and proofs of the 'admirable force and verity of celestial influences'. On one notable occasion, when the English and Dutch fleets lay close together and battle seemed imminent, he made astrological calculations and predicted that there would be no action that day. The officers standing by scoffed and were then amazed to see a wind spring up and drive the two fleets apart. Much of the story's interest lies in the bystanders' response: for instead of admitting the claims of astrology, or invoking divine providence or chance, they accused Roche of conjuring up a storm by magic to make good his prediction![175] The navy was a difficult field for missionaries of any creed.

10). For astrology and the navy in the 1790s see my *Astrology and the Popular Press* (1979), 277.

[175] B. Ingram, *Three Sea Journals of Stuart Times* (1936), 82 and *passim*. Wm. Ball, master of the *Hector* in 1627, also had some astrological knowledge: 'The Earl of Warwick's Voyage of 1627', ed. N. P. Bard, in *The Naval Miscellany*, v (NRS, 1984), 23–4.

Part III

10

The Navy and the Restoration

THE navy was very close to the centre of the political stage in the last months of the interregnum. In December 1659 Lawson's fleet played a key role in bringing down the military government and restoring the Rump, an unprecedented and probably unique achievement. Six months later the fleet, now under Mountagu, played an active part in restoring the monarchy. Though the two naval leaders ended the period as colleagues, at least in name, they viewed the Restoration through very different eyes. For Mountagu it was the fulfilment of his dreams; for Lawson it represented the failure of all his ideals, to be accepted merely as a lesser evil than the rule of the sword.

On Richard Cromwell's accession in September 1658 Mountagu quickly emerged as one of the most prominent and forceful figures in the new regime. His rise in the mid-1650s had been rapid. He held office as Councillor and Treasury Commissioner (at £1,000 apiece yearly), and as General at Sea he earned a salary of £1,095; Oliver had also made him one of the new lords in the 'Other House' and had promised him the colonelcy of a regiment of horse.[1] Mountagu naturally felt a deep sense of obligation to the Cromwells and he found Richard's moderate views and civilian background highly congenial. By contrast most of the army leaders neither liked nor respected the new Protector, and Mountagu's position soon brought him into conflict with them. They were furious when Richard gave him a colonelcy, honouring his father's promise, and demanded that Richard surrender his command of the army to Fleetwood.[2] Though the affair was smoothed over for the moment the atmosphere remained tense, and other clashes soon followed. At

---

[1] F. R. Harris, *The Life of Edward Mountagu* (1912), i. 83, 109 and n., 118; *Clarke Papers*, ii. 99, 164.
[2] Davies, 30–40; R. Hutton, *The Restoration: A Political and Religious History of England and Wales, 1658–1667* (Oxford, 1985), 23–4.

the time of Cromwell's funeral in November Desborough wanted royalists to be ordered out of London as a security measure, whereupon Mountagu allegedly retorted that 'there was no fear of any disturbance except of his [Desborough's] procurement'. A few weeks later a fierce row erupted at a Council meeting when Desborough accused Mountagu of plotting to kidnap him and Fleetwood and perhaps have them killed, a charge Mountagu dismissed as preposterous.[3] The importance of the protagonists made this feud much more than a mere personal quarrel, and a royalist agent could plausibly write that the whole army and navy were together 'by the ears' over Richard.[4]

Republicans in Richard's Parliament were also quick to challenge his control of the armed forces, as a first step towards toppling the regime. The issue surfaced in a parliamentary debate on foreign affairs in February 1659, when it was pointed out that if MPs allowed him to send a fleet to the Baltic and name its commander they would be conceding his right to command and remodel the armed forces. Sir Henry Vane urged that only a man who had demonstrated real affection for Parliament should lead such a force, a formula designed to exclude Mountagu. But the debate ended with an ambiguous vote accepting Richard's right to conduct foreign policy, 'saving the interest of this House', and a fleet sailed in March with Mountagu at its head.[5]

The royalists naturally hoped that the old Protector's death would weaken the regime. On the very next day a government newswriter had voiced fears that the Dutch would now 'break out' and renew war, and the cavaliers anticipated this prospect with relish.[6] They also believed that direct approaches to naval commanders such as Stayner or Stokes might now bear fruit, and an agent in Italy with contacts in Stokes's squadron urged the Spanish Viceroy in Naples to open the ports to English defectors.[7] But these hopes proved as illusory as ever: the navy accepted Richard's accession

---

[3] Bodl. Clarendon. MS 59, fos. 238ᵛ, 273; Harris, *Mountagu*, i. 118–19; Davies, 45–6.

[4] Clar. MS 59, fo. 355; Harris, *Mountagu*, i. 118. Desborough was still a (land-based) General at Sea, and continued to act occasionally in Admiralty affairs.

[5] Davies, 197–200; BL Lansdowne MS 823, fos. 235–6; Burton, *Diary,* iii. 376–493. Vane's comments are on p. 491.

[6] *Clarke Papers,* iii. 162–3.

[7] Clar. MS 59, fos. 86ᵛ, 186, 423; Clar. MS 60, fos. 4, 367, 371; *The Nicholas Papers,* ed. G. F. Warner (Camden Soc., 1886–1920), iv. 83; see also ch. 5, above.

without demur, and peace was maintained with the Dutch. Before long Edward Hyde, the king's chief adviser, was reflecting gloomily that Oliver's death might even have damaged the royalist cause, for he saw it was unlikely that Richard's mild regime would ever drive the landed classes to revolt. Why, he fretted, did ousted radicals such as Lawson and Overton lack the courage to challenge the regime?[8]

Cavalier spirits soon revived, however, for in April 1659 Richard's government foundered on the struggle between Parliament and the army. On 21 April he surrendered to army pressure and agreed to dissolve Parliament in return for an undertaking by Fleetwood and Desborough to stand by him, a pledge they did nothing to honour. As free elections were very unlikely to produce a parliament acceptable to the army the officers recalled the Rumpers they had expelled six years earlier, and on 7 May forty-two surviving MPs took their seats once more. Richard lingered on at Whitehall for a few more weeks and then slipped away into obscurity.[9]

The tension between the two services made the navy's response to these changes a very sensitive matter. The Rump tried to woo the ordinary seamen by promising speedy payment of their arrears, a promise it proved unable to fulfil.[10] There were some radical officers who were undoubtedly glad to see the Rump restored. The Navy Commissioner Nehemiah Bourne voiced enthusiastic approval in a letter to a friend in New England, describing the Protectorate as 'the late general apostasy' and its overthrow as 'the clearest hand of God . . . that ever was seen'. Bourne was confident the navy as a whole would share his feelings. The ships in the Downs, he explained, were under the command of his brother John, 'who hath with his squadron acknowledged and gladly embraced the change', and he had hopes of Mountagu's fleet in the Sound 'because the generality of the commanders are such who have served a commonwealth heretofore and have tasted the difference betwixt one and another government'.[11]

This analysis was far too sanguine. Apart from John Bourne's squadron none of the naval forces then at sea appear to have sent

[8] Clar. MS 60, fo. 219.
[9] Davies, 84–96; Hutton, *Restoration*, 37–41.
[10] *CJ* vii. 655.
[11] *Clarke Papers*, iii. 209, 210, 216. Nehemiah Bourne had earlier been an intimate of Lawson, signing himself 'your real servant in the bonds of love': PRO SP 18/79/191.

messages of support for the new government.[12] A major question mark hung over Mountagu's response. The official press reported that his fleet had reacted to news of the coup 'with a very calm and good temper, and generally a commonwealth is to them a most desirable change'.[13] This claim was very misleading. Mountagu had assembled a council of war to consider the situation when Pepys arrived with the dramatic news from England, bearing letters from Fleetwood and Richard each seeking the fleet's support. According to one report Vice-Admiral Goodson and one other captain were overjoyed at the change of government 'but all the rest very sad'. Though the officers cautiously resolved 'to receive the Parliament's commands' they explained that they felt it essential to remain on station to watch the Dutch, a response which allowed them to wait on events.[14] Mountagu did not bother to hide his own feelings. At the end of May, when the Rump was clearly established, he owned candidly to Speaker Lenthall that Richard's overthrow had filled him 'with fears and sorrow', though he promised to obey Parliament's orders, declaring that the mariners were faithful servants of the nation and stressing that the fleet was in good order and well governed. The Rump now felt entitled to boast of his submission, but Mountagu's seemingly anodyne phrases contained a veiled warning against any attempt to remove him or subvert his men, and his pledge of loyalty was explicitly to the nation rather than its current rulers.[15] The Venetian resident, a perceptive observer, noted that his 'expressions have a double meaning, which leaves them here disturbed and hesitating'. Mountagu's well-known attachment to the Cromwells soon prompted rumours that he would try to restore Richard by taking the fleet to Ireland, Scotland, or possibly Dunkirk, which had a Cromwellian governor. Richard himself tried to open a channel of communication to the fleet, in the hope of using it to regain power.[16] The Rump was deeply suspicious of Mountagu but dared not risk an open confrontation.

Parliament was determined however to establish its authority

[12] *The Weekly Post*, 10–17 May 1659.
[13] Harris, *Mountagu*, i. 128–9; *CSPV 1659–61*, 26, 30; *The Memoirs of Edmund Ludlow*, ed. C. H. Firth (Oxford, 1894), ii. 92; *Mercurius Politicus*, 2–9 June 1659.
[14] Clar. MS 61, fos. 19, 171–2; Sandwich, *Journal*, 31.
[15] *Clarke Papers*, iv. 279–80.
[16] *CSPV 1659–61*, 35; Harris, *Mountagu*, i. 138, 140; *CSPD 1659–60*, 19; Clar. MS 61, fo. 19ʳ⁻ᵛ; *CSP* iii. 469, 478; Lansdowne MS 823, fos. 371–2; *The Letter-Book of John Viscount Mordaunt, 1658–60*, ed. M. Coate (Camden Soc., 1945), 10.

over the rest of the navy. It began by remodelling naval administration, which had virtually collapsed in the weeks following Richard's surrender.[17] An Act of 31 May brought the Admiralty under the control of the Rumpers who had run the navy in the first years of the Commonwealth, such as Vane, Walton, and Morley. The Act dropped the usual practice of naming the Generals at Sea as Commissioners, thus removing Mountagu, though most of the other Cromwellian Commissioners were confirmed in office.[18] Parliament also asserted its supremacy over the armed forces by ordering newly appointed officers to receive their commissions in person from the hands of the Speaker. From June onwards a procession of army and navy officers filed into the Commons' chamber in a ritual the MPs must have found very satisfying.[19]

To counter Mountagu the Rump hastened to set out a new naval force under officers it could trust. By early July sixteen ships were plying off the Flemish coast under the command of John Lawson, selected as an enemy of the Protectorate and known to be popular with the seamen; his friend and protégé George Dakins held another senior post in the squadron.[20] It was no secret that one of Lawson's tasks was, in Ludlow's words, 'to balance the power of Mountagu's party, who we knew was no friend to the commonwealth'.[21] His other main function was to protect the new government from its enemies abroad, whether Spaniards, Dutch, or cavaliers. For the navy was now reverting once more to its earlier role of sheltering a precarious regime from foreign intervention, and the ambitious projects of the mid-1650s faded into the past. The Rump launched no new offensives against Spain, and allowed the war to wind down; there were even exploratory talks on peace, prompted by fears that Spain and France might intervene jointly on Charles Stuart's behalf if they reached a settlement with one

[17] PRO Adm. 2/1731, fos. 84–6.

[18] *A and O* iii. 1277–82. Desborough, also a General, was dropped too. The other members were Kelsey, Clarke, Langley, Boon, Salmon, and Say; Kelsey proved very ready to continue in service, Clarke did not: Ludlow, *Memoirs*, ii. 81.

[19] *CJ* vii. 673, 676 ff.; *The Weekly Intelligencer*, 7–14 June 1659; *The Publick Intelligencer*, 6–13, 20–7 June; B. Whitelocke, *Memorials of the English Affairs* (Oxford, 1853), iv. 351; Adm. 3/274, fos. 94–5; Davies, 105–6; Hutton, *Restoration*, 50–1.

[20] *CJ* vii. 666, 670; Adm. 2/1731, fos. 93ᵛ, 95ʳ⁻ᵛ; *The Weekly Post*, 19–26 July; *The Weekly Intelligencer*, 30 Aug.–6 Sept.; Bodl. Rawlinson MS C 179, pp. 13, 158. The other senior captains in this new force were Mackey, Fenn, Hannam, Shelley, and Potter.

[21] Ludlow, *Memoirs*, ii. 92; *CSPD 1659–60*, 19; *Nicholas Papers*, iv. 124.

another.[22] Similarly the Rump adopted a fairly conciliatory attitude towards the Dutch, very unlike the aggressive spirit it had shown in 1651–2. Nervous of its position at home, it dared not provoke new enemies abroad.[23]

The situation in the Baltic was particularly delicate, both because of Mountagu's doubtful loyalty and because he might easily come to blows with the Dutch forces there and provoke an unwanted war. The Rump therefore dispatched Commissioners to the Sound to treat with their Dutch counterparts and watch over Mountagu. The new Commissioners, led by Col. Algernon Sidney, a staunch republican MP and Councillor, arrived in the Sound on 20 July, bringing with them a fleet of victuallers.[24] Mountagu's officers had been waiting anxiously, unsure whether they would be confirmed in place or removed for the 'crime' of serving the Cromwells. They were relieved to find the Rump had opted for conciliation and had sent a batch of new commissions signed by the Speaker. To strengthen its hold it insisted that each captain, lieutenant, and master should take an engagement under the recent Act of Indemnity (12 July), promising fidelity to the government as now established without a king, Protector, or house of peers. Goodson, Stayner (the rear-admiral), and the other officers duly subscribed between 5 and 9 August.[25] Whatever their private beliefs, they were more likely to accept the new regime now their own positions were secure.

The Rump showed no such friendly spirit towards Mountagu himself, aware that blandishments would be futile. The Council took away his colonelcy and his lodgings in Whitehall, and seized many of his private papers; he was dropped from the Council and forfeited his peerage under the terms of the Indemnity Act.[26] His relations with the newly arrived Commissioners were strained from the outset. He said later that they had 'designed the taking me out of that command', and the suspicion was probably well-founded. A

---

[22] Davies, 207–8; F. J. Routledge, *England and the Treaty of the Pyrenees* (Liverpool, 1953), *passim*; *CSPD 1658–9*, 350; *CSPD 1659–60*, 31; Rawl. MS C 179, pp. 158, 202, 240–1; *CCSP* iv. 388–9; Clar. MS 60, fo. 503; *CSPV 1659–61*, 12, 25.

[23] *CCSP* iv. 287.

[24] *CSPD 1658–9*, 368, 388; Ludlow, *Memoirs*, ii. 84, 93; Clar. MS 61, fo. 172; Sandwich, *Journal*, 41. Sidney's colleagues were Sir Robert Honeywood, a Rumper and Vane's brother-in-law, and the merchant Thomas Boon, an Admiralty Commissioner, who provided some professional expertise.

[25] Sandwich, *Journal*, 42–3; *CJ* vii. 677.

[26] Harris, *Mountagu*, i. 138; Clar. MS 61, fo. 172; *CSPV 1659–61*, 42.

royalist observed at the time that the Commissioners were aiming, 'under pretence of reconciling the two kings [of Sweden and Denmark], to work upon the sea officers and, if they can, secure the navy'. They may have planned to divide him from his officers, as Sidney himself hinted, and replace him by his deputy, Goodson. If there was such a design, it failed, for Mountagu trod carefully and kept a close watch on order and discipline within the fleet.[27] Relations with Sidney, however, grew steadily worse till Mountagu came to see him as his 'mortal enemy'. This was indeed no exaggeration, for in the course of a row Sidney charged him with negotiating secretly with Charles Stuart and described his plan to take the fleet home as a piece of treachery worthy of death.[28]

From the moment of Richard's fall the royalists had looked hopefully towards Mountagu. They believed, correctly, that he would feel freed from any commitment to the Cromwell family by Richard's feeble abdication. There was even a bizarre scheme to smuggle the fallen Protector to the Sound, in the hope that both men could now be persuaded to throw in their lot with the king.[29] It was therefore decided to make an approach to the admiral, using his young cousin Edward Mountagu (who was serving with the fleet) as intermediary. Hyde wrote to Edward in June, asking him to press the king's case and promising that if the fleet came over Charles would promptly embark for England.[30] A royalist agent in London recruited another, more unlikely go-between: Cromwell's nephew, the former naval commander Thomas Whetstone. Whetstone, embittered by his disgrace a few months earlier, was eager to help, and convinced the agent that he possessed great influence among the seamen. Charles and Hyde were delighted with their catch. Whetstone made his way to Brussels, where he was knighted and given a pardon, and then set off to contact the General via Edward Mountagu. The king placed great store by the mission, directing Hyde to go to the Baltic himself if it went well. Whetstone's orders were to hand the General a letter from the king promising an

---

[27] Rawl. MS A 468, fo. 6; *Nicholas Papers,* iv. 104, 153; Clar. MS 61, fo. 325'; Harris, *Mountagu,* i. 149–51; Sandwich, *Journal,* 60–2; *Clarke Papers,* iv. 279–80.

[28] Sandwich, *Journal,* 47, 60 ff.

[29] *CCSP* iv. 191, 194; *CSPD 1658–9,* 340; Harris, *Mountagu,* i. 135–7; Pepys, *Diary,* i. 141; *CSP* iii. 478.

[30] *CSP* iii. 497–8; Clarendon, *History,* vi. 188. Ayscue was known as a royalist sympathizer but does not seem to have been used as an intermediary: *CSPD 1659–60,* 248.

earldom and any office he might ask in return for bringing over all or part of the fleet. If there was no response Whetstone was to contact other officers and seamen, and he carried with him letters from the king to the other flag-officers, Goodson and Stayner.[31]

The mission fell short of these high hopes. Whetstone duly forwarded the king's letter, with a covering letter of his own heaping abuse on the Rump (a 'new-modelled rabble of rebels') and warning that Mountagu would be sacked if he returned to England. But he lacked the most elementary skills of a secret agent, and his presence in Copenhagen soon became public knowledge. He even blundered into Mountagu and Sidney one day in the street, and Sidney, recognizing him, guessed at once what was afoot. Mountagu decided a meeting would be far too risky and had Whetstone hastily packed off back to Flanders with nothing more than a verbal message of goodwill towards the king. Edward Mountagu however also wrote directly to Hyde on 27 July, giving a frank and detailed assessment of the situation. While assuring the king of his own devotion and the General's goodwill he explained that Whetstone's mission had been badly timed. In the aftermath of Richard's fall something might have been done: the captains had been 'distracted' with fears that they would be turned out and were 'in a condition then to have received a good impression'. But now, he went on, with new commissions, protected by the Act of Indemnity, and 'not only forgiven but courted by the present power, I know no man's interest, let his inclinations be never so right, can lead any considerable part of them'. Even if half the fleet did follow the General, the most that could be hoped, the sailors would deliver up their officers once they found they had neither safe ports nor victuals. Edward was also scathing about Whetstone as an emissary, pointing out that his standing among the officers was very low.[32] The General's caution was understandable. There was no immediate prospect of winning over the fleet, and though he knew that royalist risings were being planned in England he was not prepared to risk all on so flimsy a basis. He had to consider too the hostages he had left behind: as a correspondent remarked, he had 'two thousand pounds *per annum*, with a wife and ten small

---

[31] Clar. MS 61, fos. 219, 291–2, 294, 300ʳ⁻ᵛ, 303ʳ⁻ᵛ, 385; *CSP* iii. 493–4, 497–8; Harris, *Mountagu*, i. 139–41.

[32] Clar. MS 61, fos. 280–1; Clar. MS 63, fos. 29–30; *CSP* iii. 565–6; Pepys, *Diary*, iv. 69; Clarendon, *History*, vi. 188–9; Harris, *Mountagu*, i. 144–5.

children, and it's no small matter will reward him for such a loss'.[33]

The royalists were none the less pleased with the outcome of the mission. If the General could do nothing for the present they had an indication of his support. Edward Mountagu ended his letter to Hyde with the promise: 'if there be any divisions or difference in England between the military and civil governors, or any party that will or can stand up for the king, I will venture my interest where it is most effectual'. Hyde rightly saw this as indicating the General's own intentions, and was confident that the fleet would intervene in the king's interest if risings in England did materialize.[34]

Preparations for these uprisings went ahead rapidly. But the Council was well aware of the plans and took energetic counter-measures, placing the army on alert, raising new volunteer forces, and arresting royalist suspects; the militia forces were also remodelled. As a result it was only in Cheshire that rebellion got off the ground; Sir George Booth's stand on 31 July attracted four or five thousand supporters, but his success was short-lived, for Lambert marched north and crushed the rebels at Warrington Bridge on 18 August.[35]

Naval units in home waters remained loyal throughout the crisis, helping to contain the danger. Lawson maintained a squadron off Ostend to prevent any royalist forces reaching England, and had shipping searched in the Channel for suspicious persons.[36] The agent at Plymouth, Hatsell, sent part of the western squadron to Chester Water to forestall any attempt to reinforce Booth by sea.[37] Hatsell also raised volunteer forces at Plymouth, and Benjamin Blake did the same at Bridgwater, while Nehemiah Bourne rounded up royalist supporters at Harwich.[38] The one trivial sign of royalist disaffection in the fleet was in the *Centurion*, whose surgeon declared that Charles I had died a martyr and that he was resolved to join the cavaliers if the opportunity arose.[39] It did not.

---

[33] *CSP* iii. 488; Clarendon, *History*, vi. 188–9; cf. Clar. MS 60, fo. 504.

[34] Clar. MS 63, fo. 30; *CSP* iii. 565–6; Clarendon, *History*, vi. 189.

[35] Davies, 123–43; Hutton, *Restoration*, 55–9. Lawson and the former flag-officer Edward Hall were named commissioners for Essex and Southwark respectively: *A and O* ii. 1312, 1324.

[36] *CSPD 1659–60*, 31, 101, 418; Rawl. MS C 179, pp. 158, 161, 202, 240–1.

[37] *CSPD 1659–60*, 87, 133; see also Adm. 2/1731, fo. 100ᵛ.

[38] *CSPD 1659–60*, 16, 65, 115, 119, 125, 455; Rawl. MS C 179, pp. 238, 240. All three were militia commissioners: *A and O* ii. 1322, 1326, 1332. A force was also raised at the Chatham dockyard under the master-shipwright, John Taylor: Rawl. MS C 179, p. 284; *CSPD 1659–60*, 74.   [39] *CSPD 1659–60*, 182.

Booth's rising was closely followed by the unexpected return of Mountagu's fleet. When his ships weighed anchor in the Sound on 24 August Mountagu had known of the rising but not of its failure, and his sudden, unauthorized return naturally aroused deep suspicion. Royalist agents were sure he had come to help Booth. One said the General had planned 'to block up the Thames with a squadron, and to employ the rest for the transportation of men, as occasion should require', but that finding Booth already defeated he had been forced to abandon his plans. Hyde too believed he had returned on this account. This claim cannot be proved, though if Mountagu did have such a design he would have been careful of course not to leave incriminating evidence. The reason he gave for the fleet's return to his officers and fellow Commissioners and to the Rump was the shortage of victuals, which had certainly been a major concern. He was also undoubtedly anxious to prevent the fleet from being used against the Swedes, which he feared was the drift of the Rump's policy. But if he had found a favourable situation in England it seems likely that he would have tried to use the fleet to help instal a more acceptable regime, whether under Richard or the king. (Booth himself had left his aims unclear.) The most Mountagu claimed in later years was that he had taken pains in the Sound to keep the fleet out of the Rump's hands, and that this had been of some value to the royalist cause. Whatever the truth, rumours linking his name with the royalists circulated widely, and it was soon common alehouse talk that he had engaged to serve the king. It was even whispered that he had met Charles secretly at Flushing, and that the duke of York had gone incognito to the Baltic.[40]

The Council was alarmed and angry at Mountagu's sudden return. It sent Walton and two other Admiralty Commissioners to take charge of the fleet, and they questioned him on board the *Naseby* at Southwold Bay as soon as it dropped anchor. He was summoned to London to be examined by the Council, and Parliament too debated his return. But he was then allowed to retire quietly to his estate at Hinchinbrooke; there was no firm evidence against him and the Rump had no desire to create martyrs now the

---

[40] Harris, *Mountagu*, i. 153–9; Clar. MS 61, fo. 86; Clar. MS 63, fo. 261; Clar. MS 64, fos. 178, 189, 329; Bodl. Carte MS 73, fos. 291, 306; Sandwich, *Journal*, 43, 45–7, 51; Clarendon, *History*, vi. 190; *CSP* iii. 550–1; *Clarke Papers*, iv. 292, 296–7; Rawl. MS A 468, fo. 6; Davies, 205–7. Cf. ch. 4, part iii, above.

crisis was over. His fleet was paid off, slowly and with difficulty, and the Rump breathed with relief at having control of the whole navy at last.[41] Mountagu sent a friendly message to the royal court but there was now nothing he could do to serve the king.[42]

The Rump still faced two intractable problems. One was its deteriorating financial position, which left thousands of soldiers and sailors unpaid and therefore unpredictable; as everyone knew, large-scale mutinies could play straight into the royalists' hands. Even before Oliver's death the situation had been serious, for crown and church lands had already been sold and the monthly assessment—the main tax—had been cut from a peak of £120,000 to a mere £35,000 for political reasons. The government's revenue in 1658 was about a million pounds, far short of its needs: £1.3 millions were required annually for the army and £600,000 for the navy. By the start of 1658 £714,000 was owing to the navy, more than a whole year's naval budget.[43] The Admiralty Commissioners paid several fruitless visits to the Protector in search of funds, and on Richard's accession they stated bluntly that the navy was 'on the brink of ruin', and that the summer guard was being kept out on 'dead wages' because there was no money to pay the seamen. On 1 November pressing naval debts were put at £541,000, with a further million pounds required to cover expenses over the coming year. Early in April 1659 the Commissioners gave up the struggle and resigned *en masse*, angered that naval revenues had been transferred to pay the army and tired out, they said, 'with the incessant clamours from poor men that are creditors of the navy, and with the cries and complaints of seamen and their relations for pay due to them'. The service would benefit, they added tartly, if the government sometimes heeded its own officials.[44] The restored Rump had no additional resources to help the new Commissioners it appointed in May. They reported that they would need one and a quarter

[41] Sandwich, *Journal*, 46–7; Carte MS 73, fos. 300, 304; *Clarke Papers*, iv. 102–3; *CSPD 1659–60*, 167–8, 184–5; Harris, *Mountagu*, i. 156–7. Mountagu apparently repudiated Booth's rising, though only when he already knew it had failed: *The Loyall Scout*, 26 Aug.–2 Sept.

[42] Clar. MS 66, fo. 103; cf. Clar. MS 64, fo. 178.

[43] M. Ashley, *Financial and Commercial Policy under the Cromwellian Protectorate* (2nd edn., 1962), chs. 5–9; Oppenheim, 368–70; Hammond, thesis, ch. 4; Cogar, thesis, 210, 224–5.

[44] Adm. 2/1730, fo. 250; SP 18/202/26; Adm. 3/274, fos. 56ʳ⁻ᵛ, 70ᵛ–71.

million pounds by December, whereas the anticipated revenue was only a quarter of a million, and they found themselves (like their predecessors) unable to call in the summer guard and unable to pay dockyard workers or naval contractors.[45] Their predicament is confirmed by a mass of other evidence. A list drawn up during the following winter shows ninety-three ships with wages between eight and forty-seven months in arrears. From Harwich, Dover, and elsewhere came stories of dockyard workers unpaid, resentful, and sometimes threatening violence. Contractors refused to supply new stores and the Navy Commissioners reported plaintively that their credit had grown 'low and despicable'.[46] Naval stores had been almost exhausted in sending two fleets to the Baltic and it proved impossible to replenish them.[47] Without funds naval administration would eventually collapse, followed inevitably by the gradual disintegration of the fleet; the political consequences were too alarming to contemplate.

The second and more immediate problem facing the Rump was over relations with the army leaders. The 'Grandees' showed little inclination to accept orders from a body they had called into being, and recurring tensions culminated in a showdown on 11 October, when the Rump revoked the commissions of Lambert, Desborough, and several others. This suicidal gesture merely brought about its own downfall: the officers promptly staged a coup, turning out the Rump and setting up a Committee of Safety to manage affairs while they devised a new constitution.[48]

The new military regime had little support in the nation, and even the armed forces were not solidly behind it. Monck in Scotland declared his continuing support for the Rump. In England too there was a widespread refusal to accept the new regime. A fierce remonstrance attacking the coup and calling for the Rump to be restored was published in mid-November with the endorsement of many leading army officers, both past and present, the mayor of London and many of his colleagues—and the naval leaders Lawson, Goodson, and Stayner.[49] The navy indeed remained ominously

[45] Adm. 3/274, fo. 103ʳ·ᵛ. The new Commissioners are listed in *A and O* ii. 1277.

[46] *CSPD 1659–60*, 206, 468, 471, 516.

[47] SP 18/202/26. Plans to send a force back to the Sound had to be abandoned: *CJ* vii. 773; *CSPV 1659–61*, 73.

[48] Davies, 144–58; Hutton, *Restoration*, 64–7. The new Committee of Safety included the Navy Commissioner, Robert Thomson.

[49] Davies, 162–4; *The Remonstrance and Protestation of the Well-Affected People* (Edinburgh, 1660; 1st pub. London, 1659, and dated 16 Nov.). Among the many

aloof from the new regime. The situation in some ways paralleled that of the spring: the republican Lawson posed an obvious threat to the army junta, just as the Cromwellian Mountagu had done to the restored Rump. But whereas the Rump had found in Lawson a staunch ally to counter the threat, no naval leader was likely to champion a regime which existed mainly to serve the army's own self-interest.

Though Lawson's discontent was generally known the junta dared not attempt to remove him, and it tried hard to win his support. On 15 October an Admiralty official set off for the Downs to justify the coup as an 'indispensable necessity laid upon the officers of the army'. On the same day a number of Admiralty Commissioners, including Vane and Salwey, informed him that the Council was still in being and that he should continue to follow its orders. The acquiescence of Vane, his former patron, and the survival of some part of the old regime may have dissuaded Lawson from any sudden action. More important, he had only one other ship with him in the Downs at the time of the coup, the rest being scattered on convoys and other duties, and this clearly ruled out any immediate action.[50] To keep him compliant the Commissioners sent misleading accounts of developments ashore, claiming that Monck's soldiers were so mutinous that his stand in Scotland was of no significance.[51] For the moment Lawson remained quietly in the Downs, while his seamen angrily watched the army leaders diverting revenues to pay their soldiers. Should he ever decide to challenge the junta he knew he could build on a widespread sense of resentment.[52]

In reality the new regime was of course deeply concerned about Monck's defiance, hastily sending Lambert north to block his path into England. It also took steps to secure control of the northern seas; Mackey of the *Yarmouth*, for example, was sent to the Tyne with orders to assist Lambert's forces. Sharland of the *Fox*, patrolling the northern Irish Sea, was told to prevent any contact between other sponsors were Col. Rich, Whetham, Governor of Portsmouth, William Rainborough, Henry Hatsell, William Burton, Capt. Hall (the former naval officer?), and the ex-Leveller, Petty.

[50] Adm. 2/1731, fo. 113; Clar. MS 66, fos 160, 218, 284. Monck's chaplain, Gumble, says that Monck contacted the fleet but received a cold reply. This would be surprising; Gumble was perhaps confusing Lawson's officers with those who wrote to Monck from London: T. Gumble, *The Life of General Monck* (1671), 136; Davies, 167; n. 55, below.

[51] Adm. 2/1731, fo. 119. For Vane's position see V. A. Rowe, *Sir Henry Vane the Younger* (1970), 226–9.   [52] Clar. MS 67, fo. 34ʳ⁻ᵛ; *Clarke Papers*, iv. 102–3.

Monck and the army in Ireland, whose allegiance was uncertain; a copy of the declaration justifying the coup was posted to the ship to satisfy any scruples her company might have.[53] There was a further danger that Monck, as a former General at Sea, might still have influence over some of his old naval colleagues, and the junta hastily removed former protégés serving in the North Sea who might be tempted to defect. Francis Allen of the *Advice* was sent new orders directing him to the Downs, and Edward Nixon of the *Pearl* was summoned to London for urgent consultations, while arrangements were made to secure his ship.[54]

None of the naval officers welcomed the junta, but once it was established some of them proved ready to grant it a grudging acceptance. Goodson and Stayner, who had been among those to condemn it, came to feel it would be better to negotiate a compromise settlement than risk a ruinous fraticidal war. This was the argument of a blunt, reproachful letter sent to Monck early in November by Goodson and twenty-one senior officers then in London, among them Stayner, Stokes, John Bourne, Newbery, Earning, and Myngs. They did not seek to justify the coup, they wrote, though they remarked that over the years the army had generally been faithful to the 'cause of God, and his people'; rather they begged him to see that by dividing the army he might let in the king, bringing back the 'thraldom and bondage' of earlier times. They also queried his sudden devotion to the Rump, pointing out how readily he had accepted Cromwell's dissolution in April 1653.[55] Monck's reply was friendly in tone but uncompromising. The earlier dissolution had been in the midst of war, he explained, and resistance then would have endangered the nation; moreover it had proved disastrous, leading to the oppressive rule of a single person (Cromwell), and he did not wish to see the mistake repeated. He vigorously repudiated any ties with the king, affirming 'we in our very thoughts abhor, and shall spend our blood' against Charles Stuart or any single person. 'You know my plainness and sincerity,' he added, 'that I am none of those that dare assert any thing against my conscience'. Monck was neither plain nor sincere,

---

[53] Adm. 2/1731, fos. 116ᵛ, 121.

[54] Adm. 2/1731, fos. 116, 117. For Monck as patron of the two officers see SP 18/223/25, 157; Coventry MS 98, fo. 53ᵛ; BL Add. MS 38848, fo. 30; below, n. 113.

[55] Their letter was promptly made public: *The Publick Intelligencer*, 7–14 Nov. 1659; Whitelocke, *Memorials*, iv. 370–2. Goodson and Stayner's endorsement of the *Remonstrance* must have been given some time before it appeared in print.

as the nation was soon to learn, and his conscience proved highly accommodating.[56]

The Grandees persevered in their attempts to win over Monck's army and the fleet. They sent Goodson and Stayner to treat with Lawson in the Downs, without success. The compliance of Goodson and his friends was useful propaganda for the junta but nothing more, for they had no forces under their command.[57] Talks with Monck's envoys in London made more progress, however, and led to an agreement in mid-November, by which representatives of the English, Scottish, and Irish armies and the fleet would meet early the following month to draw up a new constitution and summon a parliament. Lawson was invited to come and help choose the navy's representatives, but he refused to stir. He rejected the right of the military to make and unmake parliaments, and was also unwilling to hand over the fleet to Newbery (as directed) rather than to his own protégé, Dakins, perhaps suspecting a manœuvre to oust him.[58] On 5 December the naval officers in London went ahead without him in choosing their representatives for the constitutional talks. From their own ranks they selected Goodson, Bourne, Stayner, Stokes, Robert Blake (the late admiral's nephew), and three others, and they also nominated Lawson (though none of his friends) and Mountagu. The last two names suggest the wide range of opinion to be found within the officer corps, and they show too how personal loyalties could cut across political beliefs. Thus John Bourne, a committed radical, felt a personal attachment to Mountagu, under whom he had served, and wrote at once urging him to take part in the talks. Mountagu was slow to reply and chose to stay at Hinchinbrooke.[59]

The assembled officers pressed ahead with framing a new constitution, and by mid-December they had agreed its outlines.[60] Their plans were doomed, however, for opposition to military rule was now growing rapidly. The London apprentices expressed the

---

[56] *A Letter sent by General Monck to Vice-Admiral Goodson* ([29 Nov.] 1659: BL 669 f 22 (20)). For contrasting views of Monck's true intentions at this time see Hutton, *Restoration*, 67–74; M. Ashley, *General Monck* (1977), chs. 12–14.

[57] Clar. MS 66, fo. 218; *CSPD 1659–60*, 268.

[58] Davies, 172–4; Adm. 2/1731, fos. 121, 123–4. Monck himself did not accept the deal agreed by his agents.

[59] Carte MS 73, fos. 211, 327. (The other members were Robert Clarke, Witheridge, and Harman.)

[60] Davies, 185–6; Adm. 2/1731, fo. 123ᵛ⁻ᵛ.

mood of the capital by staging rowdy demonstrations. Still worse, the arrival of three former Rumpers in Portsmouth on 3 December prompted the Governor and garrison to declare for Parliament, and a force sent against them changed sides and joined the rebels. The Grandees' confidence was badly jolted.[61]

Portsmouth's defiance gave a new urgency to the navy's position. Disaffection in the fleet had existed before, but never with a garrisoned naval base to offer potential support. The junta's first move was to try to stop the ships based at Portsmouth from falling into rebel hands. On 6 December the Admiralty Commissioners directed the captains there to secure their ships and obey only orders from the Admiralty and the Committee of Safety. They knew the seamen were unpaid and mutinous—many had been threatening to desert and join foreign merchant ships—and they promised that an official was hastening down with money for their wages. But when the official was prevented from entering the town order among the seamen began to collapse. One of the captains (Cowes of the *Paradox*) abandoned his ship and came up to London, leaving no orders for his men, and half the crew soon followed in his wake. The Committee soon grasped that without sailors the vessel would be of no use to the Rumpers, and it promptly invited the rest of the men to come up to London too for their pay.[62]

A far more serious possibility was that Lawson's fleet would join forces with the rebels at Portsmouth. The Grandees tried hard to head off this threat. Desborough ordered him not to send ships there and added, perhaps sensing that orders were no longer automatically obeyed, that the revolt there had won little support among the citizens or seamen.[63] The army also renewed its efforts to conciliate him, sending two veteran opponents of the Protectorate (Hugh Courtney and William Allen) to the fleet for more talks.[64] The Admiralty Commissioners meanwhile bombarded him with reasons for remaining obedient to the junta. They warned that

---

[61] Davies, 180–3, 186–7; Hutton, *Restoration*, 76–80; D. Dymond, *Portsmouth and the Fall of the Puritan Revolution* (The Portsmouth Papers, xi; Portsmouth, 1971).

[62] Adm. 2/1731, fos. 122ᵛ, 123ᵛ, 125; *CSPD 1659–60*, 506–8; BL Sloane MS 970, fo. 6.

[63] Adm. 2/1731, fo. 123ᵛ; Carte MS 73, fo. 333.

[64] *Clarke Papers*, iv. 165. Courtney also took part in Vane's mission to the fleet in mid-December: *Sir Harry Vane's Last Sigh for the Committee of Safety* (1659), 4, 7.

Monck really wanted a free parliament which might bring back the king, and told him that he alone could prevent a threatened royalist invasion from Flanders. They assured him that a return to parliamentary rule was in hand, and they met his practical worries by promising that a supply of victuals was on its way.[65] In case all these arguments failed the junta also took steps to prepare a naval force for use against him. On 15 December the Committee of Safety ordered a squadron of ten ships to be set out under the command of Goodson, with Stayner, Stokes, and Bourne among its leading officers. Lawson was told this force would be used against the royalists, and would give work to unemployed sailors 'who in these unsettled and distracted times will, it's feared, be ready to join with any party that should make any insurrection'. It is unlikely that he believed this bland explanation, for the squadron's real purpose was generally known. In any case it no longer mattered: Lawson had already decided on a new course of open confrontation.[66]

The navy's break with the regime was a crippling blow for the junta, overshadowing the troubles at Portsmouth. The revolt at Portsmouth had in fact helped to trigger Lawson's action. Col. Rich, the commander of the troops who had defected and joined the rebels, was Lawson's friend and mentor and had kept closely in touch with opinion in the fleet. Once the town had taken its stand Lawson's own position hardened. On 9 December he bluntly told an emissary from Fleetwood that the only way to cure the nation's ills was to recall the Rump. The final breach came a few days later, apparently hastened by the sudden arrival in the fleet of Col. Okey and Thomas Scot, seeking refuge after the failure of their scheme to seize the Tower in the Rump's name. Lawson already had messages of support from ex-Speaker Lenthall and other MPs, and on 13 December he made a public declaration of support for the Rump, pledging to restore it by force if necessary. He also put forward a wide-ranging programme of reforms, calling for an indemnity, religious freedom, the abolition of tithes, encouragement of trade, legal reform, relief for the poor and unemployed, and, with his sailors in mind, the end of impressment and better provision for the victims of war. Lawson addressed his declaration to the Mayor and

[65] Adm. 2/1731, fos. 123–5. Desborough, Clarke, Kelsey, and Salmon were the Commissioners actively backing the junta; cf. Cogar, thesis, 236 ff.
[66] Adm. 3/274, fo. 149; Adm. 2/1731, fo. 124; *CSP* iii. 640.

corporation of London, knowing their hostility to the junta, but it found a very cold welcome. Many of the city fathers strongly favoured Charles Stuart, whereas Lawson had repudiated him and declared for the 'interest of Christ and the good and weal of all the people of God'. They also found most of his programme repugnant, and his wish to have English law brought into line with scripture revived alarming memories of Barebone's Parliament. The City therefore simply ignored his appeal.[67] No doubt it much preferred a petition from the merchant seamen, calling for a free parliament, which would be likely to bring back the king.[68] But only Lawson had the power to second his demands, and he soon showed that he was prepared to use it. The day after his declaration appeared in print his fleet left the Downs and sailed into the Thames.[69]

The junta had brazened out the defiance of Monck, the Portsmouth garrison, and the London prentices; it was Lawson's irruption, according to Clarendon, which 'brake the heart of the Committee of Safety'. The republican Ludlow agreed: Lawson's approach, he wrote, 'wrought such an alteration in them, that they expressed to us their readiness to comply with the desires of the fleet, so it might be done on convenient terms'.[70] They knew he could block all commerce in the River, and feared that once corn and coal supplies were cut off, hungry, cold, and angry Londoners would pour into the streets to sweep them away. The Committee of Safety therefore sent a powerful delegation to the fleet to seek a compromise solution; the envoys, led by Vane and Salwey, boarded the *Bristol* at Tilbury on 17 December and sailed downriver to meet Lawson and his fleet. In the event it proved difficult even to get talks started. Vane's first aim was to keep the fleet well away from London and he urged Lawson to drop anchor at once; this was refused and the fleet bore on up to Gravesend. Vane was also dismayed to find that Lawson had with him the Rumpers Scot and Okey, who had no interest in compromise; Scot refused to speak to

---

[67] *A Declaration of Vice-Admiral John Lawson* (13 Dec. 1659); Ludlow, *Memoirs,* ii. 148–9, 176, 183–4. The Speaker's agent was Col. Matthew Alured: *The Parliamentary Intelligencer,* 19–26 Dec. 1659; *CSPD 1659–60,* 591.

[68] *The Humble Petition and Address of the Sea-men* ([12 Dec.] 1659; BL 669 f 22 (8)).

[69] M. H[arrison], 'A Narrative of the Proceedings of the Fleet' (1659), in Penn, *Memorials,* ii. 187; Ludlow, *Memoirs,* ii. 175–6; Mordaunt, *Letter-Book,* 142–3; M. Guizot, *History of Richard Cromwell and the Restoration of Charles II* (1866), ii. 311.

[70] Clarendon, *History,* vi. 159; Ludlow, *Memoirs,* ii. 180.

the junta's envoys and indeed urged Lawson to arrest them. Eventually, however, Lawson persuaded everyone to take part in a general discussion the following day. The vice-admiral played a dominant role at this meeting, dashing Vane's expectation that he would be able to manipulate his old protégé. Vane and his colleagues argued that the parliament projected by the Committee of Safety would be far superior to the Rump. Lawson countered that it would be no more than a puppet of the soldiers, 'who have nothing to do with giving laws to the nation'. It would always have to serve the army's interests, and would be turned out the moment it ceased to do so. He went on to deliver a fierce diatribe against the army's past conduct, denouncing its 'horrid perjuries, breach of trust, blasting and abusing of the nation'. Lawson's outburst, in part the culmination of years of army–navy rivalry, was the clearest statement he ever made of his political creed. He argued that to be free a nation must have civilian, constitutional government; a military regime, whatever its rhetoric, was by its very nature tyrannical. He recalled how the Rump had tried in vain to shake off the army's yoke both before and since Cromwell's usurpation, and made it plain that the fleet was not prepared to allow a new sham-parliament 'to be a mask to the army's tyranny'. He carried the day, winning over four or five of his officers who had at first been swayed by Vane. The envoys went away empty-handed; Lawson did offer further talks, but only on the manner of the Rump's recall.[71]

Over the next few days the army's nerve collapsed. News came that the forces in Ireland had declared for the Rump, and troops from Portsmouth were reported to be advancing on the capital.[72] Lawson was in touch with the leaders at Portsmouth and with like-minded elements around the country. More important, his force of twenty-two ships was now blockading the capital, strangling the nation's trade, and word spread that he was prepared to send 3,000 men ashore to re-establish the Rump.[73] On 21 December he sent a second letter to the City, repeating his demands and ruling out a

---

[71] Ludlow, *Memoirs*, ii. 180–1; Harrison, 'Narrative', 186–91; *Sir Harry Vane's Last Sigh*; *Parliamentary Intelligencer*, 19–26 Dec.; *CSP* iii. 631–4; Guizot, *Richard Cromwell*, ii. 311–12.

[72] Davies, 180–1, 186–7, 248–9; Ludlow, *Memoirs*, ii. 184–5.

[73] *Clarke Papers*, iv. 216; *CSP* iii. 631, 640; Clar. MS 67, fos. 246ᵛ, 270; Clar. MS 68, fos. 11, 16; *CSPV 1659–61*, 105; *Parliamentary Intelligencer*, 19–26 Dec.; *A Particular Advice*, 23–30 Dec.

freely elected parliament. It was signed by twenty-one captains, two of whom delivered it in person to ensure a reply.[74] The City shared none of Lawson's goals, as he now realized, but it could no longer ignore his fleet. It sent back envoys with a counter-proposal, by which the City, army, and navy would formulate joint constitutional plans to be put to the Rump when it reassembled. Lawson flatly rejected this idea: Parliament was sovereign, he insisted, and all other interest-groups must accept its unqualified authority. In a further letter he brought the real issue into the open by calling on the city fathers to disavow Charles Stuart—a demand they predictably ignored. He sent a much warmer letter to the London militia, praising its zeal for 'the work of God, in securing his cause, the interest of Christ and his people'. For the moment at least, Lawson's voice carried more weight than any other: on 24 December a demoralized Fleetwood sent Lenthall the keys to the Parliament House, and on the 26th the MPs took their seats once more.[75]

The second restoration of the Rump was Lawson's finest hour. For several weeks the Rump continued to depend on him for its survival, and he remained with his fleet in the Thames to overawe the City.[76] His control over the navy was complete. There was only one commander who appeared, briefly and doubtfully, to side with the army. On the eve of the Rump's return Capt. Allgate of the *Oxford* had carried Ludlow to Ireland, and it was later alleged that when Ludlow found himself rejected at Dublin (rather unfairly) as an enemy of Parliament he and Allgate had laid plans to seize merchant shipping and form a squadron loyal to the junta. Allgate strongly denied the charge, pleading that he had believed Ludlow's claim to be a good parliamentarian; he explained that he had merely been unable 'to make a certain judgement of those late wonderful revolutions, and therefore very liable, as a poor infirm creature, to err therein'. That sounds more likely. The episode is important mainly as further evidence of Lawson's popularity among the

---

[74] *Two Letters from Vice-Admiral John Lawson* (21 Dec. 1659). It was delivered by Capts. Haddock and Harrison. One ship was represented by its lieutenant, Trafford; its captain (Robt. Nixon) appears to have died about this time.

[75] *Two Letters from Vice-Admiral John Lawson* ([30 Dec.]; BL 669 f 22 (43)); *A Common Council holden on 29 December 1659* (BL 669 f 22 (46)); *Publick Intelligencer,* 19–26 Dec.; Sloane MS 970, fo. 14; Mordaunt, *Letter-Book,* 146; Clar. MS 68, fos. 11, 48–50, 63; Davies, 188–9, 256–9.

[76] *CSP* iii. 640; *CSPV 1659–61,* 105, 107.

seamen, for the *Oxford*'s crew had forced Allgate to steer for the Downs and place the ship at his disposal.[77]

The restored Rump was immensely grateful to Lawson. The MPs voted their thanks on 27 December, sending a delegation to convey them in person. On 2 January 1660 he and Monck were elected to a new Council of State, on the 9th he came into the Commons' Chamber to be thanked once more, and on the 21st the Rump voted to settle lands worth £500 a year on him and his heirs. He was assigned Lambert's former quarters in Whitehall. The MPs naturally confirmed his command of the fleet, and approved several key appointments he had made involving his protégés Dakins, Abelson, Tearne (his former lieutenant), and Fenn.[78] Early in February he and Monck also became members of a newly constituted body of Admiralty Commissioners.[79]

Relations between Lawson and the Rump did not remain wholly untroubled. The MPs purged a number of army officers and politicians who had co-operated with the junta, and Vane and Salwey were among those to be expelled from the House. Lawson presented a petition asking for Vane to be readmitted, either swayed by old personal loyalties or perhaps realizing that the regime must be conciliatory if it was to survive. The only result was that he forfeited some of his own credit among the Rumpers.[80] Edward Hyde wondered whether he would keep his post, and one royalist agent even claimed he was now plotting rebellion with Lambert and Vane. But this was no more than wild speculation; the Rump had no wish to break with one of its saviours, and there is no sign that Lawson thought for one moment of turning against it.[81]

It was natural for the royalists to exaggerate rifts between Lawson and the Rump, for their frustration in the last months of 1659 was intense. The precarious rule of the hated army junta had created a hopeful situation for them. They believed even a small landing from the continent might now trigger a general uprising, and Lawson's

---

[77] *CSPD 1659–60*, 301–2, 311–14, 316–18; Ludlow, *Memoirs*, ii. 187–93; *Clarke Papers*, iv. 242.

[78] *CJ* vii. 707, 799, 801, 806, 818; *Occurrences from Foreign Parts*, 27 Dec.–3 Jan.; *Mercurius Publicus*, 29 Dec.–5 Jan., 5–12 Jan.; *CSPV 1659–61*, 110.

[79] *A and O* ii. 1407. The Commissioners who had accepted the army junta were naturally dropped.

[80] Davies, 260–2; Rowe, *Vane*, 230–1; *CSP* iii. 650. Pepys notes 'a picture hung up at the Exchange, of a great pair of buttocks shitting of a turd into Lawson's mouth, and over it was writ "The thanks of the House" ': Pepys, *Diary*, i. 45.

[81] *CCSP* iv. 508, 519, 521.

antipathy to the junta raised hopes that the navy could at last be won over, clearing the way for a force to cross the Channel. So from late October the cavaliers set out to woo the fleet. The duke of York ordered agents to 'feel the pulses of those which command the English ships, if by money or any other means they may be reduced to their obedience'. The king wrote to the Dover merchant Arnold Braemes, an old acquaintance of Lawson and now a royalist supporter, asking him to dangle the prospect of substantial rewards before the vice-admiral. The agents also tried to fan the mutinies which broke out during the autumn in several ships in the River over pay. This seemed a promising tactic, for angry sailors were said to have declared that 'if they cannot have it at home, they have another master to go to'. But in the event the agents had to admit they had failed to shake the officers' loyalty or the seamen's indifference.[82]

Despite these setbacks the royalists persevered, for the navy's part in the fall of the junta had underlined its political importance. Hyde asked for detailed assessments of Lawson and his colleagues, and authorized his agents to offer 20,000 pistoles to suborn five or six ships, which he thought might be enough to escort an invading force across the Channel. Braemes came up to London to work on Lawson, and the royalist Viscount Mordaunt ventured to approach the vice-admiral and several other commanders in person. But the results were again meagre. Braemes admitted he was unable to shake Lawson's 'rigid' republicanism. One frustrated agent called Lawson 'a sea-Fairfax, so sullen, so senseless, of so obstinate a courage, and so wayward obstinacy', and another concluded that 'no good is to be done with any of them'. At the end of January an agent reported that only two ships at most could be won over, and pointed out that this would be useless: the rest would blockade them wherever they went and their sailors would then simply run away. In the event not a single ship defected.[83] Hyde sent word assuring Mountagu of the king's continuing regard, but the former admiral had no forces under his command and remained quietly at home.[84]

Despairing of Lawson the royalists waited to see what Monck

---

[82] Mordaunt, *Letter-Book*, 24, 76, 79–80, 89–90; Clar. MS 66, fos. 97, 248; Clar. MS 67, fo. 34.
  [83] *CSP* iii. 628–9, 637, 640, 642, 652; Clar. MS 67, fo. 264; Clar. MS 69, fos. 30, 89, 104⁻; Mordaunt, *Letter-Book*, 164, 178. A pistole was worth about 17s. 6d.
  [84] *CSP* iii. 106.

would do. He had never accepted the junta's rule, and on 1 January 1660 his army crossed into England and began its famous march south. As the Rump was by then already back in power there was intense speculation over his motives: was he was coming to help it or to restore the old Long Parliament, by readmitting the members barred in 1648?—or to impose government by a single person, whether himself, Richard Cromwell, or Charles Stuart? Monck was extremely guarded about his intentions. He was almost certainly looking for a representative parliament to establish a lasting and conservative settlement, whatever its form, though his repeated declarations repudiating a king or any single person discouraged the royalists from placing much hope in him.[85]

Lawson was ready to welcome Monck as an old colleague, and on 28 January he took about twenty of his senior officers to St Albans, where Monck greeted them as his 'old friends'. Lawson was confident he would protect the Rump from the City, ending its dependence on the fleet and the unreliable English soldiery. Soon after the General's arrival in London Lawson took Ludlow to meet him, and in the course of their conversation Monck vowed once more to live and die for a commonwealth; as they left Lawson confided his hope that the General was the Good Samaritan who would heal the nation's wounds.[86]

In the event Monck's idea of a cure was not what Lawson had in mind. On 11 February Monck demanded that the vacant seats be filled to make the Parliament more representative, and called for a new and free parliament to meet in the spring. This, plainly, was the Rump's death-warrant. Ten days later, on 21 February, he decided to allow the moderates barred in 1648 to resume their seats, and about seventy of them promptly did so, outnumbering the Rumpers.[87]

Lawson had clearly believed in Monck's devotion to the Rump and news of the secluded MPs' return came as a shock. A royalist agent wrote that Lawson was even threatening to turn his guns on the Tower.[88] This was the decisive moment if the navy was ever to resist the turning political tide. Some radicals were standing by the

---

[85] Davies, 265 ff.; *CSP* iii. 678; Mordaunt, *Letter-Book*, 155, 162, 174, 180.
[86] *Publick Intelligencer*, 23–30 Jan. 1660; Whitelocke, *Memorials*, iv. 391; Ludlow, *Memoirs*, ii. 215–16.
[87] Davies, ch. 15; Hutton, *Restoration*, 89–96.
[88] *CSP* iii. 688.

Rump: his friend Col. Rich attempted a military rising, Overton at
Hull declared for the republic and the godly party, and Ludlow was
trying to organize a general uprising which he hoped the fleet would
assist. Lawson was unsure what to do. He confided later that he had
been strongly tempted to join these loyalists, and that he had
received assurances of support from seamen in the River and from
others in Chatham and Portsmouth.[89]

In the event Lawson did not stir. There are several possible
reasons for his failure to act, all of them probably playing some
part. First, his own position was secure and he may have thought he
could afford to wait on events. At Monck's insistence the readmitted MPs had at once confirmed him as vice-admiral and commander-in-chief, realizing that any attempt to dislodge him would
inflame the seamen.[90] Second, he seems to have believed the republican cause was not yet lost. Monck had spoken of a new parliament
to settle the nation without a king or house of Lords, and Lawson
appears to have taken this at face value. He knew the Rump could
not be a permanent solution and a new parliament, chosen with
suitable restrictions, was the natural way forward. He was still
hopeful in mid-March that MPs in the new parliament would be
strictly vetted to exclude crypto-cavaliers.[91] Third, should the king
return after all, he probably saw a monarchy bound by tight
constitutional safeguards—quite a likely outcome—as preferable to
a military regime. Braemes reported him as saying he would prefer
the king to any other single person, and this is plausible; unlike the
other possible contenders Charles would not need a large army to
sustain him. Finally, Lawson had at least one eye open to his own
survival. He knew there was little prospect of success in challenging
a Parliament backed by Monck's army and by public opinion. In
December the soldiery had been divided and demoralized, and the
Londoners had welcomed his stand; the situation by late February
was very different. Lawson was now willing to listen even to the
royalists. Though he did not succumb to Braemes's blandishments
he treated him in a friendly manner, and he even offered a safe
conduct to the notorious royalist Mordaunt. As an agent observed,

[89] Davies, 300–2; Ludlow, *Memoirs*, ii. 242–4; *CCSP* iv. 594; Pepys, *Diary*, i. 79;
Clar. MS 71, fos. 34, 185–6.

[90] *CJ* vii. 847; Pepys, *Diary*, i. 62; Clarendon, *History*, vi. 186; T. Lister, *Life and
Administration of Edward, First Earl of Clarendon* (1837–8), iii. 85–6; E. Hyde, Earl
of Clarendon, *The Life of Edward Earl of Clarendon* (with) *A Continuation of his
History* (Oxford, 1827), ii. 393; Hutton, *Restoration*, 96.

[91] *CCSP* iv. 499; SP 18/223/73.

he was 'not so obstinate as not to hear all parties speak'.[92] Lawson's first hope was still to save the republic; failing that he hoped to save himself.

The restored Long Parliament never trusted Lawson and it was determined to place the navy in safe hands as soon as it could. Mountagu was the natural choice. On 2 March Parliament named him and Monck joint Generals at Sea, designating Mountagu commander of the summer guard; Lawson retained his post as vice-admiral but lost his overall command, and he was also dropped from the Council. Rumours spread that he was now plotting against Parliament with disaffected elements ashore.[93] But on 6 March he wrote to Monck and Mountagu accepting their appointments without demur; he also thanked them for the increased salary they had tactfully secured him and for their help over the lands voted earlier by the Rump. News of his submission was quickly made public.[94] Some years later Robert Blackborne, a former colleague, called Lawson 'a stout man but a false man', who had proved to be 'the greatest hypocrite in the world'.[95] This bitter jibe has some force: like many others in the winter of 1659–60 Lawson was concerned to preserve himself. But the arguments against armed resistance were as weighty as before, and he clung even now to the possibility of a settlement without the king. He is said to have written a letter on 10 March reporting the glad (though false) news that Parliament had voted in favour of a commonwealth and against monarchy. Two weeks later an observer claimed he was still secretly hoping 'the sectaries may get up again'. And in the elections for the Convention Parliament he used his influence at Scarborough (his native town) to secure the return of the republican Luke Robinson, defeating the efforts of the moderates and crypto-royalists.[96]

[92] Clar. MS 68, fo. 204; Clar. MS 69, fos. 89, 164·; Mordaunt, *Letter-Book*, 142, 164.

[93] *CJ* vii. 849, 858, 860; Pepys, *Diary*, i. 62, 71, 75; *Nicholas Papers*, iv. 199; *CCSP* v. 743; Clarendon, *History*, vi. 186.

[94] Davies, 302–3; Carte MS 73, fos. 355, 449. Monck tried to secure £10,000 in cash for Lawson instead of £500 p.a. in land, no doubt aware how delicate the land question was likely to become: Add. MS 9300, fo. 402.

[95] Pepys, *Diary*, iv. 376.

[96] *Thurloe*, vii. 864; HMC 4, *5th Report*, 199; Lister, *Clarendon*, iii. 93; Clar. MS 71, fo. 34. Lawson's letter to Blackborne of 13 Mar. (the source of the royalist story?) expresses hope that Parliament will impose strict qualifications for MPs and militia officers: SP 18/223/73. Parliament had debated the bill for a new Parliament on 8–9 Mar.; the Act as passed barred known royalists from serving in the next Parliament but did not contain a commitment to any future form of government: *CJ* vii. 867–8; *A and O* ii. 1469–72.

At some point soon after 21 February Lawson clearly decided to acquiesce in Monck's plans, wherever they should lead—hoping this would not mean monarchy but aware that it might. At the end of March an observer judged correctly that Lawson would serve the king's interest if Monck and Mountagu did so. He probably saw no realistic alternative. Early in April Braemes felt it safe to hand him a letter of goodwill from the king, to which he responded with expressions of pleasure and gratitude.[97] His stance was crucial to the fleet's response as a whole in these critical weeks, for he alone might have been able to stir up a general revolt. Unwillingly and in part unwittingly Lawson played an important part in paving the way for the Restoration.

Mountagu's contribution to the Restoration was of a very different kind. By the beginning of 1660 he already favoured the return of monarchy, but since giving up the command of the fleet he had stayed quietly at home, taking no part in public affairs. When the secluded MPs resumed their seats, however, he was elected to the Council of State (23 February) and hastened to London; he was named a General at Sea on 2 March, and an Admiralty Commissioner the day after.[98] Though he was chosen as a conservative his precise aims were unknown; some thought he still wanted to see Richard Cromwell restored, but in the event he quickly severed ties with Richard's few remaining friends.[99] His real aim from the outset was the return of the king. He kept his royalist contacts secret but told friends that monarchy was likely to return and that a settlement without the king was impossible. (To his secretary Pepys he added that Charles would not last long unless he behaved with great circumspection.) The royalists were delighted by these indications of support. One sent word that Mountagu was going to the fleet with the fixed intention of serving the king, and the earl of Southampton, one of Charles's leading advisers, sent him a message of encouragement. An agent wrote joyfully on 21 March that 'He being engaged and Lawson too, the king may be sure of the fleet'.[100]

[97] CSP iii. 706; Clar. MS 71, fos. 185–6; CCSP v. 7.

[98] CJ vii. 849, 858, 860; Adm. 3/274, fo. 154`. He returned to London on 23 Feb.: Pepys, *Diary*, i. 68.

[99] Lister, *Clarendon*, iii. 88; CSP iii. 703; Clar. MS 70, fo. 209; Pepys, *Diary*, i. 79.

[100] Clar. MS 70, fos 118–19, 209; Rawl. MS A 468, fo. 6`; Pepys, *Diary*, i. 79; CSP iii. 703, 706. The pioneering work on the navy's part in the king's return is A. W. Tedder, *The Navy of the Restoration* (Cambridge, 1916).

In reality the position was much less settled, for the king did not know how far Mountagu's influence would extend. Neither did Mountagu himself. He was a stranger to his partner Monck, whom he regarded as a 'thick-skulled fellow', and there was very little co-operation between them. Mountagu indeed suspected him of seeking power for himself, and voiced his fears to the king.[101] He was also understandably wary of Lawson. Their only previous contact had been in 1656 when Lawson had thrown up his command, with subversive intent, at the very beginning of Mountagu's naval career. It was not until early April that he learned of Lawson's own contacts with royalist agents, and they remained uneasy colleagues.[102] Mountagu certainly had friends and clients among the sea-officers, some of whom had written to him at Hinchinbrooke pledging to 'follow him wherever he should think fit to lead them'. But these were his old Baltic colleagues, now out of employment; for the present the fleet was in the hands of Lawson's protégés, whose reliability was very uncertain.[103]

Mountagu's first hurdle came when he boarded the *Swiftsure* on 23 March to take up his command. Pepys, nervously accompanying him, was clearly relieved when Lawson and the other commanders came to pay their addresses 'and seemed very respectful'. On the 27th the *Swiftsure* fell down to Tilbury Hope, where Lawson's squadron fired so many guns in salute that all the windows in Pepys cabin were shattered. This ambiguous welcome proved appropriate, for on the evening of the 29th Pepys heard of 'a great whispering of some of the vice-admiral's captains that were dissatisfied and did intend to fit themselves to oppose the General'. Mountagu claimed later that Dakins 'had double-shotted his guns to lay me aboard', and the fact that he took no action whatever over the incident shows how precarious he felt his authority to be. It was Lawson's role that proved crucial: he refused to join the would-be rebels and eventually succeeded in restoring calm.[104] On 5 April, now in the *Naseby*, Mountagu sailed for the Downs, where the fleet was to remain for several weeks.[105]

The choice of captains and lieutenants for the summer guard was particularly sensitive in the spring of 1660. Lawson had already

[101] Pepys, *Diary*, i. 75, 118–19, 125; Clarendon, *History*, vi. 223–4.
[102] Clar. MS 71, fos. 185–6; Clarendon, *Life*, ii. 393.
[103] Clar. MS 68, fo. 161'ᵛ.
[104] Pepys, *Diary*, i. 95–6, 98, 99–100; Carte MS 73, fo. 399; Rawl. MS A 468, fo. 6ᵛ; Davies, 303.   [105] Sandwich, *Journal*, 74; Pepys, *Diary*, i. 103–5.

drawn up a list of seventeen ships and their officers as the core of the summer's fleet, and this had been presented to Parliament on 22 February, one day after the return of the secluded MPs. The timing was unfortunate, for predictably many of his nominations were repugnant to the new majority in the House. Stayner might be acceptable as rear-admiral (almost certainly named at the insistence of the Admiralty Commissioners), but the MPs would hardly want George Dakins in the next most senior post and they found that Lawson had nominated several more radicals, such as Newbery, Parke, and Higgenson, to other important commands. He had also put forward Newbery's brother and Henry Alured (probably a kinsman of the republican colonel) as lieutenants, and wanted the former commander Nicholas Foster to be lieutenant of the *London* to balance Stayner.[106] Lawson wrote to the new Generals at Sea urging that his list should stand, and even asking for Dakins to be made rear-admiral in Stayner's place.[107] Mountagu had other ideas. Parliament had given him the authority to select his officers, and he quickly prepared a revised list which the Council approved on 7 March. There were several important changes: Dakins, instead of promotion, was to have no command at all and Parke, Higgenson, and Francis Allen were also to be laid aside. Their replacements, Robert Blake, John Hayward, and Valentine Tatnel, were all clients of Mountagu. As flag-captain in the *Naseby* he appointed Roger Cuttance, who had previously served him in the same capacity. Lawson's list of lieutenants also suffered numerous alterations.[108]

Mountagu's remodelling of the other officer corps was hampered by the fact that he had to operate under strict financial constraints. The Admiralty Commissioners told him on 31 March that the rest of the summer guard would have to be made up from ships already in service, there being no money to set out any others. In deciding which ships to keep out he had to weigh up the condition of each against its officers' political views, so far as he knew them. Wherever possible he rid himself of 'Anabaptists', and he asked that if the Commissioners changed any of the ships on his list for technical reasons they should employ only officers he had already approved. The full summer guard, comprising sixty-seven vessels, was

---

[106] Carte MS 73, fo. 222; Adm. 3/274, fo. 166.   [107] Carte MS 73, fo. 355.
[108] *CJ* vii. 860–1; Carte MS 73, fo. 231; Carte MS 74, fo. 490; *CSPD 1659–60*, 547. Foster and Alured were among the lieutenants laid aside. Allen was dropped despite his ties with Monck.

approved by the Council on 7 April. In theory the other ships then at sea should have been called in and paid off but as there was no money for the men's wages they had to remain out until further notice.[109]

Mountagu thus had to contend with known malcontents who knew they were to be laid aside but whose ships could not be called in. He was particularly concerned about George Dakins in the *Worcester*, whom he regarded as far too dangerous to be left in place. His first solution was to send Dakins out of harm's way as commander of a small convoy about to leave for the Straits. But when the Commissioners decided to increase the size of this force Mountagu had second thoughts, fearing it would be unwise to entrust it to 'an Anabaptist, much discontented and busy stirring up others', especially in 'any emergency of affairs here'. Dakins must therefore be sacked. Mountagu was very reluctant to do the deed himself, fearing it would weaken his hold over the other captains. He therefore wrote to Monck begging a Council order for Dakins's removal, and that of Newbery too, who he complained was 'of the same principles, designs and humour'; in the meantime he had Pepys draw up a commission for Robert Blake to take over Dakins's command, to be ready when needed. On 17 April the Council obligingly wrote that the *Worcester* had been judged unsuitable for the Straits voyage and would be called in, and Mountagu was formally directed to place another captain in temporary command. Two days later the Council ordered Dakins's arrest. It had already summoned Newbery to London, which allowed Mountagu to replace him in the *Plymouth* with his protégé John Hayward; he also took the opportunity, he remarked later, to turn out half the ship's company.[110] The partial reshaping of the naval officer corps in the spring of 1660 is less well known than the army purges of 1659–60, but was of considerable importance. Of the twenty-one captains who helped Lawson restore the Rump in December only seven sailed with Mountagu to bring back the king in May. Three had been laid aside (Dakins, Newbery, and Hubbard), two potential trouble-makers had been sent on distant convoys (Allen to the

---

[109] Adm. 2/1731, fos. 137, 139`; Pepys, *Diary*, i. 101; SP 18/220/94; *CSPD 1659–60*, 533; Adm. 3/274, fo. 183`⁻ˇ.

[110] Adm. 2/1731, fos. 135, 139`, 142`, 144`; Carte MS 73, fos 399, 416; *CSPD 1659–60*, 405–6, 416, 574; Pepys, *Diary*, i. 109; Rawl. MS A 468, fo. 6`; Newbery had been summoned by the Council on 14 Apr.: Carte MS 73, fo. 408. Robert Blake took over the Straits convoy.

Straits, Higgenson to the Baltic), and four had been called in and
their ships paid off; the rest were left behind, to be paid off as soon
as possible, or were assigned to less sensitive duties.[111] Mountagu
was assisted by the earlier divisions within the republican ranks, for
most of the senior officers who had accepted the army junta had
remained out of employment when the Rump was restored. Had
Mountagu's fleet contained Goodson and John Bourne, or captains
such as Witheridge or Whitehorne (dubbed 'a zealous villain' by an
irate cavalier), he might have faced much greater opposition.[112]

Mountagu had kept the remodelling of the officers firmly in his
own hands. His partner Monck, fully occupied with matters
ashore, did little more than recommend some of his former clients
for employment, and Mountagu simply ignored most of these
requests. He gave no employment at all to Anthony Young, whom
Monck had recommended for one of the very best ships in the fleet,
and none to Edward Nixon, despite repeated pleas; Francis Allen,
whom Monck wanted to have promoted, was packed off to the
Straits instead. Mountagu treated many other requests with similar
disdain, and was clearly determined to rely on his own judgement
and his own dependants.[113] Monck's few successes were almost
embarrassingly trivial.[114]

While the fleet lay in the Downs Mountagu drew up a list for the
king showing 'what officers he was confident of, and of whom he
was not assured, and who he concluded would not concur with
him, and who must be reduced by force'. There were few, if any, of
the senior officers he could fully trust, and he kept his designs
hidden from even his closest colleagues. He confided to Pepys on
11 April that he had no confidence in John Stokes, the senior captain
in the fleet, and was not altogether sure of his own flag-captain, Roger

---

[111] For the fleet which brought back the king see Pepys, *Cat.* i. 256–62. The seven
were Rooth, Nutton, Parke, T. Bowry, Large, Coppin, Harrison. Mountagu did ask
for Hubbard to be given a 5th-rate; he said this was at Lawson's request, which may
have been a coded message that he would like it to be turned down, as it was: *CSPD,
1659–60*, 542.

[112] 'Might' is all we can say: Goodson for example had stood by Mountagu loyally
in the Sound in 1659 and after their return, but neither he nor Bourne served again
after the Restoration. For Whitehorne see *Nicholas Papers*, iv. 104.

[113] *CSPD 1659–60*, 378, 528, 545, 552; SP 18/223/25, 157.

[114] John Wilgress was given the *Bear* for a voyage to the West Indies, Tobias
Sackler (a gunner and Monck's distant kinsman by marriage) became captain of a
pink guarding the mackerel fisheries, and Lt. Edward Grove took command of a 6th-
rate patrolling off King's Lynn, his home town: SP 18/223/21, 106, 113, 157; Pepys,
Cat. i. 257, 263.

Cuttance; his efforts to find a command for Cuttance's son Henry look suspiciously like political bribery.[115] He was guarded even with his 'great confidant' Stayner, the rear-admiral; Stayner after all had been ready to accept the junta, had then made his peace with the restored Rump, and appears to have had few real loyalties, political or personal. Though commissions had been approved for Lawson and Stayner as flag-officers on 8 March it was not until 17 April that Mountagu handed them over, and he had them carefully worded to maximize his own authority as General.[116] None of the senior officers was likely to lead a revolt, but equally none could be trusted if the political situation were to change once more.

Mountagu was far from idle during these weeks. Parliament had dissolved itself in mid-March, arranging for a successor (the Convention) to meet on 25 April. Mountagu, who had secured the right to dispose of the writs in the Cinque Ports, was elected MP for Dover on 19 April, after a campaign managed by two of his captains who were natives of the town, Teddiman and Tatnel.[117] He had already been elected at Weymouth with the aid of his flag-captain Cuttance, a local man; the former admiral Penn (now busy once more in naval affairs) was returned as its other member.[118] Mountagu also sent an officer to Hastings to recommend his cousin Edward, though here his intervention came too late.[119] More important, Mountagu took advantage of his station to conduct a regular correspondence with the royal court. On arriving in the Downs on 9 April he had promptly dispatched his cousin with a letter to the king and there was soon a flow of messages in both directions, Mountagu expressing his devotion and Charles returning his thanks and promising more tangible rewards to follow. At first these exchanges took place amidst great secrecy, but by the end of the month Pepys noted that 'all the world' knew the stream of gentlemen visiting the flagship and going on to Holland were *en route* to the king.[120]

[115] Pepys, *Diary,* i. 107; Davies, 303 and n. On 12 Apr. Mountagu suggested turning Allgate out of the *Oxford* to make room for Henry, who eventually found a command in the *Cheriton* on 1 May: Carte MS 73, fo. 399; Pepys, *Diary,* i. 121.

[116] Pepys, *Diary,* i. 107, 110; *CSPD 1659–60,* 547.

[117] Pepys, *Diary,* i. 93, 102, 108, 110–11; Sandwich, *Journal,* 174; Carte MS 73, fos. 357, 374, 382; Carte MS 225, fo. 200; Davies, 327–8.

[118] Pepys, *Diary,* i. 103, 108; Carte MS 73, fo. 384; Carte MS 74, fo. 445; HMC 31, *Rye,* 235; Penn, *Memorials,* ii. 210. [119] Pepys, *Diary,* i. 102.

[120] Clar. MS 71, fos. 649, 651, 666–7, 687; *CSP* iii. 719, 752; Sandwich, *Journal,* 74–5; Pepys, *Diary,* i. 106, 110, 112–13, 117.

On 1 May Charles's conciliatory declaration from Breda was read out to the Convention, which thereupon declared monarchy to be England's rightful form of government. Monck forwarded a copy of the declaration to his partner, with a letter from the king expressing his good intentions towards the fleet and his readiness to pay all arrears. On 3 May Mountagu summoned the captains to consider the two documents. Nothing was left to chance: he dictated a record of their unanimous approval before they had even arrived, together with their resolution to have the king's messages read to the entire fleet. The council of war was thus a mere charade. Pepys read out the king's messages and then pretended to compose a resolution expressing the officers' joyful response, which they duly approved, though he sensed that many were really far from enthusiastic. 'Not one man seemed to say no to it,' he noted in his diary, 'though I am confident many in their hearts were against it.' He then read the king's declarations on the *Naseby*'s quarterdeck to the assembled seamen, who 'did all of them cry out "God bless King Charles" with the greatest joy imaginable'. The contrast is striking. Later in the day he visited all the other ships in the fleet, finding an enthusiastic welcome in each.[121]

Mountagu was understandably in 'a transport of joy' now that his hour had come. That evening he showed Pepys his letters from Charles and the duke of York, boasting 'how he had provided for himself so great a hold in the king'; Pepys was amazed, especially by their 'familiar style as to their common friend, with all kindness imaginable'. The days that followed were for both of them an idyllic round of merry-making and preparations, with Pepys busy writing out orders for silk flags and decorations, a rich barge, trumpeters, and fiddlers. Cromwell's effigy was torn down from the *Naseby*'s prow. Even Lawson caught the festive mood, or pretended to, calling for wine and toasting the king and duke.[122] The Commonwealth was at an end, and on 8 May Charles was formally proclaimed in London.

By the nature of the evidence the navy's role in 1660 has to be seen mainly through the words and deeds of the two leading actors,

[121] Clarendon, *History*, vi. 208–9; Pepys, *Diary*, i. 123–4; Lister, *Clarendon*, iii. 104–5. The officers present are listed in *The Diurnall of Thomas Rugg, 1659–1661*, ed. W. L. Sachse (Camden Soc., 1961), 78; *The Parliamentary Intelligencer*, 30 Apr.–7 May 1660. Cf. Davies, ch. 17.

[122] Pepys, *Diary*, i. 124–31; Harris, *Mountagu*, i. 183–4.

Lawson and Mountagu. But the response of the officer corps as a whole and of the seamen to the unfolding drama was obviously crucial, and the Admiralty officials ashore also had some part to play. The Admiralty Commissioners appointed by the Rump on 2 February were naturally firm republicans. After the return of the secluded MPs, however, Parliament added a considerable number of moderates, transforming the Admiralty's political complexion. The most committed radicals gradually dropped away and the Rumpers who remained, such as Col. George Thomson, proved willing to go along with the tide.[123] One of the most active newcomers was William Penn, the former General, who was named a Commissioner on 24 March. Monck had brought him back into naval affairs and later secured his election to the Convention, though Penn did not merely follow in his patron's wake; he had his own contacts with the royalists, and had secured promises of pardon and favour from the king before Monck wrote on his behalf. In May he was among the senior officials in the fleet bringing Charles back to England.[124]

There were some officials at all levels ready to see the king restored. Phineas Pett, clerk of the cheque at Chatham, had gone over to the cavaliers as early as December 1659 and had been working on his brother, the Commissioner. Many others, though far from eager, were swept along by the rush of events. The Admiralty secretary Robert Blackborne, a firm republican, was one such: in mid-March he was very gloomy about the king's probable return, telling Pepys that 'all good men and good things were now discouraged', but by early April he had surrendered to the inevitable and was commending Charles as 'a sober man', promising 'how quiet he would be under his government'. If resistance was hopeless, self-preservation (with a strong dash of self-delusion) was natural. By mid-May Blackborne could even write, 'Our great expectations and longings are for the safe return of his Majesty,

[123] *A and O* ii. 1407; Adm. 3/274, fos. 151-4'; Add. MS 9300, fo. 408. For Thomson see Pepys, *Diary*, i. 102.

[124] *CJ* viii. 30; Adm. 3/274, fo. 154'; Adm. 2/1731, fos. 136 ff.; Pepys, *Diary*, i. 102, 153; *CSPD 1659–60*, 427; HMC 29, *Portland*, ii. 98, 100–1; Carte MS 73, fo. 378. Monck had been in friendly contact with Penn since June 1659, and offered to bring him back into naval employment, apparently at Penn's request: BL Loan MS 29/241, fo. 291. Penn was also in contact with the royalists at least from the time of Booth's rising: *Thurloe*, vii. 739.

whom the hearts of the whole nation (as one man) are towards.' Yet underneath lay an abiding sense of bitterness and shame, evinced years later in a ferocious outburst against those he felt had betrayed the cause.[125] The Navy Commissioner Nehemiah Bourne found it still harder to come to terms with the Restoration. He claimed that sickness had prevented him from waiting on the king with the other officials, and begged Mountagu to prevent any misconstruction of his absence, but even then he could not bring himself to pretend the slightest enthusiasm for the new order. There were many senior officials in London and the dockyards who shared Bourne's distaste, as Mountagu was well aware.[126] Officials in the outports were slower to grasp the significance of what was happening in the last weeks of the interregnum. At Plymouth Hatsell was dismayed by the cavaliers' confidence in the elections to the Convention, and hoped anxiously that God would stand by his cause; it seems likely that he was unaware of any contradiction when he wrote congratulating Mountagu on his election.[127]

One important reason for the navy's general acquiescence in 1660 was the deepening financial crisis, which was inevitably compounded by the political confusion. Lack of money had undermined discipline in the English army, clearing the path for Monck, and it threatened the navy with total paralysis. No money at all arrived from the Exchequer after October 1659.[128] Only the dedication of officials and commanders kept the system alive, and the exhausting struggle sapped their will to resist the political tide. At Dover all naval work gradually came to a halt. The state's credit was dead and to secure any supplies the local agent Thomas White was forced to make himself personally liable for payment; by early 1660 he had committed himself to a sum three times the size of his estate and went in fear of a debtors' goal.[129] At Yarmouth the contractor William Burton flatly refused to supply any more goods on credit. Though a committed radical and a former Commissioner Burton explained bluntly that he 'would not trust the state for one penny, for here was one state today and another tomorrow'. The position was much the same elsewhere.[130] The prolonged crisis demoralized

[125] *Nicholas Papers*, iv. 192 (Pett); Pepys, *Diary*, i. 91, 102–3, iv. 373–6; SP 18/221/27.

[126] Carte MS 73, fo. 474; below, ch. 11.

[127] *CSPD 1659–60*, 406, 550.   [128] Ibid. 588.

[129] Ibid. 388, 393, 401–2, 408, 412, 473, 531.

[130] Ibid. 403–4; cf. 206, 338–9, 385, 391, 521.

administrators and mariners alike, and left them feeling abandoned. Anthony Rively of the *Brier*, for example, sent no fewer then ten letters from Hull setting out his men's needs and explaining that the local victualler would supply nothing without ready payment. He did not even receive a reply. By early in the new year the ship's beer had run out, the men were having to use sea water for cooking, and sickness was rapidly spreading.[131] The commander of the western squadron, Heaton, reported similarly in January 1660 that his men were desperate for food and had wages two to four years in arrears. Again the local victuallers insisted on ready cash; they distrusted the state's promises, and Heaton explained that he and the port officials had already used up their private credit. Without speedy relief, he warned, he would have to turn the men ashore, where they must either starve or rob to keep alive.[132] Even near London the situation was critical, with several crews at Chatham in a mutinous state in the last months of 1659.[133] Lawson too warned in March 1660 that many of the ships in the Downs would soon be forced to come in for lack of food. One captain came up to Whitehall to seek relief but found he could do nothing as the Commissioners rarely bothered to sit.[134] In these circumstances it is hardly surprising that some commanders proved ready to accept the king and the normality he symbolized. Some may have concluded that nothing else could end the crisis.

It does seem that Mountagu found many captains readier to go along with him than he had anticipated. Some were probably swayed by the mood ashore, and some of his own clients had promised to follow wherever he chose to lead them. They were also all aware of the total control he now enjoyed over naval patronage.[135] But in many cases this passivity reflected a sense of defeat and demoralization rather than blind loyalty to the General or any positive support for the king. Pepys leaves no doubt that their acquiescence was often slow and reluctant. The throng of visitors from London on Easter Day (22 April) had described how the king's arms were being set up in the capital once more, so few officers remained in doubt as to what lay in store; even so it was not

---

[131] Ibid. 380, 385, 391–2, 531, 550. Some supplies reached him in May through Monck's intervention.

[132] Ibid. 338–9, 383–5.

[133] Ibid. 286; *CCSP* iv. 364; Clar. MS 66, fos. 97, 284.

[134] *CSPD 1659–60*, 534, 637.

[135] Clarendon, *History*, vi. 228; see also n. 103, above.

until 2 May, after the Convention had declared in favour of monarchy, that Pepys noticed the captains beginning to speak in favour
of the king's return—'which a week ago they would not do'. They
were reluctantly bowing to the inevitable, and he remained
convinced that many were still privately against it.[136] There is no
evidence of any officers encouraging Mountagu in his design, and
he in turn kept his plans secret from all of them. According to the
royalists one captain, Jonas Poole, had been won over to their cause
the previous autumn, but even if this was so Poole played no part
in what followed, for he had left for the Straits on convoy duty in
October 1659 and continued to obey orders from London.[137] Only
Sparling of the *Assistance* jumped the gun slightly: at Flushing on 23
April he openly drank the king's health with the renegade
Whetstone (an old friend), in the presence of his officers. Sparling
seems to have been thinking mainly of his career prospects; he
advised Whetstone to find some new friends among the cavaliers,
observing that the patronage of the navy's current leaders would
soon count for little—apparently unaware that Whetstone was
already a royalist agent and that Mountagu was in high favour with
the king.[138] Most of the other commanders fell into line once the
Restoration was plainly imminent. Some, like Sparling and indeed
Lawson, hoped to keep their positions; others were simply and
sadly bowing to the inevitable, a natural if unheroic response. At
the time the cavaliers were relieved to find them so submissive,
though once the king was safely home they predictably scorned
such time-servers.[139]

Mountagu had never supposed that all commanders would be
ready to conform. As we saw, he had Dakins and Newbery turned
out and Francis Allen sent to the Straits.[140] He also had Allgate
removed from the *Oxford* for 'undutiful speeches' about Monck;
her new captain gave a pledge of personal devotion.[141] Monck too
remained very wary right up to the Restoration. Early in May he
asked Penn to assemble naval reinforcements in the River and take

[136] Pepys, *Diary*, i. 113, 122–4.
[137] Clar. MS 66, fo. 141; Adm. 2/1731, fo. 113; *CSPD 1659–60*, 243–4, 303, 501.
Poole was a kinsman and friend of Penn.
[138] Clar. MS 72, fo. 9; Carte MS 73, fo. 439. Sparling's remarks show how well
Mountagu had concealed his dealings with the king from his officers.
[139] See ch. 11, below.
[140] Sandwich, *Journal*, 74; Adm. 2/1731, fo. 144ᵛ.
[141] Carte MS 73, fo. 399; Adm. 2/1731, fo. 145ᵛ. For Allgate's successor, John
Cuttle, see *CSPD 1659–60*, 555.

them to the Downs, ordering the ships at Portsmouth to make their way there too. Monck did not explain these moves but their effect was to bring more of the commanders under the General's direct scrutiny.[142] Mountagu could not watch over the officers on other stations, of course, and it is clear that several of them were dismayed by what was happening. As late as mid-May William Barker of the *Lichfield* was pursuing the notorious royalist privateer Beach, and on the 16th he proudly reported the capture of another privateer commissioned by the duke of York—when the duke was about to return home in triumph in Mountagu's fleet! At roughly the same time Richard Potter was in trouble at Kinsale for alleged seditious words and for failing to salute the proclamation of the king.[143] Capt. Vessey of the *Constant Warwick* told his men that a storm battering their ship had been sent by God to punish England for calling back the king, though when a loose rope struck his head a bystander retorted that this was divine retribution for such disloyal words. When they next put into Plymouth they found Charles already back on the throne; so, as one of the company later recalled, 'our captain, knowing his time to be short, made the best use he could' of his place, shipping beef, butter, and woollens from Ireland to France, and bringing French wines and other goods to England.[144] Taken in isolation Vessey's merchandizing would make his attitude seem merely opportunist, but the verbal exchange on deck—the sort of evidence that rarely survives—shows how wrong it would be to assume that officers who took no public stand were therefore politically indifferent.

The views of junior officers are poorly documented. Most readily conformed. But the fleet also contained many 'Anabaptist' masters, gunners, and boatswains, and early in March the Council debated how to be rid of them.[145] The issue was important; even a handful of determined assassins might endanger the entire royal family during the crossing home. Such fears were not altogether groundless, for early in May two naval officers were arrested and sent to the Tower charged with planning to fire or blow up the ship carrying the king home. And on the 17th the House of Lords was told how the master of the *Newbury* had vowed that 'if ever the king come into

[142] *CSPD 1659–60*, 438.
[143] Ibid. 439, 442. Barker's ignorance of events ashore must have been at least partly wilful.
[144] *The Journal of James Yonge*, ed. F. N. L. Poynter (1963), 37–8.
[145] *Nicholas Papers*, iv. 198.

England, he would be the first that would take away his life'. The Speaker ordered him to be sent up at once under guard.[146] It was even rumoured that Charles had decided not to embark in the fleet, believing it would be safer to cross the Channel privately—though according to another rumour William Lilly had predicted that he was fated to be shipwrecked and drowned on the crossing![147]

Most of the ordinary seamen appear to have shared the nation's mood and were glad to welcome home the king. They had suffered most from lack of wages and shortages of food, and Charles's promise to pay all the arrears neglected by successive regimes was warmly received. When Pepys read out the king's letter on board each ship on 3 May the sailors flung their caps in the air and 'loud *Vive le Roy*'s echoed from one ship's company to another'. Other eye witnesses give similar accounts.[148]

While the fleet waited in the Downs the Convention considered the proper procedures for the king's return. Commissioners were appointed to notify Charles of his proclamation in England and formally invite him home; Mountagu would simply provide transport as directed. On 10 May however Monck sent a message urging him to fetch the king forthwith, fearing the political calm might not last. Mountagu was much taken with the idea; he spent the following day in 'high debate' with Lawson and Stayner over its propriety, and on 12 May the fleet sailed without waiting for the commissioners to arrive. Charles was also feeling anxious, and it transpired that he too had written to Mountagu the previous day urging him to sail on his own initiative if there was no order from London.[149] Mountagu was also no doubt hoping to maximize his own role in the drama, for by sailing without parliamentary order he made it clear that he was an actor, not merely an instrument. Not everyone shared the king's pleasure at the liberty he had taken, and Claren-

[146] HMC 4, *5th Report*, 149, 207. The informant refers to them as Capts. Clarke and Sparke. There was a Clarke and a Parke, but as both remained in place the report may refer to officers serving under them. For the master (Steele) see Add. MS 9300, fo. 436; *LJ* xi. 30, 33. He was found to have sailed for the Straits a fortnight before, and so escaped. The master of the *Langport*, John Croscombe, was also discharged in April, probably on political grounds: Adm. 3/274, fo. 190. See further ch. 11, below.

[147] HMC 4, *5th Report*, 207. For Lilly see *Parliamentary Intelligencer*, 14–21 May 1660.

[148] Clarendon, *History*, vi. 209; Pepys, *Diary*, i. 124, 126; Lister, *Clarendon*, iii. 104–5; *LJ* xi. 16; *Barlow's Journal of his Life at Sea*, ed. B. Lubbock (1934), 42.

[149] Pepys, *Diary*, i. 133–5; Sandwich, *Journal*, 75–6; *CCSP* v. 29; Davies, 349–50.

don indeed records that it 'was never forgiven him by some men, who took all occasions afterwards to revenge themselves upon him'.[150]

The fleet anchored off Scheveningen on the Dutch coast on 14 May and Mountagu promptly sent word of his arrival to the king. The commissioners sent by the Commons arrived that same evening, those from the Lords following next day.[151] The royal court made its way to the coast, and on the 22nd the duke of York went aboard the flagship to discuss the voyage home, visiting Lawson and Stayner later the same day.[152] Charles himself came on board the day after and greeted Mountagu very affectionately. Before the fleet weighed anchor he formally renamed several of the navy's greatest ships to symbolize the dawning of the new age: the *Naseby* became the *Royal Charles*, the *Richard* and *Dunbar* became the *James* and *Henry*, named after his brothers, and so on; the *Monck* of course kept her name, and there would soon be a *Mountagu*.[153] The short crossing was remarkable only for the 'one continued thunder of the cannons', firing in joyful salute. The royal party went ashore at Dover on 25 May, and Charles set off for London almost at once.[154]

Mountagu remained in the Downs to savour his triumph and wait for the rewards he could expect to follow. Only two days later the captains assembled in the flagship for a brief ceremony to invest him with the Order of the Garter. Other honours soon followed: he became earl of Sandwich, with an estate of £4,000 a year, Privy Councillor, and Treasury Commissioner, and received a lucrative court office as Master of the Wardrobe. He told Pepys happily 'he believed he might have anything he asked of the king'.[155] Within a few weeks Pepys found him transformed into 'a perfect courtier', anxious to find a French cook and track down some black patches—the latest continental fashion—for his wife and daughter.[156] Other officers had weightier problems on their minds. Pepys thought Lawson would soon be turned out, though 'as officious, poor man,

---

[150] Clarendon, *History*, vi. 228–9; *CCSP* v. 33.

[151] Sandwich, *Journal*, 76.

[152] Pepys, *Diary*, i. 152–3; Sandwich, *Journal*, 76.

[153] Pepys, *Diary*, i. 154; for full details of the renaming see Pepys, *Cat.* i. 256–60.

[154] Clarendon, *History*, vi. 233; Pepys, *Diary*, i. 154–8; Sandwich, *Journal*, 77–8; Barlow, *Journal*, 43.

[155] Pepys, *Diary*, i. 157–61, 258; Harris, *Mountagu*, i. 187–8, 191–2.

[156] Pepys, *Diary*, i. 269.

as any spaniel can be'; many others must have felt equally insecure, though for the moment they drank heavily and amused themselves as best they could.[157] The seamen, for their part, waited for their arrears and the extra month's pay Charles had promised the sailors of the fleet bringing him home. The men had given the king a warm welcome, but the navy's revolt in 1642 was a reminder that wages weighed more heavily with them than royalist sentiment. Till the fleet was paid off some doubt would always hang over its reliability. Everyone in the navy would have endorsed Pepys's terse comment: 'I wish we had the money.'[158]

[157] Pepys, *Diary*, i. 159, 167, 169.
[158] Ibid. i. 167. The gratuity was paid in August.

11

The Legacy of the Commonwealth

DESPITE its part in restoring the monarchy the navy presented
Charles II with considerable problems. Every ship in service was in
the hands of his former enemies, many of whom had shown little
enthusiasm over his return, and the situation was much the same in
the administrative machine and the dockyards. The challenge facing
the king was how to turn the Commonwealth navy into a royalist
one without destroying its efficiency in the process.

The process began with a sweeping reorganization of naval
administration. Early in July a Navy Board was set up under James
as Lord High Admiral to replace the Admiralty and Navy Commissioners. To help preserve parliamentary expertise Sir William Batten
and Penn were included among its members, both being seen as
converts rather than mere conformists; Pepys too found a place as
Clerk of Acts, which he owed to Mountagu's influence.[1] In general
the administrative transfer seems to have gone smoothly, partly
because the old officials were very conscious of their exposed
position; Nehemiah Bourne, for example, was aware he could face
ruinous demands arising out of his former position as a navy
victualler and saw the need for conciliatory gestures. Robert
Blackborne, the former Admiralty secretary, even succeeded in
striking up a friendship with his successor, Pepys.[2] But the Restoration was of course a bitter blow to such men, and they found it
hard to adjust to the new order. In 1662 Bourne sold his stock and
returned to New England, and his former colleague Francis
Willoughby did likewise.[3] Blackborne too was unreconciled,

---

[1] Pepys, *Cat.* i. 6–7.

[2] Chaplin, 'Bourne', 132–8; Pepys, *Diary*, i, 197; Bodl. Carte MS 73, fo. 474;
PRO Adm. 106/1, fo. 12. For Blackborne see Pepys, *Diary*, i. 193, 213, 217, iii, 28.

[3] Chaplin, 'Bourne', 135; *CSPD 1661–2*, 386; E. B. Sainsbury (ed.), *A Calendar
of the Court Minutes of the East India Company* (Oxford, 1907–38), vi. 372;
Coventry MS 96, fos. 173, 183; *CSP Col. 1661–8*, 88, 91.

though he remained in England; he was soon in trouble for attending conventicles, and nurtured a deep hatred for those he felt had betrayed the revolution.[4]

There were major changes too among dockyard personnel. A survey shortly before the Restoration had identified a number of prominent 'Anabaptists', notably the Masters Attendant at Chatham (Hill and Arkinstall) and at Portsmouth (Thoroughgood), and a senior shipwright at Woolwich (Samuel Raven).[5] Such radicals were quickly weeded out: the Commons had removed the Quaker shipwright at Harwich, Robert Grassingham, even before the king's return, and the others had been ousted by July.[6] When the oaths of supremacy and allegiance were tendered at Chatham and Deptford a further twenty-six minor officials and workmen lost their places, further evidence that radicalism had taken at least some hold at the level of ropemaker, caulker, carpenter, and labourer.[7] There was however a considerable measure of continuity in the yards: men with experience and skill were too valuable to be laid aside if they seemed conformable. The Pett clan remained firmly in control at Chatham, accepting Charles II as readily as it had abandoned his father. William Badiley was judged 'fit and honest' and stayed on as Master Attendant at Woolwich. Among others to retain their posts were John Tippett, master shipwright (and mayor) at Portsmouth, and Jonas Shish, shipwright's assistant at Deptford, both of whom went on to enjoy long and successful careers.[8]

Far more difficult was the problem of what to do with the fleet itself. It still contained many radical officers, as well as thousands of

---

    [4] Blackborne later became secretary to the East India Company. Sainsbury, *Court Minutes*, vii, p. xvii; D. L. Powell and H. Jenkinson (eds.), *Surrey Quarter Sessions Records, 1661–1663* (Surrey Record Soc., xxxvi; 1935), 59, 252, 275; Pepys, *Diary*, iv. 373–6. Nehemiah and John Bourne were also frequently cited before the court, probably on the same grounds.
    [5] Carte MS 73, fos. 402–3°. Wm. Hill (sometimes wrongly called John), an old friend of Lawson, had been appointed by the Rump on 5 July 1659 (Adm. 3/274, fo. 100). He is not to be confused with the cavalier naval captain of the 1660s, who was 'honest . . . but no seaman', and a 'papist gentleman': Coventry MS 98, fo. 53°, MS 99, fo. 91°; J. Charnock, *A History of Marine Architecture* (1801–2), i, p. lxxxvi.
    [6] *CJ* viii. 39; *CSPD 1660–1*, 307; B. Reay, *The Quakers and the English Revolution* (1985), 105; Adm. 106/1, fos. 114, 194, 196. Thoroughgood and Hill went back to sea; for Raven see below, n. 79.
    [7] Adm. 106/2, fo. 362.
    [8] Pepys, *Cat.* i. 6–11; Adm. 106/1, fo. 102; Carte MS 73, fo. 403; D. Dymond, *Portsmouth and the Fall of the Puritan Revolution* (The Portsmouth Papers, xi; Portsmouth, 1971), esp. 17; cf. Pepys, *Diary*, x. 397, 446.

unpaid seamen whose welcome for the king might quickly turn sour if he failed to keep his promises. The regime began with the officer corps. Mountagu had been able to remove only the most obvious malcontents, and once Charles was safely ashore plans were laid for a more thorough purge. As part of the process the oaths of supremacy and allegiance were tendered to the officers and men in the summer and autumn of 1660, and this disposed of a number of radicals. Capt. Joseph Ames of the *Winsby* was turned out for refusing them, as were the master of the *Happy Entrance* (a member of the Stepney congregation) and several of his colleagues, the mate and six seamen of the *Oxford*, and the Quaker gunner of the *Assistance*.[9] But overall the number of victims was surprisingly small: the surviving returns show that less than one per cent of officers and men refused to swear.[10] This hardly reflected the true extent of anti-cavalier feeling, and many had obviously sworn merely to protect their wages and jobs.

It was never likely that taking the oaths would be sufficient to make former radicals acceptable to the navy's new masters. As early as June Mountagu had gone through a list of commanders, telling Pepys to mark those he intended to put out.[11] A much wider and more searching investigation soon followed, conducted in a highly partisan spirit. Its findings were expressed in blunt terms: Anthony Earning was 'a known old enemy', Newbery 'a very high Anabaptist, infected most part of his officers', and Allen 'a violent person against the king'. Tatnel was 'most violent against his Majesty' and Coppin 'an old king-hater'. Capt. King was said to be 'ashamed of his own name'. Capt. Plumleigh was another 'known Anabaptist; if we put not him and such down, as his boatswain said, they were all such, they would assuredly put his Majesty and friends out'. Capt. Curle had grieved at the king's restoration but had remained in service by evading the oaths; he and Capt. Beer were subsequently turned out for disaffection.[12] The warrant-officers too underwent a thorough scrutiny. The carpenter of the *President* was found to have betrayed the *Marmaduke* back to Parliament after the revolt of 1648, and another carpenter was shown to be a former cornet of

[9] Adm. 2/1732, fos. 30, 59; Coventry MS 101, fo. 214 (Ames); Adm. 106/2, fo. 41 (the master, John Bannister); Carte MS 74, fo. 487. See also *CSPD 1660–1*, 456.

[10] *CSPD 1665–6*, 182. 4,211 men swore the oaths, only 31 refused—though some of the several hundred absentees may have been evading them; the figures are far from complete.

[11] Pepys, *Diary*, i. 188.   [12] Coventry MS 98, fos. 52, 67–8, 72.

horse in Parliament's army. A cook was condemned as a 'factious and utter enemy to his Majesty', and a gunner as 'a great man for the Rump'. Another gunner had said he would 'rather sink the ship' than help the Restoration. Some officers found themselves damned for having 'infectious' Quaker wives.[13]

An officer with such a label round his neck had no future in the royal navy, even assuming he wanted one. The list of radicals who never served again after 1660 is long and distinguished: at its head are the flag-officers Goodson, John Bourne, Dakins, and Benjamin Blake, and it includes Captains Ames, Blagg, Heaton, Hill, Mackey, Newbery, Plumleigh, Potter, Whitehorne, and Witheridge.

The purge of radicals naturally extended to the 'fanatic' preachers who had been serving as chaplains. With the re-establishment of the Church of England chaplains had to be episcopally ordained and willing to take the oaths, and this was sufficient to bar many of those employed in recent years. At least one 'Anabaptist' abandoned his post rather than wait to be turned out, and several others refused the oaths or were deemed 'factious and uncapable'.[14] Only a handful conformed and continued in service; one of them, Ralph Rountree, had been lucky enough to find an Irish bishop willing to ordain him without asking difficult questions.[15] Some former chaplains who had found livings ashore proved willing to conform to the Anglican Church, but most chaplains, past and present, were either ejected or silenced. Many lived in poverty, and some found it hard to adjust; Joseph Binckes, struggling to survive as a shoemaker, mixed with plotters and supplemented his income by becoming a government spy.[16]

The problem of how to pay off thousands of impatient sailors (and soldiers) was more intractable. Charles II warned in August 1660 that the soldiers were desperate and the seamen 'ready to be in a flame'. Parliament voted funds and set up a body of commissioners to tackle the problem, and by the end of the year the disbanding of the army was almost complete. Work on the navy however had

---

[13] Coventry MS 98, fos. 58–83.

[14] Ibid. fos. 68–9.

[15] Pepys, *Diary*, ii. 118; Adm. 2/1745, fo. 45. Other conformists include Harcourt, Ibbott, Roberts, A. Norwood, and Vincent.

[16] See ch. 9 n. 98. A few mechanick preachers found other occupations at sea. Robert Rose became a purser once more: Adm. 2/1732, fo. 100. For Binckes see below, n. 41.

barely begun. Parliament was responsible for the eighty-four ships in service at the king's return, plus a further twenty-five then waiting in the Thames to be paid off; by the end of 1660 only eight of this latter group had been paid, and none of the others. A sum of £128,000 was needed for the ships in the River, and £258,000 for the rest.[17] When Lawson warned early in 1661 that the sailors were growing angry and resentful James complained that Parliament's arrangements had been hasty and inadequate, though he promised a speedy settlement. Lawson himself was engaged in the task as a commissioner and treasurer-at-war—a skilful device which reassured the sailors while removing him as a possible leader if trouble were to break out.[18] In the event the state largely kept its promise this time. The newspaper *Mercurius Publicus* printed weekly reports of the number of ships paid off, and the sums involved; between February and April 1661 it listed payments to eighty-six ships at London and Portsmouth, and offered glowing tributes to the commissioners' energy and zeal. Pepys's diary gives another side to the story, noting that the officials had to sit at the Guildhall 'for fear of going out of the town into the power of the seamen, who are highly incensed against them'. The long delays, stoppages, and failure to pay arrears for service before 1659 resulted in frequent disorders.[19] None the less by the end of July 1661 the king could breathe freely in the knowledge that Cromwell's navy existed no more.

There remained the long-term problem of how to create a new officer corps with the right blend of loyalty, skill, and experience. The difficulty lay in the fact that these qualities were often mutually exclusive, for the Commonwealth veterans were politically suspect while few cavaliers had much experience except, in some cases, in small privateers. Moreover the rival groups had to be balanced and reconciled within a navy far smaller than in the 1650s; the return of peace with Spain and the king's limited resources made a large navy neither necessary nor feasible. A situation which forced former enemies to compete for slices of a much reduced cake posed obvious

---

[17] *CJ* viii. 115, 243; Pepys, *Diary*, i. 245 and n. Charles assumed responsibility from June for the 36 ships he decided to keep in service, which are listed in Pepys, *Cat.* i. 256–63.

[18] Adm. 2/1745, fo. 27ᵛ; *CJ* viii. 321; *CSPD Addenda 1660–85*, 8, 13, 20; *CSPD 1660–1*, 531.

[19] Pepys, *Diary*, ii. 45, 50; *CJ* viii. 216–17; *Barlow's Journal of his Life at Sea*, ed. B. Lubbock (1934), 48.

problems, and when former enemies had to serve side by side old antagonisms could quickly resurface. The expedition to West Africa in 1660–1 was an early case in point; its leader, the fierce royalist Robert Holmes, despised his deputy John Stokes as an 'old, fat' roundhead and noted in his journal that he would be glad to see him hanged.[20]

The king began in a conciliatory manner, by confirming the appointments Mountagu had made and giving knighthoods to Lawson and Stayner.[21] The cavaliers naturally looked for a major share in future appointments, and in August 1660 there was an early glimpse of what lay ahead: Mountagu's protégé, John Hayward, was selected to carry a new ambassador to Istanbul, only to find his appointment quashed within a week in favour of the old royalist privateer, Thomas Allin.[22] Over the next few years the character of the officer corps changed substantially. Some thirty-six parliamentarian captains and lieutenants recommissioned in 1660 received no further employment in the next three years, and half were never to be employed again.[23] Ninety-one of the men who did win commissions between 1661 and 1663 were newcomers, many clearly recognizable as staunch cavaliers; only thirty-eight were former parliamentarians.[24] This influx of cavaliers, however natural, was larger and faster than Mountagu (now earl of Sandwich) wished to see, partly because his own clients were inevitably among its victims. He complained later that he was not consulted at all over the choice of commanders and that James, the Lord High Admiral, had wanted to oust him. Though he was probably exaggerating it is clear that James leaned mainly on advice from William Coventry, his secretary, and Penn.[25] Among the serving officers he openly favoured Lawson, who had been bred to the sea and was a veteran of the Dutch war. Lawson had far more experience and professional

[20] R. Ollard, *Man of War: Sir Robert Holmes and the Restoration Navy* (1969), 67–8.

[21] Pepys, *Diary*, i. 254.　　　[22] Ibid. 217, 224; HMC 71, *Finch*, i. 80.

[23] Based on the lists in Pepys, *Cat.* i. 316–429.

[24] Ibid. The royalists include former privateers such as Allin, Beach, Cotterell, Golding, and Spragge. The parliamentarian figure would rise slightly if we included men who had served as masters in the 1650s (Heath, Poole, Wye). Cf. Davies, thesis, ch. 2.

[25] Pepys, *Diary*, ii. 169, iii. 121–2, v. 162–3; F. R. Harris, *The Life of Edward Mountagu* (1912), i. 215–16, 251–3; Bodl. Rawlinson MS A 468, fo. 6ʹ; E. Hyde, earl of Clarendon, *The Life of Edward Earl of Clarendon* (with) *A Continuation of his History* (Oxford, 1827), ii. 328–9, 354, 466–7.

expertise than Sandwich, and as an unpolished tarpaulin he could never be a rival at Court; he always remained, as Pepys noted, 'the same plain man he was'. His enemies scorned him as a sycophant but Clarendon thought him 'incomparably the modestest and the wisest man, and most worthy to be confided in', and called his death in 1665 an 'almost irreparable loss'. Lawson had put his radical past firmly behind him, whether through personal ambition or submission to the Almighty's will. He confided during a serious illness that taking up arms against the Stuarts was now the greatest regret of his life. Clarendon later recalled how he had come to play the part of poacher turned gamekeeper, using his unrivalled knowledge of naval radicals to root out those who still dreamed of the Good Old Cause. He was still immensely popular among the sailors, and his readiness to conform in both religion and politics set an admirable example of submission.[26]

With the fleet much reduced in size, Sandwich partly in eclipse, and Lawson mostly away at sea, it was probably inevitable that many Commonwealth officers would be squeezed out, however ready they were to conform. Most went back to private trade, where their experience and proven ability made then generally welcome to merchants and shipowners. Even former militants were often able to find good employment, for the same reasons; George Dakins, for example, became master of a rich vessel owned by a consortium of wealthy London merchants. Some ex-officers resumed their former trading activities across the Atlantic, among them Goodson, Bourne, Young, Heaton, and Blagg.[27] Others found employment with the East India Company, such as Earning, Whitehorne, and Haddock.[28] We find Robert Wilkinson sailing to the Levant, and Bartholomew Ketcher fetching wines from the

---

[26] Clarendon, *Life*, ii. 354–5, 391–3; Pepys, *Diary*, iv. 4, 12, vi. 138, vii. 195; Bodl. Clarendon MS 74, fos. 318ᵛ–319.

[27] Dakins: *CSPD 1661–2*, 9; Sandwich, *Journal*, 109; Pepys, *Diary*, iii. 50; HMC 50, *Heathcote*, 217. Goodson: Pepys, *Diary*, v. 30; *CCSP* v. 546; *CSPD 1667–8*, 43; PRO Cal. C 54A, 72. Bourne: HMC 50, *Heathcote*, 174; *The Journals of Sir Thomas Allin*, ed. R. C. Anderson (NRS lxxix–lxxx; 1939–40), i. 203, 209, 216. Young: Cal. C 54A, 67; *CSPD 1672*, 467; Pepys, *Cat.* iii. 276. He was an Elder Brother of Trinity House, 1676–93: W. R. Chaplin, *The Corporation of Trinity House* (1950), 56, 63. Heaton: *CSPD 1670*, 207; *CSPD 1671*, 75. The king awarded him a medal in 1674 for an action against a Sallee rover: Pepys, *Cat.* iv. 123. Blagg: Cal. C 54A, 68; *CSPD 1667–8*, 27, 29; Pepys, *Cat.* iii. 370.

[28] See Sir W. Foster, *The English Factories in India* (Oxford, 1906–27), and Sainsbury, *Court Minutes*. Wildey and Hide also continued to serve the Company.

Canaries.[29] Others traded on their own account, on a more modest scale: Joseph Ames of Yarmouth traded with France in a small vessel of his own, while Edward Tarleton bought a pink and returned to his native Liverpool.[30] A few turned to privateering as a more congenial way of life. Easily the best known—and most unlikely—of them was Sir Thomas Whetstone, the former royalist agent. Whetstone had returned to England penniless at the Restoration and was soon sending pitiful appeals from a debtors' gaol. The government eventually gave him £100 and packed him off to Jamaica, where by 1663 he was at the head of a squadron of eleven privateers; the former commanders Cobham and Blofield appear among his companions. Whetstone soon became a figure of some note in the new colony, serving as Speaker of its Assembly in 1664, and taking a leading part in the capture of Providence Island in 1666. When the Spaniards recaptured it later in the year, however, he was taken prisoner, and his picaresque career appears to have ended in a dungeon in Panama.[31] The New World appealed to many former parliamentarians, though by no means all were looking for further adventure: Lt. Thomas Trafford begged for the post of Governor of Bermuda on the grounds that he was weary of a lifetime at sea.[32]

Former officers without the capital or the contacts to succeed in trade were often anxious to remain in the navy, even if it meant dropping to a much lower level. Thus Anthony Archer, a captain throughout the 1650s, was willing to stay on as a master, while ex-lieutenant Thomas Milton reverted to his earlier position as a purser; Isaac White, who had once commanded a fire-ship, also accepted a purser's place, and Tobias Short, formerly a master, was

Wildey became Master of Trinity House in 1669 (Chaplin, *Trinity House*, 12); Hide was drowned in a wreck in 1684: [W. Smith], *A full Account of the late ship-wreck* (1684).

[29] *CSPV 1659–61*, 144; NMM AML/N/8.

[30] BL Add. MS 57491; Allin, *Journals*, ii. 16; Coventry MS 98, fo. 68.

[31] *CSPD* v. 34, 451–2; *CSPD 1661–2*, 81; *CSP Col. 1661–8*, 55, 88, 177, 244–5, 251, 287, 409, 605; Adm. 106/2, fo. 167; W. A. Shaw (ed.), *Calendar of Treasury Books, 1660–7* (1897), 132, 140, 260, 387; Bodl. Tanner MS 48, fo. 41; *Interesting Tracts relating to the Island of Jamaica* (St Jago de la Vega, 1800), 282. For Cobham and Blofield see *CSP Col. 1661–8*, 177, 332. Cf. C. Hill, 'Radical Pirates', in M. C. and J. R. Jacob (eds.), *The Origins of Anglo-American Radicalism* (1984). Jacob Reynolds, dropped earlier by Cromwell, was privateering for the Portuguese in the early 1660s; PRO HCA 13/74, 18 Jan. 1664; Clar. MS 74, fos. 318–19.

[32] *CSP Col. 1661–8*, 111. In the event Trafford's weary labours at sea continued throughout Charles's reign: Pepys, *Cat.* i. 415.

willing to serve as boatswain.[33] In general there seems to have been
more continuity among the warrant-officers than among their
superiors. Ideological considerations had, in practice, been
somewhat less important at this level in the 1650s and the vetting of
such men after 1660 was probably less thorough too. One major
consideration in the case of masters was that relatively few men
possessed the skill and experience required to handle the larger
warships. Martin Carslake, former master of the *Naseby,* soon
found himself invited back to resume his place in the ship (now the
Royal Charles), and there were many other instances.[34]

Among commissioned officers the unmistakable cavalier trend
was reinforced by the fact that mortality soon began to thin the
ranks of the former parliamentarians. Robert Blake and Eustace
Smith, prominent figures in the later 1650s, both died young in
1661. Sir Richard Stayner died the following year at Lisbon at the
age of only thirty-seven; 'a stout seaman,' Pepys commented, 'but
there will be no great miss of him for all that' — probably a reference
to his political past as much as his character.[35] Moreover several
former parliamentarians still commanding small vessels were turned
out or laid aside for fraud and embezzlement; though they were not
the only such offenders, of course, their political record inevitably
counted against them.[36]

Many cavaliers nevertheless found the political reconstruction of
the navy far too slow. Some resented every former rebel still
employed in the fleet, and Sandwich himself was the subject of
intense jealousy. The comptroller, Sir John Mennes, a veteran of
Charles I's navy, tried hard to undermine his position and told the
king that the fleet would certainly defect in a crisis unless all the old
parliamentarians were turned out. Clarendon too deplored the
number of 'infamous persons' still employed in the fleet and the dockyards, complaining that many of them were professing the same
views they had held in the 1650s.[37] By contrast James and his advisers
feared they might have gone too far in the opposite direction.

[33] Archer: Foster, *Factories*, xi. 128–9; Coventry MS 98, fo. 53. Milton: Adm.
106/1, fo. 520. White: Adm. 2/1732, fo. 28ᵛ. Short: Adm. 106/1, fo. 394.

[34] *CSPD 1661–2*, 259; cf. Adm. 3/274, fos. 50, 177; PRO SP 18/48/78.

[35] Pepys, *Diary*, ii. 73; J. H. Morrison, *Wills, Sentences and Probate Acts . . .
1661–70* (1935), 224; Pepys, *Diary*, iii. 249; *CSPD 1661–2*, 543.

[36] e.g. J. Bowry, Tatnel, Jowles, and Woolters: Adm. 2/1732, fos. 35ʳ⁻ᵛ, 38;
Adm. 2/1745, fo. 59; Adm. 106/2, fo. 19; cf. Rawl. MS A 184, fo. 88.

[37] Pepys, *Diary*, ii. 169, 216–17, iv. 169–70; Clarendon, *Life*, ii 329–30.

James remarked in 1662 that 'it must be the old captains that must do the business, and that the new ones would spoil all'. Coventry believed that very few of the cavalier officers could match the order and discipline of the parliamentarians, and Sandwich was convinced that things would 'go to wrack if ever the old captains should be wholly out, and the new ones wholly command'. Pepys agreed.[38] The strong feelings on both sides were to emerge as a major issue with the approach of a new war in 1664.

For many years the restored Stuarts lived in dread that their enemies would one day seek to topple them once more. The 1660s were marked by a long succession of rumours and plots.[39] One recurring fear was that radicals would try to subvert the navy, either from within or without, and though with hindsight this seems a remote possibility, expecially as trading voyages soon scattered them around the globe, fear fed upon rumour and there was just enough substance to give it credibility.

One of the first alarms was over the large-scale exodus of seamen to Holland early in 1661, caused by the recent demobilization of the fleet. This had flooded the labour market and driven many sailors to seek work abroad, but some took fright at reports of former Admiralty Commissioners and officers meeting in suspicious circumstances and discerned a sinister plot.[40] Some fears had a more solid foundation, for ex-naval personnel did play a part in the subversive talk and plotting rife in these years. The ex-chaplain Joseph Binckes used his close links with militant nonconformist groups in London to give the king the first hint of Venner's Fifth Monarchist rising of January 1661, and he went on to become a regular, paid informer.[41] One former captain, Richard Newbery, was gaoled in the Tower at the time of Venner's rising, and another, Thomas Elliott, was arrested later the same year for subversive activities.[42] Much of the government's knowledge of seditious talk

---

[38] Pepys, *Diary*, iii. 122, iv. 169–70, 196.

[39] R. L. Greaves, *Deliver Us from Evil: The Radical Underground in Britain, 1660–1663* (Oxford, 1986), gives a full account; two further volumes will take the story to 1670.

[40] *CSPD 1660–1*, 570.

[41] See *CSPD 1661–74*, esp. *1661–2*, 146–7, 191, 523; *1670*, 199, 344, 407–8, 427, 432, 636. He served at sea once more in the (Second?) Dutch War: *CSPD 1673–4*, 500 (probably misdated).

[42] Newbery: *Mercurius Publicus*, 10–17 Jan. 1661. Elliott: *CSPD 1661–2*, 177–8, 192. Elliott, bailiff of Aldeburgh, was also in trouble for embezzlement and drunken

among ex-naval personnel came through Capt. William Pestell, a renegade separatist, whose zeal in the role of informer helped to win him a new command through the unlikely patronage of the bishop of London.[43] In 1661 Pestell encountered the veteran commander Owen Cox, now back from service in Sweden, and a heated exchange followed. Cox denounced the Restoration, predicted that Charles II would meet the same fate as his father, and declared his sympathy for Venner's 'innocent martyrs', blaming Pestell for their deaths. These remarks were all the more alarming as he was commanding a powerful Swedish ship of seventy guns, carrying 350 barrels of gunpowder; though ostensibly bound for Portugal he allegedly showed no signs of preparing to leave the Downs. Cox was promptly arrested, but with only one witness it proved impossible to put him on trial for treason.[44] Pestell also made good use of his contacts in the West Country, reporting that the ex-captains Blagg, Heaton, Mootham, and Jefferies were among a group of radicals at Plymouth and Dartmouth openly hostile to the king and the Anglican Church.[45] Richard Potter was another former commander linked with this militant strain of nonconformity, attending a conventicle in Wapping in September 1660 where the preacher declared that only blood could satisfy God for the execution of the regicides.[46] Even some of the apparent conformists proved to be deeply discontented. Pepys found with surprise in 1663 that his sometime friend Philip Holland had 'turned almost Quaker', and a few weeks later Holland offended the commander-in-chief in the Downs by sailing past and failing to salute; he was summoned aboard the flagship for questioning and pronounced a 'fanatic'.[47]

The one serious attempt to subvert the navy was the Tonge Plot of 1662, which may well have involved far more important people

brawling; many years later he was to be Pepys's election agent, having settled perhaps for respectability: Coventry MS 96, fo. 34; *CSPD 1666–7*, 157; *The Further Correspondence of Samuel Pepys*, ed. J. R. Tanner (1929), 244–5, 252–3, 256–7, 337.

[43] Coventry MS 98, fo. 53ᵛ; Pepys, *Cat.* i. 393. He served as a master in Holmes's expedition to West Africa in 1663 and was killed at the taking of Goree early the following year: Adm. 2/1732, fo. 68ᵛ; *CSPD 1663–4*, 354; *CSPD 1664–5*, 388, 439; Ollard, *Man of War*, 285.   [44] *CSPD 1661–2*, 161, 188.

[45] Greaves, *Deliver Us*, 70; *CSPD 1661–2*, 97–8.

[46] *CSPD 1660–1*, 270. On Potter's nonconformity see also H. F. Waters, *Genealogical Gleanings in England* (Boston, Mass., 1901), 976.

[47] Pepys, *Diary*, iv. 109; Allin, *Journals*, i. 118. Holland had major financial worries too, and had made an attempt on his own life.

than the small fry who were brought to trial. Its aims were certainly ambitious: the plotters talked of killing the king, his brother, and Monck, and restoring a republic with annual parliaments and religious freedom. Many of them were disbanded soldiers, including Tonge, but there was also a strong naval element, and the paper they drew up was aimed in part at the seamen. Tonge himself may have been the man of that name who was steward of the *Lion* in 1654, and James Hinde, another active conspirator, was a former naval gunner. One of the leaders was the former chaplain Edward Riggs (now a brewer's clerk), who was described as 'zealous and active in the cause' and 'the most intelligent person among them'. A sea-captain named Brown (Zachary Brown?), who was also involved, had promised that 'Vice-Admiral Goodson was a sure man'. The plotters believed that at least one frigate would revolt from the king, and Riggs boasted that he could easily bring the garrisons in the Downs to mutiny. These bold claims were never put to the test, for Tonge and his associates were arrested in October and six of the conspirators were condemned to death.[48] Riggs saved himself by turning king's evidence; on his release in 1663 he became an effective government spy in the Netherlands, sending back a series of reports on the republican plotting which was to lead to the Yorkshire Rising of 1663.[49]

Though the plots involved fairly small numbers and flopped dismally they helped to keep alive doubts over the reliability of all Commonwealth veterans. One intelligencer claimed that Lawson himself had been aware of the 1663 design and had chosen to remain silent, and he averred that many in the fleet had favoured it.[50] There is no evidence to substantiate such claims but disaffection within the navy itself did occasionally come to light, notably in Sandwich's fleet at Lisbon in 1661. There was a drunken brawl ashore between Lt. Alured of the *Assistance* (a former officer under the Common-

---

[48] [W. Hill], *A Brief Narrative of that Stupendous Tragedie* (1662); W. Cobbett et al., *State Trials* (1809–28), vi. 226–74; *CSPD 1661–2*, 504, 530, 541, 591, 600. For a full account of the plot see Greaves, *Deliver Us*, 112–29. On Tonge the steward see Add. MS 9300, fo. 297; Hinde had long service as a gunner, and in 1655 had begged for the command of the *Cat:* SP 18/117/128–9; SP 18/134/93; SP 18/176/42; SP 18/218/90; Hill, *Brief Narrative*, sig. B. One of the plotters was John Sellers, the compass-maker and mathematician. Richard Newbery, who was seized for treasonable practices about this time, was perhaps thought to be implicated: *CSPD 1661–2*, 504.

[49] *CSPD 1663–4, passim; CSPD 1670*, 666; Greaves, *Deliver Us*, 176, 186–7, 203–4.   [50] *CSPD 1663–4*, 352.

wealth) and the lieutenant of the *Leopard*. A row also broke out on board the *Leopard* when her mate refused to drink the king's health and was accused of being a fanatic.[51] Some mariners were openly contemptuous of the new regime. A few weeks before Sandwich's arrival at Lisbon, an English shipmaster there and his mate had spoken out very freely, criticizing the king for favouring papists and handing the church back to 'Baal's priests', mocking James as a 'roaring boy', and damning most of the nobles as lewd and popish. They predicted that the regime would be short-lived: Charles would soon fall by an assassin's hand and Monck would perish within a year. The officers could not believe their hero Lawson had betrayed the cause, insisting that he was really a Fifth Monarchy man merely waiting for the right moment to strike. The consul at Lisbon had both men arrested.[52] There were other incidents of a similar nature. A veteran complained in 1663 that he could not serve as well as in the 1650s because seamen were no longer treated as well, adding that a thousand others shared his view. If another Dutch war broke out, he warned, the seamen would not fight as resolutely as before. The following year a master's mate was cashiered for drinking a satirical toast to the 'whoreson duke of York'.[53]

The approach of war with the Dutch in 1664 brought a massive expansion of the navy and intensified fears about its reliability. James had no experience of naval warfare and leaned heavily on the advice of veterans of the First Dutch War, especially Penn, Lawson, and Ayscue. They strengthened his own view that it was essential to bring back interregnum officers in large numbers, and observers were soon reporting in astonishment that the king's fleet was full of 'old Noll's captains'.[54] Coventry indeed claimed with pride in 1665 that very few Cromwellian officers had been left ashore.[55] The veterans were conspicuous even at the very highest levels. Sandwich was commander-in-chief in 1664 and part of 1665, and Monck (now duke of Albemarle) shared the supreme command with Rupert in

[51] BL Sloane MS 505, fos. 31–2, 40.
[52] Clar. MS 74, fos. 318–19`, 389. One of the offenders, Thomas Wood, was shipped back to England and gaoled: *CSPD 1660–1*, 225.
[53] Allin, *Journals*, i. 121; Coventry MS 98, fo. 124.
[54] Clarendon, *Life*, ii. 354; *CSPD 1663–4*, 597; Pepys, *Diary*, v. 293; HMC 53, *Montagu of Beaulieu*, 166.
[55] *CSPD 1664–5*, 395.

1666. Eleven of the seventeen flag-officers employed during the war were former parliamentarians.[56] Royalists were understandably dismayed at their sudden reversal. When Rear-Admiral Sansum died in 1665 his post was offered not to the fiery cavalier Robert Holmes, who had Rupert's backing, but to Sandwich's protégé Roger Cuttance; and when Cuttance chose to remain with his patron it was offered to another interregnum veteran, John Harman. Holmes resigned in disgust.[57] In all, some ninety captains in the years 1664–7 had been commanders under the Commonwealth, and a further eighteen had served as lieutenants. Several former Commonwealth masters also won commissions, and many more served again in their old role.[58] A few other new captains had served Cromwell at a humbler level, such as the former steward Stephen Pyend.[59] Even some of the old officers who remained ashore played a part in the war effort. Capt. Seth Hawley, for example, said he was too old to go back to sea but he readily placed his rope-making business at King's Lynn at the navy's disposal. William Crispin, an old associate of Penn, acted as navy agent and victualler at Kinsale.[60] The important post of resident commissioner at Harwich, revived for the duration of the war, went to Capt. John Taylor, who had been ousted as master-shipwright at Chatham at the Restoration; there were attempts to block the appointment on the grounds that he was a 'fanatic' but Coventry argued successfully that the state had 'need of all hands to the work' in a time of national crisis.[61]

The Second Dutch War did not match the triumphs of the First. An initial victory off Lowestoft in 1665 was not followed up, and the attack on a Dutch merchant fleet at Bergen later that year was a costly failure. The Four Days' Battle in June 1666, a bloody defeat, was only partly redeemed by the St James's Day victory in July. In the spring of 1667 the Dutch added a humiliating coda to the war by

[56] Pepys, *Cat.* i. 313–15.

[57] Pepys, *Diary*, vi. 122, 129; Sandwich, *Journal*, 234; Ollard, *Man of War*, 136.

[58] Pepys, *Cat.* i. 316–429. At least nine former masters served as captains and three as lieutenants. Six former lieutenants served again at the same level.

[59] Ibid. 160–3, 396. He was steward of the *Vanguard* in 1654: Add. MS 9300, fo. 290. Cf. Theophilus Scott, boatswain in 1654 and now captain: Add. MS 9300, fos. 290ᵛ–291; Pepys, *Cat.* i. 403.

[60] *CSPD 1665–6*, 87 (Hawley); ibid. 444; *CSPD 1666–7*, 441 (Crispin). Tatnel served for a time as a pressmaster: *CSPD 1664–5*, 362 etc.

[61] Pepys, *Cat.* i. 15 and n.; *CSPD 1664–5*, 68; Pepys, *Further Correspondence*, 29. For Taylor's religious affiliations see Waters, *Genealogical Gleanings*, 974–6.

sailing into the Medway and towing away or burning several major warships.[62]

The performance of the interregnum veterans was mixed. A later Admiralty survey heaped praise on many of them, and seven were knighted for their good service. Pepys too was impressed by officers such as Harman, Myngs, and Smyth.[63] But not all lived up to expectations. Edward Nixon proved so far from the 'stout' commander he had been supposed that he was sentenced to death for cowardice, and Thomas Penrose and several others were said to have 'grown debauched'.[64] Not that the cavaliers did any better overall; in the graphic phrase of one senior official, some new gentleman-captains could no more handle a ship than a horse could eat oysters.[65] None of the supreme commanders emerged with much credit. Sandwich was over-cautious, and was clearly to blame in allowing his captains to break open the holds of two captured East Indiamen and share out the booty; the row which erupted ended his part in the war and nearly destroyed his political career.[66] Monck's determination to conduct the war more vigorously led to far more serious mistakes. His sharp-tongued wife had boasted that he and his plain, fighting captains 'would make their ships swim with blood, though they could not make legs as captains nowadays can', and her dismal prophecy was soon fulfilled—if not in the way she had anticipated. Misled by his triumphs in 1653 Monck overruled the other captains and led his force out to be battered by a much stronger Dutch fleet in the Four Days' Battle.[67] Prince Rupert's conduct dealt an equally crippling blow to his reputation, too.

[62] For a brief account of the war see e.g. C. Wilson, *Profit and Power* (1957), ch. 9. For a full account of the Dutch raid see P. G. Rogers, *The Dutch in the Medway* (1970).

[63] Knighted: Harman, Jordan, Myngs, Smyth, Teddiman, Cuttance, Jennings: Pepys, *Diary*, vi. 122, 264, vii. 161–2, 165. There was praise for e.g. Clarke, Cuttance, Haddock, Hannam, Helling, Hubbard, Lloyd, Moulton, Jeffrey and John Pearce, Seaman, Wetwang: Coventry MS 99, fos. 91–2ᵛ.

[64] Nixon: *CSPD 1664–5*, 367, 387, 392, 404; Pepys, *Diary*, vi. 104; Sandwich, *Journal*, 214–15. (Nixon was reprieved.) Penrose: Coventry MS 99, fo. 102; Barlow, *Journal*, 135. It might be noted that Penrose was said to be owed £1,500 in wages at the time of his death in 1669, money never paid: D. Gilbert, *The Parochial History of Cornwall* (1838), ii. 29. Other officers who proved disappointing include E. Grove (Pepys, *Diary*, vi. 130), Jonas Poole (ibid. vi. 129; Coventry MS 99, fo. 92), Elliott (Coventry MS 99, fo. 91ᵛ: 'Stout but given to plunder'; *CSPD 1666–7*, 157), Reynolds (Pepys, *Diary*, v. 355), and Aylett (ibid. vii. 174).

[65] *CSPD 1666–7*, 96.

[66] Harris, *Mountagu*, ii, ch. 9.

[67] Pepys, *Diary*, vi. 298, vii. 11, 354, viii. 125.

The most striking feature of the war, however, was not the mixed fortunes of battle but the vicious struggle for royal favour which developed between rival factions.[68] Officers rushed to find scapegoats after every set-back, and old loyalties counted for little: former parliamentarians such as Monck, Ayscue, and Myngs joined in the attack on Sandwich in 1665, and Monck also turned on his old protégé Penn, denouncing him as a 'cowardly rogue'.[69] Monck's own failure the following year brought tensions between his supporters and Rupert's to a head; Jeremiah Smyth and Robert Holmes, the leaders of the two factions, accused each other of cowardice and only the king's personal intervention prevented a duel between them. An observer remarked that the whole fleet was behaving as if the Devil himself were in command.[70] The bitter feuding inevitably damaged the fleet's performance. It was hard for commanders to make sensible decisions when they knew colleagues and subordinates were waiting to denounce almost any course of action as either cowardly or rash. It may be that failure was bound to lead to recriminations, but some of the blame must lie with the Admiralty and the Restoration government as a whole for failing to create any sense of common purpose or discipline. The First Dutch War had also seen a high command shared between officers of very mixed temperaments and backgrounds, and had proved that it was possible for them to work together harmoniously: the contrast is glaring.

Though the factions straddled the old division between cavalier and roundhead, the memory of civil war allegiances clearly made a bad situation worse. Early in the war a lieutenant taunted Captains Hannam and Smyth as old Cromwellian rebels; he was promptly cashiered by a court martial and James took the opportunity to insist that all officers were to be 'equally esteemed good subjects'.[71] In practice it was not so easy to bury the past. Monck himself was prepared to stir up old animosities to blacken his rivals, denouncing his former ally Penn for bringing 'all these roguish fanatic captains into the fleet'. And Capt. Francis Digby, a courtier, was making a transparent attack on the old parliamentarians when he called for all the tarpaulin captains to be turned out.[72]

[68] Pepys, *Diary*, vi–viii, and *CSPD 1664–7, passim*; Davies, thesis, ch. 4.

[69] Pepys, *Diary*, iv. 260, 291; Harris, *Mountagu*, ii. 9.

[70] Pepys, *Diary*, vii. 332–3, 340, 350. viii. 42; *CSPD 1665–6*, 596; *CSPD 1666–7*, 1, 14, 15, 40, 222, 232, 236.

[71] Sandwich, *Journal*, 173.

[72] Pepys, *Diary*, vi. 291, vii. 333.

It was no secret that militant nonconformists longed for England's defeat in the war, seeing it as the best way to topple the monarchy—a mirror image of cavalier dreams in the First Dutch War. Known dissenters were therefore excluded, or excluded themselves, from the navy. Penn had drawn up a list of all the best sea-officers available in England, at James's request, and ten of those he named were barred as nonconformists; among them were Goodson, Potter, and William Hill, Lawson's former ally. It seems likely that Nicholas Heaton, a West-Countryman, was invited to serve only because the government was unaware of his strong religious views. Heaton, as a good patriot, accepted in principle (commenting tartly that he had been ignored ever since the Restoration and was still owed arrears for service in the 1650s), but he laid down the impossible condition of complete religious freedom. 'Faith and a good conscience', he declared, 'must not be parted with on any terms.'[73]

The government naturally kept a close watch on militants in England and abroad. Capt. Richard Newbery was arrested yet again in 1665 for treasonable designs.[74] Some radicals were known to be hoping for an invasion or an English defeat to trigger a republican uprising; agents reported that Col. Rich and his friends were 'hugging each other' in anticipation when the two fleets first met in 1665, and at Yarmouth wild rumours spread that James had fled and that the bishops would tumble down once more.[75] The tempo of republican activity increased sharply. The former Commissioner Nehemiah Bourne crossed the Atlantic once more to join republicans in the Netherlands, and was soon in contact with dissidents in England.[76] Militants pressed Owen Cox to use his new vessel to ferry republican exiles back to England, or to free General Lambert from his prison in Guernsey.[77] John Croscombe, a former naval master, was arrested at Chatham in July 1667 for predicting that within three months an army would rise up and seize London,

---

[73] Penn, *Memorials*, ii. 293–5; cf. *CSPD 1664–5*, 395. For Heaton see Coventry MS 96, fo. 74. John Bourne, Plumleigh, Blagg, and Dakins would also have been excluded on ideological grounds.

[74] Clarendon MS 85, fo. 330ʳ. Rich, though sent to the Tower, was in fact peaceable: *CSPD 1664–5*, 419, 483, 577. For the rumours see *CSPD 1664–5*, 408, 517, 529. For a general survey see vol. ii (forthcoming) of Greaves's study of Restoration political dissent.   [75] *CSPD 1664–5*, 259, 278.

[76] *CCSP* v. 422; Clarendon MS 85, fo. 330ʳ; *CSPD 1667–8*, 270.

[77] *CSPD 1664–5*, 234. He had been issued with letters of marque: PRO HCA 25/9. In the event he was drowned shortly afterwards when the ship foundered in a storm off Yarmouth: J. Gadbury, *Nauticum Astrologicum* (1691), 79–80.

restore the Rump, and put the king on trial. He had also been studying the fortifications at Chatham at the time of de Ruyter's raid, and it was suspected that he had been planning to help the Dutch.[78] There were undoubtedly a number of radicals willing to give such help. One of them was the shipwright Samuel Raven, who had settled in the Netherlands after the Restoration and given advice on the design of warships; in 1666 he went to sea with the Dutch, urging them to land at Harwich and promising they would find a friendly welcome.[79] Some renegades offered to serve the Dutch as pilots. Thomas Woolman volunteered in 1666 to guide them into the Thames to help them mount a blockade, and he may have accompanied the raid on the Medway the following year. De Ruyter had several offers of this kind, one from a mariner described as 'half a Fifth Monarchy man', and the former captain Philip Holland joined the Dutch during the course of the raid to tender his services.[80] In addition there were large numbers of ordinary English sailors serving with the Dutch throughout the war, most of them attracted by the higher wages on offer but some perhaps swayed by ideology too.

A more insidious fear worrying some cavaliers was that veterans who had returned to the fleet and professed to be loyal would betray it at the first opportunity. Rumours of treachery surfaced almost as soon as the war began. After the first fleet action, for example, it was alleged that many captains had held back, waiting to see if there would be a chance to defect.[81] One informant claimed that the Anabaptists had corrupted the navy and that 'no man would be firm to the king who had fought against him'. It was reported too that the militant republican Andrew Yarranton, 'as violent a villain against the king as any', had visited many of the ships to sow disaffection.[82] The Dutch themselves believed that interregnum officers might be willing to change sides. When they

[78] *CSPD 1667*, 302–3, 353.

[79] Carte MS 73, fo. 403; Carte MS 74, fo. 226; *CCSP* v. 129; *CSPD 1665–6*, 521; *CSPD 1666–7*, 146; *Samuel Pepys's Naval Minutes*, ed. J. R. Tanner (NRS, 1926), 26, 46–7. Raven had asked to return home in 1665 if he could have liberty of conscience: *CSPD 1664–5*, 537–8.

[80] For Woolman (or Woodman) see *CSPD 1666–7*, 118. He is probably identical with John or Robert Woolman, both naval masters in the 1650s. Rogers, *Dutch in the Medway*, 64–5. On Holland see Rawl. MS D 924, fos. 232–3. There were two captains named Holland, Philip and Thomas, which led to some confusion. See further *Pepys's Naval Minutes*, 19, 20, 26–7, 342, 345; *CSPD 1671–2*, 390; *CSPD 1672*, 390. [81] *CSPD 1664–6*, 151.

[82] *CSPD 1664–5*, 286; *CSPD 1665–6*, 567. For the 'Yarrington Plot' of 1661 see Greaves, *Deliver Us*, 72–7.

captured Capt. Robert Wilkinson in 1665 they promptly offered him a command, and though Wilkinson refused, his lieutenant — Sandes Temple, another former parliamentarian — proved more responsive. Temple allegedly promised republican exiles that if he could get a command after his release he would try to bring over his ship and persuade others to do the same. Temple did secure a commission in 1666 (though only as a lieutenant) before his plans came to light.[83] Philip Holland's defection to de Ruyter in 1667 was especially alarming, for the previous year he had been commanding an English warship; how many officers still serving might have a patriotism equally flimsy? The revolutionary Croscombe, for example, was found to be sharing lodgings with an officer belonging to one of the ships lying in the Medway.[84]

The parliamentary hunt for scapegoats when the war was over provided a further opportunity for trying to undermine the regime. Among the agents gathering evidence against Sir William Coventry, one of the chief targets, we find the former captain Valentine Tatnel, Gilbert Cornelius, a lieutenant in the 1650s and in the recent war, and, most striking, the veteran army agitator and Fifth Monarchist Edmund Chillenden, who had been serving as a purser. Possibly these old radicals dreamed of undermining the regime, but their sponsors were merely interested in factional struggles, and the whole affair proved a very damp squib. The petition against Coventry contained pitifully few names, Tatnel was soon exposed as a disreputable figure, and the campaign fizzled out.[85]

Despite the many alarms the Dutch war finally laid to rest the spectre of mass betrayal by the old parliamentarians. The vast majority showed themselves prepared to serve the nation loyally, whatever their private feelings about the regime. In any case their ranks were considerably depleted by the end of the war, for casualties had been heavy. Sixteen of the old commanders were killed or died of their wounds, among them the flag-officers Lawson, Myngs, and Sansum, and Lawson's associates Abelson and Tearne.[86] In addition Stokes and Penn's kinsman Jonas Poole died

---

[83] Pepys, *Diary*, vi. 118; *CSPD 1664–5*, 500, 570; *CSPD* v. 491. Temple: *CSPD 1664–5*, 500; *CSPD 1666–7*, 82, 97, 146; Pepys, *Cat.* i. 413.

[84] Pepys, *Cat.* i. 366; *CSPD 1667*, 303.

[85] Coventry MS 101, fos. 104–242; BL Egerton MS 928, fos. 66–7; V. Vale, 'The Sale of Naval Offices, 1660–8', *Cambridge Historical Journal*, xii (1956), 116–22; Davies, thesis, ch. 4, part ii. For Chillenden see Coventry MS 101, fo. 181.

[86] The others were Cadman, Coppin, Cuttle, Dare, R. Kirby, Mootham, Parker, Joseph and Robert Saunders, C. Wager, W. Wood.

from natural causes, and Gilpin was accidentally drowned.[87] The survivors, however, found their position greatly strengthened by the war. Many of those who had proved their worth were to remain in service for many years, playing a major part in the navy's development. For Jeremiah Smyth and Richard Haddock the war marked the start of a second naval career, leading in both cases to a knighthood and a place on the Navy Board.[88] Joseph Jordan and John Wetwang, who had returned to the navy after gaps of eight and eleven years respectively, stayed on to become stalwarts of the service, both earning knighthoods.[89] Willoughby Hannam found service ashore as Master Attendant at Woolwich before returning to sea once more in the next war.[90] Many of the interregnum officers had clearly convinced the Admiralty that their ability and experience were indispensable.

Several of the old parliamentarians survived to play an important part in the Third Dutch War, from 1672 to 1674. In addition to the officers already mentioned, Anthony Young returned to the navy after an absence of fourteen years, to serve as joint captain of the *Royal Charles* and then the *Sovereign*.[91] But the number of veterans still active was now much smaller, and the overall composition of the officer corps strikingly different. Only four veterans of the 1650s were appointed to flag-positions in this war, and only one of them survived it. Ayscue died in 1672 before taking up his post, Sandwich was killed at the battle of Sole Bay, and Harman died in 1673; Jordan, the sole survivor, had retired with a royal pension after the first year's campaign.[92] Several other veterans also perished in action, among them Sandwich's protégé John Hayward and Willoughby Hannam.[93]

---

[87] Stokes: *CSPD 1664-5*, 200-1; Poole: Morrison, *Wills 1661-70*, 195; Gilpin: *CSPD 1664-5*, 279. John Bourne died too, in 1667.

[88] *DNB*; Pepys, *Cat.* i. 315, 358, 406-7.

[89] *DNB*; Pepys, *Cat.* i. 314, 372, 421-2.

[90] Pepys, *Cat.* i. 359; *CSPD 1670*, 381; *CSPD 1671*, 87. Among other Masters Attendant were the Commonwealth veterans Amos Bear and Martin Carslake, who had both commanded ships in the Second Dutch War: *FDW* i. 6; Pepys, *Cat.* i. 323, 332; *CSPD 1666-7*, 396; *CSPD 1672-3*, 394, 405.   [91] Pepys, *Cat.* i. 429.

[92] Jordan was awarded a pension of £500 p.a.: *CSPD 1672-3*, 503-4. P. Le Fevre, 'Sir George Ayscue, Commonwealth and Restoration Admiral', *MM* lxviii (1982), 199-200. For Sandwich and Harman see *DNB*. Harman was in command of the fleet at one point, a remarkable position for a former Baptist! There were some doubts about his present religion; he had taken the oaths but appears to have been unwilling to take communion: A. Grey (ed.), *Debates of the House of Commons* (1769), ii. 79-80.   [93] Pepys, *Cat.* i. 359, 363.

Though the war proved as faction-ridden as the last, civil war rivalries no longer formed one of the ingredients. Most officers were products of the Restoration era itself, and the loyalty of the remaining veterans was now generally accepted. Even some of the former militants had reconciled themselves to the Stuarts. The renegade Philip Holland, who had settled in the Netherlands after joining de Ruyter, returned before the war broke out and readily told what he knew of Dutch preparations in return for a pardon.[94] Sandes Temple, despite the treachery he had earlier planned, was trusted sufficiently to be given a new commission.[95] Nehemiah Bourne figured in the records now as contractor rather than conspirator, and his brother-in-law Anthony Earning readily tendered his ship to the state.[96] Nicholas Heaton similarly found a way to serve his country without compromising his principles, as commander of a flotilla of scouts employed by the East India Company to track Dutch movements in the Channel.[97]

The dwindling band of old Cromwellians continued to play an active role during the long peace which lasted for the rest of Charles's reign. Robert Robinson, Richard Rooth, William Poole, and John Wetwang were among the linchpins of the service—though the first three also came to acquire an unsavory reputation for lining their own pockets.[98] The only flicker of political radicalism in the second half of the reign came during the Exclusion crisis, when some of the Whig militants dreamed of wresting the navy from the king's control, as in 1642. The former vice-admiral William Goodson allegedly went among the seamen in Redriff and Wapping and won assurances that 'they will be right and true Protestants, and will throw their officers overboard'. Nothing whatever came of this talk. In 1683, during another Whig scare, a shipmaster named William Blagge was tried for treason on a charge

---

[94] *CSPD 1671–2*, 390, 437–8, 609; *CSPD 1672*, 390, 683; *CSPD 1672–3*, 172. Holland was given the command of a merchant ship owned by Rupert: Pepys, *Cat.* iv. 658–9; *Pepys's Naval Minutes*, 345.

[95] Pepys, *Cat.* i. 413; *CSPD 1672*, 656, 659–60.

[96] Bourne: Chaplin, 'Bourne', 151; *CSPD Addenda 1660–85*, 305, 423, 427. Earning: *CSPD Addenda 1660–85*, 334. He served with the East India Company during the war, and was killed in 1674 in a clash with the Dutch; Chaplin, 'Bourne', 142; Pepys, *Cat.* ii. 322, iv. 204; Sainsbury, *Court Minutes*, ix. 195, x. 262. See also R. C. Anderson (ed.), *Journals and Narratives of the Third Dutch War* (NRS, 1946), 86.

[97] Sainsbury, *Court Minutes*, ix. 132, 143, 167, 186.

[98] Pepys, *Cat.* i–iv, *passim; Pepys's Naval Minutes*, 196.

of threatening to attack the Tower, though he was acquitted.[99] Religious nonconformity can be traced rather more often. The former captain Edward Moorcock, who had been invited to raise the wrecks in the Medway, took elaborate precautions to make sure his attendance at Baptist conventicles could not be used to ruin him during the operation.[100] Benjamin Blake, the old admiral's brother, held large nonconformist assemblies at his home, and when persecution intensified in the last years of the reign he emigrated with his family to Carolina.[101] A few other dissenters come to light during the brief period of religious toleration in 1672: Robert Plumleigh helped to acquire a licence for a nonconformist minister at Plymouth, and the ex-lieutenant William Rising had his own house at Lowestoft licensed as a meeting-place.[102]

None of Cromwell's veterans was still serving afloat by 1688, and they played no part in the political manœuvring at the time of William's invasion.[103] Most of the survivors no doubt welcomed the Glorious Revolution. One former officer, a young lieutenant in the 1650s, accepted a naval command from William III after holding aloof for almost thirty years. A command was even offered to the aged republican stalwart Nehemiah Bourne, almost forty years after his last service at sea![104] But the role of the surviving veterans was now mainly as repositories of naval lore and precedent. Anthony Young, for example, helped to reinforce English claims to the sovereignty of the seas by recalling what had been done sixty years earlier on Buckingham's expedition to the Île de Ré in 1627. Though Young died in 1693 Sir Robert Robinson survived till 1710, with a

---

[99] *CSPD 1680–1*, 44. For Blagge see Cobbett, *State Trials*, ix. 653–66; *CSPD 1683*, i. 385, ii. 39–40, 54–6, 71–2, 79; see also Pepys, *Cat.* iii. 273. Could he be a kinsman of Edward Blagg?

[100] *BDBR; CSPD 1667–8*, esp. 376, 401.

[101] G. Lyon Turner, *Original Records of Early Nonconformity* (1911–14), ii. 1105; C. D. Curtis, *Blake: General at Sea* (Taunton, 1934), 177; J. Oldmixon, *The History and Life of Robert Blake, Esq.* (1740), 117–18 (which confuses Benjamin with Humphrey). Blake's son Samuel became Governor of S. Carolina.

[102] Turner, *Orig. Records*, i. 207–9 (Plumleigh), ii. 912 (Rising). One of Plumleigh's colleagues was Samuel Widger, a naval chaplain in 1658 (Adm. 3/273, fo. 241; SP 18/194/33).

[103] E. B. Powley, *The English Navy in the Revolution of 1688* (Cambridge, 1928); Davies, thesis, ch. 7.

[104] J. Charnock, *Biographia Navalis* (1794), i. 58–9. (This was David Lambert, son of the Cromwellian captain John Lambert.) For Bourne see C. H. Firth, 'Sailors of the Civil War, the Commonwealth and the Protectorate', *MM* xii (1926), 255–6.

pension from Queen Anne, and Sir Richard Haddock even lived to see the Hanoverians.[105]

After the Glorious Revolution the Admiralty official Richard Gibson wrote a scathing attack on the Restoration officers, coupled with a eulogy on the parliamentarians he had known in his youth. The only contribution of the new gentlemen-captains, he mocked, had been 'to bring in drinking, gaming, whoring, swearing and all impiety into the fleet', along with their useless baggage of 'footmen, tailors, barbers, fiddlers, decayed kindred', and the like. Gibson was hardly the first veteran to feel the world had degenerated since his youth, and his analysis was strongly coloured by political and religious bias.[106] It is none the less striking that officials as diverse as Prince James, Coventry, and Pepys should have shared much of his assessment. All had recognized the danger of allowing the navy to be swamped by cavaliers lacking experience and discipline. In the climate of the 1660s it was obviously impossible to have a wholly tarpaulin, ex-parliamentarian officer corps, but James and some of his advisers had tried to limit the cavalier influx and on the outbreak of the Dutch war they had hastily recalled many of the interregnum veterans. The need for professional skills was more readily accepted thereafter. An ideal officer corps, as Pepys and some others recognized, would balance tarpaulins and gentlemen until a new breed of officer could be raised combining the best qualities of each. Halifax recommended that 'gentlemen shall not be capable of bearing office at sea, except they be tarpaulins too; that is to say, except they are so trained up by a continued habit of living at sea, that they may have a right to be admitted free denizens of Wapping'.[107] By 1688, with the Cromwellians mostly dead, the debate had lost its earlier political overtones and the lessons had been assimilated, at least in part. The career prospects for mariners of non-gentle birth had

---

[105] Young: Pepys, *Cat.* iii. 276; Adm. 7/729, pp. 251–2; *The Diary of John Evelyn*, ed. E. S. de Beer (Oxford, 1955), v. 158–9. Robinson: D. Lysons, *Environs of London* (1795), iv. 466; *CSPD 1697*, 123; *CSPD 1699*, 117; *CSPD 1703–4*, 360–1. He had ended his active career as Governor of Bermuda: S. S. Webb, *The Governor-Generals* (Chapel Hill, 1979), 473. Haddock: *DNB*.

[106] Charnock, *Marine Architecture*, i, pp. lxxxvi–xciv. Even Gibson missed the dancing-master employed in the flagship in 1666 during a critical phase of the Dutch war: *CSPD 1665–6*, 501. Gibson had first served in the navy in 1648 at the age of 13: Add. MS 11602, fo. 125.

[107] *Halifax: Complete Works*, ed. J. P. Kenyon (Harmondsworth, 1969), 160–1.

worsened, but the officer corps now contained a growing number of men from gentry backgrounds who had been bred to the sea since youth, the type which was to dominate the Hanoverian navy.[108]

The personal contribution of interregnum veterans to the Restoration navy had been very considerable. In many cases their sons and grandsons too had followed them into the service.[109] In the first ten years of Charles II's reign they had provided a backbone of experience, order, and discipline. But perhaps the greatest legacy of the 1650s was the enduring belief—half memory, half myth—that the Commonwealth navy had been honest, brave, well-ordered, and ever-victorious. Amid the failures and internecine strife of the Restoration era there survived a faith that things could be different, and had been so within living memory. The legend, almost as potent as Blake's fleet itself, was to provide a valuable yardstick for generations to come.

[108] For an important recent discussion see Davies, thesis, ch. 2.

[109] e.g. the Haddocks and Youngs. The Hanoverian admiral Sir Charles Wager was related to Goodson, Earning, and the Bournes. Admiral Sir John Leake was a descendant of the Cromwellian gunner Richard Leake; and so on.

12

Conclusion

THOUGH the Commonwealth navy served many national interests its primary function remained throughout the security of the regime. It was rightly seen by those in power as essential to their survival. The republic established in 1649 was deeply unpopular both at home and abroad, and contemporaries were less well placed than modern historians to see that a full-scale invasion from Europe was never very likely. They were aware that the Rump was also vulnerable to other pressures: English trade faced a danger of strangulation by privateers, and it was quite possible that foreign powers would back royalist incursions designed to foment risings at home. For Charles I a powerful navy had been a desirable political asset; for the Rump it was indispensable, forming the first line of defence and providing the only means of securing diplomatic recognition. By the time the Rump fell in 1653 the navy had already proved its value, destroying Rupert's squadron, recapturing English possessions overseas, and securing recognition from Spain, the Dutch, and (unofficially) France. These successes bred a confidence and belligerence among politicians and sailors alike that helped to unleash the bloody war with the Dutch. The navy was no longer merely the instrument of foreign policy: it was beginning to shape it.

Cromwell as Protector built on this inheritance. Though he brought the Dutch war to an end he still needed the fleet to secure his regime, and he set out to devise a policy by which it would pay for itself while serving both the nation's interests and his own. The fact that the French and Spaniards were competing for his friendship was delightful evidence of the new opportunities the navy was creating on the international stage. Cromwell inaugurated the age of English gunboat diplomacy with obvious relish, demonstrating the potential of naval power as none of England's rulers before him had done; his plans to seize bases such as Gibraltar and use the navy to build up a colonial empire indicated very clearly the future direction of English policy. Europeans were understandably awed by England's sudden emergence as a great maritime power. At home pride in the navy's achievements was able, eventually, to transcend party divisions. In 1660 Prince James could commend the ex-republican Lawson to the Commons for services which 'have brought so much glory to these nations'. Ten years later Monck's first biographer went out of his way to praise Blake as a national hero ('whatsoever he was otherwise') who had 'made the English courage to be both remembered and admired amongst all our neighbour nations'.[1] The lasting achievement of the interregnum navy was to reawaken the spirit of the late Elizabethan age and reassert England's maritime destiny.

The navy's most striking feature in the 1650s was the ideological and social character of its officer corps. The naval revolt of 1648 convinced the Rump that a large-scale remodelling was essential. For the first and only time in its history the navy became a stronghold of political and religious radicalism, with ideological commitment figuring prominently in appointments and promotions. The high-tide of radicalism on land, in 1653, saw a corresponding ideological surge within the fleet.

This has not been the traditional view. Most historians, noting the 1648 mutiny, have seen the navy as little affected by radical ideas and have tended to overlook its role and character thereafter. The fleet is often assumed to have stood aside from domestic political issues during the interregnum, with the Generals placing the interests of the nation above those of party and other officers loyally following their lead.[2] Some contemporaries were more cynical, depicting the mariners as tame conformists swayed merely by self-interest. In 1659 a republican mocked the 'time-serving, shuttlecock-spirited' men who had blandly accepted the Rump, Barebone's Parliament, the Protectorate, and then the Rump once more. 'What a pitiful, unconstant, weather-cock spirit is this', he

---

[1] PRO Adm. 2/175, fo. 18ᵛ; T. Gumble, *The Life of General Monck* (1671), 56, 67. Gumble also praised Lawson, Jordan, and Goodson; the inclusion of Goodson, who never served after 1660, is striking. For expressions of pride during the 1650s themselves see in particular Marvell's poem 'On the Victory obtained by Blake over the Spaniards', composed in 1657 after the attack on Santa Cruz.

[2] e.g. A. W. Tedder, *The Navy of the Restoration* (Cambridge, 1916), 16; Powell, *Blake*, 231; Laughton's article on Blake in *DNB*. Hammond, thesis, also plays down political concern in the navy before the crisis of 1659–60.

exclaimed, remarking how like the sailors were to the ever-changing element they sailed upon.[3] A cavalier writing a few months later was equally scathing. Most of the captains, he remarked, were formerly no better than 'gunners and ship carpenters; men that have no sense of honour or conscience, that will change with the winds, and keep to the strongest side as the most profitable'.[4]

These comments were ill-founded. Though the extent of radicalism among ordinary seamen was limited there is plentiful evidence of political and religious zeal among the officers, especially those recruited in and after 1649. A large and influential minority, especially the more senior commanders, were men fired by commitment to a cause. The charge of tame conformism during the subsequent political upheavals is at most a half-truth. The primary aim of many officers was to uphold the Puritan interest and keep out the Stuarts, and this goal was of course shared by all the interregnum regimes. Even so the fleet's declaration on the fall of the Rump pointedly offered no support whatever for the army's action. That there was no open protest was largely because the coup had come at a critical point in the Dutch war; had the navy tried to resist the war would have ended in disaster, perhaps playing directly into the Stuarts' hands. The Protectorate too was established while the war was still in progress. To this extent the navy did indeed place national before party interest. But once the war was over an undercurrent of dissent becomes apparent. It was harder for the government to present the subsequent war with Spain as vital to English security, and this time the appeal to patriotism was not enough to silence all opposition. Lawson and his friends were cynical about the Spanish war and regarded the Protectorate as a thinly disguised military dictatorship; Cromwell's very cautious response to their subversive talk and scheming indicates his continuing uncertainty about the regime's standing in the fleet. On the fall of Richard Cromwell ideological differences came into the open. Mountagu was not prepared to subdue, or even hide, his aversion to the restored Rump. A few months later Lawson's hatred of the rule of the army junta led to the fleet's dramatic intervention in the political crisis, which played a major part in toppling the regime.

For most of the decade the great majority of officers had proved

[3] *A True Catalogue ... of ... where, and by whom, Richard Cromwell was Proclaimed Lord Protector* (1659), 62–3.
[4] T. Lister, *Life and Administration of Edward, First Earl of Clarendon* (1837–8), iii. 92.

willing to accept successive political changes ashore. Blake gave
unswerving loyalty to the Protectorate, whatever his initial feelings
on the overthrow of the Rump. Many officers no doubt conformed
to keep their jobs, or through loyalty to their leaders. But many saw
too that faction-fighting among the parliamentarians would be a
fatal self-indulgence. This was the implicit message of the fleet's
carefully worded declaration in April 1653, and it was spelt out
clearly in the autumn of 1659. The naval officers who reluctantly
decided to accept the junta told Monck that while they did not
condone the army's actions it was essential to maintain a united
front against the Stuarts. We may be sure that the navy's course in
the months leading to the Restoration would have been very different if Blake or Deane had still been alive. Even without them it is
clear that many officers grudgingly accepted the king's restoration
only because they felt there was nothing they could do once Monck
had thrown his weight behind it. Whereas the junta had been hated
and they had the prospect of military support from Scotland and
elsewhere, they knew they would have neither popular nor military
backing if they tried to resist Monck and the royalist tide in the
spring. Lawson, the leading republican still in service, was misled
and outmanœuvred.

Royalists could never decide whether the Commonwealth naval
officer was a time-server or a fanatic. Their instinctive belief that
tarpaulins could have no sense of honour or political commitment
was hardly supported by the facts, and they had to acknowledge
that repeated efforts to win them over had failed. After 1660 many
leading tarpaulin officers either refused to serve the king or were
barred. By contrast gentleman-officers such as Monck, Mountagu,
and Ayscue had proved ready enough to switch allegiance in 1659–
60, just as a generation later in 1688 their successors readily
abandoned their old master James II.

The social character of the parliamentary navy was as distinctive
as its 'fanaticism'. This was the greatest age of the tarpaulin
officer—though even the Rump preferred to give the best ships to
substantial shipmasters rather than men of low birth. The
tarpaulins proved beyond doubt that they could fight as courage-
ously as any gentleman.[5] They faced criticism on a second count,

---

[5] The most glowing tribute was by a Dutch skipper, who told Capt. Nicholas
Foster in 1659 that the English had won because they had tarpaulin officers whereas
the Dutch fleet had many gentleman-captains intruded by the States General. Were

however, of failing to maintain proper order. It was alleged that, not being born and brought up to rule, they were over-familiar with their men and lax over standards of professional conduct. Being dependent on their modest wages they chose to exploit their places by plundering prizes, embezzling stores, and cheating their men, allowing their subordinates to do likewise.

There is indeed plentiful evidence of fraud in the navy, though this was hardly unique to the interregnum or to tarpaulin commanders. Naval captains throughout the age of sail set out to exploit their places, a practice that was generally recognized and, within limits, accepted. The plunder of prizes was similarly endemic.[6] Interregnum officers had unrivalled opportunities for plunder but there is no evidence that they were any more lax than their successors, and they may well have been less so. No hint of improper gain was made against any of the Generals at Sea or flag-officers such as Lawson, Goodson, or Bourne—in sharp contrast to the situation after the Restoration. A former colleague of Blake once remarked that the admiral was a careful man but left an estate worth only £3,000, which Pepys saw as proof that the navy was no path to riches for an honest man. Many senior officers did not in fact depend wholly on their pay, having retained their shares in merchant shipping and ventures. The charge that a tarpaulin commander was by definition less likely to check fraud among his subordinates is open to question. Being aware of all the opportunities he was far better equipped to restrain embezzlement than a gentleman ignorant of seafaring practice, and he was much less likely to regard such matters as trivia beneath his dignity. Most of the evidence of fraud relates to officers in small ships serving away from the main squadrons, and the amounts involved often appear to have been modest. There is more evidence of poverty among these men than of ill-gotten wealth. Naval pay was slow and erratic, and

the situation reversed, he added, the Dutch would win: *Samuel Pepys's Naval Minutes*, ed. J. R. Tanner (NRS, 1926), 449.

[6] The generous limits were breached so often that one historian could observe that 'the list of captains prosecuted for gross and intolerable embezzlements and frauds reads like a roster of the royal navy': R. Bourne, *Queen Anne's Navy in the West Indies* (New Haven, 1939), 219 n. It was remarked in 1668 that the senior captains had grown very rich through payments from merchantmen they had convoyed: W. E. Knowles Middleton (ed.), *Lorenzo Magalotti at the Court of Charles II* (Waterloo, Ontario, 1980), 96. See generally Pepys, *Cat.* i, introd.; *Pepys's Naval Minutes*; Davies, thesis; the works of Ehrman and Baugh, cited in ch. 7 n. 3, above; N. A. M. Rodger, *The Wooden World: An Anatomy of the Georgian Navy* (1986).

service brought many expenses as well as perks; a certain level of petty fraud by officers at every level was an inevitable lubricant to a rusty system rather than proof of boundless corruption and greed.[7]

It does appear to be true, however, that discipline in the interregnum navy was relatively relaxed. Many officers kept order by fostering a sense of harmony and community rather than by imposing a ferocious disciplinary regime. Recent studies of the Restoration and Hanoverian navies have produced rather similar findings, suggesting that the brutality of the 1790s was the exception, not the norm. Even so the regime was milder in the 1650s than after the Restoration, as many contemporaries remarked, and punishments in the 1750s which Dr Rodger calls moderate would have been unthinkable a hundred years earlier.[8] And though later seamen could still appeal to the Admiralty over their grievances the practice appears to have been far more common in the 1650s and far more acceptable to those in authority. The price of this familiarity, in the smaller ships at least, could be a weakening of the chain of command. In such a climate much depended on the personal character of the captain, and a weak or irresponsible officer was more likely to find his orders ignored than in other periods.[9] On the other hand the benefits were substantial, and the spirit of harmony, mutual trust, and co-operation which a good commander could foster help to explain the remarkable achievements of the age.

The factional strife which plagued later generations was notably absent in the 1650s. The explanation lies partly in the navy's successful record, and the sense of pride it engendered, and partly in its distinctive political and social character. The sense of fighting for a cause, ideological as well as patriotic, gave the officer corps a cohesion which the Stuart navy never matched, and Blake in particular exerted an authority none of the Restoration admirals could equal. Many of the commanders who rallied to the navy

---

[7] *Pepys's Naval Minutes*, 26 (citing Richard Haddock). Even Sir John Harman, a very senior officer, left his widow in relative poverty when he died in 1673, despite many years' service. (*The Further Correspondence of Samuel Pepys*, ed. J. R. Tanner (1929), 278–9.) See ch. 7 part ii, above.

[8] Davies, thesis, 109–16; Rodger, *Wooden World*, ch. 6. For contemporary comment see e.g. 'An Inquiry into the Causes of our Naval Miscarriages' in W. Oldys and T. Park (eds.), *The Harleian Miscellany*, i (1808), 569; E. Ward, *The Wooden World* (2nd edn., 1708), 9; J. Charnock, *A History of Marine Architecture* (1801–2), i, pp. xcii–xciv.

[9] Rodger's observation that indiscipline occurred only in port or ashore would not be true of the 1650s: *Wooden World*, 207–8.

under the Rump expected to return to civilian life when circumstances permitted, as many of them did. A more professional outlook gradually developed, as war became a permanent condition and large fleets had to be set out each year. Increasingly appointments were filled by promoting men already in the service, not by recruiting outsiders. This process continued after the Restoration, with a largely separate caste of naval officers gradually evolving, and by 1688 the navy displayed a far more professional structure and mentality. Though the advantages were many the drawbacks are also apparent in the fierce struggle among officers over jobs and promotion, and in the more rigid hierarchy within the ship's company and the service as a whole.

A Whig reformer in the early 1700s, posing as an old Cromwellian, claimed that naval officers had grown 'insupportably proud, [and] carried it towards their inferior officers with contempt (which deprived them of all authority) and treated their seamen like dogs'. Under the Commonwealth, by contrast, 'our commanders were not only civil to our seamen, but sometimes familiar with them, which procured them their love, and abated nothing of their due respect'. Officers then 'did not think it below them to return to trade again', for they fought to serve their nation rather than to advance themselves. He claimed that 'our great and good Admiral Blake' was wont to tell his men 'that the meanest of them were free-born Englishmen, as well as himself; and that officers and mariners were all fellow-servants to the government of their country'.[10] This was a very idealized view of the parliamentary navy, and Blake's words are apocryphal, but it confirms the old maxim that the best propaganda rests on a basis of fact.

---

[10] 'An Inquiry', in *Harleian Misc.* i. 570–2.

SOURCES

SELECT LIST OF MANUSCRIPT SOURCES

Bodleian Library, Oxford

Ashmole 183–4, 210, 385, 427 (astrological casebooks of Booker and Lilly)
Carte 73, 74, 103, 131, 223, 225 (Mountagu papers)
Clarendon 31–74, 85 (royalist correspondence and newsletters)
Deposit C 158–72 (Portland: Nalson papers)
Firth c 8 (royalist letters on the fleet at Helvoetsluys, 1648–9)
Rawlinson A 184–5, 187 (navy papers)
    207 (Navy Commissioners, Minute Book, Oct. 1650–June 1653)
    209 (naval pensions)
    223 (naval finance)
    224 (Parliamentary Navy Committee, Order Book, Jan.–Oct. 1649)
    225 (Admiralty Committee of the Council, Order Book, Oct. 1650–Aug. 1651)
    226 (the same, Aug. 1651–Nov. 1652)
    227 (Admiralty Commissioners, Letter-Book, Dec. 1652–Aug. 1653)
    461 (the same, Aug. 1653–Jan. 1654)
    468 (Sandwich's Journal, 1665)
Rawlinson C 94 (papers on Barbados, 1647)
    179 (Minute Book of the Council of State, May–Aug. 1659)
    381 (Whetstone correspondence, 1658)
    416 (Committee of the Admiralty, Order Book, 1645)
Rawlinson D 924 (papers on the Medway raid, 1667)
Tanner 48–58 (letters of naval officers)

British Library

Additional 4156, 4159, 4165 (miscellaneous)
    5500 (prize accounts)
    9299 (dockyards)
    9300–2, 9304 (misc. navy papers)
    9305 (Committee of the Admiralty, Minute Book, Mar.–May 1648; Admiralty Commissioners, Order Book, Apr. 1656–Mar. 1657)
    9306 (Navy Commissioners, papers and contracts, 1649–60)
    9308 (Navy Commissioners, Letter-Book, 1653–4)

9309–10 (abstracts of orders by Admiralty Commissioners, 1655–60)
11411 (West Indies papers)
11602, 11605 (treatises of Richard Gibson)
12430 (journal of Col. Wm. Beeston, Jamaica)
18986 (misc. navy papers)
19367 (the same)
19770 (letters of Charles Longland from Leghorn, 1654–6)
22546 (misc. navy papers)
38848 (the same)
57491 (letters of Joseph Ames, 1663–74)
Bath: Coventry papers 95–8, 101 (microfilm)
Egerton 928 (papers relating to Chillenden)
Harleian 1247 (forces under Goodson, Mountagu, and Ayscue sent to or at
     the Sound, 1658–9)
Lansdowne 821–3 (letters to Henry Cromwell)
Loan 29/241 (Portland)
Sloane 505 (journal of Thomas Fisher, 1661)
     970 (Common Council of London, negotiations with Lawson, Monck,
     etc., 1659)
     3926 (Journal of the West Indies expedition, 1654–5)
Stowe 427–8 (misc. navy papers)

National Maritime Museum, Greenwich

ADL/A/9–10, D/13, Q/1, X/8, Z/8 (naval letters, petitions, lists, etc.)
AGC/B/2, 7, 8 (unpublished letters of Blake and Monck, 1653)
AGC/1, 3, 7, 12, 21, 39 (letters of Blake, Deane, Lawson,
     W. Rainborough, Popham)
CAD/D/3 (naval finance, 1654; fleet lists, 1654)
GOS/3 (letter to Popham)
HSR/A/27 (papers on the *Worcester* mutiny, Jan. 1653)
JOD/1/2 (Journals of Sir John Pennington, 1632–6)
LBK/47 (Albemarle letters, 1665)
LRN/3 (ship lists)
REC/1 (misc. navy papers)
UPC/1 (naval orders)
WYN/1–18 (Wynne papers: journals, Order Books, and related papers of
     Penn)

Public Record Office, Chancery Lane

HCA 1/8–9 (High Court of Admiralty, criminal cases, 1650–62)
HCA 13/52–77 (depositions and proceedings, 1635–75)
HCA 25/9–10, 213, 227 (Letter of marque, 1651–66)

HCA 34/2 (Sentences of Reprisals, Minute Book, 1650–3)
Prob. 11 (Wills)
RG 4/2426 (Register of John Durant's church at Canterbury)
RG 4/4414 (Register of William Greenhill's church at Stepney)
SP 18 (State Papers, Domestic, Interregnum)
SP 25 (Council of State Order-Books)
SP 46/96–8, 114–21 (Navy Commissioners' and Admiralty Commissioners' papers, 1649–60)
SP 46/136–7 (Navy Papers, 1660–73)

Public Record Office, Kew

Adm. 2/1725 (Admiralty orders, 1660–6)
Adm. 2/1729 (Admiralty Commissioners, Letter-book, Apr. 1656–Mar. 1657)
Adm. 2/1730 (the same, Apr. 1657–Dec. 1658)
Adm. 2/1731 (the same, Jan. 1659–June 1660)
Adm. 2/1732 (Admiralty Order Book, June 1660–Sept. 1662)
Adm. 2/1745 (Letter-book of James Duke of York as Lord High Admiral, 1660–8)
Adm. 3/273 (Admiralty Commissioners, Order Book, Apr. 1657–Dec. 1658)
Adm. 3/274 (the same, Jan. 1659–July 1660)
Adm. 7/729–30 (naval treatises)
Adm. 7/673 (Admiralty Committee, Minutes, Oct. 1646–Feb. 1648)
Adm. 7/674 (Letters to Admiralty Commissioners, June 1653–Jan. 1656)
Adm. 82/1 (Chatham Chest)
Adm. 106/1 (Navy Board, Orders, June–Aug. 1660)
Adm. 106/2 (Admiralty papers, Sept. –Dec. 1660)

Stepney Meeting House, 135 Stepney Way, London EC1

'A Book of Church Affaires at Stepney'

Dr Williams's Library, Gordon Square, London

MS 38–208 (Records of the Congregational Church at Great Yarmouth)

Worcester College, Oxford

Clarke 1/10 (xxii), 1/12 (xxiv), 1/13 (xxv), 1/15 (xxvii) (newsletters, 1652–6)
Clarke 3/12 (xlix) (passes, warrants of Monck)
Clarke 4/4 (cclxvi) (Popham papers, 1649–51)
(consulted on Harvester microfilm; roman numbers in brackets refer to volume numbers in Worcester College library)

THESES CITED IN THE TEXT

Battick, J. F., 'Cromwell's Navy and the Foreign Policy of the Protectorate, 1653–1658', Ph.D. (Boston, Mass., 1967).

Baumber, M. L., 'The Navy during the Civil Wars and the Commonwealth, 1642–1651', MA (Manchester 1967).

Cogar, W. B., 'The Politics of Naval Administration, 1649–1660', D.Phil. (Oxford, 1983).

Davies, J. D., 'The Seagoing Personnel of the Navy, 1660–1689: Political, Religious, and Social Aspects', D.Phil. (Oxford, 1986).

Hammond, W. N., 'The Administration of the English Navy, 1649–1660', Ph.D. (British Columbia, 1974).

Kennedy, D. E., 'Parliament and the Navy, 1642–1648', Ph.D. (Cambridge, 1959).

Laurence, A., 'Parliamentary Army Chaplains, 1642–1651', D.Phil. (Oxford, 1981).

Index

Abelson, James 127 n., 143, 351, 389
able seamen 59, 259, 336, 338
Acklam, George 166 n.
Acts:
  on colonial trade (1650) 76, 105
  on crime at sea 59
  for Generals 46
  for impressment 58, 263
  Indemnity 59, 336, 338
  Navigation 75, 85–6, 105
  on prize 57–8
  for Regulators 48
  on trade with France 70
Adams, Thomas 173, 247 n.
Adderley, William 310
Admiralty Commissioners 7, 8, 16–18,
    21, 47, 108, 148–50, 156–9, 188,
    197–203, 206, 215, 222–3, 231, 234,
    235–7, 256, 258–9, 271, 278, 280–1,
    291, 311, 319–20, 341, 343, 346,
    351, 380
  composition of 16, 122–3, 126–7, 167,
    295–6, 335, 341, 356, 363, 371
Admiralty Court 76, 276, 282
Admiralty Committee (of the Council)
    47, 80, 120, 155–6, 202
Adventure 146, 221, 226, 322
Advice 283, 344
Aldeburgh 182, 265, 268
alehouses 245, 249, 283
Algiers:
  Dey of 94
  slaves in 170 n., 206, 246, 305
Allen, Francis 161 n., 170, 344, 358–60,
    366, 373
Allen, William 346
Allgate, Abraham 350–1, 361 n., 366
Allin, Thomas 167, 376
Alured, Henry 167 n., 184, 358, 382
Alured, Col. Matthew 185
Amboyna 73, 77
America, links with navy 54–6, 162,
    165–6, 295, 303, 313
Ames, Joseph 167 n., 304, 373–4, 378
Amity 126, 240, 257
Anabaptists 138–9, 147, 150, 295, 302–3,
    325, 358–9, 372–3, 388
  see also Baptists

Andrewes, Thomas 48
Andrews, Peter 166
Antelope:
  (1) 23, 28, 66
  (2) 240
anti-Catholicism 57, 58, 88, 93–4, 118,
    300
Antichrist 87, 131, 148, 301
apocalypticism 118, 125, 130–1, 300
Appleton, Henry 71, 79–80, 156, 162,
    184, 192–3
Archer, Anthony 282, 378
Arkinstall, Thomas 203, 295, 372
Arms of Holland 120
army:
  and the press 266–7, 274
  relations with navy 54, 89–90, 117,
    123–4, 135–8, 145–6, 157, 184–5,
    274–5, 285–6, 292, 331–3, 342–50
army officers, recruited to navy 18, 27,
    45–6, 54, 157, 172–5, 184–5, 206,
    208–9
Ashford, Andrew 171 n.
Assistance 366, 373, 382
Assurance 288
astrology 327–8
Axtell, Lt. 184
Ayscue, Sir George 6, 8, 24, 55, 66, 68,
    76, 78, 108, 110, 112, 132, 148,
    175–6, 246, 292, 313, 337 n., 383,
    386, 390, 398

Badcock, Heretage 315
Badiley, Richard 7, 8, 31, 55, 65, 71,
    79–80, 93, 121, 144–5, 159, 163,
    166, 176, 192–3, 198, 229, 294,
    301–3, 324
Badiley, William 56 n., 372
Baker, Daniel 58–9, 171 n., 196, 303–5
Ball, Andrew 106 n., 160 n., 173, 181 n.,
    304
Baltic, expeditions to 73, 106–12, 337–40
Baptists 126, 135, 295, 298, 305, 319,
    322, 392
Barbados 3, 43, 67–8, 76, 88, 105, 165,
    242, 265
Barbary corsairs 17, 92, 94
Barker, John 217

Barker, William 367
Barkstead, John 266
Barlow, Edward 219, 243, 248 n., 253, 327
Barrow, Henry 225
Basing 134, 289
Baskett, John 167 n.
Batten, Sir William 3, 15–17, 20–1, 26–8, 31, 33–4, 36, 38–9, 48–9, 57, 60, 120, 187, 371
Beach, Richard 139 n., 367
Bear 215, 282, 316
beer 214–15, 244–5, 247, 276
Beer, John 373
Bence, Alexander 29, 41, 46 n.
Best, John 134, 146–7, 226, 251, 322
Bethel, Henry 21, 23, 45, 53
Bethel, Slingsby 83
Bevan, Rowland 233
bigamy 252–4
Binckes, Joseph 315, 374, 380
Blackborne, Robert 125–6, 127–8, 131, 157, 187 n., 294–6, 298–9, 301, 355, 363
Blagg, Edward 90, 162, 173, 182, 198, 251, 261, 305, 371, 374, 377, 381
Mrs 251
Blagge, William 391
Blake, Benjamin 90, 162, 181 n., 183, 185, 194, 199 n., 297, 303, 311, 339, 374, 392
Blake, General Robert:
  early career 46, 175
  as General 46, 54, 116, 147, 156, 173, 190–2, 210, 214, 220, 242, 246–7, 264, 279, 281, 283, 396, 399–400
  operations against: Dutch 6–8, 77–82, 120, 129–30, 134, 195, 273; French 71, 92–3; Moors 94; royalist 62–9; Spain 3, 95, 96–9, 102, 142, 148, 272
  and patronage 173, 180, 182–3, 185, 294
  political role 46, 117, 119, 121, 124–7, 138, 142, 287, 398, 401
  and religion 62, 95, 137, 293–4, 297, 299, 300, 302, 324
Blake, Capt. Robert 182–3, 320, 345, 358–9, 379
Blake, Robert (purser) 183
Blake, Samuel 183
Blake, Shadrach 183
Blake, Thomas 183
Blake, William 183

Blith, John 166 n.
Blofield, Isaac 166 n., 378
boatswains 26, 121, 171, 204–6, 208, 238, 308 n.
Boehme, Jacob 302
Bonadventure 24
Bond, Denis 47
books, at sea 146–7, 210, 247–8
Boon, Thomas 335 n., 336 n.
Booth, Sir George 339–40
Bordeaux, Antoine de 91, 93
Borough, William 207 n., 316
Boteler, Nathaniel 160
Bourne, Bartholomew 183
Bourne, John 140, 144, 149, 163–5, 168, 177, 183, 192, 250, 294, 299–300, 333, 344–5, 347, 360, 374, 377, 390 n.
Bourne, Nehemiah 8, 56, 129, 131, 165, 173, 177–8, 182–3, 196, 240, 247, 266, 270, 273–4, 288, 291–2, 294–5, 302–3, 333, 339, 364, 371, 387, 391–2, 399
Bowen, John:
  (1) 53
  (2) 57, 222, 232, 234, 322
Bowen, Peter 225 n.
Bowry, John 159, 379 n.
Bradley, Samuel 135, 304 n., 316, 320
Braemes, Arnold 352, 354, 356
Bragge, Thomas 310
Bramble 286
Brandenburg 109–10
Brandley, William 196 n.
brawls and fights 39, 64, 206, 228, 246, 249, 323, 382
Brazil fleets 64–5, 97, 105
Brest 70, 92
Bridge, William 294–5, 296, 304, 313
Bridgewater 282
Brier 232, 278, 365
Bristol 9, 287
Bristol 298, 326, 348
Broghill, Lord 144, 208
Brookes, George 317
Brookes, Thomas 296
brothels 62 n., 252, 254, 256
Browne, Nathaniel 178, 182, 187
Brussells, Claudius 303 n., 316
Buckingham, duke of 9, 171
Bull, Richard 208
Bunn, Thomas 163, 285
Burton, William 126, 167, 188, 196, 266, 295, 304, 343 n., 364

Butler, Gregory 326
Butler, James 326
Butler, Peter 170, 171 n., 186 n.

Cadiz 69, 98–9, 117, 171, 191
Cadman, James 161–2, 243
Cane, Susan 252
Canterbury 19, 316, 320
Carew, John 80, 122, 125, 126, 157, 187, 295, 319
Caribbean, operations in 3, 9, 87–91, 95–6
carnival 301
carpenters 26, 171, 181, 204–5, 208
Carslake, Martin 379
Carteret, Sir John 120
Caryl, Joseph 320
Caton, William 243, 318, 323
Centurion 339
Challenor, Thomas 47
Channel Islands 3, 43, 67
chaplains 135, 298, 302, 306–24, 374
Chapman, Edmund 199 n., 285
Charles I 2–3, 15–17, 23, 34, 42–3, 74
Charles II 20, 23, 32–5, 43, 59, 60, 70, 74, 84, 93, 116–19, 121, 141, 144, 148, 326, 340, 353, 354–6, 361–3, 368–70, 374
Charles X of Sweden 107, 110–12
Charles:
  (1) 25
  (2) 52
Chatham 19–20, 49, 121, 196, 199, 203, 287–8, 295, 310, 363, 365, 372, 387–8
Cheare, Abraham 305
Cheyneys, Thomas 265
Chidley, Samuel 304
Chillenden, Edmund 389
Christina, Queen 107
Clarendon, earl of *see* Hyde, Edward
Clarke, Lt. Col. John 126, 335 n.
Clarke, Capt. John 203, 242, 327
Clarke, Robert 146, 215, 234, 303 n., 345 n.
Clay, Robert 171 n., 227
Clement, Gregory 45, 165
clerks of the cheque 207–8
clothing 215, 239, 244, 276, 280, 289
Cobham, Nathaniel 185, 196 n., 378
Cockayn, George 319
Cockraine, William 200
Colchester 134

Coleman, Robert 167, 169, 187, 298, 304
colliers 56, 167, 265, 269, 270, 283
commissioned officers:
  ages of 55–6, 163–4
  education of 175, 178–9
  killed and maimed 82, 195–6, 389, 390
  misconduct 199, 201, 221–5, 233–6, 241–3
  pay 57, 132, 168, 173–4, 243
  recruitment 55–6, 164–71, 172–5, 246–8
  replacement 53, 79, 120–1, 135, 195–201, 222, 358–60, 377–8
  selection 18, 30, 53, 120, 155–62, 295–6, 358–9, 387
Committee of Safety 342, 346–7, 349
Commons, House of 16–18, 24, 28, 30–2, 66
  see also Parliament
complaints and petitions 136, 214, 216, 217, 221–7, 231, 235, 272, 275–6, 278–9, 286
Concord 232
constables 240, 264–5, 267
Constant Reformation 20
Constant Warwick 23, 39, 53, 137, 317, 367
Convertine 20, 22–3, 28, 121
convoys 62, 71, 100, 103, 233, 399 n.
cooks 24, 149, 205–6, 223
Coppin, James 162
Coppin, John 28, 196, 218, 373
Coppin, William 200, 243
Corbet, Miles 45, 167, 295, 304
Cornelian 218
Cornelius, Gilbert 389
Cornelius, Lambert 217 n., 218, 282
corporals 181
Cotterell, Edward 149
Cottington, Francis, Lord 69
Council of State 46–7, 52, 60–4, 116, 119, 126, 155–6, 202–3, 234, 271, 272–5, 283–4, 288, 332, 351
Country, Jeremy 252
Country, John 172
Country, Richard 172, 181 n., 243
Courteen, Sir William 55
Courtney, Constant 309, 315
Courtney, Hugh 346
courts martial 135, 147, 150, 189, 198–9, 203, 210, 219, 220, 224, 226, 228, 240, 241, 242, 256, 285, 286, 288–9, 317, 386

Covenant 56
Coventry, Sir William 241, 376, 383, 387, 389, 393
Cowes, Richard 346
Cox, Owen 56, 108, 110, 135, 193, 200, 305, 327, 381, 387
Coxere, Edward 179, 239, 244, 250–1, 262, 270
Coytmor, Robert 159
Crandley, Richard 48–9
Cranwell, Francis 158–9, 186, 199 n.
Crapnell, George 203
Creed, Richard 125
Crescent 23, 287
Crispin, William 139, 145, 196, 207 n., 384
Cromwell, Oliver 63, 112–14, 123, 175, 210, 331
    and the Dutch 82–5, 104–6, 113
    and France 86–7, 91–3, 100
    and the navy 1, 5, 7, 10–11, 44–5, 51, 53–4, 89–90, 94–5, 97, 99, 123–4, 127–8, 132, 134–5, 138–9, 141–3, 147–8, 150, 172, 286, 288, 362, 395–7
    and Spain 86–91, 95, 97, 102, 106, 113
Cromwell, Richard 5, 108–9, 149–50, 160, 331–4, 353, 356
Croscombe, John 387, 389
Crowther, John 24, 53, 303
Cubitt, Joseph 133, 177, 196
Cullen 97
Culpeper, John, Lord 35
Curle, Edmund 198, 231, 373
Curtis, Edmund 68, 223, 261
Customs 48, 50–1, 71, 232–3
Cuttance, Henry 361
Cuttance, Roger 180, 261, 358, 360–1, 384
Cuttle, John 174, 196 n., 217

Dakins, George 56, 117 n., 138–9, 145, 272, 303, 335, 345, 351, 357–9, 373, 377
Dallington, 137
dancing 246
Dare, Jeffrey 169, 200
Dare, Robert 53
Dartmouth 177, 265, 305, 381
D'Aumont, General 101
Day, John 199 n.
Deal 20, 35, 218, 267, 287
Deane, Richard 17 n., 46, 49, 54, 59, 62,

67, 79–81, 116, 123–4, 130, 172, 175, 185, 187, 190, 195, 273, 279, 281, 293, 296, 297, 299, 300, 302, 326
Denmark, relations with 3, 79, 84–5, 106–12, 119
Dennis, Robert 55, 68, 162, 165, 202, 303
dependants, relief of 58, 59, 143, 195, 214, 347
Deptford, 275, 372
Desborough, John 89, 126, 136, 144, 172, 180, 236, 295, 332–3, 335 n., 342, 346
desertion 269, 274, 282–6
Dickenson, Samuel 247 n.
diet 244
Digby, Francis 386
discipline:
    codes of 58, 79–80, 121, 219–20, 238, 241, 284, 288, 307, 325
    practice 59, 212, 219–30, 238, 241, 256, 284, 288–9, 291, 325–6, 399–400
disease 88, 96, 195, 214, 275–6
Dolphin 229
Dorislaus, Isaac 39
Dornford, Robert 218, 298, 303
Dove, David 174 n.
Dover 177, 228, 240–1, 260, 304, 361, 364, 369
Drew, Robert 170 n.
drunkenness 199, 213, 220, 223, 224, 226, 228, 249, 317, 323
Duchess 322
Dunbar 134, 369
Dungeness, battle 6, 79–81, 120, 121, 199, 297
Dunkirk 61, 66, 70–1, 91, 100–1, 103, 105, 141, 148, 334
Dunning, Edward 204
Dunning, Henry 236–7
Duppa, John 304
Durant, John 316, 318
Dutch:
    navy 6, 77
    peace terms 83–6, 106, 113
    relations with 72–7, 100, 104–13, 332–3, 336
    wars with (1652–4) 1, 3, 4, 10, 71, 78–83, 113, 119–22, 128–34; (1665–7) 328, 383–9; (1672–4) 390–1

Earning, Anthony 180, 183, 303, 344, 373, 377, 391
East Indies traders 54–6, 73, 85, 105, 166, 377, 391
Edwin, John 166 n.
Elias 239
Eliot, Sir John 87
Elizabeth 139
Elizabeth hoy 59
Elliott, Thomas 182, 380, 385 n.
Ellison, John 322
embezzlement and fraud 7, 51, 158–9, 199–201, 232, 234–9, 241–3, 399
engagements 59, 116, 336
Entrance 137–8, 302
Estwick, Stephen 48, 50
Evans, Simon 171 n., 195 n., 207 n.
Evelyn, John 5
Expedition 202, 291

Fagons 134
Fairfax 52, 188–9
Fairfax, Thomas 17, 19, 22, 28, 44, 52, 184
Falcon 210
Fame 316, 323
Farley, Alexander 235
Farnham, Richard 254 n.
favouritism 227
Feake, Christopher 301, 319
Fearnes, Nathaniel 29, 117, 195 n.
Fearnes, Richard 31 n.
Fellowship 19, 22, 25, 30
Fenn, Henry 300, 335 n., 351
Ferrar, Edward 256 n., 321
feuds 150, 192–4, 226–7, 232, 255, 322–3, 386
Fiennes, Nathaniel 208
Fifth Monarchists 56, 125–6, 130, 135, 141, 145, 147, 294, 305, 323, 380, 383, 388–9
fire 216, 245
Firth, Sir Charles 1
fishing 245
flag, honour of the 75, 76, 85, 105
flag-officers 53–5, 79, 159, 163, 168, 195, 246, 384, 390
flags 52
Fleet, Thomas 225
Fleetwood, Charles 185–6, 331–4, 347, 350
Foresight 245
Forester 227

Foster, Nicholas 165, 178, 247 n., 253–4, 358, 398 n.
Fox 343
France:
  navy of 6, 70
  relations with 3, 70–2, 86–7, 91–3, 100–2, 109
Francis 210
Franklin, William 318
Froud, John 315
Fuller, Thomas 308
funerals 99 n., 158 n., 184, 308

Gabbard, battle 5, 81–2, 133
Gainsborough 135, 323, 327
games 242–4, 246, 247, 249 n.
Gardiner, S. R. 1, 130
Garland 23, 25, 119, 314
Garment, Joshua 298 n.
Generals at Sea 53–4, 58–9, 62–5, 79, 116, 124, 142, 147, 155–6, 168, 172–3, 175, 190–2, 202, 293–4, 301, 331
gentleman-captains 160–1, 175–7, 213–14, 385, 393–4, 398
George 30, 61
Gethings, Philip 165 n., 216 n., 224, 282
Gibraltar 97–8, 272
Gibson, Richard 175, 185, 216, 238 n., 393
Gift 247, 255
Gilbert, Eleazer 314
Gillyflower 239
Gilpin, Bernard 390
Godfrey, William 186, 228, 327
Golden Cock 188, 285
Golding, John 120, 149
Goodson, Mary 168 n., 250, 304
Goodson, William 90, 95–6, 101, 102, 108–9, 162–5, 168, 177, 182, 194, 197–8, 272 n., 280, 309, 377, 387, 396 n, 399
  political role 31, 147, 334, 336–8, 342, 344–5, 347, 360, 374, 382, 391
  and religion 294, 297, 304, 316, 387
Goose, Philip 31 n., 179 n.
Grassingham, Robert 295, 372
Graves, Thomas 165, 195 n., 242
Gravesend 121, 267, 274
Great Charity 257
Greene, John 118
Greenhill, William 296, 303–4
Greyhound 23, 28, 217, 218

Grey of Groby, Lord 208
Grimsditch, John 181 n., 183
grommets 172
Grove, Edward 222, 360 n., 385 n.
Grove, John 316
Guernsey 67, 267–8
Guinea 59, 261, 290
Guise, duke of 92–3
gunners 26, 121, 171, 181, 204–6, 236–8
Gwynne, Thomas 269

Hackwell, Robert 31, 55, 163, 166, 196, 303
Haddock, Richard:
  (1) 44, 55, 117 n., 163
  (2) 164, 177, 350 n., 377, 390, 393
Haddock family, 197
Halifax, marquis of 393
Hall, Edward 19, 55, 67, 69, 71, 72, 76, 144, 166, 339 n., 343 n.
hammocks 214, 215
Hammond, Robert 21
Hampshire 280
Hannam, Willoughby 335 n., 384, 390
Hannibal 7
Happy Entrance 373
Harbottle, Luke 262
Harcourt, Daniel 313, 374 n.
Harditch, Francis 120, 180 n.
Harman, John 178, 243 n., 305, 316, 322 n., 345 n., 384–5, 390, 400 n.
Harrington, Sir John 208
Harris, John 56, 163
Harris, Leonard 21, 29, 199
Harrison, John 309
Harrison, Mark 165, 179, 350 n.
Harrison, Maj.-Gen. Thomas 130, 135, 184, 187
Harrison, Capt. Thomas 251
Hart 59, 117, 228
Harvey, Edmund 50
Harwich 222, 232, 270, 274, 277, 288, 291–2, 295, 319, 372
Haslock, John 210
Hatsell, Henry 131, 144, 161 n., 167, 202, 249, 251, 266, 268, 279–80, 284, 291, 295, 306, 320, 339, 343 n., 364
Havana 90, 96
Hawkes, Samuel 195
Hawksworth, Walter 324
Hawley, Seth 177, 384
Haytubb, Robert 174, 182 n., 196 n.

Hayward, John 358–9, 376, 390
Heaton, Nicholas 140, 146, 172, 178 n., 182, 218, 230–1, 298, 365, 374, 377, 381, 387, 391
Hebblethwaite, Robert 314
Hector 19
Helvoetsluys 32, 36–40, 66
Henfield, Robert 171 n.
Henrietta Maria 52
Hide, Jonathan 303 n., 377 n.
Higgenson, Samuel 303 n., 358, 360
Highland, Samuel 325
Hill, William 142–4, 196, 242, 372, 374, 387
Hind 20–1, 29, 39, 57
Hinde, James 382
Hispaniola 88–9, 138, 326
Hodges, Richard 167 n., 171 n.
Holland, earl of 40, 45
Holland, Philip 232, 234, 381, 388–9, 391
Holles, Sir Frescheville 328
Hollister, Dennis 126, 295
Hollond, John 48, 50–1
Holmes, Sir Robert 376, 384, 386
homosexuality 256–7
Honeywood, Sir Robert 336 n.
Hopewell 225
Hopkins, Edward 166 n., 295
Horne, Thomas 229
Horseman, Edward 126–7
How, Daniel 315
Howett, Samuel 163, 181 n., 214 n.
Hubbard, John 359, 360 n.
Hull 146, 266
Hungerford, Lady 318
Hutchinson, Richard 48, 166, 295, 303
Hyde, Edward, later earl of Clarendon 1, 38–9, 69, 83, 121, 140 n., 333, 337–40, 348, 351, 352, 368–9, 377, 379

Ibbott, Edmund 308 n.
Iceland 161, 198, 221, 231, 233
Île de Ré 9, 171
Iles, Michael 313
Inchiquin, earl of 24–5
indemnity 169
  see also Acts
Independent churches 294–7, 302–5, 316, 319–21
Independents 15–17, 25, 27, 48
Indian 204, 228

Ingle, Richard 159
Ingoldsby, Richard 175, 273
Ipswich 182, 267
Ireland, conquest of 54, 63, 66–7, 185
Ireton, Henry 27, 45, 63, 185
Irish Sea, squadrons in 24, 54, 55, 66–7, 185, 187, 215, 233–4, 242–3, 282, 350
Isle of Man 67
Islip 227

Jamaica 88–90, 95–6, 194, 196, 263, 378
James I 73
James II, as duke of York, 38, 93, 340, 352, 362, 367, 375–6, 379–80, 383, 386–7, 393, 396
Jefferies, John 158, 223, 381
Jersey 67, 120, 122, 268
Jersey 249, 323
Jervoise, Henry 19
Jessey, Henry 319
Jews 248, 300–1
John IV of Portugal 63–5, 68, 97
John 23, 25, 28 n., 314
Johnson, Dr Samuel 212
Jones, Jenkin 319
Jones, Philip 126
Jones, Roger 180 n., 200
Jordan, Elias 28 n., 33, 34, 38–9, 60
Jordan, John 205
Jordan, Joseph 117 n., 181 n., 197, 390, 396 n.
Jowles, Valentine 171 n., 379 n.

Kelsey, Thomas 126, 127, 136, 143, 184, 295, 335 n.
Kem, Samuel 15, 20, 27
Kendall, William 275, 276
Kentish Knock, battle 78–9, 120
Kent, revolt in 18–22, 25
Ketcher, Bartholomew 377
Kiffin, William 325
King, John 179 n., 373
King's Lynn 178
Kinsale 61–3, 367, 384
Kirby, Francis 199 n., 215
Kirby, Robert 227
Knowles, William 317
Knowlman, Richard 325
Knox, Robert 248 n.

Lambert, David 163 n., 184

Lambert, Gen. John 339, 342–3, 351, 387
Lambert, Capt. John 163 n., 184
Land, Henry 157
Lane, John 311
Lane, Lionel 176, 182, 187, 197, 214 n.
Langley, John 80 n., 123, 126, 335 n.
Langport 134
Lauderdale, earl of 16, 34–5
Laurel 306, 321
law, lawyers 140, 347
Lawson, John 56, 71, 82, 85, 102, 123, 125, 134, 160 n., 164, 167, 180, 181 n., 187, 215, 226, 256, 272, 375 376–7, 382, 396, 399
   political scheming 128, 135–47, 149, 182, 196
   and religion 123, 131, 294, 296, 299, 302–3, 306, 316, 383
   and the Restoration 156–7, 331, 335, 339, 342–3, 345–59, 361–2, 365, 368–9, 397–8
Leake, Richard 237
leave 243, 248–9, 285
Leghorn 72, 79, 93, 95–6, 100, 105, 121, 170, 192–3, 300–1
Lendall, Thomas 26, 34
Lenthall, William 52, 184, 334, 347, 350
Leonard, Robert 317
Leopard 383
Levellers 16–17, 27, 118–19, 141
Liberty 50
Lichfield 367
Lidcott, Leonard 18, 54, 196 n.
lieutenants 155, 171, 173, 181, 183–4, 198, 215–16, 242
Lightfoot, John 222, 242 n., 255
Lilburne, Anthony 120 n., 161 n.
Lilburne, John 119, 120
Lilly, William 269, 327, 368
Lily 216
Limbrey, John 304
Lion 24, 298
liquor, sale of 245
Lisbon 63, 65, 67, 70, 92, 95, 97, 105
Lisle, John 184
literacy 30–1, 159, 179, 207, 250
litigation 169, 170, 198
Littlejohn, John 165, 203
Liverpool 178, 279, 282
Lizard 224
Llwyd, Morgan 319
Lockhart, Sir William 189

London:
  blockades of 2, 23, 32–3, 340, 348–9
  pressing in 264, 266, 268–9
London 270, 287, 358
Longland, Charles 102
Lords, House of 17–18, 28, 30–1
  see also Parliament
Louis XIV 70
Love 39
Lowestoft 167
Ludlow, Edmund 142, 335, 348, 350,
  353, 354
Ludlow, Philip 184
Lurting, Thomas 306, 325, 326
Lyons, Richard 130, 142, 146, 303

Mackey, Robert 161 n., 218, 267, 271,
  304, 335 n.
Maidstone 220, 289, 290
Mainwaring, Sir Henry 219, 221
Malinge, John 202
Man, John 28, 53
Manley, Nicholas 313, 315
manning 9, 96, 258–86
Mardyke 100–1, 105, 272 n.
mare liberum 104–5
Marmaduke 327, 373
Marriott, John 315
Marsh, Giles 171 n.
Marshall, Philip 26, 120
Marston Moor 134, 285
Marten, Henry 16
Martin, Robert 171 n.
Mary 316
Maryland 68
masters 26, 180, 201–4, 217 n.
Masters Attendant 196, 203, 307 n.
Mather, Nathaniel 313
Mathias 215
Mauditt, Edward 298
Mayflower 116, 217
Mayo, Richard 315
Mazarin, Cardinal 6, 71, 92–3, 100–1
Meadowe, Philip 107
medals 58, 111, 158, 377 n.
Mediterranean, operations in 3, 8, 9, 65,
  71–2, 76, 80, 92–5, 97, 100, 102,
  192–3
Mellidge, Anthony 172, 182, 196, 305
Mennes, Sir John 379
merchant shipping, hired 4, 6–9, 80, 121,
  164, 229
Merlin 149, 222, 247, 252

Mermaid 143, 288
messing 213, 216
Middleton, Hugh 171 n.
midshipmen 180–1, 206
Mihill, Tobias 181
Mildmay, John 20, 28, 70, 181 n., 183,
  195 n., 305
Milford 24–5, 67, 289
Mills, Robert 196 n.
Milton, Thomas 378
Mitchell, Andrew 26
models 245
Monck 369
Monck, George 54, 102, 137, 175, 190,
  214, 232, 259, 273, 279, 281, 287,
  288, 294, 382–3, 385–6
  and Cromwell 121, 123–4, 126, 127
  and the Dutch war 79–82, 121, 130,
    134
  and patronage 158, 173, 177, 183, 186,
    360
  and the Restoration 342–5, 347,
    351–60, 362–3, 366–8, 398
Moorcock, Edward 181 n., 305, 392
Moore, John 173 n.
Mootham, Peter 170 n., 306 n., 381
Mordaunt, Viscount 352, 354
Morley, Herbert 335
Mould, Edward 167 n., 232
Moulton, Robert:
  (1) 19, 30, 39, 44, 49, 54–5, 62, 64, 166,
    176, 185, 196
  (2) 55, 197 n.
Mountagu 369
Mountagu, Gen. Edward, later earl of
  Sandwich 101–2, 104, 107, 147,
    149–51, 160, 163, 175, 189, 210,
    247–8, 286, 293–4, 310, 321
  expedition to the Baltic 3, 107,
    109–12, 191, 332–40
  expedition to Spain 3, 96–8, 142–3,
    146, 190
  and the Restoration 156, 331–41, 345,
    352, 355–69, 397–8
  after 1660: 371, 373, 376–7, 379, 380,
    383–6, 390
Mountagu, Edward (cousin) 337–8, 361
Moxon, George 313, 315
Moyer, Samuel 48, 49, 51
music 247
musters 282
mutiny 19–40, 58–60, 215, 228–30, 248,
  274, 286–92, 350–2

Myngs, Christopher 31, 96, 105, 164, 178, 182, 240, 263, 282, 285 n., 344, 385–6, 389

Nantwich 223
Naples 92–3, 332
Narbrough, Sir John 182
Naseby 5, 101, 139, 207, 210, 253, 340, 357, 358, 362, 369, 379
naval contractors 51, 196, 342, 364–5
naval stores 79, 106–7, 342
navy:
　expansion 4–6, 9, 52, 80
　finances 9–10, 277–8, 280, 287–9, 341–2, 364–5, 374–5
Navy Board 371
Navy Commissioners 48–9, 51, 60, 123, 166, 196, 202, 215, 232, 278, 283, 286, 290–1, 295, 342
Navy Committee (of Parliament) 44, 45, 51
Navy Office 264, 277
Navy Treasurer 47, 48, 166, 277
Nayler, James 302
Nelson, Francis 308, 312, 315
nepotism 182–5, 187–9, 217
Nesfield, Nathaniel 161
Nettles 208
New Amsterdam 92
Newbery, Richard 138–9, 184, 229, 268, 302, 305 n., 344–5, 358–9, 373, 374, 380, 382 n., 387
Newbury 367
Newcastle 170, 232, 264 n., 268
Newcastle 223
Newfoundland 3, 71, 165
newspapers 247
Nicholas, Sir Edward 140
Nicholls, Josias 315
Nicodemus 21
Nieuchèse, duc de 92
Nightingale, Edward 184
Nightingale 317
Nixon, Edward 170 n., 204 n., 247 n., 344, 360, 385
Nixon, Robert 29, 225, 350 n.
Noades, Butler 171 n., 195 n., 237 n.
Nonsuch ketch 283
Norcross, Nathaniel 313, 315
Norwood, Arthur 316, 374 n.
Norwood, James 316, 320
Nutton, Michael 217 n., 282

Oates, Samuel 320
officer-corps, remodelling 53, 155–79, 359–60, 373–4, 375–6
Okey, John 145, 347–8
omens 326
Opdam, Jacob van 108–10
Oran 98, 102
Orangists 74, 75, 84, 119
Ormonde, earl of 177
Ostend 61, 101, 103, 149
Outlaw, Abel 283
Overton, Robert 137, 146, 266, 333, 354
　Mrs 146
Oxford 228, 350–1, 366, 373

Pacey, Thomas 53 n.
Packe, Henry 158, 167 n., 180
Packe, Michael 130, 158, 163, 167 n., 195 n., 305
Palmer, Jonas 204
Palmer, Thomas 321
Papachino 100
Paragon 52, 245, 297
Parke, Francis 200, 235, 303, 358
Parker, John 223
Parker, Nicholas 166 n.
Parliament:
　Long 2, 15, 21, 25, 26–7, 29
　Rump 1, 4–5, 6–7, 41, 42–5, 51, 52–3, 62, 64, 68–9, 70–3, 79–80, 116, 122–5, 128, 132, 259, 263, 288, 344, 353, 395
　Barebone's 82, 125–8, 167, 295, 348
　of 1654–5: 135–6, 138
　of 1656–8: 145
　of Richard Cromwell 106, 108–9, 332–3
　Rump (in 1659) 106, 110–12, 156, 333–6, 340–2, 346–7, 349–51
　Long (in 1660) 353, 355, 361
　Convention 355, 361
paternalism 214–15, 281–2
patronage and promotion 171–3, 179–89, 360, 366
Patterson, Edward 279–80
pay, seamen's:
　arrears 25, 229, 277–82, 285, 287–9, 333, 365, 368, 370, 374–5
　rates of 29, 57, 259, 260
Peacock, James 66, 167, 195 n., 214 n., 229
Pearce, John 216
Pearl 227, 247, 344

Pearsall, John 317 n.
Pearse, James 210
Pelham, Peregrine 46 n.
Pelican 20, 28, 216
Pell, Daniel 312, 317, 318, 323
Pembroke 316
Pendarvis, John 319
Penhallow, Richard 161 n.
Penn, William 6, 8, 24–5, 67, 76, 94,
    117, 123, 127, 131–3, 136, 172, 175,
    177, 178, 187, 190 n., 273, 281, 361,
    363, 367, 371, 376, 383, 386–7
  and patronage 181, 183, 185, 188, 217
  and religion 130, 293–4, 297, 301, 303,
    324
  and Western Design 3, 87–90, 92, 105,
    113, 138–9, 162, 183, 188, 242, 246,
    260, 281
Pennington, Sir John 171
Pennoyer, William 48, 51
Penrose, Francis 20–1, 28, 176
Penrose, Thomas 290, 298, 305, 306, 385
Penry, John 159
Penruddock's rising 40
Pepys, Samuel 6, 9, 160, 207, 234–5, 238,
    245, 247, 280, 334, 356–7, 359, 360,
    361–3, 365–6, 368–71, 375, 377,
    379–81, 385, 393, 399
Perkins, Francis 322
Pestell, William 67, 171 n., 234, 307, 381
Peter, Hugh 116, 132, 166 n., 170, 206,
    296, 303, 304, 311
Pett, Peter 19, 22, 49, 51, 249, 285,
    287–8, 363
Pett, Phineas 363
Pett family 310, 372
petty officers 171, 182, 206
Philip IV of Spain 69, 91, 92, 106, 117, 141
Phipps, William 150, 174, 302 n., 322
Phoenix 226, 253, 274, 317
Pickering, William 171 n., 181, 266
Pittock, Richard 179 n.
Plate fleets 69, 86, 89, 90, 95, 96, 97–9,
    100, 102, 113–14, 143, 147
Plumleigh, Robert 148, 162, 176–7, 183,
    197, 242, 267, 272, 275, 305, 373–4,
    392
plunder 96, 98–9, 199–201, 231–2,
    234–5, 239–44, 260–1, 282, 385, 399
Plunket, Thomas 61, 66
Plymouth 144, 167–8, 196, 230–1, 240,
    256, 261, 268, 279, 284, 287, 291,
    295, 381

Plymouth 282, 359
Poole, Jonas 100, 170–1, 183, 198, 366,
    385 n., 389
Poole, William 183, 391
Poortmans, John 121, 125, 127–8, 131,
    133, 137 n., 145–7, 247, 266, 277,
    294, 305
pope, the 93, 97, 141, 300
Popham, Edward 18, 29 n., 46, 59, 62,
    65, 66, 116, 119, 173, 175, 184, 190,
    198, 210, 228, 250, 251, 293
Portland, battle 81, 130–1, 214, 297–8
Portland 134, 138, 226, 288
Porto Farina 94, 100, 299
Portsmouth 9, 22, 27–8, 49, 136, 139–40,
    142–3, 146, 196, 218, 277, 280–1,
    287, 288, 290–1, 295, 310, 346, 349,
    372
Portsmouth 218
Portugal 3, 63–5, 68–9, 72, 97–8, 105,
    191
Potter, Richard 303, 335 n., 367, 374,
    381, 387
Powell, Henry 227 n., 243
Powell, Vavasor 319
Poyntz, John 207
President:
    Great 52, 228, 290, 373
    Little 25
press, the 32, 58, 122, 128–9, 262–72, 347
Preston 134
Pride, Col. Thomas 172, 208
Pride, Lt. 184
Pride's Purge 41, 43
Primrose 311
Prince 19–20, 52
Prior, Samuel 316, 317
privateers:
    English 76, 118, 166, 172, 263, 273,
    283–4
    Flemish 91, 101–4, 229
    French 70
    Irish and royalist 24, 45, 61–2, 66, 67,
    70, 84, 118, 120, 367
Prize Commissioners 58, 234
prize crews 232, 240, 241 n., 242
prize-money 57–8, 136, 168–9, 241,
    260–1, 276–7, 282
prizes:
    added to navy 4–5
    taken by Flemings 103
    taken from Dutch 85
Prosperous 217

Providence 20, 23, 28, 216, 322
providence, belief in 62, 95, 108, 113,
    117, 129, 140, 298–300
provisions 214, 239, 244, 275–6, 289, 290
Purefoy, William 48, 184
pursers 207–9, 236, 238–9
Purvis, John 164 n.
Pyend, Stephen 207 n., 384
Pym, John 87

Quakers 126, 266, 295, 302, 305–6,
    325–6

Rainborough, Thomas 16–21, 25, 26–8,
    45, 46 n., 56, 184, 296
Rainborough, William 119, 156, 343 n.
Ranters 298, 318
rape 256 n.
Raven, Samuel 372, 388
Reed, Nicholas 163–4, 177, 182, 196
Reeves, Jonas 167 n.
reformados 173, 180
Reformation 287
Regulators 48–52, 53
religious radicalism:
    and commissioned officers 52, 128,
        130–1, 135, 138, 157, 227, 242,
        293–307, 311, 317, 381, 387, 392
    and warrant officers and seamen 206,
        324–5, 373
    republicans and the navy 115, 117, 118,
        128, 135–47, 333–5, 358–9, 387–9,
        396–7
Reserve 276
Resolution 52, 125, 143
Reynolds, Jacob 168, 172, 200, 378 n.,
    385 n.
Reynolds, Robert 184
Rich, Jeremiah 208
Rich, Nathaniel 126, 145, 208, 295,
    343 n., 347, 354, 387
Richard 5, 134, 245, 369
Riggs, Edward 382
riots 277–8, 287–9
Rising, William 392
Rively, Anthony 181 n., 196 n., 303 n.,
    365
Robins, John 298 n.
Robinson, Luke 355
Robinson, Robert 148, 163, 216, 391–2
Robotham, 320 n.
Roche, Jeremy 328

Rochester 238, 289–90
Rockwell, Nathaniel 135, 187
Roebuck 20, 29, 65
Roe ketch 321
Rodger, N. A. M. 185, 212, 400
Rogers, John 305
Rome 88, 94
Rooth, Richard 176–7, 183, 188, 301,
    391
Rose, Robert 316, 374 n.
Rose, Stephen 174
Rosebush 224
'rough music' 238 n.
Rountree, Ralph 316, 374
Row, John 320
Rownen, Thomas 257
Rowse, William 118, 166 n.
royalists:
    and the navy 27, 115–17, 119, 121–2,
        139–41, 144, 148–50, 255, 332–3,
        337–9, 351–2, 356–7, 363, 397
    invasion plans 43, 101, 119, 148, 351–2
Rupert, Prince 3, 9, 34, 36, 38–40, 59–66,
    70, 117, 119, 383, 385–6
Russell, James 48, 80 n., 123
Ruyter, Michiel de 78, 104–5, 109, 112,
    388–9

Sabbath observance 293, 301, 302, 321–2
sabotage 64, 119–20, 139, 149, 231, 255,
    367
Sacheverell, Benjamin 148, 174, 247,
    248, 284
Sacheverell, Thomas 208 n.
Sackler, Tobias 157, 360 n.
St John, Oliver 74–5
St Kitt's 88, 105
Salmon, Edward 126, 335 n.
Saltonstall, Charles 29, 69, 165, 166, 176,
    178, 298
Salwey, Richard 80, 122–3, 343, 348, 351
Samford, Lt. 137–8, 302
Sampson 318
Sanders, Joseph 167 n.
San Domingo 88–90, 113, 170
Sandwich 20–1, 157, 354
Sandwich, earl of see Mountagu
Sansum, Robert 164, 232 n., 267–8, 384,
    389
Santa Cruz 99, 104, 192
Sapphire 182, 218, 227, 230–1, 240, 305
Satisfaction 18 n., 20, 28, 39, 282, 311
Saunders, Gabriel 290

Saunders, Robert 150, 181 n., 198, 243 n.
Savoy, duke of 300
Say, William 335 n.
Scarborough 135, 146–7, 161, 355
Scillies 43, 67, 275
Scot, Joseph 311
Scot, Thomas 347–8
Scotland:
  army in 137, 185, 342, 345
  invasion of 67
  squadron off 54, 67
Seaman, John 28
seamen:
  behaviour and ethos 213–14, 219, 226–8, 231–3, 239–41, 243–57
  political attitudes 25–8, 30–1, 115–17, 121–2, 140, 146, 149, 336–8, 362, 373
  in royalist fleet 33–5, 37–40, 63, 117
  see also pay
search, right of 75, 85, 104
sea-regiment 90, 138
Sedgwick, Robert 91, 92
Selby 146
Selden, John 73
Sexby, Edward 137, 141, 144, 147
sexual practices 249, 252–6
Shadwell, Charles 213, 249, 254
Sharland, James 343
Shelley, Giles 162, 170 n., 178, 259, 284, 335 n.
Sherwin, John 54 n., 199 n., 215, 230, 233
ship-building 9, 51, 218
ships:
  rates of 4
  (re-)naming 5, 52–3, 134, 369
ship's boys 171–2, 228 n., 246, 256–7
Shish, Jonas 372
short-allowance money 244, 246
Short, Tobias 378
Shovell, Sir Cloudesley 182
Shute, Richard 48
sick and wounded, relief of 58, 214–15
Sidney, Algernon 110, 336–8
Simmonds, John 109, 200, 318 n., 323, 327 n.
Simpson, John 319
singing 246, 247, 287
Smith, Ambrose 161–2
Smith, Edmund 167 n.
Smith, Eustace 171, 379

Smith, John 169 n., 227
Smith, Thomas 49, 51
Smyth, Jeremiah 54, 146, 173, 176, 183, 196 n., 306, 324, 385–6, 390
soldiers, serving at sea 215, 262, 272–5, 285
Sophia 227, 290
Sorlings 253
Southampton, earl of 356
Southwold 214, 267, 340
Southwood, Henry 217 n.
Sovereign 19–20, 52, 164, 172, 202, 206, 208, 255, 259, 311, 313, 390
sovereignty of the seas 60, 75, 76, 83, 85
Spain:
  navy of 6, 98
  relations with 69, 72, 86–7
  war with 3, 7, 11, 87–91, 95–106, 113–14, 143, 147–8, 335
Sparling, Thomas 101, 184, 235, 247, 366
Sparrow 232
Speaker 52, 99, 142
Spithead 136
Spradborough, Edward 318 n.
Stansby, John 53
Stapley, Anthony 47
Starbuck, William 316
Stayner, Sir Richard 98–9, 109, 148, 169, 180, 184, 192, 198, 240, 294, 320, 332, 336, 338, 342, 344–5, 347, 358, 361, 368–9, 376, 379
Stepney, church at 294, 296, 303, 307, 325, 373
stewards 207–8, 225
Stokes, John 3, 75, 100, 105, 128, 148, 150, 173, 188–9, 194, 246 n., 284, 302 n., 332, 344–5, 347, 360, 376, 389
Stone, John 126
Stoneham, Benjamin 319
Storey, Robert 139, 172 n.
Strickland, Walter 29, 39, 74
Strong, Peter 164–5, 196, 215, 303
Strutt, James 220 n., 224
Suffield, Richard 180
surgeons 209–10, 316 n., 322, 339
Sussex 274
Swallow 18 n., 20–1, 29
Swanley, Richard 24, 53, 303
swearing 323, 324
Sweden, relations with 3, 107–12, 336–40
Swiftsure 204, 357

Syms, John 314, 322, 324

tallowing 285
Tangier 98, 102
Tarleton, Edward 170 n., 178, 180, 185,
    199 n., 227, 378
tarpaulins 159–60, 175, 386, 398–9
Tatnel, Valentine 224, 228, 234 n., 236,
    260, 304 n., 311, 358, 361, 373,
    379 n., 384 n.
Taunton 142
Taylor, Commissioner John 384
Taylor, Capt. John 199 n.
Taylor, Jonathan 215
Taylor, Robert 135, 305
Tearne, Henry 351, 389
Teddiman, Thomas 177, 361
Teddiman family 304
Temple, Sandes 161 n., 389, 391
Tenth Whelp 24
Teonge, Henry 255, 326
Terry, James 196 n.
Texel, battle 82, 122, 133
Thomas, Sir Keith 163
Thompson, Edmund 131, 167 n., 217,
    304
Thomson, Edward 303
Thomson, George 80, 123, 363
Thomson, Maurice 48–9, 165, 303 n.,
    304
Thomson, Robert 49, 342 n.
Thoroughgood, Charles 118, 196, 203,
    216, 372
Thoroughgood, Thomas 287
Thorpe, Robert 204
Thurloe, John 4, 83, 90, 98–9, 101, 104,
    108, 143, 144, 189, 207–9
tickets 217, 279–80
Tickle, William 242
Tiger 23, 59–60, 229, 274
timber 9, 51
Tippett, John 372
tobacco 245
Tom, Gregory 175
Tonge plot 381–2
Torrington 150, 322
Toulon 65, 70, 92
trading, by warships 233, 367
Trafford, Thomas 181, 350 n., 378
Trapnel, Anna 133
Tredagh 5, 134
Trevythvan, Nicholas 312
Triers 320–1

Trinity House 19, 30, 49–50, 52, 264
Triumph 207
Tromp, Martin 6, 18, 37, 60, 67, 77–9,
    81, 119, 129
Truelove 289
Tucker, Anthony 138
Tunis, Dey of 94, 100
Turner, John 321
Tuscany, Grand Duke of 72, 93, 100
Tweedy, Roger 49

Unicorn 61, 288

Vane, Charles 64
Vane, Sir Henry 47, 55, 56, 72, 80,
    122–3, 128, 157, 166, 295, 310, 332,
    335, 343, 348–9, 351
Vanguard 121
Venables, Robert 87–90
Venice 5, 72, 94, 113
Venn, John 51
Venner, Thomas 145, 380–1
Venning, Ralph 320
Vessey, John 199 n., 222
Vessey, Robert 184, 233, 367
Vice-Admirals 264
Victory 269
victuallers 239, 275, 289–90, 365
Vincent, John 313, 374 n.
Virginia 3, 43, 68, 162
volunteers 213, 217–19, 227, 248,
    259–62, 283

Wager, Charles 172
Wager, John 171 n.
Waldo, 318
Walton, Valentine 45, 47, 208, 295, 335,
    340
Wapping 177, 294, 303, 316, 393
Ward, Ned 204, 239, 245, 307
warrant-officers 26, 50, 57, 121, 201–11,
    216–17, 224–6, 259, 321–3, 324–5,
    373–4, 378–9
Warren, Peter 222
Warwick, Robert Rich, earl of 3, 15–17,
    20–4, 26–7, 29–33, 36–41, 43–6, 53,
    54, 57, 87, 116, 147, 166, 216 n.,
    256 n.
Warwick 23
watermen 264, 266
Weale, John 196, 208, 216, 220, 246, 248,
    250, 300, 301, 318 n.
Wenman, Elizabeth 315

Western Design 87–91, 113, 136–9, 162
Westley, John 315
Wetwang, John 170, 176, 186, 232, 390, 391
Wexford 134
Weymouth 261, 361
Wheeler, Abraham 57, 163 n.
Wheeler, Rebecca 304
Whetstone, Catherine 188
Whetstone, Roger 188
Whetstone, Thomas 100, 161, 163, 188–9, 194, 337–8, 366, 378
White, Isaac 159, 378
White, John 308
White, Thomas 364
Whitehorne, William 104–5, 146, 158 n., 171 n., 181, 216, 311, 360, 374, 377
Whitelocke, Bulstrode 178, 250, 317, 324
Wildey, William 31, 55, 163, 196, 303, 317 n.
Wildman, John 135, 137, 141
Wilgress, John 167 n., 360 n.
Wilkes, Thomas 183
Wilkinson, Robert 179, 377, 389
William II, Stadholder 74
Willoughby, Francis 49, 144, 166 n., 280–1, 290–1, 295, 301, 371
Willoughby of Parham, Lord 34, 67
Willoughby, William 49
Wilson, Rowland 47
Winsby 373
Winslow, Edward 87

Wise, Lawrence 310, 319
witchcraft 268–9, 326–7
With, Witte de 85
Witheridge, Edward 165, 170, 303, 345 n., 360, 374
Witheridge, John 165, 170
Witt, Jan de 82, 104, 113
wives, women 22, 143, 200, 249–56, 268–9, 271, 279, 280–1, 327
Wolf 278
Wood, Walter 166 n.
Woodall, Frederick 319
Woodbridge 9, 182, 187
Woolman, Thomas 388
Woolters, John 116, 157, 304, 379 n.
Woolwich 372
Worcester 53, 134, 183, 248, 282, 359
Wright, Thomas 181 n., 196 n., 231, 252
Wyard, Robert 62, 117–18, 161 n., 221–2, 233, 322

Yarmouth, Great 9, 22–3, 29, 32, 34, 60, 126, 131, 161, 164 n., 167, 197, 218, 260, 271, 274, 284, 294–6, 304, 313, 364, 387
Yarmouth 218, 343
Yarranton, Andrew 388
Yates, Bartholomew 268
Young, Anthony 66, 129, 159, 171, 183, 302, 360, 377, 390, 392
Young, David 108, 110 n.
Young, Joseph 183